Landmark Papers in Economics, Politics and Law

The Foundations of 20th Century Economics

Prefaces by: Mark Blaug

Professor Emeritus, University of London, UK
Professor Emeritus, University of Buckingham, UK
Visiting Professor, University of Amsterdam, The Netherlands
Visiting Professor, Erasmus University of Rotterdam, The Netherlands

1. Landmark Papers in Economic Growth
   Selected by Robert M. Solow

2. Landmark Papers in Economic Fluctuations, Economic Policy and Related Subjects
   Selected by Lawrence R. Klein

3. Landmark Papers in General Equilibrium Theory, Social Choice and Welfare
   Selected by Kenneth J. Arrow and Gérard Debreu

4. Landmark Papers in Economics, Politics and Law
   Selected by James M. Buchanan

Future titles will include:

Landmark Papers in Macroeconomics
Selected by James Tobin

Wherever possible, the articles in these volumes have been reproduced as originally published using facsimile reproduction, inclusive of footnotes and pagination to facilitate ease of reference.

Landmark Papers in Economics, Politics and Law

Selected by

James M. Buchanan

Advisory General Director
Center for Study of Public Choice, George Mason University, USA

THE FOUNDATIONS OF 20TH CENTURY ECONOMICS

An Elgar Reference Collection
Cheltenham, UK • Northampton, MA, USA

Published by
Edward Elgar Publishing Limited
Glensanda House
Montpellier Parade
Cheltenham
Glos GL50 1UA
UK

Edward Elgar Publishing, Inc.
136 West Street
Suite 202
Northampton
Massachusetts 01060
USA

A catalogue record for this book is available from the British Library.

Library of Congress Cataloging in Publication Data

Landmark papers in economics, politics, and law / selected by James M. Buchanan.
p. cm. — (Foundations of 20th century economics ; 4) (Elgar reference collection)
Includes index
1. Social choice. 2. Economic man. 3. Economics. I. Buchanan, James M. II. Series.
III. Series: Elgar reference collection

HB846.8 .L36 2002
330—dc21 2001053220

ISBN 1 84064 472 9

Printed and bound in Great Britain by MPG Books Ltd, Bodmin, Cornwall

Contents

Acknowledgements

The editor and publishers wish to thank the authors and the following publishers who have kindly given permission for the use of copyright material.

American Economic Association for articles: F.A. Hayek (1945), 'The Use of Knowledge in Society', *American Economic Review*, **XXXV** (4), September, 519–30; William J. Baumol (1967), 'Macroeconomics of Unbalanced Growth: The Anatomy of Urban Crisis', *American Economic Review*, **LVII** (3), June, 415–26; Charles R. Plott (1967), 'A Notion of Equilibrium and Its Possibility Under Majority Rule', *American Economic Review*, **LVII** (4), September, 787–806; Milton Friedman (1968), 'The Role of Monetary Policy', *American Economic Review*, **LVIII** (1), March, 1–17; Mark V. Pauly (1970), 'Risk and the Social Rate of Discount', *American Economic Review*, **LX** (1), March, 195–8; Anne O. Krueger (1974), 'The Political Economy of the Rent-Seeking Society', *American Economic Review*, **LXIV** (3), June, 291–303.

Blackwell Publishers Ltd for articles: Allyn Young (1928), 'Increasing Returns and Economic Progress', *Economic Journal*, **XXXVIII** (152), December, 527–42; R.H. Coase (1937), 'The Nature of the Firm', *Economica*, **IV** (New Series), November, 386–405; Jack Wiseman (1953), 'Uncertainty, Costs, and Collectivist Economic Planning', *Economica*, **XX** (78) (New Series), May, 118–28.

Blackwell Publishers Ltd and the Canadian Economics Association for article: Frank H. Knight (1935), 'The Ricardian Theory of Production and Distribution', *Canadian Journal of Economics and Political Science*, February, 3–25 and May, 171–96.

Dott. A. Giuffre Editore S.p.A. for excerpt: Armen A. Alchian (1977). 'Some Economics of Property Rights', in *Economic Forces at Work*, Chapter 5, 127–49.

Elsevier Science for article: Marilyn R. Flowers and Patricia M. Danzon (1984), 'Separation of the Redistributive and Allocative Functions of Government: A Public Choice Perspective', *Journal of Public Economics*, **24** (3), August, 373–80.

Journal of Law and Economics and the University of Chicago for article: Ronald H. Coase (1960), 'The Problem of Social Cost', *Journal of Law and Economics*, **III**, October, 1–44.

Macmillan Press Ltd for article: Ragnar Frisch (1959), 'On Welfare Theory and Pareto Regions', *International Economic Papers*, **9**, 39–92.

MIT Press Journals for articles: Frank H. Knight (1923), 'The Ethics of Competition', *Quarterly Journal of Economics*, **XXXVII**, August, 579–624; F.H. Knight (1924), 'Some Fallacies in the Interpretation of Social Cost', *Quarterly Journal of Economics*, **38** (4), August, 582–606;

Howard R. Bowen (1944), 'The Interpretation of Voting in the Allocation of Economic Resources', *Quarterly Journal of Economics*, **LVIII**, November, 27–48; Paul A. Samuelson (1954), 'The Pure Theory of Public Expenditure', *Review of Economics and Statistics*, **XXXVI**, November, 387–9.

Oxford University Press for articles: J. Wiseman (1957), 'The Theory of Public Utility Price – An Empty Box', *Oxford Economic Papers*, **9** (1) (New Series), February, 56–74; Gordon Tullock (1967), 'The Welfare Costs of Tariffs, Monopolies, and Theft', *Western Economic Journal*, **V**, June, 224–32.

UNESCO for excerpt: Rutledge Vining (1956), *Economics in the United States of America: A Review and Interpretation of Research*, 9–62.

University of Chicago Press for excerpt and articles: Henry C. Simons (1934), *A Positive Program for Laissez Faire: Some Proposals for a Liberal Economic Policy*, Public Policy Pamphlet Number 15, 1–40; Henry C. Simons (1936), 'Rules versus Authorities in Monetary Policy', *Journal of Political Economy*, **44** (1), February, 1–30; Duncan Black (1948), 'On the Rationale of Group Decision-Making', *Journal of Political Economy*, **LVI** (1), February, 23–34; Milton Friedman (1949), 'The Marshallian Demand Curve', *Journal of Political Economy*, **LVII** (6), December, 463–95; Armen A. Alchian (1950), 'Uncertainty, Evolution, and Economic Theory', *Journal of Political Economy*, **LVIII** (3), June, 211–21; Gordon Tullock (1959), 'Problems of Majority Voting', *Journal of Political Economy*, **LXVII** (6), December, 571–9; George J. Stigler (1961), 'The Economics of Information', *Journal of Political Economy*, **LXIX** (3), June, 213–25; Amartya Sen (1970), 'The Impossibility of a Paretian Liberal', *Journal of Political Economy*, **78** (1), January/February, 152–7.

Every effort has been made to trace all the copyright holders but if any have been inadvertently overlooked the publishers will be pleased to make the necessary arrangement at the first opportunity.

In addition the publishers wish to thank the Library of the London School of Economics and Political Science, the Marshall Library of Economics, Cambridge University, B & N Microfilm, London and the Library of Indiana University at Bloomington, USA for their assistance in obtaining these articles.

Foreword

I made the initial selection of the essays in this volume with the understandings, first, that my own works were to be excluded, and, second, that my selections were being solicited along with those of others. I did not make the selections with the understanding that mine were to be the exclusive and determining suggestions for inclusion. For this reason, I made some effort to ensure that selections unlikely to be made by my peers would be advanced for consideration. Of course, I stand by the selections initially made, but my listing should be interpreted subject to the qualification noted.

One important paper by F.H. Hayek, 'Competition as a Discovery Procedure', was initially suggested for inclusion in the listing. It is omitted here because of difficulty in obtaining permission to publish.

James M. Buchanan

Preface

Mark Blaug

James Buchanan is the founder of 'public-choice theory', the economic study of nonmarket decision making or, to put it simply, the attempt to complete the theory of market exchange with a corresponding theory of the functioning of political markets. What makes public-choice theory economics, and not just fancy political science, is that it is squarely based on the standard economist's assumption of man as a rational, utility-maximising agent. Individuals agree to assign the monopoly of force in society to a government because they believe it will serve their self-interest; in so doing, they accept a set of rules, a constitution. Why and how such rules are adopted, and whether some rules are better than others, is the subject of Buchanan's and Gordon Tullock's path-breaking book, *The Calculus of Consent: Logical Foundations of Constitutional Democracy* (University of Michigan Press, 1962).

The economic analysis of constitutional choice is only part of public-choice theory. In a long series of books – *Public Principles of Public Debt* (Richard D. Irwin, 1958); *Public Finance in Democratic Process: Fiscal Institutions and Individual Choice* (University of North Carolina Press, 1966); *The Demand and Supply of Public Goods: A Defense and Restatement* (Rand McNally, 1968); *Cost and Choice: An Inquiry in Economic Theory* (Markham, 1969); *Theory of Public Choice: Political Applications of Economics* (University of Michigan Press, 1972) co-edited with R.D. Tollison; *The Limits of Liberty: Between Anarchy and Leviathan* (University of Chicago Press, 1975); *Democracy in Deficit: The Political Legacy of Lord Keynes* (Academic Press, 1977) with R.E. Wagner; *Freedom in Constitutional Contract: Perspectives of a Political Economist* (Texas A&M University Press, 1978); *The Power to Tax: Analytical Foundations of a Fiscal Constitution* (Cambridge University Press, 1980) and *The Reason of Rules: Constitutional Political Economy* (Cambridge University Press, 1985), both with G. Brennan – Buchanan has employed the theory to attack virtually every aspect of public sector economics including the political process which lies behind the determination of tax and spending levels.

One constant theme is the notion that all costs are basically subjective, that opportunity costs exist inside people's heads, that they are only identical to prices paid in the market in the long-run perfectly competitive equilibrium. This makes mincemeat out of the standard doctrine of marginal cost pricing of public utilities and more or less takes us back to square one in applied welfare economics. As a matter of fact, Buchanan takes the view that economists have not so far talked much sense about public finance.

Early in his career, Buchanan's work was deeply influenced by his study of certain nineteenth-century European and particularly Italian writers on public finance whose approach to questions of taxation was totally different from that of leading Anglo-American writers: the European authors emphasised a concept of government based on mutual agreement among citizens in which taxes are seen as 'payments' for services rendered by the government. In consequence, Buchanan has argued that unanimity is the only really defensible 'calculus of consent' but that a political democracy based on majority rule may nevertheless be freely chosen by everyone if minority rights are adequately protected. The question then becomes that of discovering those constitutional rules which preserve the original consensus. Buchanan has no difficulty in showing that the growth of government activity in recent years has departed widely from this 'optimal' constitution and his writings, therefore, abound in suggestions for additional constitutional constraints on government and its multifarious agencies. Indeed, he has called for a 'constitutional revolution' to reassess the entire spectrum of constitutional rights of individuals.

Buchanan was born in Murfreesboro, Tennessee in 1919 and has never completely lost a touch of Southern drawl in his speech. He received his BA from Middle Tennessee State Teachers College in 1940, his MA from the University of Tennessee in 1941, and his PhD from the University of Chicago in 1948. In 1955 he spent a year in Italy as a Fulbright Scholar to study the European tradition of public finance. Returning from Italy in 1956, he became a Professor of Economics and in 1985, Director of the Thomas Jefferson Center for Political Economy at the University of Virginia and proceeded to lay the foundations of public-choice theory. In 1962, having published *The Calculus of Consent*, he founded the Public Choice Society with Gordon Tullock and promoted a new journal called *Public Choice*, which stimulated others to work in the field. In 1969, Buchanan became a Professor and Director of the Center for Study of Public Choice, first at Virginia Polytechnic Institute and State University in Blacksburg, Virginia, and then at George Mason University, Fairfax, Virginia. He was President of the Southern Economic Association in 1963, Vice-President of the American Economic Association in 1971, President of the Western Economic Association in 1983 and President of the Mont Pelerin Society from 1984 to 1986. Buchanan has lectured at universities all over the world while producing a steady flow of articles and books which have gradually enlarged the scope of public-choice theory to the point where it now forms a recognised and well-defined sub-discipline within economics. In 1986 he received the Alfred E. Nobel Memorial Prize in Economic Sciences.

Some would argue that public-choice theory is too preoccupied with normative questions of how collective choices *ought* to be made instead of addressing the positive questions of the *actual* effects of government behaviour on the economy. Whatever the ultimate verdict on public-choice theory, there can be little doubt that it now forms a definite tradition connected with other straws in the wind, such as the economic theory of property rights, the economics of law and the economics of organisations.

Mark Blaug
University of Amsterdam

[1]

UNCERTAINTY, EVOLUTION, AND ECONOMIC THEORY

ARMEN A. ALCHIAN[1]
University of California at Los Angeles

A MODIFICATION of economic analysis to incorporate incomplete information and uncertain foresight as axioms is suggested here. This approach dispenses with "profit maximization"; and it does not rely on the predictable, individual behavior that is usually assumed, as a first approximation, in standard textbook treatments. Despite these changes, the analytical concepts usually associated with such behavior are retained because they are not dependent upon such motivation or foresight. The suggested approach embodies the principles of biological evolution and natural selection by interpreting the economic system as an adoptive mechanism which chooses among exploratory actions generated by the adaptive pursuit of "success" or "profits." The resulting analysis is applicable to actions usually regarded as aberrations from standard economic behavior as well as to behavior covered by the customary analysis. This wider applicability and the removal of the unrealistic postulates of accurate anticipations and fixed states of knowledge have provided motivation for the study.

The exposition is ordered as follows: First, to clear the ground, a brief statement is given of a generally ignored aspect of "profit maximization," that is, where foresight is uncertain, "profit maximization" is *meaningless* as a guide to specifiable action. The constructive development then begins with an introduction of the element of environmental adoption by the economic system of a posteriori most appropriate action according to the criterion of "realized positive profits." This is illustrated in an extreme, random-behavior model without any individual rationality, foresight, or motivation whatsoever. Even in this extreme type of model, it is shown that the economist can predict and explain events with a modified use of his conventional analytical tools.

This phenomenon—environmental adoption—is then fused with a type of individual motivated behavior based on the pervasiveness of uncertainty and incomplete information. Adaptive, imitative, and trial-and-error behavior in the pursuit of "positive profits" is utilized rather than its sharp contrast, the pursuit of "maximized profits." A final section discusses some implications and conjectures.

I. "PROFIT MAXIMIZATION" NOT A GUIDE TO ACTION

Current economic analysis of economic behavior relies heavily on decisions made by rational units customarily assumed to be seeking perfectly optimal situations.[2] Two criteria are well known—profit maximization and utility maximiza-

[1] I am indebted to Dr. Stephen Enke for criticism and stimulation leading to improvements in both content and exposition.

[2] See, e.g., J. Robinson, *Economics of Imperfect Competition* (London: Macmillan), p. 6, for a strong statement of the necessity of such optimal behavior. Standard textbooks expound essentially the same idea. See also P. Samuelson, *Foundations of Economic Analysis* (Cambridge: Harvard University Press, 1946).

tion.[3] According to these criteria, appropriate types of action are indicated by marginal or neighborhood inequalities which, if satisfied, yield an optimum. But the standard qualification usually added is that nobody is able really to optimize his situation according to these diagrams and concepts because of uncertainty about the position and, sometimes, even the slopes of the demand and supply functions. Nevertheless, the economist interprets and predicts the decisions of individuals in terms of these diagrams, since it is alleged that individuals use these concepts implicitly, if not explicitly.

Attacks on this methodology are widespread, but only one attack has been really damaging, that of G. Tintner.[4] He denies that profit maximization even makes any sense where there is uncertainty. Uncertainty arises from at least two sources: imperfect foresight and human inability to solve complex problems containing a host of variables even when an optimum is definable. Tintner's proof is simple. Under uncertainty, by definition, each action that may be chosen is identified with a *distribution* of potential outcomes, not with a unique outcome. Implicit in uncertainty is the consequence that these distributions of potential outcomes are overlapping.[5] It is worth emphasis that each possible action has a *distribution* of potential outcomes, only one of which will materialize if the action is taken, and that one outcome cannot be foreseen. Essentially, the task is converted into making a decision (selecting an action) whose potential outcome *distribution* is preferable, that is, choosing the action with the *optimum distribution*, since there is no such thing as a *maximizing* distribution.

For example, let each of two possible choices be characterized by its subjective distribution of potential outcomes. Suppose one has the higher "mean" but a larger spread, so that it might result in larger profits or losses, and the other has a smaller "mean" and a smaller spread. Which one is the maximum? This is a nonsensical question; but to ask for the optimum distribution is not nonsense. In the presence of uncertainty—a necessary condition for the existence of profits—there is no meaningful criterion for selecting the decision that will "maximize profits." The maximum-profit criterion is not meaningful as a basis *for selecting* the action which will, in fact, result in an outcome with higher profits than any other action would have, unless one assumes nonoverlapping potential outcome distributions. It must be noticed that the meaningfulness of "maximum profits—a realized outcome which is the largest that could have been realized from the available actions"—is perfectly consistent with the meaninglessness of "profit maximization"—a criterion for selecting among alternative lines of action, the potential outcomes of which are describable only as distributions and not as unique amounts.

This crucial difficulty would be avoided by using a preference function as a criterion for selecting most preferred distributions of potential outcomes, but the search for a criterion of rationality and choice in terms of pref-

[3] In the following we shall discuss only profit maximization, although everything said is applicable equally to utility maximization by consumers.

[4] "The Theory of Choice under Subjective Risk and Uncertainty," *Econometrica*, IX (1941), 298–304; "The Pure Theory of Production under Technological Risk and Uncertainty," *ibid.*, pp. 305–11; and "A Contribution to the Nonstatic Theory of Production," *Studies in Mathematical Economics and Econometrics* (Chicago: University of Chicago Press, 1942), pp. 92–109.

[5] Thus uncertainty is defined here to be the phenomenon that produces overlapping distributions of potential outcomes.

erence functions still continues. For example, the use of the mean, or expectation, completely begs the question of uncertainty by disregarding the variance of the distribution, while a "certainty equivalent" assumes the answer. The only way to make "profit maximization" a specifically meaningful action is to postulate a model containing certainty. Then the question of the predictive and explanatory reliability of the model must be faced.[6]

II. SUCCESS IS BASED ON RESULTS, NOT MOTIVATION

There is an alternative method which treats the decisions and criteria dictated by the economic *system* as more important than those made by the individuals in it. By backing away from the trees—the optimization calculus by individual units—we can better discern the forest of impersonal market forces.[7] This approach directs attention to the interrelationships of the environment and the prevailing types of economic behavior which appear through a process of economic natural selection. Yet it does not imply that individual foresight and action do not affect the nature of the existing state of affairs.

In an economic system the realization of profits is the criterion according to which successful and surviving firms are selected. This decision criterion is applied primarily by an impersonal market system in the United States and may be completely independent of the decision processes of individual units, of the variety of inconsistent motives and abilities, and even of the individual's awareness of the criterion. The reason is simple. Realized positive profits, not *maximum* profits, are the mark of success and viability. It does not matter through what process of reasoning or motivation such success was achieved. The fact of its accomplishment is sufficient. This is the criterion by which the economic system selects survivors: those who realize *positive profits* are the survivors; those who suffer losses disappear.

The pertinent requirement—positive profits through relative efficiency—is weaker than "maximized profits," with which, unfortunately, it has been confused. Positive profits accrue to those who are better than their actual competitors, even if the participants are ignorant, intelligent, skilful, etc. The crucial element is one's aggregate position relative to actual competitors, not some hypothetically perfect competitors. As in a race, the award goes to the relatively fastest, even if all the competitors loaf. Even in a world of stupid men there would still be profits. Also, the greater the uncertainties of the world, the greater is the possibility that profits would go to venturesome and lucky rather than to logical, careful, fact-gathering individuals.

The preceding interpretation suggests two ideas. First, success (survival) accompanies relative superiority; and, second, it does not require proper motivation but may rather be the result of fortuitous circumstances. Among all competitors, those whose particular conditions happen to be the most appropriate of those offered to the economic system for testing and adoption will be "se-

[6] Analytical models in all sciences postulate models abstracting from some realities in the belief that derived predictions will still be relevant. Simplifications are necessary, but continued attempts should be made to introduce more realistic assumptions into a workable model with an increase in generality and detail (see M. Friedman and L. Savage, "The Utility Analysis of Choices Involving Risks," *Journal of Political Economy*, LVI, No. 4 [1948], 279).

[7] In effect, we shall be reverting to a Marshallian type of analysis combined with the essentials of Darwinian evolutionary natural selection.

lected" as survivors. Just how such an approach can be used and how individuals happen to offer these appropriate forms for testing are problems to which we now turn.[8]

III. CHANCE OR LUCK IS ONE METHOD OF ACHIEVING SUCCESS

Sheer chance is a substantial element in determining the situation selected and also in determining its appropriateness or viability. A second element is the ability to adapt one's self by various methods to an appropriate situation. In order to indicate clearly the respective roles of luck and conscious adapting, the adaptive calculus will, for the moment, be completely removed. All individual rationality, motivation, and foresight will be temporarily abandoned in order to concentrate upon the ability of the environment to *adopt* "appropriate" survivors even in the absence of any adaptive behavior. This is an apparently unrealistic, but nevertheless very useful, expository approach in establishing the attenuation between the ex post survival criterion and the role of the individual's adaptive decision criterion. It also aids in assessing the role of luck and chance in the operation of our economic system.

Consider, first, the simplest type of biological evolution. Plants "grow" to the sunny side of buildings not because they "want to" in awareness of the fact that optimum or better conditions prevail there but rather because the leaves that happen to have more sunlight grow faster and their feeding systems become stronger. Similarly, animals with configurations and habits more appropriate for survival under prevailing conditions have an enhanced viability and will with higher probability be typical survivors. Less appropriately acting organisms of the same general class having lower probabilities of survival will find survival difficult. More common types, the survivors, may appear to be those having *adapted* themselves to the environment, whereas the truth may well be that the environment has *adopted* them. There may have been no motivated individual adapting but, instead, only environmental adopting.

A useful, but unreal, example in which individuals act without any foresight indicates the type of analysis available to the economist and also the ability of the system to "direct" resources despite individual ignorance. Assume that thousands of travelers set out from Chicago, selecting their roads completely at random and without foresight. Only our "economist" knows that on but one road are there any gasoline stations. He can state categorically that travelers will *continue* to travel only on that road; those on other roads will soon run out of gas. Even though each one selected his route at random, we might have called those travelers who were so fortunate as to have picked the right road wise, efficient, foresighted, etc. Of course, we would consider them the lucky ones. If gasoline supplies were now moved to a new road, some formerly luckless travelers again would be able to move; and a new pattern of travel would be observed, although none of the travelers had changed his particular path. The really possible paths have changed with the changing environment. All that is needed is a set of varied, risk-taking

[8] Also suggested is another way to divide the general problem discussed here. The process and rationale by which a unit chooses its actions so as to optimize its situation is one part of the problem. The other is the relationship between changes in the environment and the consequent observable results, i.e., the decision process of the economic *society*. The classification used in the text is closely related to this but differs in emphasizing the degree of knowledge and foresight.

(adoptable) travelers. The correct direction of travel will be established. As circumstances (economic environment) change, the analyst (economist) can select the types of participants (firms) that will now become successful; he may also be able to diagnose the conditions most conducive to a greater probability of survival.[9]

IV. CHANCE DOES NOT IMPLY NONDIRECTED, RANDOM ALLOCATION OF RESOURCES

These two examples do not constitute an attempt to base all analysis on adoptive models dominated by chance. But they do indicate that collective and individual random behavior does not per se imply a nihilistic theory incapable of yielding reliable predictions and explanations; nor does it imply a world lacking in order and apparent direction. It might, however, be argued that the facts of life deny even a substantial role to the element of chance and the associated adoption principle in the economic system. For example, the long lives and disparate sizes of business firms and hereditary fortunes may seem to be reliable evidence of consistent foresighted motivation and nonrandom behavior. In order to demonstrate that consistent success cannot be treated as prima facie evidence against pure luck, the following chance model of Borél, the famous French mathematician, is presented.

Suppose two million Parisians were paired off and set to tossing coins in a game of matching. Each pair plays until the winner on the first toss is again brought to equality with the other player. Assuming one toss per second for each eight-hour day, at the end of ten years there would still be, on the average, about a hundred-odd pairs; and if the players assign the game to their heirs, a dozen or so will still be playing at the end of a thousand years! The implications are obvious. Suppose that some business had been operating for one hundred years. Should one rule out luck and chance as the essence of the factors producing the long-term survival of the enterprise? No inference whatever can be drawn until the number of original participants is known; and even then one must know the size, risk, and frequency of each commitment. One can see from the Borél illustration the danger in concluding that there are too many firms with long lives in the real world to admit an important role to chance. On the contrary, one might insist that there are actually too few!

The chance postulate was directed to two problems. On the one hand, there is the actual way in which a substantial fraction of economic behavior and activity is effected. On the other, there is the method of analysis which economists may use in their predictions and diagnoses. Before modifying the extreme chance model by adding adaptive behavior, some connotations and implications of the incorporation of chance elements will be elaborated in order to reveal the richness which is really inherent in chance. First, even if each and every individual acted in a haphazard and nonmotivated manner, it is possible that the variety of actions would be so great that the resulting collective set would contain actions that are best, in the sense of perfect foresight. For example, at a horse race with enough bettors wagering strictly at random, someone will win

[9] The undiscerning person who sees survivors corresponding to changes in environment claims to have evidence for the "Lysenko" doctrine. In truth, all he may have is evidence for the doctrine that the environment, by competitive conditions, selects the most viable of the various phenotypic characteristics for perpetuation. Economists should beware of economic "Lysenkois m."

on all eight races. Thus individual random behavior does not eliminate the likelihood of observing "appropriate" decisions.[10]

Second, and conversely, individual behavior according to some foresight and motivation does not necessarily imply a collective pattern of behavior that is different from the collective variety of actions associated with a random selection of actions. Where there is uncertainty, people's judgments and opinions, even when based on the best available evidence, will differ; no one of them may be making his choice by tossing coins; yet the aggregate *set* of actions of the entire group of participants may be indistinguishable from a set of individual actions, each selected at random.[11]

Third, and fortunately, a chance-dominated model does not mean that an economist cannot predict or explain or diagnose. With a knowledge of the economy's realized requisites for survival and by a comparison of alternative conditions, he can state what types of firms or behavior relative to other possible types will be more viable, even though the firms themselves may not know the conditions or even try to achieve them by readjusting to the changed situation if they do know the conditions. It is sufficient if all firms are slightly different so that in the new environmental situation those who have their fixed internal conditions closer to the new, but unknown, optimum position now have a greater probability of survival and growth. They will grow relative to other firms and become the prevailing type, since survival conditions may push the observed characteristics of the set of survivors toward the unknowable optimum by either (1) repeated trials or (2) survival of more of those who happened to be near the optimum—determined ex post. If these new conditions last "very long," the dominant firms will be different ones from those which prevailed or would have prevailed under other conditions. Even if environmental conditions cannot be forecast, the economist can compare for given alternative potential situations the types of behavior that would have higher probability of viability or adoption. If explanation of past results rather than prediction is the task, the economist can diagnose the particular attributes which were critical in facilitating survival, even though individual participants were not aware of them.[12]

Fourth, the bases of prediction have been indicated in the preceding paragraph, but its character should be made explicit. The prediction will not assert that every—or, indeed, any—firm necessarily changes its characteristics. It asserts, instead, that the characteristics of the new *set* of firms, or possibly a set of new firms, will change. This may be

[10] The Borél gamblers analogue is pertinent to a host of everyday situations.

[11] Of course, the economic units may be going through a period of soul-searching, management training, and research activity. We cannot yet identify mental and physical activity with a process that results in sufficient information and foresight to yield uniquely determinate choices. To do so would be to beg the whole question.

[12] It is not even necessary to suppose that each firm acts as if it possessed the conventional diagrams and knew the analytical principles employed by economists in deriving optimum and equilibrium conditions. The atoms and electrons do not know the laws of nature; the physicist does not impart to each atom a wilful scheme of action based on laws of conservation of energy, etc. The fact that an economist deals with human beings who have sense and ambitions does not *automatically* warrant imparting to these humans the great degree of foresight and motivations which the economist may require for his customary analysis as an outside observer or "oracle." The similarity between this argument and Gibbsian statistical mechanics, as well as biological evolution, is *not* mere coincidence.

characterized by the "representative firm," a purely statistical concept—a vector of "averages," one dimension for each of the several qualities of the population of firms. A "representative firm" is not typical of any one producer but, instead, is a set of statistics summarizing the various "modal" characteristics of the population. Surely, this was an intended use of Marshall's "representative firm."

Fifth, a final implication drawn from consideration of this extreme approach is that empirical investigations via questionnaire methods, so far used, are incapable of evaluating the validity of marginal productivity analysis. This is true because productivity and demand analyses are essential in evaluating relative viability, even though uncertainty eliminates "profit maximization" and even if price and technological changes were to have no consciously redirecting effect on the firms. To illustrate, suppose that, in attempting to predict the effects of higher real wage rates, it is discovered that every businessman says he does not adjust his labor force. Nevertheless, firms with a lower labor-capital ratio will have relatively lower cost positions and, to that extent, a higher probability of survival. The force of competitive survival, by eliminating higher-cost firms, reveals a population of remaining firms with a new average labor-capital ratio. The essential point is that individual motivation and foresight, while sufficient, are not necessary. Of course, it is not argued here that therefore it is absent. All that is needed by economists is their own awareness of the survival conditions and criteria of the economic system and a group of participants who submit various combinations and organizations for the system's selection and adoption. Both these conditions are satisfied.[13]

As a consequence, only the method of use, rather than the usefulness, of economic tools and concepts is affected by the approach suggested here; in fact, they are made more powerful if they are not pretentiously assumed to be necessarily associated with, and dependent upon, individual foresight and adjustment. They are tools for, at least, the diagnosis of the operation of an economic system, even if not also for the internal business behavior of each firm.

V. INDIVIDUAL ADAPTING VIA IMITATION AND TRIAL AND ERROR

Let it again be noted that the preceding extreme model was designed to present in purest form only one element of the suggested approach. It is not argued that there is no purposive, foresighted behavior present in reality. In adding this realistic element—adaptation by individuals with some foresight and purposive motivation—we are expanding the preceding extreme model. We are not abandoning any part of it or futilely trying to merge it with the opposite extreme of perfect foresight and "profit maximization."

Varying and conflicting objectives motivate economic activity, yet we shall here direct attention to only one particular objective—the sufficient condition of realized positive profits. There are no implications of "profit maximization," and this difference is important. Although the latter is a far more extreme objective when definable, only the former is the sine qua non of survival and success. To argue that, with perfect competition, the two would come to the same thing is to conceal an important difference by means of a very implausible as-

[13] This approach reveals how the "facts" of Lester's dispute with Machlup can be handled with standard economic tools.

sumption. The pursuit of profits, and not some hypothetical undefinable perfect situation, is the relevant objective whose *fulfilment* is rewarded with survival. Unfortunately, even this proximate objective is too high. Neither perfect knowledge of the past nor complete awareness of the current state of the arts gives sufficient foresight to indicate profitable action. Even for this more restricted objective, the pervasive effects of uncertainty prevent the ascertainment of actions which are supposed to be optimal in achieving profits. Now the consequence of this is that modes of behavior replace optimum equilibrium conditions as guiding rules of action. Therefore, in the following sections two forms of conscious adaptive behavior are emphasized.

First, wherever successful enterprises are observed, the elements common to these observable successes will be associated with success and copied by others in their pursuit of profits or success. "Nothing succeeds like success." Thus the urge for "rough-and-ready" imitative rules of behavior is accounted for. What would otherwise appear to be merely customary "orthodox," nonrational rules of behavior turns out to be codified imitations of observed success, e.g., "conventional" markup, price "followship," "orthodox" accounting and operating ratios, "proper" advertising policy, etc. A conventionally employed type of behavior pattern is consistent with the postulates of the analysis employed, even though the reasons and justifications for the particular conventions are not.[14]

Many factors cause this motive to imitate patterns of action observable in past successes. Among these are: (1) the absence of an identifiable criterion for decision-making, (2) the variability of the environment, (3) the multiplicity of factors that call for attention and choice, (4) the uncertainty attaching to all these factors and outcomes, (5) the awareness that superiority relative to one's competitors is crucial, and (6) the nonavailability of a trial-and-error process converging to an optimum position.

In addition, imitation affords relief from the necessity of really making decisions and conscious innovations, which, if wrong, become "inexcusable." Unfortunately, failure or success often reflects the willingness to depart from rules when conditions have changed; what counts, then, is not only imitative behavior but the willingness to abandon it at the "right" time and circumstances. Those who are different and successful "become" innovators, while those who fail "become" reckless violators of tried-and-true rules. Although one may deny the absolute appropriateness of such rules, one cannot doubt the existence of a strong urge to create conventions and rules (based on observed success) and a willingness to use them for action as well as for rationalizations of inaction. If another untried host of actions might have been even more successful, so much the worse for the participants who failed, and even for those who missed "perfect success."

Even innovation is accounted for by imitation. While there certainly are those who consciously innovate, there are those who, in their imperfect attempts

[14] These constructed rules of behavior should be distinguished from "rules" which, in effect, do no more than define the objective being sought. Confusion between objectives which motivate one and rules of behavior are commonplace. For example, "full-cost pricing" is a "rule" that one cannot really follow. He can try to, but whether he succeeds or fails in his objective of survival is not controllable by following the "rule of full-cost pricing." If he fails in his objective, he must, of necessity, fail to have followed the "rule." The situation is parallel to trying to control the speed of a car by simply setting by hand the indicator on the speedometer.

to imitate others, unconsciously innovate by unwittingly acquiring some unexpected or unsought unique attributes which under the prevailing circumstances prove partly responsible for the success. Others, in turn, will attempt to copy the uniqueness, and the imitation-innovation process continues. Innovation is assured, and the notable aspects of it here are the possibility of unconscious pioneering and leadership.

The second type of conscious adaptive behavior, in addition to imitation, is "trial and error." This has been used with "profit maximization," wherein, by trial and ensuing success or failure, more appropriate actions are selected in a process presumed to converge to a limit of "profit maximization" equilibrium. Unfortunately, at least two conditions are necessary for convergence via a trial-and-error process, even if one admits an equilibrium situation as an admissible limit. First, a trial must be classifiable as a success or failure. The position achieved must be comparable with results of other potential actions. In a static environment, if one improves his position relative to his former position, then the action taken is better than the former one, and presumably one could continue by small increments to advance to a local optimum. An analogy is pertinent. A nearsighted grasshopper on a mound of rocks can crawl to the top of a particular rock. But there is no assurance that he can also get to the top of the mound, for he might have to descend for a while or hop to new rocks. The second condition, then, for the convergence via trial and error is the continual rising toward some *optimum optimorum* without intervening descents. Whether decisions and actions in economic life satisfy these two conditions cannot be proved or disproved here, but the available evidence seems overwhelmingly unfavorable.

The above convergence conditions do not apply to a changing environment, for there can be no observable comparison of the result of an action with any other. Comparability of resulting situations is destroyed by the changing environment. As a consequence, the measure of goodness of actions in anything except a tolerable-intolerable sense is lost, and the possibility of an individual's converging to the optimum activity via a trial-and-error process disappears. Trial and error becomes survival or death. It cannot serve as a basis of the *individual's* method of convergence to a "maximum" or optimum position. Success is discovered by the economic system through a blanketing shotgun process, not by the individual through a converging search.

In general, uncertainty provides an excellent reason for imitation of observed success. Likewise, it accounts for observed uniformity among the survivors, derived from an evolutionary, adopting, competitive system employing a criterion of survival, which can operate independently of individual motivations. Adapting behavior via imitation and venturesome innovation enlarges the model. Imperfect imitators provide opportunity for innovation, and the survival criterion of the economy determines the successful, possibly because imperfect, imitators. Innovation is provided also by conscious wilful action, whatever the ultimate motivation may be, since drastic action is motivated by the hope of great success as well as by the desire to avoid impending failure.

All the preceding arguments leave the individual economic participant with imitative, venturesome, innovative, trial-and-error adaptive behavior. Most conventional economic tools and concepts are still useful, although in a vastly different analytical framework—one which is closely akin to the theory of biological evolution. The economic counterparts of genetic heredity, mutations, and natural selection are imitation, innovation, and positive profits.

VI. CONCLUSIONS AND SUMMARY

I shall conclude with a brief reference to some implications and conjectures.

Observable patterns of behavior and organization are predictable in terms of their relative probabilities of success or viability *if* they are tried. The observed prevalence of a type of behavior depends upon both this probability of viability and the probability of the different types being submitted to the economic system for testing and selecting. One is the probability of appearance of a certain type of organization (mutation), and the other is the probability of its survival or viability, once it appears (natural selection). There is much evidence for believing that these two probabilities are interrelated. But is there reason to suppose that a high probability of viability implies a high probability of an action's being taken, as would be implied in a system of analysis involving some "inner directed urge toward perfection"? If these two probabilities are not highly correlated, what predictions of types of action can the economist make? An answer has been suggested in this paper.

While it is true that the economist can define a profit maximization behavior by assuming *specific* cost and revenue conditions, is there any assurance that the conditions and conclusions so derivable are not too perfect and absolute? If profit maximization (certainty) is not ascertainable, the confidence about the predicted effects of changes, e.g., higher taxes or minimum wages, will be dependent upon how close the formerly existing arrangement was to the formerly "optimal" (certainty) situation. What really counts is the various actions actually tried, for it is from these that "success" is selected, not from some set of perfect actions. The economist may be pushing his luck too far in arguing that actions in response to changes in environment and changes in satisfaction with the existing state of affairs will converge as a result of adaptation or adoption toward the optimum action that should have been selected, if foresight had been perfect.[15]

In summary, I have asserted that the economist, using the present analytical tools developed in the analysis of the firm under certainty, can predict the more adoptable or viable types of economic interrelationships that will be induced by environmental change even if individuals themselves are unable to ascertain them. That is, although individual participants may not know their cost and revenue situations, the economist can predict the consequences of higher wage rates, taxes, government policy, etc. Like the biologist, the economist predicts the effects of

[15] An anomalous aspect of the assumption of perfect foresight is that it nearly results in tautological and empty statements. One cannot know everything, and this is recognized by the addendum that one acts within a "given state and distribution of the arts." But this is perilously close, if not equivalent, to saying either that action is taken only where the outcome is accurately foreseen or that information is always limited. The qualification is inserted because one might contend that it is the "*constancy* of the state and distribution of arts" that is necessary as a *ceteris paribus*. But even the latter is no solution. A large fraction of behavior in a world of incomplete information and uncertainty is necessarily directed at increasing the state of arts and venturing into an unknown sphere. While it is probably permissible to start with a prescribed "distribution of the knowledge of the arts," holding it constant is too restrictive, since a large class of important and frequent actions necessarily involves changes in the state and distribution of knowledge. The modification suggested here incorporates this search for more knowledge as an essential foundation.

environmental changes on the surviving class of living organisms; the economist need not assume that each participant is aware of, or acts according to, his cost and demand situation. These are concepts for the economist's use and not necessarily for the individual participant's, who may have other analytic or customary devices which, while of interest to the economist, serve as data and not as analytic methods.

An alternative to the rationale of individual profit maximization has been presented without exorcising uncertainty. Lest isolated arguments be misinterpreted, let it be clearly stated that this paper does not argue that purposive objective-seeking behavior is absent from reality, nor, on the other hand, does it indorse the familiar thesis that action of economic units cannot be expressed within the marginal analysis. Rather, the contention is that the precise role and nature of purposive behavior in the presence of uncertainty and incomplete information have not been clearly understood or analyzed.

It is straightforward, if not heuristic, to start with complete uncertainty and nonmotivation and then to add elements of foresight and motivation in the process of building an analytical model. The opposite approach, which starts with certainty and unique motivation, must abandon its basic principles as soon as uncertainty and mixed motivations are recognized.[16] The approach suggested here is intellectually more modest and realistic, without sacrificing generality. It does not regard uncertainty as an aberrational exogenous disturbance, as does the usual approach from the opposite extreme of accurate foresight. The existence of uncertainty and incomplete information is the foundation of the suggested type of analysis; the importance of the concept of a class of "chance" decisions rests upon it; it permits of various conflicting objectives; it motivates and rationalizes a type of adaptive imitative behavior; yet it does not destroy the basis of prediction, explanation, or diagnosis. It does not base its aggregate description on individual optimal action; yet it is capable of incorporating such activity where justified. The formalization of this approach awaits the marriage of the theory of stochastic processes and economics—two fields of thought admirably suited for union. It is conjectured that the suggested modification is applicable to a wide class of events and is worth attempts at empirical verification.[17]

[16] If one prefers, he may believe that the suggestions here contain reasons why the model based on certainty may predict outcomes, although individuals really cannot try to maximize profits. But the dangers of this have been indicated.

[17] Preliminary study in this direction has been very convincing, and, in addition, the suggested approach appears to contain important implications relative to general economic policy; but discussions of these are reserved for a later date.

[2]

Some Economics of Property Rights

1. SCARCITY, COMPETITION, AND PROPERTY

In *every* society, conflicts of interest among the members of that society must be resolved. The process by which that resolution (not elimination!) occurs is known as competition. Since, by definition, there is no way to eliminate competition, the relevant question is what kind of competition shall be used in the resolution of the conflicts of interest. In more dramatic words designed to arouse emotional interest, What forms of discrimination among the members of that society shall be employed in deciding to what extent each person is able to achieve various levels of his goals? Discrimination, competition, and scarcity are three inseparable concepts.

2. CONSTRAINTS

That list of concepts can be expanded—scarcity, competition, discrimination, constraints, property. In other words,

Preparation of this paper was facilitated by a grant from the Lilly Endowment of Indianapolis, Indiana, to the University of California, Los Angeles, for a study of various forms of property rights.

constraints exist that prevent our individually achieving a level of want-fulfillment beyond which none of us wants more. In still other words, these constraints, even though imposed by nature, include also the constraints imposed by other people who because they achieve certain levels of want fulfillment leave other people with lower levels. (I do not mean that *all* activities that enable one person to have a greater level of goal fulfillment will also necessarily mean less for someone else; we know that some forms of exchange permit joint increases. But we also know that cooperative action is possible, and also that competitive action is also present.) If we concentrate attention on constraints and classes of permissible action we find ourselves studying the *property* aspect of behavior.

Economists are, I think, too prone to examine exchange as a cooperative act whereby the buyer and seller each act in an effort to reach a more desired position. Yet I find it more interesting (now that I understand the cooperative aspect of exchange) to examine the competitive, or property, aspect of exchange. The act of exchange is a means whereby the buyer is able to compete against other claimants for the goods being obtained from the seller. The kinds of offers, forms of competition and behavior that the members of society can employ in an endeavor to get more of the goods that would otherwise go to other people, is brought more into the focus of attention. More directly, the forms and kinds of property rights sanctioned in a society define or identify the kinds of competition, discrimination, or behavior characteristic of that society.

Yet if we look at the "fields" of economics, say as presented by the American Economic Association's classification of areas of interest or specialization, we find no mention of the word "property." Either we can infer that the profession is so obviously aware of the pervasiveness of the effects of various forms of property rights that property rights can not sensibly be regarded as merely a subfield; or else we can infer that economists have forgotten about the possibility of subjective rigorous systematic coherent analysis of the various forms of property rights. My conviction is that the latter inference is the more valid one. As evidence I cite that the only systematic analysis of choice among "goods" postulates utility maximization subject to a budget or *wealth* constraint, wherein the constraint is almost invariably a *private* property type of wealth constraint.

3. PROPERTY RIGHTS

If, in what follows, I talk as if the property rights were enforced by formal state police power, let me here emphasize that such an interpretation, regardless of what I may later say, is gross error. It seems to be a fact that individuals will not stand by idly while some other person's property is stolen. It seems to be a fact that *private* property rights are rights not merely because the state formally makes them so but because individuals want such rights to be enforced, at least for a vast, overwhelming majority of people. And yet if I recognize the number of socialist states, I must admit to some confusion (I appeal for edification).

The rights of individuals to the use of resources (i.e., property rights) in any society are to be construed as supported by the force of etiquette, social custom, ostracism, and formal legally enacted laws supported by the states' power of violence or punishment. Many of the constraints on the use of what we call private property involve the force of etiquette and social ostracism. The level of noise, the kind of clothes we wear, our intrusion on other people's privacy are restricted not merely by laws backed by the police force, but by social acceptance, reciprocity, and voluntary social ostracism for violators of accepted codes of conduct. The use of arabic numbers rather than roman, the use of certain types of clothing, or styles of speech and address, of printing from left to right and top to bottom, rather than the reverse, or keeping our garden up with Jones', all are subject to the force of social opprobrium. No laws require such behavior. Yet each of us (or nearly every one of us) will punish in one way or another those who violate these rules. Surely it is not the important rules that are left to the formal state power of enactment and compulsion. Obviously there is heated dispute as to which forms of behavior should be "enforced" by social voluntary ostracism and which by formal state police action.

By a system of property rights I mean a method of assigning to particular individuals the "authority" to select, for specific goods, any use from a nonprohibited class of uses. As suggested in the preceding remarks the concepts of "authority" and of "nonprohibited" rely on some concept of enforcement or inducement to respect the assignment and scope of prohibited choice. A property right for me means some protection against other people's choosing against my will one of the uses of resources, said to be "mine."

Often the idea or scope of *private* property rights is expressed as an assignment of exclusive authority to some individual to choose any use of the goods deemed to be his private property. In other words the "owners," who are assigned the right to make the choice, have an unrestricted right to the choice of use of specified goods. Notice, that we did not add—"so long as the rights of other people are similarly respected." That clause is redundant in strict logic. Private property owners can use their goods in any way they choose. If some of these chosen uses involve the use or destruction of other people's private property, it follows that the private property system is being violated, for this use has denied to other people the control of use over the goods classed as private property. To say I have private property rights is to say that no one else has the right to make the choice of use of that good (contained in the class of private property). This means that if I select a use for the goods said to be my private property, the selection must not affect the physical attributes of your goods. If I own some iron, I can make window frames or fence posts out of it, but if I shove a piece of iron through "your" glass window, I shall be denying you the right of choice of the physical attributes of your private property. However, if I convert the iron to a special kind of good that other people are willing to buy instead of buying what you are selling, you may find that the reduced exchange value of your goods imposes a greater loss of exchange power (wealth) than if I had simply broken your window.

Although private property rights protect private property from physical changes chosen by other people, no immunity is implied for the exchange value of one's property. Nor does it imply that my use of my goods, which may not in any way affect your goods, cannot be a use that you find objectionable on moral or emotional grounds. If I use my resources to make lewd pictures for my own use or for exchange with other people, you may find your "utility" much affected. You may be more upset, annoyed, distressed, or hurt by my action than if I had broken your window or stolen some of your wealth.

Private property, as I understand it, does *not* imply that a person may use his property in any way he sees fit so long as no one else is "hurt." Instead, it seems to mean the right to use goods (or to transfer that right) in any way the owner wishes so long as the physical attributes or uses of all other people's private property is unaffected. And that leaves plenty of room for disturbance and alienation of affections of other people. If I open a restaurant near yours and win away business by my superior service, you are as hurt as if I had burned part of your building. If I open a restaurant and pour smells and smoke over your neighboring land then I have changed the physical attributes of your property; I have violated your private property rights—incidentally, a form of violation very common in most societies.

But if the right for me to open a business were denied, this could, if it also were part of a system in which your rights to enter into various businesses were similarly restricted, be considered by you to be an undesirable restriction and one that did you more harm than would be encountered by you in a less restrictive environment.

In sum, it is only the choice over physical attributes that is constrained to owners, not the value-in-exchange effects nor the psychological, emotional effects that you may suffer in the knowledge that I am behaving in what you consider improper ways (short of changing the physical attributes of your property).

4. PARTITIONING OF PROPERTY RIGHTS

Whether or not the preceding suggested definition is useful, we examine another issue. What are the effects of various partitionings of use rights? By this I refer to the fact that at the same time several people may each possess some portion of the rights to use the land. A may possess the right to grow wheat on it. B may possess the right to walk across it. C may possess the right to dump ashes and smoke on it. D may possess the right to fly an airplane over it. E may have the right to subject it to vibrations consequent to the use of some neighboring equipment. And each of these rights may be transferable. In sum, private property rights to various partitioned uses of the land are "owned" by different persons.[1]

A lease or rental agreement partitions the rights so that the renter gets the right to make decisions about particular uses of the item by the "owner." Normally the rights of the renter to decide where the furniture will be placed or when it will be sat on, etc., are not thought of as ownership rights, because they are so frequently allocated to the renter, and because the ultimate value consequence rests on the "owner." However, our main point here is that the rights can be partitioned, divided, and reallocated on a temporary—or even on a permanent—basis, so that the "ownership" rights are partitioned among two or more persons. This kind of division is not necessarily a cross-sectional division with each owner now having equal parts of all the ownership rights. Instead it is a selective partitioning with all of some of the subrights staying with the "owner" and all of some other rights being transferred temporarily at least to the "renter." Even though this is called a rental or leasing agreement, it does contain transfers of some of the rights that are included in ownership. The fact that these partitionings of owner are temporary makes it easy to decide who is the "owner" in the conventional sense.

The partitioning of various types of rights to use, has been

[1] A different form of interpersonal sharing of rights is that in which all rights are possessed in common and jointly by the group, but the decision as to any use must be reached by the group. Rights to each different kind of use are not separated and possessed by different people. Instead the rights are commonly owned; and the problem is in devising or specifying some choice process which will "declare" the decision of the "group" of joint owners.

explored by Ronald Coase.[2] He notes that what are commonly called nuisances and torts apply to just such situations in which rights are partitioned and the exercise of one owner's rights involves distress or nuisance for the owners of other rights. For example, if a railroad spreads sparks and ignites fires in wheatfields near the tracks, the wheat grower can pay the railroad not to spread sparks (if the law gives the railroad the right to spread such sparks). On the other hand, if the right to decide about such land use is reserved to the farmer, the railroad could pay him for the right to drop sparks on the land (and save costs of spark screens, etc.). If there were no costs of *negotiating* such exchanges of rights and policing them, the initial partitioning of rights would not affect the way resources are used. (Of course, wealth would be redistributed in accord with the initial assignment of the partitioned rights.)

But when we recognize that transaction costs do exist, it seems clear that the partitioned rights will be reaggregated into more convenient clusters of rights. If so, there should be an evolutionary force toward survival of larger clusters of certain types of rights in the sanctioned concept of property rights. But I am at a loss to formulate this more precisely, meaningfully, and fruitfully. Except for rare studies like those of Glanville Williams on the development of the laws of trespass and the two-volume work of Maitland and Pollack on the development of law (and property rights) in the 12th through 14th centuries, I suspect our main alternative is to initiate studies of our own.[3] For example, a study of the property rights in Ireland during the past three hundred years and of

[2] "The Problem of Social Costs," *Journal of Law and Economics* (1960): 1–5.

[3] Frederick Pollock and Frederic Maitland, *The History of English Law Before the Time of Edward I*, 2nd ed. (Cambridge, 1952); Glanville Williams, *Liability for Animals* (Cambridge: Cambridge University Press, 1939).

water law in the United States may (and I believe, will) enable us to discover more rigorous formulation of the laws of development of property law.

5. SHARING PROPERTY RIGHTS

At this point there is a temptation to start classifying various partitioning of property rights, e.g., private, public, bailments, easements, leases, licenses, franchises, inheritances, etc. This temptation is easy to avoid, because the task is so difficult. Another temptation is to list the various ways in which property rights of owners—ownership rights, as they are called hereafter—whatever they may be, can be shared among people as joint owners or as a partnership. Or corporations can be created as a means of sharing property rights of owners among voluntary sharers. Or public property may amount to everyone having a share—although, as we shall see, I think this is not the crucial difference between public and private ownership.

The ability of individuals to enter into mutually agreeable sharing of the rights they possess is evident from the tremendous variety of such arrangements, e.g., corporations, partnerships, nonprofit corporations, licenses, bailments, nonvoting common stock, trusts, agencies, employee-employer relationships, and marriages.

Should we be surprised that the government refuses to enforce some voluntary proposed sharing of legitimate property rights among owners? Presumably the ''undesirable'' effects justify the refusal to sanction some of the ownership sharing. For example, at one time, the state refused to enforce corporate ownership—even though all the members of the corporation entered voluntarily. Will it enforce every voluntary sharing and partitioning of ownership rights among individuals?

The variety of joint sharing of property and ownership rights is a testimony to man's ingenuity. But if one asked what the difference was between any two of them, say public and private ownership, he would find the answer not so easy. In one sense it is adequate to say that the public is the owner as contrasted to a private group. But that is not very helpful if one is interested in discovering what difference it makes for behavior and use of resources. Compare a privately owned golf course with a publicly owned course (or auditorium, bus service, water service, garbage collection, airport, school, or even spaghetti factory). There are differences in the way they are operated; at least anyone who has ever compared them will think so. Why do these differences occur? Are the objectives different? Is it because the kind of people who operate one are different from those who operate the other? Is it because of the form of ownership?

I believe (on the basis of something more than casual observation) that behavior under each institution is different, not because the objectives sought by organizations under each form are different, but, instead, because even with the same explicit organization goals, the costs-rewards system impinging on the employees and the "owners" of the organization are different. And I suspect that these differences are implied by economic theory, if the trouble is taken to apply the theory. Further, preliminary speculation suggests, for example, that the difference between a privately owned corporation with 1,000 owners and a state-owned entity in a democracy with 1,000 citizens is quite significant, because the 1,000 individuals are furthering their own individual interests in each entity under two different systems of property rights, i.e., the rewards-costs schedules differ.

6. PRIVATE AND PUBLIC OWNERSHIP

How do private and public ownership rights differ? To sharpen the issue, consider a small-town theater owned by 1,000 corporate shareholders (each with one share) and an auditorium owned by the 1,000 residents as public property. This eliminates the difference of sharing and differences in the number of joint "owners." Every activity conducted at one could, in principle, just as well be held at the other building. Assume also, the city auditorium is operated to make money, not to subsidize some group, and so is the private theater.

The public auditorium and the private theater both serve the public. It is not the case that the former is designed to provide a public service and the latter not. The privately owned theater will survive only if it can provide services that the public wants at the price asked. It is a source of public service, even though its purpose from the owners' point of view is to make money. But what about the publicly owned auditorium? Is its end that of public service or to make money for the public owners? Suppose its end is public service. This does not *require* that its means of action be any different than if its ends were profits to the owners—public or private. Furthermore, assume in both cases the managers and employees were induced to take their jobs only because the salary enhances their own wealth or well-being. They take the jobs—not because they want to provide a public service or wealth for the owners; but instead because they want a better living for themselves. We can assume that those resident citizens who "own" the auditorium and voted for it did so because each felt it would make his own situation preferable—not because he wanted to benefit someone else as a charity device.

But there are differences, and we conjecture the proposition that the differences between public and private ownership arise from *the inability of a public owner to sell his share of public ownership* (and the ability to acquire a share without a purchase of the right). But let us be clear about this. We are not yet asserting that there are no other differences, nor that this difference has not been noticed before. Instead we are emphasizing the *unique* importance of this difference in the ownership rights.

We are not begging the issue by assuming away one general difference—the profit incentive or criterion. Both public and private property can seek profits. The desire to avoid or suppress the effects of the profit-making incentive is, however, often the reason society resorts to public ownership. However, the objectives sought by public ownership cannot merely be announced to the managers or operators with expectation that exhortation will be either sufficient or necessary to achieve the objective. Since our general postulate is that people, as individuals, seek to increase their utility and that wealth is a source of utility, we cannot expect people to change their goals or desires. Instead, we rely upon changes in the rewards-costs structure to redirect their activities as they seek to increase their utility or level of satisfaction of their desires.[4] And we shall try to show that many differences, that do exist between behavior in public and privately owned institutions, reflect this ownership difference—viz., the presence or the absence of the right to sell a share of ownership to someone else.

The difference can be put somewhat less euphemistically.

[4] Friends of Adam Smith will recognize this as the major postulate of his *Wealth of Nations*, a postulate which seems to have served economists well when not forgotten.

Public ownership *must* be borne by all members of the public, and no member can divest himself of that ownership. Ownership of public property is not voluntary; it is compulsory as long as one is a member of the public. To call something "compulsory" usually is a good start towards condemning it.

A person must move from one town to another to change his ownership in public property. In one sense it is not compulsory because it is not compulsory that one lives in a particular community. But so long as one does live in any community with public property he is a public owner and cannot divest himself of public ownership; but he can sell and shift private property ownership rights without also having to leave the community.

It is tempting to emphasize the possibility, under public ownership, of someone joining the community and thereby acquiring a share of public ownership, without payment to any of the existing owners. This dilution of a person's share of ownership is presumably absent in private ownership. In fact, a community could close off immigration; but public ownership would continue even if this dilution effect were an important problem. Furthermore, many corporations issue new shares without preemptive rights to former owners. Presumably this is done only when the receiver of the new shares pays the corporation something of at least equivalent value. And it is a safe assumption that the management deems the *quid pro quo* to have been worthwhile so far as present purposes are concerned. Still, it is sufficient that even if dilution of public ownership were eliminated by restriction of entry, the inability to sell one's share of public ownership remains a potent factor in the costs-reward system impinging on all members of the public and on the employees and administrators of the publicly owned institution.

7. SOME IMPLICATIONS OF TRANSFERABILITY

To see what difference is made by the right to transfer ownership shares, suppose public ownership could be sold. It would be possible for me to sell to someone else my share in the publicly owned water, or bus or garbage, or parks, or school system. To separate out the fact that public ventures are usually run without the intent of making a profit, let us suppose that the water or bus system had been instructed to be as profitable as it could. Now that its ownership has become salable, with capitalized profits or losses accruing to the owners, will incentives be any different?

The answer is suggested by two implications of the specialization of "ownership" which is similar to the familiar specialization of other kinds of skills or activities. The two derivative implications are: (1) concentration of rewards and costs *more* directly on each person responsible for them, and (2) comparative advantage effects of specialized applications of (a) knowledge in control and (b) of risk bearing.

Degree of Dependency. The greater concentration of rewards and costs means simply that each person's wealth is more dependent upon his own activities. This is brought about as follows: the more he concentrates his wealth holding in particular resources, the more will his wealth respond to his own activities in those areas. Consider the following example: Suppose there are 100 people in a community, with 10 separate enterprises. Suppose that each person, by devoting one tenth of his time to some one enterprise as an owner, could produce a saving or gain of $1,000. Since the individual is a 1/100 part owner he will acquire $10. Suppose, further, that he does this for each of the 10 different enterprises, in each of which he owns 1/100 part. His total wealth gain will be $100, with the rest of the product, $9,900, going to the 99 other people. If the 99 other people act in the same way, he will get from their activities an increase of wealth of $990,000/100=$9,900, which gives him a total of $10,000. This is exactly equal to his product most of which was spread over the other owners.

However, if everyone each owns 1/10 part of *one* enterprise only (which means that ownership has been reshuffled from pro rata equal shares in all enterprises to a concentration in one enterprise by each person, although with the same total number of enterprises), the individual will now be assumed to devote his whole time during one year to the one enterprise, so he again produces $10,000. (We assume that his productivity is proportional to the number of hours of work, and that it is the same for everyone. Other assumptions will change the arithmetic, but will not destroy the main principle being elaborated.) Of this he gets $1,000. The remainder, $9,000, goes to the owners of the other 9/10 share. Like them, he too receives portions of the other owners' products, and if all are assumed to be exactly alike, then he gets from the 9 other joint owners of his enterprise $9,000 for a total of $10,000—precisely the same as in the preceding example. The difference is that now $1,000 of this is dependent upon his own activities whereas formerly only $100 was. Or more pertinently, the amount dependent upon the activities of other people is reduced from $9,900 to $9,000.

If we go to the extreme where the 10 enterprises are divided into 100, with each person as the sole owner of one enterprise, then all $10,000 of his year's wealth increase will depend upon his own activities. The first of these three examples corresponds to public ownership, the second to corporate joint private ownership, and the third to sole proprietorship.

If public ownership rights were made salable, they would in effect become private ownership rights and there would be a movement toward concentration of ownership of the type in the second example, at least. Why? In the second case, the wealth a person can get is more dependent upon his own activities than in the first case. Many people may prefer to let the situation stay as in example 1, hoping to collect a major portion of their wealth gain from other people's activities. If this were the case, the total wealth gain would decrease since everyone would have less incentive to work. But it suffices that there be at least one person who prefers to make himself less dependent upon other people's activities than in example 1 and who prefers at least some more wealth to some more leisure. He will then be prepared to buy up some ownership rights and pay a higher price for them than they are worth to some other people. That he values them more highly is precisely another way of saying that he values independence more than they do, or that he prefers more wealth to less wealth—even if it requires some work by him.

Comparative Advantage in Ownership: Control. The preceding example did not involve interpersonal differences of abilities, knowledge, or attitude toward risk. But if people differ in any of these respects, as they in fact do, it can be shown that specialization in various tasks—including that of owning a business—will increase wealth. This demonstration is simply the logical theorem of gains from comparative advantage, which we shall not explain here.

Usually the illustrations of comparative advantage are based on "labor" productivities with no reference to "ownership" productivities. But people differ in their talents as owners. Owners bear the risk of value changes, make the decisions of how much to produce, how much to invest, and how it shall be produced and who shall be employed as laborers and managers. Ownership ability includes attitude toward risk bearing, knowledge of different people's productive abilities, foresight and, of course, "judgment." These talents differ among people according to the particular industry, type of product, or productive resource one is considering. The differences in skills of people as owners make pertinent the principle of comparative advantage through specialization in ownership. If ownership rights are transferable, then specialization of ownership will yield gains. People will concentrate their ownership in those areas in which they believe they have a comparative advantage, if they want to increase their wealth. Just as specialization in typing, music, or various types of labor is more productive, so is specialization in ownership. Some people specialize in electronics industry knowledge, some in airlines, some in dairies, some in retailing, etc. Private property owners can specialize in knowledge about electronics, devoting much of their effort and study to learning which electronic devices show promise, which are now most efficient in various uses, which should be produced in larger numbers, where investment should take place, what kinds of research and development to finance, etc. But public ownership practically eliminates possibilities of specialization among owners—though not of employees in the publicly owned venture.

A person who is very knowledgeable about woodworking and cabinet or furniture building would have an advantage as an owner of a furniture company. He would, by being a stockholder, not necessarily make the company any better, but instead he would choose the better company—as judged by his knowledge—as one in which to own shares. The relative rise in the price of such companies enables the existing owners to issue new shares, borrow money more readily, and retain control. In this way the differences in knowledge enable people to specialize in the application of that knowledge to the management and operation of the company—albeit sometimes by indirect lines.

Comparative Advantage in Ownership: Risk Bearing. A second aspect of ownership specialization is risk bearing. People's attitudes toward risk differ. If various ventures or resources represent different prospects of values, then exchange of ownership will enable a reallocation of risks among people, leading to greater utility in the same sense that exchange of goods does. This risk-bearing difference reflects not only attitudes toward risk but beliefs about the prospects of future values of the assets whose ownership can be transferred. Differences in "knowledge" can be used not only in an effort to be more productive but also as a means for distinguishing different risk situations. For example, I may be the top administrator of the Carnation Milk Company, but I may choose to hold stocks in some electronic company because I prefer the risk pattern provided by that stock to that provided by ownership in Carnation. In this way a person can separate the productivity of knowledge and effort in what he owns from the risk bearing. He can, if he wants, combine them by holding stock in a company in which he is active. This possibility of separating the *control* (effective administration or operation of the company—an activity which rewards comparative superiority in ability and knowledge) from *risk bearing* is, of course, regarded as an advantage by those who act as employed managers or administrators, and by those who choose to act as corporate stock owners without also bothering to exercise their vote or worry about control. Yet, it is often criticized as undesirable.

Not all of the owners have to think of themselves as owners who are going to exercise their voting rights so effectively as to exert an influence on management. Most of the owners may go along simply because they believe the prospects for profits and losses are sufficiently promising relative to other assets they could own. If losses eventuate, their only alternative is to sell out. To whom? To other buyers who, because of the reduced profit prospects, will offer only a lower price. These "nonactive" owners perform a very important function in that they provide the willingness to bear some of the value consequences, at least. So long as scarce resources *exist*, value changes will occur. The question left is then which particular members are to bear the reduced value. Someone has to bear them. Those changes cannot be eliminated.

Often it is said that joint ownership in the modern corporation has separated ownership and control. What this means is that risk bearing and management are more separate. This is correct in that each owner does not have the kind of control he would as the sole owner. But it is a long logical leap to decrying this. It can be a good thing. Specialization in risk bearing and in management or decision-making about particular uses of resources is now possible. Complete separation does not exist for every joint owner, for to the extent that some share owners are inactive or indifferent to alternative choices or management problems, other stockholders (joint owners) will be more influential. In effect, the "passive" owners are betting on the decisions of "active" owners; "betting" in the sense that they are prepared to pay other people for any losses produced by these "activists" and in turn collect the profits, if any. In the absence of any right to buy and sell shared ownership rights voluntarily everyone would have to bet on the activists as a group (the case of public property). The right to sell concentrates this betting on these who are prepared to pay the most (or demand the least) for the right to do so. And it concentrates the control or management with those who believe they are relatively most able at that task—and these beliefs can be tested with the less able being eliminated more surely in private ownership than in public because (1) the evidence of poor management and the opportunity to capture wealth gains by eliminating it is revealed to outsiders by the lower selling price of the ownership rights, (2) the specialization of ownership functions is facilitated, and (3) the possibility of concentrating one's wealth in certain areas permits greater correlation of personal interest and effort in line with wealth holdings.

We conjecture from the preceding discussion the theorem: *Under public ownership the costs of any decision or choice are less fully thrust upon the selector than under private property*. In other words, the cost-benefit incentives system is changed toward lower costs. The converse of this implication is that the gains to any owner resulting from any cost-saving action are less fully effective. These do not mean that the true costs are reduced. The looser correlation between the costs borne by any chooser and the costs of the particular choices he makes is what is implied. Similarly, the capturable gains to the owners of their actions are reduced.

They are *less* fully borne than they would be if the same action were taken in a private property institution, with a similar number of owners.[5] From this theorem one would expect that public agencies would, in order to offset or counterbalance this reduced cost bearing, impose special extra costs or constraints on public employees or agents. Public agents who

[5] In other words, this difference between public and private ownership does not flow from differences in numbers of owners.

are authorized to spend public funds should be more severely constrained with extra restrictions precisely because the costs of their actions are less effectively thrust upon them. And of course these extra constraints do exist. Because of these extra constraints—or because of the "costs" of them—the public arrangement becomes a higher cost (in the sense of "less efficient") than that for private property agencies.

For example, civil service, nepotism restrictions, tenure, single-salary structures for public schoolteachers, sealed bids, and "lineitem" budget controls, to name a few, are some of the costly devices used.

But it is not easy—indeed impossible—in many instances to impose "corrective" costs as offsets. How would one impose full costs upon a city manager who decided to have a garbage collection system (that turned out to be a big money loser) that the city would tolerate? By not reelecting him. But this cost is less than that borne by the private owner who decides (erroneously) to start a garbage collection system. He loses his job *and* the sunk costs. Similarly, how do we make a voter bear the costs of bad judgment in his votes? Are the prospects of costs that may be imposed on a voter equivalent to the cost-prospects that will be laid on a private owner (with share rights) voting in a private corporation? Not according to the theorem derived from our analysis.

I should, I suppose, avow at random intervals that all this is not a condemnation of public ownership any more than certain "deficiencies" of marriage, the human eye, the upright position of the human being, or smoking are to be regarded as condemnations of marriage, eyes, walking on two feet, or smoking. The "lesser" evils in some institutions—and they exist in all—are borne for the greater good in some of them. We are not arguing that private property even in its purest form is perfect in the cost-bearing sense. No standard of perfection is available. All of our statements have been comparative in degrees of cost bearing.

The converse of this "apologia" is that one should not speak of the imperfections of the marketplace, either. Nor should one assume in those instances where the marketplace is inferior in certain respects to, say, public ownership or government control, that we ought to switch from the private property market to the government. The presence of one kind of relative deficiency does not justify a switch to another agency—which has other kinds of deficiencies.

8. WE SUMMARIZE

As we suggested earlier, public and private ownership are used for different purposes, and in some cases *because* of these different behavioral implications. If public ownership in some government activity were converted to private property, the method of achieving the government objectives would be changed. If city and national parks, or golf courses owned by cities were converted to private property, they would no longer be operated as subsidies for certain groups. If the fire and police department rights were converted to private property rights, vast changes would occur in their operation. And the same goes for the postal system, the garbage collection system, the bus lines, streets, the federal mortgage insurance companies, and the army, the navy, and the air force. When "we" do not want (whatever that means) these changes to occur, these activities are conducted via public ownership instead of privately. And if the effects of greater dependence of benefits and costs on one's own actions are not wanted, resort is made to government activity. Which is not to say that government activity is therefore for that reason good or bad. The extent to which "society" reduces risks that must be individually borne and instead has them borne by society at large—thus reducing the correlation between choice of action and consequences for people as individuals—the greater is the extent of public property. How much this depends upon a *choice* to socialize certain risks, and how much reflects the voting and decision-making *process* are questions I cannot answer.

[3]

THE ETHICS OF COMPETITION

SUMMARY

The central position of the value problem in economic policy. — The necessity of formulating ideals, of an "absolute ethics," 583. — Outline of article, 584. — I. Contrast between theory and practice of laissez-faire individualism, (*a*) in its value scale and organization of resources to produce values; (*b*) in its distribution of produce, 587.— II. Business as a game, 601. — The problem of a standard for judging games, 607. — Elements of a game: ability, effort and luck, 609. — Criticism of the business game, 609. — III. Competition as a motive, 612. — It is efficient as an incentive in getting things done, 614. — The question of what things; ethical *vs.* economic view of life, 614. — Contrast of emulation with pagan ideal of perfection, 619. — With Christian ideal of spirituality, 620.

IN an earlier paper [1] the writer undertook to argue against the view of ethics most commonly accepted among economists. The argument was not directed against hedonism as such, but against "scientific" ethics of any kind, against any view which sets out from the assumption that human wants are objective and measurable magnitudes and that the satisfaction of such wants is the essence and criterion of value, and which proceeds on the basis of this assumption to reduce ethics to a sort of glorified economics. It was pointed out that any such view consistently reduces the "higher" wants to a secondary position as compared with "lower," and interprets human life in biological terms. But the fact is that human beings do not regularly prefer their lower and more "necessary" needs to those not easily justified in terms of subsistence or survival value, but perhaps rather the contrary; in any case what we call progress has consisted largely in increasing the proportion of want-gratification of an esthetic or spiritual as com-

1. Quarterly Journal of Economics, May, 1922.

pared to that of a biologically utilitarian character, rather than in increasing the "quantity of life." The facts, as emphasized, are altogether against accepting any balance-sheet view of life; they point rather toward an evaluation of a far subtler sort than the addition and subtraction of homogeneous items, toward an ethics along the line of esthetic criticism, whose canons are of another sort than scientific laws and are not quite intellectually satisfying. We cannot accept want-satisfaction as a final criterion of value because we do not in fact regard our wants as final; instead of resting in the view that there is no disputing about tastes, we dispute about them more than anything else; our most difficult problem in valuation is the evaluation of our wants themselves and our most troublesome want is the desire for wants of the "right" kind.

The purpose of the present paper is to develop and supplement the argument already given, first by re-emphasizing the necessity of a defensible criterion of values as a basis for passing judgment on questions of policy; and secondly by inquiring into the standards of value implicit in the laissez-faire or individualistic social philosophy and raising certain questions in regard to them. On the first head, fortunately, we can be brief. It is a thesis which calls for no elaborate demonstration that social policy must be based upon social ideals. An organized system must operate in accordance with a *social* standard. This standard will of course be related in some way to the values of the individuals making up the society, but it cannot be merely identical with them; it presupposes some process of organizing the various individual interests, weighing them against each other and adjudicating conflicts among them.

It is impossible to form any concept of "social efficiency" in the absence of some general measure of value. Even in physics and engineering, "efficiency" is strictly a value category; there is no such thing as mechanical efficiency. It follows from the fundamental laws of the indestructibility of matter and of energy that whatever goes into any apparatus or process comes out *in some form*. In purely mechanical terms, all efficiencies would be equal to one hundred per cent. The efficiency of any machine means the ratio between the *useful* output and the total output. In simple cases the distinction between useful and useless may be so sharp and clear as to give rise to no discussion — as in the case of the mechanical energy and the heat generated by an electric motor. But when more than one form of useful output (or costly input) is involved, the necessity arises for having a measure of usefulness, of value, before efficiency can be discussed. The efficiency relations of a steam engine may be much changed when the exhaust steam is applied to heating. In so complicated a problem as that of social efficiency, where the elements of outlay and of return are both infinitely numerous and diverse, it is no wonder that the process of valuation has become the heart and core of the study. It must ultimately be recognized that only within rather narrow limits can human conduct be interpreted as the creation of values of such definiteness and stability that they can serve as scientific data, that life is fundamentally an exploration in the field of values itself and not a mere matter of producing given values. When this is clearly seen, it will be apparent why so much discussion of social efficiency has been so futile.

Perception of these obvious fundamental principles at once cuts the ground from under one of the lines of criticism of the economic order which has attracted wide attention. It is an idea sponsored especially by Dr. Thorstein Veblen and copied by others, that there is some distinction between "pecuniary" and "industrial" employments [1] and that society ought to take the control of industry out of the hands of "financiers" and put it into the hands of "technicians." [2]

This notion rests on the same obvious fallacy, the idea that society has a choice between producing more goods and producing more value, and that it is the part of wisdom to prefer the former. It is difficult to take either part of the proposition seriously. The quantity of goods, if there is more than one kind, must so obviously be measured in value units. The proposal of leaving it to technicians in the respective fields to say how much social productive power shall be expended in each is merely grotesque; military experts would use it all for the army and navy, the medical men could usefully employ it all, and more, for health, and so on. There is no more important function of a first course in economics than to make the student see that the whole problem of social management is a *value* problem; that mechanical or technical efficiency is a meaningless combination of words.

Indeed there can be no question, as the course of the argument will show, that the valid criticisms of the existing economic order relate chiefly to its value standards, and relatively much less to its efficiency in the creation of such values as it recognizes. We shall furthermore insist that not merely a measure of value but ideals of value are prerequisite to any intelligent criticism of social processes or results. This is not, like the proposition regarding efficiency, a self-evident truth. It is quite arguable that the determination or criticism of policy involves only a comparison of alternative possibilities and a choice of that which is considered pref-

1. Publ. Amer. Econ. Assoc., 3d ser., vol. ii, 1901.

2. The Vested Interest and the State of the Industrial Arts, pp. 63, 89, 99.

erable. It is arguable, and the contention is in fact often put forward, that values are purely relative, that it means nothing to say that anything is good or bad except in comparison with a worse or better alternative. It is a practical question: does the judging faculty actually work by reasoning out alternatives and deciding which is preferable, or does it not rather formulate ideals and compare actuality and potentiality with these, and with each other indirectly, by so comparing them with an ideal? No doubt both methods are used, and are useful; but we contend that in regard to the larger and higher questions, the ultimate problems of moral and social life, the formulation of ideals is a necessary step. There is a place, and a vital place, for an "absolute" science of ethics. Its dicta will not be really absolute, for they never cut loose entirely from the real world and its possibilities of growth and transformation, and they will always grow and change. But at least they are not "merely" relative; they must be beyond the immediately attainable, and will often lie in the field of the actually impossible, patterns to be approached rather than objectives to be achieved.

We contend not merely that such ideals are real to individuals, but that they are a part of our culture and are sufficiently uniform and objective to form a useful standard of comparison for a given country at a given time. Normal common sense does judge in terms of ideals, of absolute ethics in the sense indicated, and not merely in terms of the best that can be done; else it would be linguistically equivalent to call a situation hopeless and to call it ideal, which is clearly not in accordance with usage. In what follows we shall appeal to what we submit to be the common-sense ideals of absolute ethics in modern Christendom. No pretense will be made of drawing up a code of such principles;

they are frequently not of a character to fall readily into propositions. There will be no attempt to "settle" moral questions or set up standards, but only to bring out the standards actually involved in making some familiar moral judgments in regard to the economic system, and to examine them critically. The argument will therefore be negative in tone, and the need for brevity may occasionally give it something of the flavor of an "attack"; but let it be stated here that we are not advocating or proposing change. The question of *policy* is a question of alternatives, a purely relative matter; we are concerned here with the question of *ideals*, which we assume may be carried further, into the realm of considerations at least "relatively" absolute. Even if the competitive system is better than any available substitute, a clear view of its shortcomings in comparison with conceivable ideals must be of the highest value in making it better than it is.

An examination of the competitive economic order from the standpoint of its ethical standards will fall naturally into three parts. In the first place, the contention already put forward, that wants are not ultimate data or to be identified with values, does not mean that they are not real and important. We can never get entirely away even from physical needs, requirements for life, for health and for comfort, small as such motives really bulk in civilized behavior. Moreover, at any given time and place the existing stage of culture sets minimum requirements which are imperative in character. It is true within limits that the purpose of economic activity is to satisfy wants, and the fact raises a group of questions for consideration in an appraisal of any system of economic organization. We must inquire first into its value standards, in the economic or quasi-mechanical sense, its manner of dealing with wants as they exist, its mechanism for comparing and equating and perhaps selecting among the various wants of the various persons and classes of persons which make up the society. It is hardly necessary to remark that the questions *which* wants and *whose* wants are to be satisfied are in fact closely bound up together. The system's answer to this two-fold question constitutes its social economic value scale; and very different social value scales may be formed from the same set of individual wants by different methods of selection, equation, and combination. The more distinctly ethical aspect of this issue is of course the old problem of social justice, relating to the system's treatment of the wants of persons and classes; but that is by no means separable from the question of ranking different wants of the same person. A second inquiry under the same head, of a more mechanical sort but still distinctly a problem of values, deals with the *efficiency* of the system in using its available resources in creating the values which it recognizes, that is, in producing the largest quantity of "goods" as measured by the standard which it sets up.

Another question, ethically more fundamental than these but inseparable from them, and one which must be considered in the first section of the inquiry, follows directly from recognizing the provisional character of wants and the obvious fact that the wants which an economic system operates to gratify are largely produced by the workings of the system itself. In organizing its value scale, the economic order does far more than select and compare wants for exchangeable goods and services: its activity extends to the formation and radical transformation, if not to the outright creation, of the wants themselves; they as well as the means of their gratification are largely products of the system.

An examination of the ethics of the economic system must consider the question of the kind of wants which it tends to generate or nourish as well as its treatment of wants as they exist at any given time.

The second of the three main standpoints to be considered corresponds to an aspect of economic life which is rapidly securing more adequate recognition among economists, the fact that the motive of business is to such a large extent that of emulation as such. Industry and trade is a competitive game, in which men engage in part from the same motives as in other games or sports. This is not a matter of want-satisfaction in any direct or economic sense; the "rewards" of successful participation in the game are not wanted for any satisfying power dependent on any quality which they possess as things, but simply as insignia of success in the game, like the ribbons, medals, and the like which are conferred in other sorts of contests. Our second main task will therefore be to raise the question, *what kind of game* is business? Is there anything to be said about games from an ethical point of view, any basis for judging them or ranking them as games, and if so, is business a relatively good, bad, or indifferent game?

The third division of the paper will deal briefly with the more fundamental aspects of the problem of values from the standpoint of absolute ethics. Economic activity is a large part of life, and perhaps tends to grow in relative magnitude. The issue as to the influence of the economic system on character can be treated only superficially, but should at least be raised. Emphasis will be placed on the particular phase of competitive emulation as a motive and of success in a contest as an ethical value. The competitive economic order must be partly responsible for making emulation and rivalry the outstanding quality in the character of the Western peoples who have adopted and developed it. The modern idea of enjoyment as well as of achievement has come to consist chiefly in keeping up with or getting ahead of other people in a rivalry for things about whose significance, beyond furnishing objectives for the competition itself, little question is asked. It is surely one function of ethical discussion to keep the world reminded that this is not the only possible conception of value and to point out its contrast with the religious ideals to which the Western world has continued to render lip-service — a contrast resulting in fundamental dualism in our thought and culture.

Throughout the discussion it will be necessary to keep in mind the close inter-connection among these several aspects of the economic system. Economic activity is *at the same time* a means of want-satisfaction, an agency for want- and character-formation, a field of creative self-expression, and a competitive sport. While men are "playing the game" of business, they are also molding their own and other personalities, and creating a civilization whose worthiness to endure cannot be a matter of indifference.

I

Discussion of the merits of free competition, or "laissez-faire," takes on an especial interest in view of the contrast between the enticing plausibility of the case for the "obvious and simple system of natural liberty," and the notoriously disappointing character of the results which it has tended to bring about in practice.[1] In

1. It should be stated that for simplicity we shall speak of "the" competitive system, tho the discussion relates to a "purely" competitive system, as understood by the economic theorist. It is superfluous to remark that such a system has never been closely approximated in reality, or perhaps advocated by any writer taken seriously by any large group — certainly it was not advocated by Adam Smith. The idea of a purely individualistic order is a logical device, necessary to separate for study the tendencies of individualism from those of socialism. It would go a long way toward clarifying discussion if it were generally recognized on both sides that there are no one-hundred-per-cent individualists and no one-hundred-per-cent socialists; that the issue is one of degree and proportion.

the later eighteenth and early nineteenth centuries, under the influence of the "classical economists," of the Manchester liberals, of the political pressure of the rising bourgeoisie and the general force of circumstances, rapid progress was made toward the establishment of individual liberty in economic affairs. But long before complete individualism was closely approached its consequences were recognized to be intolerable, and there set in that counter-movement toward social interference and control which has been going on at an accelerating pace ever since. The argument for individualism, as developed by its advocates from Adam Smith down, may be summarized in a sentence as follows: a freely competitive organization of society tends to place every productive resource in that position in the productive system where it can make the greatest possible addition to the total social dividend as measured in price terms, and tends to reward every participant in production by giving it the increase in the social dividend which its coöperation makes possible. In the writer's opinion such a proposition is entirely sound; but it is not a statement of a sound ethical social ideal, the specification for a utopia. Discussion of the issue between individual freedom and socialization, however, has largely centered around the truth of the proposition as a statement of the tendencies of competition, rather than around its ethical significance if true. Those who do not like the actual tendencies of the system as they appear to work out when it is tried — and that is virtually everybody — attack the scientific analysis. We propose to argue in the first place that the conditions of life do not admit of an approximation to individualism of the sort necessarily assumed by the theory, and secondly that there are in the conditions of actual life no ethical implications of the kind commonly taken for granted as involved in individualism in so far as it is possible of realization.

The careful statement of the meaning of individualism falls within the province of the economic theorist rather than that of the ethical critic. It is an accident of the way in which economic science has developed, and especially of the peculiar relation between science and practice in this field, that so little serious effort has been made to state with rigor and exactitude the assumptions involved in the notion of perfect competition, the premises of pure economics. Literary writers on economics have been interested in administrative problems, for which the results of any exact treatment of principles are too abstract to be of direct application, and have not generally been trained to use or appreciate rigorous methods. The mathematical economists have commonly been mathematicians first and economists afterward, disposed to oversimplify the data and underestimate the divergence between their premises and the facts of life. In consequence they have not been successful in getting their presentation into such a form that it could be understood, and its relation to real problems recognized, by practical economists. The critical reader of general economic literature must be struck by the absence of any attempt accurately to define that competition which is the principal subject under discussion. A clear formulation of the postulates of theoretical individualism will bring out the contrast with practical laissez-faire, and will go far to discredit the latter as a policy. In the present paper the attempt to state the presuppositions of a competitive system cannot be carried beyond a bare outline; it will be developed with reference to our special purpose of showing that in the conditions of real life no possible social order based upon a laissez-faire policy can justify the familiar ethical conclusions of apologetic economics.

1. In the first place, an individualistic competitive system must be made up of freely contracting individuals. As a matter of fact, a rather small fraction of the population of any modern nation enter into contracts on their own responsibility. Our "individualism" is really "familism"; all minors, the aged, and numerous persons in other classes, including for practical purposes the majority of adult women, have their status-determining bargains made for them by other persons. The family is still the unit in production and consumption. It is hardly necessary to point out that all arguments for free contract are nullified or actually reversed whenever one person contracts on behalf of another.

2. Moreover, the freest individual, the unencumbered male in the prime of life, is in no real sense an ultimate unit or social datum. He is in large measure a product of the economic system, which is a fundamental part of the cultural environment that has formed his desires and needs, given him whatever marketable productive capacities he has, and which largely controls his opportunities. Social organization through free contract implies that the contracting units know what they want and are guided by their desires, that is, that they are "perfectly rational," which would be equivalent to saying that they are accurate mechanisms of desire-satisfaction. In fact, human activity is largely impulsive, a relatively unthinking and undetermined response to stimulus and suggestion. Moreover, there is truth in the allegation that unregulated competition places a premium on deceit and corruption. In any case, where the family is the social unit, the inheritance of wealth, culture, educational advantages, and economic opportunities must tend toward the progressive increase of inequality, with bad results for personality at both ends of the scale. It is plainly contrary to fact to treat the

individual as a *datum*, and it must be conceded that the lines along which a competitive economic order tends to form character are often far from being ethically ideal.

3. It is universally recognized that effective competition calls for "fluidity," the perfect divisibility and mobility of all goods and services entering into exchange. The limited extent to which this assumption fits the facts of life sets limits to the "tendency" of actual competition, which in many cases nullify the principle. Here, as in the case of other assumptions, it is illegitimate to draw practical conclusions from a "tendency," however real, without taking account of contradictory tendencies also, and getting the facts as to their relative strength. One of the dangers of reasoning from simplified premises is the likelihood that the abstracted factors may be overlooked in drawing conclusions and formulating policies based thereon.

4. One of the most important prerequisites to perfect competition is complete knowledge on the part of every competing individual of the exchange opportunities open to him. A "perfect market" would involve perfect, instantaneous and costless intercommunication among all the traders. This condition is really approximated quite closely in the case of a few commodities dealt in on the organized exchanges; but the market for most consumption goods is very crude in its workings. As regards the productive services, abstract pecuniary capital does indeed flow through a highly developed market; but the market for labor, land, and real capital, and their uses, leaves wide margins for "bargaining power" and accidental aberrations. Both the organization of production and the distribution of the product diverge correspondingly from the theoretically ideal results.

5. Competition further requires that every actual or

potential buyer of every salable good or service shall know accurately its properties and powers to satisfy his wants. In the case of productive goods this means knowledge of their technical significance. In an industrial civilization as complex as that of the modern world it is clear that the divergences from this "tendency" must often be more important than the tendency. Indirect knowledge is available to offset direct ignorance in many subtle ways, and yet no individual can know enough to act very closely according to the ideal of perfect intelligence. Moreover, perfect competition does not stop at requiring knowledge of things as they are; the competitor must foresee them as they will be, often a very considerable distance in the future, and the limitations of foreknowledge are of course more sweeping than those of knowledge.

6. The results of intelligent action are the purposes to which it is directed, and will be ethically ideal only if these ends are true values. Under individualism this means that the wants of individuals must be ideal, as well as their knowledge perfect. We have commented enough on the fact that the social order largely forms as well as gratifies the wants of its members, and the natural consequence that it must be judged ethically rather by the wants which it generates, the type of character which it forms in its people, than by its efficiency in satisfying wants as they exist at any given time.[5]

5. On the character of wants, see an article by A. F. McGoun in this Journal for February, 1923. Professor McGoun appears to intend his argument in part as a criticism of my former paper already referred to; but as he begins by drawing curves to represent want-variations, whereas my main contention was that wants are not the sort of variable that can be adequately represented by curves, it would take too much space to bring the argument to a clear issue. I should not question that the observations made in his paper have great value.

Very wise and penetrating remarks on the character of various wants will be found at many points in Wicksteed's Common Sense of Political Economy. Patrick Geddes's essay on John Ruskin in the Round Table Series is a brilliant argument for the reduction of all economic values to aesthetic standards. The essay on Phases of the Economic Interest, by H. W. Stuart, in the volume on Creative Intelligence, ably emphasizes the explorative, experimental character of much of our activity, in contrast with the static

7. Another sweeping limitation to the actual workings of free competition arises from the fact that men do not have free access to such imperfect markets as exist. No error is more egregious than that of confounding freedom with free competition, as is not infrequently done. As elementary theory itself shows, the numbers of any economic group can always make more by combining than they can by competing. Under freedom all that would stand in the way of a universal drift toward monopoly is the fortunate limitations of human nature, which prevent the necessary organization from being feasible or make its costs larger than the monopoly gains which it might secure. But universal monopoly is self-contradictory, and against any such tendency social action is the only recourse. The workings of competition educate men progressively for monopoly, which is being achieved not merely by the "capitalist" producers of more and more commodities, but by labor in many fields, and in many branches of agriculture, while the producers of even the fundamental crops are already aspiring to the goal.[6]

conception of wants demanded by economic logic. Many of the "higher" wants are keenly satirized in Veblen's Theory of the Leisure Class. A sober discussion of the problems involved, of much greater scientific significance, is found in the later chapters of G. P. Watkins's volume on Welfare as an Economic Quantity.

The activity of business in the way of manufacturing wants has received much attention in the literature of late, again under the leadership of Veblen. It is a serious fallacy to condemn this sort of activity without discrimination. Whether it is good or bad to create wants depends altogether on the character of the wants created. One cannot condemn advertising and salesmanship out of hand, unless one is prepared to repudiate most of education, and of civilization in general; for most of the desires which distinguish man from the brutes are artificially created. Ethically, the creation of the right wants is more important than want-satisfaction. With regard to the facts in the case, we may observe that business is interested in the fact of change in wants more than in the character of the change, and presumably effects chiefly those changes which can be brought about most easily and cheaply. Our general moral teaching would indicate that it is easier to corrupt human nature than to improve it, and observation of the taste-forming tendencies of modern marketing methods tends perhaps to confirm the view and to substantiate a negative verdict on individualistic activity of this sort.

6. The resemblance of this argument to that of Marx is evident. There seems to be ground for treating Marx's conclusions seriously even tho his supporting logic, based on the alleged universal superiority of large-scale methods of production, must be repudiated.

8. The individualistic competitive organization of want-satisfying activity presupposes that wants and the means of satisfying them are individual, that is, that wants attach to things and services which gratify the wants of the person consuming them without affecting other persons. As a matter of fact, what is desired is more largely a matter of human relations than goods and services as such; we want things because other people have them, or cannot have them, as the case may be. Then, too, the appurtenances of civilized life can be furnished to an individual only by providing them for the community, and we want to live in a civilized community as well as to live in a civilized way ourselves. With rare exceptions exchanges or contracts between individuals affect for good and for ill persons not represented in the bargain itself, and for these the bargain is not "free." Social action is necessary to promote the exchanges which diffuse benefits on others for which the parties cannot collect payment in the market, and to suppress those which diffuse evils for which the contracting parties do not have to pay. A typical illustration is the improvement or use of property in ways which add value to or subtract value from neighboring property. In a developed social order hardly any "free exchange" between individuals is devoid of either good or bad results for outsiders.

9. An exchange system cannot work at all according to "theory" without a scientific unit for measuring values. Society has to take over or carefully control activities which have to do with the circulating medium. With the use of credit highly developed, the control of banking and currency involves a large measure of control over all business, but really free banking would soon reduce all exchange relations to chaos.

10. An economic organization must employ its available productive power in part to provide for current needs of society and in part to provide for future growth. If this second function is to be performed intelligently through individual initiative under competitive organization, each member of the system must make a correct comparison and choice between his own present wants and future social requirements. The weakness of competitive individualism in this field is well recognized, since manifestly progress is essentially a social fact. In an individualistic system provision for progress depends upon the interest of present individuals in future individuals—engendered to an uncertain extent and with uncertain consequences on the form of progress by the family system—or upon their interest in progress itself or some form of it as an ideal value, or upon some accidental connection which makes progress a by-product of activities directed toward other ends. None of these, nor all together, produce results invulnerable to criticism; but the problems of social action in the same field are likewise so difficult and the ideal of progress itself so vague that it is impossible in short compass to say anything of value about the relation of different forms of social organization to the solution of the problem. It is a fact that social interference has gone further in this field than in that of controlling current production and consumption, as witness especially the social provision for education and scientific research.

11. All human planning and execution involve uncertainty, and a rational social order can be realized through individual action only if all persons have a rational attitude toward risk and chance. But the general human attitude is proverbially irrational, and much social limitation of individual freedom is called for.

Not only is it necessary to prohibit gambling, but provision has to be made for placing control of resources and the direction of wealth-production in the hands of persons reasonably fit and competent to take responsibility; and the freedom of these individuals to take chances has to be further restricted by general regulations. Thus no society has in fact ever treated productive resources as private property in any strict sense. It seems likely, however, that a socialistic society would err rather on the side of over-conservatism than on that of recklessness.

12. The last heading in this list of reasons why individualism and competition cannot bring about an ideal utilization of social resources will be the ethics of distribution. In a competitive system distribution is effected by a marketing process, the evaluation of productive services, and is of course subject to all the limitations of marketing in general, as enumerated in the last half-dozen pages. But that is not the main point. It is a common assumption — for which the exponents of the "productivity theory" are partly responsible — that productive contribution is an ethical measure of desert. This has improperly tended to bring the theory itself, as a causal explanation of what happens in distribution, into disrepute; because those who are misled into accepting the standard, but cannot approve of the result realized, react by attacking the theory. An examination of the question will readily show that productive contribution can have little or no ethical significance from the standpoint of absolute ethics. (The question of practicability, it must be kept in mind, is eliminated by the boundaries set for this discussion; we are dealing with ideals and not inquiring whether or in what respects the possibilities of the real world may be harmonious with our moral cravings.)

The examination of productivity as a standard of desert must again be handled in outline.[7]

(*a*) In the first place, as already noted, there is only a "general tendency" to impute to each productive agency its true product. The factor of ignorance is especially important here, since correct imputation would require perfect technological knowledge and foresight. Human beings do not live on averages, and it is only to a very limited extent that a system of free exchange can make it possible for one to live this year on what he may (or may not) earn next year. To a still more limited extent, if at all, can the particular individual whom the tendency passes over live, through free exchange, on the compensating extra share of a more favored person.

(*b*) The tendency to place each productive agency in the position where it will make the greatest contribution is far less effective even than the force which adjusts remuneration to actual contribution. A social system which sets artists to shining shoes and pays them what they are worth in that occupation is no less open to condemnation than one that sets them to work at their art and pays them what they would be worth as bootblacks.

(*c*) The product or contribution is always measured

7. The "specific product" of any agency is what it enables society to produce more than could be produced without it, with no reference to what it could produce by itself. We assume that this is a correct use of the word "product," since it is generally true in cause-and-effect relations that "the cause" is only the deciding factor in the antecedent situation, and that which factor is regarded as deciding is largely a matter of point of view.

We recognize also that specific productivity is the only possible basis for organizing productive resources intelligently, since maximum specific contribution all round is the condition of maximum total product.

It should be kept in mind also that the absolute ethics of distribution are not affected by the fact of organization and the interconnection of the products of different agencies. In a society characterized by individual self-sufficiency, but recognizing the same ethical principles, the obligation of the more efficient or more industrious or more lucky individual who secured a superior share to divide up with others would be as great and as small as it is in a developed system of free enterprise.

in terms of price, which does not correspond closely with ethical value or human significance. The money value of a product is a matter of the "demand," which in turn reflects the tastes and purchasing power of the buying public and the availability of substitute commodities. All these factors are largely created and controlled by the workings of the economic system itself, as already pointed out. Hence their results can have in themselves no ethical significance as standards for judging the system. On the contrary, the system must be judged by the conformity to ethical standards of these facts of demand rather than by the conformity to demand of the actual production and distribution of goods. And the final results diverge notoriously from the ethical standards actually held. No one contends that a bottle of old wine is ethically worth as much as a barrel of flour, or a fantastic evening wrap for some potentate's mistress as much as a substantial dwelling-house, tho such relative prices are not unusual. Ethically, the whole process of valuation is literally a "vicious" circle, since price flows from demand and demand from prices.

(*d*) The income does not go to "factors," but to their owners, and can in no case have more ethical justification than has the fact of ownership. The ownership of personal or material productive capacity is based upon a complex mixture of inheritance, luck, and effort, probably in that order of relative importance. What is the ideal distribution from the standpoint of absolute ethics may be disputed, but of the three considerations named certainly none but the effort can have ethical validity.[8] From the standpoint of absolute ethics most

8. We find a fairly general agreement among serious writers that the principle of *need*, which would practically amount to equal sharing as a general rule, is the ideal basis of distribution. Among authors of general treatises at least the following have so committed themselves: Taylor, Principles of Economics, 8th ed., p. 511; Taussig (with

persons will probably agree that inherited capacity represents an obligation to the world rather than a claim upon it. The significance of luck will be discussed below in connection with the conception of business as a game. We must contend that there is a fallacy in the common position which distinguishes between the ethical significance of the income from labor and that from other factors. Labor in the economic sense may represent either a sacrifice or a source of enjoyment, and the capacity to labor productively derives from the same three sources as property ownership, namely, inheritance, luck, and effort of acquisition, and with no obvious general difference from the case of property in their relative importance.

(*e*) The value of any service or product varies from zero to an indefinite magnitude, according to the demand. It is hard to see that, even when the demand is ethical, possession of the capacity to furnish services which are in demand, rather than other capacities, constitutes an ethical claim to a superior share of the social dividend, except to the extent that the capacity is itself the product of conscientious effort.

(*f*) The value of a productive service varies from zero to indefinite magnitude, according to its scarcity. The most vital ministrations become valueless if offered in superabundance, and the most trivial performance becomes exceedingly valuable if sufficiently unique and rare, as when a human monstrosity satisfies an economic demand by letting people look at him. It is hard to see how it is more meritorious merely to be different from other people than it is to be like them — except again,

a "perhaps"), Principles of Political Economy, 3d ed., vol. ii, p. 475. In an ideal world we may assume that all men would put forth equal effort, so that distribution according to effort would become identical with the ideal. In the present writer's view, effort, — i. e, *conscientious* effort, — is a better principle; it is more in accord with common-sense ideas of desert, which hardly go to the point of treating all men as equally deserving, and is less obviously impossible of practical application.

possibly, if the capacity has been cultivated by an effort which others refused to put forth.

(*g*) Finally, it may be pointed out that modern society does accept and honor the claim of the entirely helpless to a tolerable human existence, and that there is no difference in principle between this recognition in the extreme case and admitting that differences in degree of competence form no valid basis for discriminatory treatment in distribution. But, after all, does any-one really contend that "competence," as measured by the price system, corresponds to ethical merit? Is it not obvious that "incompetence" follows just as surely if not quite so commonly from being too good for the world as from being blameworthy in character?

Thus the competitive system, viewed simply as a want-satisfying mechanism, falls far short of our highest ideals. To the theoretical tendencies of perfect competition must be opposed just as fundamental limitations and counter-tendencies, of which careful scrutiny discloses a rather lengthy list. Its standards of value for the guidance of the use of resources in production are the prices of goods, which diverge widely from accepted ethical values; and if the existing order were more purely competitive, if social control were reduced in scope, it seems clear that the divergence would be enormously wider still. Moreover, untrammeled individualism would probably tend to lower standards progressively rather than to raise them. "Giving the public what it wants" usually means corrupting popular taste. The system is also inefficient in utilizing resources to produce the values which it sets up, as brought out with startling force by the report on Waste in Industry, by a Committee of the Confederated Engineering Societies. It distributes the produce of industry on the basis of power, which is ethical only in so far as right and might are one. It is a confessed failure in the field of promoting many forms of social progress, and its functions in this regard are being progressively taken over by other social agencies. Left to itself, such a system "collapses" at frequent intervals through dilution of its value unit and through other causes which produce violent oscillation instead of the equilibrium of theory.

It is expressly excluded from the field of the present paper to pass any practical judgment upon the competitive system in comparison with any possible alternative. But in view of the negative tone of the discussion, it seems fair to remark that many of these problems are exceedingly difficult and that many of the evils and causes of trouble are inherent in all large-scale organization as such, irrespective of its form. It must be said also that radical critics of competition as a general basis of the economic order generally underestimate egregiously the danger of doing vastly worse. Finally, let us repeat that practically there is no question of the exclusive use or entire abolition of any of the fundamental methods of social organization, individualistic or socialistic. Economic and other activities will always be organized in all the possible ways, and the problem is to find the right proportions between individualism and socialism and the various varieties of each, and to use each in its proper place.

II

In turning from the want-satisfying aspect of economic activity to consider other of its value problems we enter upon a much harder task. There is little in the way of an established tradition for guidance, and the material is far less amenable to detailed subdivision or to treatment with scientific definiteness. All that can be attempted here is to raise questions and suggest lines of investigation.

It is an essential point in our criticism of established dogma that it has accepted in too narrow and final a sense the view of the economic system as merely a mechanism for satisfying those wants which are dependent upon exchangeable goods and services. Economists have given a belated and even yet not general and adequate recognition to the want-creating side of the system, and to wants as economic products at the same time that they serve as ends and guides of production. Still less attention has been paid to aspects of the organization problem which do not fall naturally under the subject of the satisfaction of wants at all, in the ordinary sense of wants for goods and services. But when we consider that productive activity takes up the larger part of the waking lives of the great mass of mankind, it is surely not to be assumed without investigation or inquiry that production is a means only, a necessary evil, a sacrifice made for the sake of some good entirely outside the production process. We are impelled to look for ends in the economic process itself, other than the mere consumption of the produce, and to give thoughtful consideration to the possibilities of participation in economic activity as a sphere of self-expression and creative achievement.

As soon as the question is raised, it becomes apparent that there are other values involved in production besides the consumption of the goods produced. Since the light of psychological criticism has been turned upon economic theory there has been a growing recognition of the inadequacy of the old treatment of production as mere sacrifice or pain undergone exclusively for the sake of consuming the product. The satisfaction derived from consumption itself is seen to be derived largely from the social situation rather than from the intrinsic qualities of the goods, while the mere fact that wealth is so largely accumulated, or devoted to all sorts of purposes manifestly not in view when its production was undertaken, is sufficient to prove that consumption is not the only motive of production. On the contrary, the persons most actively and successfully engaged in creating wealth not untypically limit their consumption to the point of living rather abstemious personal lives, which they must do to keep fit to meet the physical and mental demands which their business interests make upon them. At the bottom of the social economic scale, the satisfaction of physical needs is undoubtedly the dominant motive in the mind of the unskilled laborer. Higher up, consumption becomes less and less a matter of physiology and more a matter of esthetics or the social amenities. Still higher, this in turn becomes mixed with a larger and larger proportion of the joy of activity not dependent on any definite use to be made of its results. Traditionally, economics has been vague on the character of economic motives, implying at one time wealth-possession and at another wealth-consumption as fundamental, and never working out clearly the relations between these essentially contradictory impulses or between them and other possible motives.

Turning to look for motives attached to production as an activity rather than to the product, the most obvious is its appeal as a competitive game. The desire for wealth takes on more or less of the character of the desire to capture an opponent's pieces or cards in a game. An ethical criticism of the industrial order must therefore consider it from this point of view. In so far as it is a game, what kind of game is it? There is no doubt that a large amount of radical opposition to the system arises in this connection. The propertyless and ill-paid masses protest not merely against the privations of a low scale of living, but against the terms of what they feel to be an unfair contest in which being defeated by the stacking of the cards against them is perhaps as important to their feelings as the physical significance of the stakes which they lose. In a higher social class, resentment is aroused in the hearts of persons who do not like the game at all, and rebel against being compelled to play it and against being estimated socially and personally on the basis of their success or failure at it.

Increasing attention to this "human side" in economic relations is familiar to all in the demands of labor leaders, who talk much more than formerly of "control" and much less of wages and hours. The same shift in emphasis is manifest in the entire literature of economic discontent. When the sentiment grows strong enough, the personnel problem begins to interfere seriously with business operations, and the ruling classes are forced to pay heed to it. It is probably within the truth to say that inequality in the enjoyment of the produce is now less important as a source of opposition to the competitive system than is the far greater inequality in the distribution of economic power, opportunity, and prestige. The feeling of antagonism is no doubt accentuated by the contrast between the political rhetoric about liberty and equality, on which our citizens are so largely fed, and the facts of autocracy and servitude which laboring people (rightly or wrongly) feel to characterize their actual lives.

Economists and publicists are coming to realize how largely the efficiency of business and industry is the result of this appeal to intrinsic interest in action; how feeble, in spite of the old economics, is the motivation of mere appetite or cupidity; and how much the driving power of our economic life depends on making and keeping the game interesting. A rapidly growing literature on "incentive" is a witness to this awakening. As long as we had the frontier and there was not only "room at the top" but an open road upward, the problem was not serious. But in a more settled state of society, the tendency is to make the game very interesting indeed to a small number of "captains of industry" and "Napoleons of finance," but to secure this result by making monotonous drudgery of the lives of the masses who do the work. There are limits beyond which this process cannot be carried without arousing a spirit of rebellion which spoils the game for the leaders themselves, not to mention the effect on the output of products upon which people have become dependent.

The problem of an ethical standard or ideal in terms of which to judge the economic order is of a different and far more difficult sort when we leave the field of more or less comparable burdens and quantities of goods, to consider power and prestige as ends. In a competitive game it is absurd to speak of equality as an ideal, a fact which much radical discussion overlooks. Some of the criticisms brought against existing society amount to condemning a foot-race as unfair because someone has come out ahead. We must bear in mind, too, that the system is a want-satisfying agency at the same time that it is a competitive game, and that the two functions are inseparable, while the two sets of ideals are different. For efficiency in the production of goods a large concentration of authority is necessary. But this concentration violates the principle of equality of opportunity in the game; and when power of control carries with it the right to consume product accordingly, as it actually does, the result is flagrant inequality in this respect also. There appears to be a deep-seated conflict between liberty and equality on the one hand and efficiency on the other. There is little comfort for democratic, equalitarian idealism in the study of evolutionary biology, in which the highly centralized or "cephalized" forms have always come out ahead. Yet apparently human society is different in some degree at least, for there appears to be a tendency for autocracies, aristocracies, and systems approaching a caste organization to be beaten out in history by the apparently less efficient "democracy," tho democracies have not in practice approached closely to the equalitarian ideal.

In a system which is at the same time a want-satisfying mechanism and a competitive game we seem to find three ethical ideals in conflict. The first is the principle already mentioned, of distribution according to effort. The second is the principle of "tools to those who can use them." This is a necessary condition of efficiency, but involves giving the best player the best hand, the fastest runner the benefit of the handicap, and thus flagrantly violates the third ideal, which is to maintain the conditions of fairness in the game.

An attempt to formulate accurately the conditions of a fair and interesting game leads into difficult problems. The difference between play and work is subtle, and remains obscure after all the attempts of psychologists to deal with it. It is an old and ever-fascinating dream that all work might be converted into play under the right conditions. We know that almost any kind of work may become infused with the play spirit, as is more or less typically true of the creative arts, the higher professions to some extent, and notably business itself, as already observed. Yet definitions of play carry us little beyond the statement that it is enjoyable activity. It is usually defined as activity which constitutes its own end, is performed for its own sake.[9] But this view will hardly stand examination. We cannot think of any human activity, however "playful," which is entirely spontaneous and self-contained. Perhaps the random movements of a baby's hands and feet fit the description; but the games and recreative activities of an adult or a child look more or less beyond the mere bodily movements; they have an objective, if nothing more than to build a block house to be immediately torn down, and on it they are dependent for their peculiar interest. Perhaps we can say that in play the objective usually follows so closely upon the activity that the two are naturally thought of as a unit, or that the result occupies the attention so fully as to exclude the effort from consciousness altogether, while in work they are contrasted and the activity is presented to the mind as a means, over against the end. At least, the feeling tone of play can often be imparted to work more or less voluntarily by fixing attention upon the objective, thus crowding the effort out of consciousness. The power to induce this shift of attention in other persons seems to be an important factor in leadership.

We are here concerned rather with the special psychology of competitive games than with the general problem of play, which includes non-competitive social ceremonial as well as solitary random play and formal games played solitaire. A few general statements may be made with some confidence in regard to the difference between a good competitive game and a poor one. In the first place, there are three elements which affect the question of who is to win and thus contribute to the interest: these are ability to play, effort, and luck. It

9. For an excellent brief discussion of the use of the term "play" see C. E. Rainwater, The Play Movement, Introduction. Dewey's definition, a typical one, covers "those activities which are not consciously performed for the sake of any reward beyond themselves." See also the lecture on Work, in Ruskin's Crown of Wild Olive.

is also significant that the ability to play brought to the game on any particular occasion is, like all human capacity, a compound of innate endowment and "education" acquired from the previous expenditure of effort in play or practice, or perhaps in some closely related activity of either a recreative or a serious character. A good game must test the capacity of the players, and to do this it must compel them to exert effort. At the same time, it must involve more than a purely objective measure of capacity (assuming maximum effort). The result must be unpredictable: if there is no element of luck in it there is no game. There is no game in lifting weights, after one once knows how much can be lifted, even tho the result measures capacity. Where "records" are made, the interest centers in the unpredictable fluctuations in the powers of men (or horses, etc.) from one trial to another.

A good game calls for some reasonable, tho far from definite, proportion among the three elements, capacity, effort and luck — except that apparently most human beings are susceptible to fascination by pure chance, in spite of the obvious fact that a competitive game of pure chance involves a logical contradiction. Certainly there is general agreement that games of skill are "superior" to games of chance. Effort is called forth by interest, and intelligent interest is dependent on the fact that effort makes some difference in the result. But effort is futile or superfluous if there is too great a difference in the abilities of the players, and the game is spoiled. Even the hunter who considers himself a sportsman always gives his quarry a chance. Finally, it will no doubt be admitted that some games are "higher class" than others, depending presumably on the human qualities necessary to play them successfully and to enjoy them. The actual ranking of games would, it is true, raise the same problems of value standards which beset the path to objectivity in all fields of artistic criticism; and here also we should have to appeal to a general consensus and perhaps admit within limits the equal validity of opposing judgments.

No doubt different judges would disagree in their ranking of business as a competitive game, but the principles sketched above suggest some shortcomings. Its outcome is a very inaccurate test of real ability, for the terms on which different individuals enter the contest are too unequal. The luck element moreover is so large — far larger than fairly successful participants in the game will ever admit — that capacity and effort may count for nothing. And this luck element works cumulatively, as in gambling games generally. The effects of luck in the first hand or round, instead of tending to be evened up in accord with the law of large numbers in the further progress of the game, confer on the player who makes an initial success a differential advantage in succeeding hands or rounds, and so on indefinitely. Any particular individual may be eliminated by the results of his first venture, or placed in a position where it is extraordinarily difficult to get back into the game.[1]

Again, differences in the capacity to play the business game are inordinately great from one person to another. But as the game is organized, the weak contestants are thrown into competition with the strong in one grand

1. In the matter of luck it is even more difficult than in the case of want-satisfaction to measure the relative strength of different tendencies. Opinions will differ as to the ideal amount of luck in a game as well as in regard to the amount which there actually is in business. The cumulative working of the luck element will probably be more generally acknowledged to be a real evil. It is worth observing that the excessively crucial character of single decisions is a common phenomenon in all phases of life, a leading source of its tragedy and pathos. Rarely are we given enough "trials" in planning any feature of our careers to test the judgment which we actually possess. And when one thinks of the possibilities of developing better judgment, one is face to face with the essential tragedy of the brevity of life itself.

mêlée; there is no classification of the participants or distribution of handicaps such as is always recognized to be necessary to sportsmanship where unevenly matched contestants are to meet. In fact the situation is worse still; there are handicaps, but, as we have seen, they are distributed to the advantage of the strong rather than the weak. We must believe that business ability is to some extent hereditary, and social institutions add to inherited personal superiority the advantages of superior training, preferred conditions of entrance into the game, and even an advance distribution of the prize money.

The distribution of prizes diverges from the highest ideal of sportsmanship in another way. In a competition where the powers of the contestants are known to be unequal but the inequalities are not well enough determined to permit the classification of the players or an equalization of chances by means of handicaps, it is possible to sustain interest by offering a larger number of prizes less unequal in value. This method brings about an automatic classification of the contestants by the progress of the game itself. But in the business game the tendency is to multiply inequalities of performance in the inequality of distribution of the stakes. Let us suppose that we are organizing a foot-race among a thousand men taken at random from the general population. At one extreme they might be all lined up on a mark and made to race for a single first prize; at the other, the prize money might be distributed equally, irrespective of the results of the race. From the standpoint of sport, the one proceeding would be as absurd as the other. If the critics of competition tend to make a fetish of equality, the system itself does undoubtedly go very far to the opposite extreme.

Admitting that business success tends in the large to

go with business ability, we must face the question of the abstract merit of such capacity as a human trait, and hence of business as a game. It can hardly be denied that there is a preponderance of cultivated opinion against it. Successful business men have not become proverbial for the qualities that the best minds and most sensitive spirits of the race agree in calling noble. Business as it is and has been does not commonly display a very high order of sportsmanship, not to mention the question which will be raised presently as to whether sportsmanship itself is the highest human ideal. As to the human qualities developed by business activity and requisite to enjoyment of and successful participation in it, there is no objective measure, and no opinion will be accepted as free from "prejudice" by those who disagree with it. We shall dismiss the subject by quoting a statement by Ruskin, which can hardly be waived aside as valueless or unrepresentative. "In a community regulated by laws of demand and supply, but protected from open violence," he says, "the persons who become rich are, generally speaking, industrious, resolute, proud, covetous, prompt, methodical, sensible, unimaginative, insensitive and ignorant. The persons who remain poor are the entirely foolish, the entirely wise, the idle, the reckless, the humble, the thoughtful, the dull, the imaginative, the sensitive, the well-informed, the improvident, the irregularly and impulsively wicked, the clumsy knave, the open thief, the entirely merciful, just and godly person."[2]

However favorable an opinion one may hold of the business game, he must be very illiberal not to concede that others have a right to a different view and that large numbers of admirable people do not like the game

2. Taken from The Cry of Justice: An Anthology of Social Protest, by Upton Sinclair, p. 752.

at all. It is then justifiable at least to regard as unfortunate the dominance of the business game over life, the virtual identification of social living with it, to the extent that has come to pass in the modern world. In a social order where all values are reduced to the money measure in the degree that this is true of modern industrial nations, a considerable fraction of the most noble and sensitive characters will lead unhappy and even futile lives. Everyone is compelled to play the economic game and be judged by his success in playing it, whatever his field of activity or type of interest, and has to squeeze in as a side line any other competition, or noncompetitive activity, which may have for him a more intrinsic appeal.

III

We must treat still more inadequately our third main question, which from the point of view of pure ethics is the most important of all — the question of the ethics of competition as such. Is emulation as a motive ethically good or base? Is success in any sort of *contest*, as such, a noble objective? Are there no values which are real in a higher sense than the fact that people have agreed to strive after them and to measure success in life by the result of their striving? It seems evident that most of the ends which are actually striven after in the daily lives of modern peoples are primarily of this character; they are like the cards and checker-men, worthless (at best) in themselves, but the objects of the game; and to raise questions about the game is to make one's self disagreeable. To "play the game" is the current version of accepting the universe, and protest is blasphemy; the Good Man has given place to the "good sport." In America particularly, where competitive business, and its concomitant, the sporting view of life, have reached their fullest development, there have come to be two sorts of virtue. The greater virtue is to win; and meticulous questions about the methods are not in the best form, provided the methods bring victory. The lesser virtue is to go out and die gracefully after having lost.

We do not mean to beg the question whether the spirit of rivalry is ethically good, but only to state it in a form which raises it sharply. It cannot be denied that appeal to the competitive motive may be a source of interest in activity. The issue raised is in part the old and doubtless scientifically unanswerable one of pleasure *versus* discipline as the fundamental moral value. The hedonist would say that, as a matter of course, whatever adds to the pleasure adds to the value, and would ask only whether more is added than is taken away.

But here we appear to run into the obverse of Mill's paradox of hedonism, which is perhaps the paradox of life. It is in fact much easier to argue that the introduction of the contest motive into economic life has made it more efficient than that it has made it more pleasurable! Candid observations of industrial operatives at work, and of their frenzied, pathetic quest for recreation when off duty, alike fail to give the impression of particularly happy existence. As already observed, economic production has been made a fascinating sport *for the leaders*, but this has been accomplished by reducing it to mechanical drudgery for the rank and file. In the large is the competitive urge a lure, or is it rather a goad? Is it positive or negative, especially when we recall that for the masses the competition is in the field of consumption, with production regarded purely as a means? From the standpoint of pleasure, does the normal human being prefer a continuous, unquestioning, and almost deadly competition, or the less strenuous atmosphere of activity undertaken for ends that seem intrinsically worth while, with a larger admixture of the spectator attitude of appreciation? Current comment on the rush of life and the movement toward gilds and medievalism indicate a widespread feeling of opposition to the competitive tendency.[3]

If on the other hand one adopts the view that the end of life is to get things done, the case for competition becomes much stronger; but even here misgivings arise. It is hard to avoid asking, *what things*. If it is thought to be important which things are done, competition may be entirely indifferent and unselective, equally effective as a drive toward worthy and unworthy ends. If so, the selection of ends must be left to accident or to some other principle. There seems to be a tendency, however, for competition to be selective, and not in a very exalted sense. It is hard to believe that emulation is as effective in the "higher" fields of endeavor as it is in relation to material concerns or mere trivialities.

It is possible to hold that it does not matter what is done, that all activity develops personality equally, or that action and change as such are what make life worth living. From the point of view of mere interested activity, if we are to bring into question neither the character of the result nor that of the interest (beyond the fact that it is an "intelligent" interest, the result a foreseen result), the organization of life on a competitive basis would seem to be abundantly justified. Perhaps the organization tends to foster a philosophic attitude

3. Bertrand Russell, in his Principles of Social Reconstruction, makes the distinction between competitive and non-competitive values virtually equivalent to good and bad, the devotion to the former the primal sin of the modern world. H. G. Wells, in an early book, In the Days of the Comet, drew an idyllic picture of a world with competition eliminated. On the other hand, modern socialism has perhaps more commonly accepted competitive emulation as a motive, claiming only that under socialism it would be moralized and turned toward social welfare instead of private gain.

which will justify itself; and if so, we have a sufficient "economic interpretation" of the vogue of pragmatism. Interpreting life in terms of power as such, including "intelligence" as a form of power, there can be little question that competitive business has been an effective agency in bringing the forces of nature under human control and is largely responsible for the material progress of the modern era.

It is in terms of power, then, if at all, that competitive economics and the competitive view of life for which it must be largely accountable are to be justified. Whether we are to regard them as justified at all depends on whether we are willing to accept an ethics of power as the basis of our world view. And as Fichte said, "Was für eine Philosophie man wählt hangt davon ab was für ein Mensch man ist." But like most aphorisms this may be turned around without ceasing to be equally true: the sort of person one is depends on the sort of philosophy one chooses. It is the eternal law of reciprocal cause and effect; as just suggested, the system tends to mold men's minds in the channels which will justify the system itself, and in this sense there is a partial truth in the "economic interpretation," which we have gone to such lengths to attack and repudiate.[4] But the matter does not, cannot, rest there. The whole question is, are we to accept an "ethics of power" à la Nietzsche, or does such an acceptance involve a contradiction in terms and really mean the rejection of any true "ethics" altogether? Most of us have been taught in various connections not only that there is some sort of contrast between ethics and power, between right and might, but that the contrast is fundamental to the nature of morality. In these days it is eminently respect-

4. See the paper above referred to: "Ethics and the Economic Interpretation," in the Quarterly Journal of Economics for May, 1922.

able to hold that all ideas of this sort belong to those childish things which one must put away on becoming a man. It is a part of the modern scientific world view, and a legitimate part. To many of its "tough minded" advocates, one who calls it in question must class himself as not merely "tender-minded," but "feeble minded" as well.

And "logically" they are inevitably right! A strictly scientific discussion of general world problems leads inexorably to fatalism, to a mere question of power, to the relegation to a land of dreams of any ethics which involves questions of another sort than that as to which of two forces is the greater in magnitude. The question at issue must be clearly recognized to be precisely this: whether the logic of science itself is universally valid; whether there is or is not a realm of reality which is not comprehended in factual categories and describable in terms of definite meaning combined in propositions subject to empirical verification. Or, more accurately, it is the question whether knowledge of any such reality is possible, or whether it can be intelligently discussed. The tough-minded scientist, if candid, will admit that there *may be* such a reality, but will insist that we cannot talk about it "intelligently." Which of course is true, in the nature of the case, if to talk intelligently means to talk scientifically, which are to him equivalent terms. To the modern mind any attempt to argue such a question is fraught with the greatest difficulty, since the modern mind itself is molded into conformity with the scientific view of what is meant by intelligent discourse. Two facts, however, must apparently be accepted. The first is that one may also find "respectable" company in the belief that the scientific world view not only finds no place for many of the most fundamental data of human experience, but that, tested by the canons of its own logic, it is ultimately riddled with contradictions; numerous minds of demonstrated competence in the field of science itself hold this view. The second fact is that people do manage to "understand each other" more or less, in conversation about things which are not matters of scientific fact, but of interpretation, as in discussions of art and of character or personality.

Assuming that all ethical standards other than that of quantity of accomplishment, the ideal generated by the institution itself, are not to be dismissed *a priori* as manifestations of incompetence to discuss the question, we may close the discussion by referring briefly to the relation of some historic types of ethical theory to the problem of the evaluation of competition. From the standpoint of hedonism, the question would be simply whether competition has added to the pleasure of living. This question has been raised above, and we shall recur to it presently. In our view the nineteenth-century hedonists were not ethical hedonists anyway. They held, or assumed, the position of psychological hedonism, which involves the question-begging procedure of using pleasure as a synonym for motive in general, and to attack or criticize it at this day would be to slay the slain. They were really utilitarians in the sense in which the term was used by Paulsen, referring to the judgment of human actions by their consequences and not in accordance with formal rules. On the crucial question, how to judge the consequences, they were commonly silent or vague. But examination will show that nineteenth-century utilitarianism was in essence merely the ethics of power, the "glorified economics" to which we have referred before. Its outcome was to reduce virtue to prudence, its ideal the achievement of the greatest *quantity of desired results*. It was scientific, intellectual, in the naturalistic, pragmatic conception of knowledge as instrumental to power, that is, as power itself. As to the purposes for which power *ought* to be used, the true problem of ethics, they had nothing to say in any definite or systematic way; the fact of desire was tacitly accepted as the essence of value. Spencer bravely reduced the whole system to an ethical absurdity by explicitly carrying desire back to an ultimate justification in the desire to live, postulating that any species "must" desire what is good for it in a biological sense; and for all the group, survival power was in fact the final measure of rightness.

It seems to the writer almost superfluous to deny the appropriateness of the term "ethics" to any such conception. The conditions of survival are merely the laws of biology. It may well be the part of prudence to act in accordance with them, assuming that one *wants* to survive, but it can hardly be associated with the notions of right or duty, and if these have no meaning beyond prudence the whole realm of ethics is illusory.[5] Ethics deals with the problem of choosing between different kinds of life, and assumes that there is real choice between different kinds, or else there is no such thing as ethics. The ethical character of competition is not decided by the fact that it stimulates a greater amount of activity; this merely raises the question of the ethical quality of what is done or of the motive itself.

With this so-called ethics of scientific naturalism may be contrasted, as general types of ethical thought, true ethical hedonism or eudemonism, the Greek and the Christian views. From the standpoint of the first, the happiness philosophy, little need be added to what has already been said. Competition may form an added source of pleasure in activity, especially to the winner

5. These writers could find no place for and would have to reject an ethical obligation to live.

or, in the progress of the game, to those who stand some chance to win. But it is more likely to become a goad, especially when participation in the contest is compulsory. There is a fairly established consensus that happiness depends more on spiritual resourcefulness, and a joyous appreciation of the costless things of life, especially affection for one's fellow creatures, than it does on material satisfaction. A strong argument for coöperation, if it would work, would be its tendency to teach people to like each other in a more positive sense than can ever be bred by participation in a contest — certainly in a contest in which the means of life, or of a decent life, are felt to be at stake. The dominance of salesmanship in the business world, as well as the spirit of economic rivalry, must also tend to work against the appreciation of the "free goods."

It should be observed also that while the principle of "whom the Lord loveth he chasteneth" is hard to apply as a maxim of practical morality, it is generally admitted that human nature is likely to show up morally finer under adversity than in security and ease; also that few people can be trusted with much power without using it to the physical damage of others and their own moral discredit.

Surely no justification of competition as a motive is to be found in the Aristotelian conception of the good as that which is intrinsically worthy of man as man, or the Platonic idea of archetypal goodness. The outstanding characteristic of Greek ethical thought was the conception of the good as objective, and of the moral judgment as a cognition. A thing should be done because it is the thing to do, not because it is or is not being done by others. Virtue is knowledge, and the good is intellectually conceived, but the meaning of these statements contrasts as widely as possible with the modern reduction of virtue to prudence and of choice to a calculation of advantage. The intellectual quality in Greek ethics is the capacity of discrimination between true and false values, which is a wholly different thing from the ability to foresee changes and adapt means to ends. The one runs in terms of appreciation as the other runs in terms of power. The ideal in the one case is perfection, in the other that of bigness. To be sure, the Greeks were far from indifferent to recognition and glory, and the contest spirit played a large rôle in the life of the people, as shown in the national games. But the ideal seems always to have been the achievement of perfection, and the education of the people to recognize superior merit, not merely to win. Certainly it was not the mere winning of power.

Christianity has been interpreted in so many conflicting ways that one must hesitate to bring it into a scientific discussion; yet even this wide range of uncertainty will not admit competitive values into Christian thought. If there is anything on which divergent interpretations would have to agree, it would be the admission that the Christian conception of goodness is the antithesis of competitive. We are by no means forced to believe that the central figure of the Gospels was an ascetic; he never condemned pleasure as such, and seems to have had his own pleasure in life. But his participation in any sort of competitive sport is not to be imagined. Among his most characteristic utterances were the fervent exhortations that the last should be first and that he who would be chief should be the servant of all. The Christian ethical ideal contrasts as sharply with the Greek as either does with modern ideas derived from natural science and political economy. We have said that any *ethical* judgment of activity must be based not upon its efficiency, the quantity of results accomplished, but on either the character of those results or the character of the motive which led to the action. The Greek view fixes attention upon the character of the result, and gives an essentially esthetic conception of ethical value; Christianity centers attention upon the motive, and its ideal of life may be summed up in the word "spirituality," as the Greek ideal is summed up in "beauty" or "perfection." As the Greek identified virtue with knowledge, assuming it to be inconceivable that one should recognize true values and not act in accordance with them, Christianity (more explicitly as formulated by Paul — Romans 7: 15; Galatians 5: 19–23) makes virtue consist in conscientiousness, in doing what one believes to be right, rather than in the correct perception of objective goodness. It must be admitted that if it is hard to describe or define beauty, it is enormously more difficult to discuss spirituality in terms that seem at all intelligible to a scientific age. Both ideals agree in differing from economic (scientific, pragmatic) ethics in that they are *qualitative* in their ideals, whereas the last is merely quantitative. It seems fairly clear to the writer that it is from Christianity (and from Kant, who merely systematized Christian, or Pauline, principles) that modern common sense derives its conceptions of what is ethical when that point is explicitly under discussion.

The striking fact in modern life is the virtually complete separation between the spiritual ethics which constitutes its accepted theory of conduct and the unethical, uncriticized notion of efficiency which forms its substitute for a practical working ideal, its effective values being accepted unconsciously from tradition or the manipulations of commercial sales managers, with a very slight admixture of esthetic principles. For "spirituality" is reserved in practice a smaller and smaller fraction of the seventh day, by a smaller and smaller fraction of the population; and even that is more and more transformed by organizations into a mere contest in membership and display, with a larger or smaller admixture of the element of esthetic diversion and a smaller or larger admixture of pure commercialism. The spirit of life in the "Christian" nations and the spirit of Christianity offer an interesting study in the contrast between theory and practice. And all the while there are multiplying evidences of a genuine spiritual hunger in the modern peoples. They have got away from the spiritual attitude toward life, and do not know how to get back. Science is too strong for old beliefs, and competitive commercialism too strong for old ideals of simplicity, humility, and reverence.

Thus we appear to search in vain for any really ethical basis of approval for competition as a basis for an ideal type of human relations, or as a motive to action. It fails to harmonize either with the Pagan ideal of society as a community of friends or the Christian ideal of spiritual fellowship. Its only justification is that it is effective in getting things done; but any candid answer to the question, "what things," compels the admission that they leave much to be desired. Whether for good or bad, its esthetic ideals are not such as command the approval of the most competent judges, and as for spirituality, commercialism is in a fair way to make that term incomprehensible to living men. The motive itself has been generally condemned by the best spirits of the race. In academic life, for example, though every (American) institution feels itself compelled to use credits, marks, and honors, they are virtually never defended as intrinsically worthy incentives to effort.

Whether it is possible to bring about improvement by substituting some other basis of social organization for competitive individualism, is beyond the scope of this paper. Its purpose has been merely to bring out fundamental weaknesses of competition from the standpoint of purely ideal standards, and so to establish bases for comparison with any other possible system. Summarizing the argument, it was first emphasized by way of introduction that any judgment passed upon a social order is a value judgment and presupposes a common measure and standard of values, which must be made as clear and explicit as possible if the judgment is to be intelligent. Efficiency is a value category and social efficiency an ethical one. Now the standards which underlie a competitive system, according to orthodox economic theory, are the actual desires of the individual members of society. Competition is supposed to effect a comparison of these, and to organize the resources of society in such a way as to satisfy them to the greatest possible extent in order of magnitude — that is, it is supposed to "tend" to do so. The first main task of the paper was therefore to enumerate the more fundamental and obvious limitations on this tendency, or counter-tendencies which are in many cases quite as important as the tendency itself. Economic theory must isolate the ideal tendencies with which it can deal most readily; but no practical conclusions as to the real beneficence of the system can be drawn until the actual relative importance of the tendencies recognized by the general theory—which in endeavoring to explain always seems to justify—are measured in comparison with divergent tendencies and taken into account.

In the second division of the paper it was pointed out that the competitive economic life has value implications on the production side, the most notable of which is its appeal as a competitive game. An examination from this point of view reveals notable shortcomings of business considered purely as a game. There is also a certain ethical repugnance attached to having the livelihood of the masses of the people made a pawn in such a sport, however fascinating the sport may be to its leaders.

Finally, we have called in question from the standpoint of ideal ethics the predominance of the institution of sport, or action motivated by rivalry, and in particular have contrasted it with the Pagan ethics of beauty or perfection and the Christian ideal of spirituality.

FRANK H. KNIGHT.

THE UNIVERSITY OF IOWA.

[4]

SOME FALLACIES IN THE INTERPRETATION OF SOCIAL COST

SUMMARY

Arguments for social interference developed by Pigou and Graham illustrate common misinterpretations of the meaning of cost and its variation with output, 582. — I. The private owner of a natural opportunity secures maximum return from it by charging that rent which halts the application of investment at the point which is socially most advantageous, 584. — II. The notion of decreasing cost is a fallacy; competitive price fixation under decreasing cost or increasing returns an impossible situation, 592. — III. The law of comparative advantage in international trade is fundamentally sound, 599. — Importation a method of using resources to produce the imported good, and will be employed under competitive conditions only when more efficient than a direct method, 603. — The competitive system has important defects, but they lie outside the mechanical theory of exchange relations, 605.

In two recent articles in this Journal,[1] Professor F. D. Graham of Princeton University has developed an ingenious argument to prove that the classical theory of comparative cost as a demonstration of the economic advantage of trade between nations is "all wrong." He contends that a protective tariff may, after all, be a wise national policy in that it may enable the nation which adopts it to secure a larger product from its resources than would be secured if free trade were permitted. It is the opinion of the present writer, and the contention of this paper, that it is Professor Graham's argument which is fallacious, tho the way in which the classical theory has been formulated in many instances leaves much to be desired. The matter is of the greater importance because the most important argument, from the standpoint of general theory, in Professor A. C.

1. February 1923, November 1923.

Pigou's monumental work on *The Economics of Welfare* [2] is, as I shall also try to show, marred by the same, or a very similar, fallacy.

If economic theory is interpreted as a critique of the competitive system of organization, its first and most general problem is that of determining whether the fundamental tendencies of free contractual relations under competitive control lead to the maximum production of value as measured in price terms. The problems of the validity of the price measure of "real value," and of the distribution of the value produced, are larger but subsequent problems, and belong to ethics as much as to economics; while the detailed comparison of the theoretical tendencies of perfect competition with the facts of any actual competitive society lie in the field of applied economics rather than that of theory. The theory of international or inter-regional trade is a special case under the more general problem, whether "society" can increase the production of exchange value by interfering with free bargaining relations: the case, namely, of bargains between its own members and members of some other society possessing a distinct body of productive resources. The peculiarity of international trade as compared with domestic lies in the immobility of population viewed as labor power. Natural resources are immobile even within a country, and capital goods enter into international commerce in the same way as goods ready for consumption.

2. The Macmillan Co., 1918. This paper was written and submitted to the editor of the Quarterly Journal before the appearance of the March number of the Economic Journal. In that number, Professor D. H. Robertson has an article covering some of the same ground and treating it with his usual analytic penetration and stylistic brilliancy. Moreover, in a rejoinder appended to that article, Professor Pigou admits the particular error in his analysis and states that it is to be eradicated in a forthcoming revised edition of his book. It seems inadvisable to recast and enlarge the present paper so as to include a discussion of Professor Robertson's argument, which is notably divergent from that presented herewith. I trust it will not be thought presumptuous to print without change the few pages which in some sense cover ground already covered by Professor Robertson.

Both Professor Graham and Professor Pigou reason to the conclusion that freedom of trade between regions may reduce the production of wealth in one or even both; and Professor Pigou extends essentially the same logic to cover the relations between different industries, irrespective of regional separation. The contention is that individual profit-seeking leads to an excessive investment of resources in industries of increasing cost (decreasing returns), part of which would yield more product if transferred by social action in some form to industries of constant or decreasing cost. The fallacy to be exposed is a misinterpretation of the relation between social cost and *entrepreneur's* cost. It will be convenient to take up first Professor Pigou's argument, which presents the more general problem.

I

In Professor Pigou's study the argument that free enterprise leads to excessive investment in industries having relatively upward-sloping cost curves is developed with the aid of a concrete example, the case of two roads.[3] Suppose that between two points there are two highways, one of which is broad enough to accommodate without crowding all the traffic which may care to use it, but is poorly graded and surfaced, while the other is a much better road but narrow and quite limited in capacity.[4] If a large number of trucks operate between the two termini and are free to chose either of the

3. Economics of Welfare, p. 194.

4. For simplicity, no account is taken of costs involved in *constructing* the two roads. The aim is to study the effects of the two types of "cost" — that which represents a consumption of productive power which might have been put to some other use, and pure rent or the payment for situation and opportunity. The assumption adopted is the simplest way of making the separation. The conclusion will not be changed if various types of cost are taken into account, so long as one of the roads has a definite situation advantage while the investment in the other can be repeated to any desirable extent with equivalent results in other locations.

two routes, they will tend to distribute themselves between the roads in such proportions that the cost per unit of transportation, or effective result per unit of investment, will be the same for every truck on both routes. As more trucks use the narrower and better road, congestion develops, until at a certain point it becomes equally profitable to use the broader but poorer highway. The congestion and interference resulting from the addition of any particular truck to the stream of traffic on the narrow but good road affects in the same way the cost and output of all the trucks using that road. It is evident that if, after equilibrium is established, a few trucks should be arbitrarily transferred to the broad road, the reduction in cost, or increase in output, to those remaining on the narrow road would be a clear gain to the traffic as a whole. The trucks so transferred would incur no loss, for any one of them on the narrow road is a marginal truck, subject to the same relation between cost and output as any truck using the broad road. Yet whenever there is a difference in the cost, to an additional truck, of using the two roads, the driver of any truck has an incentive to use the narrow road, until the advantage is reduced to zero for all the trucks. Thus, as the author contends, individual freedom results in a bad distribution of investment between industries of constant and industries of increasing cost.

In such a case social interference seems to be clearly justified. If the government should levy a small tax on each truck using the narrow road, the tax would be considered by the trucker as an element in his cost, and would cause the number of trucks on the narrow road to be reduced to the point where the *ordinary cost, plus the tax,* became equal to the cost on the broad road, assumed to be left tax free. The tax could be so adjusted that the number of trucks on the narrow road would be such as to secure the maximum efficiency in the use of the two roads taken together. The revenue obtained from such a tax would be a clear gain to the society, since no individual truck would incur higher costs than if no tax had been levied.

It is implied that the same argument holds good over the whole field of investment wherever investment is free to choose between uses subject to cost curves of different slope. Take, for example, two farms, one of superior quality, the other marginal or free land. Would not labor and capital go to the better farm, until the product per man became equal to the product to be obtained from the marginal land? If so, it is clear that the total product of all the labor and capital could be increased, as in the case of the roads, by transferring some of it from the superior to the inferior farm. This application of the reasoning will probably suggest the fallacy to any one familiar with conventional economic theory. The statement does in fact indicate what would happen *if no one owned the superior farm.* But under private appropriation and self-seeking exploitation of the land the course of events is very different. It is in fact the social function of ownership to prevent this excessive investment in superior situations.

Professor Pigou's logic in regard to the roads is, as logic, quite unexceptionable. Its weakness is one frequently met with in economic theorizing, namely that the assumptions diverge in essential respects from the facts of real economic situations.[5] The most essential feature of competitive conditions is reversed, the feature namely, of the private ownership of the factors practically significant for production. If the roads are

5. For the edification of the advocates of "inductive economics" it may be observed that the "facts" are not in dispute; that what is needed in the case is not more refined observation or the gathering of "statistics," but simply correct theorizing. There is, of course, also a large field in which the crucial facts are *not* obvious.

assumed to be subject to private appropriation and exploitation, precisely the ideal situation which would be established by the imaginary tax will be brought about through the operation of ordinary economic motives. The owner of the broad road could not under effective competition charge anything for its use. If an agency of production is not subject to diminishing returns, and cannot be monopolized, there is, in fact, no incentive to its appropriation, and it will remain a free good. But the owner of the narrow road can charge for its use a toll representing its "superiority" over the free road, in accordance with the theory of rent, which is as old as Ricardian economics. An application of the familiar reasoning to this case will show that the toll will exactly equal the ideal tax above considered, — tho the application may need to be more careful and complete than that made by many of the expositors of the classical theory.

The owner of a superior opportunity for investment can set the charge for its use at any amount not greater than the excess of the product of the first unit of investment above what that unit could produce on the free opportunity. Under this charge investment will flow into the superior road up to the point where congestion and diminishing returns set in. (It is better in such a simple case to use the notion of diminishing returns than to use that of diminishing costs, since in the large the practical objective is to maximize the product of given resources and not to minimize the expenditure of resources in producing a given product.) By reducing the charge, the owner will increase the amount of traffic using his road (or in general the amount of investment of labor and capital in any opportunity). But obviously the owner of the road will not set the charge so low that the last truck which uses the road secures a return in excess of the amount which it adds to the total product of the road (that is, of all the trucks which use it). This is clearer if we think of the owner of the road hiring the trucks instead of their hiring the use of the road. The effect is the same either way; it is still the same if some third party hires the use of both. The toll or rent will be so adjusted that *added* product of the last truck which uses the narrow road is just equal to what it could produce on the broad road. No truck will pay a higher charge, and it is not to the interest of the owner of the road to accept a lower fee. And this adjustment is exactly that which maximizes the total product of both roads.

The argument may be made clearer by the use of simple diagrams.[6]

Chart A and B

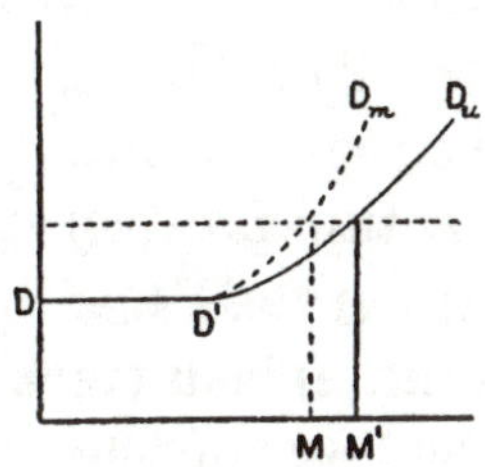

Chart C

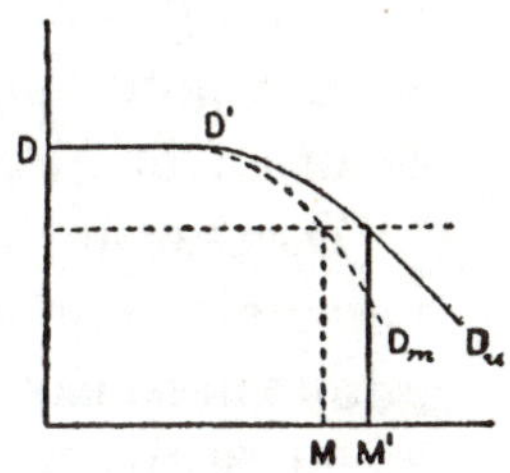

Chart D

Chart A and B represents the case of constant cost or constant returns, the cost of successive units of output or the return from successive units of investment on the broad road. In Chart C, the curve $DD'D_u$ is a *cost* curve for the narrow road, showing the cost of successive units of output. It starts at a lower level than the cost on the broad road, but at a certain point D′, congestion sets in and increasing cost appears. Curve $DD'D_m$ is a curve of *marginal* costs on the narrow road, as Professor Pigou uses the term marginal cost; the marginal cost of the *n*th unit of product is the difference

6. Cf. Pigou, op. cit., Appendix iii, pp. 931–938.

between the total cost of producing n units and the total cost of producing $n + 1$ units. When costs begin to increase, the marginal cost will increase more rapidly than the cost of the added unit, since the production of each additional unit raises the cost of the earlier units to a level with that of the new unit. It must be observed that the cost of the additional unit is always the same as the cost per unit of the whole supply produced; much economic analysis is vitiated by a spurious separation of these two conceptions of cost.

Chart D represents the same facts as Chart C, but in terms of the product of successive units of investment instead of the cost of successive units of output, that is, as curves of "diminishing returns" instead of "increasing costs." The output begins at a higher level than on the broad road, but at the point D′, which corresponds to the point of the same designation on Chart C, the return from investment begins to fall off. The curve $D'D_u$ shows the actual product of the added unit of investment, and the curve $D'D_m$ its marginal product, its addition to the total. The latter decreases more rapidly, because the application of the additional unit reduces the yield of the earlier ones to equality with its own. The argument is the same, but stated in inverse or reciprocal form. As indicated, the viewpoint of Chart D is to be preferred, and it may be surmised that, if Professor Pigou had put his argument in this form, he would probably have avoided the error into which he was very likely misled by measuring efficiency in terms of cost of output instead of output of resources.[7]

The owner of the road will adjust his toll so that the

7. It may be noted that Robertson makes the opposite contention, that the concepts of increasing and decreasing costs are to be preferred to those of decreasing and increasing returns. Loc. cit., p. 17. He gives no argument for this position. It seems to me that this is the entrepreneur's point of view, while that of either the investor or society is the inverse one advocated in the text above, and is distinctly to be preferred for general analysis.

traffic will take his road out to the point M in Chart C or D. It will *not*, under conditions of profit-seeking exploitation, be continued to M′, as argued by Professor Pigou. The actual output is the same as the "ideal" output, but it is the "ideal" output which is wrongly defined in Pigou's treatment (p. 937). Evidently, the adjustment is correct when the *marginal* product of the last unit of investment on the superior road is equal to the product of a similar unit on the free road. Confusion arises in translating this condition into terms of cost and selling price of product. Selling price will be determined by cost on the free road, or at least these two will be equal, however the causal relation is conceived. That is, the *money* cost of any unit of product is the value of the investment which is necessary to produce it on the free opportunity, where cost is constant, or, in general, at an opportunity margin where rent does not enter. Comparison of the two viewpoints shown by our Charts C and D above shows that under competitive conditions the application of investment to the superior opportunity will be stopped at the point where *marginal real cost* (cost in terms of the transferable investment) is equal to real cost on the free opportunity. When equal additions to investment make equal additions to output, equal units of output have the same cost. But the condition of equilibrium cannot be stated in terms of money cost and money selling price of product on the superior opportunity, *because these would be equal however the investment might be distributed*, whatever rent were charged, or whether the opportunity were appropriated and exploited at all. The condition of equilibrium is that the rent on the superior opportunity is maximized as an aggregate. The rent per unit of output is a variable portion of a total unit cost which is fixed.

Extension of the foregoing argument to the general case of land rent involves no difficulties and will not be carried out in detail. The point is that any opportunity, whether or not it represents a previous investment of any sort, is a productive factor if there is sufficient demand for its use to carry into the stage of diminishing returns the application to it of transferable investment. The charge made by a private owner for the use of such an opportunity serves the socially useful purpose of limiting the application of investment to the point where *marginal* product instead of product per unit is equal to the product of investment in free (rentless) opportunities; and under competitive conditions this charge will be fixed at the level which does make marginal products equal, and thus maximizes productivity on the whole. [8]

It is pertinent to add that in real life, the original "appropriation" of such opportunities by private owners involves investment in exploration, in detailed investigation and appraisal by trial and error of the findings, in development work of many kinds necessary to secure and market a product — besides the cost of buying off or killing or driving off previous claimants.

8. It is a theoretically interesting fact that the rent on an opportunity which maximizes the return to its owner and brings about the socially correct investment in it is its "marginal product," in the same sense as used to describe the competitive remuneration of other productive factors transferable from one use to another or ultimately derived from labor and waiting. It is exactly the amount by which the product of the whole competitive system would be reduced if the opportunity were held out of use or destroyed, and the investment which would be combined with it were put to the next best possible use. This point is brought out in Professor Young's chapter on Rent in Ely's Outlines of Economics (pp. 409, 410 in the fourth edition). Professor Young also pointed out the essential fallacy in Professor Pigou's argument, in a review of the latter's earlier work on Wealth and Welfare (Quarterly Journal of Economics, August 1913).

The relation between "investment" and "opportunity" is an interesting question, by no means so simple as it is commonly assumed to be. In the writer's view there is little basis for the common distinction in this regard between "natural resources" and labor or capital. The qualities of real significance for economic theory are the conditions of supply and the degree of fluidity or its opposite, specialization to a particular use. In a critical examination neither attribute forms a basis for erecting natural agents into a separate class.

Under competitive conditions, again, investment in such activities of "appropriation" would not yield a greater return than investment in any other field. These activities are indeed subject to a large "aleatory element"; they are much affected by luck. But there is no evidence proving either that the luck element is greater than in other activities relating to economic progress, or that in fact the average reward has been greater than that which might have been had from conservative investments.

II

While Professor Pigou constantly refers to industries of decreasing cost, or increasing returns, the principles at issue do not necessarily imply more than a *difference* in the way in which efficiency varies with size from one industry to another. Some of Professor Graham's reasoning in regard to international trade and international value depends upon decreasing cost as such. It seems advisable, before taking up his argument concretely, to devote a few paragraphs to this conception, which the writer believes to involve serious fallacies, and to the meaning of cost and its variation.

Valuation is an aspect of conscious choice. Apart from a necessity of choosing, values have no meaning or existence. Valuation *is* a comparison of values. A single value, existing in isolation, can no more be imagined than can a single force without some other force opposed to it as a "reaction" to its "action." Value is in fact the complete analogue of force in the interpretation of human activity, and in a behavioristic formulation is identical with force—which is to say, it is an instrumental idea, metaphysically non-existent. Fundamentally, then, the cost of any value is simply the value that is given up when it is chosen; it is just the reaction or resistance to choice which makes it choice. Ordinarily we speak of cost as a consumption of "resources" of some kind, but everyone recognizes that resources have no value in themselves; that they simply represent the products which could have been had by their use in some other direction than the one chosen.

The notion of cost suffers greatly in logical clearness from confusion with the vague and ambiguous term "pain." In the broad true sense every cost is a pain, and the two are identical. Little or nothing can be made of the distinction between pain and the sacrifice of pleasure, or between pleasure and escape from pain. The subject cannot be gone into here from the point of view of psychology; it is enough to point out that the way in which a particular person regards a particular sacrifice depends mainly upon the direction of *change* in the affective tone of his consciousness or upon the established level of expectations. The essential thing is that the pleasure-pain character of a value is irrelevant, that the universal meaning of cost is the sacrifice of a value-alternative. This is just as true of the "irksomeness" of labor, as of a payment of money. The irksomeness of digging a ditch reflects the value of the loafing or playing which might be done instead. And there is no significant difference between this irksomeness or pain and that of using the proceeds of the sale of a liberty bond to pay a doctor's bill when it might have been used to procure a fortnight's vacation.[9]

9. Besides confusion with the notion of pain, which has at last obtained in psychology a definite meaning independent of unpleasantness, the notion of cost encounters in economics another source of obscurity. This is in the relation between those values which do not pass through the market and receive prices and those which do. The "loafing" which underlies the irksomeness of labor is such a value, and there is a tendency to associate the notion of cost with these non-pecuniary values. In this connection it should be noted that not merely labor but all types of productive service are subject to the competition of uses which yield their satisfactions directly and not through the channel of a marketable product. Thus land is used for lawns as well as for fields, and examples could be multiplied at will.

The natural and common rule in choice is necessarily that of increasing cost. In the exchange of one good for another at a fixed ratio, the further the exchange is carried, the more "utility" is given up and the less is secured. This is merely the law of diminishing utility. It is only when one commodity is given up in order that another may be produced by the use of the common and divertible productive energy that we ordinarily think of the variation of cost. If two commodities are produced by a single homogeneous productive factor, there is no variation of cost as successive portions of one are given up to procure more of the other by shifting that factor—except in the sense of increasing utility cost as met with in the case of exchange. Ordinarily, however, new considerations enter, as a matter of fact. If we wish to produce more wheat by producing less corn, we find that the further the shift of production is carried, the more *bushels* of corn (as well as corn value) have to be given up to produce a *bushel* of wheat (and still more for a given amount of wheat value). This is the economic principle of increasing cost (decreasing returns) as generally understood, reduced to its lowest terms and freed from ambiguity.

When costs are measured in value terms and product in physical units there are two sorts of reasons for increasing cost, one reflecting value changes and the other technological changes. The first would be operative if all productive resources were perfectly homogeneous and perfectly fluid. But this is not, in general, the case, and technological changes supervene which work in the same direction and add to the increase which would otherwise take place in the cost of a unit of the product which is being produced in larger volume. Principal among these technological changes is the fact that some of the resources used to produce the commodity being sacrificed are not useful in the production of that whose output is being increased, and in consequence the resources which are transferred are used in progressively larger proportions in the second industry and in smaller proportions in the first, in combination with certain other resources which are specialized to the two industries respectively. The consequent reduction in the physical productive effect of the transferred factors is what is meant by diminishing returns in one of the many narrower uses of that highly ambiguous expression. Another technological cause still further aggravating the tendency to increasing costs arises from the fact that productive factors are not really homogeneous or uniform in quality. As productive power is transferred from corn to wheat, it will be found that the concrete men, acres, and implements transferred are those progressively more suitable for corn-growing and less suitable for wheat. Thus each unit suffers a progressively greater reduction in its value in terms of units of either commodity, or it takes more units to represent in the wheat industry the value of a single unit in the corn industry, and value costs of wheat mount still higher for this third reason.

All three changes so far noted clearly involve increasing cost in the real sense, the amount of value[1] outlay or sacrifice necessary to produce an additional physical unit of the commodity whose production is increased. In addition to these we have to consider two further possible sources of increased cost. The first is that, when an additional unit of, say, wheat is produced, and the factors transferable from other industries to wheat are raised in price, the quantities of these factors already used to produce wheat will rise in price along with those

1. Value as used in this discussion means "real" value, relative significance or utility. No assertion as to exchange value or price is implied.

added to the industry. Should all this increase in cost be charged up to the production of the last unit of wheat produced, which causes it to appear? In a sense, this is in truth a social cost of this last unit. Yet the transfer of productive energy will not take place unless there has been a shift in the market estimate of wheat in comparison with competing commodities such as to justify it. That is, as the exchange system measures values, making all units of the same good equal in value, the increase in the total value of the wheat must be greater than the decrease in the value of the output of competing commodities. (A discrepancy — *in either direction* — may result from considering the potential significances of infra-marginal units commonly designated as consumers' surplus.) The second additional possible source of increased cost is the increased payments which will be made for the specialized factors used in producing wheat,[2] the cost elements which are of the nature of rent or surplus. These payments evidently do not represent social costs at all, but redistributions of product merely. Such redistributions may be "good," or "bad," depending on the moral position, according to some standard, of the owners of the two classes of factors respectively.

Decreasing cost (or increasing returns) is alleged to result in several ways, which can be dealt with but briefly. The most important is the technological economy of large-scale production. When the output of a commodity is increased, the cost of the productive services used to produce it will be higher; but this increase in their cost per unit may, it is held, be more than offset by economies in utilization, made possible by larger-scale operations, which increase the amount of product

2. The fallacy of identifying specialized factors with natural agents and transferable factors with labor and capital has been referred to above. It will not be elaborated in this paper.

obtained from given quantities of materials and resources consumed.[3] But technological economies arise from increasing the size of the productive unit, not from increasing the total output of the industry as a whole. The possibility of realizing such economies — by the distribution of "overhead," or more elaborate division of labor, or use of machinery — tends to bring about an increase in the *scale* of production, but this may happen independently of any change in the output of the industry. If competition is effective, the size of the productive unit will tend to grow until *either* no further economies are obtainable, *or* there is only one establishment left and the industry is a monopoly. When all establishments have been brought to the most efficient size, variation in total output is a matter of changing their *number*, in which no technical economies are involved.

The rejoinder to the above argument is the doctrine of "external economies," which surely rests upon a misconception. Economies may be "external" to a particular establishment or technical production unit, but they are not external to the industry if they affect its efficiency. The portion of the productive process carried on in a particular unit is an accidental consideration. External economies in one business unit are internal economies in some other, within the industry. Any branch or stage in the creation of a product which offers continuously a chance for technical economies with increase in the scale of operations must eventuate either in monopoly or in leaving the tendency behind and establishing the normal relation of increasing cost with increasing size. If the organization unit is not small

3. Professor Graham says (p. 203, note) that decreasing cost is an "aspect of the law of proportionality." This is a form of statement frequently met with, but rests on a misconception sufficiently refuted in the text. It is true only accidentally, if it is true in any general sense at all, that a more elaborate technology is associated with a change in the proportions of the factors.

in comparison with the industry as a whole, a totally different law must be applied to the relation between output, cost, and price.

Two other alleged sources of decreasing cost are the stimulation of demand and the stimulation of invention. Neither can properly be regarded as an effect of increasing output, other things being equal. Producing a commodity and distributing it at a loss might result in developing a taste for it, but would be no different in principle from any other method of spending money to produce this result. Inventions tend to enlarge the scale of production rather than large-scale production to cause inventions. It is true that an increase in demand from some outside cause may stimulate invention, but the action takes place through first making the industry highly profitable. The result is not uniform or dependable, nor is it due to increased production as such.

These brief statements form a mere summary of the argument that, with reference to long-run tendencies under given general conditions, increasing the output of a commodity must increase its cost of production unless the industry is, or becomes, a monopoly. They also indicate the nature of the relation between social cost and entrepreneur's money cost. Under competition, transferable resources are distributed among alternative uses in such a way as to yield equal marginal[4] value product everywhere, which is the arrangement that maximizes production, as measured by value, on the whole. Non-transferable resources secure "rents" which equalize money costs to all producers and for all units of product under the foregoing condition; or, better, the rents bring about that allocation of resources which maximizes production, under the condition that money costs are equalized.

4. "Differential" is the term in use in other sciences for the idea commonly referred to as a marginal unit in economics.

A further major fallacy in value theory which suffuses Professor Graham's argument will be pointed out in general terms before proceeding with detailed criticism. The reference is to the notorious "law of reciprocal demand." This so-called law, that the prices of commodities exchanged internationally are so adjusted that a country's exports pay for its imports, is at best a truism. To say that what one gives in exchange pays for what one gets is merely a statement of the fact that one is exchanged for the other. What calls for explanation in the case is the process which fixes *how much* of one thing will be parted with, and *how much* of the other received in return.

III

We are now ready to take up concretely the proposed refutation of the law of comparative advantage. Professor Graham begins by assuming two countries, which he calls A and B, but which it appears simpler to designate as England and America respectively. Suppose then that in England

10 days' labor produces 40 units of wheat
10 days' labor produces 40 watches;

in America

10 days' labor produces 40 units of wheat
10 days' labor produces 30 watches.

America has a comparative advantage in wheat, England in watches.[5] According to the accepted theory, trade at any ratio intermediate between the two cost

5. The use of labor as equivalent to productive power, or the treatment of labor as the only factor which may be transferred from one industry to the other, is a simplification likely to mislead the unwary, but it will not be criticized here. It is of interest to note, however, that historically the whole doctrine of comparative cost was a prop for a labor cost theory of value.

ratios will be of advantage to both countries. Our author assumes it to begin at the ration of 35 watches for 40 units of wheat. Then, for each ten days' labor devoted to producing wheat and exchanging for watches, America can get 35 watches instead of the 30 which could be produced by using the same labor in producing the watches. England, for each ten days' labor devoted to producing watches and exchanging for wheat can secure $\frac{40}{35} \times 40$ ($= 45\frac{5}{7}$) units of wheat, instead of the 40 units which could be directly produced with the same labor.

So far, well and good for the theory. But at this point Professor Graham's blows begin to fall. Assuming that wheat-growing is an industry of increasing, and watch-making one of decreasing costs, it will come to pass, as the two countries progressively specialize, that the cost of both commodities is decreased for England and increased for America. It clearly follows, first, that if the process goes on long enough, America will begin to lose, and just as clearly, from the assumptions of the article, that the process will go on forever! For the further it is carried, the greater becomes England's comparative advantage in the production of watches and the greater becomes America's comparative advantage in the production of wheat. Yet this conclusion must arouse a suspicion that there is something wrong in Denmark.

First, in accordance with the argument above, drop the assumption of decreasing cost as a permanent condition in the watch-making industry; then the two cost ratios in the two countries must come together instead of separating as the specialization of productive efforts progresses. Under any assumption whatever, *either* this must happen, *or else* one country must entirely cease to produce one of the commodities. In the first event, the exchange ratio will be the common cost ratio of the two countries (transportation costs being neglected, as usual in these discussions). If the second result ensues, — that one country abandons one of the industries, — *the exchange ratio will be the cost ratio in the country which still produces both commodities* (assuming, always, that monopoly is absent). Professor Graham "assumes" that the comparative advantage has become progressively greater as the result of specialization and then "assumes" (page 210) that, with the cost ratio in one country half what it is in the other, the market price may be established at any ratio between the two. In reality the only possible result under the cost conditions he states would be that America would stop producing watches at once and would exchange wheat for watches at the ratio of 40 for 40 (the cost ratio in England), thus making a *gain* of 20 watches on each ten days' labor so employed as compared with using it to produce the watches in America.

Next, the author proposes to consider the effect of interpreting his cost figures as representing marginal cost instead of cost per unit. He gets no further, however, than to average up the marginal with assumed inframarginal costs, which amounts merely to a slight change in the numbers assumed for cost per unit. He nowhere gives an explicit statement of what he means by cost, and must be suspected of not having clearly faced the difficulties and ambiguities in the notion, as brought out in the argument of the first and second parts of this paper. Certainly it will not do to recognize a possible permanent difference under competition in the money cost of different units of a supply, or in their marginal real cost. The money costs which represent real costs differ in different situations, but the rent element always equalizes them, or produces *coincidence* between equality of money cost, which would result in any case, and equality of marginal real cost, which is the social desideratum. Value and cost are like action and reaction, axiomatically equal, and as in an exchange system the value of all similar units must be equal, so must their costs.

In the writer's opinion this also is socially and morally correct. We do not, and should not, value the first slice of bread more highly than the last, nor systematically value anything at more or less than its necessary cost. As between units of supply consumed by different persons, the case is different, because different persons do not come into the market with equal exchange power in the form of productive capacity. But the question is one of ethics, entirely outside the field of exchange as a mechanical problem. The famous surpluses have the same kind of significance as potential energy in physics. They relate to possible changes in fundamental conditions, but have nothing to do with the conditions of equilibrium in any particular situation. With reference to relations among actual magnitudes, cost curves and utility curves should always be interpreted to mean that, as supply varies, the cost, or utility, of every unit changes in the manner shown by the curve.

Marginal money cost, in the sense in which it is used by Professor Pigou, is meaningless with relation to competitive conditions. It is true that under monopoly the supply is so adjusted that the contribution of the last unit to total selling price (marginal demand price) is equal to the addition to total cost incurred in consequence of producing it (marginal supply price); but this is a mere equivalent of the statement that the difference between total cost and total selling price is made a maximum. Professor Graham seems to use the expression marginal cost to mean the particular money expense of producing the last unit of supply; but, as already stated, there cannot in the long run under competitive conditions be a difference between the cost of this unit and that of any other, or the cost per unit of producing the whole supply.

Professor Graham's article makes use at several points of the effects of different elasticities of demand for different goods, especially as between agricultural products and manufactures. He fails to recognize that, with reference to large and inclusive groups of commodities, demand, which is an exchange *ratio*, is merely a different view of a production ratio, and hence of a cost ratio. In discussing the sale of a single commodity in a complicated economic society and with reference to small changes, it is permissible to treat money as an absolute; but in reducing all exchange to barter between two classes of goods, this procedure is quite inadmissible.

Moreover, consideration of the actual course of events when trade is opened up will show that elasticity of demand has little to do with the special theory of international trade or international value. Each country continues to specialize in the commodities in which it has a comparative advantage, until there is no gain to be secured from further specialization; that is, until it will cost as much to secure the next unit of the imported good by exchange as it will to produce it within the country. Now at a certain point, a country will obtain as much of the imported good as it would have produced for itself under an equilibrium adjustment within itself if foreign trade had been prohibited; and in consequence of the saving of productive power effected by the trade, a part of the resources which in its absence would be used to produce that commodity will be left to be disposed of. *Beyond this point*, that is, in the disposition of the saved productive power, elasticities of demand come into operation. This fund of saved productive power will not all be used to produce either of the commodities concerned in the exchange with the foreign nation, but will be distributed over the whole field of production in accordance with the ordinary laws of supply and demand.

The foregoing paragraphs are believed to cover the main points in the writings criticized which involve fallacies in the interpretation of cost and so come under the title of this paper. The entire argument of Professor Graham's second article falls to the ground, as he has stated it, as soon as the principles of cost are applied to the determination of international values instead of "assuming" the latter. Many further points in his first article are especially inviting to criticism, but fall outside the scope of the present paper. It suffices for the solution of the essential problem of international trade to recognize that the production of one good to exchange for another is an *alternative method of producing* the second commodity. Under competitive conditions, productive resources will not be used in this indirect process of production unless the yield is greater than that obtained by the use of the direct method. The task of economic analysis is to show why the profit-seeking motive impels the private producer to put resources to the use which brings the largest yield. Now to the entrepreneur producers of wheat and watches, in a case like that used in the illustration, the choice is not a question of comparative advantage, but of absolute profit or loss. If ten days' labor will produce a quantity of wheat which can be exchanged for more than 40 watches, then that amount of labor will be *worth more* than 40 watches, and the business enterprise which uses it to produce the watches will simply lose money. It is an example of the common fallacy of thinking in terms of physical efficiency, whereas efficiency is in the nature of the case a relation between value magnitudes.

That free enterprise is not a perfectly ideal system of social organization is a proposition not to be gainsaid, and nothing is further from the aims of the present writer than to set up the contention that it is. But in his opinion the weaknesses and failures of the system lie outside the field of the mechanics of exchange under the theoretical conditions of perfect competition. It is probable that *all* efforts to prove a continued bias in the workings of competition as such, along the lines followed by Professors Pigou and Graham, are doomed to failure. Under certain theoretical conditions, more or less consciously and definitely assumed in general by economic theorists, the system would be ideal. The correct form of the problem of general criticism referred to at the outset of this paper is, therefore, that of bringing these lurking assumptions above the threshold into the realm of the explicit and of contrasting them with the facts of life — the conditions under which competitive dealings are actually carried on.[6]

When the problem is attacked from this point of view, the critic finds himself moving among considerations very different from the logical quantitative relations of such discussions as the foregoing. Human beings are not "individuals," to begin with; a large majority of them are not even legally competent to contract. The values of life are not, in the main, reducible to satisfactions obtained from the consumption of exchangeable goods and services. Such desires as people have for goods and services are not their own in any original sense, but are the product of social influence of innumerable kinds and of every moral grade, largely manufactured by the competitive system itself. The productive capacities in their own persons and in

6. The great bulk of the critical material in Professor Pigou's Wealth and Welfare is of this character.

owned external things which form the ultimate stock in trade of the human being are derived from an uncertain mixture of conscientious effort, inheritance, pure luck, and outright force and fraud. He cannot be well or truly informed regarding the markets for the productive power he possesses, and the information which he gets has a way of coming to him after the time when it would be of use. The business organizations which are the directing divinities of the system are but groups of ignorant and frail beings like the individuals with whom they deal. (In the perfectly ideal order of theory the problem of management would be non-existent!) The system as a whole is dependent upon an outside organization, an authoritarian state, made up also of ignorant and frail human beings, to provide a setting in which it can operate at all. Besides watching over the dependent and non-contracting, the state must define and protect property rights, enforce contract and prevent non-contractual (compulsory) transactions, maintain a circulating medium, and most especially prevent that collusion and monopoly, the antithesis of competition, into which competitive relations constantly tend to gravitate. It is in the field indicated by this summary list of postulates, rather than in that of the mechanics of exchange relations, that we must work out the ultimate critique of free enterprise.

F. H. Knight.

The University of Iowa.

[5]

THE RICARDIAN THEORY OF PRODUCTION AND DISTRIBUTION[1]

I. Introductory: Basic Misconceptions

ON the assumption that the primary interest in the "ancients" in such a field as economics is to learn from their mistakes, the principal theme of this discussion will be the contrast between the "classical" system and "correct" views. The system is taken in the sense indicated by the title, with little regard to other writers than Ricardo's own great master and the two successors most competent and closest to his own spirit, Senior and Mill. While our special interest is distribution theory, it is useful to have in the background clear views of essential doctrines or points of view in the authors' theory of value or price; for these are often closely connected with fallacies in the other field. It will be appropriate to give by way of introduction a kind of formal list of main deficiencies and sources of error in the system as a whole. At least seven such "aberrations" appear to have vital importance.

The *first* to be noticed is the unfortunate conception of value, in negative terms—cost, interpreted as "pain"—instead of positive terms—desire or utility. This fallacy occurs explicitly in the parts of the argument which have come to be referred to in the literature as the "philosophical" account of value. Specific discussion of the determination of value (price) as a quantity (the "empirical account") runs, indeed, largely in other, more "correct" terms, of the equalization of return from productive expenditure in different fields through correct allocation. But the negative view of the ultimate nature and causes of value clearly shows through in many places as a source of confusion. It is, of course, completely wrong. Speaking "philosophically" the basis of value in human life is the necessity of making choices among alternatives more or less preferred in a purely relative sense, and also, where there is an economic problem, more or less subject to combination in varying proportions under a principle of diminishing value-effectiveness. For any one individual, all the alternatives chosen should theoretically be equally "pleasant" or "painful" ("at the margin") depending upon his arbitrary zero point; but for purposes of economic analysis, they are simply points on a scale of preference. Thus the *cost* of any value is the alternative

[1]The second instalment of this article will be printed in the May number.

value given up in choosing it.[2] In general, the ground of the necessity of choice—at least in any case which gives rise to "economic" value—is limitation of *resources* of some kind, which are to be *economized* by correct allocation among the open alternatives of use. That *maximum* return from any resource is obtained by *equalizing* the increments of return from equal small increments of the resource in all the alternative modes of use is the axiom underlying all economic reasoning and may be called *the economic principle*.[3]

The *second* main aberration is a false conception of *production*, another aspect of which is a fallacious view of the nature of wealth or capital. Production was defined as production of *wealth*. But in fact, primary production consists in the rendering of *services*. Wealth is an agency by which services are rendered, not a product in the primary sense. (As a quantity it is abstract capacity to render service, not a collection of con-

[2]The classical cost theory is a strange and interesting mixture of theories based on two different assumptions as to the character of economic life. The pain-cost theory would fit a society in which productive resources are completely immobile or specialized as between different money income yielding uses, but in which each resource is employed in its income yielding use at the "cost" of sacrificing some "non-pecuniary" employment. The most familiar case, and the only one recognized at all clearly by the classical economists, is that of labour and "irksomeness". Irksomeness reflects the possibility of using one's personal powers for some purpose other than that of creating exchange value. The same principles apply to all, or virtually all, resources. (Regarding the classical doctrine of abstinence as the pain cost involved in the use of capital, see below, p. 23.) On the other hand, there is a large bulk of discussion of valuation more or less explicitly in terms of the mobility of resources between industries producing different commodities, and value determination through the *equalization* of yield of resources. Both views assume, though in different contexts, and unconsciously, that value is determined by utility, which varies inversely with supply. But, in general, the argument runs in terms of equalization of reward for equal *sacrifice* rather than of yield on *resources*. Since in either case the "sacrifices" are generally made by different individuals, this doctrine is subject to sweeping limitations, and Mill even pointed out (p. 388) that, in fact, the values produced by labourers at different wage levels about as typically bear an inverse ratio as a direct one to the presumptive sacrifice (see next footnote).

[3]In practice the individual makes a two-fold apportionment of his productive resources: first, between money-earning uses and direct uses, and second, as regards the part used for money-making, among different industries or occupations. In consequence of specialization, especially the division of labour, an individual does not do much apportioning under the second head, and, in fact, the first is rather rigidly determined by circumstances. These and related facts—especially the fact that the principle and motive of economy applies in various degrees to different behaviour, with no definite boundaries—set limits to the clarity and accuracy with which it is possible to formulate cost theory. This argument is briefly developed in the writer's paper, "The Common-Sense of Political Economy: Wicksteed Reprinted" (*Journal of Political Economy*, October, 1934), and more fully in two articles in the *Zeitschrift für Nationalökonomie*, the first in the issue for January, 1935,

crete things.) Wealth. axiomatically is "produced", either to *replace* some item which is used up in rendering its service, or to *add* to the total stock of service-rendering agencies. Wealth replacement is properly a detail of *maintenance*, and (simultaneous) maintenance is an essential part of the production of the services of wealth which are consumed in any interval, however short. No consumption corresponds to the "production" of *additional* wealth in any period, either during that period or at any subsequent time—unless the wealth itself is consumed by "disinvestment", which in a free market means a net decrease in total social wealth or capital through under-maintenance. The use of the new wealth increment (throughout future time, or until it is used up without replacement in a general liquidation of the social "plant") constitutes production of the services contemporaneously rendered; and the same services cannot be produced twice.

These two observations or fallacies are combined in the view that "labour produces all wealth" (meaning here "want satisfaction"). Obvioulsy, individuals render enjoyable services to others either through personal activities or through the use of their "property" (usually both combined).[4] Social economic life is essentially a matter of the exchange of services among individuals; it is only more or less accidentally that the exchange and consequent valuation of service-rendering things, or their production, in a technical economic sense, enters into the economic process, under "stationary" conditions.

The economic theory of progress or growth in the total means of want satisfaction is rather a separate branch of inquiry, and the activities ministering to current satisfaction, and those leading to growth, interact in complicated ways. The failure to separate clearly and sharply these two branches of the study is so important as to merit listing as the *third* major aberration in the system.[5]

The *fourth* deficiency or aberration to be noted is a methodological one. The classical writers had no clear conception of causality in the mechanistic, or "positive" sense of function and variable, or, in less technical language, the relation between a continuously varying cause and its effect varying (quantitatively) in some *corresponding* way. This

[4]It is perhaps more than a fancy to find a source as well as a picture of these two basic misconceptions in the classical system in the "curse of Adam": "In the sweat of thy face shalt thou eat bread" (Genesis 3: 19). This suggests that cost is pain rather than the sacrifice of an alternative, and again, bread is a false and misleading illustration of the nature of economic value or production. Because it has practically no durability, it invites the confusion of consumption of services and consumption of things rendering services.

[5]As to the meaning of wealth and its increase, and the other problems in connection with the second aberration and the third, see below, part II.

failure is manifested in, or closely connected with, a number of more specific errors; perhaps most directly in the failure to apply the "law of diminishing utility". (In a real sense they did *see* it, especially Senior.[6]) In connection with the principle of uniformity of price in a market and that of uniformity of significance of interchangeable units of a supply to an individual, this law is essential to value analysis, including the rôle of cost (which, as Senior also saw, functions through limiting supply.[7]) The principle could not be understood without at least an elementary grasp of the notion of increments, if not of the refinement of this in the theory of rates of change.

Fifth in the list is ignorance of the principles of *analysis*, closely related to the elementary mathematical or logical conceptions suggested under the previous number. Before Adam Smith was born, it was understood by students of physical science that causes and effects must be brought into relation through another application of the principle of small increments or rates of change. All causes and all effects in nature are complexes. The effect of any cause must be measured as a variation in a total effect associated with a small variation in that cause other elements in the complex of which it is a part being held constant; and similarly, *mutatis mutandis*, for the cause of any element of effect. Only after the passing of the older classical economics and the rise of the "subjective value" school has the theory of *imputation* (really partial differentiation) gradually come to be more or less understood in connection with production and distribution;[8] it is only now fairly beginning to be understood that all valuation, including direct utility, involves the same process.

Sixth: ignorant of mathematical concepts, the classical writers had no clear or definite conception of the meaning of *economy* as a process of *maximizing* a value return from given limited resources of whatever kind.

Of particularly direct and vital interest to our topic here is the *seventh* aberration. The problem of *distribution*, the sharing of a joint product among an indefinite number of agencies (owners) co-operating in its creation, not merely was not seen as a problem of imputation, but was not approached as a problem of valuation at all.[9] This is really myster-

[6]*Political Economy* (octavo ed.), p. 12.

[7]*Op. cit.*, p. 24.

[8]There is one remarkable partial exception to this general statement in the Ricardian theory of rent which involves a "rudimentary" recognition of the notion of increments, and of imputation. See below, part III.

[9]In this connection, see the remarkable statement by Ricardo in a letter to McCulloch: "After all, the great questions of Rent, Wages and Profits must be explained by the proportions in which the whole produce is divided between landlords, capitalists and labourers, and which are not essentially connected with the doctrine of value" (Hollander ed., letter XV, p. 72).

ious, in view, first, of the unescapable fact that the shares in the social income are received by individuals as money payments for services rendered; and it is even more so because in some parts of the discussion of the value problem all the writers, but especially Smith, were on the very threshold of a correct general conception of the organization of production and distribution in society as a whole through price competition.

It may be listed as a corollary of this observation (and perhaps of that under number six) that the classical writers had no conception of the nature of the economic organization in which alone a pecuniary distribution problem arises, the system or order best called "enterprise economy". In an "exchange" economy, where individuals (families) secured their livelihood by the production and exchange of products (services or direct-service-rendering goods), the categories of rent, wages, interest, and profits would have no existence. In an enterprise economy, the individual gets his livelihood by selling productive services to one or more *enterprises*, individual or corporate, for money, and with the money buying from enterprises the products consumed. The organization as a whole is worked out through two interacting systems of markets and prices, one for products, in which individuals are buyers and enterprises sellers, and one for productive services, in which the relation is reversed. The classical economists give no picture of a system of prices, and practically no hint of a system of economic organization worked out and directed by price forces.[10] As noted under the first two aberrations, they failed to see the *relativity* of all values and of all costs; still less did they grasp the identity of costs with distributive payments and the functional rôle of the two interacting sets of prices.

[10]Let it be observed here, once for all, that general negative statements are to be taken subject to interpretation. They mean that the "system" expounded by the writers does not take account of the facts in question. To say that they absolutely failed to see anything essential to a sound theory is generally too strong. One of the mysteries of economic theory is the fact that most of the essentials are things of which no fairly intelligsnt adult living in a world where exchange relations are at all developed could possibly be ignorant. The problem is to build these unescapable facts into a coherent system of relations. Such general negative statements are in no wise disproved by citing particular passages in which the fact or principle in question is, or seems to be, recognized. But it is sometimes a matter of interpretation whether they are taken into account where they need to be. In general, our discussion deals with the chapters treating systematically the problems under discussion, and passages from other chapters are doubtfully, if at all, in point.

References to authors by pages are to the following works, unless otherwise stated:
Smith, *Wealth of Nations* (Cannan ed.), 2 vols.
Ricardo, *Principles of Political Economy and Taxation* (Gonner ed.).
Senior, *Political Economy* (octavo ed.).
Mill, *Principles of Political Economy* (Ashley ed.).

II. Production: The Product and the Productive Agents

The best approach to discussion of the classical system is afforded by the last of the "aberrations" noticed in the introductory section, the failure to give any picture of the social-economic process as a whole, especially from the standpoint of the organization of production. Economic theory is nothing, or is significant only as an intellectual curiosity, unless it shows how, in a price economy, the price system works out: (a) in the assignment of productive capacity in society to different uses or "industries"; (b) in the technical organization of productive agents within each industry; and (c) in the sharing of the joint product among the co-operating individual owners of productive capacity. What is called "distribution theory" has to do with the pricing of productive services. These prices are significant in connection with the division of the product, but their prior and even more fundamental function is the dual one of apportioning productive capacity in the various forms among industries and among financial and technical productive units within each industry. It is the competition between producers in the same industry which provides the pressure to increase technical efficiency as well as to keep prices down to the level of costs.

As a first step in discussing the theory of distribution in these functional aspects, it is necessary to devote considerable space to the logically prior question of the meaning of production itself, especially the meaning of product and the conception of the agencies by which product is created. The classical writers viewed production as the creation "of" *wealth* "by" *labour*; other agencies (capital, or stock, and land) were recognized, but their rôle was auxiliary, not co-ordinate. On the other hand, labour which does not produce capital was explicitly and emphatically called "unproductive". Part III of this paper will deal with productive organization and distribution. In this part, we are concerned with the meaning of product, and especially with the confusion involved in treating production as production of wealth.

What is in fact *consumed*[11] in economic life is exclusively *services*, and accordingly, the *primary* meaning of production is the *rendering* of service. A service is a magnitude of the nature of *intensity*. It inherently involves

[11]The classical writers had no theory of consumption, and Mill even excluded it from the province of the economist. See *Essays on Some Unsettled Questions*: Essay V, "On the Definition of Political Economy, etc.", p. 132, footnote. They took it for granted that it is wealth which is consumed as well as produced and that wages are paid out of past, not current, product.

In modern discussion we have, of course, the "theory of diminishing utility", which was really implicit in the classical discussion, and was also given clear statement by Senior, although it was not explicitly built into his version of the classical system.

time, and care must be used in giving it a time "dimension". The relation between quantity and rate of flow is here, to begin with, like that involved in light, in contrast with a stream of water. Water exists, and can be measured, apart from any flow in time; but with light, and services, this is not true. A *quantity* of service, or of light, is derivative from flow, and is obtained by aggregating a "rate" of flow over some time interval. But the service has an additional and complicating peculiarity. In practice, we rarely care about the quantity of the service as such, but rather the value (in exchange) of a specified service over some interval of time, which is either in the future or in the past with reference to the point in time at which the value is struck. Streams of service—of some intensity, constant or variable, and over some interval, from zero to infinity as limits—are the things valued, and exchanged in the market. The value of any service stream is affected by *discounting* if paid for in advance, and by interest accumulation if paid for after it is rendered and consumed. (The problem of the *rate* of discount and of interest will be considered later.)

A service in the economic sense is physically defined by reference to some agency which renders it (and sometimes further by the specification of a particular physical use or performance of the agency). But the value of the physical service (in comparison with any other service) depends in the first place on its relative subjective appeal or "utility" to some consumer. More accurately, since all similar units are valued alike, it depends on the appeal of a single unit or increment (of flow) considered as an addition to the total flow—for both of any two services being compared. In accord with the familiar "law of diminishing utility", the relative utility of any increment of service (flow) decreases as the relative supply increases. Thus utility and value become a matter of the "scarcity" of services, which in turn involves the scarcity of the economic agencies rendering them. Immediately, this is a matter of the (limitation of) supply of some economic agency in the particular use of rendering the service whose value is in question. But from the economic standpoint, this scarcity is *always* a result of the competition of some other use, or uses, for the agency or agencies; otherwise, no "economic" problem arises, though a technical, or "technological", problem may. In "free" society, economic agencies, or "resources", include human beings and external things "owned" by human beings. Postponing detailed consideration of the relations between the two classes of resources, we are concerned at the moment with the owned things, or what is ordinarily designated as "wealth".

Many (not all) of the owned economic agencies in use at any time have limited life, in various degrees and for various reasons. In consequence, provision for the continuity of the service or services which they render must include provision for the replacement of the agency at the end of its life. In fact, if the consumption of any product (service) during any interval, long or short, is not accompanied during that interval by the complete *maintenance* of any scarce agencies involved in rendering (producing) it, the service cannot be said to be produced during that interval; instead, it will represent, wholly or in part, the consumption of "supply" on hand at its beginning. It should also be evident without discussion that there is no difference in principle between maintenance in the routine sense of, say, the oiling and care of a machine, and replacement, either bit by bit, or as a whole at a particular time. In fact, no very definite meaning can be given for a "whole" agency, in distinction from a part, and replacement of parts is naturally included in routine maintenance.[12]

The owned agencies of limited life which render directly consumed services are typically "made" with the aid of other "indirect" owned agencies, and these, of course, must also be replaced as fast as they lose for any reason their power to function economically, or the final service currently consumed is not currently produced. Thus a considerable part of actual productive activity, in the primary sense of rendering consumed services, comes to be, in a physical view, *indirect*; it takes the immediate form of making things, to be used either to render services or to make other things, in an almost infinitely complex sequence and interrelationship. In other words, a large part of production in its true, primary, meaning does *physically* take the form of producing "wealth". But the maintenance of an existing stock of wealth (including any necessary re-

[12]The necessity of providing for maintenance of capital before counting any result of its use as product was seen, if not understood, by the classical writers (*cf.* above, p. 7, note 10). In Smith it appears in the confused discussion of "capital" and "revenue" in book II, chapter iii (*cf.* also book I, chapter viii, on revenue and stock, p. 71). Ricardo refers to it more explicitly several times, and in his first edition (*op. cit.*, pp. 32-3) he even set up an annuity to provide for replacement. As to Senior, there are few more puzzling passages in all the literature than his argument as to how to classify the replacement fund (pp. 94-5). Strange to say, Mill seems hardly to refer to the point directly, though he mentions capital as a perpetual fund (p. 72) and discusses its "perpetual consumption and reproduction" (pp. 74-5) and his definition of production (productive labour) restricts this to additions to total wealth (p. 49).

The maintenance of social capital was of the profoundest concern to all the writers and this interest underlies the doctrine of productive and unproductive labour. This, however, involves the fallacy of failing to impute product. The labourer who does not directly produce capital produces whatever he does produce, which is presumably worth his wages to whoever pays them, and worth at least as much as any other possible product. Failure to maintain capital means non-productivity of capital, not of labour. The reasons for not deducting the maintenance of the labour from apparent gross product will be considered presently.

placements) does not represent the creation of any economic value in addition to the value of the services simultaneously consumed, but appears in their value and hence, in the economic sense, replacements are not "product".

In addition to maintenance (including replacements), the making of fairly regular and considerable additions to the *total social stock* of owned economic agencies, or "plant", has been typical of the period of history in which enterprise economy has prevailed, and must be considered as a "normal" feature in the working of such a system. Moreover, the increase in the social plant is typically associated with considerable changes in the form and kind of agencies used, brought about through replacement of one kind by another, presumably embodying a more effective way of using the *same* "productive capacity". This fact makes it practically impossible to distinguish sharply between the maintenance and the increase of the plant as a whole, though none the less necessary to make the distinction analytically. A further source of confusion is that the specialized producer who secures his income by making material agencies or "equipment goods" cannot know, and individually has no reason to care, whether they are destined for replacement or expansion.

For practical reasons, the creation of *additions* to the social plant is included in the economic production of a given time interval. But it is essential to understand that this is production only in an accounting sense. There is no consumption corresponding to such production, either in the interval in which it takes place, or at any other time. The specialized producer receives what he consumes through "abstinence" on the part of some *saver*. An addition to plant will presumably be used in the future for production in the primary sense (*i.e.*, to render consumed services). But unless the process of social growth is reversed, the plant itself is never consumed; its subsequent use to render services constitutes the production of those services simultaneously with their consumption, and the same service cannot be produced twice.[13] Moreover, even if the

[13]Treating capital growth as income involves a serious theoretical confusion, for it represents double counting (as Professor Fisher in particular has emphasized and as we have indicated). The wealth as a quantity is a capitalized service value, the "present worth" of a future income stream; logically its production *is* the production of this income stream. Yet it is unquestionably necessary in practice to treat an addition to wealth made in any interval as product and the activity as production in that interval, *and* to treat the use of the wealth to produce consumed service as production in later time. This is especially because the wealth rarely, if ever, in an organized economy, either yields its return or maintains itself automatically, but requires constant management. The student must simply be careful to recognize at all times that such product and income do not represent consumption, and reflect accounting convenience rather than economic reality.

process of social growth is at some future time reversed, it will never be possible to say when or in what connection any particular increment of wealth, described by the time and process of its creation, is "disinvested" and there will be no definite correspondence between the consumption of plant and its "production".

The notion of an "addition" to plant has no meaning, especially if associated with any change whatever in form, unless it is possible to *measure* plant. We must now consider this problem, and here we have to do with another fallacy, as egregious and as persistent as that of viewing production as production of wealth. Wealth must be a quantitative concept, and indeed it is always treated as such, but commonly without recognizing what is necessarily involved in its quantification, which is inconsistent with the notion of it as a collection of concrete things. It is certainly obvious (as in the case of most general economic principles) that an aggregate is measured, or viewed as a quantity, only in terms of some common quality or attribute. And it is likewise self-evident that an *economic* magnitude is based upon the quality or capacity of contributing to some end, rendering some service (to some "subject", an individual, or possibly a group). The notion of a quantity of service has already been mentioned; a service is measured, and so reduced to a common denominator with other services, by its "relative marginal utility". It goes without saying that the consumed service may take various forms, including the "utility" of mere miserly possession; but the value which makes a thing "wealth" can only be the value of some *anticipated use*, which, to the user, is at least as important as any other service of equal market value, or he would exchange.[14]

Since the product of any agency in any interval is reckoned only after complete maintenance of the agency, including any eventual replacement (which may mean replacement by a physically similar or dissimilar agency), it follows that productive plant is measured by the *perpetual* service income which it can be counted upon to yield. In other words, plant itself, in its quantitative aspect, is perpetual (regardless of changes in physical form), except for a possible net disinvestment in society as a whole. Perpetual service income is the primary magnitude in economic

[14]The measurement of service income is subject to limitations of a theoretically serious nature, and accurate measurement is impossible practically. In fact, the very notion of a total of value, in connection with either service flow or capacity to render service, is subject to serious conceptual limitations, value being relative. But these difficulties cannot be gone into here. It is necessary to distinguish analytically between larger and smaller (perpetual) service income streams, whatever the margin of error in objective discrimination may be. The character of the problem may be suggested by noting that what is involved is the definition of money of unchanging purchasing power. (This does not necessarily imply "ideal" money in an ethical or practical sense.)

analysis. (It is necessary to specify "service" income if the word "income" is used because an increase in wealth, or "assets", is regularly considered as income.) Quantitatively speaking, any two pieces or items of wealth are to be compared as perpetual incomes in monetary units, say dollars per year. But in this connection, two observations are necessary.

In the first place, a matter of relatively minor importance, it is unrealistic and impracticable to treat very short segments of service flow, or short-lived items of material wealth, in this way. Only relative durable things, or contractual income streams, are treated as wealth by separating, in practice or in thought, the source of a flow of service from the service itself. The classical economists were practically right in treating "food" and similar forms of wealth as products; where they were wrong was in treating *such* products as the type of wealth or capital in general. Very short-lived material "consumption goods" are best viewed as representing the services of the (human beings and) more durable material agencies which produce them.

The second observation is fundamental. As already noted, relatively few items of concrete wealth directly yield perpetual service income, or money income, to the owner. A thing either "wears out" in some sense, in a more or less definitely foreknown period, or it is problematically "liable" to supersession in connection with shifts in demand or technological advance. In either case, the effect is that to secure perpetuity in the return, provision must be made for *replacement* of the physical thing by another individual, of the same or different (physical) kind as the case may be. In accounting terms, the item must be depreciated, or written off, out of its gross yield. But the process or calculation of depreciation involves a rate of return on capital. Such a rate thus comes into the problem of capital quantity (value) in two ways, the determination of the perpetual income to be capitalized as well as the capitalization.

As to what this rate would mean and how it would be determined in a world of a different kind from that in which we live—one in which durable wealth could not actually be produced, or could not be exchanged—we need not speculate here. In the actual world, income-yielding goods are freely and competitively produced by the use, in large part, of resources which would otherwise yield current service income; and they are freely exchanged. In consequence, the cost of perpetual income, in terms of current service value sacrificed, is carefully reckoned, and is known for a given market at a given time, more accurately than most economic magnitudes. Under such conditions, the value of income-bearing goods must "equal" their cost. That identical applications of resources create equal increments of value in alternative employments, is an immediate consequence, or case, of the "economic principle".[15]

[15]See above, p. 4.

But there is a technical difficulty in carrying out this analysis, arising from the fact that the production of a durable agency requires time and in consequence must include an element of "interest". Accumulation, as well as discounting, is involved. However, the difficulty is not serious. It is also a corollary of the economic principle that the rate of interest and the rate of discounting must be equal. It is, then, merely necessary to set up an equation expressing the equality of the two values of any wealth item, one the discounted value or present worth of the stream of services it will yield—reduced to a basis of perpetuity, if not originally perpetual—and the other the cost of producing any new item yielding an equal stream of perpetual money income. Both sides of the equation involve the rate, and the equation is to be solved for the rate as the unknown. The rate of interest being known, the quantity of wealth, represented by any source of a known money value, is then found by the operation of "capitalization". ("Capital" is measured wealth, considered in relation to a measured income.)

The capitalization operation is a matter of very simple arithmetic (dividing the yield by the rate) when the "capital good" under consideration directly yields a perpetual income. It is not so simple when the good is one of limited life as is, of course, more usually true. In that case, the perpetual yield may be computed as suggested, by "depreciating" the item, *i.e.*, reducing its imputed income during life by an amount sufficient to accumulate to a sum equal to its cost and so provide for its replacement. Both in capitalizing and in the more complex calculation determining the rate, it happens to be somewhat simpler algebraically not to make this conversion formally, but to express the present worth of the time-limited income stream directly. The two operations, however, are exactly equivalent, and either form of algebraic expression may be converted into the other by a few simple steps.[16]

[16](1) *Discounting Method*: Total Cost = Present Worth of Yield

Let: Cost of Capital good be $S per year for c years, and its yield be $R per year for l years

Accumulation of $1 per year for n years at $i\% = \frac{(1+i)^n - 1}{i}$

Present worth of $1 per year for n years at $i\% = \frac{(1+i)^n - 1}{i(1+i)^n}$.

Let $(1+i) = A$

Then: Total cost $= \frac{S(A^c - 1)}{i}$

Present worth of yield $= \frac{R(A^l - 1)}{iA^l}$

$$\frac{S(A^c-1)}{i} = \frac{R(A^l-1)}{iA^l} \quad or \quad SA^l(A^c-1) = R(A^l-1) \qquad (1)$$

Especially because of the simpler form of the direct calculation, where income has limited duration, there is likely to be objection to the definition of capital as perpetual income. But certain facts seem decisive in favour of this view. The first is the universally understood meaning of interest in everyday usage, which is that of a net rate of return after maintaining the principal intact. The second is the *fact* of perpetuity. Unless society as a whole becomes decadent with respect to its stock of capital, no increment of capital viewed as a quantity ever is disinvested; the physical item worn out or superseded is always replaced by an "equal" item or quantity in items of some kind. If an individual owner wishes to "liquidate", he does so by sale to another owner. Moreover, even if the individual owner of a concrete item plans to "eat it up" without replacement, he can only know what he is doing by separating the interest element in the imputed yield from the amortization element, which involves calculating depreciation.[17] And if individuals disinvest, society will have no capital, or practically none.

---

(2) *Sinking Fund Method:* Interest = Perpetual Income ÷ Cost

$$i = \left\{R - \left[\frac{S(A^c-1)}{i} \cdot \frac{i}{A^l-1}\right]\right\} \div \frac{S(A^c-1)}{i}$$

$$= \frac{R(A^l-1) - S(A^c-1)}{A^l-1} \div \frac{S(A^c-1)}{i}$$

$$= \frac{iR(A^l-1) - iS(A^c-1)}{S(A^l-1)(A^c-1)}$$

or

$$S(A^l-1)(A^c-1) = R(A^l-1) - S(A^c-1)$$

$$SA^l(A^c-1) - S(A^c-1) = R(A^l-1) - S(A^c-1)$$

$$SA^l(A^c-1) = R(A^l-1) \qquad \text{(2) same as (1)}$$

For continuous compounding

Amount of \$1 for n years at $i\% = e^{in}$

Then e^{in} replaces $(1+i)^n$

Formula becomes: $Se^{il}(e^{ic}-1) = R(e^{il}-1)$.

[17]This is not the place for any extended discussion of interest theory; but it is in order to note that it is not properly a part of *distribution* theory at all. The special problem of interest is that of the *rate*, which is entirely a matter of the valuation of the wealth item, or its quantification as wealth. The yield, either in perpetuity or as a known duration (and, more generally, the shape) of income stream, is a *datum*; in other words, the distribution problem must be solved before the interest problem can be attacked. We shall later have occasion to notice the peculiar fallacy of the classical theory, still generally persistent to-day, that rent and interest are different distributive "shares" arising from different sources or in connection with different economic functions.

The equality of the two expressions suggested above constitutes an explanation of the interest rate (and capital quantity) in the conditions obtaining in a capital market

Summing up: The significance, for the history of doctrine, of this long discussion of the relation of material things to the concept of product is that in general they are not products, but means of production. But two exceptions are to be allowed, and carefully understood. When a material thing is so short-lived that it must practically be treated as the embodiment of a certain quantity of service, not appreciably affected by the distribution of the service in time, it should be regarded as product. The source in this case would be the more permanent productive agencies producing the "perishable" item, whose service is considered as the service of these agencies. The second exception is that the creation of net additions to a total stock of wealth, or "plant", must for accounting and managerial purposes be treated as production, and the wealth increment itself as product, in the time interval for which accounts are kept. But such production is logically double counting, as there is no corresponding consumption.

. . . . .

Further analysis of the concept of product confronts the question of other productive instruments, *i.e.*, other than "artificial" owned things. The greatest difficulty arises in connection with the theoretical position

at a moment of time, assuming freedom of investment, perfect competition, and full knowledge of all circumstances and conditions affecting the prospective yield of investments to the infinite future, on the part of all parties interested in capital transactions. In such a market, the rate of interest is simply the demand price for capital, set by the productivity of the increment of investment about to be made. Further discussion of the problem of interest would deal with the possible changes in demand and supply conditions as investment goes forward. That analysis cannot, however, be given the form of demand and supply curves or functions in the ordinary sense, because the changes have a time dimension, which the curves for demand and supply of a commodity do not have. The situation at a moment can be represented by supply and demand curves, but they have practically no meaning; for, as further analysis would indicate, the demand for capital is indefinitely (at a moment, infinitely) elastic, and the supply, even over time, is practically inelastic—if there is any functional relation between saving and the interest rate, which is questionable. For a brief discussion of the matter, see the article, "Interest", in *The Encyclopaedia of the Social Sciences*. See also the writer's article, "Capital, Time and the Interest Rate", in *Economica*, August, 1934. On "abstinence" as subjective or pain cost in relation to interest, see below pp. 23*ff*.

In viewing interest as the marginal productivity of capital, as above, it must be recognized that capital quantity itself involves the interest rate. But the rate can be derived very simply in terms of perpetual income without reference to capital quantity. Whether income is paid continuously (if that is conceivable) or in instalments on any plan, the rate of interest, per cent. per annum, is the ratio of the additional perpetual income creatable by investing a one-year segment of any given perpetual income to the given income itself. Of course, both incomes must be realized on the same plan in relation to accrual, and investment made instantly (presumably at the highest rate which available investment opportunities offer).

of human beings. It is necessary to consider each human member of an economic society (non-producers are not members) in the three aspects of: (a) a bundle of wants; (b) a bundle of capacities, his technical knowledge and skill, which the individual "owns" and uses to satisfy wants as he uses other physical agents; and (c) his (productive) "property" in the ordinary sense of external things which he owns. It is the "capacities" that we are concerned with here. From the standpoint of causality, the productive capacity in one's person is generally the result, more or less, of activity on his own part, which has, more or less, the character of investment, and, in addition, every human being is originally "created" by the use of "resources" belonging to other persons, most of which resources might have been used in other ways, and whose use in this way represents, *prima facie*, an economic choice.

But all this does not mean that the human being as a source of economic services can be treated in theory as wealth or capital, or additions to human productive capacity treated as product, or the act of making them as production, as in the case of material wealth. There is a fundamental difference, in the form of a somewhat paradoxical *limitation* to the individual's ownership of himself. The principle of "inalienable rights", recognized in all free societies, means not merely that one cannot sell himself outright, but that he cannot so much as give a valid lien on his services or make an enforceable contract to deliver them for any considerable time in the future. In other words, he cannot "capitalize" his earning capacity. Having no economic value to anyone but himself, he has in effect none at all. He cannot keep a capital account with himself, with any degree of accuracy, and has little incentive to do so, and it would have little meaning, if he could. And the same is true of parents in relation to their children. Because of these facts, the human being as a producer is in a different position from property or capital, and activity expended upon him, by himself or another, must be treated (in so far as it comes into the economic reckoning) as the rendering of services instantly and finally consumed. This we actually know to be partly false to the facts; much effort and expense laid out on human beings, by themselves and even by others, is clearly, as to motivation, investment for the sake of a future return, on a par with the construction of income-yielding implements and materials. Professional education—often carried out with borrowed money—is the typical example. But the exigencies of accounting, which embody the rationale of management, preclude analytical treatment in these terms.[18]

[18]It is true that at various points in the classical writings (not to mention modern expositors) we find explicit or implicit reference to a supply function for labour, and a cost of production. Also, that in recent history efforts have been made (*cf.* Fisher,

The third type of agency recognized in the classical writings in connection with production, namely land, was really defined as "unproduced"—"The original and indestructible powers of the soil".[19] This is the difference between land and "stock" or capital goods. The view, though so largely followed even down to the present and by the best economists, is a tissue of fallacies. In the first place, the historical question is irrelevant to economic theory in the strict sense, because the economic point of view is forward-looking: "bygones are forever bygones". And the notion that what are called "natural agents" are not produced (in the sense in which any material agents are produced) is false and reflects a false conception of production. In so far as economic conditions have held good in the past, *i.e.*, to the degree that people knew what they were doing, and there was effective competition, the use of labour and property in pioneering and all exploration and development activities could not yield a return smaller or greater than that obtainable in any other use. That is, the result must be equal in value to its cost. This is true even if possession be obtained by a mere contest or fight, and not less so because such activity would not be socially necessary or useful.

As to the facts, economic conditions have obtained in a country like

---

Huebner, and many others) to define and measure the capital value of human beings. These notions cannot be given critical examination here. Our conclusion must be that it is "impossible" to separate in the expenditure upon human beings the elements which represent respectively (a) want-satisfaction or consumption proper, (b) maintenance, and (c) growth of productive capacity, hence that it is "necessary" to treat all such expenditure as representing current final consumption.

The question whether the creation of human productive capacity is to be treated as "production" is explicitly discussed only by Mill of the four writers considered here, and he takes both positions (*cf.* pp. 46 and 48 *vs.* 51-2). The kinship of labour capacity with capital is referred to by Smith in various connections (*e.g.*, vol. I, pp. 103, 123). In his general analysis of capital (book II, ch. i, pp. 264-5) Smith explicitly includes in fixed capital "the acquired and useful abilities of all the inhabitants or members of the society". But these "abtiliies" are certainly not included in the "value" product which distinguishes productive labour in the definition with which chapter iii of book II begins (p. 313). Senior makes much of the relation, analysing nominal wages into "all three" types of return: wages proper (payment for direct sacrifice), profit (payment for training acquired at a cost), and rent (costless surplus) (see pp. 128*ff*., also pp. 61, 69). Ricardo gives no discussion of production—in classical terms productive *vs.* unproductive labour—but his allusions to the topic show that he accepts Smith's position (see especially chaps. vii and xx).

[19]As to whether land "produces" or not, the writers take contradictory positions. The crucial point is that they had no clear notions of production or the (symmetrical) relations between agencies in production, because they had none of mechanical causality. See above, part I, on the fifth aberration, and the argument of part III, below, *passim*.

the United States in as high a degree as in other fields of activity, and the social utility of the activities challenges comparison with any whatever. It is no doubt true that in comparison with *many* other types of capital creation, the results of expenditure of productive capacity in the natural-resource field as a whole are less accurately foreseeable, and in consequence may be expected to show a wider dispersion from the competitive norm of equality. In so far as the divergence follows the ordinary law of error, it will be equal in both directions. But in fact, the well-known principles of gambling psychology may be expected to skew the distribution as a whole in the *unfavourable* direction. In the more highly "aleatory" subdivisions of the field, such as prospecting for precious metals, this result is a familiar and undisputed fact, and there is no reasonable question about it in the field as a whole. But again, some other types of capital creation also present a high degree of uncertainty, and no *general* difference between "natural resources" and other types of capital goods can be defended. "Land" is capital merely; defined in any realistic way, it presents an infinite variety of conditions as to maintenance and replacement requirements, and possibilities of increase in supply, as does any other general class of capital instruments.[20]

There are numerous other forms or embodiments of "capital" besides material agencies, such as "inventions" of every sort and various "special advantages" in production. The relation of most of these to monopoly is fairly evident as a fact, but its precise character defies general formulation. The question whether their creation is "production" can only be mentioned. The same applies to other vital but difficult problems in the meaning and scope of production. It would be reasonable to restrict all *economic* production to the creation of salable value under "economic conditions", meaning that the activity is deliberate and is carried on in view of, and motivated exclusively by, a perfectly correct anticipation of its consequences, all measured in exchange value terms by a perfectly competitive market. In reality, the "capacity" of most economic resources is allocated in some vague way between the production of exchange value and other (non-pecuniary) uses, in infinitely complex variety, of which the "leisure" uses of men's personal powers (the basis of the "pain" cost of labour) is the type. There are no definite boundaries,

[20]In a physical analysis, as we have seen, labour power is also produced at a cost, and it has to a considerable extent the other properties of capital. The classification of types of productive agents and of productive capacity is a technological problem, and also a sociological and "human" one; but economic theory is concerned only with the fact that there are different kinds, which co-operate in production, and with general characteristics, not with descriptive classification. See below, pp. 22*ff*.

either: (a) to the activities organized through the price system; or (b) to those of an individual which it is realistic to regard in "economic" terms as involving the rational allocation of resources. The activities of government would also constitute a special problem. In general, the difficult problems of production and product arise largely in connection with economic growth—the "production" of productive capacity (so called only for reasons of accounting necessity).[21] There is little of all this in the writings of the classical economists—and not much that seems to the writer very much to the point in any later economic literature with which he is familiar!

. . . . .

The question of the conception and classification of productive agencies, to which we now turn, overlaps extensively with that of the meaning of product, and relatively little need be added to what has already been set down. The historical problem is that of explaining the origin (and persistence) of the indefensible "trinity" of "factors".[22] As a classification of agencies, the theory might have been derived by distinguishing first between human beings and non-human things, and then dividing the non-human, but not the human, group, into two sub-classes, the unproduced or natural, and the produced or artificial. Reasons which seem to justify the first dichotomy have already been given in the differences in ownership relations and facts which follow from these.[23] It may be added that because human beings are not property in the full sense of capital, and investment in them is not made under approximately economic conditions, there is no effective tendency for such investment to yield a return equal to the general market rate, *i.e.*, for value to equal cost. But the basic distinction between labour and other factors is "institutional", rather than theoretical-economic. In a society where all labour was performed by slaves, it would obviously be pointless.

[21]It is common usage in economics to refer to phenomena of growth or change in the given general conditions of a stationary economy as "dynamic" and to this general branch of study as "economic dynamics", in contrast with "economic statics". This is misleading, because entirely different from the meaning of the terms statics and dynamics in the field of theoretical mechanics, from which they are taken. Dynamics deals with motion, and the working of a *stationary* economic system involves the analogue of motion. The process of establishing a moving equilibrium under stationary conditions might more reasonably be called economic dynamics. Changes in these given conditions (wants, resources, and technology) are analogous with nothing dealt with in the science of mechanics, and should be designated by some other term, such as "historical" or "evolutionary" economics.

[22]This term was not used by the British classical writers, and is said to come from J. B. Say.

[23]See above, pp. 16-7.

Moreover, neither labour nor capital, as a class of things, is properly a "factor of production". This term suggests internal homogeneity, with effective distinction from other, similar "factors", and fluidity, calling for a high degree of divisibility. The description is somewhat applicable to unskilled labourers as a separate group, and in less degree to other particular groups. Specialized, or skilled, workers are likely to be more or less attached to a locality and conditioned to a particular enterprise. Mobility of labourers over long periods of time is a matter of social stratification—the "non-competing groups" of Cairnes, though in more recent times and newer regions the groups or strata tend to fuse into a continuum. The degree to which this stratification rests on biological differences, in comparison with social institutions and conventions, is a matter on which learned as well as popular opinion has gone through several cycles since Smith so confidently asserted the eighteenth-century view that it is almost entirely a result of "nurture". In a causal sense, all human capacity is socially and artificially created; in so far as its creation is under control and is controlled by economic motives, labour and its mobility form a sub-head under the capital problem. A quantity of labour has meaning only in terms of value, which is the imputed share of product value.

On the "capital" or "property" side of the division, the outstanding fact is the contrast between short-run and long-run conditions. For capital *goods*, as they stand at any moment, homogeneity and distinctiveness of classes and other qualities are questions of brute fact, and the predominant fact is specialization, complementarity, and immobility, in almost infinite variety. In the long run, the question is one of the fluidity of *capital* between different *forms* of *investment*. On the side of exodus from any employment, fluidity beyond that of the concrete agency depends (inversely) upon durability, while on the side of entry into an employment it depends (inversely) on the period of construction. But mobility in the abstract is far less a problem than foreknowledge of conditions calling for movement, making it possible to plan for it a sufficient time in advance. In addition, mobility is not a matter of an individual agency or item, which, indeed, has little meaning, but of an interrelated complex in space and time. Specialized goods are complementary to other specialized goods and to specialized labourers and are produced by other specialized goods, and labourers. Again, mobility is a composite of elements—time, or speed of transfer, and cost, which in turn includes direct outlays of many sorts, and loss of efficiency. The mobility of the capital invested in any item is dependent on facts in infinite detail. None of the factors in it can be measured at all definitely, for there is no economic magnitude available as a standard which is not changed by any shift in the productive organization. Yet analysis has to recognize such differences, and the production manager must estimate them as accurately as he can.

"Capital" is the ideal "factor of production" and is "theoretically" (meaning in a society completely economic) all-inclusive. Groups of concrete things approximate more or less to its empirical characteristics, while they exist as such. Obviously, capital is something very different from a class name for a group of things. The entire treatment of the subject of productive agencies has been vitiated by a confusion between the classification of things and the analysis of types or sources of productive capacity. This is particularly evident in the distinction between "natural" and "artificial". The productive capacity of any concrete agent may be more or less realistically analysed into qualities resulting from previous human activity and those given by nature, and the previous human activity will have been more or less "economic" in intention and result. But to the extent that human activity in general is "economic", *all* the *exchange value* represented by any agency will be accounted for in terms of that source, the "natural" attributes contributing nothing. Human beings might be similarly analysed, or they might be classified, quite as realistically as non-human things, according to the predominance of the one or the other source of their productive capacity.[24]

To explain the origin of the three-factor theory, we should go back to the historical conditions in which our economic conceptions were formed. General usage has long, and properly, recognized the three forms of income—wages, land rent, and return on capital (originally thought of as including profit[25] as well as interest). In post-feudal Europe, when our economic terminology was taking shape, the recipients of these three forms of income were fairly distinct social classes—labourers, landlords, and the middle class. The idea of distribution as a division of the total product among such classes is undoubtedly the point on which the classical economists "went wrong".[26] But discussion of this

[24]As regards "natural resources", the political interest is a further source of confusion. There is no contradiction between complete equality between value and economic cost of all such resources within any "country", and the greatest difference between countries is the effectiveness with which existing productive capacity can be employed in "producing" these types of "capital goods".

[25]The classical treatment of the *entrepreneur* function and the corresponding type of income (or lack of such treatment) will call for notice in part III.

[26]See Ricardo, preface, first paragraph; Senior, p. 88, heading. Mill's reference to classes is more casual and uncertain in meaning (*cf.* pp. 353, 417). Smith speaks of the different "ranks" of the people, in his heading to book I, and of "ranks and conditions of men" in the brief "Introduction and Plan" (pp. 4, 2). None of the writers had any notion of a class as scientifically defined by sociologists.

topic belongs to the treatment of productive organization (see part III). The three social classes have no comparable reality to-day, particularly in the "newer" parts of the world, and in any case, if distribution is a phenomenon of competitive valuation, classes have nothing to do with it.

Another vital factor in the genesis and persistence of the three-factor view is undoubtedly the influence of the doctrine of pain cost as an explanation of the prices of products. The division might be systematized in these terms. Land would be defined by the absence of affection by pain, presumably in both use and origin. The fallacy as regards use has been indicated when it was pointed out that the meaning of the pain of labour is the competition of non-pecuniary employments, and this obviously applies to land as well. The same reasoning fits the "production" of land also, as soon as it is seen to be produced, and the general relation of pain to production is understood.

Labour, of course, was virtually defined as pain, undergone for the sake of production, which was taken as the universal basis of value. This view has been criticized above.

As regards capital, one of the great inventions of the classical school was Senior's doctrine of abstinence. This functioned as a pain cost, corresponding to the interest element in the value of a product in a manner analogous to the pain of labour in relation to the wage element.[27] But there is much confusion here, which has also persisted to the present. Senior is emphatic that "abstinence" is the sacrifice incurred in *creating* capital. After capital "has become, whether by gift or by inheritance, the property of a person to whose abstinence and exertions it did not owe its creation", the profit ceases to be distinguishable from rent (p. 129). For Mill, however, "As the wages of the labourer are the remuneration of labour . . . the profits of the capitalist are . . . the remuneration of abstinence . . . what he gains by *forbearing to consume* his capital for his own uses . . ." (p. 405, our italics). Neither of them clearly saw the relation between the cost of capital in this sense and the direct, contemporary subjective cost of its use involved in giving up the *use* of *existing* capital for non-pecuniary enjoyments. The latter is the meaning of the "pain" involved in labour, and is the only subjective sacrifice which can

[27]See Senior, pp. 59, 89. Note the inconsistency in the definitions of abstinence, one calling it an agent, the other a kind of conduct. The germ of the abstinence idea is visible in Ricardo's repeated references to the time required to bring products to market and to the effects of the durability of capital on product value. In *Economica* for February, 1933, Mr. Victor Edelberg ingeniously argues that Ricardo expounded a "sound" theory of capital, *à la* Böhm-Bawerk. The present writer is unable to find in Ricardo's discussion very much *either* of Böhm-Bawerk's analysis or of a sound one, which to him mean very different things (*cf.* below, note 29).

be held to be remunerated or motivated by the current money payment of interest.

This is most easily shown in relation to the non-consumption of existing capital. Assuming an interest rate of 5 per cent., one could enjoy double his net return by consuming the capital over about fifteen years. But to regard the $5 (per year on each $100) as pay for giving up $10 is palpably absurd. The only pecuniary incentive for not eating up the investment is the *anticipation* of having the net income beyond the fifteen years (or other period). But when this time arrives, as "now", the interest will, at the margin, exactly balance the day-to-day subjective cost of renouncing the use of the capital (viewed as permanent) for direct (non-pecuniary) satisfactions. That is, the capitalist never gets any pecuniary remuneration for non-consumption, and similar reasoning will show, *a fortiori*, that a saver never gets any for the original sacrifice of current consumption during the period of accumulation.[28]

Saving involves *abstinence*, not "waiting", as later writers have erroneously preferred to call it, following Marshall, who took the term from Macvane. Mill himself glimpsed the fact (p. 405) that, even apart from the considerations brought out above, the capitalist could "often" increase his consumption during his own lifetime by consuming the capital. In fact he could always do so, on the average more than doubling it, and in a majority of cases the saver decreases his absolute total consumption by saving.

Senior makes no attempt to connect the quantity of capital with the

[28]The paradox is identical with that raised, but not analysed, by Marshall, in meeting Nicholson's objection to consumers' surplus (*Principles*, p. 127, note). The choice involved in saving is analogous to that of moving from Africa to England in Marshall's illustration. If one lives in Africa on an income of £1,000 per year, spending it rationally, one's total utility *and its subjective cost* is £1,000 per year, and in England, it is the same. Yet there may obviously be a gain in moving, *at a cost*, because of the difference in the composition of the utility stream purchasable with the same money. Similarly, there may be a sufficient incentive to save in the privilege of securing in the future an enlarged utility stream at an equally increased cost (though that is not in any important degree the real motive of saving).

The notion of maximizing "total utility" (defined as whatever men do maximize in behaving rationally) will serve to explain the expenditure of a *given* income among *given* alternatives of choice. But any attempt to use it to explain movement from one economic situation to another seems to run inevitably into a "double-counting" paradox. For a present act must be explained by a present motive; and psychologically, it seems that the books actually do balance from moment to moment—and not merely "at the margin", either. If we give up using quantity of utility to explain changes taking place over time, we are released from assuming that consumers' surplus is "real", and our reasoning harmonizes with the *fact* that no one in a routine situation experiences the free satisfaction pictured by the theory.

quantity of abstinence, or to define quantity of capital in any way. It was left for Böhm-Bawerk and his successors to develop in this direction Senior's clear references to the interval, or period, which elapses between the employment of the labour, or the labourer and natural agent (p. 111, *vs.* p. 93), and the sale or completion of the product.[29]

In addition to the pain relation, it might be argued on purely general grounds that labour and capital depend for their continued existence upon their receiving a remuneration, while this is not true of land; and traces of this view may be found in the classical writers. The precise relation between the quantity of remuneration and the requirement for the existence of the factor is, of course, not discussed, but the same is true in the pain theory, and quantitative relations could not be discussed intelligently without bringing in the "marginal" principle.

In relation to land, we find clear evidence of another distinction, in the assumption that land is available for only one use, *i.e.*, produces only one product, while labour and capital are subject to competition from a plurality of uses. There is, in fact, a fundamental difference between specialized and unspecialized agencies, but there is no correspondence between this distinction and that between "natural resources" and "capital goods", or labour. (And agriculture represents more a stage in production than even a distinct *group* of products.) Only an arbitrary classification of productive agencies can be made on the basis of specialization, which is purely a matter of degree. To discuss the fallacies in these views would require taking up in detail the separate questions of supply curves for productive agencies, for the services in pecuniary production of existing agencies, and for agencies or their services in particular pecuniary uses.

(*To be continued.*)

FRANK H. KNIGHT

The University of Chicago.

[29]The main argument of this part should suffice to make it clear that there is no relation between the quantity of capital used in a society and the length of any "production period" or interval between production and consumption. Real production is simultaneous with consumption, while the time taken to build up the capital of society is its entire period of historical growth. The production period and service life of concrete things have no definite relation to the quantity of capital. *Cf.* also articles by the writer in *Economic Essays in Honour of Gustav Cassel* and in *Economica* for August, 1934, and one scheduled to appear in *The Economic Journal* for March, 1935; and also, part III of the present essay.

THE RICARDIAN THEORY OF PRODUCTION AND DISTRIBUTION[1]

III. Productive Organization and Distribution

Introductory: Implications of Natural Price Doctrine

The "correct" approach to the theory of distribution in economics is by way of a theory of productive organization; in fact, a sound distribution theory is hardly more than a corollary or footnote to an exposition of the mechanism by which resources are apportioned among different uses, and organized in each use, under the forces of price competition. The "sense" in economics as a subject for study is derived from the idea of increasing the efficiency of action (*i.e.*, of "economy of resources") through mutual rendering of services by individuals. Historically, the development of the science may be imputed to the realization that purchase and sale represent and mediate such an exchange of services;[2] with a few individual exceptions, men seem never to have

[1]This is the second and concluding instalment of a paper, the first instalment (parts I and II) of which appeared in the preceding issue of this Journal (February, 1935). As in the previous instalment, references in the text to authors by pages relate to the following works:

Smith, *Wealth of Nations* (Cannan ed.), 2 vols. Vol. I unless specified.
Ricardo, *Principles of Political Economy and Taxation* (Gonner ed.).
Senior, *Political Economy* (octavo ed.).
Mill, *Principles of Political Economy* (Ashley ed.).

In a few cases I have used decimals in page references to indicate the approximate position of the statement in question on the page, where this seemed desirable.

Some apology seems in order for the absence of references to previous writers. A critique of previous critiques would be another labour equal to the survey itself, and I should not care to undertake it. Acknowledgements are also beyond my ability to state. I have learned from the better known historians of economic thought, but am not conscious of indebtedness to any one in particular for any of the main interpretive ideas (such as they are) presented here. Except for running through a few chapters of Cannan's history of production and distribution theories, I have made no direct use of published work in preparing the essay, which presents the results of an effort through years of teaching to get at "what it is about", and makes no pretence to scholarship. I should be more interested in making acknowledgements to students who have written suggestive "papers", but that also is out of the question. For a general check on the argument and aid in connection with references, I have relied upon an able graduate assistant, Miss Rose Director, who has lately been working over the material intensively in connection with a more specialized study in the history of the theory of capital.

[2]Services may be rendered "personally" or by granting to another the use of some external thing which one owns. There is no important analytical difference between the two sorts, either in economic theory, in social psychology, or in ethics.

had this realization before the eighteenth century, but to have regarded it as axiomatic that what anyone gains in a pecuniary transaction, some-one else must lose. Under analysis, a socially general effort to profit by exchange relations takes the form of a tendency toward a maximum (viewed as a state of equilibrium for the society as a whole) through the attraction of every increment of service capacity into its "best" use for the mutual advantage of both parties, *i.e.*, the owner of the increment of capacity and the consumer of its service (who gets the service in exchange for that of some increment of capacity owned by him). If it is seen that this urge on the part of individuals as owners of service capacity is the organizing force in all price relations, and in the economic life which prices mediate and reflect, it becomes truistical to remark that the distribution of the product of all service capacity, considered as acting jointly, is on the basis of increments of yield.[3]

Distribution really presents no special problem, unless the fact of indirect instead of direct demand may be regarded as such. The special theory of distribution usually given in our text-books is simply a theory of *joint demand*, but, in fact, the demand for final products is over-whelmingly of that nature. The notion of indirect demand itself is purely a matter of degree; the designation of a really final product must be more or less arbitrary, and results must be treated as final for the purposes of discussion which are technically removed in various

[3]All such statements should be accompanied by others emphasizing the considerations which tend to make "nonsense" (instead of sense) out of the study if they are not carefully taken into account: (1) The individual, including productive capacity in personal and property form on the one hand, and knowledge, taste, and judgment as consumer on the other, is taken as an absolute *datum*. (The severe limitations of this procedure cannot be developed here.) (2) The individual as a datum includes also his comparisons of present and future, and (3) either includes his attitude toward un-certainty (security *vs.* adventure), which cannot conceivably be formulated accurately, or else we are forced to make the impossible assumption of universal omniscience of the future. (4) It is assumed that individuals behave in a purely individualistic way, without collusion and without antagonism. This assumption, too, is highly unrealistic; in particular, it is theoretically impossible for two individuals in a system simultaneously to act intelligently in a way which at once takes the system as a set of given conditions of action and modifies it in any way, unless the action is fully preconcerted, which, of course, means collusion. It should be noted, too, that practically any aggregate of individuals within an economic system can profit by collusion; the only question is whether the gain will be greater than the cost of "organization", which is a conception so subtle that analysis in general terms cannot be carried very far. (5) Finally, and perhaps "worst" of all, it is not true that the things really and finally wanted by human beings are typically, or in a major degree, physically measurable or that value-experience is a mathematical function of physically measurable causes or sources. Economic values are really instrumental to values inherent in process rather than result, and in a social context rather than the physical world.

degrees from the theoretically final result of "psychic income"—or whatever it is called. Moreover, distribution theory has little meaning apart from a theory of general equilibrium. For, obviously, the effective demand for any resource-service depends on the distribution of income itself; and it is, of course, a reflection of the price of products, while the price of the service is a more or less price-determining element in the cost of the products. All the relations in question are relations of mutual determination in a framework of given conditions.

We should keep in mind, too, that a sound distribution theory must rest upon clear notions (*a*) of the meaning in quantitative terms of the resource-services priced, and (*b*) of the mathematical-logical principles of a functional connection between variables, of small increments and variable proportions. On all such matters the classical writers were either unsuspecting or utterly confused.

. . . . .

The problem of interpreting the classical works in their treatment of distribution is more obscure than it would be if all theory of organization were absent. What we find, however, is that the discussions of value theory give, in connection with natural price, a fair indication of the general nature of the organization mechanism and process under price competition, but that the chapters on distribution ignore this reasoning and approach the subject from an entirely different point of view. In other words, the discussion of cost of production in relation to price is in general realistic, even if seriously incomplete, but the writers had little or no comprehension of the fact that the costs of production are identical with the distributive payments—that the two are simply the prices of productive services under different names. In the chapters dealing with distribution, *i.e.*, with the various "shares", there is no approach to the subject in terms of competitive pricing or of supply and demand; also, there is little explicit theory of organization, while such organization theory as is stated or most clearly implied is of another sort than the analysis of allocation and co-ordination of resources through price competition.

It is in Smith that we find much the clearest view of the organization process developed in connection with the theory of natural price.[4] Smith explicitly places the three types of productive agencies—"land, labour, and capital"—in the same position and role in the process of economic readjustment, and treats them all as productive capacity, not as "pain".[5] Smith makes it fairly clear that the process of adjustment

[4]See *Wealth of Nations*, book I, chapter vii, "Of the Natural and Market Price of Commodities".

[5]The question of the nature of cost of production, especially its relation to pain, or sacrifice, was, of course, one of the main sources of controversy and of confusion in the

is one of transferring resources of any of the three kinds (individually) from less to more remunerative uses until the remuneration in all competing fields is equalized. In Ricardo and his followers, the essential phenomenon is the equalization of the return on *capital*, which is supposed automatically to equalize at the same time the return to labour.[6]

whole body of classical literature. Two questions were really involved: (1) what it is that the money outlays of the producers really pay for, and (2) the meaning of sacrifice. On both points, the classical writers were in general wrong. What any outlay pays for is a service to the person making the payment, and not a pain; and to the person rendering the service a sacrifice which is voluntary, or connected with a choice, is, in any rational view, simply the giving up of one alternative to get another, which must be equal or greater, or the choice would not be made.

Regarding pain as the basis of production and of value, it is interesting to note that even Ricardo clearly recognized (ch. i, sec. 2) that the wage payments themselves do not correspond at all to the pain of the labourer, and Mill emphasized (p. 388) the tendency to an inverse correspondence where the wages go to different labourers in different wage groups. In the face of the unescapable facts, the related dogmas that "labour" is a homogeneous factor, rather than an indefinite plurality of kinds, and that prices must correspond with a meaningless pain cost, forced the writers into absurdity. The culmination in connection with labour was Cairnes's theory of value in terms of the "non-competing groups". As already noted, Senior's great "contribution" was the interpretation of capital as pain in the form of abstinence; the dimensional confusions in this notion were also pointed out above (see this JOURNAL, February, 1935, pp. 23 *ff*.).

[6]Chapter iv in Ricardo gives the argument corresponding to book I, chapter vii in Smith, under practically the same title, "Natural and Market Price". In Senior, we have no separate section on the subject, but see his emphatic statements, especially on pages 97, 101 *ff*. (He uses here the expression "labour and capital", but the argument as a whole will show that the meaning is not different from that of Ricardo; the heart of the matter is that a fixed amount of capital always "supports" a fixed amount of labour.) In Mill, the equalization process receives relatively little attention in connection with the discussion of value, but is discussed at length in connection with labour and capital (wages and profits) separately (see below).

Mill's discussion in the first section of his chapter on cost of production (pp. 451-2) is thoroughly muddled as to the meaning of cost. He says (p. 452.6): "As a general rule, then, things tend to exchange for one another at such values as will enable each producer to be repaid the cost of production with the ordinary profit; in other words, such as will give to all producers the same rate of profit on their outlay. But in order that the profit may be equal where the outlay, that is, the cost of production, is equal, things must on the average exchange for one another in the ratio of their cost of production: things of which the cost of production is the same, must be of the same value." This seems to be a reworking of Ricardo's statement (p. 50) to the effect that if a manufacturer should continue in a trade, "it would be only on condition that he should derive from it the usual and general rate of profits on stock; and that could only happen when his commodity sold for a price proportional to the quantity of labour bestowed on its production".

Ricardo seems at least to make his meaning intelligible, however untenable his doctrine, which can hardly be said of Mill. Ricardo's position, as we must repeatedly emphasize, is that a fixed amount of capital always employs a fixed amount of labour; capital cost and wages paid are identical, and measure "labour cost".

All the Ricardian writers put land in a special role in relation to cost (as does Smith, *in part*, in his chapter on rent, in contrast with the chapter on natural price). The details of the theory will be taken up presently.

Apart from his notion of three homogeneous factors, Smith falls short in two respects of giving a real theory of distribution. In the first place, and of chief importance, there is no clear recognition of the fact that his "ordinary or average rates" of wages, profits, and rent are themselves variables determined by the adjustment, being merely the rates at which the remuneration of each factor respectively is equalized among all competing uses when the available (or forthcoming) supply is fully employed in the best way. He seems to think of the transfer of any productive service into or out of any industry as affecting the price of that product (through quantity, a demand curve being implied but not clearly recognized) and of that service in that use, bringing both into harmony with the general average price paid for the productive service, taken as given. In the second place, there is no recognition of what is now generally treated as the central problem of distribution, namely the derivation of demand prices of factors separately through the "imputation" of the joint product, or its value, among the various agencies which co-operate in producing it (in connection with variable proportions in any productive unit).[7]

Smith, of course, gives, following his chapters on wages and profits and preceding the chapter on rent, a separate discussion of differences in wages and profits in different employments. The same general pattern is followed by Mill, while Senior concludes his book with such a discussion. Ricardo gives only brief notice to the fact of differences, incidental to the argument of chapter iv (on natural price). All the treatments suffer from the theoretical defects just noticed; they fail to recognize that the process of equalization determines the general level, or to explain the mechanism by which the factors separately are allocated among uses and among producers (and combined in each use and each productive unit). Indeed, the notion that labour and capital are separately movable contradicts the doctrine, so often stated or clearly implied, that the proportions of the two are fixed. And, of course, all the authors are wrong in not applying the same principles of equalization to land—which would force recognition, actually lacking,

[7]This omission may be connected with Smith's earlier acceptance of the dogma that labour produces all wealth (related to the doctrine of pain cost) with which the chapter as a whole is in outright contradiction. The inferiority of the treatment in the later writers may also be due to their being still more influenced by this dogma.

of the fact that uniformity of return in any connection has meaning only to the degree that the base is homogeneous.

General View of the System

When the classical writers, in their chapters treating of the distributive shares, turned away from the near approach to a realistic view of production and distribution presented in their discussion of value theory (natural price), and expressly took up our subject, they did not give up the notion of a "system" of distribution or even one of productive organization. Their theory is of little value as an explanation, because it ignores the essential phenomena of price competition and of economic organization through price competition, but this does not mean that it is false to the facts, still less that it is uninteresting. Beginning almost unconsciously with the idea of three shares, corresponding to the three social classes,[8] and presumably to three social functions and three distinct sources of income, they attempted to picture a *social* process of division. The matter of most direct concern in the exposition seems to be the order in which the shares are assigned to the respective classes. In the very nature of their approach, the actual mechanism has to be inferred, and any exposition of the system must involve debatable interpretations of diverse statements which can hardly be reconciled into consistency. It must be based chiefly on Ricardo and later writers, for Smith's strength was not in "system" but in realism of detail; but Smith provided practically all the materials used later.[9]

In form, the resulting "Ricardian system" of distribution is a double dichotomy. The social product as a whole is first divided between the land on the one hand and the labour-and-capital on the other, and then the labour-and-capital share is divided between its two claimants. The primary fact, in Ricardo's view, is the peculiar character of rent as not entering into the price of the produce.[10] The view of rent as a

[8]See above, this JOURNAL (February, 1935, pp. 22 *ff*.).

[9]Except the idea of an increment of product associated with an increment of resource, of which there seems to be no clear trace in his thought.

[10]If this doctrine meant what it said, that rent does not "enter into" or "form a part of" (Hume) price, it would imply that the aggregate value of the produce would be equal only to the sum of wages and profit, and the source from which rent would come is a mystery. What was meant was, of course, that the money payment for rent, and land use itself, are not causal in relation to price.

The general problem of interpreting Ricardo is too large and difficult to be attacked here, but one or two observations may be worth noting. Ricardo's primary interest in value theory was to make the theory of value "monistic", and we might say "absolute", in contrast with what seemed to him the pluralism and circularity (relativity) of Smith's reasoning. The task he set himself was two-fold: to get rid of all use of prices to explain price, and to find some one thing, not itself a price, to which the price

"surplus" taken by the landlord as a first claimant superficially simplifies the problem to a dichotomy; only one "share" need be really explained; the other is fixed by subtraction. The one more or less independently explained is wages, leaving profit as a residuum. Thus the treatment of distribution falls, or should fall, into two parts, the theory of rent and the theory of wages—in that order of sequence; and the organization mechanism must fit the same scheme.

The general conception of productive organization, in relation to distribution, is worked out by the classical writers only in connection with agriculture, and with that only in a primitive form or aspect. Regarding every other phase of economic life, only extremely long-range and dubious inference is possible. In the situation the lines of which we can draw with some confidence, capital is thought of as in the literal sense "supporting" labour, and the two are "applied to" land. Production is carried on and directed by the "capitalist", who in the first instance owns all the product.[11] Production must be thought of as

of a product must be equal. For fairly simple reasons, he picked quantity of labour. To explain price in this way, he had to explain away the price-determining roles of capital and land (or their remunerations) and to overcome the further difficulty that for common sense the price of labour as paid by the *entrepreneur* does not correspond to its quantity. Only one aspect of his procedure calls for notice here. He emphatically asserts (ch. i, sec. 2), that he is not concerned to explain the "absolute" value of commodities, but only the "variations in the relative value", which he says are not affected by the differences in remuneration of different grades of labour. The misuse of words is characteristic; he means that he is concerned with changes in relative value, not with actual relative value at any given time. In other words, his contention is that he is concerned with historical changes and not with equilibrium relations or tendencies, a position characteristic of many modern writers. The difficulty (as with his later emulators) is that a large part of what he says makes sense only in connection with a theory of equilibrium.

If we could view Ricardo's system in a purely historical light, as an explanation of contemporary events, it would, in a general way, fit the facts as to the outstanding changes in England during the half-century prior to the date of his book. The main fact was an increase of several fold in the prices of agricultural relative to manufactured products. And it would be correct to explain this, in the main, and speaking superficially, by the increase in the efficiency of "labour" in manufactures through inventions, and its decrease in agriculture, in consequence of the pushing outward of the margin of cultivation. (See especially Ricardo's *Essay on the Influence of a Low Price of Corn on the Profits of Stock.*) The latter change was a consequence of the increase of population and the disruption of foreign trade by the wars. The first was a phase of the Industrial Revolution, which also underlay the growth of population.

[11]See especially Senior, pp. 93, 94; Mill, pp. 417-8; in Ricardo and Smith the assumption is clear beyond doubt. We find abundant recognition of lending at interest, but no separation of *entrepreneur* and capitalist functions. Karl Marx, who in so many respects is more classical than the classicals themselves, had abundant historical justification for calling—*i.e.*, miscalling—the modern economic order "capitalism". Ricardo

carried on in an annual cycle. At the end of the year, when the harvest is in, the capitalist-employer first pays his *rent*—if he uses any land superior to that at the margin of cultivation. He then divides the remaining product into two parts, one for his own use in consumption, and the other for the support of labour the next year. This second part replaces, continues, and constitutes his "capital", which is each year "advanced" to labourers. The rent or landlord's share (like that of the capitalist himself) is *not* thought of as advanced or paid out of capital. This can be rationalized only by assuming that the labourer is paid for his services (or the pay set aside and earmarked) at the beginning of the year, before they are rendered, while the landlord is paid at the end of the year. (In the writers' own exposition, none of the shares is treated as payment for services, not even wages, though they all, even rent, are occasionally referred to as such, especially by Smith and Senior; but it is now impossible to think of distribution in any other way.) We now take up the classical analysis in detail, beginning with the share which was first segregated, *i.e.*, rent.

Rent and Land Utilization

Ricardo's treatment of rent is brief, and in spite of the declaration in his preface, is oriented primarily toward the problem of rent in its relation to value and price rather than that of a distributive share. From the standpoint of this primary interest, it serves the purpose of eliminating an obstacle in the way of a labour theory of value. But in spite of these facts, it is in connection with rent that we find the nearest approach in the classical writings to a real theory of distribution, meaning a process of imputation on the basis of final increments. In the theory, rent has two aspects; from the standpoint of production it is a *surplus*, an excess of the yield of *capital*, meaning capital-and-labour, over the yield in a situation where no rent is paid, while from the standpoint of distribution, it is a *residuum* after capital-and-labour get their

and his followers certainly thought of the system as centring around the employment and control of labour by the capitalist. In theory, this is of course "diametrically" wrong. The *entrepreneur* employs and directs both labour and capital (the latter including land), and labourer and capitalist play the same passive role, over against the active one of the *entrepreneur*. It is true that *entrepreneurship* is not completely separable from the function of the capitalist, but neither is it completely separable from that of labour. The superficial observer is typically confused by the ambiguity of the concept of ownership. The "owner" of an enterprise may not "own" any of the "property" employed in it; and further reflection will show that the same item of property may in different senses be owned entirely, or in widely overlapping degrees, by a considerable number of proprietors.

joint share, determined by marginal productivity (pp. 48-9).[12] All through the chapters on wages and profits, as well as that on rent, Ricardo consistently develops his rent theory in these terms; capital-and-labour, viewed as a single, homogeneous factor, are applied to land in successive *doses* ("portions"), and their remuneration is determined by the product of the last increment, the land receiving the remainder of the product, if any. It is made fairly clear, too, that the order of application is such as to keep the product of equal final increments uniform in all locations. This reasoning obviously involves variable proportions of labour and capital with land, in two senses of the word.

Though it may seem hypercritical, careful reflection on the text as a whole forces us to raise the question as to how clearly Ricardo really grasped the meaning of the incremental principle. In spite of his consistency in making fairly correct statements (in terms of his assumptions), we find on analysis a staggering number of essential things that he certainly did not understand. (1) He did not see that all this is, or would be, under his assumptions, the condition for maximizing the product as a whole. (2) The absurdity of treating capital-and-labour as a homogeneous factor has been mentioned, and the underlying theory will receive attention in the next section, dealing with wages and profits.[13] (3) It is equally absurd to treat land as homogeneous except for differences in grade. If Ricardo had attempted to give a definition of land "quality" (in the sense of grade) he would surely have been forced to see that its only test or measure is precisely the rent (*per acre*—see below), and cannot be used to explain rent—unless one gives a thoroughgoing productivity theory.

(4) Ricardo has no real notion of proportions between capital-and-labour and land, for he has none of quantity of land. He never connects rent with any particular quantity of land, or in general with land at all;

[12]The use of the terms surplus and residuum in this technical sense appears later, though all our writers refer to rent as the surplus product of land. See, *e.g.*, Smith, pp. 146, 147; Ricardo, p. 52; Senior, pp. 90, 91; Mill, pp. 427, 472.

[13]Ricardo says expressly (p. 59.6) that using less capital is the same thing as using less labour. As far as the duality of the capital-and-labour factor is concerned, we must recognize that if the proportions are assumed to be fixed (which generally seems to be the assumption, in the discussion of rent), or if the use of more capital with a given quantity of labour through the payment of higher wages occurs but does not increase the total product (which is the assumption at some other points), then the grouping of two factors as one would not be illicit. (See next section.) The fallacy of treating labour as a factor would remain, and the treatment of capital in the same way would have to be justified by a clear explanation of capital quantity, which is certainly not found in the classical writers (and can be justified only with complex and fairly serious limitations).

it is the capital-and-labour (or "capital") applied to the land which yields the rent[14] (p. 49). He generally refers to the total quantity of land of a given grade in a society; but on page 48.6 a clear reference of this sort is immediately followed by an illustration of a particular tenant and "his" land, without reference to the conditions under which the second £1,000 of capital would be applied to such a particular piece of land.

(5) We may group here some other "indications" that Ricardo did not really understand the principle of variable proportions. (*a*) His "increments" are enormously large, instead of negligibly small as a sound analysis requires. (*b*) The notion that it becomes "necessary" to take up new land or apply more "capital" to that already in use (p. 47), and equivalent expressions, are not to his credit. (This usage is even more typical of other writers and of modern text-books.) Even when Ricardo does refer to an "increase in demand" for agricultural products, his case is not improved, for it is hardly possible to read into his text any economically defensible interpretation of the phrase. (His general usage of the term demand is hopelessly confused and inconsistent; see especially chapter xxx). (*c*) It is difficult to interpret the famous discussion of two kinds of improvements in agriculture (pp. 57-9) in such a way that it does not deny the possibility of varying the proportions between capital and land.

(6) Another point of major importance is that Ricardo (and his school) did not so much as glimpse the reversibility of the entire apparatus of dosing, diminishing returns, and residuals, with the consequence that the reasoning is circular, and is a "vicious" circle unless and until it is developed as a theory of mutual determination and of equilibrium in a system under stated given conditions. Of course, our criticism of the writers in this regard might be tempered by the fact that such notions only began to come into economic science the better part of a century after Ricardo's death and have been slowly making headway since that time.[15] A modern analysis would recognize that the entire theory

[14]His doctrine as a whole undoubtedly requires that only labour be considered productive, though in the preface and in the second paragraph of the chapter on rent, he refers to "the produce of the earth". Other classical writers make occasional statements more explicitly to the effect that rent is the value of the land-use, or its "product", which, of course, is a lapse into common sense inconsistent with the general position. (See Smith, p. 344). Senior (p. 136) in one of his characteristic flashes of insight really commits himself to a productivity theory (*cf.* also p. 181), though he gives no hint of an imputation process. But on page 140 he says that the amount is subject to no general rule, and has neither a maximum nor a minimum.

[15]The notion of "dosing" an entire supply of one factor or group of factors on to the given total supply of other factors is as unnecessary as it is unrealistic. Even the

can be turned upside down and viewed as a productivity theory of rent, with the capital-and-labour share as residual; and indeed this is closer to the underlying logic of the treatment, since the rent share is taken out first.

To see this, we need only fix our attention upon the form of the Ricardian statement (p. 47) which is followed by Mill (p. 425), viewing rent as the difference between the product of the same capital-and-labour when applied to a rent-yielding piece of land and when applied under no-rent conditions at the extensive or intensive margin, but with no statement as to proportions. (It must be the "best" amount of capital-and-labour for the particular piece of superior land, and the comparison must lie between the product in that use and the product when applied to the "best" amount of submarginal land, or in the "best" way at the intensive margin—"best" being defined in accord with the economic law that maximum total effect is secured through equalizing final increments.) It will be evident that the residuum left to the given piece of superior land after paying the capital-and-labour what it could produce at the margin is identical with the marginal or incremental product of the land itself, considered as a final small "dose" of its given kind and grade. For, under competitive conditions, if any (*small*) piece of land were held out of use, the labour and the capital properly belonging to it, *would be* applied at the margin of cultivation. But at the margin of cultivation, each small increment of labour and of capital adds the same amount to the total product as the "last unit" on the superior land.[16]

(7) A more technical, but quite fundamental, criticism is that Ricardo and the other writers had no clear or accurate understanding of the principle of diminishing returns, even in the limited and one-

postulate of continuity in the proportions of combination is superfluous. The correct notion is one of the increment of total effect secured by adding any concrete agency, or bargaining unit of a "factor", to an organization as a whole. (The consequences of the actual finite size of the increment of productive capacity is a question to be examined on its merits in view of the facts in any case.) As for the residual theory in general, it practically reduces to saying that the effect of any change in a causal complex is the difference between what it is and zero, and that this fact is a causal explanation.

It may be worth noting that the analysis of distribution in the form of a double dichotomy with both rent and profit as "residual" does not involve the fallacy of two residuals in the same system, which is found in some later expositions, egregiously in that of F. A. Walker. (My own teaching was wrong on this point for years.) But as we shall see, the fallacy of plural residuals does occur in the classical theory of profits and wages, which reduces to the absurdity that each claimant gets what is left after the other is paid.

[16] *Cf.* Allyn A. Young, in Ely's *Outlines of Economics*, ed. 4, p. 410 (end of fine print section).

sided connection of the application of other factors to land, and overlooking the undefined and undefinable character of the variables they assumed. (This also is a recent achievement of the leaders of the science, which is still slowly making headway in the treatise literature.) It is true that Ricardo consistently speaks of the product (clearly meaning the increment of product) due to an increment of capital and labour in a combination. But in view especially of his controversial relations with other writers in his own day, it seems more than suspicious that the form of statement common in the literature at that time and since is a confused reference to different "proportional" changes in factor and in product. A correct formulation must, of course, distinguish two entirely different principles with no direct or necessary interconnection. One is the *proportional* law, stating that a given ratio of increase in a variable factor will give rise to a smaller ratio of increase in the total product. This principle is axiomatically true if the factors are combined intelligently, but has no great importance for analysis, since it affords no standard for selecting and using any particular proportions of the factors. For this we must have recourse to a different principle, the *incremental* law, stating that equal successive increments of a variable factor yield decreasing increments of product.[17] It is also necessary for valid analysis to distinguish between, and interrelate the effects upon, physical product and value product, and in this connection, to distinguish carefully between a competitive industry and one in which there is but a single enterprise, *i.e.*, a monopoly.[18]

(8) Although the fact has been mentioned, it should be listed as a separate item that Ricardo's ablest followers clearly do not at all understand the significance of increments, even in the narrow and special setting in which Ricardo himself employs the concept. Senior, indeed, gives at one point a formally correct exposition of the Ricardian theory, though in connection with the express treatment of rent as a phenomenon of monopoly (see p. 115, table and explanatory text at bottom of page).

[17]In a graph showing total product from a given amount of some fixed factor or factors, as a function of the amount of a variable factor, the proportional law finds expression in the fact that the curve at a given point has a positive slope less than that of a line connecting the point with the origin of co-ordinates, *i.e.*, a tangent at the point cuts the vertical or variable-factor axis. The incremental law is expressed by the fact that the curve of total product bends toward the base line (the fixed-factor axis).

[18]Monopoly is, of course, almost always a matter of degree, a fact which has lately attracted a somewhat strange amount of attention. The views of the classical writers, including Ricardo, on monopoly value or price were absurdly confused (and they have no discussion of monopoly in connection with distribution); and of the authors under consideration here, only Ricardo failed explicitly to treat land as a monopoly.

But later (p. 126) he uses the absurd assumption that equal areas of land of different grades yield different amounts of produce at the same "expense"; and his discussion in connection with distribution (pp. 135 *ff.*) gives no definite theory, and ends with the statement already quoted (p. 140) that the amount of rent is not subject to any general rule. (He makes the same assertion regarding monopoly price in general; pp. 97, 104, 111.)

In Mill's treatment of rent, there is no definite recognition of the incremental principle at all. He merely repeats (p. 425) the Ricardian formula that rent is the difference in the productivity of a given amount of capital on the rent-yielding land in comparison with that which yields no rent; but there is no clear reference to dosing or increments,[19] and no explanation whatever of the process by which the quantity of "capital" to be applied on any particular amount of land of any quality is determined, which is the essential point for the theory of organization, and so for a sound theory of distribution. He does emphasize the equalization of the return on capital through competition, but gives no evidence that he understands the meaning of this as equalization of increments of return from equal increments of capital. The natural inference would be that he thinks of it as equalization of total return *per unit*, which is a *fatal* error. Mill's numerous references to diminishing returns are always to the proportionality form of the law.[20]

. . . . .

Smith's treatment of rent properly lies outside the scope of this essay, as he does not give anything like the Ricardian theory. But a

[19]He does refer in the chapter on rent (p. 429) to a "portion" of capital applied to agriculture yielding "only the ordinary profits"; and in his chapter on "Distribution as Affected by Exchange" his language is "the least productive instalment of the capital employed on the better lands". Just what should be read into this is a typical problem of interpretation. It may be argued that the process of dosing and equalization is taken for granted. But should it, or would it, be in such an exposition? The difficulty, as already pointed out, is that practically all the fundamentals of economic analysis are too obvious to be really overlooked by any observer who thinks about the problems at all.

[20]There is an obviously accidental exception on page 181. The first sentence on the page says that "the produce of land increases, *caeteris paribus*, in a diminishing ratio to the increase in the labour employed. . .". This is really the incremental principle. But before finishing the next sentence the author quotes H. C. Cary as holding that "the produce increas[es] in a greater ratio than the labour". Senior also makes a similar accidentally correct statement of the incremental principle (pp. 105-6).

Both Senior and Mill treat capital-and-labour as a single homogeneous factor, referring to it indifferently as capital, or labour, or joining the two words in either order. (I have not noticed a statement by either paralleling that of Ricardo (p. 59.6) saying expressly that the two always vary together.)

few points in his treatment seem to be worth setting down. The first is the glaring inconsistency between his chapter on rent, especially the introductory section, and the treatment of rent as a cost in the chapter on natural price.[21] In the second place, Smith has no statement or clear implication of the principle of diminishing returns in any form.[22] Third, and most important of all, Smith shows at various points some recognition of the role of competition of different uses for land, and in particular emphasizes the special significance of unique or highly specialized land, in contrast with that which is subject to competition from various ordinary uses.[23]

Labour and Capital: Wages and Profits

The classical theory of wages and profits contrasts with that of rent in that it continued to be controversial, while the rent doctrine was, from the "beginning", accepted as definitive.[24] This, at least, is a "good

[21]See final paragraph of introduction to book I, chapter xi; also the change made in the second edition in chapter vi (p. 51, n. 7). Ashley suggests that this was done at the suggestion of Hume (see his abridged edition, p. 46, note). In the chapter on rent, Smith relapses by implication into an "absolute" labour theory of value, like that which Ricardo assumes in his book subsequent to chapter i, where the explicit argument is subject to a much more reasonable interpretation. Smith nowhere really argues for such a labour theory as cause or determinant of value, not even in chapter v. Moreover, his chapter on rent itself runs largely in other terms, and is much more realistic than those of the other writers.

[22]Perhaps an exception should be made for two or three sentences relating to economic progress in colonies in the chapter on profits (book I, ch. ix, p. 94.7).

[23]The references are chiefly to vineyard land on the one hand, and to competition between tillage and grazing on the other. Similar passages occur in the discussion of natural and market price (book I, ch. vii, pp. 62-3) and in the chapter on rent (book I, ch. xi, p. 156 on vineyard land; pp. 149-50, 150, 153, 157-9 on competing uses). The passage dealing with payment of rent above a "natural rate" (p. 63) is especially significant. The argument as to which particular use "determines" the value in all other uses is, of course, confused.

It might be noted, too, that in at least one place (in book II, see p. 344) Smith takes a productivity view of rent, saying that it "may be considered as the produce of those powers of nature, the use of which the landlord lends to the farmer".

[24]Cairnes's brief parenthetical reference to rent (*Leading Principles*, pp. 58-9) might well be placed alongside Mill's oft-quoted reference to value theory as a topic on which nothing remained to be said. But as a matter of fact, the "controversy" in question raged around the composition of the "wages-fund", which is by no means the central conception in the doctrine of wages and capital; and on the other hand, as shown above, the different writers did not really state the same theory of rent, though they were unconscious of the fact.

It will be recalled that it was really after the "downfall" of the older classical school (under the impact of the theory of subjective value) that Cairnes wrote his main treatise; also, that he wrote it for the purpose of rehabilitating the wages-fund theory (after the recantation by Mill), along with the other "leading fallacy" in the classical position, the labour theory of value.

sign", for the theory sheds no light whatever on the economic principles of distribution, and is an amazing tissue of inconsistency and irrelevance. These reasonings are interesting and important, not merely because they illustrate the workings of the "best minds" in one of the most important fields of thought, and have, needless to say, some relation to facts and to real problems, but especially because they serve to warn against types of fallacy which seem to be perennially "natural" to minds not trained to be on guard against them. Modern discussion has recognized that the theory of profit does not get beyond the arithmetical truism of the residual idea; our examination will show, what is not so generally recognized, that the theory of wages is in no better case. The only sense in which the entire treatment gets beyond the narrow and vicious circle of each claimant getting what the other does not get, lies in the idea that labour gets what it "has to have". This is not only meaninglessly indefinite, but is in no defensible sense true, and moreover, the same principle is advanced for the profit share also.

Viewed from the standpoint of a real analysis, the fundamental difficulty is, as already emphasized, the failure to treat the shares in distribution as competitively determined prices. But they have to be prices "of" something, which must be a measurable commodity. The absurdity of treating land-use as a homogeneous magnitude has been commented upon above; regarding labour, the fallacy has been pointed out often enough—quite typically by writers who go ahead to discuss "wages", in general, as if the concept had meaning. Ricardo, whose main interest was the promotion of a quantity-of-labour theory of value, was not altogether blind to the latter difficulty, and his mode of evading it has been indicated above (p. 177, n. 10). For present purposes, we may follow the classical assumption that "labour" is a homogeneous and fluid fund, of which common agricultural labour may be taken as a type. But as regards capital, the entire discussion runs in terms of a *rate* of return, and it is necessary to have some conception of the meaning of a quantity of capital, homogeneous both in itself and with its return, if we are to talk sense about the problem at all.[25]

[25]On the treatment of capital, it might perhaps be observed first of all that the writers have nothing to say about the yield or income of concrete "capital goods". This would, of course, tie up with rent theory; it conforms to the sense in which the term rent is used in everyday life, and recognition of the realities here would have gone far toward straightening out the entire system of concepts. (If "rent" is to be used in economics in a more specialized sense, to represent a theoretically peculiar sort of income, it should be the "price-determined" payment for the services of completely specialized productive agencies—which would naturally include a large fraction of wages.) But while the classical writers have much to say in various connections about various capital instruments—machines, buildings, *etc.*—they neither have anything to

The problem of capital is crucial for distribution theory because of the fact that so much income is received in the form of interest, reckoned as a rate of return on a principal sum. It is strange, however, that anyone ever failed to see that the "capital" is always the *value* of some concrete thing endowed with earning power, and is a distinct source of income, or class of sources, only in the sense that it is restricted to things which are allowed to be owned and bought and sold, *i.e.*, to "property", excluding "free" human beings. Capital *is* the productive capacity of such things, except that it is measured by salable value at a moment of time, while the product of capital is a perpetual flow or stream of value. As already explained (in part II) its quantity must be found by "capitalizing" a stream of value return, using a formula in which the chief unknown is a *rate of interest*, determined by the "cost" of creating additional income-sources under the existing technical and economic conditions. (The "cost" of a capital item about to be created is also derived from an income-stream of some volume for some period, by a formula involving the rate of interest, but inverse to capitalization, namely accumulation; the yield must be viewed as a *perpetual* income-stream, since no yield can be counted until after complete maintenance is provided for.)

Nothing of this is to be found in the classical analysis of distribution. The notion of capital there assumed is simply a quantity of ordinary consumable product, accumulated as a "stock". In this way the writers side-tracked any special problem of capital quantity, apart from the exchange value of a product for consumption use.[26] The distinguishing mark of capital is for them a special use of produce, its consumption in the special connection and for the special purpose of production, *i.e.*, its own reproduction with an additional product, which is profit. But since in the classical system only labourers produce, capital is limited in the first place to product consumed by labourers. However, not all labourers were considered productive, but only those actually engaged in reproducing capital, which they necessarily consumed, and so providing

---

say about the earnings of such concrete things nor give any explanation of how they are quantified as abstract capital. The same statement holds for human beings, and also for land; everything is abstract quantity, yet, of course, there is no indication of definitions in quantitative terms. Even the conception of rent as a surplus falling or accruing to the "original and indestructible powers of the soil" treats these powers as a homogeneous fund, though an attribute possessed in different degrees by different examples of "land".

[26]That is, they seemed to themselves to do so; to be accurate, they would still have required a rate of interest to define a quantity of capital. This is true under any conditions in which capital exists at all, and is to be kept in mind as a special reservation whenever we speak of the incremental productivity of capital.

for the perpetual continuation of the production process. Thus capital is also limited to products suited for the consumption of labourers. But there are two further restrictions. First, labourers were supposed to live exclusively on *material products*, specifically excluding all "services"; and secondly, in strict theory, only that consumption of products which actually enabled the labourer to work was held to be "productive consumption", and only that part of actual consumption could count as capital.[27]

But in classical theory there are still two additional circumstances necessary to give rise to capital, as distinct from other produce. Produce is employed productively (*a*) because the process of production requires time, and the producer (labourer) has to be supported during the period by produce previously accumulated and (*b*) because society is so organized that the labourer himself does not make this prior accumulation, but has it done for him by another person, who thereby becomes a capitalist. Now, since the capitalist is the *entrepreneur* and manager, and since, moreover, the "activity" of saving received so much emphasis, it is hard to give any reason for the view that the share of the produce consumed by the capitalist is not productively consumed, and is not capital in the same sense as that which is advanced to labourers. None the less, it is plainly an essential part of the system expounded by Smith and the Ricardians.[28]

[27]Of course, this notion of what is "necessary" to enable the labourer to produce is indefinite at best. As remarked at the outset, the classical writers did not understand the notion of functionally related variation and cannot be expected to recognize a detail like difference in degree. Logically, the line would be drawn at consumption which *increased* production by *more* than the product consumed, and so yielded a profit. Such principles would have significance for a slave economy under perfectly rational exploitation, but it is hard to see their relevance to any free society. Needless to say, the writers, being human beings and endowed with common sense, did not stick to their definitions. Even apart from extensive animadversions on machines and other forms of capital which are not products in the sense here in question, and are not fitted into the theory of a rate of return, they always treated as capital whatever is actually paid ("advanced") to labourers as wages.

In discussing the notion of unproductive consumption, Senior makes an observation (p. 56) which contains much realistic economic insight, and deserves especially to be brought to the attention of social reformers devoted to the equalitarian ideal: "We do not, of course, mean it to be inferred that all personal expenditure beyond mere necessaries is necessarily unproductive. The duties of those who fill the higher ranks in society can seldom be well performed unless they conciliate the respect of the vulgar by a certain display of opulence." Senior illustrates the point by the magistrate and ambassador, but the extreme paradoxical example is the minister of such a religion as Christianity.

[28]Malthus held a diametrically opposite view, which was "refuted" by Senior (p. 64). *Cf.* also Smith, p. 58.

Exclusion from capital of the share of produce consumed by the landlord (when

The classical writers' general theory of productive organization and of distribution may now be restated with explicit reference to the division between wages and capital, and to profit as a rate of return. All production takes place in an *annual cycle*, starting anew from zero at the beginning of each year. During the year, all classes live on the produce of the previous year. The current year's produce comes at the end of the year into the hands of the capitalist. This functionary first pays his rent (if any) as already explained; then from the produce-less-rent, he sets aside a part—what is "necessary"—as "capital", replacing his advances of the previous year and to be advanced to labour as wages during the next year. The final "residue" is his own share or "profit", which is reckoned as a fraction or percentage of the annual advance, the capital. Thus the capital of society is a "wages fund", and the rate of wages is found by dividing the amount of the fund by the number of the working population.

Such a general view of organization and distribution must be sought in the chapters or sections dealing with profit; the fundamental conceptions met with in the explicit discussion of wages are utterly different as we shall see. The theory as sketched was first given a fairly clear formulation in Smith's chapter (book II, ch. iii) bearing the significant title, "Of the Accumulation of Capital, *or* Of Productive and Unproductive Labour" [our italics]. Interestingly enough, Ricardo gave no explicit treatment of the topic of productive and unproductive labour. It is, however, referred to in terms which make it clear that he accepted it as established. It comes up several times in the first few pages of the

rent is paid) would be easier to justify, since the landlord was supposed to play a strictly passive role. (In fact, our authors discuss the division between labour and capital only at the land margin.) From the standpoint of a correct analysis, the landlord, of course, furnishes productive services to industry in a sense theoretically indistinguishable from similar activities on the part of the labourer, and is subject to a "sacrifice", in the same sense, of giving up one valuable alternative to get another. The capitalist, as shown above (part II), is in a somewhat different position, in so far as he not merely furnishes the use of capital, but "abstains" from consuming the capital itself, and perhaps saves it in the first place. But, of course, where land is private property in the complete sense, the individual land owner is in identically the same position as the owner of any other salable productive agency (ignoring the deeper similarities between land and other agencies). But, from the standpoint of a really correct analysis, all of the contributors to production receive their remuneration instantly out of current production and not out of "advances" or "capital".

Some writers, but not in general those here being considered, identified the rate of return with the fraction of the produce accruing to the capitalist. The rent share is, of course, ignored, or eliminated by thinking of production at a land margin, but the statement is still inaccurate, unless the capitalist's own share is considered as capital. But the statement is approximately true since the profit share may be assumed to be small in comparison with that of wages.

chapter on taxes (ch. viii), where the wording is "productive and unproductive consumption" (pp. 131, 132, 133); but on page 135 we have "unproductive labourers". The latter is also the usage in chapter xx on value and riches (p. 263—on p. 264 it is the "reproductive" use of revenue); in chapter xxvi on gross and net revenue (p. 336) we find "unproductive labour". It does not appear that Ricardo attached any meaning to the difference in terminology.[29]

Accepting the general approach, and framework of assumptions, of the system, two main problems leap out at once from the classical writers' pages treating of capital, wages, and profits. The first is, what actually determines the division of the produce-less-rent between capitalists and the labourers, or, stating the question in the form set by the treatment itself, what determines the amount which the capitalist must pay as wages, before he gets his own share, fixed by subtraction. The other problem is the more complex one of fitting into the theory of capital and profit the other forms of capital, so often and fully discussed, represented by things which cannot be viewed as reproduced in an annual cycle starting anew from zero each year.

On the first point, we get a fairly positive answer, if we consider only the treatment of wages which forms the body of the treatment of profits, leaving the latter as a residual. It is a very unsatisfactory answer, but is at least verbally definite. Wages are determined by what is "required" for the support of the labourer (see Ricardo, p. 105.3; Senior, p. 191.2; Mill, p. 416.8). That is, we have a "subsistence theory" of wages. But the definiteness is purely verbal; the substance raises a number of crucial questions, and really answers no questions at all. Since the theory purports to explain, and must explain, the division of the joint labour-capital share which actually takes place, it must be a short-run or momentary theory, and not one which merely states or explains a long-run tendency; the labourer must obviously get what he has to have, "now". (The very different question of long-run tendencies will be taken up presently.) In the absence of any impersonal mechanism of market competition fixing wages,[30] the logic of the situation

[29]The expositions of Senior (pp. 51-7) and of Mill (book I, ch. iii, secs. 5-6) are somewhat easier to follow. Smith has a different arrangement of the material, but except for the "refinement", his wages and profit doctrine is that of the later writers. His main discussion of the phenomena of capital is segregated from that of price and distribution theory in a short second book (book II, "Of the Nature, Accumulation and Employment of Stock"), in chapter iii of which the doctrine in question is developed. His chapter on profits in book I is brief and says little about general theory. (Its main theoretical point will be noticed later.)

[30]Fixing them, of course, at the economic value of the service to the *entrepreneur*, which is their value to the consumer, under the given conditions. But no ethical

would be that the employer should pay what it pays him to pay; any individual labourer should receive the wage which yields the employer the maximum product. That is, wages would be fixed on the same principles as the feed and care of a beast of burden.[31] Thus the subsistence theory of wages rests on the deeper assumption that the employer-capitalist makes the division arbitrarily, and this is the clear import of the text. The minimum subsistence requirement sets the limit in that direction to which it pays him to go, and in the absence of forces setting any other limit, his self-interest makes the minimum the maximum and the actual wage. For those interested in raising wages, the suggestion of policy is obvious: it is only necessary to provide some form of compulsion in order to secure to the labourer "the whole product of his labour", which, again in accord with the principles of the classical economics, is taken to be the whole product of industry. But the notion that wages might be raised by bringing pressure to bear on those who pay them is, as we shall presently emphasize, antithetical to the dearest conclusion on policy of the classical writers themselves.

The deeper aspect of this theory, that capitalists make the division between themselves and their labourers by arbitrary fiat, is strongly confirmed by the tone of the discussion in Smith (book II, ch. iii) and Mill (book I, ch. v, sec. 9), which is one of downright fear lest they may not choose to "destine" to the support of *productive* labour enough of the product to maintain the social capital. Smith is obviously preaching (if not scolding), as well as analysing motives, in his emphasis on the "uniform, constant, and uninterrupted effort of every man to better his condition" (p. 325).[32]

---

implication attaches to the notion of the economic value of a service as a remuneration for the service, without a special examination of the whole problem from an ethical standpoint. All competitive values depend, as a matter of course, on the distribution of ownership of productive capacity (human and non-human) and on the knowledge and tastes of its owners as they affect the supply of services for various uses and the demand for various products. Persons who do not own some productive capacity in some form are outside the economic system altogether. See also, above, p. 172, n. 3.

[31]With the interesting exception, that since the workers are not actually slaves by inheritance, there is no reason why the individual employer should provide the worker with maintenance for a family. But this might be explained by assuming that the employer cannot prevent the worker from having a family and sharing his wages with them, and so must support the family to get the services of the worker. From a social-ethical standpoint, it is an interesting feature of the system that provision for all contingencies in the lives of the workers and their families becomes a responsibility of the workers individually, and one which they cannot adequately meet. But all "individualistic" societies alleviate some of the worst consequences of this inadequacy through various organizations for relief.

[32]Senior and Mill make similar appeals, but Ricardo's preaching generally relates

The other phase of the theory, that wages depend on subsistence requirements is supported by the fact that it has been taught ever since by the radical schools of economics, especially the Marxists, as the "iron law of wages", and is fervently believed to-day, with unessential modifications, by labour leaders and a very large section of the general public. Even when it is held in the form of a "standard of living" theory, the "necessary" standard is viewed as effective at the moment, and not over some long-run of generations.[33] If Marx and the radicals are clear and emphatic about anything, it is the repudiation of Malthusianism and all its works. The theory then takes a "bargaining power" form; but there is no change in economic principles, the essential point being that there are no general impersonal forces determining wages and that, short of the whole product, the individual employer pays what he is somehow "compelled" to pay.[34]

Yet, viewed in the light of the whole text, even of the chapters on profit, Smith and Ricardo and their followers clearly do not really think either that wages ordinarily correspond to, or approximate, a literal minimum subsistence requirement, or that they are fixed by an arbitrary fiat of the employer—in spite of the fact that they often seem to be trying to state these principles as unequivocally as possible. They believed strongly in the fixing of wages by impersonal forces, even by competitive forces, as the chapters on wages (to be considered presently) clearly show. Yet they failed to give any analysis of competitive process, hence any real distribution theory. The reason is simply that they

---

to public policy such as taxation, protective duties, and the poor law, rather than to private behaviour. We should not leave the topic without noting that Ricardo and Mill also expressly state that profit must be at a level which will enable the capitalist to live! (Ricardo, p. 100.9; Mill, p. 450.5). Smith also calls profit the capitalist's fund of subsistence (pp. 57-8).

33 See below, on the classical long-run subsistence theory based on Malthusian population doctrine. This "Malthusian" doctrine is quite adequately stated by Smith (ch. viii, esp. pp. 81-3), along with characteristically sensible observations on the direction of the causal relation between scale of living and wages at a given time (pp. 77-8).

34 The practical conclusion which motivates the wish-thinking back of this theory—namely, that to raise wages it is only necessary to find some way to "build a fire under" the individual who pays them—illustrates a basic human trait. We seem to crave some "enemy" whom we can blame for anything that seems to be wrong, and can attack, as a method of correcting the evil. It is often implied, if not explicitly stated, that it would only be necessary to eliminate ("liquidate"?) the employer and place "the workers themselves" (meaning the propagandists as their "representatives") in charge of production in order to pay wages equal to the income which (successful!) employers receive under competition.

were discussing a problem which, self-evident as its main principles are, they only half saw, and did not at all understand.[35]

The classical writers' explicit discussions of wages, to which we now turn (preceding their treatment of profit) develop two main explanations of wages, one for the short run and one for the long run; both are utterly different from the theory developed as the content of the discussion of profit, in arriving at that share as a residual. The short-run theory, or theory of actual wages, runs in terms of "supply and demand". The supply of labour is the labouring population (not separated from the population as a whole). The demand for labour is the "funds destined for the payment of wages", or "wages fund". As in the discussion of profit, so generally in that of wages, this fund is identical with the capital of society (sometimes only proportional); and, *assuming an annual turnover of capital* (without which it has no meaning), the wage rate is given by the simple formula, "capital divided by population". But capital itself is merely the portion of the produce-less-rent which is actually employed in the payment of wages; and, in the absence of a *momentary* subsistence theory of wages, we simply have no principle of division. Yet the argument clearly assumes both that wages are definitely above the minimum of subsistence, and that the wages fund has some sort of objective reality, though subject to changes. The conclusion which the writers are evidently concerned to establish is that wages can be increased only by increasing the wages fund relative to the number of labourers. But two "burning issues" are raised: first, why should the wages fund increase?[36] and second, if it does increase,

[35]As already noted, they make it clear that competition compels all employers to pay the same wages, and equalizes the rate of profit among them all. (Generally in a separate discussion, not dealing with the general levels of wages and profits, but *cf.* Senior, pp. 191.6 *ff*. Ricardo, in chapter iv, talks constantly about the competition of different uses for capital, but only once uses the word, at p. 68.9.) This, of course, clashes directly with the notion of an arbitrary division between the employer and labour—but in no wise prevents their asserting the latter fact.

Smith repeatedly speaks of increased competition lowering the rate of profit. See pp. 89, 129-30, 335.3, 335.6. At the point of the last reference, he also has the competition raise the wages of labour (*cf.* also Mill, p. 343). The paragraph in Smith containing the last two references occurs in the chapter on interest in book II. It is especially interesting as giving what is perhaps the fullest discussion to be found in his work of a demand function for a productive service, and as completely failing to give any indication of the real mechanism of competition, based on variable proportions and the significance of increments.

[36]One of the puzzling features of the classical exposition is the absence of any clear suggestion that an increased amount of capital, even in the primitive use of raising wages, should within some limits increase the output of given labourers. Smith's remarks at page 88.4 do not invalidate this observation, as it is the increased division

will the effect be to raise wages, or to increase the number of labourers? On the first issue, we are left almost completely in the dark. (It is the first main unanswered question already referred to.) On the second issue we get both alternatives as answers, and also (most clearly in Smith) a third, more defensible view, that it depends for the time being on the *relative rates of increase* in "capital" and "population"; but it is made clear that the rate of increase of capital cannot permanently be the greater, so that the final result is an increase in the supply of labour.[37]

---

of labour which increases the product, and the increase in wages referred to simply raises the question, "why", discussed in the text. At page 259.5f. there is a parallel statement with no reference to an increase in wages. On p. 84, Smith raises the question whether higher real wages *lower* efficiency, as the mercantilist writers generally held. Senior's discussion in particular (p. 188 *ff.*) is put in a form to give him every opportunity and suggestion for mentioning such an effect, but it is conspicuously absent. In order to rationalize a raise in wages from the employers' standpoint, it would seem necessary to assume either that the labour supply responds instantly (see below) or that they deliberately maintain the higher rate for at least a generation in order to make possible an increase in the supply of labourers (which is supposed always to be tending to happen). But such conduct is out of the question under an individualistic system.

In the view of the classical conception of capital, an increase in wages is the same thing as an increase in the proportion of capital to labour. Only Senior of the writers under consideration seems to refer expressly to changes in the proportions of capital and labour as a condition affecting the division between them (pp. 140, 188, 189, 190); but even he makes no mention in this connection of a principle of diminishing returns or the significance of increments. Smith, in his discussion of colonial conditions, in his chapter on profits, mentions the proportion of stock to territory and of people to stock (p. 94). (The classical discussions of changes in the proportions of fixed and circulating capital have possible implications for this topic, and for the theory of capital in general; but the problem is too intricate to take up here. But see below.)

[37]The writers generally did not know whether they were talking about quantities or rates of change. When Smith says, at the beginning of the second paragraph of the chapter on profits, that "the increase of stock . . . raises wages", he means a "sufficient" *rate* of increase. The third answer above may sometimes be used to interpret the other two, but often the context makes this very difficult, definitely implying that more labour will always be on hand to consume more capital.

For the purpose of this essay, we must cut short the discussion of the wages fund with a note on its relation to the facts. The writers' objective, as already observed, was to show that wages cannot be raised by arbitrary action, or by any method which does not increase the amount of capital in proportion to the labouring population—or by "inventions", which they treated in a strangely parenthetical tone. Of course, the application of inventions is generally connected with an increased use of capital, and with this qualification, the conclusion of the older economists was sound, though their reasoning was fallacious. Their major premise was that the employer's share in the product is either negligible or fixed. In recent years, statistical investigation has more and more impressed us with the narrow limits of the possibility of raising wages at the expense of interest and profit. With rent (in accord with any probable estimate) excluded, and allowance made for taxes, gifts for charitable and benevolent purposes,

We have repeatedly referred to the long-run theory developed in the classical writers' treatment of wages, a theory based on the Malthusian doctrine of population. It cannot be subjected to critical examination here, and is mentioned primarily to emphasize again its complete divergence from the short-run subsistence theory already discussed. Careful analysis must distinguish at least three different versions of the subsistence theory of wages in the classical writings. The first of the three (already discussed) is the notion that actual wages are determined by the subsistence requirements of the workers. The second is the doctrine just referred to, that in the long run, wages are controlled by a "standard of living", through the tendency of population to increase or decrease whenever they are above or below the workers' "psychological" requirements which regulate reproduction. A standard of living, to operate in this way, must obviously itself remain stationary, or at least change slowly in comparison with the population changes which bring the supply of labour into equilibrium with reference to it. But thirdly, Smith and the Ricardians clearly recognize historical changes in the standard of living, which is normally under continuous pressure through the tendency of population to outrun the supply of provisions. It is natural to think of the movement as tending toward an ultimate equilibrium, set perhaps by the actual physical requirements of life (if the conception of a physiological minimum can be made to mean anything for human beings). The three equilibrium levels of wages implied in the three theories are all highly indefinite. Furthermore,

---

and necessary savings, the total share now falling to capital and *entrepreneurship* would not raise total wages by any large percentage, and it would have been much smaller a century or two ago. Of course, deductions from the capital share would make more difference if used to raise only the lowest wages. The amount of saving which ought to be provided for is indeed a large political question. As to rent, the modern disposition (with the exception of some Roman Catholic writers) would be to throw the landlord to the wolves first of all. But in Europe, under the feudal tradition, the rent of land was the chief means of payment for public services and for the maintenance of all cultural activities.

Even the distinction between types of product consumed by labourers and by capitalists, suggested by Senior, has vastly more significance for the problem of transfer of income than he recognized; a large part of the difference between large and small incomes would disappear under equalization in relative changes in the prices of "choice cuts" and those less choice, where the proportions in production are relatively inflexible.

From the standpoint of economic theory, the conception of capital as a fund for the support of labour over an interval between production and consumption is still profoundly important. It was reworked by Böhm-Bawerk, who combined elements from Ricardo and Senior to make the amount of capital a matter of the length of the production process, and in his form is still generally accepted and taught. For the fundamental fallacies involved, see above, part II and references, this JOURNAL, vol. I, no. 1, p. 25, note.

the notion of currently "necessary" wages is ambiguous, and might be subdivided into various shorter and longer-run conceptions.

. . . . .

On the second major unanswered question in classical wages and profit theory, we must be very brief. This has to do, as will be recalled, with the treatment of capital in other forms than the annual wage advances to labour, especially with the question of the quantity of "capital" in various "capital goods", relatively permanent in comparison with food, and other things which may be thought of as used up and replaced in an annual cycle. The question is especially insistent and perplexing, not merely because of the prominence given to these other forms (more or less corresponding to the division between "fixed" and "circulating", in the general discussions and classifications of capital) but even more because in the illustrations used in explaining distribution theory the more durable forms are so largely involved.

The general position taken more or less explicitly by the writers is that the rate of return in other fields is "determined" by the rate on capital used to pay wages in agriculture at the land margin.[38] But in the first place, any view of the determination of a price in one section of a market by the price in another section is indefensible, as the causal relation in such a case is necessarily mutual.[39] But secondly, and more important, such reasoning is worthless without an explanation of the meaning of a quantity of capital "in" an instrument which is not a consumable product but has "indirect utility". For the value is struck "now" while the product (*a*) is to be enjoyed in the future, and (*b*) must be isolated by imputation. This is the central problem, almost the whole problem, of capital as a base for a rate of return; the classical economists never glimpsed the problem itself and, of course, have no light to shed upon it. All that it seems possible to say is that they had a fixed idea that all capital is the accumulated product of labour (or labour itself—the same thing in their minds), and that consequently the same principles which fit the advance of subsistence to labourers would fit all other cases (*cf.* esp. Mill, p. 418).

[38]See Ricardo, "Essay on the Influence of a Low Price of Corn on the Profits of Stock, etc.", in *Works*, p. 372 and second footnote; Senior, p. 188.7; Mill treats agriculture and manufactures together, failing to see that his theory approximately fits only the former (book II, ch. xv).

[39]It could at most be approximately correct if the demand for capital in the particular part of the market supposed to control were overwhelmingly large in comparison with all other demand. (It seems legitimate to say that the level of the water in the ocean "determines" the level in some particular bay.) Moreover, Ricardo's argument that a change in the level of profit in agriculture will change the level in manufacturing industry without a movement of capital from one field to the other is rank fallacy (see *Essay*, in *Works*, pp. 379-80).

However, given a market rate of interest, the concept of capital quantity as cost, including interest, is so simple and obvious that no one who knew anything about business management and accounting could possibly be unfamiliar with its meaning. Consequently, it is easy, and no doubt justifiable, to read roughly correct general conceptions into the illustrations involving "fixed" capital which are used by Ricardo and other writers. They undoubtedly understood even the nature of capital maintenance as well as men need to do to administer capital intelligently in practice.

This suggests the fact that their crucial error lay in the theory of the "primary" case, the interpretation of the nature and role of capital in the use of paying wages in agriculture, and at the land margin. Even under the absurd assumption of a strictly *annual* and *synchronous* agricultural cycle in the production and using-up of physical materials, it is still true that in correct accounting, the "quantity of capital" is theoretically constant; the writers simply forgot that the growing crop is capital! Perhaps conditions can be imagined under which their theory would be valid; but these issues cannot be further considered here.[40] The outstanding fact is the absurd unrealism of a periodic or episodic view of capitalistic production. Capital is inherently continuous, because production is continuous, as is all activity directed by thinking. It is the essential nature and task of rational accounting to make this continuity explicit.[41]

FRANK H. KNIGHT

The University of Chicago.

[40]They have been broached above in part II. The first requisite which comes to mind is that the physical cycles should not overlap, the capital-creation phase of one coinciding with the capital consumption phase of the next. We may revert again to Böhm-Bawerk, to note that his error was the same as that of the classical writers; that is, it lay not in assimilating the other forms of capital to the wages fund, but in failing to give an accurate analysis fitting any case, under anything like real conditions.

[41]In a deeper analysis, the error in the whole classical position (including, of course, Böhm-Bawerk) roots in the special character and role assigned to labour. More generally still, it consists in confusing conceptual analysis with ethical evaluation. From the former standpoint, labour and capital instruments, including land, are all alike, simply productive resources. It is in the contrast between capital as "supporting" and "aiding" labour, and labour as "using" and "reproducing" capital, that the immediate fallacy lies. The relation is symmetrically mutual. All the productive agencies use each other (or are used jointly by the enterprise), and all are jointly maintained and reproduced by all, in a continuing process.

[6]

Economics in the United States of America

A Review and Interpretation of Research

PART I

PRELIMINARY REMARKS REGARDING THE NATURE OF AN ECONOMIC PROBLEM

AN ECONOMIC PROBLEM ALWAYS A PROBLEM OF CHOICE

In these preliminary remarks I shall try to make clear the point of view which I have adopted in the organization of this review. Economic research and analysis presuppose formulations of economic problems, and it is in the forms in which the problems are considered, as well as in the development of methods of dealing with the problems, that we may observe the trends of economic research. I shall accordingly explain my understanding of the essential nature of an economic problem.

In brief, to economize is to choose, and the possibility of a choice implies the existence of alternatives. Hence, by economic problem we shall always refer to a problem of choice among alternatives, and the burden of the discussion of a particular economic problem will be the description of alternatives and the designation or discovery of an acceptable criterion by which a selection is made. Three types of choice problems readily come to mind. First, if there is a given end to be attained and if there are alternative means of attaining the end, there is a problem of choosing a particular means. This type includes only conditional problems, the choice being conditioned by a well-defined end. Decisions made by the management of a business firm are examples of choices of this type. Second, each individual as a free agent chooses his own ends. A consumer will have made a choice of this type when he decides upon the allocation of his budget. Third, the individuals constituting a group or society of free agents jointly choose the constraints and regulations which they impose upon their individual actions. The decisions made by a legislative body in the drafting of legislative acts are examples of choices of this third type.

A considerable part of recent theoretical and applied research has been devoted to the first type of choice problem. These problems are technical in that they do not involve social conflict; and in this sense a problem belonging to this first type is not a social problem. Economic analysis of the conventional sort, however, does not directly deal with problems of this first type, but is rather concerned primarily with problems of the third type, which are social problems in that social conflict and the seeking for consensus are essential elements. In recent times the discussion of this third type of problem has had to do with the farm problem, the labour problem, the employment problem, the problem of trade restrictions, and the like. To name them is to realize that these are problems inherent in the idea of a social organization of free individuals. The touchstone, it is said, of any legislative constraint upon individual action that may be imposed lies in the question whether a rational people could have imposed such a law on itself. Social discussion is always a discussion of this question. It was the question at the base of Adam Smith's and David Ricardo's discussions and analyses, no different in any respect from the essential question involved in any contemporary issue of public policy. In this sense, the third type is the classical economic problem.

In the remainder of this Part, I shall discuss the nature of these first and third types of economic problems. In doing so I shall propose an interpretation of what economists do as analysts and advisers. In Parts II and III I shall discuss what they have recently done in these roles, the nature of their theoretical and applied work, and this discussion will be presented under headings referring to these two types of problems.

THE FIRST TYPE OF PROBLEM: THE CHOICE OF MEANS FOR A WELL-DEFINED END

The management of a business concern is a choosing agency which is supposed to review continually the performance of the concern and to make any alterations which will improve this performance. When we say this, what is the nature of this that we have in mind as being subject to alteration by the management? It is the performance of what that is to be analysed, predicted, and evaluated.

If we were asked to point to the accounting system that has been adopted by the management, we could do no more than point to a set of rules indicating what the operating personnel are to do in all conceivable situations. When we speak of the accounting system of a firm we do not refer to particular human beings and physical equipment. We refer to a system of rules of action, which includes a designation of required equipment and operating personnel. To change this accounting system is to change this set of rules, and generally a new system involves the use of different personnel and equipment. If a new accounting system is adopted, the management will have reached a judgment that the performance of the old system is not good enough; i.e. the management will have made a choice among the respective performance properties of alternative systems of rules of action.

Similarly, a production scheduling system is a system of rules which governs the actions of certain operating personnel. The scheduling system does not consist of the employees. It consists of the system of rules. Likewise, the inventory control system is a system of rules, as is the procedure for assigning men or equipment to jobs or the procedure for producing the product or for the assignment of quotas or for the control of finances. The description of any particular procedure which may be singled out within the firm would take the form of a statement of a set of rules stipulating the conditions and governing the actions of operating personnel.

With these considerations in mind, we may say that the organization for the performance of which the management is responsible is simply the system of all these sets of rules of action. The management is a decision-making agency, and the firm is its organization for decision-making at all levels of operation. The business organization in this sense is one vast decision-function. To use another current expression to convey the same idea, it is a strategic plan of operations which the management controls. A strategic plan of operations is described by the sets of rules of action such as those to which we have referred. A plan of operations requires personnel and equipment for its implementation; but in essence it is simply a system of rules of action. And the choice problem of the management is that of selecting the best performing system of rules.

In considering the choice problem in this form, I am following the tendency of a vigorous contemporary development in theoretical statistics and in the theory of strategic behaviour. I may go too far in supposing that every economic problem can be regarded as a problem of finding an optimum set of rules of action. But I do not think I go too far in this. To economize is to choose an action which in some sense is regarded by the chooser as best for the observed situation. But if we attempt to set forth the explicit grounds for the choice, we do not talk about the particular action as such. Rather, we analyse the rule or principle which would prescribe the action for this particular situation. And our discussion consists primarily of a comparison of how different rules of action would work out in repetitions of this kind of situation.

The advantage that I see in adopting this formulation is that certain theoretical developments have clarified the problem of choice and the nature of rational action when viewed in this light. I do not mean to suggest that this recently developed body of theory provides a ready technical device for solving problems of choice in general. To many or most people the kinds of problems to which the theory has been applied will appear relatively unimportant. Furthermore, the fundamental theorems would be looked upon by many as applying to aspects of the problem which are of small practical interest. A choosing agency in a real situation is not concerned with whether or not a 'solution' exists in the sense defined in the theory. It must take action in any event, and it may find little help in a theory which presupposes information which is virtually unattainable. In order to apply the theorems, the problem must be formulated in well-defined terms. But the practical solutions of many problems of choice would become almost obvious if they could be formulated in carefully defined terms. That is, it is the definition of the terms which in many instances gives the trouble.

However, it is a clarification of choice problems in general if this is understood. In an application of this theory, alternative systems of rules are accounted for, measures of performance are clearly defined, the performance of each possible system is predicted, and a criterion for the ordering of the systems with respect to the goodness of their performances is made explicit. Much experience has been gained in the doing of these tasks for certain kinds of problems. If the procedure that is being critically reviewed were a quality control system, we should know pretty well how the specialist would approach his tasks—how he would analyse a particular system, the measures he would propose for describing the performance characteristics, the theoretical basis for his predictions of the performances of alternative systems. The basic theory which he would apply would be the theory of probability. These methods and measures would not be applicable for a similarly critical study of an accounting system. But the same kinds of tasks would have to be performed, for it is the same kind of problem of choice among alternative systems of rules of action. The same would be true for other control procedures. The specialization of any expert who tenders advice on problems of choice lies in his ability to analyse special kinds of rules of action, and the statements which he makes as a specialist have reference to one or another of the above tasks.

THE SECOND TYPE OF CHOICE: THE LEGISLATIVE CHOICE OF CONSTRAINTS UPON INDIVIDUAL ACTION

We have envisaged the management of a firm as continually reviewing the performance of its organization. It is never quite satisfied with this performance, and it is forever making observations which induce it to judge tentatively that one part or another of its system of rules can be improved upon. That is, the management is continually selecting and choosing, and so is any other individual agency.

Let us consider now some of the conditions under which individual agencies make their choices. While the individual can at any time alter his rules of action and procedures, he does so subject to physical and institutional constraints which he looks upon as not alterable by his personal decision. But while not alterable by actions of individuals acting independently from the point of view of personal interests, some of these institutional and physical conditions are subject to change by the joint action of the group or society of individuals. For example, the actions of all individuals are constrained by the particular monetary and banking system which exists within a nation. This national financial system is not subject to change by the act of an individual, but the society of individuals, through a legislative process, takes action from time to time to alter it.

A major alteration of the monetary and financial system was made in 1913, and we may use this case as an illustration. Prior to 1913, stringencies in the money markets were observed in the spring and in the autumn of nearly every year, and every few years or so one of these stringencies would turn into something severe enough to be looked upon as a financial panic. This kind of behaviour was interpreted as indicative of a 'flaw' and as 'poor' performance of the financial system. That is to say, just as the individual management in the above discussion observed something which induced it to judge tentatively that it could improve upon the performance of a procedure which it was using, so in this case members of the society were induced by what they observed to judge tentatively that the performance of the monetary system of the nation could be improved upon.

In the previous section we undertook to explain the sense in which it is said that a quality control system, or any other procedure being used by an individual management, is described by a specification of a set of rules which govern the actions of operators. What, now, in this present case do we mean to convey by the term 'monetary and banking system'? That is, how do we go about describing that which we have in mind when we speak of the monetary system in force at that time within this nation? When we consider how we may alter the monetary system, we raise in our minds possible forms of legislative acts which might be enacted. To change the system is to substitute an alternative legislative act for the act which is currently in force. The alternative monetary systems then are the alternative formulations of legislative acts and regulations. Hence, I suggest that the financial system would be described by a listing of all the laws and regulations bearing upon what individuals can and cannot do in regard to financial matters and bearing upon what designated administrators of the system are required to do. In the sense that the laws and regulations are rules, the system that we have in mind is a system of rules.

Again, as in the case of a choice by an individual agency, to say that a system can be improved upon is to say that the performance characteristics of another system of rules and constraints are preferable. What is it that the members of the society were observing when they were induced to review and re-evaluate the performance of the established monetary system? That is, taking 'system' to mean the set of constraints and prescriptions laid down in the legislative acts in force, how were the performance characteristics of the monetary system observed?

The performance was observed in the behaviour of selected variable quantities: interest rates, price indexes, bank loans, bank reserves, bank deposits, the quantity of money in circulation, business failures, etc. For example, when short-term money rates are plotted by weeks or months for the years before 1913, the graph shows a tendency for two extreme peaks to appear in each year—in the spring and in the autumn. When bank and general business failures are plotted in the same way for those years, peaks again appear within each year, and these series concur with the money rate series in reflecting the occurrence every few years or so of a virtual financial panic. In connexion with these observations, it was argued that there was a 'perverse elasticity' of the quantity of money—that the actions of individuals at certain periods of the year resulted in relatively large net withdrawals of deposits from banks located in the agricultural areas of the nation and that the system was such that this resulted in a geographical flow of money and reserves, which in turn, as the system stood, sharply reduced the total quantity of money available for the commerce of the nation during these periods of the year. This regular and pronounced seasonal reduction in the quantity of money was attributed to the monetary and banking system as an inherent working property.

Thus, the characteristic performance of the system was described in the statements that were made about the behaviour of and relationship among a selection of variable quantities. Such statements, describing regularities and associations among variables, go beyond a simple description of what may have been historically observed. They are essentially analytical inferences and refer not merely to the real system that had been in operation but to any system having the same essential features. This is what is meant by a theoretical model, and the identification of the essential features in the real system under observation is the empirical element in the work of the analysts. It is stated in effect that the performance characteristics which are described as being observed are necessary properties of the system under review, and this represents a prediction of what will be observed if the system continues in operation. The validity of the predictions of course rests upon the validity of the empirical judgments pertaining to observed regularities and upon the truth of the analytical inferences.

The argument went on to contend that this marked seasonal variation in the availability of liquid funds made private risk and hardship greater than they need be. The latter contention expresses an evaluation indicating that the performance properties of the system in force are not so good as those which would characterize some alternative which may possibly be designed. Although a defined criterion was not explicitly stated, essentially a criterion was applied when a choice was made among the conceivable alternative systems. Those who favoured a redrafting of banking legislation, in order to reduce this 'private risk and hardship', did not propose merely to establish an authority directed to take whatever action it saw fit to take in order to iron out certain seasonal variations. They proposed the selection of a banking system designed specifically to perform better than the old one, irrespective of the particular members of the administrative personnel.

It may be noted in this connexion that the drafting of this reform legislation raised theoretical controversies which involved essentially the same issues as those in the banking school-currency school controversies of the mid-nineteenth century in Great Britain. These controversies had to do with how to design the system in such a way that it would be characterized by certain working properties. The side which prevailed in the drafting of the original Federal Reserve Act relied, for the automatic control of the quantity of money, upon a rule which would restrict rediscounting privileges to 'self-liquidating' commercial loans. The predicted performance of this rule was not borne out by later experience. Whatever the actual outcome, however, the explicit attempt on the part of the reformers was to draft a new set of rules constituting a new monetary and banking system which would perform better than the system then in operation.

We might have referred to the discussion of any public policy issue to illustrate the nature of an economic problem of the type which we are now considering. In the case of the agricultural problem, it is the pricing system which many members of the society regard as faulty. The discussion of any such issue—the tax problem, the monopoly problem, the problem of employment instability, etc.—follows the same general pattern. In any case, the economic problem is posed when members of the society are induced by what they observe to inquire into the possibility of improving the performance of the system currently in force. To change the system means to alter certain legislative acts and regulations. There is thus a choice to be made by legislators among the respective performance characteristics of systems of laws and regulations. Hence, there are three essential stages in the formulation and solution of an economic problem: first, the specification of a set of possible alternative systems of constraints; second, to each system there is to be attributed its performance characteristics; and, third, there is to be determined the relation 'better-than-or-as-good-as' between the respective performances of any pair of alternative systems.

THIS SECOND TYPE OF CHOICE INTERPRETED AS THE SUBJECT MATTER OF CLASSICAL POLITICAL ECONOMY

We are using the term 'economic system' to mean a system of legislative constraints upon individual action. In the sense that laws and regulations are rules, an economic system is a system of rules, and legislators are confronted always with the problem of finding a better-working system of rules. While this is perhaps a somewhat novel use of the term economic system and although this formulation of the problem of political economy corresponds in general outline with the contemporary formulation of a decision problem, our conception of political economy is nevertheless strictly classical.

Adam Smith regarded political economy 'as a branch of the science of a statesman or legislator'. His treatise, *The Wealth of Nations*, was in its entirety a critical review of the performance characteristics of various 'systems of political economy'. He began by noting that 'Nations . . . have followed very different plans in the general conduct or direction [of their affairs]; and those plans have not all been equally favorable to the greatness of its produce.' The 'greatness of its produce' was the basis upon which he proposed to judge the performances of these different systems of political economy. The expected average 'welfare' of the members of the society, i.e. per capita income, would be different depending upon the particular system adopted. That is, to each alternative system there would correspond a characteristic 'average welfare' or 'per capita income', and the analytical and predictive problem was to compare systems of political economy with respect to this measure or quantity. This comparison and evaluation is the essential subject-matter of his work. The price and value theory, the monetary theory, the economic history are all developed and presented as incidental to the discussion of this main topic. He outlined and explained what he regarded as the conditions favourable to the improvement of 'welfare'. He argued that under any circumstances which allow freedom of action within a system of constraints, there will be variation among the values of the outputs and incomes of the members of a society. Hence, the presence *per se* of differences among the prices of commodities and among the incomes of individuals is not to be interpreted necessarily as indicative of faulty performance of a political economy. His theory of value and of price and distribution was presented in the development of this argument. But while there will be observed variations among incomes of families and among prices of commodities under any particular system of legislative constraints, average income and output will be different for different systems. This led up to the main part of his work, the consideration of 'different systems of political economy', by which he meant alternative systems of legislative constraints. He considered 'two different systems. . . . The one may be called the system of commerce, the other that of agriculture'. These were the Mercantilist and Physiocratic systems. He reviewed critically the measures of performance proposed by the proponents of these systems, and he analysed the arguments that were presented purporting to show that one or the other was a 'best' performing system. The statements made in these arguments were descriptive and predictive or else evaluative, and Smith applied logical and empirical tests, such as these were understood in that day, in order to arrive at judgments regarding their truth or falsity. Reaching judgments that the arguments were unsound, he concluded his discussion by proposing the general outlines of a third legislative policy.

As his discussion now appears, he took for granted much that now would be questioned. For example, 'welfare' as a variable has many dimensions, and the variation of a one-dimensional quantity such as per capita income reflects only one aspect of what the term welfare is supposed to connote. A change in a system of legislative constraints will result in changes in the values of many quantities. Smith implied that the adoption of his legislative programme would result in a set of values for all these quantities other than per capita income which would be no less preferred by the group and that, in addition, the effect would be to increase per capita income. But he presented no argument to this effect.

We would seem to be today scarcely better prepared than Smith to develop a compelling argument in regard to such matters. Our measures of performance are still ambiguous and controversial and we have scant theoretical basis for predicting performance characteristics. Had Smith been evaluating alternative designs for a quality control system, he would have had the same kinds of problems of observation, definition, and analysis; for in this simple case the ultimate problem is also to evaluate the performances of alternative systems of rules. For dealing with problems of the latter sort, a present-day technician would have at hand generally accepted definitions of measures of performances and analytical techniques for the confident prediction of performance characteristics. Smith's problem of political economy, however, is enormously more complex.

INCIDENTAL PROBLEMS OF MEASUREMENT AND OF DEFINITION OF CRITERIA

It is a peculiarity of a problem of political economy that there must be a popular understanding of its nature and formulation; for the choice to be made is ultimately by the joint action of all the members of the society. Not only must a large number of individuals of varying capacities understand the formulation. It is a much more complicated problem to formulate than is the first type. The management of a business firm recognizes a well-defined end to be attained, and the continuing task is the evaluation of alternative means. Conceptually, for each alternative there is a corresponding 'pay off', and the measure of this 'pay off' is given in the formulation of the problem. It is an easily understood means-end problem which is presented. But legislators who act on behalf of the members of a society do not have before them a well-defined end for which there are alternative means. There is no generally accepted measure of the 'pay off' corresponding to each of the alternatives confronting legislators in a problem of political economy.

I wish now to develop this distinction between the two types of choice problems.

An individual owns service-yielding assets which he is free to dispose of as he sees fit, subject to a system of constraints which he has had a part in legislating and which he continually participates in judging. A firm is a decision-making agency organized by such individuals for the management of assets assigned to it by these individuals. The quantity of these assets is measured in terms of a common unit called the monetary unit, and this quantity measures the net worth of the firm. The firm's operations with this net worth involve purchasing physical resources and services, transforming these resources and services into a product, which in turn is exchanged for financial resources. This exchange of money for resource services, on the one hand, and produced goods and services for money, on the other, is a continuing process; and the firm's objective in managing this process is to add to the net worth which individuals have put at its disposal.

For any period of time, the 'result' or 'outcome' of the firm's operations is given by the difference between its net worth at the beginning of the period and its net worth at the end of the period prior to any distribution among the individual owners of the firm. This difference is equivalent to the difference between the firm's financial expenditures and its financial receipts, after appropriate allowance has been made for changes in the capital accounts—for example, an allowance for depreciation as a 'cost expenditure' and for changes in the value of inventories as a 'financial receipt'. The task which is assigned to the firm is that of maintaining a 'best' use of the net worth available to it. 'Best' or 'optimum' use is understood to be that use which maximizes the growth rate of the net worth of the firm; or, equivalently, that use which maximizes the firm's net revenue.

Hence, when the firm considers whether or not a particular procedure should be adopted, it has a criterion at hand. It asks what its net revenue would be on the assumption that one of the possible procedures were substituted for the one presently in use. If the adoption of this possible substitute may be expected to result in a larger net revenue, then the substitute is designated as 'better' than the procedure being used. The end or objective of the management's actions in selecting a procedure is to maximize this variable quantity called net revenue, and the value or worth of each alternative is measured by the expected increment to net revenue which would result from its adoption.

However, it is only by virtue of the individual's having accepted a quantifying procedure for measuring 'costs' on the one hand and 'receipts' on the other and having defined the end to be the maximizing of the difference between these quantities that this problem of selecting an 'optimum' alternative may be regarded as objectively technical. The individual in accepting the quantifying procedures and the method of measuring the ' pay off' chooses to enter into the play of a 'game'; and he engages technical personnel to select and operate an 'optimum strategy'. The technicians in designating a 'best' procedure do not strictly choose. They measure and arrange, and they have no other alternative than to select the 'best' as this is defined.

Unlike the firm, the individual is not a technical instrument for the attainment of a predetermined end. All that can be said in this regard is that the individual is his own end. We all understand that as individuals we do not make our choices in order simply to maximize income or to minimize hours of labour or to minimize days of sickness or to maximize years of life, or to minimize or maximize any particular one-dimensional variable. What are believed to be the effects upon these and an undetermined number of other variables have a bearing upon the choices which an individual makes. Presumably, there is a system of rules of action which corresponds to a preferred combination of the values among a set of variables which an individual recognizes as pertinent. This system of rules would be the individual's 'plan of living'. But there is no variable quantity which can be said to be maximized by the choice of the system.

We speak of an individual as striving to maximize his 'welfare', and the way in which we use the term 'welfare' seems to imply that it refers to some variable quantity. But there is no one-dimensional variable which measures welfare. When I speak of my welfare or satisfaction as being higher if I follow one course of action than if I follow another, I am asserting how I would locate on a one-dimensional continuum the respective consequences which I expect to follow from two courses of action. To say that I like one set of consequences better than the other is to say no more than that I place the first set to the right of the second. This is a statement referring to a simple ordering of the alternatives, and it is location along a non-numerical scale and not quantity which is expressed.[1]

It may be that through some scaling analysis,[2] technicians may discover approximately what an individual does when he responds to the stimuli of the alternatives,, and thus may predict this individual's ordered arrangement of alternatives. But this prediction is a different kind of operation from that performed by technicians in the case of the firm. In the latter case, 'net revenue' is a well-defined quantity, and the technicians are instructed to find the set of rules of action which maximizes this quantity. The prediction is of how a designed set of rules will perform. In the other case, 'welfare' is not a measurable quantity, and optimum is undefined so far as the technician is concerned. The task is that of finding out what rules an individual is in fact following in arriving at an ordered arrangement of alternatives. The prediction is of the rules which the individual will use in the future. There is no further analysis of the worth of the rules, for there is no well-defined end for which the individual is a means.

Similarly, a society of individuals is not a means to an end. The society is not a designed instrument for a designated purpose. A society of individuals is simply a collection of persons who mutually recognize situations calling for joint action. The term 'society' is not to be identified with the term 'Government' or 'State'. The latter term refers to a collection of agencies and services presumably designed for the attainment of ends more or less well defined. The rules and procedures adopted by these agencies, i.e. by police, fire, health, welfare, and other governmental departments, are subject to evaluation as means for attaining ends, just as the worth of a procedure adopted by a firm is subject to objective measurement; and it makes sense to speak of such an agency as more or less efficient just as it is operationally meaningful to state that a private firm has increased its efficiency. But the society of individuals is a collection of individuals rather than a collection of these agencies; and no meaning can be attached to the concept of efficiency when the reference is to this collection of jointly choosing individuals.[3]

By joint action, the persons constituting the society choose the details of their economic system—by which term we mean the collection of all the enactments and rules which constrain and prescribe the individual actions of the members of the society. The individuals who jointly choose the constraints are the same individuals whose actions are constrained; and they are continually engaged in reviewing the performance of these enactments, just as an individual continually reviews the performance of his personal rules which he has adopted for the

1. Cf. C. H. Coombs, 'Mathematical Models in Psychological Scaling', *Journal of the American Statistical Association*, December 1951, pp. 480-9.
2. Cf. W. G. Madow, 'The Measurement and Prediction of Attitudes', ibid., pp. 508-14. This is a review article of the book *Measurement and Prediction*, by S. A. Stouffer, L. Guttman, *et al.*
3. Further remarks are made below, pp. 32 et seq., regarding the use of concept of 'efficiency' as this concept is applied by 'welfare economists' in their efforts to appraise 'the economic organization of a society'.

guidance of his private actions. Also analogously with the case of an individual, we speak of a society of individuals as striving to maximize 'social welfare'. But again this is not a variable which can be plotted as a quantity upon a numerical scale. Per capita income, calculated in accordance with some specified set of definitions, is not infrequently used as an indicant of the 'welfare' of a society, and this can be plotted upon a numerical scale. But we can all imagine circumstances such that even though the per capita income be smaller the 'social welfare' would be regarded as the greater; and hence we must conclude that if per capita income measures one dimension of social welfare, there must be other dimensions. It would seem then that social welfare is not a one-dimensional variable in terms of which an end is defined, but rather is an expression having approximately the same meaning as the term 'performance'.

The performance of an economic system is observed in the behaviour of certain variable quantities such as: measures of aggregate income or output, of the degree of equality of distribution of income among families, of the standard of living, of the rate of change in the standard of living, of the instability of employment, of the freedom of individual action. Corresponding to a particular system, a set of expected values, as measures of these and other variables, would describe the characteristic performance. When an individual states a preference for one system over another, he, again, is stating how he would locate the set along a non-numerical scale—placing one to the right of the other. But in this case, he only participates in the making of a choice. The members of the society must reach a consensus, and the choice is based upon a joint evaluation. This involves the resolution of conflicting evaluations through argument and discussion.

There being no end for which the society is a means, there is no defined criterion which technicians can apply to designate an 'optimum' system. The system must be jointly chosen by the members of the society, and the technical problem, beyond the measurement and prediction of performance characteristics, is that of facilitating the social inter-action and communication leading to a consensus.

THE INDIVIDUAL OBLIGATION IMPLICIT IN THE IDEA OF INDIVIDUAL FREEDOM

One can never propose an alteration in an economic system on the explicit grounds that he will gain personally from the alteration—at least he can never do so with any hope that he will be listened to. The proposal must be made on the grounds that the result will be generally more satisfying or else that what now exists is unfair. Party platforms contain assertions of this sort, and the process of legislative enactment is the procedure of social discussion by which joint judgments are made upon the validity of the criticisms and the value of the proposals. How is it that we say that social criticism in order to be valid must necessarily be devoid of personal motive? And how is it that the individuals constituting the society may feel a binding obligation to pursue the process until consensus is reached and to conform to the rules and constraints which are the outcome of the process? That is, what is the source of the obligation that may be felt by each member of the society to abide by the laws established by the group?

These obligations—to reach judgments which are independent of personal interests and to conform to the system of laws which results from the process of social discussion—are implied in the idea of a political organization of individuals each of whom recognizes all of the others as equally free each to act as he wills. To be free to act as one chooses and at the same time to recognize the freedom of others to do likewise can only mean that all participate equally in setting the constraints upon individual action. For no one is free unless all abide by the rules of conduct which all can be brought to accept as appropriate constraints upon individual action. The establishment of a corps of policemen whose function it is to restrain individuals from impairing the freedom of other individuals who are less strong or less crafty, is not an impairment of the freedom of these strong or crafty individuals. For if the strong and crafty are free to impose their wills upon the less endowed, then too the less endowed are free to band together to impose their will upon the stronger individuals. To require of each individual that he takes no action which impairs the freedom of any other individual is to accept the moral principle that no individual should treat another simply as a means to an end. Each individual chooses the rules and principles for the guidance of his conduct, but he does so under the general principle that no rule of action will be adopted which could not be universally adopted by all individuals. In deciding whether an action is compatible with the assumption of freedom for all, he will apply a test to the rule which would call for this action under the contemplated conditions, asking, not how the rule will work from the point of view of his own personal interests, but how the rule will work if all individuals adopted it as a principle of action.

Hence, when we think of a free and rational individual we do not envisage an individual unconstrained by law but rather an individual who acts in accordance with rules of conduct which he has chosen. The statement that a free man enacts his own laws expresses only the principle[1] that he chooses no rule of action which he would not accept as universal law to be acted upon by all individuals.

We have considered rules of action which may be chosen for the attainment of a specified end. These are conditional rules, and they prescribe what the individual must do in order best to attain the end. The other kind of rule of action is unconditional and prescribes what one must do or what one must refrain from doing without regard to any personal end. This type of rule is of the nature of law, and it enjoins certain kinds of actions to correspond with certain kinds of situations, let the consequences be what they may.

The idea of each individual regarding himself as one who enacts law and who judges himself and his actions from this point of view leads to the notion of a commonwealth of individuals—a systematic union of different human beings living under common laws. The social problem confronting these individuals is that of jointly choosing this system of laws.

INDIVIDUAL FREEDOM A FUNDAMENTAL ASSUMPTION OF THE CLASSICAL TYPE OF THEORETICAL ECONOMICS

The ideas expressed above were presented as implications of the concept of individual freedom at about the time this nation was formed; and the political structure of the U.S.A. reflects this conception of freedom and rationality. It was at this time also that Hume and Smith were writing the essays and books which

1. The discussion of this section will be recognized as a paraphrase of Kant's analysis of the concept of freedom as presented in his *Groundwork of the Metaphysics of Morals*. A remark may be added here regarding political procedure. How does an individual see to it that the laws which he recognizes as binding upon his actions are of his own choosing? Is a majority vote to be interpreted as an expression of 'consensus'? The answer to this latter question is clearly no. The majority rule is no more than a device constituting a part of a political procedure which is accepted by the individual. There is no implication that he accepts as right and just a particular law which results from a particular application of this device. It is understood that the resulting law is only tentative, that the search for consensus continues, that the rule will be applied to proposed revisions of the law at the next opportunity, and that the joint action taken was expedient action rather than necessarily right. The individual accepts the political procedure for seeking a consensus and by implication the results which may be observed at any particular point in time.

set the pattern for the classical tradition in economic theory. Their works, and the works of those who followed them, were directed to problems of choice of our third type—where free men are reviewing the working properties of alternative systems of laws as constraining rules to apply to all alike. This continuing review and rewriting of enactments with the intent to improve, presents economic problems in the classical sense, and these problems are implicit in the growth of knowledge and the idea of a union of free rational beings under common laws.

The historical development of this classical type of theoretical economics has not altered its essential character; and the more or less recent developments outside this tradition have not dealt with the problems which gave rise to this tradition. These newer developments have been directed at problems of choice of the first kind, the technical problems of determining best means for the attainment of well-defined ends. The classical type of theoretical economics has virtually nothing to contribute to a solution of this kind of problem. For example, a solution is not even sought for the firm's problem of choosing a 'best' way of producing a given rate of output—as solution is understood and as the problem would be formulated in the recently developed decision theory. The assumption is simply that the managing agency, for any given set of prices of resource services, knows how to find for each rate of output that combination of resources which renders the cost of producing that output a minimum. On the hypothesis of competitive conditions, the implication of the firm's having chosen a least cost combination of resources is that for each pair of resources the ratio of their respective marginal productivities is equal to the ratio of their prices. But this equality of ratios is not presented as a rule for the guidance of an economizing agency in its search for this optimum combination. The equality is inferred from the assumption of rational action and is not itself a guide to that action.

Such conditions—e.g. that the ratio of the price of a factor service to the marginal productivity of the service be made the same for all factor services—are called equilibrium conditions. From the equilibrium conditions, other relations are inferred among variable quantities in terms of which the working properties of a system of legislative enactments are described. The fundamental assumption underlying the structure of the theory is that free men choose among alternative ways of using their respective assets, and that they are constrained in these choices by technological and institutional conditions. The derived theorems describe implications of this fundamental assumption with respect to the relationships among such quantities as prices, outputs, inputs, incomes, revenues, costs. The observed performance of the system of constraints is described in terms of measures calculated from these quantities; and when members of the society consider ways and means of improving the system of laws under which they make their individual choices, they attempt to analyse and predict the effects upon the performance of the system brought about by changes in the relations implied in proposed legislative changes in the system of laws.

THE SUBJECT MATTER OF THE FOLLOWING TWO PARTS

The theoretical work of recent years which seems to have received most notice has dealt with the first type of choice problem—problems of choice in which ends are well-defined. These contributions fall under the heads of game theory, statistical decision theory, the theory of linear-programming, and the like. It may be noted here that the political economist, who specializes in the other type of choice problem—the problem confronting a community of individuals who are jointly making a choice of conditions which they will mutually impose as constraints upon their individual actions—may or may not find these contributions relevant for his research and applications. And yet the methodological introductions to some of the more prominent contributions would lead one almost to believe that the new techniques proposed for dealing with problems of the first type represent a culmination of the long historical development of theoretical economics. I believe this to be questionable and somewhat misleading, and in my opinion a political economist must search with care in order to find within this work techniques or materials directly applicable to the study and analysis of economic problems of the 'classical' type.

In the following parts, an elaboration of this point will be presented. In Part II, theoretical and applied work dealing with choice problems of the first type will be considered. In Part III, an effort will be made to judge the trend of thought on the part of political economists in their work upon the 'classical' type of economic problems. These include the problem of employment instability, the agricultural problem, the problem of monopoly, the labour problem, the international trade problem, and such problems of social conflict as are inherent in a political system in which a community of free individuals continually reviews and evaluates the performance of the prevailing system of legislative enactments,

PART II

AN INTERPRETATION OF RECENT THEORETICAL WORK UPON THE FIRST TYPE OF CHOICE PROBLEM—THE CHOICE OF MEANS FOR A WELL-DEFINED END

THE CONCEPTS OF 'PROBLEM' AND 'SOLUTION' IN THE THEORY OF GAMES

Von Neumann and Morgenstern explain as follows the 'problem which the theory of "games of stategy" is mainly devised to meet'.[1]

Let us look . . . at the type of economy which is represented by the 'Robinson Crusoe' model, that is, an economy of an isolated single person. . . . Crusoe is given physical data (wants and commodities) and his task is to combine and apply them in such a fashion as to obtain a maximum resulting satisfaction. . . . He controls exclusively all the variables upon which this result depends—say, the allotting of resources, the determination of the uses of the same commodity for different wants, etc. . . . Thus Crusoe faces an ordinary maximum problem. . . . its difficulty depending on the number of variables and on the nature of the function to be maximized, but this is more of a practical difficulty than a theoretical one . . . of a purely technical—and not conceptual—nature. . . .

Consider now a participant in a social exchange economy. His problem has, of course, many elements in common with a maximum problem. But it also contains some, very essential, elements of an entirely different nature. He too tries to obtain an optimum result. But in order to do this, he must enter into relations of exchange with others. If two or more persons exchange goods with each other, then the result for each one will depend in general not merely upon his own actions but on those of the others as well. Thus each participant attempts to maximize a function (his above-mentioned 'result') of which he does not control all variables. This is certainly no maximum problem, but a peculiar and disconcerting mixture of several conflicting maximum problems.

This kind of problem is nowhere dealt with in classical mathematics. We emphasize at the risk of being pedantic that this is no conditional problem no problem of the calculus of variations, of functional analysis, etc. . . .

The difference between Crusoe's perspective and that of a participant in a social economy can also be illustrated in this way: apart from those variables which his will controls, Crusoe is given a number of data which are dead; they are the unalterable physical background of the situation. . . . Not a single datum with which he has to deal reflects another person's will or intention . . . based on motives of the same nature as his own. A participant in a social exchange economy, on the other hand, faces data of this last type as well: they are the product of other participants' actions and volitions (like prices). His actions will be influenced by his expectation of these, and they in turn reflect the other participant's expectation of his actions.

Thus, the study of the Crusoe economy and the use of the methods applicable to it, is of much more limited value than has been assumed even by the most radical critics. . . . We hope that the reader will be convinced by the above that we face here and now a really conceptual—and not merely technical—difficulty. And it is this problem which the theory of 'games of strategy' is mainly devised to meet.

1. Von Neumann and Morgenstern, *Theory of Games and Economic Behavior*, 3rd ed., 1953, Princeton University Press, p. 915.

The authors go on to point out that the features of their problem which they emphasize are those which show most prominently when the number of participants is small; and they express the hope that a more conventional type of economic theory will emerge as game theory is developed to cover cases of large numbers of participants. But this is only a hope.

> The problem must be formulated, solved and understood for small numbers of participants before anything can be proved about the changes of its character in any limiting case of large numbers, such as free competition.
>
> A really fundamental reopening of this subject is the more desirable because it is neither certain nor probable that a mere increase in the number of participants will always lead to the conditions of free competition. The classical definitions of free competition all involve further postulates besides the greatness of that number. E.g. it is clear that if certain great groups of participants will . . . act together, then the great number of participants may not become effective; the decisive exchanges may take place directly between 'large coalitions', few in number, and not between individuals, many in number, acting independently. Our subsequent discussion of 'games of strategy' will show that the role and size of 'coalitions' is decisive throughout the entire subject. . . . Any satisfactory theory of the 'limiting transition' from small numbers of participants to large numbers will have to explain under what circumstances such big coalitions will or will not be formed—i.e. when the large numbers of participants will become effective and lead to a more or less free competition. Which of these alternatives is likely to arise will depend on the physical data of the situation. Answering this question is, we think, the real challenge to any theory of free competition.[1]

I wish first to suggest that there are two problems, rather than one, that the authors pose in the above quotations. In their subsequent discussion, when these problems are analysed, the authors present two different concepts of 'solution' corresponding to these two different problems. On the one hand, the problem is to determine a 'best' course of action for each participant in a well-defined contest. It is generally accepted that for the class of situations considered (zero-sum, two-person games), the theory provides intuitively appealing concepts of 'optimal behaviour' and of 'solution'; and for this class of situations, the theory is operational (at least in principle and to some extent in practice), in that a participant may apply the theory in order to find the particular course of action which would yield for him the 'best' result.

But there are nuances, and familiar ambiguities, about the other problem which set it apart. This second problem posed by von Neumann and Morgenstern is to 'show [how] the role and size of coalitions is decisive' in considering the change in the character of the 'problem' (which presumably means their first problem) as the number of participants increases indefinitely. They seek a 'satisfactory theory of the "limiting transition" from small numbers of participants to large numbers [in order] to explain . . . when the large numbers of participants will become effective and lead to a more or less free competition. . . . Answering this question is, we think, the real challenge to any theory of free competition'.

It is not altogether clear what an answer to this question would look like, but, from the arrangement of their book and the drift of the discussion as they develop their arguments, I get the impression that it was this kind of question which the authors conceived to be the major subject of their studies. Their consideration of the first problem seems to be incidental to their attack upon this main second question. This has apparently been disconcerting to mathematicians;[2] for the first problem and the concept of its solution are clear cut and well defined, and in the mathematical development of the theory one has an easy and confident feeling that he understands where he is headed. The second question, however,

1. Von Neumann and Morgenstern, op. cit., p. 15.
2. Cf. J. C. C. McKinsey, *An Introduction to the Theory of Games*, New York, 1952, pp. 303, 332, 339, 343, 358.

is not well defined, and it is not obvious at all where one is headed as he pursues the new concept of 'solution' which the authors introduce when they begin their consideration of 'coalitions' i.e. when they undertake their study of the main question. To mathematicians and to technicians primarily interested in the first kind of individual choice problem, the abrupt transition from the clear-cut first concept of 'solution' to the obscure second concept is confusing. Confronted with a 'solution' of the second sort, the practitioner concerned with the problem of individual choice is inclined to say: 'But how does this help? How does this inform a player in regard to how he might best proceed?' This obscurity and confusion, in my opinion, arise from a failure on the part of the authors to distinguish clearly between the fundamentally different types of choice problems discussed above.[1] Although devoting a considerable part of a 45-page introductory chapter to a criticism of the 'classical' type of economic theory, they failed to clarify and make explicit the peculiarities of the type of problem which gave rise to the development of this theory. I do not mean to suggest that their second concept of 'solution' corresponds to a solution of the kind of choice problem which in Part I above we called the 'classical' type. But whatever practical relevance is to be found for this concept would apparently refer to a process of discussion in which a 'solution' is being sought for this much more complex type of problem of political economy.

Von Neumann and Morgenstern consider their first problem only in connexion with the simplest class of contests—two-person games in which the winnings of one participant are identical with the losses of the other. A game consists of, or is completely described by, a set of rules which describe conditions and which indicate the alternative actions open to each player. A strategy is a set of rules which prescribe a definite action for each possible situation which may confront a player. 'The rules of the game should not be confused with the strategies of the players. . . . Each player selects his strategy . . . freely. While any particular strategy may be good or bad . . . it is within the player's discretion to use or to reject it. The rules of the game, however, are absolute commands'[2] If a player chooses a particular strategy, the outcome of his play will depend, of course, upon the choice of strategy by his opponent. It is assumed that he will seek to make his gains as great as possible, realizing that his opponent will try to thwart his efforts. If he knows the possible alternatives open to his opponent, he knows the least possible value of his gains for each strategy that he may choose, and it is assumed that he chooses the strategy which makes this least possible expected value of his gains as great as possible. The opponent, on the other hand, is assumed to be seeking to make the first player's gains (which is the second player's losses) as small as possible. Knowing the possible alternative strategies of the first player, he knows the greatest possible expected value of his losses for each strategy that he may choose; and it is assumed that he chooses the strategy which makes this greatest possible value of his losses as little as possible. The first player chooses his strategy so that he maximizes the smallest gain to which his opponent (through an appropriate choice of strategy) may restrict him. The second player makes his choice so that he minimizes the largest loss which the first player may impose upon him. If when the choices of strategies are thus made, it is found that these two values are identical, then the point corresponding to this value is called a 'saddle-point', where a maximum in one direction is at the same time a minimum in the other direction; and the game is said to have a solution. Neither player could do better than to respectively choose these strategies—the one to maximize

1. See pp. 9 et seq.
2. Von Neumann and Morgenstern, op. cit., p. 49.

his expected gains and the other to minimize his expected losses. The fundamental theorem of the theory of games establishes the existence of a saddle-point for any two-person, zero-sum game and hence shows that there exist optimal strategies for the players of such a game. The value corresponding to this saddle-point—which is simultaneously the expected gain of player one and the expected loss of player two when they choose their optimal strategies—is called the value of the game. The designation of the optimal strategies and of the value of the game constitutes the solution of the two-person, zero-sum game. The theory of this class of games provides methods for determining these optimal strategies. Essentially, the solving of such a game involves the solution of a system of linear equations and inequalities.

The analysis of the two-person, zero-sum game has been enormously interesting to applied mathematicians and to mathematical statisticians. The mathematical contributions of von Neumann in his dealing with this part of this problem have been found to be applicable to a wider class of problems. Wald,[1] following the earlier work of Neyman, formulated the general problem of theorical statistics as a decision problem. A statistical decision function is a rule which prescribes an action to correspond to each possible observation upon a specified set of random variables. A quality control system is a decision function, as is any design of an experiment. So is a sample survey design. These are the conventional applications, but the idea of statistical decision functions applies in any situation in which an action is induced by observations upon random variables.[2] Theoretical statistics is thus conceived of as a theory of choice that provides methods for determining 'best' rules of action for specified situations. Wald developed the theory of statistical decision functions as a special case of von Neumann's theory of two-person, zero-sum games, letting 'Nature' correspond to player 1 and the decision-maker to player 2. A recent textbook in theoretical statistics[3] follows this development. Also, as will be noted below, the solving of a linear programming problem[4] is shown to be formally equivalent to a problem of solving a two-person, zero-sum game, and the mathematics developed for the latter is applicable to the analysis of the former.

This part of their work—having to do with the analysis of the simplest possible game situations and concerned with the determination of 'best' rules of action for the guidance of individual decision-making agencies—has been and is now an inspiration to a host of applied mathematicians to whom our first type of problem is *the* 'economic problem'. But von Neumann and Morgenstern devoted only the first third of their book to this analysis. Having completed their discussion of the two-person, zero-sum situation, they passed to the case of three or more persons, and here for the first time 'coalitions' become possible. From henceforth in their book, their primary attention is directed to the phenomena of 'coalitions' that is, to their second question. They do not approach this question, as they did their first, from the point of view of the individual players. That is, they do not attempt to develop methods by which an individual, in a well-defined game situation, may determine the particular form of collusion which it would be 'best' for him to engage in. If this were their approach, then the concept of 'solution' for an *n*-person game would have been the same as for the two-person game, for the designation of the form and detail of a 'best' alliance or coalition would be a

1. A. Wald, *Statistical Decision Functions*, New York, 1950.
2. For example, Littauer *et al.*, 'On the Inventory Problem', *Journal of the American Statistical Association*, December 1943, pp. 717-32.
3. Blackwell and Girshick, *Theory of Games and Statistical Decision*, New York, 1954.
4. Gale, Kuhn and Tucker, 'Linear Programming and the Theory of Games', and Dantzig, 'A Proof of the Equivalence of the Programming Problem and the Game Problem', *Activity Analysis of Production and Allocation*, edited by T. C. Koopmans, New York, 1951.

preliminary step in the designation of a 'best' strategy to be followed by the individual, the remaining steps being the rules to be followed by the group of individuals who are to act in concert.

This, however, was not done by the authors. It will be recalled that conventional economic theory presupposes that individual economizers know how to economize and goes on to pursue questions pertaining to the behaviour properties of an economic system. In a way somewhat suggestive of this feature of economic theory, the ǝoɥʇɹʎ of *n*-person games, as developed by von Neumann and Morgenstern, takes for granted that the players know how to choose their respective optimal courses of action and pursues primarily the question of what the results may possibly be with respect to the formation of coalitions. For these situations in which coalitions are possible, a second concept of 'solution' was defined.

Suppose there are n players, and assume that these n players organize themselves into two groups or coalitions with n_1 players in the first group and n_2 in the second. Now consider the two groups as the two players of a two-person, zero-sum game, so that all that was said about the latter class of game may now be applied to the situation where the two groups are playing against one another. A 'best' strategy exists for each group, considered as a single choosing agency, and the game, as a two-person, zero-sum game, has a value, representing the expected value of the gain for group one and the expected value of the loss for group two. There is no discussion or illustration, beyond that in the first third of the book, in which the two-person zero game is the primary subject of the analysis, of methods for determining the optimal strategies and the value of the game to the coalition, and there is introduced no concept of a value of the game for the individual player who may choose an optimal individual strategy. Coalition 1, consisting of n_1 individuals, may possibly contain 2 players or 3 players or 4 or . . . $n - 1$ players, and n_2 is always $n - n_1$. And there are many combinations of 2 or of 3 or of 4, etc., that may be formed out of the total of n. Each of these combinations constitutes a possible coalition; and for each coalition there would be an optimal strategy and an expected gain or loss, for such strategies exist for two-person, zero-sum games, into which the n-person situation has been artificially transformed.

Consider now that for a given pair of coalitions of n_1 and n_2 players the optimal strategies and the terms of the alliances are such that the n players receive gains and losses represented by $x_1, x_2, x_3 \ldots x_n$. This latter set of values is called an 'imputation'. No method is developed for calculating these values from the specified conditions of a game. But nonetheless the imputation exists whatever the values constituting it are, and a similar imputation corresponds to every possible pair of specified coalitions. An individual player is assumed to prefer one imputation to another if his gain is greater in the one than in the other; and a particular coalition of n_1 players is assumed to prefer one imputation to another if the gain of each of the members is greater in the one than in the other. Now, the statement that one possible imputation 'dominates' another with respect to a coalition containing n_1 members is defined to mean: first, that the gain of each of the n_1 players is greater in the one imputation than in the other; and second, that the value of the gain by the coalition acting as a single player is at least as great as the sum of the amounts assigned to each of the members of the coalition by the preferred imputation. This latter condition is to assure that the preferred imputation can be insisted upon by the particular coalition.

In terms of this idea of the domination of one imputation over another, the authors define their concept of the solution of an n-person game. Suppose that there exists a coalition consisting of n_1 players which can enforce an imputation that dominates any other imputation which it might enforce or which any other coalition might propose. Then, the determination of this imputation would constitute von Neumann and Morgenstern's solution of the n-person game. The coalition corresponding to this imputation would be the 'coalition which would tend to arise'. However, it is shown that there is no single imputation which dominates all the rest. This being the case, a solution of an n-person game is defined as a set of imputations no member of which dominates any other member and at least one member of which dominates any imputation which is not a member. Von Neumann and Morgenstern's development of the theory of n-person games is essentially an inquiry into the properties of this concept of 'solution', the ultimate objective (which has not been attained) being the discovery of methods for determining what kinds of coalitions 'will tend to arise' under various kinds of circumstances.

Non-zero sum games—two-person as well as games for more than two—are treated similarly, in the sense that the problem and the concept of solution are substantially the same as for n-person, zero-sum games. In the case of non-zero-sum games, a fictitious player is introduced who is assumed to receive as a gain or loss, for any set of strategies chosen by the n players, an amount which is exactly the negative of the sum of the pay-offs to the n players. The n-person, non-zero-sum game is thus transformed into a $(n + 1)$-person, zero-sum game. For example, a two-person, non-zero-sum game (which would correspond to the kind of situation described by the term 'bilateral monopoly') is treated as a special form of a three-person, zero-sum game. A solution of a non-zero-sum game, as for all games where $n > 2$, is defined as a set of imputations no member of which dominates another member and some one or more members of which dominate any imputation not included within the set. A solution in this sense, again, conveys no information to the players regarding what they should do in order to maximize the expected value of their gains. It purports only to present a set of possible results of a play of the game.

As indicated above, this treatment of the theory of n-person games for $n > 2$ and of non-zero-sum games in general has appeared quite unsatisfactory to the applied mathematicians who have found the two-person, zero-sum game theory so fruitful and stimulating. This point of view is expressed by the author of what is generally regarded as an exceptionally good textbook in this field:

> For this wider class of games [for more than two players] there is not available, unfortunately, any theory which is intuitively as acceptable as is the theory for two-person games. Although a large part of von Neumann and Morgenstern's book (roughly 400 out of 600 pages) is devoted to games with more than two players, mathematicians generally seem to have been dissatisfied with the theory there developed. Comparatively little research has been done in this branch of game theory during the last few years. . . .
>
> . . . .
>
> In von Neumann's development of the theory of n-person games, the notion of 'solution'. . . occupies the central position one would expect from the name. The theory consists essentially in a search for solutions and a discussion of their properties.
>
> The intuitive justification of the use of the word 'solution' is, of course, now different from what it was in the case of two-person [zero-sum] games. In the former case, a solution meant [a set of rules] . . . with which the player should play. . . in order to maximize his expectation of gain. But in the case of n-person games (for $n>2$), a solution purports merely to give a set of possible ways in which winnings can be divided at the end of a play.
>
> Some people have felt dissatisfied with the intuitive basis of this notion, however, and the question has been raised as to whether knowing a solution of a given n-person game would enable a person to play it with greater expectation of profit than if he were quite ignorant of this theory . . . [moreover, it is not known] that every n-person game has a solution (in the given sense) . . .; we know only that certain special games have solutions (for example, it is known that all three-person games and all four-person games have solutions, but it has never been shown that all five-person games have solutions). . . .
>
> . . . .
>
> It might be thought that in order for the definition of a solution to be regarded as

satisfactory, it would also be necessary that a given game have a unique solution. However, von Neumann dissents from this view and holds that a given solution represents merely a socially accepted standard of behaviour and consequently that there can, and should, be many solutions—corresponding to the many possible stable organizations of society. . . .

. . . in the case of the essential three-person game [for example] we have an embarrassing richness of solutions. In addition to the finite solution (consisting of three imputations) with which we started our discussion, we have also found an infinite collection of infinite solutions. . . . Von Neumann accounts for this situation, as was mentioned earlier, by regarding the various solutions as representing various standards of social behavior. In the case of the three-person game in question . . . [he suggests grounds for calling one of the solutions] the 'non-discriminatory' solution and the others 'discriminatory'.

It seems hard to believe that knowing [the solutions as formally specified in the analysis of the three-person game] would enable a man to play the game more smoothly or profitably. . . . Thus it appears that the theory of n-person games is not yet in a completely satisfactory form. . . .

. . . .

Although parlor games are ordinarily [zero-sum], the games which do not satisfy the zero-sum condition are very important from the point of view of applications to economic theory. Thus, if we consider, for example, the mutual interactions of a labor union with an industrial company as a two-person game, it is clear that this game is not zero-sum. . . . Thus the theory of games which are not zero-sum occupies an exceedingly important position so far as regards the development of the social sciences. . . .

Unfortunately it happens that, despite the great importance of [non-zero-sum] games for the social sciences, there is not available so far any treatment of such games which can be regarded as even reasonably satisfactory. . . .

The most crying need in game theory at the present time . . . is for a more satisfactory theory of non-zero-sum games and n-person games (for $n>2$). . . . Despite the great ingenuity that has been shown in the various attacks on the problem of n-person and non-zero-sum games, we have not yet arrived at a satisfactory notion of a solution of such a game.[1]

Now it is evident that the difference between the confident claims and promises voiced in the long methodological chapter with which von Neumann and Morgenstern began their book and the complaints of the specialist in the mathematics of game theory quoted above is very great indeed[2]. But while admitting that the statements in the first chapter are somewhat confusing in the light of the authors' subsequent development of their theory and while possibly experiencing a sense of anti-climax and disappointment in going from the first chapter to the illustrative 'economic' applications at the end for the book (pp. 555-86), a political economist may nevertheless suggest that such a critic would seem to have an excessively restricted concept of 'economic problem'. It may be noted that the above-quoted criticism of the second concept of 'solution' is essentially that it is not the first concept of 'solution': the second concept does not provide for the player information in regard to the rules which he should adopt in order to maximize his expected gains. But on the basis of their considerable heuristic and interpretative discussion in the last two-thirds of their book, I believe that von Neumann and Morgenstern should reply that they really did not intend to place such an emphasis upon this first problem as their introductory chapter might have led one to understand; that the theory of choice of individual strategies for the more complicated situations involving more than two persons may be developed by technicians primarily concerned with this first type of problems; that in writing their book, however, they were primarily interested in the changing properties of game situations as circumstances are changed in a specified

1. J. C. C. McKinsey, op. cit., pp. 303, 332, 335, 339, 343, 358.
2. The difference between the tone of the introductory remarks in Mr. McKinsey's first chapter and the tone of the above quotations taken from the last part of his book also seems great; for his comments in which he characterizes conventional theoretical economics are such as to suggest that game theory has attained to a power which the above quotations deny. Also, Mr. McKinsey has taken too seriously what appear to me to be loose and historically misleading remarks of von Neumann and Morgenstern about 'Robinson Crusoe economics'.

way; that is, that their ultimate interest is in contributing to the continuing search for ways and means of improving the economic and social system or, expressed in the terminology of games, to provide an analysis useful for the evaluation of alternative sets of rules defining the game itself rather than of the rules describing possible strategies that the players might adopt; that a consideration of the circumstances under which different forms of coalitions might arise is relevant in discussions among legislators who are confronted with the problem of evaluating the laws and regulations under which economizing firms and individuals make their choices of actions.

From this point of view, their theory of two-person, zero-sum games, with the corresponding first concept of 'solution', is analogous to the theory of the firm as presented in conventional theoretical economics. The so-called equilibrium conditions of the firm would provide the firm with information regarding what it should do in order to 'best' conduct its affairs, provided that circumstances and motivations are as they are assumed to be and provided that the situation is so specified that the equations, in terms of which the equilibrium conditions are expressed, can be solved. These provisions are never satisfied, however, and while textbooks ordinarily include problems which have numerical solutions for the 'optimum' output of a firm, no one should take these illustrative examples seriously. They are like the parlour games, which, if sufficiently simple, can be numerically solved. The theory should not be regarded as operational and as an end in itself but only as a first step in the development of a theory of social organization.

But the traditional theories of the firm and of individual consumer choice represent only a stage in the development of the theory of the market; and market equilibrium is a second concept of equilibrium which is defined in terms not directly referring to any particular decision-making agency's problem of finding a 'best' course of action. The problem of general equilibrium is said to be 'solved' when the values of all the defined variables (prices, rates of output, rates of consumption, etc.) are shown to be formally 'determined' by the system of equations defining the conditions of market equilibrium. The formal proofs in theoretical economics, to the extent that they are proofs, lead to a sort of existence theorem asserting that there exists a set of values for the variables (which would include an 'imputation' in the sense of von Neumann and Morgenstern) uniquely satisfying the conditions assumed in the specification of the system. This is a second concept of 'solution' and from Mr. McKinsey's point of view it would be open to his objection that it does not inform anyone how to find out what these values are and it does not inform an economizer in regard to how he should run his business. But no such purpose motivated this definition of the concept. Instead, this theory of the market is simply a second stage in the development of a theory of social organization: the equilibrium conditions and the so-called stability conditions being the basis for the derivation of what are called the 'laws of the working of the system'. The latter refer to behaviour properties of the 'system'. The firm and its problem of finding a 'best' course of action have by now been left behind, it being taken for granted that it knows how to choose among alternative courses of action. The theory is ultimately concerned with a different kind of problem from that confronting the firm. In Mosak's *General Equilibrium Theory in International Trade*,[1] the traditional type of theory is systematically developed in these stages; and, like von Neumann and Morgenstern, Mosak gives illustrative examples of the application of the theory. In these applications he discussed the effects, under fixed exchange rates and under free exchange rates,

1. Cowles Commission Monograph No. 7, Bloomington, Indiana, Principia Press, 1944.

of reparations payments, of capital movements, of foreign trade restrictions, et cetera. The discussion, like von Neumann and Morgenstern's illustrations of applications, is somewhat anti-climatic ; but it deals with matters clearly relevant for the problem confronting legislators who are considering the effects of changing the 'rules of the game'.

Similarly, I should say that the theory for which von Neumann and Morgenstern's first concept of 'solution' was defined is simply a first stage in the development of a theory analogous in general purpose to the traditional theory of the market. The second concept of 'solution' corresponds in this analogy to the 'equilibrium conditions for the market'; and the theory of coalitions and imputations (i.e. prices) corresponds to the theory of the market. The analysis of the properties of this second concept of solution is then analogous to the traditional inquiry into 'the laws of the working of the system'.

But if this is a valid interpretation of von Neumann and Morgenstern's theory of *n*-person, non-zero-sum games, then we must conclude that as a theory of social organization it is at present in an exceedingly crude state of development. Whereas the mathematics of their theory of two-person, zero-sum games has been an excitement and an inspiration to specialists and technicians whose primary interest is in the first type of choice problem, where conditions and ends are well defined, the rest of their discussion, covering two-thirds of their book, has had no influence that I can detect upon discussions of economic problems. Recent books on mathematical statistics make operational use of the mathematics of two-person, zero-sum games. But recent descriptions of the 'tendencies toward coalitions' and recent discussion of the problem of devising regulations for monopoly and competition, which one might expect would draw upon a 'theory of coalitions', refer not at all to von Neumann and Morgenstern's analysis. In saying this, I have in mind the papers presented at the Conference on Business Concentration and Price Policy,[1] sponsored by the National Bureau of Economic Research, and at the conference on monopoly and competition and their regulation,[2] edited by E. H. Chamberlain and sponsored by the International Economic Association. It of course is not a substantive criticism of an original and highly sophisticated theoretical development to say that it is scarcely more than an embryo as a theory of social organization and that it has yet to be established as even ultimately applicable in discussions of problems of political economy. But the introductory chapter would seem to lead one to expect too much.

A NEW PROFESSIONAL SOCIETY DEDICATED TO THE MEANS-END TYPE OF CHOICE PROBLEM

In 1952 a new professional organization was founded in this country under the name of the Operations Research Society of America. A year or so earlier a similar society had been formed in Great Britain, and a professional journal was launched, *The Operational Research Quarterly*. Within the last few years courses in operations research have been introduced by certain universities, and curricula leading to advanced degrees have been organized.[3] The founders of this branch of study have been natural scientists and engineers, and the first president of the

1. *Business Concentration and Price Policy. A Conference of the Universities National Bureau Committee for Economic Research*, Princeton University Press, 1955.
2. E. H. Chamberlain (ed.), *Monopoly and Competition and their Regulation. Papers and Proceedings of a Conference held by the International Economic Association*, London, Macmillan, 1954.
3. F. N. Trefethen, 'A History of Operations Research', *Operations Research for Management*, edited by J. F. McCloskey and F. N. Trefethen, Baltimore, John Hopkins Press, 1954.

Operations Research Society of America was Philip M. Morse, professor of physics of the Massachusetts Institute of Technology.

Professor Morse describes the subject matter of this newly organized field of study as follows:[1]

Operations research . . . is concerned with an attempt to understand something, in the scientific sense of the word understanding. It is an effort to discover regularities in some phenomenon and to link these regularities with other knowledge so that the phenomenon can be modified or controlled, just as other scientific research does. The difference comes in the phenomena which are studied, the subject matter. Instead of studying the behavior of electrons or metals or gasoline engines or insects or individual men, operations research looks at what goes on when some team of men and equipment goes about doing its assigned job. A battalion of soldiers, a squadron of planes, a factory, or a sales organization is more than a collection of men and machines; it is an activity, a pattern of operations. These operations can be studied; their regularities can be determined and related to other regularities; they can be eventually understood and they then can be modified and improved.

That is to say, our first type of choice problem defines the subject field of operations research. The problem situation envisaged is this: A group of men have an assigned objective. An executive decision-maker exists who is in charge of the group and responsible for the efficiency of its operations. 'How the group goes about doing its assigned job' may be described by writing out the 'programming' which governs the activities or operations of the members of the group. The decision-making agency continually reviews this 'programme of operations' with the possibility of improvement in mind. There being many different programmings, each of which would attain the objective, and new conditions and circumstances always emerging, there is a continuing problem of choice. This choice problem defines the subject field of operations research. Professor Morse goes on to say:

As with any research, the development of understanding of the subject matter is intimately bound up in the techniques of investigation used. The understanding, of course, is the important thing; to obtain it one uses any technique of measurement or of calculation, any portion of a basic science which will produce results. We should expect that the techniques of the theory of probability and of statistics would be very useful tools. . . . This does not mean that operations research is applied statistics. . . .

Though the techniques are less important than the understanding, nevertheless it is worth while studying the techniques. . . . New areas of understanding have always been opened up, in basic sciences, by the perfection of a new research technique, either observational or theoretical. In a new field the development of research techniques may well appear to be more studied and discussed than is the basic accumulation of understanding; this is chiefly because the understanding is as yet scanty and fragmentary. It is not necessarily an unhealthy development, as long as most workers keep clearly in mind that methodology is but a means to the sought-for understanding.[1]

He then briefly describes certain mathematical models which have been used in the analysis of actual problems—e.g. queueing theory, information theory, and other probabilistic models—and certain techniques which seem promising for the analysis of choice problems of this type—e.g. linear programming and game theory. In the rest of the volume[2] containing Professor Morse's discussion there are expository essays which explain and illustrate in some detail these mathematical models, techniques, and theories: 'Linear Programming and Operations Research', by Joseph O. Harrison, Jr., 'Game Theory', by David H. Blackwell, 'Information Theory', by David Slepian, etc. The volume also

1. P. M. Morse, 'Progress in Operations Research', ibid.
2. *Operations Research for Management*, op. cit.

includes case histories of a number of actual operations research problems, and it ends with an eighteen-page bibliography under the headings: I. History and Methodology; II. Military Applications; III. Industrial Applications; and IV. Government Planning.

Here then is a newly organized professional field of study which deals specifically and exclusively with our first type of choice problem. The subject matter is the phenomenon, 'the operations of a group whose activities are directed toward the attainment of a well-defined objective.' Operational procedures are described by a 'programming of activities'—i.e. by a system of rules of action. There are alternative possible programmings from among which an executive agency makes a choice. The analysis is of the respective performances of the alternatives. To improve the operations of a group is to substitute a better performing programming of activities. To describe 'betterness' is to apply an agreed-upon criterion in ordering quantitative measures of the performances of alternatives.

How would one be trained for this profession? That is, what formal courses of instruction would be taken by a student working toward professional standing in this field of analysis and study? So far as analytical theory is concerned, I should say (and this would seem also to be what Professor Morse would say) that the study would include courses in the theory of probability, the theory of statistical decision functions and the theory of games; and there would be applied courses in all of these fields of theory. The construction of probabilistic models for the analysis of observed phenomena would represent applications of the theory of probability[1]. There would be the familiar applications of mathematical statistics and decision theory—the designing of quality control systems, sample surveys, tests of hypotheses, etc. There are the various kinds of situations in which the mathematics of two-person zero-sum game theory is said to be applicable—the various illustrative applications of the method of linear programming: assignment problems,[2] mixing problems,[3] scheduling problems.[4] These studies would presumably induce a problem-solving frame of mind in the student and an understanding of the conceptual elements of the problems falling within his subject-field. Along with or after the analytical work, there would be experimental[5] and case history studies of patterns resulting from the operations of 'task-oriented groups'.

The recognition and formal organization of this special field of study devoted exclusively to the means-end problems confronting the managements of 'task-oriented groups' is an important development for the traditional field of economics. It clarifies the nature of the latter to have these problems set apart as the subject-field of a distinct profession. The new profession definitely has a natural science and engineering orientation, for the means-end problem is an engineering kind of problem. Professor Morse, a physicist at Massachusetts Institute of Technology, and Professor Kimball, a chemist at Columbia University, have written a textbook[6] for the study of methods 'of providing executive departments with a quantitative basis for decisions regarding the operations under their control';

1. Numerous applications of this sort are found in William Feller, *Probability Theory and its Applications*, New York, John Wiley & Sons, 1950.
2. e.g. Votaw and Orden, 'The Personnel Assignment Problem', *Symposium on Linear Inequalities and Programming*, Planning Research Division, Director of Management Analysis Service, Comptroller, Headquarters, U. S. Air Force, April 1952, pp. 155-63.
3. e. g. Charnes, Cooper, and Mellon, 'Blending Aviation Gasolines', ibid., pp. 115-46.
4. J. F. Magee, *Studies in Operations Research. I: Application of Linear Programming to Production Scheduling*, Cambridge, Mass.; Arthur D. Little, Inc., n. d.
5. e.g. Alex Bavelas, 'Communication Patterns in Task-Oriented Groups', *Journal of the Acoustical Society of America*, November 1950.
6. Morse and Kimball, *Methods of Operations Research*, The Technology Press Massachusetts Institute of Technology and John Wiley & Sons, New York, 1951.

and, while drawing upon the natural sciences and engineering, they found no occasion at all to mention any work of an economist or to make use of any principle or concept of theoretical economics. So far as their problems are concerned, the traditional theories of production and of the firm are without operational content, whereas mathematical statistics, game theory, and the method of linear programming do have operational content for their purposes. On the other hand, the problems of operational research are not of the type that gave rise to the development of traditional theoretical economics. Professeur F. H. Knight has devoted much of his energies to explaining the importance of keeping the two types of problems from becoming confused and the pernicious results of confusing them.[1] The recognition of a professional society for each of the types of choice problems will presumably help to keep them distinct.

A question may be raised with respect to courses in econometrics: Would not such courses be included in the operations research curriculum? We may note first that nothing definite is conveyed by the expression 'courses in econometrics'. In my opinion, no distinct problem-field and subject matter has been delineated for the professional members of the Econometric Society in the sense that this has been done for the Operations Research Society. In practice, those who regard themselves as econometricians have been concerned primarily with techniques of analysis and calculation. Professor Morse drew a sharp distinction between the study of the phenomena which constitute the subject matter of an empirical science and the development of techniques of analysis; and he went on to state the obvious—that in operations research there will of course be used 'any technique of measurement or of calculation, any portion of a basic science which will produce results'. Hence, if the techniques of estimation and calculation taught in an econometrics course are shown to be useful for the analysis of problems of the type studied in operations research, then the course is appropriate for inclusion in the operations research curriculum. Over the past few years, there has been great interest among econometricians in the method of linear programming. Every issue of *Econometrica* over the recent past has contained one or more articles on the subject, and several conferences on linear programming are reported in these recent issues. As indicated above, this work refers to the type of choice problem studied in the fields of operations research. There has also been great interest shown by econometricians in the development of the technique called input-output analysis. While the method of linear programming has to do with the problem of determining 'optimum' values for specified variables under the control of a decision-making agency with a well-defined objective, the technique of input-output analysis as it has been presented does not deal directly with this problem of finding an optimum. It is a technique for predicting the effects upon certain specified variables resulting from the alteration of certain other variables. If this technique were shown to be useful for the study of the operations research type of problem then by that token it would of course be relevant for operations research analysis. The reliability and usefulness of the technique is still a matter of conjecture, however, nothing having been demonstrated in this regard.[2]

1. Cf. G. H. Knight, *Freedom and Reform*, Harper & Brothers, 1947; especially the essays: 'Pragmatism and Social Action', 'Science, Philosophy and Social Procedure', 'Fact and Value in Social Science', and 'The Sickness of Liberal Society'.
2. For a review of the state of research upon this technique see Carl F. Christ, 'A Review of Input-Output Analysis' and the comment by Milton Friedman, included in *Input-Output Analysis. An Appraisal* (*Studies in Income and Wealth*, Vol. 18), National Bureau of Economic Research, Princeton University Press, 1955, pp. 137-74.

QUESTIONS REGARDING VALIDITY OF CERTAIN CONCEPTS OF WELFARE ECONOMICS

We may note, in closing this part that in the literature of econometrics and welfare economics there are suggestions of a confusion of the two types of problems we have been discussing. For example, T. C. Koopmans, in introducing the papers presented at a conference on linear programming,[1] states as the 'fundamental problem of normative economics: the best allocation of limited means toward desired ends'; and he speaks of the converging lines of applications in widely different fields of study as indicating 'the fundamental unity of the economic problem'. In his discussion (in the introduction and in his essay, 'Analysis of Production as an Efficient Combination of Activities') he uses such terms as 'efficiency of allocation [of the resources of an entire economy]', a 'general transformation function for an [entire] economy' representing 'the most favorable relationship between the inputs of individual primary factors of production and the final outputs of individual commodities'. At various places in his essay, one is confronted with the idea of an 'optimum (efficient) allocation of the manpower and other resources of an entire economy'. By 'efficient allocation of a society's resources' he means 'an allocation such that an increase in the output of any one good can be obtained only at the cost of a decrease in some other good'.

Now, if the entire society of individuals is regarded as a 'task-oriented group', the objective being well-defined, and if there is presupposed some will or decision-maker who controls the activities of the group directed toward the objective, then the notion of an optimum allocation or efficient use of the manpower and equipment of the society is meaningful. Also, if the finding of this optimum allocation is the 'fundamental problem of economics', then the problem field of economics is identical with that of operations research. This is the confusion that Professor Knight has attempted to clarify. A society of people is not regarded by him as a task-oriented group with a well-defined objective, and no operational meaning can be assigned to the idea of an 'efficient use of a society's resources'.

Consider the idea in a slightly different form—an 'optimum' geographic distribution of a society's population or an 'efficient' spatial orientation of a nation's cities and towns. The concepts of 'optimum' and 'efficiency' imply a choosing agent confronted by a well-defined objective, a set of alternative ways of attaining the objective, and a criterion by which an order number or value may be assigned to each alternative. Who would be the chooser of the location of a town or of the spatial distribution of a population? A town is a concentration of individually chosen locations. If there were a decision-making agency with the power to choose the location of a town, by this act this agency would be choosing a *combination* of locations, of families and firms. Its problems would be formally of the nature of an assignment problem, a class of problems which are studied in applications of game and linear-programming theory. But there is no choosing agency which directly and primarily selects a particular *combination* of the possible locations of the human beings which make up a society. The legislative agency of a society of individuals is concerned primarily with the problem of choosing a system of laws and institutions which constrain the choices made by individuals. Within these constraints, imposed by the individuals acting jointly, each individual chooses the locations of those things within his power. There are thus millions upon millions of individual choices of locations and not an overriding choice of a *combination* of all locations. There being no agency which evaluates alternative combinations of individual locations, there is no meaning, at least

1. T. C. Koopmans (ed.), *Activity Analysis of Production and Allocation*, New York, John Wiley & Sons, 1951.

in any ordinary sense, of 'best' or 'optimum' in the context of a discussion of the location of a town. Hence, such phenomena as those observed in the spatial distribution of a society's population and industry do not present an optimizing linear-programming type of problem, as econometricians and welfare economists in general would seem to imply.

There is no choosing agency which directly and primarily selects a combination of all individual locations. But nonetheless a spatial orientation of human beings and activities results from the free actions of individuals within the constraints of a system of legislative acts. This system is subject to alteration and choice by the joint action of all individuals; and the legislative agency, which is the means by which such joint action is taken, continually seeks to find reforms which will improve these constraints upon individual actions. In considering the merits of any proposed legislative change, this choosing agent arrives at judgments with regard to many measurable aspects of the expected performance of the new system. Some of the quantities measuring this expected performance will refer to the spatial orientation of the population of individuals and activities. The evaluation, by this choosing agent, of the alternative systems of constraints involves the arranging and ordering of sets of quantities, those pertaining to locational aspects being included within the set of all quantities deemed relevant by the choosing agent. The analytical problem is not that of maximizing or minimizing some particular variable that conceivably may be plotted upon a one-dimensional scale (the idea, mistaken in my view, being to determine an 'optimum' location of a city or an 'efficient' spatial orientation of cities and towns). Rather, the problem is that of analysing a process implicit in a sequence of actions by many individuals all taken within a specified system of constraints. The quantitative and qualitative characteristics of this process are among the features that are subjectively considered by the society of individuals, through its legislative procedures, in its evaluation of alternative forms which its laws and institutions might take.

This then seems to be the confusion in the work of 'welfare economists': these analysts presuppose that there exists a decision-making agent which chooses a particular distribution of products among families, or a particular allocation of jobs among the working population, *et cetera*; they further presuppose that there is an objective to be attained in the choice of an allocation of a population among jobs or a distribution of products among families, and of such a nature that a test may be applied by a technician for determining how well a particular allocation or distribution attains the objective. But there exists no such choosing agent which selects an allocation of a national population or a distribution of a national product. These latter result from millions of individual choices each made under a given system of constraints which apply to all individuals; and it is the system of constraints, and not the resulting allocation or distribution, which is chosen by the joint action of the individuals constituting the society.

The method and problems of welfare economics are essentially similar to the method and problems of scale analysis, which is being developed by social psychologists.[1] The scale analyst is a measurer and predictor of attitudes or preferences which are manifested in the actions of individuals. He has a systematic way of studying an individual's observed reactions to a given set of situations. From an analysis of the observations, he infers how the individual will react when confronted with a situation which is different from those covered by the observations.

1. Brief reference was made on page 17 above to this type of analysis. The book referred to was *Measurement and Prediction*, Samuel A. Stouffer, Louis Guttman, Edward A. Suchman, Paul F. Lazarsfeld, Shirley A. Star, and John A. Clausen. Vol. IV of *Studies in Social Psychology in World War II*, Princeton University Press, 1950.

The objective of his analysis is to predict the reactions or preferences or attitudes of an individual or of a group of individuals.

The 'welfare economist's' point of view and method would seem to be not essentially different. He begins with a formal statement of certain general properties of the preference function of any individual and of the transformation function of any firm. A statement of these properties and their implications is simply a formal statement of how any individual or any firm will react when confronted with a specified situation requiring his making a choice. On the basis of these properties attributed to any individual's preference function and any firm's transformation function, the 'welfare economist' infers the preferences or attitudes of individuals toward situations not explicitly covered in the statement of the properties of the preference and transformation functions.

Now consider the respective tasks of the two types of technicians: the scale analyst, on the one hand, who analyses and predicts attitudes and preferences of individuals; and the quality control engineer, on the other, who predicts and measures the *efficiency* of a quality control system. In the latter case, there is a well-defined end, and the technician applies mathematical statistics in order to instruct the management upon whether or not a particular system of rules constitutes an optimum or efficient quality control system. For the task of the scale analyst, however, the concept of optimum or efficiency has no meaning at all. He attempts simply to predict preferences, having no basis for an evaluation of these preferences. But whereas the 'welfare economist' begins with a point of view and problem similar to those of the scale analyst, before he has done he has undertaken a task resembling that of the mathematical statistician for whom the concept of efficiency or optimum is fundamental. In making this transition, he confuses the problem of political economy with the technical means-end problem and presents his theory as a technical device for objectively evaluating the efficiency of an economic system.

The following quotations, taken from Scitovsky's *Welfare and Competition*, illustrate this transition of ideas:

> In Chapters IV and V we appraised the efficiency of distribution among consumers and of specialization and job allocation among workers; but we never appraised the economic efficiency of the individual person's behavior. The reason is obvious. Since economic efficiency means conformity to people's wishes, the individual's behavior is economically efficient when it conforms to his own wishes. But it would be absurd for us to appraise the degree of conformity between the individual's wishes and his behavior because... we assumed that his wishes and his behavior are in conformity. This is why we never applied the criterion of efficiency to the individual's behavior and applied it only to economic organization among individuals—distribution among consumers and specialization and job allocation among workers.[1]

Now if one reviews Scitovsky's application of the criterion of efficiency to the 'economic organization among individuals', he will find no operationally specified 'organization' that is appraised. He will find a comparison of two formally described allocations, the postulated conditions being such that one of the allocations may be inferred to be preferable to all individuals. But there is no consideration of a specified 'organization' which would generate either of these allocations. A description of such an organization would consist of a detailed cataloguing of the laws and binding custom subject to change by the joint action of the individual members of society. One sees such an organization being appraised at Congressional Hearings—e.g., on the 'farm problem'—at which proposed amendments of the existing laws are being considered and jointly

1. Tibor Scitovsky, *Welfare and Competition*, Chicago, Richard D. Irwin, Inc., 1951, p. 159.

evaluated by the representatives of the individuals constituting the society. The welfare economist's allocations and distributions may possibly be observed as aspects of the outcome of a process consisting of millions of individual actions within a system of constraints. But there are many other performance features, qualitative as well as quantitative; and a choice, by the group of individuals, of a particular system of legislative constraints constitutes a choice not only of observable allocations and distributions but also of the many other characteristics. Hence, it makes no sense to consider how well an allocation of a population 'conforms to the wishes of the people', for 'the people' do not choose or exercise their wishes in regard to an allocation. And there is no sense in applying the words 'optimum' or 'efficient' to that which they do choose—i.e., a system of legislative constraints—for there is no well-defined end as an objective of this system.

Scitovsky goes on to say:

> The position of the individual firm is entirely different from that of the individual person. It is true that the firm's behavior conforms to the wishes of its owner in much the same way in which a person's behavior conforms to his wishes; but the firm, in addition to being a source of profit to its owners, is an economic organization which affects the welfare also of other members of society . . . and it is from their point of view that we shall now appraise the economic efficiency of the firm. In particular, we shall discuss whether and under what conditions the firm's choice of factors, products, and rate of output is desirable from society's point of view.[1]

In this quotation, 'economic efficiency' does not refer to a measure of how well the firm's procedures and methods serve the purposes of the firm. It refers to how well the firm's decisions serve the 'purposes' of society. All that was said above may be said here. The actions of an individual person affect the 'welfare' of other members of society in the same sense that the actions of a firm affect this 'welfare'. The actions of a firm are the actions of a group of individuals. The choices of this group are no more subject to outside evaluation than are the actions of a single individual. What is evaluated is the system of legislative enactments under which individuals organize firms for joint action. This is a joint evaluation representing a joint expression of preference by all members of the society. The analytical problem has to do with the prediction of performance characteristics in terms of the values of numerous parameters and variable quantities. The joint evaluation involves the reaching of a consensus by the members of a society with respect to an ordering of sets of values. 'Efficiency' can be given no more meaning in this situation in which a group choice is being made than in a situation in which an individual preference is being expressed. And to use the concept as welfare economists do use it is to lend the false impression that the management of a society's affairs is something to be dealt with as a problem of positive science and engineering.

1. op. cit., p. 160.

PART III

THE PROBLEM OF APPRAISING AN ECONOMIC SYSTEM—THE CLASSICAL TYPE OF ECONOMIC PROBLEM

SELECTION OF AN ILLUSTRATIVE EXAMPLE—THE PROBLEM OF THE BUSINESS CYCLE

In this final part, I shall attempt to interpret the trend of thought of economists who are primarily concerned with the 'classical' type of economic problem. Due to limitations of space, I shall use but one economic problem as an illustration. Perhaps the farm problem would have been the better one for my purpose, for this would have illustrated the more or less natural emergence of a 'classical' type of value theory as the discussions proceed on 'what if anything is wrong' and of how whatever it is that is judged to be wrong should be 'fixed'. With this illustration the point would have been made that, if the operating procedures of a farm management are regarded as analogous to a strategy for the playing of a game, and if the problem of this management is thus analogous to that of finding an optimum strategy, then the corresponding analogy for the farm problem as a public issue is that of evaluating the rules of the game. Or we would see that, while a farm management is confronted by a linear programming type of problem, this is not the kind of problem confronting a national legislature engaged in the framing of an Agricultural Act. However, I have chosen for my purpose the problem of employment instability, for this has been the dominant issue over the past twenty-five years, strongly influencing the discussion of all other economic problems of public policy.

AN INTERPRETATION OF METHODS OF ANALYSIS PROPOSED BY ECONOMETRICIANS

I shall begin with what to me seems a representative statement of the point of view of the econometrician, using statements of Marschak and Koopmans for this purpose. First, with respect to the meaning of certain terms:[1]

> The construction of dynamic economic models has become an important tool for the analysis of economic fluctuations and for related problems of policy. In these models, macro-economic variables are thought of as determined by a complete system of equations.

1. I know of no test or experience with an econometric model which would substantiate the statement in the first sentence of the quotation. In the only systematic test of which I am aware. the econometric model showed up poorly. Cf. Carl Christ, 'A Test of an Econometric Model for the United States, 1921-1947', and the discussion by Milton Friedman in: *Conference on Business Cycles*, Universities National Bureau Committee for Economic Resea ch New York, National Bureau of Economic Research, 1951, pp. 35-114.

. . . At present it may suffice to describe a complete system as one in which there are as many equations as endogenous variables, that is, variables whose formation is to be 'explained' by the equations. The equations are usually of, at most, four kinds: equations of economic behavior, institutional rules, technological laws of transformation, and identities. We shall use the term structural equations to comprise all four types of equations. . . . In many practical situations it is required to predict the values of one or more economic variables, either under changes in structure that come about independently of the economist's advice, or under hypothetical changes in structural parameters that can be brought about through policy based in part on the prediction made.[1]

Some readers may find it more convenient to give the set of exogenous variables and structural paramenters a more general name: 'conditions'. Similarly, the set of jointly dependent variables can be renamed 'results'. Conditions that undergo changes during the period of observation correspond to 'exogenous variables'. Conditions that remain constant throughout the observation period but may or may not change in the future constitute the 'structure'. Conditions that can be controlled are called 'decisions'. Given the conditions, the result is determined. The decision-maker ranks the various achievable results according to his preferences: some results are more desirable than others. The best decision consists in fixing controlled conditions so as to obtain the most desirable of all results consistent with given non-controlled conditions.

For the economy as a whole, endogenous variables can be roughly identified with what are often called 'economic variables'. These are usually the quantities and prices of goods and services, or their aggregates and averages, such as national income, total investment, price level, wage level, and so on. The exogenous variables and the structural parameters are, roughly, 'non-economic variables' (also called 'data' in the economic literature) and may include the weather and technological, psychological, and sociological conditions as well as legal rules and political decisions.[2]

Next, with respect to the nature of government policy:

Policy consists in changing those elements of the structure and those exogenous variables that are under the policy-maker's control. Given the values of the uncontrollable features of the structure and of the uncontrollable exogenous variables, the technician's task is to predict which stochastic processes will be generated by the various proposed policies. The variables that are thus predicted are the potentially observable values of some economic quantities of interest to the policy-maker. To make his best decision, the policy-maker ranks these alternative outcomes according to his preferences.[3]

Finally, why it is that knowledge of structural relations in the econometric sense is necessary for policy decisions:

. . . Knowledge of past structure is necessary if the policies under consideration and the expected changes of uncontrolled conditions involve not only changes in exogenous variables but also changes in the structure itself.

To the extent to which economic fluctuations are regarded as an evil, policies can be suggested that will dampen such fluctuations. Through an appropriate change of controlled exogenous variables or controlled structural parameters, the jerky path described by national income and other economic aggregates in the last hundred years or so may be replaced by a smoother one in the future. . . . If the existing structure is known, one can attempt to find the extent to which a given and feasible change in the institutional characteristics of the structure would affect certain properties of the oscillatory path of an important economic variable, such as the wave frequency, or the so-called damping ratio between the amplitudes of two successive waves in the absence of new impulses. . . .

Economic history knows [examples of institutions which have stabilized economic quantities without a knowledge of economic structure in this econometric sense; and policy proposals are made in the form of guiding rules for the stabilizing actions of these agencies. For example], in the discussion of the stabilization of employment and of the price level, institutional rules [have been] proposed that would obligate the monetary or fiscal authorities to take specified measures that would nip deflations and inflations in the bud. It has been argued that the formulation of such rules need not presuppose any

1. T. C. Koopmans, 'Identification Problems in Economical Model Construction', *Studies in Econometric Method*, New York, John Wiley & Sons, 1953, pp. 26-47.
2. Jacob Marschak, 'Economic Measurements for Policy and Prediction', *Studies in Econometric Method*, New York, John Wiley & Sons, 1953, p. 10.
3. Jacob Marschak, op. cit., p. 23.

knowledge of economic structure or, in particular, of its numerical characteristics. . . . The motorist [it is said], ignorant of the car mechanism, steers his wheel quite successfully, responding instantaneously to changes in the surface and the direction of the road. Other economists have even suggested what we may call 'pilotless' devices. Thus, income tax receipts, at a tax rate fixed once and for all, will rise and fall with money income, thus counteracting inflation or deflation. . . . Again, it has been argued that the knowledge of economic structure is not necessary if one wants to stabilize the economy by such devices . . . [called by some 'built-in stabilizers'].

[But] there is a difference between changing the exogenous variables and changing the structure. If a certain rule of fiscal or monetary action in response to changes in national income or in price level has been tried out long enough, in various doses and with various delays, such experience can indeed suffice to determine when and how intensely the measure should be applied. If an income tax has been operating in various situations and at various tax rates, it is possible to estimate the tax rate that would best fulfil the task of damping fluctuations of national income. . . . The case is then indeed analogous to that of . . . the motorist, or, for that matter, to the case of the firm that [has] collected experience on the effect of output upon profit without ever bothering to explain this effect by the existing behavior of buyers, the cost structure, and the rate of the excise tax on the firm's product.

Suppose, however, that the institution in question is to be introduced for the first time. To fix in advance the rule of monetary action that will stabilize prices and national income most quickly and effectively . . . it is necessary to know, e.g. the lags and elasticities involved in the relation describing consumers' response to changes in national income, prices, cash balances, etc., and the lags and elasticities involved in other structural relations at a time when the institution was not in force. To experiment with the institution would require too much trial and error.[1]

Let us now review what is being said. A legislature chooses among alternative ways of changing the system; and a rational choice implies that judgments have been reached regarding how each alternative will work. The task of the economist is to assist the legislature in arriving at these judgments. So far, there is no difference of view between the econometricians and the economists who are not called by this name, this being the task performed by the political economist throughout the history of the subject. The econometricians, however, typically make extraordinary claims in regard to how much the particular techniques which they propose can help in this respect; they apparently go further, asserting even the necessity of the use of their particular techniques in order that a rational choice be made by a policy-maker. What is it, in brief, that they urge economists to do?

They propose that what is to be called the structure of an economic system be specified in a system of linear equations, the number of variables being equal to the number of equations. Judgment is to be exercised by the economist in the selection of the variables and of the particular relationships described by the equations. The adoption of a particular equation relating certain variables is the adoption of a particular 'theory'. The economist is not restricted in this regard, and his 'test' of a theory is obtained in the observed 'fit' of his equation system to the data of the observation period. There is not a single equation system describing a unique structure as a character of an observable economic system. There could be an indefinitely large number of structural equation systems which, by various econometricians working independently, might be found to 'fit' the data. The constants in the equations making up a system are regarded as estimates of what are assumed to exist as 'structural parameters' of the economic system. Familiar concepts such as the propensity to consume, elasticities of one sort or another, etc. are defined in terms of the structural parameters, and these are assumed to be stable during the observation period, although on what grounds is not clear.

1. Jacob Marschak, op. cit., pp. 24-5.

In the favoured equations systems, lags and leads are introduced—i.e. the value of a particular variable is assumed to depend upon the values of other variables in previous periods. By virtue of such lagged effects the value of, say, the 'national income' variable is determined for a given period, except for a random component, if the values of all the variables for previous periods are known. If nothing happens to the structural equations or the values of the exogenous variables, then, in such a model, the values of this variable designated as national income are determined period by period into the future; and an analysis of the equation system will indicate the character of the fluctuation of the variable: whether it is oscillatory; if so, the amplitude of its oscillation and the expected value of its period; its growth trend, etc. If the policy-maker should seek a way (and why should he not?) of rendering the system more stable—that is, of reducing the amplitude of the oscillations of this variable in the model—then, say the econometricians, we may investigate all the possible alterations in the equation system or in the controlled exogenous variables which will result in a reduced amplitude. Thus informed of what he may possibly do—the different ways that structural equations and exogenous variables may be altered in order to attain the objective—and of the respective 'costs' of his doing this or that, the policy-maker arrives at a subjective ordering of alternatives and hence makes a rational choice. This is the only way, they say, to reach a judgment regarding the effects of a specified change of structure. By the very meaning of structure, there will have been no experience of the effects of such a change upon which to base an empirical estimate. But with the structural equations before us, we simply see what happens to the properties of the model when we alter the equation system in accordance with the proposed change of structure.

But what, we may ask, of all the changes of 'structure' that we can easily recall as having been decided upon and without resort to these econometric methods of analysis? What of the recent and current changes and proposals of change of 'structure' designed for some particular objective? The econometricians, so far as I am able to interpret them, answer that, where judgments are reached in regard to the effects of proposed structural changes, the responsible persons are doing intuitively or else consciously but with weak and clumsy methods what they could be doing systematically with the more powerful and reliable econometric methods. The same logical arrangement of relationships is necessarily involved, they say, even though one does not use these mathematical methods of analysis.[1] By using them, one is able to apply mathematical tests for the logical consistency of his argument and statistical tests to his empirical hypothesis. The econometric method can only be an improvement over other methods of analysing the effects of policy changes in the economic system.

All of this is hard to accept. A game theorist does not tell a chess player that an application of game theory in the solution of a game is simply a systematic way of doing what the player must do 'intuitively' in any case, and that he may as well apply the powerful mathematical methods of game theory in choosing his strategy rather than depend upon a relatively weak and untested conjecture. The reason that he does not tell the chess player this is that the game of chess is too complicated a game for an application of his theory. While there are players of chess who do remarkably well in finding strategies that are better than those found by other players, there are no known mathematical methods that can be shown to be useful to any of the players. Or a mathematical statistician who specializes in the design of experiments and tests of hypothesis does not tell a

1. e.g. Jacob Marschak, op. cit., p. 25, and T. C. Koopmans in his comment on the paper, 'Reformulation of Current Business Cycle Theories as Refutable Hypotheses', *Conference on Business Cycles*, New York, National Bureau of Economic Research, 1951, p. 144.

medical diagnostician that an application of the theory of tests of hypothesis is simply a systematic way of doing what the diagnostician must do 'intuitively' in any case, and hence that in all possible situations he can improve upon his uncontrolled judgment by applying the powerful methods of mathematical statistics. He may demonstrate to him that for certain situations that have been studied and carefully specified there are systematic tests that are useful and an improvement over other methods of reaching a decision. For such situations, the mathematical methods would certainly be used. But the statistician knows that the situations typically dealt with by diagnosticians are not problems to be turned over to a technician in statistical methods and are far too complicated, for an application of any presently known mathematical theory.

In a similar way, one may simply reserve judgment on the usefulness of the proposed econometric methods until there are demonstrations of this usefulness. Moreover, it should be noted that the analogies with the chess player and with the diagnostician are not at all complete. I believe no one would doubt that the chess player and the diagnostician do in fact do 'intuitively' what would be formally involved in an application of the principles of game theory and the principles of the theory of tests of hypothesis. But there are many who would decline to accept the statement that in reaching a judgment regarding the effects of a new legislative act one necessarily must do in some way or another what would be done systematically and more reliably in an application of the kind of technique proposed by econometricians.[1] However, there is no call for nor profit in an argument over the validity of the claims made on behalf of a proposed technique of analysis. All that need be done by an innovator of a new technique is simply to present empirical demonstrations of its superiority in use. Other methods could not long compete with the demonstrably superior technique.

In my judgment, the most important econometric paper that has been recently published is the report by Carl Christ describing an empirical test of an econometric model.[2] It was a revision of L. Klein's econometric model for the United States that was tested, and the somewhat heated interchange between the two econometricians, Christ and Klein, is quite instructive in regard to the role of 'non-mathematical (non-rigorous?) thinking' in the construction of econometric models. This interchange is a distinct addition to econometric literature. But more instructive, I think, are the remarkably cogent comments by Milton Friedman on the various points raised in Christ's study. In the tests which were applied in the study, the econometric model showed up poorly as a predictor of the economic variables involved, and it was judged to be of no use for business cycle analysis. But the importance of the paper, and of the extended discussion by Friedman, lies in its raising, for the first time so far as I know, the general and crucial problem of designing critical tests of the performance of econometric techniques of analysis. The 'confidence intervals' for the 'structural parameters', calculated on the basis of what would seem to many persons as quite artificial assumptions regarding the 'population' from which a sample has been drawn, do not provide such a test of performance. These cannot measure one's confidence in the model's capacity to predict the future values which will be observed in the set of time series; for these confidence intervals refer to different variables and to a different experimental operation than that of observing the empirical process which generates the time sequences. Nor do they measure one's confi-

1. On this point, see especially the discussion by Milton Friedman in *Conference on Business Cycles*, New York National Bureau of Economic Research, 1951, p. 111.
2. Carl Christ, *A Test of an Econometric Model for the United States, 1921-1947*, with comments by Milton Friedman, Lawrence Klein, and Geoffrey Moore, and a reply by Christ to the comments of Klein, *Conference on Business Cycles*, New York, National Bureau of Economic Research, 1951, pp. 36-129.

dence in the model's capacity for predicting the effects of policy-decisions. The econometrician speaks of introducing 'greater stability in the economy by indirect inducements', and he explains the meaning of 'indirect inducements' by showing the effects of various changes in the 'structural parameters' or of a 'suppression of a structural equation' upon the behaviour of certain variables in his equation system. He would translate possible legislative changes in the actual economic system into corresponding alterations of his equation system, and he would predict the behaviour properties of the altered economic system by identifying these with the behaviour properties of his altered equation system. So far as I know, there is only disputed conjecture and no empirical evidence at all on which one may base a belief that the behaviour properties of the new equation system constitute reliable predictions of the behaviour properties of the altered economic system. No measure of performance of an econometric model for this purpose of prediction has ever been developed.

There is no instance, so far as I know, where policy-decisions have been based upon an application of the econometric technique of business cycle analysis. It seems reasonable to suppose that such an application will only come after the development of generally convincing tests of performance of the technique. The paper of Christ, together with Friedman's comments, represents at least a beginning of work directed at this problem of measuring the performance of econometric models for the purpose of prediction.

PRELIMINARY REMARKS REGARDING SUBSEQUENT REVIEW OF CONGRESSIONAL DISCUSSIONS OF THE BUSINESS CYCLE PROBLEM

We have found in the econometric literature conceptual experimentation but no substantive gain in the understanding of the business cycle problem. Let us now consider certain other discussions of this problem.

We regard all discussions of public policy to be of this general form: the seeking for an improved set of rules for the constraint and prescription of individual actions. The grounds for proposing a rule which obligates a public agency to act in a certain way are found in the belief held by the proposers that the performance of the economic system will thereby be improved. Controversy arises when the validity of these grounds is questioned. Ever since the business cycle has been recognized as a public problem, there has been a continuing effort to introduce 'stabilizers' into the system and to remove from the system those features which contribute to 'instability'. An introduction of a 'stabilizer' or a removal of an 'unstabilizer' consists of a legislative or administrative change of rules. The controversies have to do with the prediction and evaluation of the effects of a proposed change of rules.

I shall review some of these discussions as they have been recorded before Congressional Committees. The point which I shall attempt to make is that the conceptual ambiguities which prevailed in the discussions of thirty years ago seem still to persist today. These ambiguities have primarily to do with the meaning of the concept of 'stability'. In the quotation with which we began this Part, a well-known analogy is mentioned: that between a motorist steering his automobile and a monetary and fiscal authority 'steering' an economic system. All that either need have, concludes the user of this analogy, is a 'feel' for the response of the mechanism to the various possible actions of the steerer. This analogy begs the crucial questions of the specification of the steering mechanism and of how to observe a state of economic stability and how to recognize an incipient departure from this state. The steerer of the automobile knows how to determine whether or not he is on the road, whether his direction at any point in time will lead him off the road; he is determined to stay on the road, and he has the requisite understanding for the operation of the steering mechanism. The road and the steering mechanism are there before him in all their concreteness. But what these are for the 'steerer' of an economy are not defined. Over the past twenty-five years there has been a proliferation of new 'steering techniques'. The invention of such techniques has absorbed much of the energies of economists. But we seem no nearer now than before to a general understanding and consensus in regard to how the 'steerer' is to recognize a state of 'being on the road', how he is to recognize an incipient departure from this state, and what he should do to arrest each of the various forms of 'departure' which he may possibly observe. That is to say, the meaning of stabilization, in the sense of a rule to be followed by the 'stabilizer', has been and is now the bone of contention in discussions of business cycle policy.

I shall first review this problem of instability as it was presented in the 1920s. The controversial issues of this earlier period will then be compared with the issues as they are presented today. Discussions by responsible Authorities and before Congressional Committees will be used to illustrate the points of controversy. I shall then briefly review what appears to me to be promising empirical work on the business cycle.

AMBIGUITIES IN THE OFFICIAL DISCUSSIONS OF BUSINESS CYCLE POLICY DURING THE 1920S

During the 1920s, the agency responsible for doing whatever was to be done about the business cycle was the central bank—in this country, the Federal Reserve Authorities. There was strong support among economists for a simple rule to guide—in fact, to bind—the actions of this agency; and recommendations were made to Congress that legislation be passed amending the Federal Reserve Act to incorporate this rule of administrative action. The proposed rule called for actions directed to the stabilization of a specified price index—an expansion of Federal Reserve credit when the price index showed a tendency to decline and a contraction when there appeared a tendency for the price index to rise.

The Federal Reserve Authorities vigorously opposed the adoption of this rule, maintaining that the Act as it stood stipulated a rule which was better than the one being proposed. As we shall see, however, they essentially opposed any rule whatsoever which would bind the actions of this agency, for what was being interpreted as a rule of action was stated in undefined terms and left the Administrator virtually free to interpret his responsibilities as he saw fit. In their annual report for 1923, the Federal Reserve Authorities discuss their view of the matter. From this report, the following statements have been taken as representative of the thinking of the Federal Reserve Authorities of that time:

> Particular prominence has been given in discussions of new proposals to the suggestion . . . that the credit issuing from the Federal Reserve Banks should be regulated with immediate reference to the price level, particularly in such manner as to avoid fluctuations of general prices. Entirely apart from the difficult administrative problems that would arise in connection with the adoption of the price index as a guide . . . , there is no reason for believing that the results attained would be as satisfactory as can be reached by other means economically valid and administratively practicable. . . .
>
> Credit administration must be cognizant of what is under way or in process in the movement of business before it is registered in the price index. The price index records an accomplished fact. Good credit administration in times of active business expansion should not assist the excessive accumulations of forward commitments in business . . . which only

later on will reflect the rate at which they have been taking place in changes of price levels; and in times of business reaction should discourage enforced liquidation, which also will only later on reflect the rate at which it has been taking place in price levels. The problem of efficient credit administration is, therefore, largely a question of timeliness of action.

No statistical mechanism alone, however carefully contrived, can furnish an adequate guide to credit administration. Credit is an intensely human institution and as such reflects the moods and impulses of the community. . . . The business situation at any particular time is weighted and charged with these invisible factors. They are factors which must always patiently and skillfully be evaluated as best they may . . . In its ultimate analysis credit administration is not a matter of mechanical rules, but is and must be a matter of judgment—of judgment concerning each specific credit situation at the particular moment of time when it has arisen or is developing.

. . . By what means may it be known whether the volume of credit provided by the Federal Reserve Banks is in any given set of circumstances adequate, excessive, or deficient? The problem in good administration under the Federal reserve system is not only that of limiting the field of uses of Federal reserve credit to productive purposes, but also of limiting the volume of credit within the field of its appropriate uses to such amount as may be economically justified. . . . The Federal Reserve Act itself suggests the nature of the tests, guides, or indicators—whatever they may be called—to be used in gauging the need for and the adequacy of Federal reserve credit. The provisions of the Act indicate that the needs for credit which are recognized by the Act as appropriate are those derived from agriculture, industry, and trade. It is the belief of the Board that there will be little danger that the credit created and contributed by the Federal Reserve Banks will be in excessive volume if restricted to productive uses. A characteristic of the good functioning of the economic system is to be found in the smooth unobstructed movement of goods from the producer through the channels of distribution to their several ultimate uses. The characteristic of the good functioning of the credit system is to be found in the promptness and in the degree with which the flow of credit adapts itself to the orderly flow of goods in industry and trade. . . .[1]

With the benefit of hindsight, no more than a second reading of the above quotation is required for one to see that nothing at all is said except that the Federal Reserve Authorities opposed any rule whatsoever which would bind their actions. The proposed rule would call for an expansion of money and credit if the price index were observed to decline and a decrease of money and credit if it were observed to rise. Little discretion would be left to the Federal Reserve Authorities—at any rate, this was the intention of the proposers of the rule. The Authorities' actions would be determined by what they observe when they collect specified data and arrange it in a specified way. These Authorities opposed this categorically; and although they said and presumably believed they did, it is clear now that they did not indicate any rule or guide at all which would limit their discretion.

They spoke as though they did not have the technical means to stabilize the price index, but they were willing to assume responsibility for the maintenance of the 'smooth, unobstructed, orderly flow of goods in industry and trade'. They laid down the principle that excessive accumulation of forward commitments should not be assisted; but they did not explain how they proposed to recognize 'excessiveness' in what they could observe nor what action they would take if they thought they observed it. Enforced liquidation should be discouraged, but there was no explanation of how this quality of being 'enforced' is to be recognized when 'liquidation' is observed. They stated that timeliness of action is paramount, but they suggested no way of recognizing when and what action should be taken. They asserted that the good functioning of the economy is to be observed in the 'smooth unobstructed movement of goods' and that the good performance of the banking and monetary system is to be observed in the 'prompt-

1. *Tenth Annual Report of the Federal Reserve Board, 1923*, Washington, Government Printing Office, 1924, pp. 31-5.

ness with which the flow of credit adapts itself to the orderly flow of goods'. But one may yet ask what actions the Authorities propose to take as induced by what observations. The Authorities did not explain themselves and said in effect: Leave these matters to us.

Several bills were introduced in Congress during the later 1920s which would have written into the Federal Reserve Act this rule which the Federal Reserve Authorities opposed. There was a Congressional Committee on Stabilization, and Governor Strong of the Federal Reserve Bank of New York for the Committee described a kind of dilemma which a 'steerer' of an economic system is constantly having to deal with.

> Assume that we here are the directors of the Federal Reserve Bank trying to determine what to do about the discount rate. We have this feeling that there is a growth of speculation; possibly a feeling that it ought to be curbed by the Federal Reserve system in some way. On the other hand, we are faced with a clear indication of some decline in the price of farm commodities. Now, if great concern had been felt about the price of farm commodities, and we felt that the introduction of credit into the market or lowering interest rate might correct the prices of those individual commodities, what might the consequences be in speculation? There you are between the devil and the deep sea.[1]

Here is an example, said Governor Strong, of how responsible authorities must use their judgment. Something may be observed which looks unstable. And yet, the actions required to stabilize this situation may unstabilize something else. Governor Strong was undoubtedly unable to describe explicitly what general stability would look like. He would not have been able to specify what data should be collected and how they should be arranged in order that a test be applied for the stability of the system at a given time. He felt intuitively, however, that what he would regard as a situation calling for remedial action of some sort is consistent with the stability of a price index; and he could give examples which illustrated to his satisfaction the possibility that actions taken to arrest a downward tendency in the general price index could be wrong actions for the authorities to take. In brief, the price index rule, he thought, grossly over-simplifies matters. He goes on to say:

> I believe that there is a tendency to look at the price-level as though it operated up and down against a counter-weight of credit, and as if you could open a spigot when prices are declining and put a little more credit in the counter-weight and raise prices, and if prices are going up you could drain a little credit out of the counter-weight and let prices go down. But I am afraid the price problem is a little more complicated than that.
>
> Take the situation for the present and for quite a period past. We have had a remarkably stable level of prices for general commodities, with the exceptions within the last few months of a decline in grain and cotton prices. Prices of cattle and hogs have remained pretty steady. There has been a decline in agricultural prices sufficient to bring about a gradual reduction in the index number of general prices. Now, take the problem of today. Is the Federal Reserve System to step in and attempt to regulate this movement which seems to have started; and if so, how? That is the practical thing that the price regulatory would face from time to time.
>
> If we had such a severe decline in the value of cotton and all the commodities that are influenced by world market prices as to cause a decline in the general price level, and we should attempt to remedy it just by buying securities and making cheap money, it would not cause an advance, certainly not immediately, in the prices of those commodities whose prices are fixed by world markets and world competition. It would have an inflationary effect which might indeed affect price-levels of purely domestic commodities; and, if it did, it would be thereby advancing the price of everything the farmer consumed, at the same time that the selling price for what he produces was being reduced.[2]

1. Quoted in J. M. Keynes, *Treatise on Money*, New York, 1930, pp. 340-3; and drawn from the testimony of Governor Strong before the Committee of the United States Congress on Stabilization. The testimony is found on pp. 295, 359, 550 and 557 of the Evidence presented before this Stabilization Committee.
2. Ibid.

Governor Strong observed that some prices were rising while others were falling during a period when the index was stable. I am inclined to think that the meaning which he intended to convey by his statement, 'I am afraid the price problem is a little more complicated than that', is that stability cannot be maintained by stabilizing an average; and this raises the question of what the term 'stability' is to mean—that is, of how we are to recognize in the data that we may assemble the presence or absence of the state of affairs called stability. Governor Strong saw cross-currents in that which he observed, and he thought he could describe situations in which the variety of movements and counter-movements of individual economic series would call for actions by the monetary Authority that would not be prescribed by a simple rule requiring a stable average. However, he was apparently unable to formulate a rule that would prescribe the actions he would deem appropriate for the conceivable situations.

We may note that the terms which the Authorities of that day used to describe what they proposed to do were undefined and empty, and their statements reduced essentially to: Rely upon us to handle the situations as they arise. We may also note that at the time these monetary authorities were making the statements they were sitting upon a desperately weak financial system without apparently recognizing the weaknesses. There are prominent students of the business cycle—such men as Simons, Knight, Friedman, Schumpeter, among others—who have expressed the opinion that the extraordinary severity of the depression beginning in 1929 may be attributed to the mechanical defects of the financial system and to the bad judgment of men not constrained by rules. The bank failure epidemics and the wholesale farm mortgage foreclosures occurring during the later 1920s and early 1930s were a gravely demoralizing experience and virtually paralysed the economies of large areas of the nation. Since that day, laws pertaining to banking, farm financing, security exchanges, house construction financing, and the like have been enacted which are regarded as having strengthened the financial system. Other laws have been passed which are thought to have altered the fiscal system in such a way as to render the economic system inherently more stable. A decline in business activity is now automatically offset to some extent: as personal incomes and business net revenues decline, personal and business tax payments are reduced; as unemployment increases, social security payments increase; as farm prices fall, government farm payments increase; etc. The economists to whom I now refer do not think in terms of an absolute concept of 'stability' or 'balance'. They would define a measure of the 'degree of instability' and they would consider that some 'degree of instability' is to be associated with any system allowing individual freedom of action. The enactment of such laws as those mentioned above, in their judgment, will have brought about an observable reduction in the degree of instability of the economic system. Certain of these economists[1] propose that further alteration be made in the fiscal and monetary system and such as to remove discretionary powers from monetary and fiscal authorities. Business cycle policy would be a part of the general legislative problem—the seeking for a 'best' performing system of laws, the degree of instability being regarded as one aspect of performance. In this scheme, no administrative agency would have discretionary authority to take the actions it sees fit to take in order to 'stabilize' the system or in order to maintain 'maximum levels of employment'. The legislature itself would continually strive to improve the performance of the system; and this would entail the reduction of the instability of the system so long as ways may be found for doing this which are consistent with other objectives.

1. Cf., e.g., Milton Friedman, 'A Monetary and Fiscal Framework for Economic Stability', *The American Economic Review*, June 1948.

THE INTRODUCTION OF NEW TERMINOLOGY DURING THE 1930S

But this is not the prevailing view. In some circles, as we shall see, to speak of an economist as 'believing' in this kind of policy would be virtually to speak of him as believing in misery and distress and as 'abandoning sound economic analysis'. During the 1930s, a new set of terms became current, and business cycles policy has been discussed primarily in these terms. It was Keynes who fitted the terms to the times and gave them their immense popularity, but the point of view was an established attitude in this country.[1]

Very briefly and in its popular form the idea is something like this: With the technology, capital equipment, and labour force which exist during a given period of time, there is an aggregate value of total output which would be forthcoming if all the labour force were fully employed. This total value of output is identical with the total income available for expenditure by the spending units; for everything that is produced is owned by some person or agency. Let the spending units be classified in three broad groups: there are the family and individual units who are the private buyers of consumer goods; there are the business firms who are the private buyers of investment goods; and there are the governmental agencies. Assume that at the income level corresponding to a fully employed labour force, as at any other level, there is a predictable amount of consumer spending. For short periods ahead, the spending by private business firms may be estimated. By subtracting the amount of the consumption and investment expenditures by these private spending units from the figure representing the 'maximum value of output', one obtains, so goes the argument, the amount of the expenditure by governmental units which is required in order to induce the production of the 'maximum output of the economy'.

In such terms as these, persons in positions to wield great influence over popular thinking express their views. But few if any of the ambiguities of the earlier Federal Reserve Board statements are avoided. The Employment Act of 1946 is couched in such terms. It does not, however, define the terms. Rather it demands that the administrator define them; and this he cannot do without raising the unresolved controversies and ambiguities of the 1920s. It will be recalled that the Federal Reserve Authorities of 1923 observed the 'good functioning of the economic system . . . in the smooth unobstructed movement of goods from the producer through the channels of distribution to their several ultimate uses', and they observed the adequacy of their actions 'in the promptness and in the degree with which the flow of credit adapts itself to the orderly flow of goods in industry and trade'. Mr. Leon Keyserling, the chairman of President Truman's Council of Economic Advisers, is no less specific. He explains that:

> Maximum production means a sufficient level of output and demand to be consistent with maximum employment. . . . Maximum purchasing power means, in the final analysis, a flow and dispersion of income among various sectors of the economy which will promote equilibrium at maximum levels of employment and production. . . . The ultimate purpose of national economic policies and programs, manifestly, is to promote the utilization of our labor force and other resources in ways which avoid excess waste of manpower and excess waste of opportunity for enjoying maximum output. It would seem obvious beyond the need for argumentation that no systematic formulation or evaluation of such policies and programs can have any sound point of departure, unless that point be a definition of what quantities of employment and production connote maximum employment and production, and what allocations of purchasing power are consistent with maximum employment and production.[2]

1 Cf. 'Suggestions of Keynes in the Writings of Veblen', *Journal of Political Economy*, October 1939.
2. *Hearings before the Joint Committee on the Economic Report, Eighty-fourth Congress, First Session*, Washington D.C., Government Printing Office, 1955, pp. 167-8.

Just as we would all hold with the Federal Reserve Authorities of the 1920s that a disorderly, rough, and obstructed flow of goods is something to be avoided, we can now take a stand opposing 'excess waste of manpower and excess waste of opportunity for enjoying maximum output'. But from the contemporary controversies it would seem clear that agreement upon how to define 'potential maximum production' and how to use this definition in formulating a rule of administrative action is as remote as agreement upon a definition of 'smooth unobstructed movement of goods from the producer through the channels of distribution to their several uses'. A chairman of the President's Council of Economic Advisers like Mr. Keyserling would apparently be prepared to exercise his judgment in taking actions that would have seemed fantastic to Governor Strong. But from Governor Strong to Mr. Keyserling, it is difficult to detect a growth of knowledge and understanding of the phenomena with which these high officials dealt.

THE AMBIGUITY OF THIS TERMINOLOGY IN DISCUSSIONS DURING THE 1950S

The Federal Reserve Authorities in 1923 regarded[1] Section 14, paragraph (d) of the Federal Reserve Act of that time (which stated that credit facilities shall be used only for 'accommodating commerce and business') and Section 13 (which restricted Federal Reserve credit to 'agricultural, industrial, or commercial purposes') as providing adequate guidance and restraint for monetary authorities. In the light of experience we can now see that these sections provided virtually no guidance at all and that the responsible officials exercised questionable if not poor judgment in the use of their discretion.

Just as the Reserve Authorities of 1923 were satisfied with what they looked upon as the rule of action set forth in the Federal Reserve Act of that day, now Mr. Keyserling, as a man of contemporary official experience, regards[2] 'the meaning of the Employment Act' of 1946 as 'unmistakably clear' with respect to the rules of action which it imposes upon the administrators of the Act. These rules are laid down in Sections 2 and 3 of this Employment Act of 1946:[3]

Declaration of Policy

Sec. 2. The Congress declares that it is the continuing policy and responsibility of the Federal Government to use all practicable means consistent with its needs and obligations and other essential considerations of national policy, . . . to coordinate and utilize all its plans, functions, and resources for the purpose of creating and maintaining, in a manner calculated to foster and promote free competitive enterprise and the general welfare, conditions under which there will be afforded useful employment opportunities . . . for those able, willing, and seeking to work, and to promote maximum employment, production, and purchasing power.

Economic Report of the President

Sec. 3. (a). The President shall transmit to the Congress at the beginning of each regular session an economic report setting forth (1) the levels of employment, production, and purchasing power obtaining in the United States and such levels needed to carry out the policy declared in section 2; (2) current and foreseeable trends in the levels of employment, production, and purchasing power; (3) a review of the economic program of the Federal Government and a review of economic conditions affecting employment in the United States or any considerable portion thereof . . .; and (4) a program for carrying out the policy declared in section 2. . . .

1. *Tenth Annual Report of the Federal Reserve Board, 1923*, Washington, D.C., Government Printing Office, 1924, pp. 32-3.
2. *Hearings before the Joint Committee on the Economic Report*, op. cit., p. 168.
3. *Economic Report of the President, January, 1954*, Washington, D.C., Government Printing Office, 1954, pp. 129-32.

In the recently held Hearings before the Joint Committee on the President's Economic Report, the present administration of the Act was strongly criticized. Senator Douglas and his Democratic colleagues were heavily critical, as were Mr. Keyserling, the previous chairman of the President's Council of Economic Advisers, Messrs. Reuther and Ruttenberg of the CIO, Mr. Colm of the National Planning Association, and many others, academic and non-academic alike. From the criticism, one may get the impression that the Act sets forth a definite rule of action which the Administration is reluctant to follow. In some respects, the discussion is remindful of the Congressional Hearings on Stabilization held in the 1920s. But there is this difference: In the 1920s, the proposed rule, which was never enacted, would have required the governmental agency to stabilize a price index; and the responsible authorities vigorously opposed the adoption of this rule. In the 1950s, the critics of the Administration seem to suspect that the responsible authorities, more or less surreptitiously, are following this very rule, in defiance of the mandate of the Act—which these critics interpret as requiring the stabilization of unemployment at a 'minimum level'. The spokesman for the Administration, on the other hand, denies this interpretation of the Act, points out crucial ambiguities, and, much as did Governor Strong in the 1920s, calls attention to the dilemma which would confront an administrator who was bound by a simple rule requiring a strict stabilization of unemployment at a specified 'minimum level'. The following quotations illustrate these remarks.

Mr. Reuther sees in the Administration's behaviour a banker's mentality at work, selfishly or foolishly fearful of inflation. He sees the intent of the Act being frustrated in the Administration's concern for the stability of the price level, when its mandate is to stabilize at a minimum the level of unemployment.

Now in reading the Employment Act of 1946 . . . we find in Section 3 (a) that the President has certain basic obligations of responsibility. . . . We would like to suggest . . . that your Committee ask the President to comply with the law and . . . to present Congress with the estimated required goals of employment, production, and purchasing power for attaining maximum employment in 1955 . . . and to present Congress and the American people with a program for carrying out the declared policy under the law. . . .

Now what bothers us about the President's report is that we believe it reflects a kind of banker mentality, and we believe that the people who are primarily the architects of the Administration's economic fiscal policies are operating as bankers instead of operating in terms of the basic needs of the American people. . . .

Mr. Humphrey, the Secretary of the Treasury, is undoubtedly the chief architect of the economic and fiscal policies of this administration, and we are disturbed by the fact that Mr. Humphrey would have us believe that the most important and compelling problem that we need to meet in America on the economic front is to fight the threat of inflation. There is no serious inflation in America, and yet all of the efforts being made would have us believe that the No. 1 problem is fighting inflation.

You get the testimony of Mr. Martin, head of the Federal Reserve Board . . . and there you get a reflection of this same attitude, that the problem, the threat, is inflation. Therefore, we have to tighten up. When Mr. Martin is asked what do you mean, how do you measure when we have an inflationary threat, he says the minute we get beyond any point that may approach economic growth of more than 3 per cent a year, we put the brakes on. . . . This is obviously an effort to make money more valuable so that the bankers will get the benefit of money with greater value. . . .

Now, we believe that your committee ought to insist upon a definition of what we consider to be maximum employment. We in the CIO believe that in a free economy you have to have a normal float of workers who are seeking jobs. That is a part of the normal process of a free economy in a free society. We believe that the level of the amount of unemployment required to facilitate the movement and the healthy shift in job opportunities should not exceed 2 to 2.5 per cent of the civilian labor force, which means that 1.5 million people in that category would be adequate to meet the mobility needs of our free economy. . . . I believe that at the current rate of labor force growth and technological progress, we need from 2.5 to 3.5 million new jobs a year. . . . The combination of those two factors means that we are in trouble if we do not begin to find a way to expand and facilitate economic growth to take up the slack.[1]

Mr. Keyserling criticized the Administration for not abiding by the mandate of the Act as he interprets it; and he warns that the Act was designed to correct what he regards as a confirmed performance characteristic of the economic system as it stood and as it now would stand without the Act—viz., a persistent trend toward under-employment of resources:

You cannot find in [the Economic Report of the President for 1955] the measurements of need which respond to the Employment Act of 1946, which I think is a good law. There is nothing in the report which says what the needed level of employment is . . . nothing which says what the needed level of production is . . . nothing which says or analyses seriously what the needed level of farm income or consumer income, or of business income, might be to restore a lower level of unemployment. . . . I do not think this is responsive to the Employment Act. The Employment Act does not set the target of having a reasonably good economic year for some people. It sets a target of good conditions for the great majority of people in our country, and no serious hardship for the others. . . .

. . . .

I think we are threatened by a long-term trend of rising chronic unemployment. . . . According to my calculations . . . we would need in 1955 an expansion of about 6 per cent in total output above the 1954 level to reduce unemployment to what I would regard as tolerable levels under the standards of the Employment Act. . . . Now, what has actually happened since the beginning of 1953 is that our economy has shown what I firmly believe to be a long-term chronic trend of failure to absorb increases in productivity and increases in the labór force.[3]

Mr. James G. Patton, the President of the National Farmers' Union, expressed his annoyance with the present administrators of the Act:

The President's 1955 Economic Report reaches a new low. . . . It highlights the wrong facts; it misconstrues the facts that it highlights. . . . The Economic Report is supposed to be a great interpretative document. . . . Here are a few of the questions that the report makes no attempt to answer. . . . Is employment too high or too low? . . . Is production sufficient? . . . Is purchasing power sufficient, and is it well distributed? . . .

These are not merely random questions. They are the core of intelligent consideration of economic policy. They are the central questions that the statute directs be answered in the Economic Report. The report does not even raise these questions. It abandons the field of sound economic analysis. It cuts the ground from under intelligent discussion of economic policy. And specifically it flouts not only the spirit but the very letter of an explicit mandate of the Employment Act.[4]

The Democratic majority of the Congressional Committee reacted similarly. Representative Kelley of Pennsylvania, for example, showed his impatience with the President and his economic advisers and their concern with 'inflation . . . at the price of misery and distress':

I have contended that the authors of the Economic Report for 1955 have exercised more than the normal amount of ingenuity in missing the point, and the point is this: there is a mandate in the Full Employment Act to provide maximum employment, maximum production, and maximum purchasing. The report misses that pretty much, as I said. . . .

There is no use in having maximum production if you do not have maximum purchasing power. In many areas of the country today there is a great deal of unemployment. . .. It appears that those in authority in this Government are satisfied, in order to balance the budget and to prevent inflation, to do so at the price of misery and distress in these areas, and that calls, I think, for some very dynamic action to be taken in order to aid

1. *Hearings*, op. cit., pp. 1152-4; also cf. p. 1200 *et seq.*
2. *Hearings*, op. cit., pp. 102-3.
3. *Hearings*, op. cit., pp. 66-7, 80.
4. *Hearings*, op. cit., p. 1169.

those areas, and I might add this, too, that while we uphold this prosperity in the country generally, there is not a very great distribution of this prosperity.[1]

Representative Patman of Texas was disturbed by what he saw as an undue emphasis placed by the present Administration upon price stability:

Maintenance of a stable price level seems to be given the highest priority in administration declarations dealing with economic policies. Does this mean that the behavior of some price index rather than, say, the amount of unemployed, is used as a guide for economic policy decisions? . . .

Does the mere stabilization of a wholesale price index mean that there are no imbalances developing in the economy? Does not the experience of the 1926-29 period raise questions concerning the validity of this assumption? Does not the experience of 1953-54 indicate that unsound structural dislocations have taken place underneath the cover of a stable-price level?[2]

Spokesmen for depressed areas and industries were critical of the Administration's neglect of the 'victims of industrial change'. Representative Gray of Illinois appeared before the Committee and described the needs of his district.

The people of our great country may be enjoying, by and large, what the present administration calls a growing prosperity; but that is not true of the people of southern Illinois. . . . We are predominantly coal mines . . . and we are experiencing not only a recession but a full-fledged depression in southern Illinois. . . . The people sent me to Congress to stand up and speak out in behalf of their wants and needs. . . . Is it not time to do more than lend a sympathetic ear? . . . Is it not time to balance the human budget before balancing the monetary budget? . . . The people of southern Illinois have a right to work; they have a right to live with their own families in their own homes. . . . My home town of West Frankfort, Illinois, had a population of 15,000 in 1940. The population today is 8,000. . . . I have studied with great interest the Economic Report of the President of the United States, but I find no place in this report where they make mention of such districts as the 25th Congressional District in southern Illinois, which I represent.[3]

Along similar lines, Mr. Soloman Barkin, of the Textile Workers Union of America, called in question the 'philosophy underlying the President's Economic Report'.

The textile industry has been in a depressed state since 1951 and has not yet recovered. . . . As textile mills are generally located in nonmetropolitan areas, frequently comprising one-industry communities, alternative employments in the locality are lacking. The slump in textile employment therefore depresses entire communities and leaves workers and their families stranded. . . . The inability of these communities to get out of this chronic state is attested by the fact that they have remained distressed for long periods of time. . . .

. . . .

The current administration promised much but has done little to relieve distress in the textile industry. The President's Economic Report acknowledges that 'some industries and localities suffered from serious unemployment' but we are reassured that 'the recovery was largest in the . . . textile industries'. There are no suggestions in the report of means for aiding the revival and reinvigoration of the industry and its expansion. The only recommendation is for assistance to 'depressed communities to develop workable solutions of their problems'. . . . But we are cautioned against expecting much help since 'these programs can make only a limited contribution to relieving 'spot unemployment'. Moreover, the adjustment is to be left to 'the local citizens themselves'. Major reliance is to be placed upon policies that 'promise a high and stable level of employment in the Nation at large'.

But it is quite obvious, as the Economic Report declares in the preceding paragraph,

1. *Hearings*, op. cit., p. 1171.
2. *Hearings*, op. cit., p. 13.
3. *Hearings*, op. cit., pp. 197, 265.

that 'although the economy as a whole was prosperous, some communities suffered from sizable unemployment'. Certainly the philosophy underlying the President's Economic Report, which sets its goal at high rather than full employment, offers us no confidence that these industrial and geographical difficulties will be relieved. A government which does not seek to assure a job opportunity for all will only provide verbal solace to the victims of industrial change, unenterprising industrial managers, and unfair competition built upon wage cutting and substandard labor conditions.

It prescribes the encouragement of 'enterprise and innovation' but not in a volume sufficient to overcome the distress of local communities. Its unfounded presumption that full employment will threaten the 'integrity of the money in which contracts are expressed and payments made' has stopped it in its tracks. It has desisted from aiding the communities and industries in need as it is fearful of action which will impart 'an immediate upward thrust to economic activity'. Economic policies inspired by this philosophy are not likely to generate a full employment economy essential to the solution of the problems of the economic 'sore spots' in our country.[1]

The above quotations come, so to speak, from the front line of policy discussions. The persons quoted (and many more might have been included) are able men, representing large segments of the electorate; and they are presumably seeking a solution to the problem and not simply special privileges for those whom they represent. But a simple underlining of undefined concepts, begged questions, and untenable implications provides a measure of the poverty of political economy as an intellectual discipline in the social discussion of this issue.

The Employment Act of 1946 provides no well-defined rule of administrative action, any more than did the Federal Reserve Act of the 1920s. It will be recalled that the Federal Reserve Authorities of 1923 maintained that they were able to observe the 'good functioning of the economic system . . . in the smooth unobstructed movement of goods . . . through the channels of distribution to their several ultimate uses', and that they measured the adequacy of their actions 'in the promptness and in the degree with which the flow of credit adapts itself to the orderly flow of goods in industry and trade'. The critics of the present Administration seem to say, paraphrasing these expressions used in 1923, that 'the characteristic of the good functioning of the economic system is to be found in levels of production, employment, and purchasing power at maximum potentials' and that 'the measure of the adequacy of a national economic policy is to be found in its effectiveness and sufficiency for the maintenance of these maximum potentials'. 'Maximum potential level' would seem to have approximately the same content as 'smooth, unobstructed flow' and 'effectiveness and sufficiency of a policy' has about as much content as 'promptness of the adaptation to an orderly flow'. In the years since the 1920s, the popular understanding of political economy has attained a level such that the spokesmen for the public demand of the Government that it 'take the dynamic action required for maintaining an employment level which is not too low and production and purchasing power which are sufficient and adequately distributed in order to meet the needs of local communities'.

That this emptiness and conceptual ambiguity are not confined to popular discussions of this issue may be illustrated by a colloquy which took place at these Hearings between two recent presidents of the American Economic Association, Professor Calvin Hoover and Senator Paul Douglas. Professor Hoover was asked a question by Representative Mills: 'What rates of national economic growth should government economic policy attempt to facilitate in the coming year?' Senator Douglas commented, 'That is a very good question'. Professor Hoover had already testified in much the same vein as Messrs. Keyserling and Ruttenberg, and to this question he responded promptly in definite terms, just

1. *Hearings*, op. cit., pp. 267-70.

as did Mr. Keyserling: '. . . a rate of something like 4 to 5 per cent.' He added further that ' we may need more stimulus than present policies provide if we are to attain this rate of growth'. But then, as the discussion proceeded, he abandoned this definiteness and ended by admitting that such statements convey virtually no meaning:

Professor Hoover: . . . Having said that, fairness compels me to go on and say that we should not forget that this is a very delicate matter, to know how stimulative or how restrictive our economic policy should be in order to attain this growth rate. I could be quite wrong in my estimate of what degree of stimulation the economy needs just now. It must be noted, too, that at one time there was, I think, quite a real problem of stopping inflation. . . .

Senator Douglas: When did you think that the problem of stopping inflation occurred? Was it in 1953 or had it been in 1951?

Professor Hoover: It well may have been 1951, but on my part this is largely hindsight. If you had asked me in 1951 I doubt whether I would have given that answer.

I hope everybody else knows the answer better than I do on these matters, you see, because unfortunately I do not. I have to admit a very large margin of error. Yet we must repeatedly make value judgments and act or refrain from acting. . . .

Senator Douglas: A very wise man. But you would say a failure to grow at a rate of 4 or 5 per cent should be a matter of concern?

Professor Hoover: Yes. However, I would point out that you cannot be sure about it. If my recommendation were followed, it might well turn out that you would get more inflation than we would want. As you ask me right now, I gave a recommendation. That recommendation might result in action which would be wrong.

Senator Douglas: Does anybody want to comment on that statement?

With the above colloquy in mind, let us recall the testimony of Governor Strong before the Congressional Committee on Stabilization in the 1920s. Governor Strong described a dilemma which confronts stabilizers when recession and inflation are simultaneously observed. He was testifying adversely upon the advisability of adopting a rule directing the monetary authorities to take the actions required for stabilizing a price index. Professor Hoover, as near as I can make out, was testifying more or less favourably upon the interpretation of the 1946 Act as a 'mandate' for the stabilization of an index of unemployment at a 'minimum level'. But his answers to the questions lead one to suppose that if he were in charge of things in the 1950s he would find himself almost continually facing the situation described by Governor Strong and with no more confidence about what to do. With only a few changes in the words used by Governor Strong in the quotations presented earlier we may obtain a statement such as we may imagine Professor Hoover making. For example we may paraphrase Governor Strong's statement in the terms now current:

I believe there is a tendency to look at the employment level as though it operated up and down against a counter-weight of expenditure, and as if you could open a spigot when unemployment is rising and put a little more expenditure in the counter-weight and raise employment, and if unemployment is going down to the point where inflation develops you could turn expenditure off a little. But I am afraid the employment and inflation problem is a little more complicated than that.

Take the situation for the present (late '53 and early '54). We have had a remarkably stable level of income and consumer expenditure and total employment, with the exception of recent employment and production declines in certain industries primarily concentrated in certain North Central and Eastern industrial communities. Consumption expenditures and private investment expenditures are increasing. There has been a decline in defense expenditures and of employment in defense industries. Now take the problem of today. Is the Federal Administration to step in and find something to do that will increase the employment in the communities where unemployment is found; and if so, how?

As Mr. Hoover said, one must act or refrain from acting, and the crucial question is what to do.

AN INTERPRETATION OF THE STUDIES OF THE PRESENT CHAIRMAN OF THE COUNCIL OF ECONOMIC ADVISERS

These Hearings were held during January and February of 1955. The six months that have passed since then have generally shown the critics of the 1955 *Economic Report of the President*[1] to have been poor forecasters of business cycle movements; and the changes that have taken place have borne out the judgments presented by the authors of the report. The last two reports, for 1954 and 1955, have substantially been the work of A. F. Burns, the present chairman of the Council of Economic Advisers. Mr. Burns, I am inclined to think, knows more about business cycle phenomena and about how an economic system grows and develops than any other economist of this country, and his appointment to the post he occupies was a remarkable one.

He has spent his life as an economist studying the fluctuations and growth of economic activity; and he and his associates at the National Bureau of Economic Research have developed methods for describing the enormously complex cross-currents and counter-movements that may be observed in any phase of the business cycle—the hard-pressed firms and industries and communities during periods of prevalent prosperity; the prosperous firms, industries, and communities during periods of depression. His earlier study[2] of the growth tendencies in American production laid similar emphasis upon the great divergencies and variation among the growth rates of the many different industries which are the components of the 'nation's industry'. In all of his work, he has concentrated upon the study of the nature and form of the variation in growth and change which is implicit in the idea of freedom of individual action within the constraints of a system of laws.

In a sense, this is a 'classical' type of inquiry, which ultimately comes to questions that are fundamental to the 'classical' type of economic problem. In Part I, we reviewed the framework of Adam Smith's argument and presented an interpretation of his theory of social organization. The fundamental supposition underlying this 'classical' argument is that under any circumstances allowing freedom of individual action within a system of laws there will be variation among the values of commodities and among the outputs and incomes of the members of society. The formal theory of value purported to explain the character of this inherent variation among values. Faulty performance of an economic system is observed not in variation *per se* but in a particular kind of variation that in principle can be set conceptually apart. It is in such terms that the monopoly problem and the problem of trade restriction have been discussed: an observed price which is judged to be 'too high' is so judged by a sort of virtual comparison with what the price would be were there 'free entry' or 'free access', etc. In the case of the business cycle problem, we do not deal with the classical value problem, which involves comparisons of price and incomes at points of time. Rather, the observed variables are those describing relative changes in production, relative changes in family incomes, relative changes in net revenues of firms, in the employment rate of firms, in the growth of communities, etc.; and it is not simply the rates of changes of great aggregates that are observed, but rather the rates of change of the millions of possible components of these aggregates. The classical type of price theory does not come into the discussion. But there is involved a 'classical' kind of problem nevertheless. For it is evident that the

1. *Economic Report of the President.* Transmitted to the Congress, January 1955, Washington, Government Printing Office, 1955.
2 A. F. Burns, *Production Trends in the United States since 1870*, New York, National Bureau of Economic Research 1934.

mere existence of a lower end of a range of variation of some variable—like relative change of ouput by firm or industry or area, or relative change of family income by area or industry source, or percentage of labour force employment by industry or area or quarter—does not in itself indicate a fault in the system prevailing at the time; for under any system of laws a range of variation for any such variable would be observed. In order to judge the observed variation, divergencies of growth, and differences among individual conditions, it is essential that there be some conception of the form and character of the variation and divergencies inherent in the operation of any system of this general class. Insofar as it may be established that some specifiable form of variation of individual conditions is an inherent characteristic of a government of laws, then in judging the performance of a particular system of laws the attention is to be directed to the kind of variation which is not inherent in any government of laws—i.e. to the kind which may be altered by an alteration of the system of laws.

No such theory has been developed which explores this aspect of the implications of the idea of freedom of individual action under a system of laws. And Burns has never intimated that he has this sort of thing in mind in planning his empirical investigations. But his work seems to me to be in this direction, and he has provided arrangements of data yet to be accounted for by a theoretical argument. In his studies of economic growth,[1] he observed at all times new industries being introduced, established industries growing at declining rates, and old industries dying out. In this welter of divergency of industrial growth rates, he was able to discern statistical regularities in terms of which he described the processes of growth and change within an economic system—and the process which he described was more or less invariant with respect to the technological and institutional changes over the period of sixty years.

In his more comprehensive studies of the cyclical fluctuation of economic activity, his approach has been similar. He has worked with a large number of series, and his arrangements of the data show again the striking divergency of economic change which can be observed at any point of time. Always there are firms, industries, and areas which are experiencing expansions, and always there are others showing contractions. The rate of change of an aggregate like Gross National Product is a kind of average of the rates of change shown by components of this aggregate. In any observation period, there are firms, industries, and areas that are reaching a peak of activity. Along with these there are others that are reaching their troughs. One arrangement of Mr. Burns' data shows for each successive period the percentage of all the series studied which reach a peak in that period.[2] This percentage itself rises, reaches a peak, declines, reaches a trough, rises, and so on. A 'national business cycle peak' corresponds to the peak of this percentage of individual series reaching peaks. In such a 'national peak period' there is always a sizable percentage of series reaching troughs. Another arrangement of the data shows for each successive period the percentage of the series which are undergoing expansion during that period. This percentage shows an approximately regular cyclical fluctuation. About 50 per cent of the series are showing expansion in each peak period of 'national economic activity'. The percentage declines from this figure during a national contraction, reaches a trough about midway during the 'national contraction', then expands and passes the 50 per cent mark in the period which we recognize as the 'national trough period', continues to expand and reaches a peak about midway in the 'national expansion'. In his data, this percentage, rarely gets above 75 and

1. A. F. Burns, op. cit.
2. A. F. Burns, 'New Facts on Business Cycles', *The Frontiers of Economic Knowledge*, National Bureau of Economic Research, Princeton University Press, 1954, pp. 108-33.

rarely below 25; and it follows a cyclical, roughly periodic course. Another arrangement of data shows percentage changes of such a variable as output or income payments classified by industry or by area and arranged in the form of a frequency distribution. For each period there is such a frequency distribution of these measures of activity, and national expansion and contraction are seen as a development in time of these relative frequency distributions.

These descriptions, then, are in terms of stable patterns of relative frequencies and of stable forms of frequency distributions. The 'things' being measured or observed are not 'at rest', nor are they ever tending to a 'state of rest'. There is a continuing state of motion among the individual units. Yet the frequency distributions of the individual observations suggest a regular form into which the variation fits period by period—and again the stable features extend over long periods, suggesting invariance properties with respect to technological and institutional changes. This is the kind of situation described by the idea of statistical equilibrium,[1] referring to stable forms of frequency distributions of measures made upon individual entities that are themselves in a continual state of motion; and its analysis would involve an application of probability theory. No one has yet attempted to develop a conceptual model for the analysis of the kind of probability phenomena suggested in Burns' arrangements of data. But this, I think, will come, and it will be a 'classical' kind of contribution. In the real population, each individual during his waking life apparently is engaged in a decision-making process. He consciously weighs and judges the expected consequence of alternative actions which are possible under a system of physical and institutional constraints. But in the construction of a theory of economic development that will account for the kind of regularity of distribution described by Burns, this individual decision-making may perhaps be abstracted from—for this does not pose the social problem—and perhaps it may be assumed that the results of millions of individuals making rational choices are essentially the same as though the individual movements were chance events. The social problem is posed not by the necessity of an individual making a choice under a given system of constraints but rather by the necessity of a society making a choice among alternative possible systems of constraints. To evaluate a system of constraints which is subject to change and improvement through legislation is to compare the working properties of this system with the working properties of alternative systems. These are population characteristics that may possibly be described in terms of limiting forms of distributions such as are suggested by Burns' arrangements of business cycle data. The analytical problem is that of determining the working properties of a model 'experiment' which has been made to satisfy the conditions laid down in a system of constraints. This is a problem of analysing a time-dependent stochastic process.[2] Presumably, legislative policy changes are designed to alter the conditions of the process so as to affect the limiting forms of the various distributions.

THE TESTIMONY OF THE PRESENT CHAIRMAN BEFORE CONGRESSIONAL HEARINGS ON THE PROBLEM OF INSTABILITY

A theory of economic change and growth in this sense has yet to be developed, however, and the scientific contribution of Burns lies in his discovery of highly suggestive arrangements of data. But in his extensive empirical work, he has

1. I have briefly discussed this idea from this point of view in 'A Description of Certain Spatial Aspects of an Economic System', *Economic Development and Cultural Change*, Vol. III, No. 2, January 1955, pp. 185-95.
2. Cf., e.g., William Feller, *An Introduction to Probability Theory and Its Applications*. Ch. 17, 'The Simplest Time-dependent Stochastic Processes'. John Wiley & Sons, New York, 1950.

reached what I would think is the deepest understanding, among the economists of this country, of business cycle phenomena. His testimony at the recent Congressional Hearings thus merits special mention in this review.

The testimony of Mr. Burns was diametrically opposed to that presented by his predecessor in office, Mr. Keyserling. He was asked the same questions as were put to the others who were quoted above. For example, Representative Mills asked him the question which elicited such a confident answer from Mr. Keyserling and which Senator Douglas thought to be such a good question:

Representative Mills: What rates of national economic growth should government economic policy attempt to facilitate?

Mr. Burns: That is a question to which neither I nor, if I may be so bold as to say, any other person can give a responsible quantitative answer.

I am inclined to think that we ought not to be satisfied with any rate of growth that we attain. We ought to try to better it. But I would hesitate about expressing that thought in a numerical phrase.[1]

Senator O'Mahoney asked a series of questions which undoubtedly would have led Mr. Keyserling or Mr. Reuther, or any of the many critics of the report, to make definite statements regarding the 'needed levels of production, employment, and income' and the 'required program of Government expenditures' for the coming months. But the questions led Mr. Burns only to a characterization of the prevalent use of the Keynesian terminology as question-begging exercises in arithmetic:

Senator O'Mahoney: Then you would agree that if the military budget were severely cut there would have to be substituted for it substantial expenditures of a civilian sort, of a public works nature or something in the normal category of peacetime operations to maintain employment and profits on anything approximating their present levels?

Mr. Burns: Well, as you put the question, it is purely a matter of arithmetic, is it not?

Senator O'Mahoney: I think so.

Mr. Burns: That if one part of the Nation's total of expenditure, namely, that devoted to military purposes, is reduced, then if we are to maintain economic activity at an unchanged level, surely other parts of other categories of expenditures will have to show increases. If this is what you mean, of course, you are right.[2]

Mr. Burns elaborated his point of view in a written answer to a more comprehensive question asked by Representative Bolling. This statement constitutes an answer to his critics, and it would seem to be of sufficient interest and importance to be quoted in full.

Question: The Employment Act, in section 3 (a), states that the Report of the President shall set forth 'the levels of employment, production, and purchasing power obtaining in the United States and such levels needed to carry out the policy declared in section 2'. The President's Economic Report, on page 24, states: 'With economic activity continuing to expand, it is reasonable to expect that the Nation's output within the coming year will approximate the goals of 'maximum employment, production, and purchasing power' envisaged by the Employment Act'.

What are these levels or goals for 1955 in terms of employment, unemployment, production, and purchasing power?

What specific forces do you see operating in the economy that will raise levels of demand sufficient to meet the goals of the Employment Act?

Mr. Burns: Section 3 (a) of the Employment Act states that the Economic Report of the President shall set forth 'the levels of employment, production, and purchasing power obtaining in the United States and *such levels needed to carry out the policy declared in section* 2'. The Act does not clarify the italicized phrase. Its interpretation is left to the President and his Council of Economic Advisers. The phrase can be interpreted as calling

1. *Hearings*, op. cit., p. 24.
2. *Hearings*, op. cit., pp. 27-8.

for a numerical specification of economic goals, or it can be interpreted as calling for as good a specification of objectives, whether in terms of numbers or otherwise, as can be made. In the former case, one would assert that 'to carry out the policy declared in section 2' employment must be X, production must be Y, etc. In the latter case, one might answer that 'to carry out the policy declared in section 2', employment must be a little higher, or substantially higher, etc.; the drop in employment and production, if any, during the recent past, after allowing for an increment of growth, would suggest the general order of the magnitudes that are involved.

For internal purposes the Council utilizes and makes all sorts of quantitative estimates. It seems unwise, however, to publish near-term estimates that rest heavily on assumptions and conjecture, and that is bound to be the case with numerical 'goals' or 'targets'. The use of such estimates by the President in his Economic Report would not render a useful service to the nation.

The present Economic Report, like its predecessor, does not specify numerical goals for the coming year. If these had been presented, neither the economic analysis of the report, nor its recommendations of policy, would have been improved in any way. The impression might, however, have been created that economists or Government officials can reliably estimate how much our economy is able to produce under conditions of full employment, that they can reliably judge what the numerical magnitude of employment should be, and that they can reliably estimate the quantitative effects of specific public policies or programs. All this may become true in the future; it is not true today.

It is important to recognize the limitations of economic knowledge, and how difficult it is to make useful economic predictions or projections. Serious uncertainties surround even historical descriptions, such as the average rate of growth of production during the past decade or the gross national product during a particular year or quarter. Under ideal conditions of measurement, the gross national product should be the same, whether measured from the expenditure side or the income side. In current practice the two figures are sometimes very different, and it is impossible to tell which is the more accurate. According to the figures from the expenditure side, the annual rate of the gross national product decreased $14.4 billion between the second quarter of 1953 and the third quarter of 1954. If, instead, we take figures estimated from the income side, we find that the drop in the gross national product was at a rate of $7.4 billion during this period.

Economists who are familiar with statistical vagaries such as this, and who know how difficult it is to measure with tolerable accuracy even experiences of the past will hesitate to specify numerical goals for the Nation's economy over the next 6 months or year or two. They know that in setting goals some arbitrary assumptions must be used and that alternative assumptions, which often are no less reasonable than the particular ones selected, can lead to such a wide range of results that the calculated goals cannot have great value for policy decisions.

For example, if we are to specify numerically what the gross national product would be in a later period under conditions of full employment, we must rely on a great variety of assumptions. The most important of these relate, first, to the increment of the labor force, second, to the increment of productivity, using this term in the sense of a ratio of output to labor input. The basis for such assumptions is past experience, very largely. But what do statistics tell us about the increment of the labor force between, say, the final quarters of successive years? For the civilian labor force, the figures range from about 100,000 to 1.4 million between 1947 and 1954, excluding the drop between 1950 and 1951. For the total labor force, the figures range from 50,000 to 1.5 million. If we attempt to look a year ahead, which figure within the indicated range shall we use? Not being content with any of them, we might take their average, but what reasons have we for supposing that the year ahead will be an average year? This variability of economic experience is, of course, reflected also in the case of productivity increments. We might assume that the gain in productivity will be 2.5 per cent, as some historical averages suggest. But statistical estimates recently made by the staff of the Joint Committee show that in years that have immediately followed business-cycle troughs since 1911, the increment in productivity has ranged from a minus 4.4 to a plus 7.9 per cent.

The Council's appraisal of the economic outlook for 1955 is indicated in the Economic Report. After noting that the economy has recently been operating at a high level and analysing the forces now at work, the report proceeds to appraise what seem to be the likely developments. It points out that the annual rate of the gross national product increased by about $5.5 billion (6.5 according to more recent estimates) between the third and fourth quarters of 1954, and that the current recovery has some momentum. It describes the economic forces now in motion and concludes: (a) That they hold out the promise that we shall achieve a high and satisfactory level of employment and production within the current year, and (b) that if this expectation is not fulfilled the Government must be ready to revise its policies so as to help to bring this result about as promptly as feasible. This is a reasonably clear indication of how the economic situation is judged. It admittedly leaves room for discussion concerning the interpretation of some of the phrases used, but this difficulty could not be overcome by specifying numerical targets.

In handling problems of economic policy, nothing is more important than full recognition of the limitations of economic forecasting, and therefore of the need, first, for flexible policies, second, of being in a position of preparedness to meet various economic contingencies. These are the matters that the Council has repeatedly stressed. And let it be said here that, although 4 per cent of the labor force is nowadays widely regarded as an approximate measure of the average amount of frictional and seasonal unemployment, the Council has not favored this or any other rigid figure to serve as a trigger to governmental action or as a measure of good performance. When the President's Economic Report of January 1954 was presented, the latest figure of unemployment then available stood at 3 per cent. Yet that report counseled the Congress that it was essential 'to avoid the adverse consequences that existing uncertainties might generate', that 'it makes a vital difference whether an unemployment rate of 3 per cent is reached by rising up to that figure or declining to it', and that 'prudence as well as zeal for economic improvement require that public policy contribute both to the immediate strength of the economy and to its long-term growth'.[1]

In the latter part of the above statement, Mr. Burns expresses his opposition to any rule of action which would rigidly require the Federal Administration to keep unemployment below some stated figure. In his written answers to questions asked by Representative Patman, he expressed a generally adverse opinion regarding the advisability at present of a legislature's attempting to set forth definite rules of action for the administrator of a nation's business cycle policy. In some respects these questions and answers are remindful of the Federal Reserve Board's Annual Report for 1923. Representative Patman asked whether the mere stabilization of a price index precluded the 'development of imbalances in the economy', and 'what thinking had been done . . . about divergent movements of prices within a stable level of average prices'; and he called attention, much as did Governor Strong in the 1920s, to the rising 'prices of industrial supplies while the prices of farm commodities have been dropping'. Mr Burns used the following expressions in his answer:

Mere stability of an average of prices . . . does not of itself give assurance that there are no serious imbalances in the economy. . . . In fact, no single indicator can be used as a test of the degree of balance or imbalance. . . . In reaching decisions concerning economic policy, consideration must be given to a large number of factors. These include the state of employment, unemployment, prices, production, sales, inventories, new orders, the rate of saving, and many others. Neither prices nor unemployment, important as they are, can be taken as the sole guide for economic policy. To confine attention to an index of prices or to the level of unemployment would impede the search for adequate measures to reduce unemployment or to prevent its increase.

This bears a resemblance to the statements of the monetary authorities of 1923. These men stated that 'no statistical mechanism alone, however carefully contrived, can furnish an adequate guide to credit administration', that 'administration is not a matter of mechanical rules, but is and must be a matter of judgment', that administrators must be cognizant of what is under way or in process in the movement of business before it is registered in any statistical mechanism that can be observed, that the good functioning of the economic system is to be observed in the 'smooth unobstructed movement of goods from the producers to their several ultimate uses'. Mr. Burns does not go so far as these administrators of 1923 in disposing of the idea of explicit rules of action for the control of administrative decisions. But he rejects each of the two rules proposed, and he neglects to discuss specifically how consideration is to be given to the large number of factors mentioned.

1. *Hearings*, op. cit., pp. 43-5.

When one says that 'judgment, and not rules, must be relied upon in determining what to do in a given situation', what meaning is supposed to be conveyed? Is it not obvious that any action which is induced by empirical observations implies some rule of inductive action? The statement could not deny that conscious action implies a rule of action. Rather, it would seem to mean simply that for the particular area of responsibility in question it is physically impossible to list the millions upon millions of possible combinations of events constituting possible 'situations'. But there is a clear implication in the context of a statement of this sort that if the list could be made there would be an appropriate action corresponding to each 'situation'.

Perhaps the analogy would be with the practice of a medical diagnostician. Judgment and intuition are exercised in reaching a final diagnosis, although the decision is induced in some way by the empirical observations made. Similarly, the administrator of a nation's economic policy is a sort of diagnostician who uses judgment and intuition in 'reaching decisions' after giving 'consideration . . . to a large number of factors'. This analogy, however, fails at a crucial point.[1] The concepts of 'healthiness' and 'disease' are well-defined in medicine in the sense that there are objective and agreed upon tests which may be applied to distinguish between the observable states of affairs to which the terms correspond. The cumulation of medical knowledge includes a cumulation of tests for the classification of different forms of disease. The objective of medical research is to assign to each 'situation' a best action or treatment—i.e. to formulate an administrative rule of inductive action. When the expert prescribes for a case, he is applying this rule to the extent that he can recognize its applicability. Judgment and intuition are exercised when the tests give ambiguous results or when agreement has not been reached upon the performances of various possible tests and treatments. But in the field of economic policy, what are supposed to be the analogues of the concepts of 'healthiness' and 'disease'? Is such a concept as 'economic balance' or 'balanced growth' or 'a production level which meets the needs of the people' the counterpart of 'healthiness', and is 'serious imbalance' the analogue of 'disease'? But these are just the concepts that are still undefined—in the sense that there are no agreed-upon objective tests which technicians may apply to distinguish between the observable states of affairs to which the terms refer. Medical research begins with the recognition of a 'natural' distinction between 'healthiness' and 'disease'. Our crucial controversies are at this very beginning. By the inherent nature of social problems there is no such 'natural' distinction between 'healthy performance' and 'pathological performance' of an economic system. These are not 'natural' states. Their distinction turns upon the outcome of a process of group discussion and choice, and in the essence of this distinction there is continual social controversy.

But certainly the quality of social discussion can be improved. If such a term as 'imbalance' is to be used, and if minds are to meet upon matters of diagnosis and prescription, we must do better toward specifying the empirical state of affairs to which such a term refers. In our field, as in the other, the cumulation of knowledge is a cumulation of tests for distinguishing different perceptual states of affairs. If it is taken for granted that there will be freedom of individual action within the constraints of a system of laws, some of these observable states of affairs are inherent in the class of system and hence are not 'pathological' under any admissible set of criteria. There has been little cumulation of knowledge here, however. Mr. Burns states that no single indicator that has been

1. Cf. F. H. Knight, 'Economic Theory and Nationalism', *Ethics of Competition* New York, Harpers, 1936, p. 284 (footnote).

proposed can be used as a 'test of imbalance', implying in his discussion that a consistent use of any one of them would involve an application of inadmissible criteria. That is, any one of the rules would fail to distinguish between performance which necessarily must be accepted as 'healthy' (given the postulates of the system) and performance which may possibly be designated as 'pathological'. I believe this point should be developed explicitly and at length. His mention of the 'many factors which must be considered' undoubtedly refers to his arrangements of data showing at once the behaviour of large numbers of indicators. In these arrangements of statistical data, there are suggestions of systematic forms and developments in time of frequency distributions, and there are further suggestions of stabilities of shapes that have persisted over periods during which great changes in technology and institutions have taken place. His descriptions call to one's mind the probability concept of statistical equilibrium. Burns uses a clinical approach in his study of the performance of an economic system. His inferences, however, imply conceptual analysis, and I believe that a development of his argument will ultimately involve a mathematical analysis of the essentially probabilistic phenomena which he has begun to describe.

[7]

THE ECONOMIC JOURNAL

DECEMBER, 1928

INCREASING RETURNS AND ECONOMIC PROGRESS [1]

My subject may appear alarmingly formidable, but I did not intend it to be so. The words economic progress, taken by themselves, would suggest the pursuit of some philosophy of history, of some way of appraising the results of past and possible future changes in forms of economic organisation and modes of economic activities. But as I have used them, joined to the other half of my title, they are meant merely to dispel apprehensions, by suggesting that I do not propose to discuss any of those alluring but highly technical questions relating to the precise way in which some sort of equilibrium of supply and demand is achieved in the market for the products of industries which can increase their output without increasing their costs proportionately, or to the possible advantages of fostering the development of such industries while putting a handicap upon industries whose output can be increased only at the expense of a more than proportionate increase of costs. I suspect, indeed, that the apparatus which economists have built up for dealing effectively with the range of questions to which I have just referred may stand in the way of a clear view of the more general or elementary aspects of the phenomena of increasing returns, such as I wish to comment upon in this paper.

Consider, for example, Alfred Marshall's fruitful distinction between the internal productive economies which a particular firm is able to secure as the growth of the market permits it to enlarge the scale of its operations and the economies external to the individual firm which show themselves only in changes of the organisation of the industry as a whole. This distinction has been useful in at least two different ways. In the first place it is, or ought to be, a safeguard against the common error of assuming that wherever increasing returns operate there is necessarily an effective tendency towards monopoly. In the second

[1] Presidential Address before Section F (Economic Science and Statistics) of the British Association for the Advancement of Science, Glasgow, September 10, 1928.

place it simplifies the analysis of the manner in which the prices of commodities produced under conditions of increasing returns are determined. A representative firm within the industry, maintaining its own identity and devoting itself to a given range of activities, is made to be the vehicle or medium through which the economies achieved by the industry as a whole are transmitted to the market and have their effect upon the price of the product.

The view of the nature of the processes of industrial progress which is implied in the distinction between internal and external economies is necessarily a partial view. Certain aspects of those processes are illuminated, while, for that very reason, certain other aspects, important in relation to other problems, are obscured. This will be clear, I think, if we observe that, although the internal economies of some firms producing, let us say, materials or appliances may figure as the external economies of other firms, not all of the economies which are properly to be called external can be accounted for by adding up the internal economies of all the separate firms. When we look at the internal economies of a particular firm we envisage a condition of comparative stability. Year after year the firm, like its competitors, is manufacturing a particular product or group of products, or is confining itself to certain definite stages in the work of forwarding the products towards their final form. Its operations change in the sense that they are progressively adapted to an increasing output, but they are kept within definitely circumscribed bounds. Out beyond, in that obscurer field from which it derives its external economies, changes of another order are occurring. New products are appearing, firms are assuming new tasks, and new industries are coming into being. In short, change in this external field is qualitative as well as quantitative. No analysis of the forces making for economic equilibrium, forces which we might say are tangential at any moment of time, will serve to illumine this field, for movements away from equilibrium, departures from previous trends, are characteristic of it. Not much is to be gained by probing into it to see how increasing returns show themselves in the costs of individual firms and in the prices at which they offer their products.

Instead, we have to go back to a simpler and more inclusive view, such as some of the older economists took when they contrasted the increasing returns which they thought were characteristic of manufacturing industry taken as a whole with the diminishing returns which they thought were dominant in agriculture because of an increasingly unfavourable proportioning of labour and land. Most of them were disappointingly vague with respect to the origins and the precise nature of the " improvements " which they counted upon to retard somewhat the operation of the tendency towards diminishing returns in agriculture and to secure a progressively more effective use of labour in manufactures. Their opinions appear to have rested partly upon an empirical generalisation. Improvements had been made, they were still being made, and it might be assumed that they would continue to be made. If they had looked back they would have seen that there were centuries during which there were few significant changes in either agricultural or industrial methods. But they were living in an age when men had turned their faces in a new direction and when economic progress was not only consciously sought but seemed in some way to grow out of the nature of things. Improvements, then, were not something to be explained. They were natural phenomena, like the precession of the equinoxes.

There were certain important exceptions, however, to this incurious attitude towards what might seem to be one of the most important of all economic problems. Senior's positive doctrine is well known, and there were others who made note of the circumstance that with the growth of population and of markets new opportunities for the division of labour appear and new advantages attach to it. In this way, and in this way only, were the generally commonplace things which they said about " improvements " related to anything which could properly be called a doctrine of increasing returns. They added nothing to Adam Smith's famous theorem that the division of labour depends upon the extent of the market. That theorem, I have always thought, is one of the most illuminating and fruitful generalisations which can be found anywhere in the whole literature of economics. In fact, as I am bound to confess, I am taking it as the text of this paper, in much the way that some minor composer borrows a theme from one of the masters and adds certain developments or variations of his own. To-day, of course, we mean by the division of labour something much broader in scope than that splitting up of occupations and development of specialised crafts which Adam Smith mostly had in mind. No one, so far as I know, has tried to enumerate all of the different aspects of the division of labour, and I do not propose to undertake that task. I shall deal with two related aspects only: the growth of indirect or roundabout methods of production and the division of labour among industries.

It is generally agreed that Adam Smith, when he suggested that the division of labour leads to inventions because workmen engaged in specialised routine operations come to see better ways of accomplishing the same results, missed the main point. The important thing, of course, is that with the division of labour a group of complex processes is transformed into a succession of simpler processes, some of which, at least, lend themselves to the use of machinery. In the use of machinery and the adoption of indirect processes there is a further division of labour, the economies of which are again limited by the extent of the market. It would be wasteful to make a hammer to drive a single nail; it would be better to use whatever awkward implement lies conveniently at hand. It would be wasteful to furnish a factory with an elaborate equipment of specially constructed jigs, gauges, lathes, drills, presses and conveyors to build a hundred automobiles; it would be better to rely mostly upon tools and machines of standard types, so as to make a relatively larger use of directly-applied and a relatively smaller use of indirectly-applied labour. Mr. Ford's methods would be absurdly uneconomical if his output were very small, and would be unprofitable even if his output were what many other manufacturers of automobiles would call large.

Then, of course, there are economies of what might be called a secondary order. How far it pays to go in equipping factories with special appliances for making hammers or for constructing specialised machinery for use in making different parts of automobiles depends again upon how many nails are to be driven and how many automobiles can be sold. In some instances, I suppose, these secondary economies, though real, have only a secondary importance. The derived demands for many types of specialised production appliances are inelastic over a fairly large range. If the benefits and the costs of using such appliances are spread over a relatively large volume of final products, their technical effectiveness is a larger factor in determining whether it is profitable to use them than any difference which producing them on a large or a small scale would commonly make in their costs. In other instances the demand for productive appliances is more elastic, and beyond a certain level of costs demand may fail completely. In such circumstances secondary economies may become highly important.

Doubtless, much of what I have said has been familiar and even elementary. I shall venture, nevertheless, to put further stress upon two points, which may be among those which have a familiar ring, but which appear sometimes to be in danger of being forgotten. (Otherwise, economists of standing could not have suggested that increasing returns may be altogether illusory, or have maintained that where they are present they must lead to monopoly.) The first point is that the principal economies which manifest themselves in increasing returns are the economies of capitalistic or roundabout methods of production. These economies, again, are largely identical with the economies of the division of labour in its most important modern forms. In fact, these economies lie under our eyes, but we may miss them if we try to make of *large-scale* production (in the sense of production by large firms or large industries), as contrasted with *large* production, any more than an incident in the general process by which increasing returns are secured and if accordingly we look too much at the individual firm or even, as I shall suggest presently, at the individual industry.

The second point is that the economies of roundabout methods, even more than the economies of other forms of the division of labour, depend upon the extent of the market—and that, of course, is why we discuss them under the head of increasing returns. It would hardly be necessary to stress this point, if it were not that the economies of large-scale operations and of "mass-production" are often referred to as though they could be had for the taking, by means of a "rational" reorganisation of industry. Now I grant that at any given time routine and inertia play a very large part in the organisation and conduct of industrial operations. Real leadership is no more common in industrial than in other pursuits. New catch-words or slogans like mass-production and rationalisation may operate as stimuli; they may rouse men from routine and lead them to scrutinise again the organisation and processes of industry and to try to discover particular ways in which they can be bettered. For example, no one can doubt that there are genuine economies to be achieved in the way of "simplification and standardisation," or that the securing of these economies requires that certain deeply rooted competitive wastes be extirpated. This last requires a definite concerted effort—precisely the kind of thing which ordinary competitive motives are often powerless to effect, but which might come more easily as the response to the dissemination of a new idea.

There is a danger, however, that we shall expect too much from these "rational" industrial reforms. Pressed beyond a certain point they become the reverse of rational. I have naturally been interested in British opinions respecting the reasons for the relatively high productivity (per labourer or per hour of labour) of representative American industries. The error of those who suggest that the explanation is to be found in the relatively high wages which prevail in America is not that they confuse cause and effect, but that they hold that what are really only two aspects of a single situation are, the one cause, and the other effect. Those who hold that American industry is managed better, that its leaders study its problems more intelligently and plan more courageously and more wisely can cite no facts in support of their opinion save the differences in the results achieved. Allowing for the circumstance that British industry, as a whole, has proved to be rather badly adjusted to the new post-war economic situation, I know of no facts which prove or even indicate that British industry, seen against the background of its own problems and its own possibilities, is less efficiently organised or less ably directed than American industry or the industry of any other country.

Sometimes the fact that the average American labourer works with the help of a larger supply of power-driven labour-saving machinery than the labourer of other countries is cited as evidence of the superior intelligence of the average American employer. But this will not do, for, as every economist knows, the greater the degree in which labour is productive or scarce—the words have the same meaning—the greater is the relative economy of using it in such indirect or roundabout ways as are technically advantageous, even though such procedure calls for larger advances of capital than simpler methods do.

It is encouraging to find that a fairly large number of commentators upon the volume of the American industrial product and the scale of American industrial organisation have come to surmise that the extent of the American domestic market, unimpeded by tariff barriers, may have something to do with the matter. This opinion seems even to be forced upon thoughtful observers by the general character of the facts, whether or no the observers think in terms of the economists' conception of increasing returns. In certain industries, although by no means in all, productive methods are economical and profitable in America which would not be profitable elsewhere. The importance of coal and iron and other natural resources needs no comment. Taking a country's economic endowment as given, however, the most important single factor in determining the effectiveness of its industry appears to be the size of the market. But just what constitutes a large market? Not area or population alone, but buying power, the capacity to absorb a large annual output of goods. This trite observation, however, at once suggests another equally trite, namely, that capacity to buy depends upon capacity to produce. In an inclusive view, considering the market not as an outlet for the products of a particular industry, and therefore external to that industry, but as the outlet for goods in general, the size of the market is determined and defined by the volume of production. If this statement needs any qualification, it is that the conception of a market in this inclusive sense—an aggregate of productive activities, tied together by trade—carries with it the notion that there must be some sort of balance, that different productive activities must be proportioned one to another.

Modified, then, in the light of this broader conception of the market, Adam Smith's dictum amounts to the theorem that the division of labour depends in large part upon the division of labour. This is more than mere tautology. It means, if I read its significance rightly, that the counter forces which are continually defeating the forces which make for economic equilibrium are more pervasive and more deeply rooted in the constitution of the modern economic system than we commonly realise. Not only new or adventitious elements, coming in from the outside, but elements which are permanent characteristics of the ways in which goods are produced make continuously for change. Every important advance in the organisation of production, regardless of whether it is based upon anything which, in a narrow or technical sense, would be called a new "invention," or involves a fresh application of the fruits of scientific progress to industry, alters the conditions of industrial activity and initiates responses elsewhere in the industrial structure which in turn have a further unsettling effect. Thus change becomes progressive and propagates itself in a cumulative way.

The apparatus which economists have built up for the analysis of supply and demand in their relations to prices does not seem to be particularly helpful for the purposes of an inquiry into these broader aspects of increasing returns. In fact, as I have already suggested, reliance upon it may divert attention to incidental or partial aspects of a process which ought to be seen as a whole. If, nevertheless, one insists upon seeing just how far one can get into the problem by using the formulas of supply and demand, the simplest way, I suppose, is to begin by inquiring into the operations of reciprocal demand when the commodities exchanged are produced competitively under conditions of increasing returns and when the demand for each commodity is elastic, in the special sense that a small increase in its supply will be attended by an increase in the amounts of other commodities which can be had in exchange for it.[1] Under such conditions an increase in the supply of one commodity *is* an increase in the demand for other commodities, and it must be supposed that every increase in demand will evoke an increase in supply. The rate at which any one industry grows is conditioned by the rate at which other industries grow, but since the elasticities of demand and of supply will differ for different products, some industries will grow faster than others. Even with a stationary population and in the absence of new discoveries[2] in pure or applied science there are no limits to the process of expansion except the limits beyond which demand is not elastic and returns do not increase.

If, under these hypothetical conditions, progress were unimpeded and frictionless, if it were not dependent in part upon a process of trial and error, if the organisation of industry were always such as, in relation to the immediate situation, is most economical, the realising of increasing returns might be progressive and continuous, although, for technical reasons, it could not always proceed at an even rate. But it would remain a process requiring time. An industrial dictator, with foresight and knowledge, could hasten the pace somewhat, but he could not achieve an Aladdin-like transformation of a country's industry, so as to reap the fruits of a half-century's ordinary progress in a few years. The obstacles are of two sorts. First, the human material which has to be used is resistant to change. New trades have to be learnt and new habits have to be acquired. There has to be a new geographical distribution of the population and established communal groups have to be broken up. Second, the accumulation of the necessary capital takes time, even though the process of accumulation is largely one of turning part of an increasing product into forms which will serve in securing a further increase of product. An acceleration of the rate of accumulation encounters increasing costs, into which both technical and psychological elements enter. One who likes

[1] If the circumstance that commodity *a* is produced under conditions of increasing returns is taken into account as a factor in the elasticity of demand for *b* in terms of *a*, elasticity of demand and elasticity of supply may be looked upon as different ways of expressing a single functional relation.

[2] As contrasted with such new ways of organising production and such new "inventions" as are merely adaptations of known ways of doing things, made practicable and economical by an enlarged scale of production.

to conceive of all economic processes in terms of tendencies towards an equilibrium might even maintain that increasing returns, so far as they depend upon the economies of indirect methods of production and the size of the market, are offset and negated by their costs, and that under such simplified conditions as I have dealt with the realising of increasing returns would be spread through time in such a way as to secure an equilibrium of costs and advantages. This would amount to saying that no real economic progress could come through the operation of forces engendered *within* the economic system—a conclusion repugnant to common sense. To deal with this point thoroughly would take us too far afield. I shall merely observe, first, that the appropriate conception is that of a *moving* equilibrium, and second, that the costs which (under increasing returns) grow less rapidly than the product are not the "costs" which figure in an "equilibrium of costs and advantages."

Moving away from these abstract considerations, so as to get closer to the complications of the real situation, account has to be taken, first, of various kinds of obstacles. The demand for some products is inelastic, or, with an increasing supply, soon becomes so. The producers of such commodities, however, often share in the advantages of the increase of the general scale of production in related industries, and so far as they do productive resources are released for other uses. Then there are natural scarcities, limitations or inelasticities of supply, such as effectively block the way to the securing of any important economies in the production of some commodities and which impair the effectiveness of the economies secured in the production of other commodities. In most fields, moreover, progress is not and cannot be continuous. The next important step forward is often initially costly, and cannot be taken until a certain quantum of prospective advantages has accumulated.

On the other side of the account are various factors which reinforce the influences which make for increasing returns. The discovery of new natural resources and of new uses for them and the growth of scientific knowledge are probably the most potent of such factors. The causal connections between the growth of industry and the progress of science run in both directions, but on which side the preponderant influence lies no one can say. At any rate, out of better knowledge of the materials and forces upon which men can lay their hands there come both new ways of producing familiar commodities and new products, and these last have a presumptive claim to be regarded as embodying more economical uses of productive resources than the uses which they displace. Some weight has to be given also to the way in which, with the advance of the scientific spirit, a new kind of interest—which might be described as a scientific interest conditioned by an economic interest—is beginning to infiltrate into industry. It is a point of controversy, but I venture to maintain that under most circumstances, though not in all, the growth of population still has to be counted a factor making for a larger *per capita* product—although even that cautious statement needs to be interpreted and qualified. But just as there may be population growth with no increase of the average *per capita* product, so also, as I have tried to suggest, markets may grow and increasing returns may be secured while the population remains stationary.

It is dangerous to assign to any single factor the leading rôle in that continuing economic revolution which has taken the modern world so far away from the world of a few hundred years ago. But is there any other factor which has a better claim to that rôle than the persisting search for markets? No other hypothesis so well unites economic history and economic theory. The Industrial Revolution of the eighteenth century has come to be generally regarded, not as a cataclysm brought about by certain inspired improvements in industrial technique, but as a series of changes related in an orderly way to prior changes in industrial organisation and to the enlargement of markets. It is sometimes said, however, that while in the Middle Ages and in the early modern period industry was the servant of commerce, since the rise of "industrial capitalism" the relation has been reversed, commerce being now merely an agent of industry. If this means that the finding of markets is one of the tasks of modern industry it is true. If it means that industry imposes its will upon the market, that whereas formerly the things which were produced were the things which could be sold, now the things which have to be sold are the things that are produced, it is not true.

The great change, I imagine, is in the new importance which the *potential market* has in the planning and management of large industries. The difference between the cost per unit of output in an industry or in an individual plant properly adapted to a given volume of output and in an industry or plant equally well adapted to an output five times as large is often much greater than one would infer from looking merely at the economies which may accrue as an existing establishment gradually extends the scale of its operations. Potential demand, then, in the planning of industrial undertakings, has to be balanced against potential economies, elasticity of demand against decreasing costs. The search for markets is not a matter of disposing of a "surplus product," in the Marxian sense, but of finding an outlet for a potential product. Nor is it wholly a matter of multiplying profits by multiplying sales; it is partly a matter of augmenting profits by reducing costs.

Although the initial displacement may be considerable and the repercussions upon particular industries unfavourable, the enlarging of the market for any one commodity, produced under conditions of increasing returns, generally has the net effect, as I have tried to show, of enlarging the market for other commodities. The business man's mercantilistic emphasis upon markets may have a sounder basis than the economist who thinks mostly in terms of economic statics is prone to admit. How far "selling expenses," for example, are to be counted sheer economic waste depends upon their effects upon the aggregate product of industry, as distinguished from their effects upon the fortunes of particular undertakings.

Increasing returns are often spoken of as though they were attached always to the growth of "industries," and I have not tried to avoid that way of speaking of them, although I think that it may be a misleading way. The point which I have in mind is something more than a quibble about the proper definition of an industry, for it involves a particular thesis with respect to the way in which increasing returns are reflected in changes in the organisation of industrial activities. Much has been said about industrial integration as a concomitant or a natural result of an increasing industrial output. It obviously is, under particular conditions, though I know of no satisfactory statement of just what those particular conditions are. But the opposed process, industrial differentiation, has been and remains the type of change characteristically associated with the growth of production. Notable as has been the increase in the complexity of the apparatus of living, as shown by the increase in the variety of goods offered in consumers' markets, the increase in the diversification of intermediate products and of industries manufacturing special products or groups of products has gone even further.

The successors of the early printers, it has often been observed, are not only the printers of to-day, with their own specialised establishments, but also the producers of wood pulp, of various kinds of paper, of inks and their different ingredients, of type-metal and of type, the group of industries concerned with the technical parts of the producing of illustrations, and the manufacturers of specialised tools and machines for use in printing and in these various auxiliary industries. The list could be extended, both by enumerating other industries which are directly ancillary to the present printing trades and by going back to industries which, while supplying the industries which supply the printing trades, also supply other industries, concerned with preliminary stages in the making of final products other than printed books and newspapers. I do not think that the printing trades are an exceptional instance, but I shall not give other examples, for I do not want this paper to be too much like a primer of descriptive economics or an index to the reports of a census of production. It is sufficiently obvious, anyhow, that over a large part of the field of industry an increasingly intricate nexus of specialised undertakings has inserted itself between the producer of raw materials and the consumer of the final product.

With the extension of the division of labour among industries the representative firm, like the industry of which it is a part, loses its identity. Its internal economies dissolve into the internal and external economies of the more highly specialised undertakings which are its successors, and are supplemented by new economies. In so far as it is an adjustment to a new situation created by the growth of the market for the final products of industry the division of labour among industries is a vehicle of increasing returns. It is more than a change of form incidental to the full securing of the advantages of capitalistic methods of production—although it is largely that—for it has some advantages of its own which are independent of changes in productive technique. For example, it permits of a higher degree of specialisation in management, and the advantages of such specialisation are doubtless often real, though they may easily be given too much weight. Again, it lends itselt to a better geographical distribution of industrial operations, and this advantage is unquestionably both real and important. Nearness to the source of supply of a particular raw material or to cheap power counts for most in one part of a series of industrial processes, nearness to other industries or to cheap transport in another part, and nearness to a larger centre of population in yet another. A better *combination* of advantages of location, with a smaller element of compromise, can be had by the more specialised industries. But the largest advantage secured by the division of labour among industries is the fuller realising of the economies of capitalistic or roundabout methods of production. This should be sufficiently obvious if we assume, as we must, that in most industries there are effective, though elastic, limits to the economical size of the individual firm. The output of the individual firm is generally a relatively small proportion of the aggregate output of an industry. The degree in which it can secure economies by making its own operations more roundabout is limited. But certain roundabout methods are fairly sure to become feasible and economical when their advantages can be spread over the output of the whole industry. These potential economies, then, are segregated and achieved by the operations of specialised undertakings which, taken together, constitute a new industry. It might conceivably be maintained that the *scale* upon which the firms in the new industry are able to operate is the secret of their ability to realise economies for industry as a whole, while presumably making profits for themselves. This is true in a way, but misleading. The scale of their operations (which is only incidentally or under special conditions a matter of the size of the individual firm) merely reflects the size of the market for the final products of the industry or industries to whose operations their own are ancillary. And the principal advantage of large-scale operation at this stage is that it again makes methods economical which would be uneconomical if their benefits could not be diffused over a large final product.

In recapitulation of these variations on a theme from Adam Smith there are three points to be stressed. First, the mechanism of increasing returns is not to be discerned adequately by observing the effects of variations in the size of an individual firm or of a particular industry, for the progressive division and specialisation of industries is an essential part of the process by which increasing returns are realised. What is required is that industrial operations be seen as an interrelated whole. Second, the securing of increasing returns depends upon the progressive division of labour, and the principal economies of the division of labour, in its modern forms, are the economies which are to be had by using labour in roundabout or indirect ways. Third, the division of labour depends upon the extent of the market, but the extent of the market also depends upon the division of labour. In this circumstance lies the possibility of economic progress, apart from the progress which comes as a result of the new knowledge which men are able to gain, whether in the pursuit of their economic or of their non-economic interests.

ALLYN A. YOUNG

NOTE

IN the accompanying construction (which owes much to Pareto), a collective indifference curve, I, is defined by the condition that, at equal cost, there would be no sufficient inducement for the community to alter an annual production of x units of one commodity and y units of another in order to secure the alternative combination of the two commodities indicated by any other point on the curve.[1] Each commodity might be taken as representative of a special class of commodities,

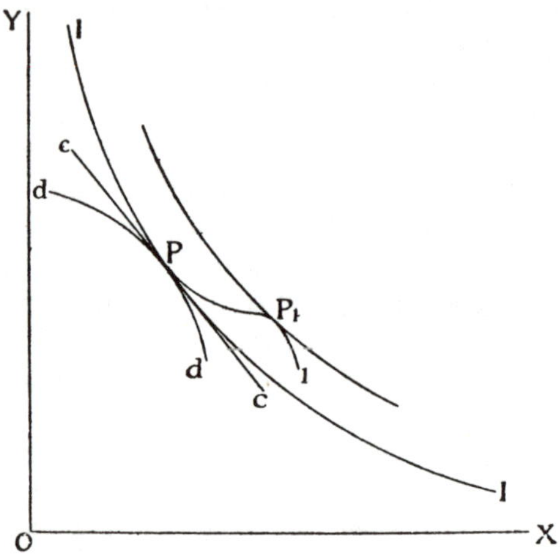

produced under generally similar conditions. Or one commodity might be made to represent "other goods in general," the annual outlay of productive exertions being regarded as constant. Alternatively, one commodity might represent "leisure" (as a collective name for all non-productive uses of time). The other would then represent the aggregate economic product.

There will be equilibrium (subject to instability of a kind which will be described presently) at a point P, if at that point a curve of equal costs, such as d, is tangent to the indifference curve. The curve of equal costs defines the terms upon which the community can exchange one commodity for the other by merely producing less of the one and more of the other (abstraction being made of any incidental costs of

[1] The collective indifference is to be taken as an expository device, not as a rigorous conception. The relative weights to be assigned to the individual indifference curves of which it is compounded will depend upon how the aggregate product is distributed, and this will not be the same for all positions of P.

change). Negative curvature, as in *d*, reflects a condition of decreasing returns, in the sense that more of either commodity can be had only by sacrificing progressively larger amounts of the other. Although a sufficient condition, the presence of decreasing returns is not a necessary condition of equilibrium. There would be a loss in moving away from P if equal costs were defined by the straight line *c*, which represents constant returns. Increasing returns, even, are consistent with equilibrium, provided that the degree of curvature of their graph is less than that of the indifference curve. It might happen, of course, that returns would decrease in one direction and increase in the other. Curve *d*, for example, might have a point of inflexion at or near P.

Consider now the conditions of departure from equilibrium. The curve *i* is drawn so as to represent *potential* increasing returns between P and P_1, which lies on a preferred indifference curve. If these increasing returns were to be had merely for the taking, if *i* were, for example, merely a continuation of the upper segment of *d* or *c*, P would not be a point even of unstable equilibrium. The advance from P to P_1 would be made by merely altering the proportions of the two commodities produced annually. To isolate the *problem* of increasing returns it is necessary to assume that P is a true point of equilibrium in the sense that it is determined by a curve of equal costs, such as *d* or *c*. The problem, then, has to do with the way in which the lower segment of *d* or *c* can be transformed into or replaced by such a curve as *i*. This requires, of course, that *additional* costs be incurred, of a kind which have not yet been taken into account. To diminish the amount of the one commodity which must be sacrificed for a given increment of the other, some of the labour hitherto devoted to its production must be used indirectly, so that the increase of the annual output of the one lags behind the curtailing of the output of the other.

This new element of cost might be taken into account by utilising a third dimension, but it is simpler to regard it as operating upon Δx, the increment in x accompanying the movement from P to P_1, so as to move the indifference curve upon which P_1 lies towards the left. It would be an error, however, to think that the combinations of x with y and $x +$ (Δx) with $y - \Delta y$ (where (Δx) is the contracted form of Δx) are themselves indifferent, so that P_1 is, in effect, brought over on to the original indifference curve, I, and no advantage is reaped. The path from P to P_1 is a *preferred* route, not merely a segment of an indifference curve. The cost of moving along that route is a function of the *rate* (in time) of the movement. An equilibrium rate (which need not be constant), such as would keep the movement from P to P_1 continuous and undeviating, would be determined by the condition, not that (Δx) and $- \Delta y$ should negate one another, but that either an acceleration or a retarding of the rate would be costly or disadvantageous. Because a mountain climber adjusts his pace to his physical powers and to the conditions of the ascent, it does not follow that he might as well have stayed at the foot. Or, alternatively but not inconsistently, the movement from P to P_1 may be conceived as made up of a series of small steps, each apparently yielding no more than a barely perceptible advantage, but only because the scale of reference for both costs and advantages depends at each step upon the position which has then been reached.

Several sets of circumstances will affect the amount and direction of the movement. (1) Even if i has no point of inflexion, such as has been indicated at P_1 (merely to simplify the first stages of this analysis), it will sooner or later (taking into account the " contraction " of Δx) become tangent to an indifference curve. In the absence of any other factor making for change, progress would then come to an end. (2) There may be another possible alternative path of increasing returns extending upwards from P and curving away from I. The most advantageous route will then be a compromise between (or a resultant of) the two limiting alternatives. In such circumstances the only effective limitation imposed upon the extent of the movement may come from the failure of elasticity of demand on one side or the other. (3) Successive indifference curves cannot be supposed to be symmetrical, in the sense that dy/dx remains the same function of y/x. If, for example, the slope of successive indifference curves at points corresponding to given values of y/x decreases (indicating that the demand for the commodity measured in units of y is relatively inelastic), freedom of movement in the direction of P_1 is reduced, while it becomes advantageous to move a little way in the opposite direction along even such a path as c or d. Under inverse conditions (with $-dy/dx$ increasing relatively to y/x for successive indifference curves) the extent of the possible movement in the direction of P_1 is increased. This conclusion amounts to no more than the obvious theorem that the degree in which the decreasing returns encountered in certain fields of economic activity operate as a drag upon the securing of increasing returns in other fields depends upon the relative elasticities of demand for the two types of products. But this consideration, like the others of which note has been made, serves to make clear the general nature of the reciprocal relation between increasing returns and the " extent of the market." (4) Discoveries of new supplies of natural resources or of *new* productive methods may have either or both of two kinds of effects. They may tilt the curves of equal cost and they may modify their curvature favourably. In either event a point such as P is moved to a higher indifference curve, and the paths along which further progress can be made are altered advantageously.

[8]

A POSITIVE PROGRAM FOR LAISSEZ FAIRE

SOME PROPOSALS FOR A LIBERAL ECONOMIC POLICY

This is frankly a propagandist tract—a defense of the thesis that traditional liberalism offers, at once, the best escape from the moral confusion of current political and economic thought, and the best basis or rationale for a program of economic reconstruction. This view has been widely ridiculed of late, by communists and fascists, by most of our "liberal" reformers and politically ambitious intellectuals. Old-fashioned liberals, and the more orthodox economists especially, have responded meagerly to the attack; only their position is inadequately represented in the welter of current controversy. Consequently, one is impelled to try, humbly but uncompromisingly, to state that position, and to indicate specifically how economic reconstruction might be achieved along lines dictated by a faith in liberty.

There is in America no important disagreement as to the proper objectives of economic policy—larger real income, greater regularity of production and employment, reduction of inequality, preservation of democratic institutions. The real issues have to do merely with means, not with ends (or intentions); but the future of our civilization hangs in balance as these issues are decided; and those whom the recent crisis has brought to positions of political and intellectual leadership seem to lack insight as to the nature of our economic ills or the effects of their own prescriptions.

We have witnessed abroad the culmination of movements from constitutional government to dictatorships, from freedom back to authority. This spectacle, for most of us, is revolting; and the experience, something to be avoided at all costs. Yet, faced with the same problems, we adopt measures and accept political slogans which call explicitly for an "American compromise," that is to say, for more authority and less freedom here and now. Thus do we justify and rationalize a policy of accelerating movement in a direction which we overwhelmingly disapprove.

The real enemies of liberty in this country are the naïve advocates of managed economy or national planning; but with them we must agree on one vital point, namely, that there is now imperative need for a sound, positive program of economic legislation. Our economic organization is perilously near to disintegration and collapse. In earlier periods, it could be expected to become increasingly strong if only protected from undue political interference. Now, however, it has reached a condition where it can be saved only through adoption of the wisest measures by the state. Modern democracy arose under conditions which made only negligible demands for intelligence in economic legislation; it remains soon to be seen whether democracy can survive when those demands are very great.

It is the main purpose of this tract to criticize current policies, simply by defining the main elements of a vitally different program. Part I undertakes to present the minimum of general analysis or diagnosis which seems essential for exposition of the program and specific proposals presented in Part II.

PART I

Much significance has been, and should be, attached to the simultaneous development of capitalism and democracy. Indeed, it seems clear that *none of the precious "freedoms" which our generation has inherited can be extended, or even maintained, apart from an essential freedom of enterprise—apart from a genuine "division of labor" between competitive and political controls.* The existence (and preservation) of a competitive situation in private industry makes possible a minimizing of the responsibilities of the sovereign state. It frees the state from the obligation of adjudicating endless, bitter disputes among persons as participants in different industries, and among owners of different kinds of productive services. In a word, it makes possible a political policy of laissez faire.

This policy and the correlative political philosophy, nineteenth-century liberalism, have been subjected latterly to gross misrepresentation and to shallow satirical jibes in the "new economics." The representation of laissez faire as a merely do-nothing policy is unfortunate and misleading. It is an obvious responsibility of the state under this policy to maintain the kind of legal and institutional framework within which competition can function effectively as an agency of control. The policy, therefore, should be defined positively, as one under which the state seeks to establish and maintain such conditions that it may avoid the necessity of regulating "the heart of the contract"—that is to say, the necessity of regulating relative prices. Thus, the state is charged, under this "division of labor," with heavy responsibilities and large "control" functions: the maintenance of competitive conditions in industry; the control of the currency (of the quantity and value of the effective money); the definition of the institution of property (especially with reference to fiscal practices)—not to mention the many social-welfare activities.

The great errors of economic policy in the past century may be defined—and many of our present difficulties explained—in terms of excessive political interference with relative prices, and in terms of disastrous neglect of the positive responsibilities of government under a free-enterprise system. Our governments have tinkered interminably with relative prices (witness the tariff). On the other hand, they have never really tried to maintain effectively competitive conditions in industry (witness the "rule of reason" and the absurd grants of powers to corporations). They have evaded—when they have not abused—their responsibility of controling the currency (witness the growth of private banks which provide, and potentially can destroy, all but a small percentage of our total effective circulating media). Moreover, they have scarcely recognized the obligation, or the opportunities, of mitigating inequality through appropriate fiscal practices—that is to say, through appropriate definition of the institution of property. Consequently, the so-called failure of capitalism (of the free-enterprise system, of competition) may reasonably be interpreted as primarily a failure of the political state in the discharge of its minimum responsibilities under capitalism. This view may suggest reasons for skepticism with reference to currently popular schemes for curing our ills.

It seems clear, at all events, that there is an intimate connection between freedom of enterprise and freedom of discussion, and that political liberty can survive only within an effectively competitive economic system. Thus, *the great enemy of democracy is monopoly, in all its forms:* gigantic corporations, trade associations and other agencies for price control, trade unions—or, in general, organization and concentration of power within functional classes. Effectively organized functional groups possess tremendous power for exploiting the community at large and even for sabotaging the system. The existence of competition within such groups, on the other hand, serves to protect the community as a whole and to give an essential flexibility to the economy. The disappearance of competition would almost assure the wrecking of the system in the economic struggle of organized minorities; on the political side, it would present a hopeless dilemma. If the organized economic groups were left to exercise their monopoly powers without political restraint, the result would be a usurpation of sovereignty by these groups—and, perhaps, a domination of the state by them. On the other hand, if the state undertakes to tolerate (instead of destroying) such organizations and to regulate their regulations, it will have assumed tasks and responsibilities incompatible with its enduring in a democratic form.

Thus, for one who prizes political liberty, there can be no sanguine view as to where the proliferation of organization leads. If the state undertakes, under popular government (or perhaps under any other form), to substitute its control for competition in the determination of relative prices and relative wages, the situation must soon become chaotic. Congressional meddling with relative prices through tariff legislation has never hurt us severely, for we have had within our tariff walls an enormous free-trade area. The legislative history of the American tariff, however, does suggest most clearly the probable outcome of an experiment in the political manipulation of the whole structure of internal prices. That our political system could endure either the economic effects of such control, or its consequences for political morality, is at least highly improbable.

If popular government did for a time achieve that infinitely wise and effective control which would be necessary merely to prevent economic collapse, the system could not survive. Political determination of relative prices, of relative returns from investment in different industries, and of relative wages in different occupations, implies settlement by peaceful negotiation of conflicts too bitter and too irreconcilable for deliberate adjudication and compromise. The petty warfare of competition within groups can be kept on such a level that it protects and actually promotes the general welfare. The warfare among organized economic groups, on the other hand, is unlikely to be more controllable or less destructive than warfare among nations. Indeed, democratic governments would have hardly so good a chance of arbitrating these conflicts tolerably as have the League of Nations and the World Court in their field.

Suppression of the competitive struggle within economic groups, and their organization into collective fighting units, will create conditions such that only ruthless dictatorship can maintain the degree of order necessary to survival of the population in an economy of intricate division of labor. Under these circumstances, the distribution of power among nations is likely, by the way, to be altered drastically in favor of those people best disciplined to submission and least contaminated with dangerous notions about the rights of man. In the Western world, the price of short-run security under such political arrangements is likely to be greater insecurity in the long run; for Western peoples will probably insist on changing dictators occasionally, even at the expense of catastrophic upheavals, disintegration of national units, and progressive political and economic separatism.

It seems nowise fantastic, indeed, to suggest that present developments point toward a historic era which will bear close resemblance at many points to the early Middle Ages. With the disappearance of the vestiges of free trade among nations will come intensification of imperialism and increasingly bitter and irreconcilable conflicts of interest internationally. With the disappearance of free trade within national areas will come endless, destructive conflict among organized economic groups—which should suffice, without assistance from international wars, for the destruction of Western civilization and its institutional heritage.

Thus, the increasing organization of interest groups (monopoly) and the resurgence of mercantilism ("planning")[1] promise an end of elaborate economic organization (of extensive division of labor, nationally and internationally), and an end of political freedom as well. If the situation is not yet hopeless because of the technical difficulties of turning back (and I refuse to believe it is), one finds abundant reason for despair in the fact that our sophisticated generation seems simply not to care. It has become unfashionable to reveal affection for democracy; and the meager curiosity about the future of our institutions leads only to the publication of our cheapest romantic literature in the guise of economics.

Competition and laissez faire have not brought us to heaven. The severe depression, regarded as resulting from competition *instead of from the lack of it*, naturally produces an impairment of our affection for the system. But the widespread disposition to deprecate our institutional heritage seems explicable only in terms of general unwillingness and inability to consider seriously what the actual alternatives are—where new roads lead—or, whatever their destination, how much human suffering must be endured on the way. Few people are now interested in assessing the opportunities for remodelling the old system without destroying its foundations. Worst of all, perhaps, is the popular disposition to accept from zealous "uplifters" devices for salvaging our institutions which are, in fact, the most effective means for undermining them irreparably.

Let us consider now what circumstances are most inimical, within the old system, to production of a large social income (to economic efficiency). The effective functioning of our economic organization requires full utilization of existing resources—including labor, use of the best available technical methods, and, less obviously, economical allocation of resources among available, alternative uses. This latter aspect of the problem may well be emphasized here.

Any judgment of efficiency implies a standard or scale of values—merely physical efficiency is an absurd conception. For economic analysis, such a scale of values is available in the market values (prices) of commodities. These market values, being the result of competitive purchase by persons free to utilize purchasing power as they please, may be accepted as measuring roughly the relative importance (for the community) of physical units of different things. To be sure, these prices are the result of free disposition of purchasing power by individuals of widely different income-circumstances. But the problems of efficiency and of inequality may usefully be separated for purposes of discussion—and properly, if one accepts the view that the appropriate measures for improving efficiency and for mitigating inequality are, within fairly wide limits, distinct and independent.

Efficient utilization of resources implies an allocation such that units of every kind of productive service make equally important (valuable) contributions to the social product in all the different uses among which they are transferable. Such allocation will be approximated if, by virtue of highly competitive conditions, resources move freely from less productive (remunerative) to more productive employments. It is an essential object of monopoly, on the other hand, to maintain an area of abnormally high yield (productivity), and to prevent such influx of resources as would bring the monopolized industry down to the common level. Any effectively organized group may be relied upon to use to this end the power which organization brings.

Monopoly thus means the exclusion of available resources from uses which, on the market-value standard, are more important, and, therefore, means diversion of resources to less important uses. Every organized group, whether of employers or of workers, possesses great power, both for exploiting consumers and for injuring other groups of producers to whose industries resources are diverted by virtue of the monopoly restrictions.

Such characterization fits best the case of the strongest and most nearly complete monopolies. For the more typical, partial monopolies (the organization basis for which the National Recovery Act has sought to establish everywhere), the situation is somewhat different, and possibly worse from the viewpoint of the community at large. The looser forms of organization for price maintenance and output control (cartels, trade associations), while able to enforce output limitation upon existing firms, are seldom able to restrict the growth of investment (to control the number and size of firms); nor does their position permit them to withhold output quotas from newcomers in the industry. Such arrangements lead to gross wastage of investment as well as to exploitation of consumers. New firms, attracted by the high returns resulting from price maintenance, will construct plants; and they will be drawn into the organization and given their appropriate quotas (presumably on the basis of "capacity"). This means reduction in the quotas of other firms, and increasingly meager utilization of plant capacity throughout the industry. Finally, producers within the organization may obtain, in spite of the price maintenance, no higher return on investment than prevails in competitive fields. But consumers will be paying heavily, in higher prices, for the policies of the organization; and the industry will end up with much smaller production, in spite of much larger total investment, than would have obtained under competitive conditions. In technical language, equilibrium under the cartel or trade association form of monopoly means equality between average cost and price, in spite of enormous discrepancy between marginal cost and price. This, in general terms, describes the goal toward which "planners" unwittingly direct us.

The situation is strikingly similar with respect to trade-union monopoly, which usually involves a similarly partial monopoly power. The main device of trade-union strategy is the maintenance of the standard rate of pay, through collective bargaining. The raising of rates of wages in a particular field above the competitive level, by whatever methods of coercion, serves to diminish the volume of employment available within that field—inducing economy of such labor by substitution (of machinery and of other labor) and relative contraction of the industries requiring such labor. If the organization admits newcomers freely and rations employment, the occupation may continue to grow in numbers, or fail to decline, in spite of decline in the total amount of employment available—the increased rate of pay more than offsetting, for a time, the reduction in employment available per man. As with the trade association, numbers may increase until the members are no better off than they would have been without any organization at all. Yet product prices in the industries concerned will be higher; and a large part of the community's labor resources will be wasted—a situation which roughly describes, except for the denoument, recent conditions in coal mining in the Midwest. If the union can prevent entrance into the trade, if the older members are given full employment before newcomers are employed at all, or if the demand for this kind of labor is highly elastic, the effects of the wage control in this particular field will manifest themselves largely in diversion of labor into less important *and less remunerative* occupations. In any case, the diseconomies for the community are sufficiently evident.

The gains from monopoly organization in general are likely,

of course, to accrue predominantly to the strong and to be derived at the expense of the weak. Among producers, organization is least expensive and most easily achieved, as well as most effective, within groups whose members were unusually large and prosperous at the outset. Among workers, the bias is not less striking. The most highly skilled and most highly remunerated trades are the trades where organization is least difficult and where the fighting strength of groups once organized is greatest. Little evidence, inductive or analytic, can be conjured up to support the popular conception of trade unionism as a device for raising incomes at the bottom of the scale. Its possibilities lie mainly in the improvement of the position of labor's aristocracy[2]—and largely at the expense of labor generally. Here as elsewhere the gains from monopoly are exploitative. The restriction of employment in the more remunerative occupations injures other laborers, both as consumers and as sellers of services rendered more abundant in other areas by the restriction.

Another major factor in the inefficient allocation of resources is to be found in government regulation and interference. Tariff legislation is again the main case in point; for the protective tariff is essentially a device for forcing resources from uses of higher to uses of lower productivity. Moreover, there are good reasons for believing that political controls will generally work out in this way. Government interference with relative prices is in the nature of arbitration of conflicts of interest between minority producer groups and consumers (the whole community); and such interference inevitably involves decisions which have regard primarily for the interests of the minorities. Producers are, from a political point of view, organized, articulate groups; and it is in the nature of the political process to conciliate such groups. Anyone may detect the notorious economic fallacies, and thus see the dictates of sound policy, if he will look at every issue from the viewpoint of consumers; but no politician can be expected to do this, or to act on his conclusions if he does, except in a world where legislators are motivated primarily by the desire to be retired at the next election. People as consumers are unorganized and inarticulate, and, representing merely the interests of the community as a whole, they always will be. This fact, perhaps, suggests the decisive argument for laissez faire and against "planning" of the now popular sort.

While the tariff is the example par excellence of how the political process works in the control of relative prices, our experience with regulation of the so-called "natural monopolies" is also instructive. With the railroads, the abuse of private monopoly power led finally to real control over the prices of services. We have developed in the Interstate Commerce Commission an unusually competent and scrupulous public body. Even here, however, the preposterous system of relative charges (freight classification), and the disastrous rigidity of freight rates during the depression, testify eloquently to the shortcomings of the regulation expedient; the intrenched position of the Railway Brotherhoods indicates clearly how governments reconcile the interests of small, organized groups and those of the community at large. In the field of local utilities, a half century of effort at regulation yields up a heritage of results, a cursory inspection of which should suffice to dampen anyone's enthusiasm for a system of private monopoly with superimposed government regulation.

Public regulation of private monopoly would seem to be, at best, an anomalous arrangement, tolerable only as a temporary expedient. Half-hearted, sporadic, principle-less regulation is a misfortune for all concerned; and systematic regulation, on the basis of any definite and adequate principle, would leave private ownership almost without a significant function or responsibility to discharge. Analysis of the problem, and examination of experience to date, would seem to indicate the wisdom of abandoning the existing scheme of things with respect to the railroads and utilities, rather than of extending the system to include other industries as well. Political control of utility charges is imperative, to be sure, for competition simply cannot function effectively as an agency of control. We may endure regulation for a time, on the dubious assumption that governments are more nearly competent to regulate than to operate. *In general, however, the state should face the necessity of actually taking over, owning, and managing directly, both the railroads and utilities, and all other industries in which it is impossible to maintain effectively competitive conditions.* For industries other than the utilities, there still remains a real alternative to socialization, namely, the establishment and preservation of competition as the regulative agency.

Turning now to questions of justice, of equitable distribution, we may suggest that equitable distribution is at least as important with respect to power as with reference to economic goods or income; also, that the cause of justice, perhaps in both directions, would be better served if well-intentioned reformers would reflect seriously on what their schemes imply with respect to the distribution of power. Surely there is something unlovely, to modern as against medieval minds, about marked inequality of either kind. A substantial measure of inequality may be unavoidable or essential for motivation; but it should be recognized as evil and tolerated only so far as the dictates of expediency are clear.

If we dislike extreme inequality of power, it is appropriate to view with especial misgivings the extension of political (and monopoly) control over relative prices and incomes. Either socialization or the mongrel system of "national planning" implies and requires extreme concentration of political power, under essentially undemocratic institutions. A system of democratic socialism is admittedly an attractive ideal; but, for the significant future, such a system is merely a romantic dream. On the other hand, it seems unlikely that any planners or controllers, with the peculiar talents requisite for obtaining dictatorial power, would be able to make decisions wise enough to keep an elaborate economic organization from falling apart. Even if one regards that prospect as not unpromising, the implied division of power between controllers and controllees would seem an intolerable price for increased efficiency.

An important factor in existing inequality, both of income and of power, is the gigantic corporation. We may recognize, in the almost unlimited grants of powers to corporate bodies, one of the greatest sins of governments against the free-enterprise system. There is simply no excuse, except with respect to a narrow and specialized class of enterprises, for allowing corporations to hold stock in other corporations—and no reasonable excuse (the utilities apart) for hundred-million-dollar corporations, no matter what form their property may take. Even if the much-advertised economies of gigantic financial combinations were real, sound policy would wisely sacrifice these economies to preservation of more economic freedom and equality.

Another cardinal sin of government against the free-enterprise system is manifest in the kind of institution of property which the state has inflicted upon that system. It has lain within the powers of the political state, in defining rights of property and inheritance, to prevent the extreme inequality which now obtains; and the appropriate changes might still be effected without seriously impairing the efficiency of the system. In a practical sense, there is not much now wrong with the institution of property except our arrangements with respect to taxation. Instead of collecting their required revenues in such manner as to diminish the concentration of wealth and income, governments have relied on the whole upon systems of levies which actually aggravated inequality. Until recently (and the situation is not strikingly different now) governments have financed their activities largely by conglomerations of miscellaneous exactions which have drawn funds predominantly from the bottom of the income scale. Modern fiscal arrangements, like those of medieval barons, must be explained largely in terms of efforts to grab funds wherever they could be reached with least difficulty—to levy upon trade wherever tribute could most easily be exacted—and with almost no regard for consequences in terms of either economic efficiency or personal justice.[3]

The problem of stabilization, of maintaining reasonably full employment of resources, calls for emphasis mainly upon two factors, one of which again is monopoly. If all prices moved up and down with substantial uniformity, changes in the general level of prices would have only unimportant effects upon the volume of production or employment. A major factor in the cycle phenomenon is the quite unequal flexibility of different sets of prices and, more explicitly, the stickiness of prices which, for the bulk of industry, determine out-of-pocket, operating (marginal) costs. This stickiness of prices reflects, first, competition-restraining organization, and, second, a widespread disposition to sacrifice volume to price—which is the characteristic exercise of monopoly power. Decisively important in the total situation is the exceeding inflexibility of wages—the explanation of which would require attention to many factors, of which effective labor organization is but one. To some extent it reflects merely a subtle sort of defensive co-operation among workers to protect themselves in a market which is often only nominally competitive on the employers' side. To some extent it involves employer deference to an attitude of the public, which condemns wage cutting and yet accepts wholesale discharge of employees as unavoidable and unreprehensible. More interesting than the stickiness of wages, if not more important, is the price policy in depression of those basic industries which have long since disciplined themselves along lines now widely approved, against "unfair"(!) competition. Equally significant, or more so, is the depression behavior of railroad rates and the charges in other public utilities subject to government regulation, especially freight rates. At all events, the existence of extreme inflexibility in large areas of the price structure is one of the primary factors in the phenomenon of severe depression. This inflexibility increases the economic loss and human misery accompanying a given deflation, and it causes deflation itself to proceed much farther than it otherwise would.

The major responsibility for the severity of industrial fluctuations, however, falls directly upon the state. Tolerable functioning of a free-enterprise system presupposes effective performance of a fundamental function of government, namely, regulation of the circulating medium (money). We should characterize as insane a governmental policy of alternately expanding rapidly and contracting precipitously the quantity of paper currency in circulation—as a malevolent dictator easily could do, first issuing currency to cover fiscal deficits, and then retiring currency from surplus revenues. Yet that is essentially the kind of monetary policy which actually obtains, by virtue of usurpation by private institutions (deposit banks) of the basic state function of providing the medium of circulation (and of private "cash" reserves). It is no exaggeration to say that the major proximate factor in the present crisis is commercial banking. This is not to say that private bankers are to blame for our plight; they have only played the game (and not so unfairly, on the whole) under the preposterous rules laid down by governments—rules which mean evasion or repudiation by governments of one of their crucial responsibilities. Everywhere one hears assertions of the failure of competitive controls, of the chaos of unplanned economy, when the chaos arises from reliance by the state upon competitive controls in a field (currency) where they cannot possibly work. Laissez faire, to repeat, implies a division of tasks between competitive and political controls; and the failure of the system, if it has failed, is properly to be regarded as a result of failure of the state, especially with respect to money, to do its part.

We have reached a situation where private-bank credit represents all but a small fraction of our total effective circulating medium. This gives us an economy in which significant disturbances of equilibrium set in motion forces which operate grossly to aggravate, rather than to correct, the initial maladjustments. When for any reason business earnings become abnormally favorable, bank credit expands, driving sensitive product prices farther out of line with sticky, insensitive costs; earnings become more favorable; credit expands farther and more rapidly; and so on and on, until costs finally do catch up, or until some speculative flurry happens to reverse the initial maladjustment. When earnings prospects are unpromising, credit contracts and earnings become still smaller and more unpromising. In an economy where costs (especially wages, freight rates, and monopoly prices in basic industries) are extremely inflexible downward, the deflation might continue indefinitely (until everyone was unemployed) if governments did not intervene (inflate) to save the banks or to mitigate human suffering.

Thus, the state has forced the free-enterprise system, almost from the beginning, to live with a monetary system as bad as could well be devised. If, as seems possible, both capitalism and democracy are soon to be swept away forever by a resurgence of mercantilism (by the efforts of persons who know not whither they lead), then to commercial banking will belong the uncertain glory of having precipitated the transition to a new era. Such is likely to be the case, even if our institutions survive this time the attentions of their misguided, if well-meaning, guardians. Capitalism seems to retain remarkable vitality; but it can hardly survive the political rigors of another depression; and banking, with the able assistance of monopoly, seems certain to give us both bigger and better depressions hereafter—unless the state does reassume and discharge with some wisdom its responsibility for controlling the circulating medium.

PART II

We shall now try to define, for present conditions, the main features of a genuinely liberal program, in the traditional sense of liberalism. Such a program, if it could be realized politically, would suffice to permit tolerable functioning of a free-enterprise system, and to prevent (or postpone) revolutionary change in our whole institutional framework. The time has come (some will say it has already passed) for close co-operation between those interested in making capitalism a better system and those of less liberal persuasion who merely dislike revolutions. Consequently, we hope that the proposals described below may receive consideration, both from liberals who are not naïvely romantic, and from conservatives who are not stupidly reactionary.

The proposals, of necessity, are rather drastic. A liberal-conservative movement must now resist and overcome long-established, cumulative trends; it must set itself against the forces of history. We are drifting rapidly toward political and economic chaos. Consequently, a political movement which is conservative in its objectives must be radical in terms of its means. Those who hope for dictatorship, whether under proletarian or fascist symbols, may rather fittingly refer to us as the impractical visionaries. It is they who may now complacently embrace the faith that what is going to be is good, merely because it so obviously is going to be—in spite of us. The cause of economic liberalism and political democracy faces distinctly unfavorable odds and, therefore, requires above all a strategy boldly and intelligently conceived.

The main elements in a sound liberal program may be defined in terms of five proposals or objectives (in a descending scale of relative importance):

I. Elimination of private monopoly in all its forms
 1. Through drastic measures for establishing and maintaining effectively competitive conditions in all industries where competition can function as a regulative agency (as a means

for insuring effective utilization of resources and for preventing exploitation), *and*

2. Through gradual transition to direct government ownership and operation in the case of all industries where competition cannot be made to function effectively as an agency of control

II. Establishment of more definite and adequate "rules of the game" with respect to money, through

1. Abolition of private deposit banking on the basis of fractional reserves[4]
2. Establishment of a completely homogeneous, national circulating medium, *and*
3. Creation of a system under which a federal monetary authority has a direct and inescapable responsibility for controlling (not with broad discretionary powers, but under simple, definite rules laid down in legislation) the quantity (or, through quantity, the value) of effective money

III. Drastic change in our whole tax system, with regard primarily for the effects of taxation upon the distribution of wealth and income

IV. Gradual withdrawal of the enormous differential subsidies implicit in our present tariff system

V. Limitation upon the squandering of our resources in advertising and selling activities

The case for a liberal-conservative policy must stand or fall on the first proposal, abolition of private monopoly; for it is the *sine qua non* of any such policy. Reasonable differences of opinion may appear as to methods; but there can be no intelligent dispute, among liberals and conservatives, as to the objective.

This proposal contemplates deliberate avoidance of the regulation expedient—or, if you please, adherence to the kind of regulation which works only through the preservation of competitive controls. It implies that every industry should be either effectively competitive or socialized; that governments should plan definitely on socialization of the railroads and utilities, and of every other industry where competitive conditions cannot be preserved. On the other hand, it should be a main objective of policy to prevent the development, in the case of other industries, of conditions which would necessitate political control of prices, or socialization. It must suffice here merely to sketch some of the requisite measures.

There must be outright dismantling of our gigantic corporations, and persistent prosecution of producers who organize, by whatever methods, for price maintenance or output limitation. There must be explicit and unqualified repudiation of the so-called "rule of reason." Legislation must prohibit, and administration effectively prevent, the acquisition by any private firm, or group of firms, of substantial monopoly power, regardless of how reasonably that power may appear to be exercised. The Federal Trade Commission must become perhaps the most powerful of our governmental agencies; and the highest standards must be maintained, both in the appointment of its members, and in the recruiting of its large technical staff. In short, restraint of trade must be treated as a major crime, and prosecuted unremittingly by a vigilant administrative body.

As a main feature of the program, *there must be a complete "new deal" with respect to the private corporation.* As many writers have pointed out, the corporation is simply running away with our economic (and political) system—by virtue merely of an absurd carelessness and extravagance on the part of the states in granting powers to these legal creatures. The following proposals, while tentative in detail and obviously inadequate in scope, will suggest the kind of reform which seems imperative:

I. Transfer to the federal government of the exclusive power to charter ordinary, private corporations, and subsequent annulment of all charters granted by the states

II. Enactment of federal incorporation laws, including among others the following provisions:

   1. That no corporation which engages in the manufacture or merchandising of commodities or services shall own any securities of any other such corporation

   2. Limitation upon the total amount of property which any single corporation may own

      a) A general limitation for all corporations, *and*

b) A limitation designed to preclude the existence in any industry of a single company large enough to dominate that industry—the principle being stated in legislation, the actual maxima for different industries to be fixed by the Federal Trade Commission[5]

3. That corporations may issue securities only in a small number of simple forms prescribed by law, and that no single corporation may employ more than two (or three) of the different forms
4. Incorporation of investment corporations under separate laws, designed to preclude their becoming holding companies or agencies of monopoly control—with limitations on their total property, on percentage holdings of securities of any single operating company, and on total investment in any single industry (again under the immediate control of the Federal Trade Commission)
5. That investment corporations shall hold stock in operating companies without voting rights, and shall be prohibited from exercising influence over such companies with respect to management
6. That no person shall serve as an officer in any two corporations in the same line of business, and that no officer of an investment corporation shall serve as an officer in any operating company
7. That corporate earnings shall be taxed to shareholders in such manner as to prevent evasion of personal-income tax with respect to undistributed earnings (see below, p. 27)

The corporation is a socially useful device for organizing the ownership and control in operating companies of size sufficient to obtain the real economies of large-scale production under unified management. It should not be made available, however, for financial consolidation of operating enterprises which are (or which, without serious loss of efficiency, might be) essentially independent as to production management. Horizontal combinations should be prohibited; and vertical combinations (integration) should be permitted only so far as clearly compatible with the maintenance of real competition. Few of our gigantic corporations can be defended on the ground that their present size is necessary to reasonably full exploitation of production economies; their existence is to be explained in terms of opportunities for promoter profits, personal ambitions of industrial and financial "Napoleons," and advantages of monopoly power. We should look toward a situation in which the size of ownership units in every industry is limited by the minimum size of operating plant requisite to efficient, but highly specialized, production —and even more narrowly limited, if ever necessary to the maintenance of freedom of enterprise.

Only a special class of investment corporations should be permitted to hold stock in other corporations; and their powers should be circumscribed narrowly, in order to assure that they confine themselves to performing the important and legitimate functions of the investment trust. These corporations should be merely passive investors, protecting their own stockholders by diversification, rather than by exercising control over operating companies; and full precautions should be taken against their becoming, in effect, holding companies or devices of producer organization.

All corporations should be held to a Spartan simplicity in their capital structures. There should be the sharpest distinction between owners and creditors; and, where this distinction becomes impaired through financial adversity, reorganization should be compulsory and immediate. It would seem wise, indeed, to require the maintenance of a predominant residual equity, and to limit narrowly (say to 20 per cent) the percentage of contractual obligations to total assets.

The establishment and preservation of effective competition throughout the labor market is a difficult and forbidding task. Given real competition among employers, one might wisely advocate application to labor organizations of the general prohibitions upon restraint of trade. If trade unions could somehow be prevented from indulging restrictive monopolistic practices, they might become invaluable institutions. They might then assume their proper rôle as agencies for making labor articulate politically, for preventing arbitrary and oppressive treatment of individual workers, for rendering special services to their members, and for promoting consumer cooperation with respect to both commodities and the various forms of social insurance. Such policy, however, may seem politically fantastic. The community regards unions as representing the interests of labor generally, rather than as agencies for exploitation within the ranks of labor. Even the weaker groups who largely bear the brunt of such exploitation co-operate with their organized brethren and applaud their conquests.

The best one may hope, perhaps, is that labor monopolies, if not fostered and supported by the state, will cease to grow, and even decline in power. Developments of recent years afford some grounds for this hope. Moreover, if genuinely competitive conditions were established among employers, and if we had an efficient system of public employment exchanges, labor monopoly would probably have to face a more hostile public opinion. Full publicity, through the employment exchanges, as to the numbers of qualified workers unable to obtain employment in various trades would create some pressure, in normal times, against unreasonable wage demands. Greater stabilization of production and employment, under a sound system of money and credit, should eliminate the boom periods in which organization proliferates, and also minimize the need for pressure to overcome the lag of wage rates when costs of living are rising.

One scarcely need remark that the establishment of good public employment exchanges is immensely important, on other grounds, for the strengthening and improving of our economic system.

The proposal for abandonment of the regulation expedient in the case of the railroads and utilities requires little comment here. We can worry along with existing arrangements, to be sure, for a considerable time. It seems imperative, however, that we recognize the inherent limitations of these arrangements and plan toward gradual change. Mere recognition of the ultimate difficulties should help to dissuade us from extending needlessly the range of regulation.

Much can be said for early socialization of the railroads, if only for the training of governments in the discharge of such functions, and for the light which experience would throw upon the expediency of extending gradually the scope of public ownership. The feasibility of public ownership and operation of the other utilities will vary from locality to locality, according to the efficiency of public administration and the level of political morality. A good case can be made for extensive experimentation, however, if only because the present system of regulation is failing so completely.

The proposals with reference to banking and currency arise out of the conviction that extreme fluctuations of production and employment may be prevented by rather simple (if drastic) measures with respect to money and credit. The proposals may be defined tentatively in terms of the following measures:

1. Outright federal ownership of the Federal Reserve Banks.
2. Annulment of all existing bank charters (as of a date, say, two years in the future), and enactment of new federal legislation providing for complete separation, between different classes of corporations, of the deposit and lending functions of existing deposit banks.
3. Legislation requiring that all institutions which maintain deposit liabilities and/or provide checking facilities (or any substitute therefor) shall maintain reserves of 100 per cent in cash and deposits with the Federal Reserve Banks.
4. Provision during the transition period for gradual displacement of private-bank credit as circulating medium by credit of the Federal Reserve Banks.

   (This implies enormous increase in the investments and in the demand obligations of the Reserve Banks—i.e., long continued open-market purchases which would serve to inject the substitute credit medium and also to facilitate gradual liquidation of the investments of existing deposit banks. At the end of the transition, the Reserve Banks should find themselves in possession of investments amounting to a substantial portion of the federal debt—or, perhaps, in possession of the greater part of the debt itself—thus eliminating the burden of the debt, to that extent, without taxation and without inflation.)
5. Displacement by notes and deposits of the Reserve Banks of all other forms of currency in circulation, thus giving us a completely homogeneous national circulating medium.

(This implies permanent retirement of all U.S. notes ["greenbacks"], all silver dollars and silver certificates, all gold coin and gold certificates, and all national bank notes. Subsidiary silver might be retained [though it might better be replaced by coins of a cheaper and more durable metal]. Monetary gold would be held exclusively by the Reserve Banks, in the form of bars, and utilized only for settlement of international balances.)

6. Prescription in legislation of an explicit, simple rule or principle of monetary policy, and establishment of an appointive, administrative body ("National Monetary Authority"), charged with carrying out the prescribed rule, and vested with no discretionary powers as regards fundamental policy.
7. Abolition of reserve requirements against notes and deposits of the Reserve Banks, and broad grants of powers to the "National Monetary Authority" for performance of its strictly administrative function.

(The foregoing measures contemplate an economy in which the rules of the game as to money are definite, intelligible, and inflexible. They are intended to avoid both the "rulelessness" of the present system and the establishment of any system based on discretionary management. "Managed currency," without fixed rules of management, appeals to me as among the most dangerous forms of "planning." To establish, as part of a free-enterprise economy, a monetary authority with power to alter vitally and arbitrarily the position of parties to financial contracts, would seem fantastic.)

There will be wide differences of opinion as to what the specific rule of monetary policy, within such a system, should be; but this is not the place to discuss the relative merits of different possible rules. Two observations, however, may be submitted dogmatically: (1) That the adoption of one among the several definite and unambiguous rules proposed by competent students is more important than the choice among them. (2) That rigid stabilization of exchange rates on other (gold-standard) countries is totally inadequate and undesirable as a rule of national currency policy. The various rules which merit consideration differ with respect to the amount of change in the quantity of circulating medium proposed. At one extreme is the rule of fixing the quantity (M) or the total turnover (MV); at the other is the rule of stabilizing some index of commodity prices. The former contemplates ultimately a policy of balancing federal expenditures and federal tax revenues; the latter would require continuous financing of expenditures (or retirement of outstanding debt) to some extent by mere issue of currency. It is important to consider how different possible rules would operate, given the basic inflexibilities in the price structure; but it is equally important that the rule be chosen with regard for the political possibilities of securing adherence to it over long periods without substantial modification. (The rule must be such that strong sentiments against "tinkering with the currency" can be regimented around it.)

The proposals with reference to banking contemplate displacement of existing deposit banks by at least two distinct types of institutions. First, there would be deposit banks which, maintaining 100 per cent reserves, simply could not fail, so far as depositors were concerned, and could not create or destroy effective money. These institutions would accept deposits just as warehouses accept goods. Their income would be derived exclusively from service charges—perhaps merely from moderate charges for the transfer of funds by check or draft. Given generous co-operation on the part of the Reserve Banks, the deposit banks should be able to offer their facilities at quite reasonable cost to their customers. Incidentally, a good case could be made for extending the facilities of the Postal Savings System for the provision of something like checking accounts.

A second type of institution, substantially in the form of the investment trust, would perform the lending functions of existing banks. Such companies would obtain funds for lending by sale of their own stock; and their ability to make loans would be limited by the amount of funds so obtained. Various types of agencies, for bringing together would-be borrowers and lenders, would of course appear. In a word, short-term lending would be managed in much the same way as long-term lending; and the creation and destruction of effective circulating medium by private institutions would be impossible.[6]

These banking proposals define means for eliminating the

perverse elasticity of credit which obtains under a system of private, commercial banking, and for restoring to the central government complete control over the quantity of effective money and its value. The success of such measures, to repeat, requires the adoption of sound rules of monetary and fiscal policy, effective administration under those rules, and a high degree of stability in the rules themselves. But no monetary system, however perfectly conceived and administered, can make a free-enterprise system function effectively, in the absence of reasonable flexibility in the price structure—i.e., in the absence of effective price competition among enterprisers and among owners of productive services.[7]

Our proposal with reference to taxation is based on the view: (1) that reduction of inequality is per se immensely important; (2) that progressive taxation is both an effective means and, within the existing framework of institutions, the only effective means to that end; (3) that, in a world of competitive, invidious consumption, the gains at the bottom of the income scale can be realized without significant loss to persons of large income, so long as their rank in the income scale is unchanged; and (4) that drastic reduction of inequality through taxation is attainable without much loss of efficiency in the system, and without much impairing the attractiveness of the economic game.[8]

Taxation must affect the income distribution, whether we will it so or not. Actually, it has operated to increase inequality, except for a slight opposite effect at the upper extremes of the income scale. The proposal here is simply that tax systems be ordered in such a way as to diminish income differences all along the line; that the funds which governments require be obtained through a system of levies which is actually progressive throughout the income scale.

Such a policy requires the establishment of the personal-income tax as the predominant element in our whole fiscal system, and the rescue of inheritance taxation from its miserable failure. The following measures may be suggested as among the important steps in this direction:

1. Elimination of all exemptions of income by kind, establishment

of the tax as a purely personal levy, and clear recognition in the law that the tax is a tax upon persons according to their incomes, not a tax upon income as such.

a) Abolition of "tax-exempt securities," and inclusion of all interest and salary items in the calculation of taxable income, whether such items are received from governmental bodies or from private persons.

b) Elimination of all special treatment for "capital gains" (and for "capital losses"), but with introduction of rebates under a simplified averaging system, to avoid undue penalty on persons of widely fluctuating annual incomes.

(For example, rebates might be made every five years to persons whose actual tax payments had exceeded by more than 5 per cent what their total tax payments would have been if their taxable income each year had been their average income for the period.)[9]

c) Levy upon estates under the income tax with respect to all "unrealized" appreciation of investment assets—i.e., levy of income tax upon the estate just as though the decedent had sold all his property at the time of his death at the appraised value as of that date.

(This would eliminate, except for non-rational behavior, the unfortunate, but exaggerated, effects during booms of taxes upon capital gains. There is now a strong incentive for elderly people to hold on to appreciated investments, merely because the appreciation may be realized without becoming subject to taxation as income *as soon as the owner dies.* This is the rational explanation of why stocks remain in big strong-boxes during stock-market booms—instead of being peddled out to the lower middle class! By such arrangement, moreover, we might eliminate the worst practical fault of income calculation according to the "realization criterion"—i.e., according to the anomalous, but practically useful, rule that "unrealized income is not income until it is realized through sale.")

d) Effective provision against evasion of personal-income tax by stockholders with respect to the undistributed earnings of corporations.

(The objective here should be that of taxing shareholders in corporations in exactly the same manner as members of partnerships. This is, perhaps, altogether impractical under existing conditions; but, given the "new deal" proposed above with respect to corporation law, it would be feasible.)

e) Provision for inclusion, in the calculation of taxable personal income, of the net use value of all real estate used by the owner for consumption purposes (residence, etc.).

(The unhappy omission of this item is peculiar to income taxes in America. Such income-in-kind must be accounted for if the income tax is to be equitable among individuals. For the best solution, we might well follow the Australian practice of measuring this item of income by taking a fixed percentage (say 5 per cent) of the capital value of the property. This would eliminate the complications of depreciation and maintenance allowances. It would be an enormous improvement over existing arrangements, even if this item of income were measured merely on the basis of existing local assessments of real property.)

2. Treatment of all inheritances, bequests, and (large) gifts *inter vivos* as personal income of the recipient for the year in which received.

(This, a cardinal feature among these proposals, is conceived as the only practicable method of securing effective application of the principle of inheritance taxation—i.e., for successfully avoiding evasion through distribution of property prior to death. Its adoption should be accompanied by repeal of existing inheritance taxes; a case could be made for retention of moderate estate taxes.)

3. Reservation of estate, inheritance, and personal-income taxes for levy exclusively by the federal government, but with provision for generous sharing of revenues with the states.

(One may suggest, tentatively, the return of 50 per cent of the revenues to the states, on the basis of collections—i.e., on the basis of the residence of the individual taxpayers. Herein lies, perhaps, the only real opportunity for eliminating antiquated and regressive elements in our state and local tax systems.)

4. Drastic alteration in the rate structure of the personal-income tax, with more rapid progression, and above all with the introduction of really substantial levies upon the so-called middle and lower income brackets.

(Something may be said for retaining the present exemptions, but in the "vanishing" form—i.e., with the exemptions expressed in terms of amounts of tax, instead of in terms of amounts of income. A good case can be made for requiring every income receiver to file a return and perhaps to pay a small fee. With present exemptions, we should have an initial rate (normal tax) of at least 20 per cent, and the rates should rise rapidly to at least the present maximum. Whether the rates should be higher in the upper brackets than at present is of minor importance from a revenue point of view. If these heavy levies on middle-class incomes seem objectionable, one should remember that the alternative is the retention, as a major element in the system, of the drastically regressive levies on commodities of wide and general consumption. The really important question, as I see it, is whether government revenues shall be derived largely from the middle class or pumped largely out of the bottom of the income scale by excise levies.)

These proposals look toward arrangements whereby something like 10 per cent of the whole national income would pass, via personal-income taxation, into the hands of government. They contemplate abolition of all excises on commodities of wide and general consumption, and ultimately of the innumerable miscellaneous levies which have no justification in terms of broad considerations of policy. Levies like the gasoline taxes might well be retained indefinitely—being eminently defensible as charges for special services of government to a class (or to a form of consumption) which does not merit subsidy. Taxes upon real property also might properly be retained without diminution of long-established rates. These levies are largely in the nature of fixed charges, representing an established equity of the state in real property. Such property has long been bought and sold subject to the prospect of continued taxation; to reduce the levies would involve a large gift by the community (through increase in capital value) to persons who happened to be in possession at the time.

On the expenditure side, we may look forward confidently to continued augmenting of the "free income" of the masses, in the form of commodities and services made available by government, either without charge or with considerable modification of prevailing price controls. There are remarkable opportunities for extending the range of socialized consumption (medical services, recreation, education, music, drama, etc.) and, especially, for extending the range of social-welfare activities. The prospects in these directions, however, must remain somewhat unattractive so long as the expenditures involved must be covered by the kind of taxes on which we have relied in the past—i.e., so long as what the government gives to the masses with one hand is largely taken away with the other.

Opposition to tariffs is, of course, a cardinal element in the liberal creed. Our tariff system is essentially a system of subsidies financed by means of commodity taxes. The precisely equivalent system of explicit subsidies and taxes would surely look like a monstrosity to every reasonable person—with subsidy expenditures exceeding all other federal expenditures, and with an enormous burden of highly regressive excise levies. Two arguments especially may be urged against our tariff: (1) if we are to have enormous subsidies, they ought not to be borne by consumers in proportion to their consumption; and (2) there is something absurd about wholesale subsidizing of particular industries by the government. An "equitable" subsidy system, whereby every producer group both shares and contributes uniformly, is, of course, merely ludicrous. Tariff subsidies, to be sure, can never be uniform, being available only to producer groups whose products might otherwise be imported; but that only raises the question of why public subsidies should be confined to such groups (and the question of why the inevitable burdens should be inflicted upon producers for export).

Thus, our tariffs serve both to reduce substantially the total of our real national income and to increase markedly the degree of income inequality. But two other points may be especially emphasized here.

In the first place, drastic tariff reduction is an important and perhaps indispensable element in a program for eliminating private monopoly and restoring reasonable flexibility in the price structure. There are technical difficulties, in the case of some industries, in establishing adequately competitive conditions merely within national boundaries. With a high tariff wall, it might be necessary, in order to assure real competition, to enforce an otherwise undesirable smallness of firms which would be quite unnecessary with freedom of importation. Though we do have strong international cartels, the fact remains that it is much more difficult to enforce price maintenance on an international scale. Moreover, it is difficult to imagine a thoroughgoing political program which undertook to introduce competition and flexibility internally, while freezing the economy against competition from abroad.

The second point has to do with the general argument against public regulation of prices in private industry, and its consequences for political morality and the future of democracy. A nation which wishes to preserve democratic institutions cannot afford to allow its legislatures to become engaged on a large scale in the promiscuous distribution of special subsidies and special favors. Once this occurs, there is no protecting the interests of the community at large and, what is more important, there is no protecting the political institutions themselves. Tariff legislation is politically the first step in the degeneration of popular government into the warfare of each group against all. Its significance for political morality is, moreover, quite patent. Against the tariff, all other forms of "patronage" and "pork-barrel legislation" seem of minor importance.

The way to reduce the tariff is simply to reduce it. There is, to be sure, a decisive case in favor of gradualness. One must recognize legitimate vested interests in even the most objectionable subsidies. An ideal program would call for a continued scaling down of duties, with the announced objective of getting rid of them all, over, say, a ten-year period.[10] If some reciprocal reductions can be obtained from other nations, well and good. But let us understand that, given an independent national currency administered according to sound rules, the gains to this country from reduction of its tariff are nowise conditional upon reduction of tariff duties abroad.

The fifth proposal must be dealt with briefly here, and left somewhat unprecise. It is a commonplace that our vaunted efficiency in production is dissipated extravagantly in the wastes of merchandising. This economic system is one which offers rewards, both to those who direct resources into industries where the indirect pecuniary demand is greatest, and to those who divert pecuniary demand to commodities which they happen to be producing. Profits may be obtained, either by producing what consumers want, or by making consumers want what one is actually producing. The possibility of profitably utilizing resources to manipulate demand is, perhaps, the greatest source of diseconomy under the existing system. If present tendencies continue, we may soon reach a situation where most of our resources are utilized in persuading people to buy one thing rather than another, and only a minor fraction actually employed in creating things to be bought.

Firms must spend enormous sums on advertising, if only to counteract the expenditures of competitors; and, finally, all of them may end up with about the same volume of business as if none had advertised at all. Moreover, every producer must bribe merchants into pushing his product, by providing fantastic "mark-ups," merely because other producers are doing the same thing. Consumers must be prohibited access to wholesale markets and prices, in order to protect the "racket" of retailers whose co-operation the individual producer requires; and there follows inevitably the absurd proliferation of small retail establishments which spring up to exact on small volumes of trade the large percentage tribute which existing arrangements allow to those who can classify as dealers rather than as consumers. There appears to be no significant limit, along these lines, to the potential accumulation of economic waste; for every producer must at least keep up to the pace which others set.

In these practices of merchandising, moreover, one finds an outstanding incentive to combination and producer organization. Firms acting co-operatively may spare themselves the expense of competitive selling activities; and organization permits of profitable joint enterprise in building up demand for their common product, at the expense of other industries. Thus, organization of competing firms tends to change the form of advertising, rather than necessarily to reduce the total of such outlays; selling activities become competitive among industries instead of merely within industries; the battle of advertising becomes a battle between organized groups, instead of between competing producers of similar commodities. While organization has little or nothing to offer by way of merchandising economies for the community, it has much to offer to the individual participants. Besides, advertising intrenches monopoly by setting up a financial barrier to the competition of new and small firms. Consequently, an appropriate remodeling of the system with respect to merchandising would do more than free wasted resources for useful employment; it might remove one of the main factors working to destroy real competition in industry.

The reform of merchandising offers immense economic rewards; but, unlike the other proposals, it is not immediately indispensable for survival of our economic and political system. Moreover, there is prospect of substantial and continued improvement in merchandising, even in the absence of any deliberate political action to that end. The unfortunately wide differentiation between wholesale and retail prices, and the sharp separation between wholesale and retail markets, may be regarded as a vestigial remainder of the mercantilist system (as a colossal system of restraint upon trade) which has only recently begun to be undermined. The growth of mail-order houses and of large-scale retailing through chain stores is salutary and (given not too much foolish legislation) abundantly promising—offering great economies through increase in the size of units, and without raising any real problem of monopoly.

Enterprises like Consumers Research, Inc., may represent the beginnings of an almost revolutionary development. We may hope that such undertakings may flourish, and that their growth may be promoted through private endowment. (It is hard to imagine a more worthy philanthropy.) Perhaps we shall see the establishment of endowed, non-profit-making institutions, of unimpeachable disinterestedness, which will offer to manufacturers (freely or with moderate charges) the use of the institutions' certification or recommendation in the labeling of approved products. Ultimately, we may see the labeling and classification of the more staple goods on the basis of Bureau of Standards specifications, so that consumers may know (and insist on knowing) which brands of goods meet requirements for government purchase. Perhaps we may still hope for substantial development of consumer co-operatives, organized for collective research and consumer education.

Early correction of merchandising evils by restrictive legislation is perhaps impossible; and one resents the conviction that many proposed remedies would prove worse than the disease. The strongest case can be made for heavy taxation of advertising, provided rates can be made much higher than revenue considerations would dictate. There are interesting possibilities in progressive taxes on manufacturers and jobbers according to the percentage of selling expenses to total expenses. The important objective, however, is that of breaking down, first, competitive advertising and, second, the artificial separation between wholesale and retail markets. Consumers should be free to purchase commodities either with or without the services offered by existing retail establishments —just as they should be free to purchase milk, at substantially different prices, with or without doorstep delivery.

Little has been said so far about the immediate problems of the depression. Our first and second proposals indicate appropriate methods for preventing the recurrence of extreme depressions. For the moment, however, attention must be focused on the task of escaping from the present affliction of extreme unemployment and underproduction. Unless the immediate crisis can be dealt with, there is no sense in talking about long-run policy.

The depression is essentially a problem (1) of relative inflexibility in those prices which largely determine costs, and (2) of contraction in the volume and velocity of effective money. The crucial characteristic of the situation is maladjustment between product prices and operating costs; and, given this condition, there is no necessary limit to the possible deflation and decline of employment. Sound policy will look, first, toward pulling the more sticky prices down and, second, toward pulling the flexible prices up, in order to create favorable prospects with respect to business earnings. Little can be accomplished quickly in the first direction; consequently, main reliance must be placed on "reflationary" government spending.

Inflationary fiscal policy is dangerous, to be sure—but not so dangerous as the alternatives. It should be undertaken with definite preliminary announcement of an objective, stated, perhaps, in terms of *moderate* increase in a specified price index. The program should be planned with an eye to maximum flexibility, for prompt attainment of the price-level objective, and to assure checking of the inflation within the limits designated. Measures of this kind must be undertaken, merely to keep running a system which banking and monopoly have brought to its present plight.

Such a program contemplates bringing the more flexible prices back into line with the prices which prove most resistant to downward change (freight rates, prices of steel rails, electrical equipment, and aluminum, wages in strongly organized trades, etc.), and it looks toward general increase in the volume of production. If the prices which have been most inflexible downward prove highly flexible in an upward direction with inflation, the whole undertaking will fail calamitously. While there may not be much which governments can do to bring the relatively high prices down, it is the supreme folly of a recovery program to facilitate their increase. If the uncompetitive prices are pushed up continually with inflation,[11] the effects of the stimulant will be counteracted, and more and more inflation will become politically inevitable. No diabolical ingenuity could have devised a more effective agency for retarding or preventing recovery (or for leading us away from democracy) than the National Recovery Act and its codes.

It is easy to devise phrases for denouncing the Roosevelt program and the so-called New Deal. On the other hand, one hesitates to condemn, knowing that condemnation will invoke applause from persons whose political philosophy has nothing in common with one's own. Moreover, one hesitates to alienate that now large group of earnest persons with whose general purposes and aspirations one has the deepest sympathy—whatever one may feel about their conception of means to the ends on which it is so easy to agree.

One cannot criticize the policies of the present administration without seeming to approve those of its predecessors. In fact, one must condemn the Democrats mainly for their wholesale extension of the worst policies of the past. The N.R.A. is merely Mr. Hoover's trust policy and wage policy writ large. The agricultural measures and many other planning proposals are the logical counterpart and the natural extensions of Republican protectionism. The gold policy and the silver legislation, like the Federal Reserve System, lead from a bad monetary and banking system only into something worse.

There is little point, however, merely in condemning particular measures and proposals. Real negative criticism must be judged in terms of, and will be significant for, the critic's conception, express or implied, of sound policies. In these pages we have tried to express criticism of current trends in economic policy in terms of definite specifications for a sound liberal program. For those who accept understandingly the position here outlined, it would be gratuitous to point in detail to the dangers of the spuriously liberal proposals which receive the benediction of our political leaders and journalist-economists; and for others, it would be pointless indeed.

The program here outlined should afford adequate outlet for all the enthusiasm and genuine idealism which might now be canalized so effectively. It seems drastic enough to satisfy the most ardent reformers; and it offers abundant opportunity for real economic planning. There is the whole field of transportation and public utilities for the gradual expansion of government enterprise. Competition enforcement and the reform of merchandising call for a generous measure of government control over private business. The designing and building of a mighty engine of income and inheritance taxation is an undertaking big enough and hard enough to occupy the capable people who are really concerned about inequality. There are endless possibilities for increasing and improving the community's "free income" in the form of governmental services, especially through extension of social-welfare activities. Finally, and perhaps most difficult of all, is the task of constructing a sound monetary and banking system.

There cannot, of course, be general agreement in detail on the measures here proposed. No reader is likely to find all of them acceptable. (I must confess to serious misgivings myself at many points.) However, it has seemed desirable, if only for conciseness, to define problems in terms of possible solutions, and to define the general objectives of a liberal policy in terms of fairly specific measures. We hope that there may be agreement, within a significant group, on these general objectives; and that, starting from such agreement, we may be able to formulate specific proposals which are less inadequate and less ambiguous.[12]

This tract is submitted in the hope of promoting a concensus of opinion within a group which might now perform an invaluable service in intellectual leadership. The precious measure of political and economic freedom which has been won through centuries may soon be lost irreparably; and it falls properly to economists, as custodians of the great liberal tradition out of which their discipline arose, to point the escape from the chaos of political and economic thought which warns of what impends.

NOTES

1. The reference here, of course, is merely to that kind of planning which, like mercantilism, implies elaborate regulation of trade, both foreign and domestic, and extensive political control of relative prices, relative wages, and investment.

2. It is, perhaps, easy, from this general viewpoint, to see both advantages and serious practical difficulties in the development of labor organization along industrial, as against occupational, lines.

3. For the disillusioned economist-liberal, a certain bitter satisfaction may be found in the spectacle of capitalism, and the whole institution of property, collapsing under the feet of distinguished propertied gentlemen addressing their brethren on the remarkable virtues of the sales tax.

4. The essential practice of modern banking is that of maintaining obligations payable on demand, or on short notice, while holding "cash" amounting to only *a small fraction* of those obligations.

5. It will be necessary to revise notions commonly accepted (especially by courts) as to the maximum size of firm compatible with effective competition. The general rule and ultimate objective should be that of fixing in each industry a maximum size of firm such that the results of perfect competition would be approximated even if all firms attained the maximum size. One may suggest, tentatively, that in major industries no ownership unit should produce or control more than 5 per cent of the total output. Any such rule, of course, raises the difficult question of what is "a commodity"—of how industries or significant classes of commodities should be defined. A period of several years should be allowed for orderly readjustment, the full restrictions coming into effect only gradually. Special arrangements would be necessary, of course, in the case of new industries and new products.

6. It should be clear that *the measures here proposed have no affinity whatever with schemes for socialization or nationalization of banking*. Indeed, they contemplate a financial system under which there would be the least danger and the least occasion for government control over the lending function, i.e., over the allocation of investment funds. One of the great faults of the present banking system is that it is peculiarly exposed to socialization, merely because of its instability. If we could isolate the lending and investment business from deposit banking, we might eliminate a real danger of government control or socialization in an area where it is most important to avoid it.

7. Any treatment of the problem of monetary and banking reform, within space limits appropriate to this tract, must suffer from serious omissions and oversimplification. Correction of these faults would require extended discussion of the following considerations, among others:

a) There is likely to be extreme economic instability under any financial system where *the same funds* are made to serve at once *as investment funds for industry and trade* and *as the liquid cash reserves of individuals*. Our financial structure has been built largely on the illusion that funds can at the same time be both available and invested—and this observation applies to our savings banks (and in lesser degree to many other financial institutions) as well as commercial, demand-deposit banking. Thus, any reform which dealt merely with demand deposits and checking accounts might largely fail to accomplish the results intended—might lead, indeed, to a merely nominal transformation of demand deposits into the savings account form.

b) A major source of instability is also to be found in the widespread practice of borrowing at short term. Most of the capital requirements which are met by such borrowing are of a permanent, continuing character. Indeed, under modern conditions there are few types of enterprise where funds, once invested, are or can be promptly disinvested again, in the ordinary course of business. The existence of a large volume of short-term commercial debt is thus peculiarly inimical to stability, since any general demand for repayment forces industry into an effort at liquidation which cannot succeed and cannot fail to produce serious disorder. Short-term debts, moreover, are, like time deposits, closely akin to money and demand deposits, since they provide in normal times an attractive and effective substitute medium in which the liquid "cash" reserves of individuals may be held.

In the interest of economic stability, it would be desirable to bring about conversion of all investment (property) into the residual-equity form. A large volume of contractual obligations, with maturities, is inherently dangerous in an economy where orderly liquidation on a large scale is simply impossible. But the problem of long-term debt is less serious. Adequate reform of our monetary and financial system does call, however, for the sharpest separation between money and money substitutes, on the one hand, and investments, on the other—between debts which are regarded as convertible into money by demand upon the debtor (or by refusal of renewal), and debts which may be realized upon only by sale to third parties. It is the rôle of banking, and of the Federal Reserve System especially, to obscure this distinction.

c) Effective administration, through a monetary authority, of any sound rule of monetary policy would be impossible apart from the closest co-operation, on the part of the Treasury and Congress, with respect to fiscal practices. Ultimate control of the currency (and the banks) lies in the management of government expenditure, taxation, and borrowing; and the establishment of a separate monetary authority implies a division of powers which would be workable only with thoroughgoing co-ordination and co-operation. Every change in the relation between taxation and expenditure, in either the amount or form of the public debt, and even in the character of tax levies, has monetary effects of first magnitude. Thus, specifications for sound monetary and banking reform cannot be drawn without reformulation of the whole problem of government finance. Monetary policy must ultimately be implemented through fiscal arrangements.

8. Some students would justify the reduction of inequality on the ground that it is essential to the political stability of the system; others, on the ground that it is important for the reduction of unemployment and for the mitigation of industrial fluctuations. The former position, while tenable, involves an unhappy confusion of means and ends. The latter, in my opinion, is open to the same objection, and also to the characterization of completely spurious economics. Moreover, the methods proposed by exponents of this now widely accepted position (widespread unionization, reduction of hours, and increase of wage rates *in a depression*) are the immediate occasion for the assertion that progressive taxation is the only effective means for improving the distribution of income.

9. Considerations of equity clearly demand provision for further rebates in the more extreme cases, especially where persons pay large income taxes and later lose practically all their income and property.

10. It is worth noting that the recent sharp reduction in the gold value of the dollar is likely to create the ideal conditions for (and, internationally, the necessity of) gradual, continued tariff reduction—and, thereby, for raising the prices of export products, notably cotton and wheat, *relative* to other prices.

11. The recent phenominal rise in building costs, with almost no building going on at all, is a case in point.

12. There remains one point which has not been properly emphasized, namely that genuinely liberal reform must aim primarily at explicit changes in the rules of the economic game and must minimize reliance on control or regulation through nominally administrative bodies with large discretionary, policy-determining powers. The point has already been noted with respect to monetary and banking reform; but it is of decisive importance in many other fields. There is now profound significance in the distinction between a government of men and a government of rules; and to the extent that we move toward the former we are accepting or inviting fascism. One highroad to dictatorship lies in the creation of a large number of petty, specialized authorities in particular fields. For an old-fashioned liberal, it is terrifying to reflect on the amount of arbitrary power which has recently been delegated to the President, the Secretary of the Treasury, the N.R.A., the A.A.A., the R.F.C., the S.E.C., etc. However reasonable this expedient in an acute emergency, we must face the fact that emergency measures are unlikely to prove entirely temporary, and also the fact that we were making substantial strides in this direction long before the emergency arose.

A substantial measure of administrative discretion is obviously essential to good government; but it must be economized. If large latitude must often be allowed in the administration of new reform measures, we should seek afterward to reduce the powers of the administrative authorities as rapidly as experience provides the basis for more definitive legislative rules.

[9]

THE JOURNAL OF
POLITICAL ECONOMY

Volume 44 FEBRUARY 1936 *Number 1*

RULES VERSUS AUTHORITIES IN MONETARY POLICY

HENRY C. SIMONS
University of Chicago

THE monetary problem stands out today as the great intellectual challenge to the liberal faith. For generations we have been developing financial practices, financial institutions, and financial structures which are incompatible with the orderly functioning of a system based on economic freedom and political liberty. Even more disturbing, perhaps, than the institutional trend is the trend of thinking and discussion among special students of money—the fact that economists have become accustomed to deal with monetary problems in a manner which impliedly belies their professed liberalism.

The liberal creed demands the organization of our economic life largely through individual participation in a game *with definite rules*. It calls upon the state to provide a stable framework of rules within which enterprise and competition may effectively control and direct the production and distribution of goods. The essential conception is that of a genuine division of labor between competitive (market) and political controls—a division of labor within which competition has a major, or at least proximately primary, place.

A liberal system adapted to modern conditions would be, of

course, exceedingly complex, by comparison with an authoritarian collectivism. It would involve a large measure of political control: outright collectivism in some areas; deliberate enforcement of competition in others; prevention of extreme inequality, largely via taxation, in the distribution of property, income, and power. Moreover, such a system is attainable, through economic reconstruction, only by years of careful planning and wise legislation; and, once realized, however perfectly, it would require continuous modification, with at least minor changes in the rules, to meet new developments and new conditions.

There is thus little point in contrasting a liberal system and a planned economy—except for the coincidence that the latter phrase has been appropriated by reformers who have little sympathy with, and less understanding of, the liberal position.

There is imminent danger, however, that actual governmental policies will undermine irreparably the kind of economic and political life which most of us prefer to the possible alternatives. This danger manifests itself mainly in three ways: (1) in the displacement of price competition by political (governmental or monopoly) control in many areas where such competition, if established, preserved, and properly canalized, is peculiarly competent for promoting the general welfare; (2) in the neglect of the unquestioned positive responsibilities of governments under the free-enterprise system; and (3) in measures and policies which involve delegation of legislative powers and the setting-up of *authorities instead of rules*.[1]

It is this danger of substituting authorities for rules which especially deserves attention among students of money. There are, of course, many special responsibilities which may wisely be delegated to administrative authorities with substantial discretionary power; health authorities, for example, cannot well be limited narrowly in their activities by legislative prescriptions. The expedient must be invoked sparingly, however, if democratic institutions are to be preserved; and it is utterly inappro-

[1] These views have been presented more fully by the writer in a tract entitled *A Positive Program for Laissez Faire: Some Proposals for a Liberal Economic Policy* (Public Policy Pamphlet No. 15; Chicago: University of Chicago Press, 1934).

priate in the money field. An enterprise system cannot function effectively in the face of extreme uncertainty as to the action of monetary authorities or, for that matter, as to monetary legislation. We must avoid a situation where every business venture becomes largely a speculation on the future of monetary policy. In the past, governments have grossly neglected their positive responsibility of controlling the currency; private initiative has been allowed too much freedom in determining the character of our financial structure and in directing changes in the quantity of money and money-substitutes. On this point there is now little disagreement. In our search for solutions of this problem, however, we seem largely to have lost sight of the essential point, namely, that definite, stable, legislative rules of the game as to money are of paramount importance to the survival of a system based on freedom of enterprise.

Indeed, it may be said that economists, as students of money and banking, have accepted and propagated the first serious heresy among liberals. Managed currency (along with protectionism) is the prototype of all current "planning" schemes—in the sense of all the illiberal connotations of planning. To be sure, many economists still protest vigorously against proposals for currency management; but they and their teachers before them joined zealously in the movement for central banking—and it is precisely here that the heresy is clearly manifested.

This unwitting defection among custodians of the liberal faith is explicable, and may be apologized for, in terms of an unfortunate habit of distinguishing too sharply between currency and banking problems, and in terms of a disposition to look upon banking arrangements as merely a detail or subsidiary system within the supposedly automatic mechanism of the gold standard. Only of late is it clearly realized that the money problem has been swallowed up in the credit problem, or that gold has long been reduced largely to the status of a decorative symbol within a welter of national policies as to central banking, government finance, and foreign trade.

Economist-liberals are now on the defensive. On most fronts, however, their position is, or can be made, very strong intellectually. Conspicuous weakness is to be found only with respect to the problems of money and banking. There is little agreement, and not much relevant discussion, as to how the monetary rules of the game might effectively be altered to prevent or greatly to mitigate the affliction of extreme industrial fluctuations. We cannot effectively answer radical critics of the present system, or expose the stupid schemes of plausible reformers, by saying that the problems which they find in other areas are really just problems of money (although this observation is usually correct and pointed), when we have no good solutions to propose, with some unanimity, in the money field.

Our problem is that of defining an adequate monetary system based on simple rules and of finding the way toward such a system. We cannot seek merely to return to some arrangement of the past. The monetary problem was never solved in the past. There is no adequate system of rules to be found in earlier arrangements—except in the sense that the specific form of the rules was formerly, in a more flexible economy, a matter of less importance. Moreover, we have become so habituated to the fact and to the idea of "management," especially with respect to banking, that we shall find it hard either to reject the palliatives which management offers or even to face squarely our intellectual task.

It is significant that the most stimulating contribution to recent discussion, namely, the conception of a neutral money, comes from a group of economists who have held most firmly to the essential tenets of old-fashioned liberalism. In this conception we have, perhaps, a clue as to how the practical problem may ultimately be solved—although it must be conceded that the conception rather defies precise definition or easy translation into concrete proposals.

An effort at such translation was made recently by a group, including the present writer, in connection with some tentative proposals for banking reform.[2] These proposals contemplated (*a*) putting demand-deposit banking on a 100 per cent reserve basis

[2] See mimeographed memorandum on "Banking and Currency Reform" (with Supplement and Appendix), prepared and circulated by several Chicago economists in November, 1933. See also the pamphlet mentioned above, n. 1.

and, more tentatively, (*b*) eventual fixing of the total quantity of circulating media (currency plus demand deposits).[3]

The fixing of the quantity of circulating media is attractive as a principle of monetary policy for several reasons: (1) it avoids reliance on discretionary (dictatorial, arbitrary) action by an independent monetary authority and defines a statutory rule which might be enacted by the competent legislature without substantial delegation of its powers; (2) it provides automatically for downward adjustment of commodity prices as output expands through improvement in technical efficiency; (3) it represents a rule which, from the viewpoint of a contractual, enterprise economy, is ideally definite and simple; (4) it is clear enough and reasonable enough to provide the basis for a new "religion of money," around which might be regimented strong sentiments against tinkering with the currency. It requires little or no judgment in its administration; it defines a policy in terms of means, not merely in terms of ends; it is compatible with the rule of balancing governmental revenues and expenditures; and it gives to "inflation" a simple meaning which would be conducive to long-term stability in, and observance of, this section of the rules of the economic game.

With all its merits, however, this rule cannot now be recommended as a basis for monetary reform. The obvious weakness of fixed quantity, as a sole rule of monetary policy, lies in the danger of sharp changes on the velocity side, for no monetary system can function effectively or survive politically in the face of extreme alternations of hoarding and dishoarding. It is easy to argue that something would be gained in any event if perverse changes were prevented merely as to quantity, but the argument is unconvincing. The fixing of the quantity of circulating media might merely serve to increase the perverse variability in the amounts of "near-moneys" and in the degree of their general acceptability, just as the restrictions on the issue of bank notes presumably served to hasten the development of deposit (checking-account) banking.

[3] The two features of the scheme are clearly separable, each calling for appraisal on its merits. The banking proposals might be adopted along with many different monetary arrangements, including the international gold standard.

This possibility is clearest in the case of savings accounts (time deposits), where one faces a real difficulty of preventing, and even of defining, effective circulation.[4] The questions which may be raised in this case alone are, indeed, sufficiently involved to dictate one's passing immediately, in discussion, to a broader and less practical approach.

The problem of synchronous industrial (employment) fluctuations is a problem (*a*) of rigidities in crucial areas of the price structure—of adjustments made through output and employment instead of through prices and wage-rates—and (*b*) of perverse flexibility in the total turnover (quantity and velocity) of effective money. Assuming now a limited flexibility in prices and wages, let us try to see what would be the nature of better or ideal conditions on the financial side. What arrangements as to the financial structure would be conducive to lesser or minimum amplitude of industrial fluctuations?[5]

An approximately ideal condition is fairly obvious—and unattainable. The danger of pervasive, synchronous, cumulative maladjustments would be minimized if there were no fixed money contracts at all—if all property were held in a residual-equity or common-stock form. With such a financial structure, no one would be in a position either to create effective money-substitutes (whether for circulation or for hoarding) or to force enterprises

[4] All reform proposals which depend on or imply a categorical distinction between circulating media (say, demand deposits) and non-circulating near-moneys (time deposits, savings accounts, treasury bills, commercial paper of large corporations) are exposed to serious criticism on that account. Moreover, those who argue that the 100 per cent reserve system need not be a seriously disturbing innovation, because of the opportunities for expansion of savings-deposit banking, are in effect proposing that we undertake radical institutional changes for utterly trivial gains. Indeed, they are really arguing for drastic reform on the grounds that its intended effects would never be realized.

[5] If one finds this question unclear, and the following discussion confusing, for lack of definite assumptions regarding currency, one may assume, for the moment, any monetary system which does not provide for the deliberate offsetting of velocity changes by wholesale changes of quantity. The intention, however, is to focus attention on monetary factors outside the central field of currency and to inquire as to the conditions in the field of private finance which would be most (and least) conducive to stability under any particular set of rules as to the currency.

into wholesale efforts at liquidation.[6] Hoarding and dishoarding (changes in velocity) would, to be sure, still occur; but the dangers of cumulative maladjustment would be minimized.[7]

Not far short of the ideal is a financial system in which all borrowing and lending takes the form of contracts in perpetuity—contracts on which repayment of principal can never be demanded. Given a large volume of financing on such contracts, the mere

[6] It might be argued that the emphasis here is misplaced, and that what may be called "voluntary liquidation" is quantitatively more important than liquidation forced by creditors. Undoubtedly, there have been enormous accumulations of cash and near-moneys, and wholesale reductions of debts which might easily have been renewed or refunded, by firms which could anticipate no threat of bankruptcy in the significant future. Whatever the facts, however, the observation is hardly in point, as the following comments may indicate:

1. We are concerned in this paper with monetary factors—with the financial structure as a source of aggravation in booms and depressions. Voluntary liquidation (as evidenced by voluntary reduction of debts and by the augmenting of reserves of cash and near-moneys) must be regarded, on the other hand, as induced essentially by relative-price maladjustments, i.e., as attributable to monopoly and other sources of price rigidity. The distinction between monetary and non-monetary factors seems indispensable analytically; and, from the viewpoint of practical policy, it is certainly useful to separate the factors which have to do with currency, banking, fiscal practice, and business finance from those which have to do with industrial monopoly, the labor market, and public regulation of utility charges. To suggest that monetary factors be conceived and defined very broadly, as relating to other phases of private finance as well as to banking, is not to question the importance of non-monetary factors.

2. Given monopoly and limited flexibility of prices, the efforts of even a small percentage of firms to meet unrenewable and unrefundable obligations of early maturity, or to guard against prospective difficulties, may create or greatly aggravate the maladjustments which dictate liquidation (suspension of investment, hoarding) by firms whose debts represent no threat whatever to continued solvency. It may be appropriate to ask how much voluntary liquidation has been "caused" by involuntary liquidation elsewhere, whatever the difficulties of answering the question quantitatively.

[7] Even with such a simple financial structure, decentralization of security markets would be further conducive to stability. The concentration of security trading in a few large centers greatly facilitates hysterical mob movements of bullishness and bearishness; and it is dangerous, indeed, to have such sensitive and conspicuous barometers of speculative temper in a system where they easily create the conditions which they predict. The maintenance of ready markets (liquidity) for investment assets is possible only with great risks and costs; we have probably gone much too far in facilitating gambling in property rights and in fostering the dangerous illusion of general liquidity of investments.

burden of the fixed annuity charges might occasionally lead to extensive effort among enterprisers to become more liquid. The protection against demands for payment of principal, however, leaves the total of fixed claims relatively small. Moreover, these perpetuities, being subject to substantial change of selling prices, would be relatively unattractive as money-substitutes in hoards.

Only a little farther away from the best system is one where all borrowing and lending contracts are entered into for long periods —say, for at least fifty years. Here there would be the added danger that such maturities as did occur during a depression would be availed of to augment money hoards,[8] but the percentage of total obligations falling due in any critical period would probably be small.

[8] To some critics it may seem a mistake to emphasize the possibilities of depression-aggravation from bond maturities without mentioning the possible aggravation of booms through new issues. Here, however, an appearance of elegant symmetry would conceal a real distortion. Obligations of distant maturity (as already implied) are subject to substantial changes of selling-prices, even apart from changing prospects of their discharge. At the time of issue, bonds are little nearer to money, and hardly more acceptable as media for use in hoards, than are other property rights generally. They come close to the money category, or become significant as money-substitutes, only as they approach maturity—i.e., only as they become short-term debts. (These distinctions obviously relate merely to differences of degree along a continuous scale, as is inevitable with reference to any realistic and useful conception of money and money functions.) At all events, the possible inflationary effect of bond flotation is simply not of the same order of magnitude as the possible deflationary effect of their retirement. The issue of long-term bonds during a boom is unlikely, in itself, to alter much the velocity of circulating media; but the discharge of such obligations in a depression may induce the former holders to increase their cash reserves by something like the amount of the funds so received, i.e., to hoard on a scale which otherwise would have been difficult or impossible. Bond issues might be concentrated heavily in periods of speculative optimism, and they might be absorbed largely by inflationary dishoarding; but the form of issue (whether of bonds or stocks or partnership equities) could hardly be regarded as an important independent factor.

Under the existing financial organization, of course, bond flotations of large magnitude are likely to be coincident with general credit expansion and dishoarding; and thus, whatever the qualitative control of banking and whatever the actual content of bank portfolios, the increase of deposit currency will serve to absorb such issues. Moreover, a merely empirical study of industrial fluctuations (especially of the so-called "long cycles") may easily lead to unfortunate inferences as to causation or (evading a slippery conception) to gross underestimate of the importance of banking and of the results attainable by reform in that area.

Coming on down the scale, the economy becomes exposed to catastrophic disturbances as soon as short-term borrowing develops on a large scale. No real stability of production and employment is possible when short-term lenders are continuously in a position to demand conversion of their investments, amounting in the aggregate to a large multiple of the total available circulating media, into such media. Such an economy is workable only on the basis of a utopian flexibility of prices and wage-rates. Short-term obligations provide abundant money-substitutes during booms, thus releasing money from cash reserves; and they precipitate hopeless efforts at liquidation during depressions. The shorter the period of money contracts, the more unstable the economy will be; at worst, all money contracts would be in the form of call loans.

Thus we move rapidly out of sight of ideal or even tolerable conditions if there develop special institutional arrangements for financing a large volume of investment commitments (which are, or, to permit steady and efficient functioning of the economy, would have to be, essentially permanent and continuing) through intermediaries (banks) which obtain funds for lending by issuing demand and near-demand claims to the original lenders (depositors). If the state gives special status to banking corporations, if their obligations become the established medium of payment, and, what is perhaps more important, if these obligations come to be considered as good as (or, for convenience, better than) currency for use as reserves, then the banking system acquires in effect the prerogative of currency issue and places the government under the practical necessity of giving these private obligations virtually the status of public debts. Demand-deposit banking represents a gigantic development of call-loan financing; moreover, the practical difference between demand deposits and time deposits (savings accounts) is slight indeed.

The fact that such a system will be exposed repeatedly to complete insolvency is perhaps not a matter of primary concern, for government intervention to protect at least the great majority of banks may be taken for granted. What matters is the character of the financial structure which banking creates—and the fact that, in the very nature of the system, banks will flood the economy with money-substitutes during booms and precipitate futile efforts at general liquidation afterward.

Two special circumstances serve to make such a financial system still more sensitive to disturbances: (1) the maintenance by banks of relatively small cushions of owner equities; and (2) the practice of making short-term loans which represent secondary, unsecured claims. Thus, a relatively small decline of security values properly raises question as to the solvency of banks and induces widespread effort to improve the quality of bank assets. Moreover, bankers as holders of unsecured claims naturally respond to signs of unfavorable business conditions with sharp contraction of loans. Certainly, it is an unhappy arrangement whereby those who can demand prompt repayment (can discontinue lending) are, because of the preferred position of other creditors in bankruptcy, compelled to attempt immediate liquidation in the face of the slightest uncertainty.

The notion has somehow become prevalent that banks ought to invest only or largely in short-term commercial paper; indeed, one finds here the rationale of a great enterprise in banking reform. Anyone who is not something of an economist can see that banks, acquiring funds subject to call, should lend only upon promise of early repayment; but the notion, while plausible, is entirely spurious. Indeed, the adherence to this cardinal rule of conservative lending serves (would serve), not to mitigate the affliction of banking, but to compound it; for banks thus increase the volume of short-term debts, not merely in acquiring funds, but in lending them as well. It must be accounted one of the most unfortunate effects of modern banking that it has facilitated and encouraged the growth of short-term financing in business generally.[9]

[9] If banks were to confine their investments to long-term obligations, several benefits would accrue. Business would be less exposed to paralyzing withdrawals of working capital; and the banks would largely lose the power, dangerous to themselves as well as to the community, of precipitating chaotic liquidation. Bankers, freed from the illusion of liquidity, would have to face more squarely the necessity of meeting demands for cash by transferring (selling) their investments; thus, their own judgment, if not the demands of depositors, would probably lead them to maintain more nearly appropriate cushions of stockholder equities. There might be significant gains, moreover, in better allocation of investment funds, for investment in long-term securities would probably mean more fundamental and more thorough analysis of

The penultimate step away from the ideal financial system carries us to one under which all matured (demand) and maturing obligations are legally convertible into some particular commodity like gold, whose total available supply is only a trivial fraction of the amounts which creditors are in a position to demand. And finally, the worst financial structure is realized when many nations, with similar financial practices and institutions and similar credit pyramids (and narrowly nationalist commercial policies), adopt the same commodity as the monetary standard. When one thinks of the total potential creditor-demands for gold for hoarding, in and after 1929, it seems almost beyond diabolical ingenuity to conceive a financial system better designed for our economic destruction. The anomaly of such a system is perhaps abundantly evident in the strong moral restraints and inhibitions which dissuade many people from exercising their legal rights under it.

Given the vagaries of commercial, fiscal, banking, and currency policies in the various countries, and given the character of national financial structures and price rigidities, it is to the writer a source of continued amazement that so many people of insight should hold unwaveringly to the gold standard as the best foundation of national policies.[10] The worship of gold, among obviously

---

the debtor enterprises. Certainly there are disadvantages in a system under which large volumes of funds are allocated primarily with respect to the borrower's immediate outlook and the opportunities for liquidation ahead of other creditors.

Of course, there would also be some disadvantages for the banks. Thorough analysis of prospective investments would be expensive. Moreover, short-term paper has one attractive feature, namely, that one can seldom be expected to tell what it is worth. Thus owners, depositors, and examiners are frequently spared for considerable periods the awareness that banks are insolvent—usually, indeed, until that distressing condition has passed. With portfolios of securities, on the other hand, the magnitude of stockholder equities would be seriously exposed to the bitter test of prices on the security exchanges.

It seems, at all events, that desirable changes in the content of bank portfolios might be defined roughly in terms of transfer from earlier to later kinds of assets in the following list: (1) short-term commercial paper; (2) long-term private obligations; (3) federal securities; (4) legal-tender currency.

[10] This is not the place to argue the matter in any detail. See the writer's memorandum to the Commission of Inquiry into National Policy in International Economic Relations (Hutchins Commission), published in their report, *International Economic Relations* (Minneapolis: University of Minnesota Press, 1934), pp. 344–49.

It may be noted that the gold-standard arrangement simply does not define a

sophisticated people, seems explicable only in terms of our lack of success in formulating specifications for a satisfactory, independent national currency—and certainly not in terms of the need of stable exchange-rates for orderly international commerce. Indeed, it indicates how little progress liberals have made in showing, by way of answer to revolutionists, what kind of money-rules might be adopted to make capitalism a more workable system.

On the other hand, the desire to hold to something, in the face of perplexity, invites understanding sympathy—for certainly we have made little progress in defining attractive alternative systems. Some students propose pure dictatorship, under powerful monetary authorities; others, the stabilization of various price-indexes; not to mention the many irresponsible proposals for indefinite inflation, based on the notion that our ills are traceable to deficiency of consumer-purchasing-power. Of all these schemes, those which contemplate stabilization of price-indexes are least illiberal; but they, too, are unsatisfying. They define programs in terms of ends, with little discussion of appropriate means; they call for an authority with a considerable range for discretionary action, and would require much intelligence and judgment in their administration; and they would leave us exposed to continuous legislative (if not administrative) tinkering, since no particular price-index has much greater inherent reasonableness than many others, and since most of them would serve badly the end of profit stability.[11]

---

monetary system based on rules in any sense consistent with our usage in this paper. It defines a policy merely in terms of its end or objective, and not in terms of means —not in terms of rules of operation. To be sure, such rules might be established. To illustrate, Congress might establish a monetary authority with large powers and with a definite mandate (1) to buy and sell gold freely at a fixed price and (2) to maintain a fixed, constant proportion between the amount of its gold holdings and the total amount of money (including demand deposits) in circulation. It is doubtful whether much enthusiastic or intelligent support could be recruited for such a scheme—or for any other which would establish real rules for the operation of the gold-standard system.

[11] The choice of a particular price-index, as the basis of a definitive rule of policy, presents serious difficulties. If monetary uncertainties are to be minimized and the monetary authority limited to a strictly administrative function, the commodities whose prices are included in the index must be (1) commodities which can (with a

In a free-enterprise system we obviously need highly definite and stable rules of the game, especially as to money. The monetary rules must be compatible with the reasonably smooth working of the system.[12] Once established, however, they should work

minimum of difficulty) be sharply defined in terms of physical specifications, (2) commodities which (as so defined) are and probably will continue to be actively traded in highly organized and highly competitive markets. The index must be highly sensitive; otherwise, the administrative authority would be compelled to postpone its actions unduly after significant disturbances or (Heaven forbid!) obliged to use discretion in anticipating changes. All prices subject to deliberate regulation, whether by producers or governmental agencies, obviously should be excluded—and all prices which are likely to fall into this class in the significant future!

If a reasonably inclusive, representative index could be designed in accordance with these specifications, it would still be very unsatisfactory. Such an index, governed predominantly by the prices of standardized, basic commodities, would give us an excessively "inflationary" rule, for the production of these commodities is likely to be affected most markedly by the progress of technical efficiency; with such an index we should depart far indeed from the ideal of a neutral money. Moreover, an index of this kind would be peculiarly sensitive to changes and disturbances originating abroad; thus, it might often dictate monetary measures which would be undesirable and merely disturbing domestically. It would seem best to employ an index made up primarily of prices of "domestic," rather than of internationally traded, goods; but it would probably not be possible to construct an index of this kind which would be at all satisfactory in terms of the other considerations which we have noted.

The writer's notion as to how these conflicting considerations should be weighed, for a judicious, practical decision, may be inferred roughly from the order in which they are mentioned above.

[12] The literature of money, however, seems on the whole greatly to overstress this consideration and to minimize the prospects of automatic adjustment through anticipations, under a definite and stable monetary constitution. This may be the result of the widespread practice of discussing the question of what monetary policy should be, in terms of an implied assumption that knowledge of that policy is to be the exclusive possession of an inscrutable monetary authority. The outcome, at all events, is a critical appraisal of possible rules of policy which relates mainly to difficulties of the transition period rather than to the operation of these rules as established bases of anticipations.

This criticism is conspicuously applicable to the usual discussions of "justice" as between debtors and creditors. It is clear that, given a minimum of uncertainty as to money, differences in the monetary rules would tend to be compensated by differences in interest yields. The same point is relevant, moreover, if less obvious and decisive, with respect to "forced saving" and induced maladjustments generally. If the monetary constitution called for a rising, instead of a stable or a declining, price-level, economic behavior would be modified considerably in every sphere—in the labor market, among employers and labor leaders as well; in the determina-

mechanically, with the chips falling where they may. To put our present problem as a paradox—we need to design and establish with the greatest intelligence a monetary system good enough so that, hereafter, we may hold to it unrationally—on faith—as a religion, if you please. The utter inadequacy of the old gold standard, either as a definite system of rules or as the basis of a monetary religion, seems beyond intelligent dispute. But if that system lacks peculiarly the virtues which now seem important, they are also patently lacking in most of the systems proposed as substitutes.

Thus, traditional liberalism, if not hopelessly or more fundamentally decadent for other reasons, is at least seriously embarrassed by the difficulty of answering urgent monetary questions in a manner consistent with its central tenets. It is the purpose of this paper, not to present any simple answer or solution, but merely to define the problem more closely and perhaps to provide some basis for ultimate consensus on definite proposals.

The problem of booms and depressions is one which must be attacked from both sides, (*a*) by policies designed to give us a more flexible price structure and (*b*) by measures which will minimize the aggravations attributable to the character of the monetary system and financial structure. The former attack, however, must always be regarded as primary. With adequate price flexibility, we could get along under almost any financial system; with extreme rigidities (reflecting widespread partial monopoly), the most drastic monetary and financial reform, even an ideal financial structure, could not protect us from serious disturbances of production and employment.

tion of the "administered" prices, by both public and private agencies; and, of course, in the money markets.

Generally speaking, it is very difficult to judge the merits of any precise rule of monetary policy on the basis of experience in an economy where no such rule has obtained and where economic behavior has been profoundly influenced by the extreme monetary uncertainty. (The common criticism of price-level stabilization, on the basis of our experience during—and after—the twenties, is thus without much force.) The primary objective of reform should be that of minimizing this kind of uncertainty for the future. From the point of view of ultimate operation, it seems likely that many different rules would serve about equally well. Thus, it is appropriate to focus attention on the difficulties of transition—explicitly.

For the present, we obviously must rely on a large measure of discretionary money management—on a policy of offsetting and counteracting, by fiscal and banking measures, the effects of monopoly and custom upon prices and wage-rates. Such a policy, however, must be guided by a more fundamental strategy and by the need for early abandonment of temporizing expedients;[13] otherwise, political control must degenerate into endless concessions to organized minorities, with gradual undermining of the "constitutional structure" under which free-enterprise economy and representative government can function.[14]

The possibilities of genuine economic reconstruction, and the requirements of sound liberal strategy, may be defined in terms of three objectives: (1) restoration of a maximum of competitiveness in industry (including the labor markets); (2) transition to a less preposterous structure of private money contracts; (3) ulti-

[13] The alternative position would hold that sheer temporizing is less dangerous than definite commitment to any precise, inflexible monetary rule. Given stabilization of a price-index, organized groups might establish the "administered" prices and wage-rates at a level which would prohibit tolerable functioning of the economy as a whole. To guard against this contingency, the monetary authority might be set up as a kind of agency of monopoly control, with an implied policy of countering every general increase of monopoly prices and wages with deliberate inflation of the whole price-level.

Such therapy would alleviate the patient's distress by eliminating possibility of his recovery. We cannot long preserve existing political and economic institutions by countering the infection of monopoly with the opiates of monetary dictators. The uncertainties of business as to, notably, wage-rates and freight-rates may be as serious as those relating to money; but it would seem sheer folly deliberately to create monetary uncertainties in the hope of salutary counteraction or offsetting effects. Especially alarming, along these lines, is the possibility of a long-continued struggle between the monetary authority, raising the price-level to diminish unemployment, and labor organizations seeking, with able assistance from the Department of Labor, to advance wage-rates ahead of price-level changes—and even, avowedly, to assist the monetary authority by increasing purchasing power! At all events, under such a monetary scheme, the controlled parts of the price structure would probably be manipulated in such manner as to require an indefinite, revolution-creating inflation; indeed, this seems to define the real threat of Fascism in this country and the likely route toward it. If monopoly proves fatal to capitalism, inflation will be the announced cause of death.

[14] As evidence of the grave moral dangers of present policies, one only need mention two superlative contributions of our legislature and executive to the degradation of representative government: the silver legislation and the Guffey-Snyder Bill.

mate establishment of a simple, mechanical rule of monetary policy. As regards this third objective, the writer feels that his earlier persuasion as to the merits of the rule of a fixed quantity of money was fundamentally correct, although the scheme is obviously too simple as a prescription under anything like present conditions. Its limitations, however, have to do mainly with the unfortunate character of our financial structure—with the abundance of what we may call "near-moneys"—with the difficulty of defining money in such manner as to give practical significance to the conception of quantity.

Under what financial conditions would the simple rule of fixed quantity become reasonably satisfactory? In principle, the answer is easy: under the ideal financial structure described above. If this seems to be a counsel of despair, one may add that perfection is not necessary practically. On the other hand, it requires some temerity to specify how far the ideal conditions might safely be sacrificed.

To propose abolition of all borrowing, or even of all borrowing at short term, is merely to dream. It would seem feasible, however, to undertake gradual and systematic reordering of financial practices, to the end of limiting quite narrowly the amount and the possible quantity fluctuations of the generally acceptable near-moneys. This would mean, above all, the abolition of banking, i.e., of all special institutional arrangements for large-scale financing at short term. Demand-deposit banking would be confined (in effect, at least) to the warehousing and transferring of actual currency. Savings banks would be transformed into strictly mutual institutions or investment trusts. Narrow limitation of the formal borrowing powers of other corporations would obviously be necessary, to prevent their effectively taking over the prerogatives of which banking corporations as such had been deprived. Further limitations might also be necessary with respect to financing via the open account (book credit) and instalment sales, although other prohibitions might provide adequate protection indirectly against these evils. If such reforms seem fantastic, it may be pointed out that, in practice, they would require merely drastic limitation upon the powers of corporations (which is eminently desirable on other, and equally important, grounds as well).[15]

Banking is a pervasive phenomenon, not something to be dealt with merely by legislation directed at what we call banks. The experience with the control of note issue is likely to be repeated in the future; many expedients for controlling similar practices may prove ineffective and disappointing because of the reappearance of prohibited practices in new and unprohibited forms. It seems impossible to predict what forms the evasion might take or to see how particular prohibitions might be designed in order that they might be more than nominally effective. But we perhaps approach insight when we conceive the problem broadly as that of achieving a financial structure in which the volume of short-term borrowing would be minimized, and in which only the government would be able to create (and destroy) either effective circulating media or obligations generally acceptable as hoards-media. More narrowly (with reference to depressions), the problem is one of moving toward a system in which creditors would be unable quickly to demand, and to require enterprises generally to undertake, rapid and impossible liquidation.

Whatever the best-detailed solutions as to financial practices and their control, it seems that some arrangements compatible with rigid fixing of the quantity of effective money may be feasible as a long-term objective of reform. Given such arrangements, the danger of alternate hoarding and dishoarding tendencies, to be sure, would still remain; but it would remain as a problem to be dealt with exclusively via efforts to obtain greater flexibility (competitiveness) in the economy. The problem of industrial fluctuations cannot be solved, and should not be attacked, exclusively by monetary devices. The best monetary system, so to speak, would tolerate occasional disturbances without alleviation, accepting them as a reasonable cost of maintaining the best structure of relative prices and as a means for preventing a continued

[15] These other grounds, of course, have to do mainly with the monopoly problem. For the writer's views, see the pamphlet mentioned in n. 1.

accumulation of basic maladjustments which could only issue politically in disruption of the system itself.[16]

In the present critical situation we should not balk at bold schemes for restoring the free-enterprise system to a securely workable basis. The requisite measures, radical in the money field and more radical elsewhere, will become possible politically only with the revival or development of a real religion of freedom, of a strong middle-class movement, and of values (and revulsions) of a rather intense sort. These necessary conditions, however, might soon appear, through popular disillusionment with respect to recently popular economic nostrums and policies, as the perhaps natural alternation in a cycle of opinion and prejudice.

If this favorable climate of opinion does appear, it will behoove liberals to make the most of the opportunity (otherwise probably their last) and, avoiding plausible compromises, to focus their efforts on basic reforms. In particular, this may be interpreted to

[16] That the fixed-quantity policy would go too far in this direction, however, is a contention to conjure with. Speculative movements with respect to money will always be somewhat cumulative and self-aggravating, even given the most drastic reforms in the field of private finance. Thus, conceding the merits of long-run fixity in the quantity of money, one may argue that provision should be made for temporary changes to offset changes in velocity. But this view, however commendable in principle, has not been, and probably cannot be, translated into significant practical proposals. The difficulties of drafting satisfactory rules based on elaborate statistical measures of velocity seem decisive. On the other hand, if one wants a system based on rule, it would be folly to enact legislation calling for secular constancy in the quantity of money but leaving the administrative authority free to make "temporary" changes at its own discretion.

These considerations emphasize one great advantage of a price-index rule, namely, that it defines, within a definite long-term rule, appropriate measures for dealing with velocity changes. However, it is possible that, with a more flexible price structure and a narrowly limited amount of short-term financing, the anchor of a fixed quantity of circulating media might suffice to induce prompt reversal of hoarding and dishoarding movements. And moderate cyclical fluctuations might wisely be accepted as the price paid for the conspicuous superiority of the fixed-quantity rule in terms of other considerations. Substantial sacrifice might well be made to obtain greater simplicity and definiteness; to avoid the inherent limitations of index numbers, especially as elements in permanent legislation; to escape the continuing disturbance of positive monetary action; and to dispense with powerful administrative authorities. On the other hand, the price-index rule is eminently preferable for the immediate future—and certainly will remain the more expedient solution unless and until a highly competitive economy is realized and the structure of private money contracts drastically modified.

mean (*a*) that no concessions can be made as regards the restoration of highly competitive conditions and (*b*) that few concessions can be made in the effort to remodel our permissible financial practices to the end of making feasible and easily workable a definite, mechanical set of rules of the economic game as to money.[17]

For the moment, of course, we must be reconciled to pure management in the money field. We must rely on government action —on political efforts to bring down the prices which remain far out of line; on such injections of fiscal stimulants as may be necessary to prevent recurrence of wholesale liquidation; and, above all, on the prompt and drastic measures for debt retirement which may soon become imperatively necessary to prevent a disastrous inflationary boom. It should be feasible, however, increasingly to concentrate the monetary powers of governmental agencies in fewer hands and, later on, to bring the appropriate agencies more closely within the control of law, through the adoption of rules, expressed perhaps in terms of price indexes. Such measures, at all events, seem essential in a program for avoiding revolutionary changes in economic and political institutions.[18] For the most san-

[17] The so-called 100 per cent scheme of banking reform can easily be defended only as the proper first step toward reconstruction of our whole financial organization. Standing by itself, as an isolated measure, it would promise little but evasion—small effects at the price of serious disturbance—and would deserve classification as merely another crank scheme.

[18] Indeed, the time seems fully ripe for a declaration by Congress and the Administration against further increase in the American price-level. This does not imply that early and rapid recovery is now assured or that the federal budget should promptly be balanced; but it does mean that the gravest dangers are involved in relying upon further reduction in the commodity-value of the dollar for correction of the relative-price maladjustments which still impede recovery. A sound program must now undertake to bring about reduction of those controlled prices and wage-rates which remain high relative to other prices. The problem of relative-price maladjustments must be worked out along the line of the present general level, if reasonable precautions are to be taken against a chaotic boom, wholesale dishoarding, and uncontrollable inflation.

There may now be little agreement on the merits of price-index stabilization as a permanent rule of monetary (fiscal) policy; but there would probably be a surprising unanimity among reputable economists on the proposition that fiscal and banking policy henceforth should not permit any further rise of prices generally. At all events, announcement by the Administration (with supporting Congressional resolu-

guine view, however, they define only a proximate objective in monetary reform—a way of escape from present chaos and a step toward a more satisfactory ultimate solution.

The shortcomings of price-index stabilization, as the fundamental basis of a monetary system, are numerous and serious from either an analytical or an empirical viewpoint. It is easy to maintain that such a rule falls far short of the ideal in monetary arrangements—far too easy, indeed, when those who criticize are not obliged or inclined to define the better rules by comparison with which the one in question is so defective. The advocates of a stable price-level (with all the irritating excesses of their advocacy) are proposing a solution which is genuinely consistent with traditional liberal principles—and, precisely on that account, are faring rather badly in the debate which the proposal has provoked among professional economists and journalists. The most vigorous and pungent criticism comes from specialists who themselves have no intelligible solutions to offer and who generally have been spared the suspicion that a solution in terms of definite rules is of any importance.[19]

---

tions) of its intention to use all its powers to prevent a further rise in the level of prices is the first important step which can be taken to reduce uncertainty as to monetary conditions in the near future. With such an important beginning, we might move on afterward to more and more definitive rules, as political and economic developments permit.

To appreciate the danger of our present position, a moment's reflection should suffice: simply contemplate the political fate of any leader who, in the midst of the credit inflation now imminent, would try to stand in the way or to impose real checks. As a mob, we have probably learned much less than nothing since 1929; the long depression has only put us in the mood to draw and quarter anyone who would deny us the release of an exciting prosperity. And, incidentally, those political leaders who talk most about balanced budgets and sound currency would, by virtue of the magnificent simplicity of these nostrums, probably do least to check wholesale dishoarding and expansion of private credit. But a reasonable rule of policy, erected now, might save us where nothing else would.

[19] In the writer's opinion, the same issue is, or rather ought to be, fundamental in the current controversy as to qualitative versus quantitative control of credit. Qualitative control not only implies avoidance of all definite, meaningful rules; but, while espoused by persons peculiarly hostile to government interference with private business, it also implies a much broader range of political interference and a less specialized conception of appropriate governmental function. Indeed, qualitative control of credit essentially amounts to political control over the *direction*

If price-level stabilization is a poor system, it is, still from a liberal viewpoint, infinitely better than no system at all. And it seems now highly questionable whether any better system is feasible or possible at all within the significant future. Given the present financial structure, and given the present multitude of uncoordinated monetary measures and monetary authorities, is there any other rule of policy around which some order and system might be achieved? How else may the present chaos of private financial practices, central-bank action, fiscal measures, and tariff changes be pulled together into something which resembles a

---

of private investment. Control over the quantity of media, on the other hand, is consistent with the narrowest conception of the proper rôle of political control—with the narrowest definition of control of the currency. Those who argue for greater and more direct control of quantity by political agencies would argue quite as vigorously that the *allocation* of investment funds should be directed only by the freest competition—that this allocation should be entirely freed from the influence of Congress, the Treasury, any monetary authority, or any organization of bankers in the form of bankers' banks.

The so-called 100 per cent scheme was suggested, at least by its Chicago proponents, largely, if not primarily, with the notion that reform along such lines would serve to minimize the danger of increasing political control over the direction of investment, i.e., the danger, both of socialization of banking in its present form and of "financial planning" administered by organizations of private banks. From this viewpoint one may deplore the mass of legislation which has given special status to banking corporations and the development of many kinds of supervision and regulation (qualitative control) which has served to differentiate the obligations of banks from other private obligations and to facilitate their use as money. If a rigid separation could be achieved between the business of warehousing and transferring funds and that of mobilizing funds for lending and investment, the state might properly limit its regulation of the latter type of business to the provision of ordinary safeguards against fraud and the maintenance of competitive conditions in the investment markets.

The 100 per cent banking scheme has been characterized as socialistic; and advocates of quantitative control have been charged with the intention of turning the banking business over to politicians. While both observations are intellectually beneath notice, they might be countered, for purposes of vulgar debate, with the remark that most defenders of qualitative control are impliedly espousing syndicalist ideas and, for their own purposes, a corporative state. At all events, the task for serious students, here as elsewhere, is that of defining carefully the proper spheres for competitive and political controls and of discovering how each may best be implemented in its own sphere. If the 100 per cent scheme has any merit, it is largely that of directing attention to this problem in connection with the reform of a financial system which has acquired a functional complexity that renders useful analysis as difficult as it is important.

monetary system? How else can we possibly escape from a situation where monetary policy is merely the composite of the uncertain daily actions of an indefinite number of agencies, governmental and private? Some ordering of this chaos is imperative. It may be achieved, either by setting up a superior, independent authority or by bringing the totality of monetary measures under the discipline of some rule; and only the advocates of price-index stabilization have offered a feasible way out along the latter lines.

This solution, if unsatisfying, is likewise not simple administratively. Question is often raised as to whether stabilization of a price-level is possible. The problem is better formulated, however, when we ask by what agency it might best be undertaken and what methods would be appropriate in its execution.

The task is certainly not one to be intrusted to banking authorities, with their limited powers and restricted techniques, as should be abundantly evident from recent experience. Ultimate control over the value of money lies in fiscal practices—in the spending, taxing, and borrowing operations of the central government. Thus, in an adequate scheme for price-level stabilization, the Treasury would be the primary administrative agency; and all the fiscal powers of Congress would be placed behind (and their exercise religiously limited by) the monetary rule. The powers of the government to inject purchasing power through expenditure and to withdraw it through taxation—i.e., the powers of expanding and contracting issues of actual currency and other obligations more or less serviceable as money—are surely adequate to price-level control. At present, monetary powers are dispersed indefinitely, among governmental agencies and private institutions, not to mention Congress itself. Since the powers of the legislature are ultimate and decisive, a program looking toward co-ordination and concentration of responsibility must focus on fiscal policy as its mode of implementation.

The scheme clearly requires the delegation of large administrative powers. The Treasury might be given freedom within wide limits to alter the form of the public debt—to shift from long-term to short-term borrowing or vice versa, to issue and retire demand obligations in a legal-tender form. It might be granted some control over the timing of expenditures. It might be given limited power to alter tax rates by decree and to make refunds of taxes previously collected. How wide and numerous these powers should be, need not concern us here. Any legislation granting such authority, however, must also impose the duty and responsibility of exercising that authority in accordance with a sharply defined policy.[20]

Given the suitable mandate, the grant of administrative powers should err, if at all, on the side of generosity. The more adequately implemented the rule of monetary policy, the easier will be its actual execution. The greater the powers available for its execution, the smaller will be the probable demands for their exercise. If it is clear that the administrative authority is adequately equipped to make the rule effective, then the rule will be, to some extent, self-enforcing, in so far as the actions of enterprisers and speculators come to be predicated upon its enforcement.

Not only must the price-level rule be implemented through fiscal

[20] Congress would really be the administrative agency in any event. It could always revoke the powers of the monetary authority or nullify that agency's efforts to execute the price-index rule. Observance of the rule would require appropriate budgetary practice and thus would depend basically upon revenue and appropriation measures. The administrative function of the monetary authority might therefore be conceived mainly in terms of temporary devices for checking or ironing out small aberrations of the index. Its main responsibility, properly, would be that of giving advice and making recommendations to the executive and to the legislature with respect to the budget.

It may be interesting, if gratuitous, to note some features of fiscal practice under a properly executed price-index policy. The old perversity of fiscal changes would, of course, disappear. We should have to get accustomed—assuming continued increase in "physical production"—to the novel phenomenon of chronic budget deficits accompanied by declining interest charges or, at least, not accompanied by corresponding growth of the interest-bearing debt. (That this experience might induce widespread financial insanity is perhaps an argument in favor of a quantity-rule.) The Treasury would systematically borrow when interest rates were high and reduce its interest-bearing debt when rates were lowest; in other words, it would consistently make open-market purchases of its obligations when their prices were highest and sell them when their prices were abnormally low.

Under either a price-index or a quantity rule, by the way, there would presumably be no justification for a complex structure of federal debt. Treasury obligations might properly be confined to two simple forms, lawful money and consols or perpetuities (which would facilitate deletion of the usual textbook observations about benefits to future generations and probable service-life of public improvements).

measures; it must also serve as a control upon all governmental measures which have significant monetary effects. In other words, it must be accepted by the community, and obeyed by legislatures, as the guiding principle of government finance—as the basic criterion of sound fiscal policy.[21] While the rule cannot wisely be

[21] It may be interesting to note that the whole argument of this paper might properly be developed with primary emphasis upon problems of government finance. With the growth of deposit currency and central banking, not only has monetary policy been left without substantial foundation in legislative rule and without adequate implementation but fiscal policy also has lost its appropriate orientation. Nominally, of course, it has been ordered in terms of the requirements of the gold standard—and it may be conceded that the prestige of gold has occasionally enforced some discipline in government finance. But the rule of maintaining convertibility or redemption has the obvious limitation of any legislative policy which is defined merely in terms of its end. There was no assurance that budgetary arrangements (or the behavior of the banking authorities) would actually be consistent with continued adherence to the rule—and even little prospect that blame for its violation would fall upon those really responsible. Whatever the other limitations of the gold-standard system (see n. 10), its administration, at all events, was left largely to the banking authorities, with only vague recognition that reckless accumulation of federal indebtedness might give rise to difficulties.

One consequence is the conspicuous absence, in both popular and academic discussion, of anything that might seriously be called principles of sound fiscal practice. (For eloquent testimony on this point, see the textbooks on public finance.) There are no accepted criteria for criticism; there is no real basis for intelligent public opinion and, thus, little opportunity for effective democratic control. Moreover, within the uncertain limits set by the requirements of the gold standard, there are indefinitely large opportunities for doing things backward in the field of government finance (as well as in banking)—and political pressures assure that these opportunities will be fairly well exhausted.

Just as the financial system is conducive to utterly perverse changes in the quantity of credit, so likewise does it lead almost inevitably to extreme perversity in fiscal changes. During periods of expanding profits and credit inflation, tax rates are reduced, expenditures increased, and long-term obligations retired (instead of being refunded and increased to permit the impounding of currency). In the face of declining production and employment, taxes are increased (especially the critical excises), expenditures are usually curtailed, and money is obtained by borrowing (instead of being created by the Treasury or released from previously accumulated balances). Moreover, little real comfort can be found in recent recognition of this perversity, for it promises only temporary, one-sided correction in the case of expenditures and, thus, perhaps greater ultimate confusion.

It may seem a counsel of sheer cynicism or of utter despair to suggest that all our established fiscal practices should be entirely reversed—and, as regards the possibilities of reform within our present financial organization, it is so intended. Sound fiscal policies are impossible (cannot even be defined) without precise and firmly established rules of monetary policy; but the early adoption of, or rapid movement toward, such rules is entirely feasible.

written into our fundamental law, it must provide the same sort of limitation and mandate as would a constitutional provision. As things stand now, there is almost nothing which a dominant party may not do or leave undone financially, without rebuke. (There is still some moral pressure, to be sure, against outright issue of paper money; but this only invites evasion through the use of short maturities and through resort to the inelegant expedient of paying the banks to create money for the Treasury.) A federal administration can now spend far beyond its revenues, and grossly debase the currency, without even placing itself on the defensive before public opinion. On the other hand, the "principles" to which reactionaries would have us return are perhaps worse than none at all. That the old moral prohibitions have lost their force is here not altogether an occasion for regret. But we cannot get along without some such rules—without some moral sanctions and mandates which politicians must obey in matters of finance. And there is probably nothing more promising than the idea of a stable price-level as a symbol articulating deep-rooted sentiments and as a source of discipline in fiscal practice.[22]

A serious practical shortcoming of stable money programs lies in the fact that they are sponsored most vigorously by persons who want the price-level raised sharply before it is stabilized. Thus the scheme is likely to be realized, if at all, on the basis of dangerously large concessions to the demands of debtors, in terms of stabilization at a level involving serious maladjustments and internal strains, and under conditions which would present great difficulties in administration and execution. If the undertaking is to get under way auspiciously, it is imperative that the level chosen should be low enough to require only the minimum of action and display of power by the monetary authority during the trying first years. (The possibility that the level would be fixed too low is of theoretical, rather than practical, interest.) Drastic adminis-

[22] To assure popular approval, strong moral support, and thus political stability, it would be desirable, under a price-index rule, to employ an index whose changes would correspond roughly to changes in living-costs for families of modal income. Some weight certainly should be given to this consideration; but, adding it to those mentioned in n. 11, one sees that the best attainable index must fall far short of what is desirable on this, or on any other, particular criterion.

trative measures to overcome the inertia of an upward movement would jeopardize the political security of the rule and would also involve unfortunate disturbances in lines of business exposed to the direct impact of such measures. The advocates of stable money will do well not to offer the community one last big spree after the pledge is taken, and not to promise a perpetuity of blissful inebriation.

The issues which such proposals raise with respect to gold are issues which may largely be neglected for some years to come. In the United States we might stabilize on the basis of a price-index, while maintaining indefinitely the present gold price. Indeed, unless the orgy of devaluation which we invited in 1933 does finally occur, we shall, with world-recovery, find it easy both to maintain the present price of gold and to reduce continuously the enormous barrier to trade which our tariff legislation has erected. The possibilities of such a program are indicated in the report of the Commission of Inquiry into National Policy in International Economic Relations:[23]

It may be argued that, while there is unlikely to be any occasion for justifiable increase in the dollar price of gold, it might soon be expedient to lower the price: (*a*) to prevent a wastefully large accumulation of gold by the United States; (*b*) to promote distribution of our surplus stock among countries which have real need for additional reserves; (*c*) to check an over-rapid recovery or a potentially dangerous boom at home; or even (*d*) as one means of putting pressure on the reserves of a too rapidly expanding banking system. To any of these ends, however, a more attractive means is at hand, namely, reduction of our tariff duties, even beyond those already recommended. This strategy would afford us a better protection against an unhealthy boom and against over-large investment in gold; it would affect other nations in the same manner economically as would a lowering of our gold price; and it would probably be even more effective toward improving the spirit of international commercial relations.

Not least of the merits of this procedure is the prospect it offers for raising the internal prices of export products (notably, cotton and wheat) relative to other prices. Indeed, it might in the end prove to be an adequate justification of our recent gold policy, that it created this opportunity for gradually and systematically repairing the injury of our past tariff policy to agriculture. Our drastic devaluation, whatever its short-term effects, is

[23] *International Economic Relations*, pp. 96–98.

likely to lead, slowly and over a long period, to a rise of our price level which could serve no good purpose and might work serious injury. However, if we undertake by tariff reductions systematically to correct favorable balances of payments, and even to send abroad part of our present stock of gold, we could avoid the upward pressure on many industrial prices, while allowing our export staples to enjoy the full effect of the devaluation.

The scheme here proposed is perhaps more elegant in principle than it could ever be in actual application. But it may be worth noting that, just as devaluation offered to post-war France a means for returning to gold without internal deflation, so devaluation offers to the United States a means for scaling down its barriers to trade *without internal deflation*. This opportunity, moreover, presents itself, fortunately from the viewpoint of domestic politics, at a time when there is widespread demand for just the assistance to agriculture that it so clearly offers. Furthermore, an expression by our government of the intention to prevent, by this procedure, any enduring injury to foreign countries from our devaluation, would do much to smooth the way for future international understandings as to both monetary and commercial policy.

In this connection two observations are especially in point. (1) It is likely, in view of the condition of our balance of payments prior to devaluation, and in view of the prospect that many of the foreign measures for resisting gold drains will disappear with world recovery, that our present price of gold will prove distinctly excessive, unless measures are taken to offset the long-term effects of its sharp increase. (2) There are many strong considerations, not heretofore invoked in these pages, against resorting to reduction of our gold price in the future. Many of those who bitterly condemn our devaluation program will readily agree that little is now to be gained by trying merely to retrace our steps. If the rise in the price of gold may be held to have worked injury and injustice, it is still unlikely that reduction of that price at a much later date would accomplish much toward repairing the inequities. Those who lost (or gained) by the increase would be largely a different group from those who gained (or lost) from the reduction. Thus, all in all, a number of strong considerations appear to support the proposal for utilizing systematically the potentially large opportunities for tariff reduction which our recent devaluation promises to yield in the future. On this view, tariff reduction might be regarded as an agency of monetary stabilization for the near future and, quite consistently, as a means for helping agriculture at the same time.

The whole argument here may be regarded as supporting the position that our bargaining efforts should be directed especially toward concessions with regard to exchange controls, quota limitations, and similar barriers to our exports. These barriers, largely the product of the acute emergency, may be regarded in part as compensatory to our emergency gold policy. The prospect of their removal will depend partly on our willingness to make the concessions necessary to preservation of reasonable balance. The only major or equivalent concessions which we could offer are (1) reduction of our gold price and/or (2) lowering of our tariff barrier. There are reasons for our preferring the second of these, and no apparent reasons why it should not be equally attractive to other nations.

Price-level stabilization thus seems, on the whole, extremely attractive as the basis of a liberal-conservative policy in the field of money and government finance for the next decade. Whether the price-index rule would be as satisfactory under conditions which could be realized only over a longer period as the rule of a fixed quantity of money, may merit discussion in academic circles and may provide a promising point of departure for analysis and exposition; but the question is not of practical significance now. Given the inevitable limitations of any particular index, however, the former rule might ultimately acquire or manifest serious shortcomings. It is thus appropriate to observe that all the changes in our financial structure which seem necessary to make feasible the adoption of the fixed-quantity rule are changes which would also facilitate the operation of the price-index rule. The existence of a large volume of privately created money-substitutes, with alternate expansion and contraction, might tax seriously the powers of a monetary authority seeking to prevent price-level changes. Thus, if the stability of an index is to be maintained with the least resistance and the minimum of disturbing administrative measures, it is essential that the power to issue money and near-money should increasingly be concentrated in the hands of the central government.

As regards policies for the significant future, it therefore matters little whether price-level stabilization is conceived as a definitive reform or as a transition expedient in a long-term program pointed toward ultimate stabilization of the quantity of money. On either view, the same radical (if not drastic) changes in the field of private finance are clearly appropriate. Most of them, moreover, are necessary, on other grounds as well, for the preservation of economic freedom and political democracy.

CONCLUSIONS

The following observations may now be submitted, to define the author's general position and to guard against misinterpretation:

1. A democratic, free-enterprise system implies, and requires for its effective functioning and survival, a stable framework of definite rules, laid down in legislation and subject to change only gradually and with careful regard for the vested interests of participants in the economic game. It is peculiarly essential economically that there should be a minimum of uncertainty for enterprisers and investors as to monetary conditions in the future—and, politically, that the plausible expedient of setting up "authorities" instead of rules, with respect to matters of such fundamental importance, be avoided, or accepted only as a very temporary arrangement. The most important objective of a sound liberal policy, apart from the establishment of highly competitive conditions in industry and the narrow limitation of political control over relative prices, should be that of securing a monetary system governed by definite rule.

2. To assure adequate moral pressure of public opinion against legislative (and administrative) tinkering, the monetary rules must be definite, simple (at least in principle), and expressive of strong, abiding, pervasive, and reasonable popular sentiments. They should be designed to permit the fullest and most stable employment, to facilitate adjustment to such basic changes (especially in technology) as are likely to occur, and, secondarily, to minimize inequities as between debtors and creditors; but the problems here, while of first importance, should be conceived and dealt with mainly as problems of a transition period. Once well established and generally accepted as the basis of anticipations, any one of many different rules (or sets of rules) would probably serve about as well as another.

3. The responsibility for carrying out the monetary rules should be lodged in a federal authority, endowed with large administrative powers but closely controlled in their exercise by a sharply defined policy. The powers of the monetary authority should have to do primarily or exclusively with fiscal arrange-

ments—with the issue and retirement of paper money (open-market operations in government securities) and perhaps with the relation between government revenues and expenditures; in other words, the monetary rules should be implemented entirely by, and in turn should largely determine, fiscal policy.

4. Political control in this sphere should be confined exclusively to regulation of the quantity of money and near-money, the *direction* of investment (the allocation of investment funds) being left to the control of competition and kept as far as possible outside the influence of political agencies (or central banks).

5. A liberal program of monetary reform should seek to effect an increasingly sharp differentiation between money and private obligations and, especially, to minimize the opportunities for the creation of effective money-substitutes (whether for use as circulating media or in hoards) by private corporations. The abolition of private deposit-banking is clearly the appropriate first step in this direction, and would bring us in sight of the goal; but such a measure, to be really effective, must be accompanied, or followed closely, by drastic limitation on the formal borrowing-powers of all private corporations, and especially upon borrowing at short term.

6. A monetary rule of maintaining the constancy of some price-index, preferably an index of prices of competitively produced commodities, appears to afford the only promising escape from present monetary chaos and uncertainties. A rule calling for outright fixing of the total quantity of money, however, definitely merits consideration as a perhaps preferable solution in the more distant future. At least, it may provide a point of departure for fruitful academic discussion.

[10]

THE INTERPRETATION OF VOTING IN THE ALLOCATION OF ECONOMIC RESOURCES

Economic goods are of two types: individual goods and social goods. The two types are similar in that each serves the needs of human beings and each is produced only through the use of scarce resources. They differ, however, in the character of their demand. Individual goods are characterized by *divisibility*. They can be divided into small units over which particular persons can be given exclusive possession (e.g. carrots, sewing machines, barber services). Such goods are amenable to individual demand and to free consumer choice. The amount consumed by any individual can be adjusted to his particular tastes. Social goods, on the other hand, are not divisible into units that can be the unique possession of individuals. Rather, they tend to become part of the general environment — available to all persons within that environment (e.g. education, protection against foreign enemies, beautification of the landscape, flood control). Consequently, these goods cannot easily be sold to individual consumers and the quantities available to different individuals cannot be adjusted according to their respective tastes. The amount of the good must be set by a single decision applicable jointly to all persons. Social goods, therefore, are subject to collective or political rather than individual demand.

Economists have, on the whole, been preoccupied with the portion of economic activity relating to the production of individual goods. They have developed an impressive body of theory describing the enterprise economy under various conditions, and have formulated a set of principles for determining the most economical outputs of individual goods. But no comparable body of theory exists for social goods, despite the fact that the production of the latter — even in peacetime — uses up no less than a fifth of all available resources and that the relative importance of social goods is steadily growing. The purpose of the present paper is to show

how certain portions of conventional economic theory may be adapted to problems relating to the production of social goods.

According to accepted theory, a maximum of human satisfactions will be attained, through the use of a given supply of factors, if: (1) production is carried on in response to the free choices of individual consumers (providing the consumers make the "right" choices and income is distributed "correctly"),[1] (2) all units of each good and of each factor are priced uniformly, (3) the output of each constant- or increasing-cost industry is adjusted so that the price of the product is equal to average cost, and the output of each decreasing-cost industry is adjusted so that the price of the product is equal to marginal cost, (4) production is carried on with the least costly known methods, and (5) the price of each factor is set so that the demand for it is equal to the supply.[2]

The first three of these principles are not entirely relevant to the production of social goods, because such goods are not suitable for individual consumer demand. It will be shown, however, that these principles can be modified for use in determining the ideal output of social goods. The argument will proceed in three steps: (1) formulation of the basic principles to guide the production of social goods, (2) practical application of these principles, and (3) examination of problems in the distribution of costs.

Quantitative Measurement of Social Goods

In discussing the ideal output of social goods, it is necessary at the outset to establish meaningful units in which quantities of social goods may be measured. This raises certain difficulties, because most of the things ordinarily regarded as social goods are highly complex. Each comprises whole congeries of particular goods which can be provided in many different ways and in

1. By "right" consumer choices I mean simply those choices which make for proportionality between prices and marginal rates of substitution; by "correct" distribution of income, a distribution such that marginal satisfactions from income are equal, in terms of socially accepted valuations, for all persons.

2. See A. C. Pigou, Economics of Welfare, 4th ed., London, 1933; Oskar Lange et al., On the Economic Theory of Socialism, Minneapolis, 1938; Harold Hotelling, "The General Welfare in Relation to Problems of Taxation and of Railway Rates and Utility Rates," Econometrica, July, 1938, pp. 242–269; J. R. Hicks, "The Foundations of Welfare Economics," Economic Journal, December, 1939, pp. 696–712.

different combinations. For example, an increase in the "quantity" of education available in a given community may take the form of additional buildings, changes in curricula, inclusion of a greater number of students, addition of new educational units such as kindergartens or junior colleges, raising of minimum teacher requirements, etc. Thus, quantities of "education" cannot be measured in simple physical units of volume, time, or weight. There are, however, other practicable quantitative measures of education and other such similar complex social goods.

One approach is to treat separately each component element of the complex social good. Thus, instead of dealing with quantities of "education" taken as a whole, attention would be centered on buildings, equipment, number of teachers, training and grade of teachers, hours devoted to particular subjects, number of students participating, hours of instruction per day, days of instruction per year, etc. Reasonably satisfactory quantitative measures could be assigned to each of these components. This solution is essentially similar to that which is ordinarily applied in measuring quantities of individual goods. Here the good is defined, not in terms of complexes such as food, but in terms of particular components such as cane sugar or No. 2 red wheat. Another possible approach is to measure the quantity of complex social goods simply in terms of their money cost. This solution is based on the principle that any decision to change the quantity of a complex social good may be resolved into two distinguishable parts: (1) a decision as to the relative priorities of various particular component services, and (2) a decision as to the amount of the over-all increase or decrease. If the scale of priorities is established so that it is known what particular services are to be added with increasing expenditure and what services are to be dropped with decreasing expenditure, then the quantity of the complex social good can be usefully measured in terms of the amount of money expended.

Each of the two approaches is useful and each is applicable to certain practical situations. Whenever the scale of priorities is not definitely established or agreed upon, the separate treatment of each component in terms of physical units would be preferred. On the other hand, whenever the scale of priorities is clearly established or whenever the determination of the scale is to be referred to experts or representatives, the second approach of measuring quantities in terms of cost would be preferred.

The following analysis is arranged so that either of the two measures may be employed alternatively. If physical units are used, increasing, constant, or decreasing cost may apply, whereas if cost units are used, only constant cost may apply. It should be emphasized that the quantity of a social good, whatever measure is used, refers to the quantity available in the community as a whole, not necessarily to the amount available to any particular person or consumption unit.

Ideal Output of Social Goods

Suppose that the citizens of a given community are faced with the task of deciding how much public education should be made available. It is inevitable that the citizens will differ regarding this question. Some, perhaps, will wish to have no education under any circumstances, some will want no more than the three R's, and others will desire a highly developed system of schools. Assuming a "correct" distribution of income, each person's taste can be expressed by a curve indicating the amount of money he would be willing to give up in order to have successive additional quantities made available in the community. Such a curve would be analogous to an individual demand curve. It would express, for different possible quantities of education, the individual's marginal rate of substitution between education and other goods (money). A series of such curves of individual marginal substitution is shown in Figure 1 for a community which is assumed to contain three persons (MS_a, MS_b, MS_c). The marginal rates of substitution of the three individuals, for each quantity of education, can be added to give the total marginal rate of substitution of the entire population. In this way a "curve of total marginal substitution" (TMS in Figure 1) can be constructed, expressing the amount of money the members of the group collectively would be willing to give up in order to obtain successive units of education. This curve corresponds, as closely as is possible under the conditions, to the familiar curve of total demand.[3]

3. It must be noted that this curve differs from the familiar curve of total demand, which denotes the amount of a good that individuals are willing to buy at each of several prices. The demand curve is obtained by adding the number of units of the good that would be purchased by the various individuals at each possible price (horizontal addition); whereas the curve of total marginal

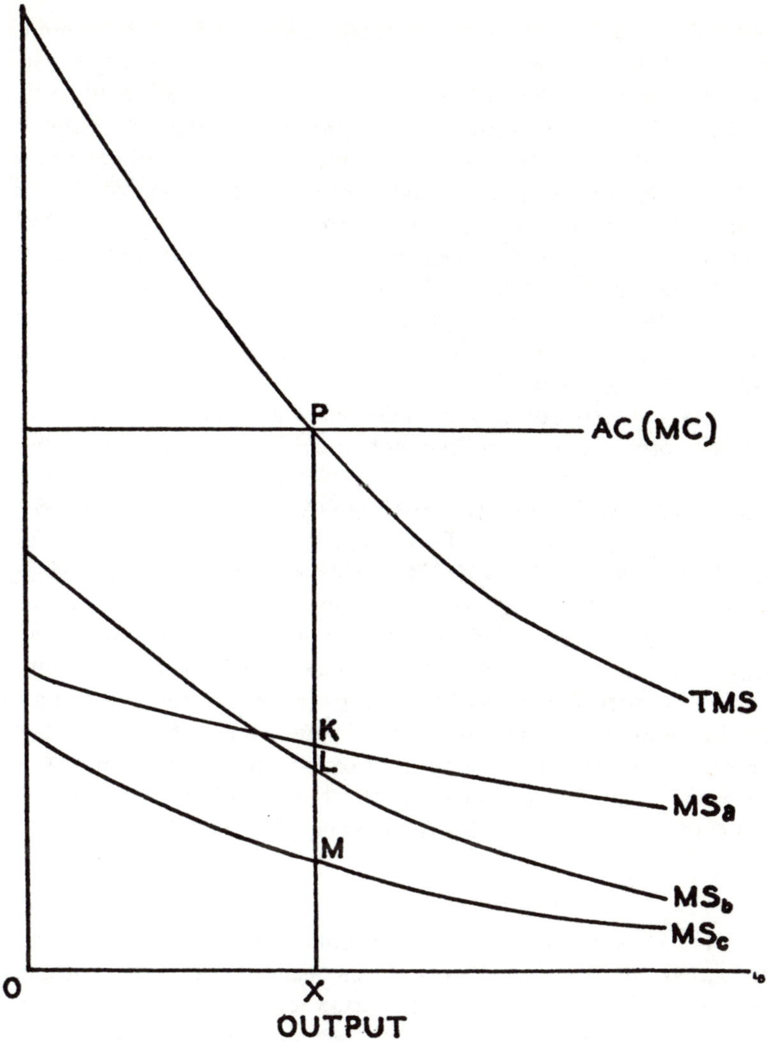

FIGURE 1

One of the cardinal principles in determining the output of an individual good is that price should equal cost, i.e. average cost or marginal cost, whichever is lower. This implies that the ideal out-

substitution is obtained by adding the marginal rates of substitution (expressed in money) of the various individuals at each possible quantity of the social good (vertical addition).

put is indicated by the point of intersection between the demand curve and the appropriate cost curve. Through the use of the curve of total marginal substitution, this principle can be adapted to the problem of determining the ideal output of a social good. Thus, to continue with our illustration, the ideal output of education is indicated by the point of intersection between the curve of total marginal substitution and the appropriate cost curve — which one depending upon whether increasing or decreasing cost prevails at relevant outputs. This is shown in Figure 1 (assuming constant cost) by the point of intersection (P) between the curve of total marginal substitution (TMS) and the curve of average cost (AC). OX is the ideal output.[4]

Ideal output can also be indicated in another way, which will prove more useful for subsequent analysis. For this, three new curves are required: (1) a curve expressing the average marginal rate of substitution per person (TMS/N), (2) a curve expressing average cost per person (AC/N), and (3) a curve expressing marginal cost per person (MC/N). These curves are derived by dividing the total marginal rate of substitution, average cost, and marginal cost, respectively, by the number of people (N). Ideal output, originally defined as the output at which the total marginal rate of substitution is equal to average (or marginal) cost, can also be designated as the output at which the average marginal rate of substitution is equal to average cost per person (or marginal cost per person). This follows since, at the output where AC (or MC) equals TMS, AC/N (or MC/N) must equal TMS/N. See Figure 2.

Individual Voting on Outputs

It has been shown that the optimum output of social goods is indicated by the intersection of the curve of average marginal substitution (TMS/N) and the appropriate curve of cost per person (AC/N or MC/N). If this formulation is to be practically useful, something must be known — directly or by inference — about marginal rates of substitution and costs. It is, of course, no more difficult to obtain information on the cost of producing social goods than to get similar data on individual goods; but to estimate marginal rates of substitution presents serious problems,

4. If there were no point of intersection between the two curves, i.e. if average cost were at all outputs greater than total marginal substitution, the service should not be offered at all.

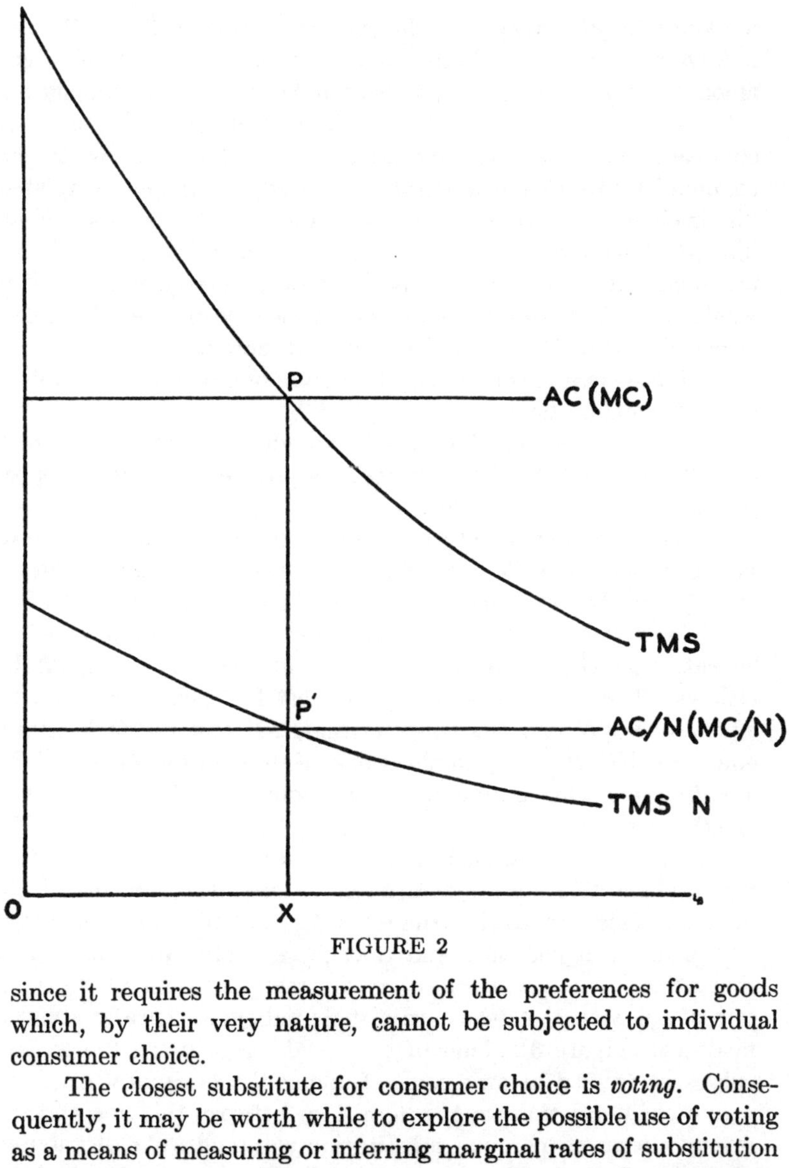

FIGURE 2

since it requires the measurement of the preferences for goods which, by their very nature, cannot be subjected to individual consumer choice.

The closest substitute for consumer choice is *voting*. Consequently, it may be worth while to explore the possible use of voting as a means of measuring or inferring marginal rates of substitution and hence of determining ideal output. Suppose that our community, faced with the problem of determining the precise quantity of education to provide, allows each individual to indicate, by means of voting, the amount of education that he prefers. Each individual's preference will depend upon two factors: (1) the relative amount of satisfaction *he* expects to derive from different amounts of education — as indicated by his curve of marginal substitution, and (2) the cost *to him* of different amounts of education. The latter will depend partly on the total cost to the community of different amounts and partly on the contemplated distribution of that cost among different individuals. Each individual will, of course, vote for that quantity at which *his* marginal rate of substitution is equal to *his* marginal cost. This would be indicated by the point of intersection between his curve of marginal substitution and his curve of marginal cost.

At this point it is necessary to digress briefly in order to introduce four assumptions:

First, it is assumed that all individuals in the community actually vote and that each expresses a preference which is appropriate to his individual interests.

Second, it is assumed that the cost to the community of providing various possible quantities of education is known. Curves AC, AC/N, MC and MC/N can then be constructed.

Third, it is assumed that the cost of whatever amount of education is to be "produced" will be divided equally among all the citizens. Thus the curve of average cost for each citizen will be equal to AC/N and the curve of marginal cost for each citizen equal to MC/N. The implications of this assumption will be analyzed in a later section on the distribution of the cost of social goods.

Fourth, it is assumed that the several curves of individual marginal substitution are distributed according to the normal law of error. This implies that there is a large number of such curves — one for each person — and that these curves are arranged so that at *each quantity of education* the marginal rates of substitution of the several persons are distributed symmetrically about a mode (see Figure 3). Thus, if a vertical line, cutting the several curves, is erected at any point Z along the horizontal axis, the points of intersection (a, b, c, d, e, f, g) between this line and the several curves of marginal substitution will tend to be distributed along the line according to the normal law of error. Most of the intersections will occur near the mode (d), but some will occur at varying distances above and below the mode. Indeed, a modal curve can be drawn indicating the position of the mode at each

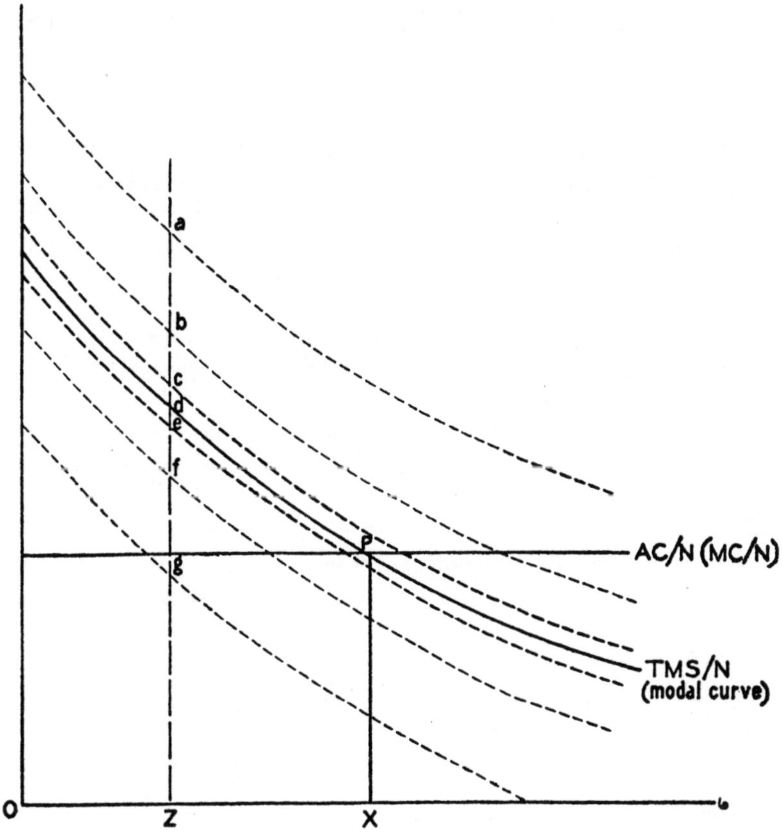

FIGURE 3

quantity of output, and this modal curve will, still assuming a symmetrical distribution of the curves, coincide with the curve of average marginal substitution (TMS/N).[5]

This assumption can conform to the facts of individual preference only if two conditions are met. (*a*) The tastes or desires of

5. In a symmetrical distribution the mode and the arithmetic mean are identical. It is to be noted, however, that the symmetry of a frequency distribution may be disturbed by the fact that zero is the lower limit of the data. In terms of the present problem, zero represents the lowest possible marginal rate of substitution (except in cases where the commodity is so abundant as to be a nuisance). At relatively large outputs, therefore, the marginal rate of substitution of some individuals would be zero, and the modal marginal rate of substitution would be less than the average per capita.

individuals must actually be distributed according to the normal law of error. Whether this condition is realized in practice is not known definitely, but available information suggests that it is not an unreasonable hypothesis. For example, the data in the Consumer Purchases Study of the United States Department of Agriculture indicate that consumer tastes for individual goods are distributed normally. Three series from this study, selected from hundreds of similar series, are shown in Table I. (*b*) All individ-

TABLE I

PERCENTAGE DISTRIBUTION OF FAMILIES BY EXPENDITURES FOR VARIOUS PURPOSES: WHITE, NON-RELIEF, NATIVE-BORN FAMILIES, 1935–36[1]

Annual Expenditures for Food: farm families with three or more children, and with incomes from $1,000 to $1,499 per year, Middle Atlantic and North Central States[2]		Annual Expenditures for Clothing: village families with two young children and with incomes from $1,500 to $1,999, Pennsylvania and Ohio[3]		Total Annual Expenditure for Family Living: small city families with incomes from $2,000 to $2,249, North Central States[4]	
Expenditure	Percentage of Families	Expenditure	Percentage of Families	Expenditure	Percentage of Families
$50–$99	4%	Under $50	4%	$750– $999	2%
100–149	16			1,000–1,249	8
150–199	25	$50–$99	15	1,250–1,499	13
200–249	17	100–149	28	1,500–1,749	21
250–299	19	150–199	33	1,750–1,999	29
300–349	9	200–249	16	2,000–2,249	17
350–399	5	250–299	4	2,250–2,499	5
400–449	3			2,500–2,999	4
450 or over	2			3,000–3,499	1
Total	100	Total	100	Total	100

1 Data based on Consumer Purchases Study made by the United States Department of Agriculture in coöperation with the Work Projects Administration.
2 U. S. D. A., Miscellaneous Publication, No. 405, 1941, p. 14.
3 U. S. D. A., Miscellaneous Publication, No. 422, 1941, p. 17.
4 U. S. D. A., Miscellaneous Publication, No. 396, 1940, p. 33.

uals must be potentially in an equal position to benefit from the social good. This condition is not always realized in practice. For example, childless persons may be less interested in education than families with children. Thus, even though the curves of marginal substitution of either class of persons might be arranged symmetrically, the distribution of the curves for the two classes together might be significantly skewed or multi-modal. However, most social goods are or can be made available on relatively equal terms to all persons, e.g. health services, protection from foreign enemies, maintenance of law and order, etc. For the moment, therefore, we shall postulate that all individuals are equally able to benefit from the social good under consideration. In this way, we may continue with the assumption that individual marginal substitutions are distributed according to the normal law of error. Later we shall take up the problem of social goods which are not equally available to all.

Under the conditions assumed, if the citizens are allowed to vote on the quantity of education to be provided, each person will vote for the quantity indicated by the intersection between his individual curve of marginal substitution and his curve of marginal cost (MC/N). Since the various individuals will presumably be interested in education to varying degrees, as indicated by the dispersion of the individual curves of marginal substitution, a wide variety of preferences will be indicated. Referring to Figure 3, those whose curves of marginal substitution lie in the lower left part of the diagram will favor a relatively small amount; those whose curves of marginal substitution lie in the upper right will favor a relatively large amount. But, assuming that the curves of marginal substitution are distributed according to the normal law of error, one intermediate amount (OX) will be voted for by more individuals than any other single amount. The individuals voting for this quantity are those whose marginal rates of substitution are modal, and the amount voted for by this modal group may be presumed to indicate the point of intersection (P) between the curve of marginal cost per person (MC/N) and the modal or average curve of marginal substitution (TMS/N). Thus voting makes possible the location of one point (P) on the curve of average marginal substitution (TMS/N), namely, the point at which the curve of individual marginal cost (MC/N) intersects with (TMS/N).[6] See Figure 3.

If education is "produced" under conditions of constant cost, as shown in Figure 3, marginal and average cost will be identical. Hence the modal vote will indicate not only the point of intersection between TMS/N and MC/N but also the point of intersection between TMS/N and AC/N. This latter point, as stated above, occurs at the optimum output. Hence the modal vote pro-

6. In order to designate this point of intersection, it is not necessary that the majority of *all* the voters should prefer this amount. It is only necessary that more persons vote for this amount than for any other.

vides direct information as to the most economical amount of education to provide.

If education is "produced" under decreasing cost, the modal vote will also give the desired information directly. In this case the marginal cost curve (MC/N) lies below the average cost curve (AC/N). However, the most economical output is that at which the marginal rate of substitution and marginal (rather than average) cost are equal. Thus the modal vote directly indicates the most economical output.

If, however, education is produced under conditions of increasing cost, the modal vote cannot directly denote optimum output. It can indicate only the point of intersection between MC/N and TMS/N, not the point of intersection between AC/N and TMS/N which is required. A further elaboration of our technique is therefore necessary.

This case requires a different procedure of taxation. The cost must be raised by means of a tax levied upon each individual in the form of a "price" per unit of the social good, it being understood (1) that the price is to remain constant regardless of output, and (2) that the price is to be uniform for all individuals. From the point of view of any one individual, this "price" represents his marginal cost. His marginal cost curve would appear, therefore, as a horizontal line, the height of which would be determined by the "price." Moreover, since the same "price" would be charged all individuals, the marginal cost curve would be the same for all. This curve is shown in Figure 4 as IMC (individual marginal cost).

Let us now suppose that the "price" of education is set, and that the citizens are asked to vote on the quantity of education they prefer. Each person will, of course, vote for the quantity indicated by the intersection between his curve of marginal substitution and the curve of marginal cost (IMC), and the modal vote will locate the point of intersection (R) between TMS/N and IMC. The optimum output, however, is determined by the intersection of TMS/N and AC/N; the modal vote does not locate this point. From the position of point R relative to curve AC/N, it can be ascertained, however, whether the intersection of TMS/N and AC/N lies to the right or to the left of point R.

If R is above curve AC/N, then the point of intersection lies to the right of R,[7] and output should be increased beyond the

7. Assuming that curve TMS/N slopes negatively.

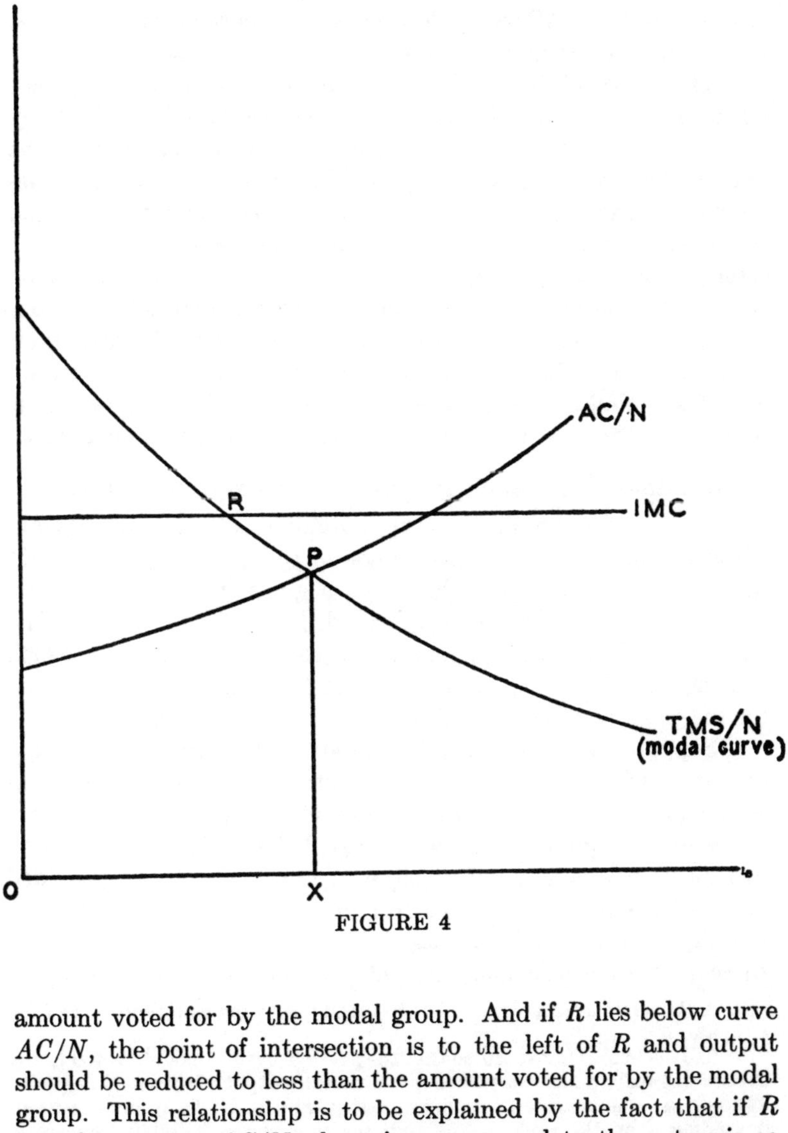

FIGURE 4

amount voted for by the modal group. And if R lies below curve AC/N, the point of intersection is to the left of R and output should be reduced to less than the amount voted for by the modal group. This relationship is to be explained by the fact that if R lies above curve AC/N, the price announced to the voters is so high that (at this price) the modal group prefer less than the optimum amount of the good; and if R is below curve AC/N, the price is so low that the modal group prefer more than the optimum amount. Only when R lies on curve AC/N (i.e., when curves

AC/N, *IMC*, and *TMS/N* all intersect at the same time) will the vote of the modal group indicate the optimum output.

The result of the voting depends entirely on the price announced. The question arises, then, whether there is any rule by which the correct price could be ascertained in advance of the voting. The answer is in the negative. However, as a result of successive trials and errors over a period of time the correct price could be closely approached, especially since (1) the direction of the error is known after each trial, and (2) more than one point on the *TMS/N* curve would be known after several trials.[8] It is conceivable, moreover, that the voters might be asked to indicate their preferences at each of several possible prices, so that the position of *TMS/N* could be ascertained along several points and the intersection of *TMS/N* and *AC/N* could be located immediately.[9]

Individual Voting on Increments to Existing Outputs

Let us now assume that the individuals of a community are permitted to vote, not on how much of the good they prefer, but rather on whether or not they wish a given increment or decrement to the quantity already provided. This situation is illustrated by school elections, common in the United States, in which citizens are asked to vote "yes" or "no" on a proposed bond issue for the purpose of constructing a new school building.

Suppose the community is composed of seven persons whose marginal substitution curves are distributed symmetrically, as shown in Figure 5, and that the cost of education (or any increment in the quantity) is to be divided equally among them. Assume that quantity OX (Figure 5) is actually being provided and that the people are asked to vote on the question whether or not they wish a small increase in the quantity up to OX_2. All those persons whose marginal rates of substitution at quantity

8. This raises a problem similar to that of deducing a demand curve from a time series.

9. It is tempting to assume that the average of the amounts voted for by the several individuals represents the optimum output. In fact, it does not. The average amount voted for will be greater or less than the optimum output, depending upon the slope, shape, and position of the individual curves of marginal substitution. Similarly, the assumption that the curves of marginal substitution are distributed according to the normal law of error in no way implies that the results of the *voting* will also be distributed in the same way. The distribution of the vote may be skewed in either direction — depending on the shape of the curves — without violating the assumption that the curves are distributed according to the normal law of error.

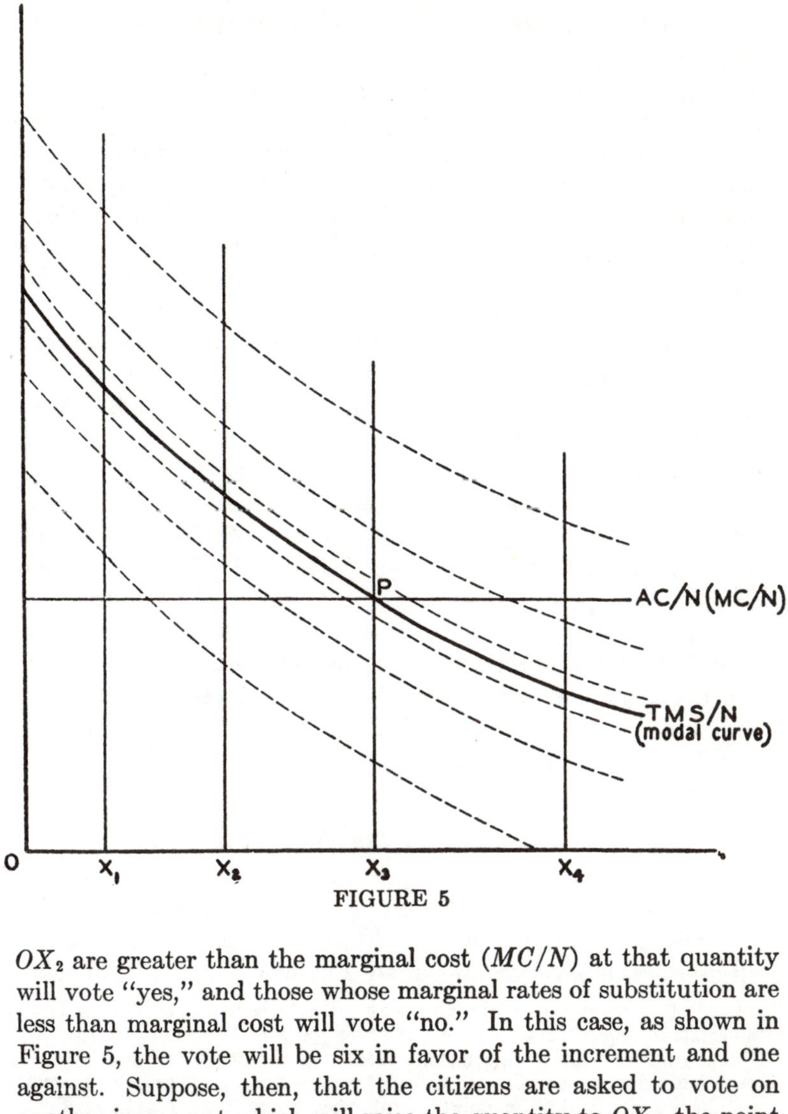

FIGURE 5

OX_2 are greater than the marginal cost (MC/N) at that quantity will vote "yes," and those whose marginal rates of substitution are less than marginal cost will vote "no." In this case, as shown in Figure 5, the vote will be six in favor of the increment and one against. Suppose, then, that the citizens are asked to vote on another increment which will raise the quantity to OX_3, the point at which MC/N and TMS/N are equal. On this question, one-half the citizens will vote "yes" and one-half "no." Finally, suppose the citizens are asked to vote on still another increment which will increase the quantity to OX_4. This time, six persons will vote against and one will be in favor.

From these illustrations it may be seen that as the quantity of education is increased, bit by bit, a majority of the voters will favor each additional increment until a quantity is reached such that the average marginal rate of substitution (TMS/N) is equal to marginal cost (MC/N). At this point the vote is equally divided. Beyond this point, the majority of the voters are opposed to additional increments. Thus it is possible to locate the point of intersection between curves TMS/N and MC/N by finding an increment (or decrement), through trial and error, which is favored by one-half of the voters and opposed by the other half.

This procedure makes possible the direct determination of optimum output for "industries" subject to constant cost and decreasing cost. In these cases, the intersection of TMS/N and MC/N determines the most economical quantity of the social good. This procedure does not, however, directly give the answer for "industries" of increasing cost. For them, it is the point of intersection between curves TMS/N and AC/N (not between TMS/N and MC/N) which must be located. This can be done, but only by a procedure so awkward as to be virtually useless.[1]

On the whole, the procedure of voting on increments does not lend itself well to the determination of optimum output. For constant and decreasing cost "industries" it is somewhat more complicated than the method of asking voters to indicate the quantities they prefer, and for increasing cost "industries" it is hopeless.

Alternatives to Voting

In a society which has outgrown the town-meeting stage, it is seldom practicable to decide on the output of specific social goods by means of popular voting. More commonly, public officials (legislators, elected or appointed administrators, dictators, etc.)

1. Several separate trial and error procedures would be involved. First an arbitrary fixed "price" per unit of education would be set, so that the curve of marginal cost for the individuals (IMC) would be a horizontal line. Then each individual would be asked to vote "yes" or "no" on successive increments or decrements, until the point of intersection between IMC and TMS/N could be determined. It would be located at the increment for which one-half the voters are in favor and one-half opposed. After that, in order to find the intersection of AC/N and TMS/N, it would be necessary to adjust the price and again ask voters to express preferences on increments (or decrements), so that other points on the curve TMS/N could be located. By a wearisome process, it might ultimately be possible to find enough points on curve TMS/N so that the intersection between that curve and AC/N could be located.

are endowed with the power to make such decisions and are expected to act in the "general interest." This means that such officials, if they are to carry out their duties, must have methods of finding out what the people want, i.e. how much of each social good should be produced.

The people can be consulted by letting them vote on particular questions, or perhaps letting them vote for candidates who identify themselves with particular policies. In this case, if the issues are clearly understood, the results of the election can be interpreted as suggested in the preceding sections. In practice, however, the issues are seldom clear-cut. The result of an election can seldom be regarded as an unequivocal indication of public desires. Hence there is a real need for other techniques of gauging public opinion, i.e. finding the points of intersection between the curves of total marginal substitution and average (or marginal) cost. It is for this reason that a number of writers have recently suggested the possibility of using polls, questionnaires, interviews, budget investigations, and other devices involving samples, to study the desires of the individuals who compose the public. Indeed, with the increasing emphasis upon economic planning, it is imperative that these and other techniques for discovering individual tastes and preferences be developed and employed.[2]

If a poll is based on a representative sample of the population, and if the questions are put in the same way as if the entire citizenry were voting, the results can of course be interpreted in exactly the same way. For such a poll to be as reliable as the results of actual voting, however, several conditions would have to be met.[3] First, it would be necessary that the issue had been discussed sufficiently to enable the pollees to become informed. Second, in order to be sure that the individual pollees would use thought and discretion in reaching their decisions, it would be necessary for them to have a sense of responsibility, i.e. to feel that their choices would actually influence policy.

2. See Maurice Dobb, Review of Economic Studies, February, 1935, pp. 137–148; and Barbara Wootton, Lament for Economics, London, 1938, Chapters 5 and 6, especially pp. 289–291.

3. The polling of a "scientifically" selected sample might produce more accurate results than general voting, unless arrangements were made to insure that every person would actually vote. If voting is voluntary, it is possible that the results may represent the preference of a biased sample of the population, including a relatively large proportion of, perhaps, the "politically minded," the well-to-do, or the better educated.

It is conceivable that techniques involving polls and questionnaires would yield information in greater detail than could be obtained through large-scale voting. It might be possible in this way to carry on minute studies of individual preferences, so that actual curves showing marginal rates of substitution, instead of merely a few isolated points on curves, could be obtained.[4]

Distributing the Cost of Social Goods

In the discussion of voting it has been consistently assumed that the cost of providing social goods is to be divided equally among all individuals. This assumption requires further examination. If income were distributed "correctly," so that apportionment of the cost of social goods would not be designed for the purpose of redistributing income, the benefit principle would provide the ideal basis for assessing the costs of social goods. Each person would contribute according to the benefit received by him, and the distribution of real income would be unaffected. In applying the benefit principle, each individual would be charged *as if* he were paying a price per unit for the social good, the price being equal to his marginal rate of substitution at the particular amount of the good being produced. Thus, instead of applying a uniform price to all individuals and allowing each to adjust his consumption according to that price, as with individual goods, a uniform amount of the social good would be provided, and the "price" charged individuals would vary according to their marginal rates of substitution. Referring to Figure 1, if quantity OX were being provided, Individual A would pay a "price" equal to XK, and his contribution would be equal to this price multiplied by the number of units of the good provided (OX). The "price" charged Individual A under this arrangement would be such that, if free individual consumer choice were possible, he would choose the particular quantity of the social good that is actually available.[5] In this way his marginal contribution to the cost of the social good would correspond to his marginal rate of substitution, and his real income would remain

4. The work of Professor L. L. Thurstone in deriving the indifference schedules of actual individuals is suggestive. See his article "The Indifference Function," Journal of Social Psychology, 1931, pp. 139–167. The difficulty with this approach is that individuals must be asked what they would do under various hypothetical conditions. There is always the possibility that verbal preferences would differ significantly from actual choices in a real situation.

5. If the social good were financed in this way, all individuals would vote for the same output, namely, the most economical quantity.

unchanged. Any other arrangement would result in his being made worse or better off. Similarly, the "price" charged Individual B would be *XL*, and the "price" charged Individual C would be *XM* (Figure 1). Thus the total amount paid by the three individuals would be equal to the total cost of the service.[6]

The application of the benefit principle is difficult, however, because of problems involved in the measurement of benefit. To determine the cost that should be assessed against an individual, if the benefit principle is to apply, requires that something be known about his marginal rates of substitution. At first thought it might be supposed that this information could be obtained from his vote (or other expression of preference). But the individual could not vote intelligently, unless he knew *in advance* the cost to him of various amounts of the social good, and in any case the results of the voting would be unreliable if the individual suspected that his expression of preference would influence the amount of cost to be assessed against him. Moreover, the practical administrative problem of making nice adjustments between individual benefit and cost would be insuperable.

On the whole, the possibility of distributing costs according to benefit is not very promising. It seems clear that some more or less arbitrary alternative method must be adopted. The problem is to find that arbitrary method which will involve the least error and the fewest practical problems. With an initially "correct" distribution of income, an *equal* distribution of cost seems most practicable. This means, of course, that the provision of social goods may involve the redistribution of income. Those individuals who are forced to pay more in taxes than they get back in benefits will find their real incomes diminished, whereas those who pay out less than they receive in return will enjoy an addition to their real incomes. The seriousness of this redistribution is greatly lessened, however, by the fact that many social goods are ordinarily produced simultaneously. Thus the gain to any one individual from the

6. An exception to this solution for the problem of distributing the burden of costs must be made in the case of a social good provided under conditions of decreasing cost. Here economy requires that output be increased to the point where total marginal substitution is equal to marginal cost. At this output, however, if each individual beneficiary were to contribute an amount equal to his marginal rate of substitution times the number of units of the good produced, total revenue would be insufficient to defray total cost. In this case, therefore, it would be necessary to devise an alternative method that would raise sufficient revenue and yet leave the distribution of incomes unaffected.

provision of a particular social good may be counterbalanced by a loss to him resulting from the provision of another social good, and on balance the redistribution of income may be slight.

The great advantage of the equal distribution of cost is that it involves only random errors, whereas any other arbitrary distribution introduces a constant bias in favor of some particular group or class. It also has the advantage that it helps to clarify the desires of the public regarding the distribution of social goods. If costs are not distributed equally, variations in amounts voted for by different individuals would depend quite as much upon differences in individual marginal costs as upon differences in individual marginal rates of substitution, and the modal vote would not necessarily indicate the point of intersection between the curve of marginal (or average) cost per capita and the curve of average marginal substitution. Indeed, if the output of social goods is to be determined by the preferences of individuals, it must be possible to obtain expressions of individual preferences unalloyed by differences in individual marginal costs. In other words, a necessary condition to the use of individual preferences in determining the ideal output of social goods is that the cost of social goods be distributed equally. Since equal distribution of cost is desirable on other grounds, as pointed out, this condition does not necessarily render the technique of voting impracticable or objectionable.

It must also be recognized that the condition of equal distribution of cost does not in any way preclude the use of taxation for purposes of redistributing income. It is required only that redistributive taxes be levied independently of taxes for the purpose of financing the production of social goods. This is, of course, at variance with present practice. Commonly the functions of redistributing income and of providing funds for public services are merged into a single tax system. Under these conditions, any expressions of preference on the part of individual citizens are ambiguous in that they reflect not only marginal rates of substitution but also (different) marginal costs.

Neither does the condition of equal distribution of cost require that incomes be distributed equally. The only assumption is that the distribution of income is "correct" in the sense that it is socially accepted. Thus, if some individuals have more income than others, they may well vote for more of a particular social good than others, with less income — if the cost of the social good is uniformly dis-

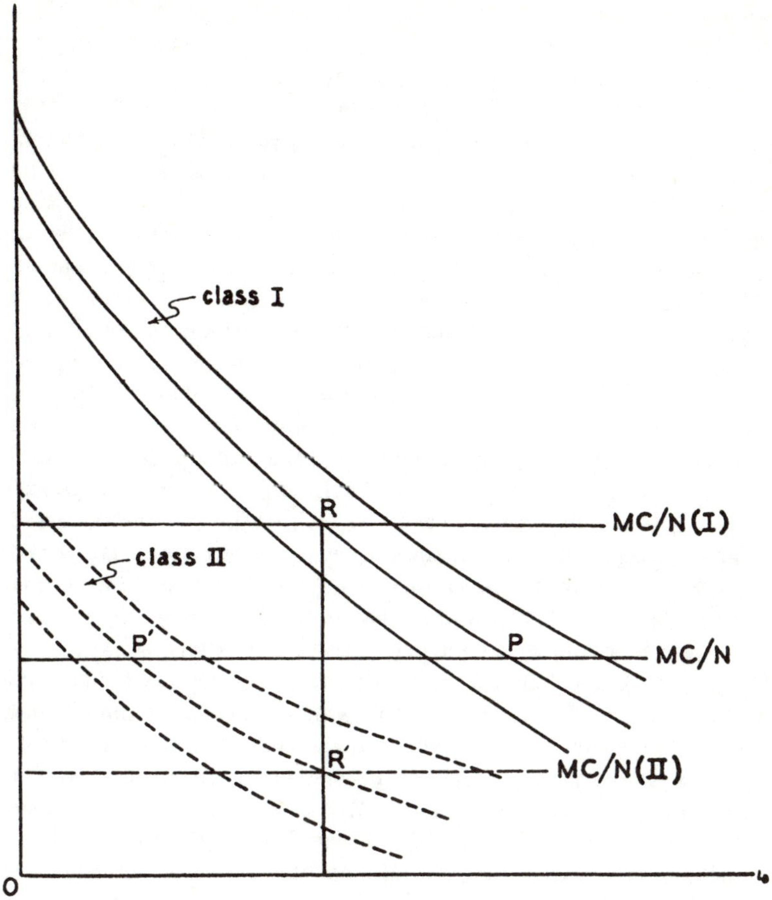

FIGURE 6

tributed. This corresponds exactly to the fact that the individuals with larger incomes buy more individual goods than persons with smaller incomes. The fact that such differences in income are socially sanctioned implies that the preferences of richer persons ought to count for more than that of the poorer persons in determining the allocation of the society's resources.

SOCIAL GOODS NOT EQUALLY AVAILABLE TO ALL VOTERS

Up to this point it has been assumed that any social good voted upon is accessible to all voters upon equal terms, and that differences in individual preferences are to be accounted for solely by differences in taste. This postulate, however, does not always conform to practical reality. When it does not, recourse to the benefit principle becomes more necessary and at the same time more practicable. It would then be desirable to classify the voters according to the amount of potential benefit that they would be expected to derive from the social good, and to tabulate the voting separately for each class. The intersection of the modal curve of marginal substitution and the curve of marginal cost per person (MC/N) could then be located for each class. For example, in Figure 6, the curves of marginal substitution for a group of citizens (Class I) who are in a position to benefit greatly from a social good are shown in solid lines, and the curves of marginal substitution for those able to benefit to a much smaller degree (Class II) are shown in dotted lines. The modal vote of the first group is indicated by P and of the second group by P^1. In such a situation, application of the benefit principle would require that the cost assessed against citizens of Class I should be increased and that levied against citizens of Class II decreased, until two conditions are satisfied: (1) the modal output voted for by persons of Class I (indicated by point R) is equal to that voted for by persons of Class II (point R^1), and (2) the entire cost of providing the social good is covered. The difficulty with this solution is that if the citizens realize that their voting affects the amount of cost they will be expected to bear, individually or as a class, the results of the voting will tend to be unreliable. Hence the cost to be levied on the several groups must be determined (apparently or in fact) without reference to the voting. Hence other methods of estimating potential benefit — drawing heavily upon common sense — are undoubtedly necessary. Such techniques are illustrated by the methods used in many American cities of distributing special assessments for street improvements. By such methods only very rough adjustments, for obvious and clear-cut differences in potential benefit, can be made.

Howard R. Bowen.

Washington, D. C.

[11]

THE PURE THEORY OF PUBLIC EXPENDITURE

Paul A. Samuelson

1\. *Assumptions.* Except for Sax, Wicksell, Lindahl, Musgrave, and Bowen, economists have rather neglected the theory of optimal public expenditure, spending most of their energy on the theory of taxation. Therefore, I explicitly assume two categories of goods: ordinary *private consumption goods* $(X_1, \cdots, X_n)$ which can be parcelled out among different individuals $(1, 2, \cdots, i, \cdots, s)$ according to the relations $X_j = \sum_1^s X^i_j$; and *collective consumption goods* $(X_{n+1}, \cdots, X_{n+m})$ which all enjoy in common in the sense that each individual's consumption of such a good leads to no subtraction from any other individual's consumption of that good, so that $X_{n+j} = X^i_{n+j}$ simultaneously for each and every ith individual and each collective consumptive good. I assume no mystical collective mind that enjoys collective consumption goods; instead I assume each individual has a consistent set of *ordinal preferences* with respect to his consumption of all goods (collective as well as private) which can be summarized by a regularly smooth and convex utility index $u^i = u^i(X^i_1, \cdots, X^i_{n+m})$ (any monotonic stretching of the utility index is of course also an admissible cardinal index of preference). I shall throughout follow the convention of writing the partial derivative of any function with respect to its jth argument by a j subscript, so that $u^i_j = \partial u^i/\partial X^i_j$, etc. Provided economic quantities can be divided into two groups, (1) *outputs* or goods which everyone always wants to maximize and (2) inputs or factors which everyone always wants to minimize, we are free to change the algebraic signs of the latter category and from then on to work only with "goods," knowing that the case of factor inputs is covered as well. Hence by this convention we are sure that $u^i_j > 0$ always.

To keep production assumptions at the minimum level of simplicity, I assume a regularly convex and smooth production-possibility schedule relating totals of all outputs, private and collective; or $F(X_1, \cdots, X_{n+m}) = 0$, with $F_j > 0$ and ratios F_j/F_n determinate and subject to the generalized laws of diminishing returns.

Feasibility considerations disregarded, there is a *maximal* (ordinal) *utility frontier* representing the Pareto-optimal points — of which there are an $(s-1)$fold infinity — with the property that from such a frontier point you can make one person better off only by making some other person worse off. If we wish to make normative judgments concerning the relative ethical desirability of different configurations involving some individuals being on a higher level of indifference and some on a lower, we must be presented with a set of ordinal interpersonal norms or with a *social welfare function* representing a consistent set of ethical preferences among all the possible states of the system. It is not a "scientific" task of the economist to "deduce" the form of this function; this can have as many forms as there are possible ethical views; for the present purpose, the only restriction placed on the social welfare function is that it shall always increase or decrease when any one person's ordinal preference increases or decreases, all others staying on their same indifference levels: mathematically, we narrow it to the class that any one of its indexes can be written $U = U(u^1, \cdots, u^s)$ with $U_j > 0$.

2\. *Optimal Conditions.* In terms of these norms, there is a "best state of the world" which is defined mathematically in simple regular cases by the marginal conditions

$$\frac{u^i_j}{u^i_r} = \frac{F_j}{F_r} \qquad \begin{matrix}(i = 1, 2, \cdots, s;\ r, j = 1, \cdots, n) \text{ or} \\ (i = 1, 2, \cdots, s;\ r = 1;\ j = 2, \cdots, n)\end{matrix} \qquad (1)$$

$$\sum_{i=1}^{s} \frac{u^i_{n+j}}{u^i_r} = \frac{F_{n+j}}{F_r} \qquad \begin{matrix}(j = 1, \cdots, m;\ r = 1, \cdots, n) \text{ or} \\ (j = 1, \cdots, m;\ r = 1)\end{matrix} \qquad (2)$$

$$\frac{U_i u^i_k}{U_q u^q_k} = 1 \qquad \begin{matrix}(i, q = 1, \cdots, s;\ k = 1, \cdots, n) \text{ or} \\ (q = 1;\ i = 2, \cdots, s;\ k = 1).\end{matrix} \qquad (3)$$

Equations (1) and (3) are essentially those given in the chapter on welfare economics in my *Foundations of Economic Analysis*. They constitute my version of the "new welfare economics." Alone (1) represents that subset of relations which defines the Pareto-optimal utility frontier and which by itself represents what I regard as the unnecessarily narrow version of what once was called the "new welfare economics."

The new element added here is the set (2), which constitutes a pure theory of government expenditure on collective consumption goods. By themselves (1) and (2) define the $(s-1)$-fold infinity of utility frontier points; only when a set of interpersonal normative conditions equivalent to (3) is supplied are we able to define an unambiguously "best" state.

Since formulating the conditions (2) some years ago, I have learned from the published and unpublished writings of Richard Musgrave that their essential logic is contained in the "voluntary-exchange" theories of public finance of the Sax-Wicksell-Lindahl-Musgrave type, and I have also noted Howard Bowen's independent discovery of them in Bowen's writings of a decade ago. A graphical interpretation of these conditions in terms of *vertical* rather than *horizontal* addition of different individuals' marginal-rate-of-substitution schedules can be given; but what I must emphasize is that there is a different such schedule for each individual at each of the $(s-1)$fold infinity of different distributions of relative welfare along the utility frontier.

3. *Impossibility of decentralized spontaneous solution.* So much for the involved optimizing equations that an omniscient calculating machine could theoretically solve if fed the postulated functions. No such machine now exists. But it is well known that an "analogue calculating machine" can be provided by competitive market pricing, (a) so long as the production functions satisfy the neoclassical assumptions of constant returns to scale and generalized diminishing returns and (b) so long as the individuals' indifference contours have regular convexity and, we may add, (c) so long as all goods are private. We can then insert between the right- and left-hand sides of (1) the equality with uniform market prices p_j/p_r and adjoin the budget equations for each individual

$$p_1X^i_1 + p_2X^i_2 + \cdots + p_nX^i_n = L^i \quad (i = 1, 2, \cdots, s), \qquad (1)'$$

where L^i is a lump-sum tax for each individual so selected in algebraic value as to lead to the "best" state of the world. Now note, if there were no collective consumption goods, then (1) and (1)′ can have their solution enormously simplified. Why? Because on the one hand perfect competition among productive enterprises would ensure that goods are produced at minimum costs and are sold at proper marginal costs, with all factors receiving their proper marginal productivities; and on the other hand, each individual, in seeking as a competitive buyer to get to the highest level of indifference subject to given prices and tax, would be led as if by an Invisible Hand to the grand solution of the social maximum position. Of course the institutional framework of competition would have to be maintained, and political decision-making would still be necessary, but of a computationally minimum type: namely, algebraic taxes and transfers $(L^1, \ldots L^s)$ would have to be varied until society is swung to the ethical observer's optimum. The servant of the ethical observer would not have to make explicit decisions about each person's detailed consumption and work; he need only decide about generalized purchasing power, knowing that each person can be counted on to allocate it optimally. In terms of communication theory and game terminology, each person is motivated to do the signalling of his tastes needed to define and reach the attainable-bliss point.

Now all of the above remains valid even if collective consumption is not zero but is instead *explicitly set* at its optimum values as determined by (1), (2), and (3). *However no decentralized pricing system can serve to determine optimally these levels of collective consumption.* Other kinds of "voting" or "signalling" would have to be tried. But, and this is the point sensed by Wicksell but perhaps not fully appreciated by Lindahl, now it is in the selfish interest of each person to give *false* signals, to pretend to have less interest in a given collective consumption activity than he really has, etc. I must emphasize this: taxing according to a benefit theory of taxation can not at all solve the computational problem in the decentralized manner possible for the first category of "private" goods to which the ordinary market pricing applies and which do not have the "external effects" basic to the very notion of collective consumption goods. Of course, utopian voting and signalling schemes can be imagined. ("Scandinavian consensus," Kant's "categorical imperative," and other devices meaningful only under conditions of "symmetry," etc.) The failure of market catallactics in no way denies the following truth: given sufficient knowledge the optimal decisions can always be found by scanning over all the attainable states of the world and selecting the one which according to the postulated ethical welfare function is best. The solution "exists"; the problem is how to "find" it.

One could imagine every person in the community being indoctrinated to behave like a "parametric decentralized bureaucrat" who *reveals* his preferences by signalling in response to price parameters or Lagrangean multipliers, to questionnaires, or to other devices. But there is still this fundamental technical difference going to the heart of the whole problem of *social* economy: by departing from his indoctrinated rules, any one person can hope to snatch some selfish benefit in a way not possible under the self-policing competitive pricing of private goods; and the "external economies" or "jointness of demand" intrinsic to the very concept of collective goods and governmental activities makes it impossible for the grand ensemble of optimizing equations to have that special pattern of zeros which makes *laissez-faire* competition even *theoretically* possible as an analogue computer.

4. *Conclusion.* To explore further the problem raised by public expenditure would take us into the mathematical domain of "sociology" or "welfare politics," which Arrow, Duncan Black, and others have just begun to investigate. Political economy can be regarded as one special sector of this general domain, and it may turn out to be pure luck that within the general domain there happened to be a subsector with the "simple" properties of traditional economics.

[12]

THE JOURNAL OF
POLITICAL ECONOMY

Volume LVII DECEMBER 1949 *Number 6*

THE MARSHALLIAN DEMAND CURVE

MILTON FRIEDMAN[1]

ALFRED MARSHALL's theory of demand strikingly exemplifies his "impatience with rigid definition and an excessive tendency to let the context explain his meaning."[2] The concept of the demand curve as a functional relation between the quantity and the price of a particular commodity is explained repeatedly and explicitly in the *Principles of Economics:* in words in the text, in plane curves in the footnotes, and in symbolic form in the Mathematical Appendix. A complete definition of the demand curve, including, in particular, a statement of the variables that are to be considered the same for all points on the curve and the variables that are to be allowed to vary, is nowhere given explicitly. The reader is left to infer the contents of *ceteris paribus* from general and vague statements, parenthetical remarks, examples that do not purport to be exhaustive, and concise mathematical notes in the Appendix.

In view of the importance of the demand curve in Marshallian analysis, it is natural that other economists should have constructed a rigorous definition to fill the gap that Marshall left. This occurred at an early date, apparently without controversy about the interpretation to be placed on Marshall's comments. The resulting definition of the demand curve is now so much an intrinsic part of current economic theory and is so widely accepted as Marshall's own that the assertion that Marshall himself gave no explicit rigorous definition may shock most readers.

Yet why this particular interpretation evolved and why it gained such unquestioned acceptance are a mystery that requires explanation. The currently accepted interpretation can be read into Marshall only by a liberal—and, I think, strained—reading of his remarks, and its acceptance implicitly convicts him of log-

[1] I am deeply indebted for helpful criticism and suggestions to A. F. Burns, Aaron Director, C. W. Guillebaud, H. Gregg Lewis, A. R. Prest, D. H. Robertson, G. J. Stigler, and, especially, Jacob Viner, to whose penetrating discussion of the demand curve in his course in economic theory I can trace some of the central ideas and even details of this article. The standard comment that none is to be held responsible for the views expressed herein has particular relevance, since most disagreed with my interpretation of Marshall as presented in an earlier and much briefer draft of this article.

[2] C. W. Guillebaud, "The Evolution of Marshall's *Principles of Economics*," *Economic Journal*, LII (December, 1942), 333.

ical inconsistency and mathematical error at the very foundation of his theory of demand. More important, the alternative interpretation of the demand curve that is yielded by a literal reading of his remarks not only leaves his original work on the theory of demand free from both logical inconsistency and mathematical error but also is more useful for the analysis of most economic problems.

Section I presents the two interpretations of the demand curve and compares them in some detail; Section II argues that a demand curve constructed on my interpretation is the more useful for the analysis of practical problems, whatever may be the verdict about its validity as an interpretation of Marshall; Section III demonstrates that my interpretation is consistent with Marshall's monetary theory and with his work on consumer's surplus; and Section IV presents the textual evidence on the validity of my interpretation. Finally, Section V argues that the change that has occurred in the interpretation of the demand curve reflects a corresponding change in the role assigned to economic theory.

I. ALTERNATIVE INTERPRETATIONS OF MARSHALL'S DEMAND CURVE

The demand curve of a particular group (which may, as a special case, consist of a single individual) for a particular commodity shows the quantity (strictly speaking, the maximum quantity) of the commodity that will be purchased by the group per unit of time at each price. So far, no question arises; this part of the definition is explicit in Marshall and is common to both alternatives to be discussed. The problem of interpretation relates to the phrase, "other things the same," ordinarily attached to this definition.

In the first place, it should be noted that "same" in this phrase does not mean "same over time." The points on a demand curve are alternative possibilities, not temporally ordered combinations of quantity and price. "Same" means "same for all points on the demand curve"; the different points are to differ in quantity and price and are not to differ with respect to "other things."[3] In the second place, "all" other things cannot be supposed to be the same without completely emasculating the concept. For example, if (*a*) total money expenditure on all commodities, (*b*) the price of every commodity other than the one in question, and (*c*) the quantity purchased of every other commodity were supposed to be the same, the amount of money spent on the commodity in question would necessarily be the same at all prices, simply as a matter of arithmetic, and the demand curve would have unit elasticity everywhere.[4] Different specifications of the "other things" will yield different demand curves. For example,

[3] Of course, when correlations among statistical time series are regarded as estimates of demand curves, the hypothesis is that "other things" have been approximately constant over time or that appropriate allowance has been made for changes in them. Similarly, when correlations among cross-section data are regarded as estimates of demand curves, the hypothesis is that "other things" are approximately the same for the units distinguished or that appropriate allowance has been made for differences among them. In both cases the problem of estimation should be clearly distinguished from the theoretical construct to be estimated.

[4] Yet Sidney Weintraub not only suggests that Marshall intended to keep *a*, *b*, and *c* simultaneously the same but goes on to say: "Clearly Marshall's assumption means a unit elasticity of demand in the market reviewed and no ramifications elsewhere; that was why he adopted it" ("The Foundations of the Demand Curve," *American Economic Review*, XXXII [September, 1942], 538–52, quotation from n. 12, p. 541). Weintraub even adds the condition of constant tastes and preferences to *a*, *b*, and *c*, speaking of a change in tastes as shifting the demand curve. Obviously, *a*, *b*, and *c* together leave no room for tastes and preferences or, indeed, for anything except simple arithmetic.

one demand curve will be obtained by excluding *b* from the list of "other things"; another, quite different one, by excluding *c*.

a) THE CURRENT INTERPRETATION

The current interpretation of Marshall's demand curve explicitly includes in the list of "other things" (1) tastes and preferences of the group of purchasers considered; (2) their money income, and (3) the price of every other commodity. The quantities of other commodities are explicitly considered as different at different points on the demand curve, and still other variables are ignored.[5]

On this interpretation, it is clear that, while money income is the same for different points on the demand curve, real income is not. At the lower of two prices for the commodity in question, more of some commodities can be purchased without reducing the amounts purchased of other commodities. The lower the price, therefore, the higher the real income.

[5] Explicit definition of the demand curve in this way by followers of Marshall dates back at least to 1894 (see F. Y. Edgeworth, article on "Demand Curves" in *Palgrave's Dictionary of Political Economy*, edited by Henry Higgs [rev. ed.; London: Macmillan & Co., Ltd., 1926]). Edgeworth's article apparently dates from the first edition, which was published in 1894. While Edgeworth does not explicitly attribute this interpretation to Marshall, it is clear from the context that he is talking about a Marshallian demand curve and that he does not regard his statements as inconsistent in any way with Marshall's *Principles*. Though no explicit listing of "other things" is given by J. R. Hicks, *Value and Capital* (Oxford, 1939), the list given above is implicit throughout chaps. i and ii, which are explicitly devoted to elaborating and extending Marshall's analysis of demand. For statements in modern textbooks on advanced economic theory see G. J. Stigler, *The Theory of Price* (New York: Macmillan Co., 1946), pp. 86–90, and Kenneth E. Boulding, *Economic Analysis* (rev. ed., New York: Harper & Bros., 1948), pp. 134–35.

b) AN ALTERNATIVE INTERPRETATION

It seems to me more faithful to both the letter and the spirit of Marshall's writings to include in the list of "other things" (1) tastes and preferences of the group of purchasers considered, (2) their real income, and (3) the price of every closely related commodity.

Two variants of this interpretation can be distinguished, according to the device adopted for keeping real income the same at different points on the demand curve. One variant, which Marshall employed in the text of the *Principles*, is obtained by replacing "(2) their real income" by (2*a*) their money income and (2*b*) the "purchasing power of money." Constancy of the "purchasing power of money" for different prices of the commodity in question implies compensating variations in the prices of some or all other commodities. These variations will, indeed, be negligible if the commodity in question accounts for a negligible fraction of total expenditures; but they should not be disregarded, both because empirical considerations must be sharply separated from logical considerations and because the demand curve need not be limited in applicability to such commodities. On this variant, all commodities are, in effect, divided into three groups: (*a*) the commodity in question, (*b*) closely related commodities, and (*c*) all other commodities. The absolute price of each commodity in group *b* is supposed to be the same for different points on the demand curve; only the "average" price, or an index number of prices, is considered for group *c;* and it is to be supposed to rise or fall with a fall or rise in the price of group *a*, so as to keep the "purchasing power of money" the same.

The other variant, which Marshall employed in the Mathematical Appendix of the *Principles*, is obtained by retaining "(2) their real income" and adding (4) the average price of all other commodities. Constancy of real income for different prices of the commodity in question then implies compensating variations in money income. As the price of the commodity in question rises or falls, money income is to be supposed to rise or fall so as to keep real income the same.

These two variants are essentially equivalent mathematically,[6] but the assumption of compensating variations in other prices is easier to explain verbally and can be justified as empirically relevant by considerations of monetary theory, which is presumably why Marshall used this variant in his text. On the other hand, the assumption of compensating variations in income is somewhat more convenient mathematically, which is presumably why Marshall used this variant in his Mathematical Appendix.

On my interpretation, Marshall's demand curve is identical with one of the constructions introduced by Slutsky in his famous paper on the theory of choice, namely, the reaction of quantity demanded to a "compensated variation of price," i.e., to a variation in price accompanied by a compensating change in money income.[7] Slutsky expressed the compensating change in money income in terms of observable phenomena, taking it as equal to the change in price *times* the quantity demanded at the initial price. Mosak has shown that, in the

[6] Let x and y be the quantity and price, respectively, of the commodity in question; x' and y' the quantity and price of a composite commodity representing all other commodities; and m, money income. Let

$$x = g(y, y', m, u) \tag{1}$$

be the demand curve for the commodity in question, given a utility function,

$$U = U(x, x', u) , \tag{2}$$

where u is a parameter to allow for changes in taste, and subject to the condition

$$xy + x'y' = m . \tag{3}$$

From eq. (3) and the usual utility analysis, it follows that eq. (1), like eq. (3), is a homogeneous function of degree zero in y, y', and m; i.e., that

$$g(\lambda y, \lambda y', \lambda m, u) = g(y, y', m, u) . \tag{4}$$

On the current interpretation, a two-dimensional demand curve is obtained from eq. (1) directly by giving y' (other prices), m (income), and u (tastes) fixed values. A given value of y then implies a given value of x from eq. (1), a given value of x' from eq. (3), and hence a given value of U (i.e., real income) from eq. (2). The value of U will vary with y, being higher, the lower y is.

On my alternative interpretation, u and U are given fixed values and x' is eliminated from eqs. (2) and (3). This gives a pair of equations,

$$x = g(y, y', m, u_0) , \tag{5}$$

$$U_0 = U_0\left(x, \frac{m - xy}{y'}, u_0\right) , \tag{6}$$

where the subscript o designates fixed values. The two-dimensional variant involving compensating variations in other prices is obtained by eliminating y' from eqs. (5) and (6) and giving m a fixed value; the variant involving compensating variations in income, by eliminating m from eqs. (5) and (6) and giving y' a fixed value.

The homogeneity of eqs. (5) and (6) in y, y', and m means that x is a function only of ratios among them. Thus eqs. (5) and (6) can be written:

$$\left.\begin{aligned} x = g(y, y', m, u_0) &= g\left(\frac{y}{m}, \frac{y'}{m}, 1, u_0\right) \\ &= g\left(\frac{y}{y'}, 1, \frac{m}{y'}, u_0\right) , \end{aligned}\right\} \tag{5'}$$

$$\left.\begin{aligned} U_0 &= U_0\left(x, \frac{m - xy}{y'}, u_0\right) \\ &= U_0\left(x, \frac{1 - x\frac{y}{m}}{\frac{y'}{m}}, u_0\right) \\ &= U_0\left(x, \frac{m}{y'} - x\frac{y}{y'}, u_0\right) . \end{aligned}\right\} \tag{6'}$$

The choice of price-compensating variations is equivalent to selecting the forms of these two equations in the next to the last terms of eqs. (5') and (6'); of income-compensating variations, to selecting the forms in the last terms.

[7] Eugenio Slutsky, "Sulla teoria del bilancio del consumatore," *Giornale degli economisti*, LI (1915), 1–26, esp. Sec. 8.

limit, the change in income so computed is identical with the change required to keep the individual on the same level of utility (on the same indifference curve).[8] It follows that a similar statement is valid for compensating changes in other prices. In the limit, the change in other prices required to keep the individual on the same indifference curve when his money income is unchanged but the price of one commodity varies is identical with the change in other prices required to keep unchanged the total cost of the basket of commodities purchased at the initial prices, i.e., to keep unchanged the usual type of cost-of-living index number.

c) COMPARISON OF THE INTERPRETATIONS

The relation between demand curves constructed under the two interpretations is depicted in Figure 1. Curve *Cc* represents a demand curve of an individual consumer for a commodity *X* drawn on the current interpretation. Money income and the prices of other commodities are supposed the same for all points on it; in consequence, real income is lower at *C* than at *P*, since, if the individual sought to buy *OM* of *X* at a price of *OC*, he would be forced to curtail his purchases of something else. As the curve is drawn, of course, he buys none of *X* at a price of *OC*, spending the sum of *OHPM* on other commodities that his action at a price of *OH* shows him to value less highly than he does *OM* units of *X*. The ordinate is described as the ratio of the price of *X* to the price of other commodities. For the demand curve *Cc* this is a question only of the unit of measure, since other prices are supposed to be the same for all points on it.

From the definition of the demand curve *Cc*, *OC* is obviously the maximum price per unit that an individual would be willing to pay for an infinitesimal initial increment of *X* when his money income and the prices of other commodities have the values assumed in drawing *Cc*. Let us suppose him to purchase this amount at a price of *OC*, determine the

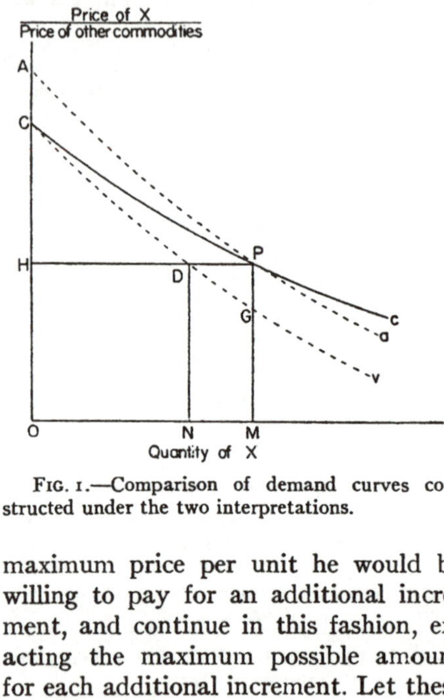

FIG. 1.—Comparison of demand curves constructed under the two interpretations.

maximum price per unit he would be willing to pay for an additional increment, and continue in this fashion, exacting the maximum possible amount for each additional increment. Let these successive maximum prices per unit define the curve *Cv*. The consumer obviously has the same real income at each point on *Cv* as at *C*, since the maximum price has been extracted from him for each successive unit, so that he has gained no utility in the process.

Cv is now a demand curve constructed according to my interpretation of Marshall. If other prices are supposed to be the same, the necessary compensating

[8] Jacob L. Mosak, "On the Interpretation of the Fundamental Equation of Value Theory," in O. Lange, F. McIntyre, and T. O. Yntema, *Studies in Mathematical Economics and Econometrics* (Chicago: University of Chicago Press, 1942), pp. 69–74, esp. n. 5, pp. 73–74, which contains a rigorous proof of this statement by A. Wald.

variations in money income as the price of X falls are given by triangular areas exemplified by HCD for a price of OH: OH is the maximum price per unit that the individual will give for an additional infinitesimal increment of X when he has spent $OCDN$ for ON of X out of his initial income of, say, m; but his situation is exactly the same if, when the price of X is OH, his income is $(m - HCD)$ and he spends $OHDN$ on X; he has the same amount left to spend on all other commodities, their prices are the same, and he has the same amount of X; accordingly, his demand price will be the same, and he will buy ON of X at a price of OH and an income of $(m - HCD)$.[9]

If compensating variations in other prices rather than in money income are used to keep real income the same, the absolute price of neither X nor other commodities can be read directly from Figure 1. For each ratio of the price of X to the price of other commodities, the quantity of X purchased will be that shown on Cv. But the prices of other goods will vary along Cv, rising as the relative price of X falls, so the absolute price of X can no longer be obtained by multiplying the ordinate by a single scale factor.

Figure 1 is drawn on the assumption that X is a "normal" commodity, that is, a commodity the consumption of which is higher, the higher the income. This is the reason Cv is drawn to the left of Cc—at every point on Cv other than C, real income is less than at the corresponding point on Cc; hence less X would be consumed.

Curve Aa represents a demand curve on my interpretation of Marshall for a real income the same as at point P on Cc; it is like Cv but for a higher real income. Real income is higher on Aa than on Cc for prices above OH, lower for prices below OH, which is the reason Aa is to the right of Cc for prices above OH and to the left of Cc for prices below OH.

d) WHY TWO INTERPRETATIONS ARE POSSIBLE

The possibility of interpreting Marshall in these two quite different ways arises in part from the vagueness of Marshall's exposition, from his failure to give precise and rigorous definitions. A more fundamental reason, however, is the existence of inconsistency in the third and later editions of the *Principles*. In that edition Marshall introduced the celebrated passage bearing on the Giffen phenomenon. This passage and a related sentence added at the same time to the

[9] In the notation of n. 6, except that u is omitted for simplicity, the quantities of X and X' that will be purchased for any given values of y and y' and any given real income, U_0, are obtained by solving simultaneously:

$$\frac{U_x}{U_{x'}} = \frac{y}{y'}, \quad (1)$$

and

$$U(x, x') = U_0, \quad (2)$$

where U_x and $U_{x'}$ stand for the partial derivatives of U with respect to x and x', respectively, i.e., for the marginal utility of X and X'. The solution of these equations gives the demand curve on my interpretation of Marshall, using compensating variations in money income.

$U_0(0, m/y')$ is the utility at C in the diagram. For any given amount of X and given value of y', the amount of X' purchased is obtained by solving

$$U(x, x') = U_0\left(0, \frac{m}{y'}\right), \quad (3)$$

which is identical with eq. (2). The amount paid for X (the area under Cv) is

$$m - x'y'. \quad (4)$$

The maximum price that will be paid per unit of X is the derivative of eq. (4), or

$$y = -\frac{dx'}{dx}y' = \frac{U_x}{U_{x'}}y', \quad (5)$$

which is identical with eq. (1). It follows that Cv is a demand curve constructed on my interpretation of Marshall.

Mathematical Appendix fit the current interpretation better than they fit my interpretation. Although these are the only two items that I have been able to find in any edition of the *Principles* of which this is true, they provide some basis for the current interpretation. A hypothesis to explain the introduction of this inconsistency into the *Principles* is offered in Section IV*e* below.

II. THE RELATIVE USEFULNESS OF THE TWO INTERPRETATIONS

The relative usefulness of the two interpretations of the demand curve can be evaluated only in terms of some general conception of the role of economic theory. I shall use the conception that underlies Marshall's work, in which the primary emphasis is on positive economic analysis, on the forging of tools that can be used fairly directly in analyzing practical problems. Economic theory was to him an "engine for the discovery of concrete truth."[10] "Man's powers are limited: almost every one of nature's riddles is complex. He breaks it up, studies one bit at a time, and at last combines his partial solutions with a supreme effort of his whole small strength into some sort of an attempt at a solution of the whole riddle."[11] The underlying justification for the central role of the concepts of demand and supply in Marshall's entire structure of analysis is the empirical generalization that an enumeration of the forces affecting demand in any problem and of the forces affecting supply will yield two lists that contain few items in common. Demand and supply are to him concepts for organizing materials, labels in an "analytical filing box." The "commodity" for which a demand curve is drawn is another label, not a word for a physical or technical entity to be defined once and for all independently of the problem at hand. Marshall writes:

> The question where the lines of division between different commodities should be drawn must be settled by convenience of the particular discussion. For some purposes it may be best to regard Chinese and Indian teas, or even Souchong and Pekoe teas, as different commodities; and to have a separate demand schedule for each of them. While for other purposes it may be best to group together commodities as distinct as beef and mutton, or even as tea and coffee, and to have a single list to represent the demand for the two combined.[12]

a) THE DISTINCTION BETWEEN CLOSELY RELATED AND ALL OTHER COMMODITIES

A demand function containing as separate variables the prices of a rigidly defined and exhaustive list of commodities, all on the same footing, seems largely foreign to this approach. It may be a useful expository device to bring home the mutual interdependence of economic phenomena; it cannot form part of Marshall's "engine for the discovery of concrete truth." The analyst who attacks a concrete problem can take explicit account of only a limited number of factors; he will inevitably separate commodities that are closely related to the one immediately under study from commodities that are more distantly related. He can pay some attention to each closely related commodity. He cannot handle the more distantly related commodities in this way; he will tend either to ignore

[10] Alfred Marshall, "The Present Position of Economics" (1885), reprinted in *Memorials of Alfred Marshall*, ed. A. C. Pigou (London: Macmillan & Co., Ltd., 1925), p. 159.

[11] Alfred Marshall, "Mechanical and Biological Analogies in Economics" (1898), *ibid.*, p. 314.

[12] Marshall, *Principles of Economics* (8th ed.; London: Macmillan & Co., Ltd., 1920), p. 100 n. All subsequent page references to the *Principles*, unless otherwise stated, are to the eighth and final edition.

them or to consider them as a group. The formally more general demand curve will, in actual use, become the kind of demand curve that is yielded by my interpretation of Marshall.

The part of the Marshallian filing box covered by *ceteris paribus* typically includes three quite different kinds of variables, distinguished by their relation to the variable whose adaptation to some change is directly under investigation (e.g., the price of a commodity): (*a*) variables that are expected both to be materially affected by the variable under study and, in turn, to affect it; (*b*) variables that are expected to be little, if at all, affected by the variable under study but to materially affect it; (*c*) the remaining variables, expected neither to affect significantly the variable under study nor to be significantly affected by it.

In demand analysis the prices of closely related commodities are the variables in group *a*. They are put individually into the pound of *ceteris paribus* to pave the way for further analysis. Holding their prices constant is a provisional step. They must inevitably be affected by anything that affects the commodity in question; and this indirect effect can be analyzed most conveniently by first isolating the direct effect, systematically tracing the repercussions of the direct effect on each closely related commodity, and then tracing the subsequent reflex influences on the commodity in question. Indeed, in many ways, the role of the demand curve itself is as much to provide an orderly means of analyzing these indirect effects as to isolate the direct effect on the commodity in question.

The average price of "all other commodities," income and wealth, and tastes and preferences are the variables in group *b*. These variables are likely to be affected only negligibly by factors affecting primarily the commodity in question. On the other hand, any changes in them would have a significant effect on that commodity. They are put into the pound in order to separate problems, to segregate the particular reactions under study. They are put in individually and explicitly because they are so important that account will have to be taken of them in any application of the analysis.

Price changes within the group of "all other commodities" and an indefinitely long list of other variables are contained in group *c*. These variables are to be ignored. They are too numerous and each too unimportant to permit separate account to be taken of them.

In keeping with the spirit of Marshallian analysis this classification of variables is to be taken as illustrative, not definitive. What particular variables are appropriate for each group is to be determined by the problem in hand, the amount of information available, the detail required in results, and the patience and resources of the analyst.

b) CONSTANCY OF REAL INCOME

It has just been argued that any actual analysis of a concrete economic problem with the aid of demand curves will inevitably adopt one feature of my interpretation of Marshall—consideration of a residual list of commodities as a single group. For somewhat subtler reasons this is likely to be true also of the second feature of my interpretation of Marshall—holding real income constant along a demand curve. If an analysis, begun with a demand curve constructed on the current interpretation, is carried through and made internally consistent, it will be found that the demand curve has been subjected to shifts that, in effect, result from failure to keep real income constant along the demand curve.

An example will show how this occurs. Let us suppose that the government grants to producers of commodity *X* a subsidy of a fixed amount per unit of output, financed by a general income tax, so that money income available for expenditure (i.e., net of tax and gross of subsidy) is unchanged. For simplicity, suppose, first, that no commodities are closely related to *X* either as rivals or as complements, so that interrelations in consumption between *X* and particular other commodities can be neglected; second, that the tax is paid by individuals in about the same income class and with about the same consumption pattern as those who benefit from the subsidy, so that complications arising from changes in the distribution of income can be neglected; and, third, that there are no idle resources. Let *DD* in Figure 2 be a demand curve for commodity *X*, and *SS* be the initial supply curve for *X*, and let the initial position at their intersection, point *P*, be a position of full equilibrium. The effect of the subsidy is to lower the supply curve to *S′S′*. Since we have ruled out repercussions through consumption relations with other markets and through changes in the level or distribution of money income, it is reasonable to expect that the intersection of this new supply curve and the initial demand curve, point *P′*, will itself be a position of full equilibrium, involving a lower price and larger quantity of *X*. Yet, if the demand curve is constructed on the current interpretation and if the supply curve is not perfectly inelastic,[13] point *P′* is not a position of full equilibrium. This can be seen most easily by supposing *DD* to have unit elasticity, so that the same amount is spent on *X* at *P′* as at *P*. The same amount is then available to spend on all other commodities, and, since their prices are supposed to be the same for all points on *DD* under the current interpretation, the same quantity of each of them will be demanded. But then where do the resources come from to produce the extra *MN* units of *X?* Obviously, our as-

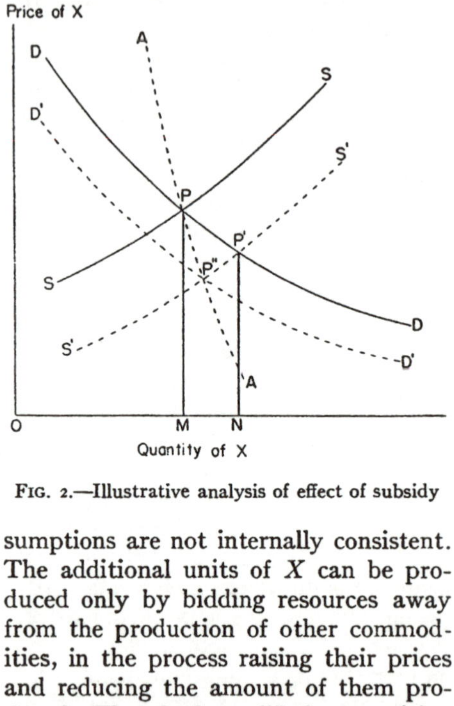

FIG. 2.—Illustrative analysis of effect of subsidy

sumptions are not internally consistent. The additional units of *X* can be produced only by bidding resources away from the production of other commodities, in the process raising their prices and reducing the amount of them produced. The final equilibrium position will therefore involve higher prices and lower quantities of other commodities. But, on the current interpretation, this means a shift in the demand curve for *X*—say, to *D′D′*—and a final equilibrium position of, say, *P.″*[14]

[13] If it is perfectly inelastic, neither the price nor the quantity of *X* is changed, so the new position of equilibrium coincides with the old; but the demand curve will pass through the initial position of equilibrium whether constructed on the current interpretation or on mine; hence the two coincide at the one point on them that is relevant.

[14] *D′D′* will not necessarily be to the left of *DD* even for a "normal" commodity. The reason is that the ordinate of Fig. 2 measures the absolute price of *X*, so that ordinates of the same height on *DD*

The assumption that the elasticity of *DD* is unity is not, of course, essential for this argument. If the elasticity of *DD* is less than unity, a larger amount than formerly is available to spend on other commodities; at unchanged prices this means a larger quantity demanded. In consequence, while the additional amount of resources required to produce the increased amount of *X* demanded is smaller when *DD* is inelastic than when it has unit elasticity, this is counterbalanced by increased pressure for resources to produce other commodities. Similarly, when *DD* is elastic, the additional amount of resources required to produce the increased quantity of *X* demanded is larger than when *DD* has unit elasticity, but some resources are released in the first instance from the production of other commodities.

No such internal inconsistency as that just outlined arises if the demand curve is constructed by keeping real income the same. Curve *AA* is such a demand curve. At prices of *X* less than *PM*, prices of other commodities are supposed to be sufficiently higher than at *P* to keep real income the same, which involves the release of just enough resources so that the position of final equilibrium, P'', lies on the demand curve so constructed—at least for small changes in the price of *X*.[15]

The fundamental principle illustrated by this example can be put more generally. The reason why a demand curve constructed under the current interpretation fails to give the correct solution even when all disturbing influences can be neglected is that each point on it implicitly refers to a different productive capacity of the community. A reduction in the price of the commodity in question is to be regarded as enabling the community, if it so wishes, to consume more of some commodities—this commodity or others—without consuming less of any commodity. But the particular change in supply whose consequences we sought to analyze—that arising from a subsidy —does not make available any additional resources to the community; any increase in the consumption of the commodity in question must be at the expense of other commodities. The conditions for which the demand curve is drawn are therefore

and *D'D'* represent different ratios of the price of *X* to the price of other commodities. If the ordinate measured the ratio of the price of *X* to the price of other commodities, *D'D'* would always be to the left of *DD* for "normal" commodities, always to the right for "inferior" commodities.

[15] Let X' be a single composite commodity representing all commodities other than X; x and x', the quantities of X and X'; and y and y', their prices. Let the subscript 1 refer to values at the initial position of equilibrium, P; the subscript 2, to values at the final position, P''. The condition of constant total expenditures means that

$$x_1y_1 + x_1'y_1' = x_2y_2 + x_2'y_2' \,. \tag{1}$$

As was pointed out above (Sec. I*b*), in the limit, holding real income constant is equivalent to holding constant the cost of a fixed basket of commodities. Thus, if P'' is considered close to P,

$$x_1y_1 + x_1'y_1' = x_1y_2 + x_1'y_2' \,. \tag{2}$$

In the neighborhood of P, y_1 can be regarded as the cost per unit of producing X; y_1', as the cost per unit of producing X'. The condition that sufficient resources be released to permit the production of the requisite additional amount of X is therefore

$$(x_2 - x_1)y_1 = -(x_2' - x_1')y_1' \,, \tag{3}$$

which is equivalent to

$$x_1y_1 + x_1'y_1' = x_2y_1 + x_2'y_1' \,. \tag{4}$$

But, in the limit, eqs. (1) and (2) imply eq. (4), as can be seen by subtracting eq. (2) from eq. (1) and replacing y_2 and y_2' in the result by $(y_2 - y_1 + y_1)$ and $(y_2' - y_1' + y_1')$, respectively.

More generally, constant real income involves keeping a price index unchanged; constant use of resources involves keeping a quantity index unchanged; and, in the limit, a constant price index and constant total expenditures imply a constant quantity index.

Note that *AA* need not be steeper than *DD* in a graph like Fig. 2. The point in question is that commented on in n. 14.

inconsistent with the conditions postulated on the side of supply. On the other hand, if the demand curve is constructed by keeping "real income" the same, no such inconsistency need arise. True, constant "real income" in the sense of "utility" and constant "real income" in the sense of outputs attainable from a fixed total of resources are different concepts, but they converge and can be treated as the same in the neighborhood of a position of equilibrium.

Of course, not all shifts in supply that it is desired to analyze arise in ways that leave the productive capacity of the community unaltered. Many involve a change in productive capacity—for example, changes in supply arising from improvements in technology or the discovery of previously unknown resources. Even in these cases, however, a demand curve constructed on the current interpretation will not serve. There is no reason to expect the differences in productive capacity implicit in constant money income and constant prices of other goods to bear any consistent relation to the change in productive capacity arising on the side of supply.[16] The better plan, in these cases, is to allow separately and directly for the increase in productive capacity by redrawing the demand curves to correspond to an appropriately higher real income and then to use a demand curve on which all points refer to that higher real income.

The main point under discussion can be put still more generally. The opportunities open to a consumer to satisfy his wants depend principally on two factors—the total resources at his disposal and the terms on which he can exchange one commodity for another, that is, on his real income and on relative prices. The form of analysis that is now fashionable distinguishes three effects of changes in his opportunities—the income effect arising from changes in his money income; the income effect arising from changes in the price of a commodity, with unchanged money income and prices of other commodities; and the substitution effect arising from a change in the relative price of a commodity, with unchanged real income.

The distinction between the so-called "substitution" and "income" effects of a change in price is a direct consequence of defining the demand curve according to the current interpretation of Marshall. Its basis is the arithmetic truism that at given prices for all commodities but one, a given money income corresponds to a higher real income, the lower the price of the remaining commodity—at a lower price for it, more of some commodities can be purchased without purchasing less of others. In consequence, a decline in the price of a commodity, all other prices constant, has, it is argued, two effects: first, with an unchanged real income, it would stimulate the substitution of that commodity for others—this is the substitution effect; second, if the money income of the consumers is supposed to be unchanged, the increase in their real income as a result of the decline in price causes a further change in the consumption of that commodity as well as of others—this is the income effect.[17]

[16] Note the difference from the previous case of constant productive capacity. As stated above, there is reason to expect constant real income along a demand curve to bear a consistent relation to constant productive capacity in the neighborhood of equilibrium. The reason, in effect, is provided by one of the conditions of equilibrium: the tangency of consumption and production indifference curves,

[17] See Slutsky, *op. cit.*; Henry Schultz, *The Theory and Measurement of Demand* (Chicago: University of Chicago Press, 1938), pp. 40–46; J. R. Hicks and R. G. D. Allen, "A Reconsideration of the Theory of Value," *Economica*, XIV (1934), 52–76 and 196–219; Hicks, *op. cit.*, Part I.

The two different kinds of income effects distinguished in this analysis—one arising from a change in money income, the other from a change in the price of one commodity—are really the same thing, the effect of a change in real income with given relative prices, arising in different ways. It is hard to see any gain from combining the second income effect with the substitution effect; it seems preferable to combine the two income effects and thereby gain a sharp contrast with the substitution effect.

It has often been stated that Marshall "neglected the income effect."[18] On my interpretation of his demand curve, this statement is invalid. One must then say that Marshall recognized the desirability of separating two quite different effects and constructed his demand curve so that it encompassed solely the effect that he wished to isolate for study, namely, the substitution effect. Instead of neglecting the income effect, he "eliminated" it.

The conclusion to which the argument of this section leads is identical with that reached by Frank H. Knight in a recent article, in which he says:

> We have to choose in analysis between holding the prices of all other goods constant and maintaining constant the "real income" of the hypothetical consumer. . . . The treatment of the Slutzky school adopts the assumption that . . . the prices of all other goods (and the consumer's money income) are constant. Hence, real income must change. Of the two alternatives, this seems to be definitely the wrong choice. . . . The simple and obvious alternative is to draw the demand curves in terms of a change in *relative* prices, i.e., to assume that the value of money is held constant, through compensating changes in the prices of other goods, and not that these other prices are held constant.[19]

III. THE CONSISTENCY OF THE ALTERNATIVE INTERPRETATION WITH OTHER PARTS OF MARSHALL'S WORK

Marshall's demand curve is part of a coherent body of thought; it is designed to fit into the rest of his structure of analysis; and it is used extensively in developing and applying this structure. It would take us too far afield to demonstrate in detail that my interpretation of his demand curve is consistent with the rest of his work. However, two special topics call for some explicit consideration: (1) the relation between the demand curve and Marshall's theory of money, because, in my view, this explains the particular device that he adopted for holding real income constant; and (2) the concept of consumer's surplus, because this is one of the most important applications of the demand curve and certainly the most controversial and because the passages in the later editions of the *Principles* that are inconsistent with my interpretation were introduced into the discussion of consumer's surplus.

a) THE THEORY OF RELATIVE PRICES AND THE THEORY OF MONEY

Granted that real income is to be held constant along the demand curve, why do so by holding money income and the purchasing power of money constant rather than, for example, by holding prices of other goods constant and permitting compensating variations in money income? What reason is there to treat the prices of all other commodities as moving inversely to the price of the commodity in question?

The answer to these questions is given, I think, by one of Marshall's basic or-

[18] Hicks, *op. cit.*, p. 32.

[19] "Realism and Relevance in the Theory of Demand," *Journal of Political Economy*, LII (December, 1944), 289–318, esp. Sec. III, "The Meaning of a Demand Curve," pp. 298–301. Quotation from p. 299.

ganizing principles, namely, the separation of the theory of relative prices from monetary theory, the theory of the level of prices. The *Principles* is devoted to the theory of relative prices under given monetary conditions; *Money, Credit, and Commerce* to the analysis of monetary conditions and their effect on the "purchasing power of money." With *given monetary conditions*, is it possible for the prices of all commodities other than the one in question to remain the same, on the average, while the price of this one rises or falls? Will not a rise or fall in the price of the commodity in question set in motion *monetary* forces affecting other prices? A complete answer requires explicit specification of the content of "given monetary conditions" and perhaps also of the source of the initial price change.

Marshall's selection of a constant purchasing power of money as a means of impounding monetary forces is presumably the end-result of a chain of reasoning about the influence of monetary forces, not the direct content that he gave to "given monetary conditions." The beginning of the chain of reasoning may well be his own version of the quantity theory of money. According to this version, "the value of money is a function of its supply on the one hand, and the demand for it, on the other, as measured by 'the average stock of command over commodities which each person cares to keep in a ready form.' "[20] Given monetary conditions would then imply a given stock of money and a given desired "average stock of command over commodities." A decline in one price alone, all other prices remaining the same, is inconsistent with these "givens." It would increase the real value of a fixed (nominal) stock of money, leave the community with a larger "stock of command over commodities" than previously, and establish an incentive (reflecting "monetary" forces) to increase expenditures and thereby raise prices until the fixed stock of money again represented the same "stock of command over commodities," i.e., until the "purchasing power of money" reached its former level.[21] This argument suggests that not only was constant purchasing power of money a device for separating the theory of relative prices from monetary theory, it was also a bridge between the two. Marshall separated the two theories in his attempt to reduce problems to manageable proportions, but he constructed them in such a way as to make them mutually consistent and thus facilitate ultimate combination.[22]

[20] J. M. Keynes, "Alfred Marshall, 1842–1924," *Memorials*, p. 29.

[21] C. W. Guillebaud has pointed out to me that Marshall typically supposed the desired "stock of command over commodities" to be a given fraction of real income (see *ibid.*) and that the argument in the text might not apply if this fraction were taken as the fundamental given. The monetary effects of a change in one price, other prices given, would then depend on the source of the initial price change. If this involved no change in aggregate real income (e.g., arose from a shift in demand), the argument in the text would remain unchanged. If it did involve a change in aggregate real income (e.g., arose from an invention reducing the cost of producing the commodity in question), no inconsistency need arise, since the desired "stock of command over commodities" would change in proportion to the change in real income. These considerations account for the phrase "perhaps also of the source of the initial price change" at the end of the preceding paragraph of the text.

[22] This interpretation would, of course, be contradicted if Marshall had devised his theory of money after he had substantially completed his theory of relative prices, as might be inferred from the fact that *Money, Credit, and Commerce* was not published until 1923, thirty-three years after the first edition of the *Principles*. But in Marshall's case, the order of publication is a poor guide to the order of construction. Keynes tells us that the essence of his quantity theory of money is contained in a manuscript "written about 1871"; that "by 1871 his progress along" the lines of the material

Marshall was, of course, very much aware of the interaction between real and monetary factors. The 1879 *Economics of Industry* contains an extremely interesting discussion of the trade cycle, part of which Marshall thought sufficiently important to quote at length in 1886 in answering questions circulated by the celebrated Royal Commission on the Depression of Trade and Industry.[23]

Marshall's decision to keep the purchasing power of money the same for different points on a demand curve may not be the device best suited to abstract from monetary factors. It serves, however, to emphasize the necessity of considering explicitly the monetary arrangements under which the forces affecting relative prices are supposed to operate. The best apparatus for tackling problems of relative prices cannot be determined independently of these arrangements and of their mode of operation. Though price theory and monetary theory can be separated, they are not basically independent. From this point of view it is entirely natural that the recent development of alternative monetary theories should have stimulated re-examination of price theory.

b) CONSUMER'S SURPLUS

Marshall's discussion of consumer's surplus constitutes one of the most extensive applications that he made of his demand curve and has probably given rise to more controversy and discussion than any other part of his theory. Recently, consumer's surplus has come in for renewed attention, primarily as a result of J. R. Hick's attempt to rehabilitate and reinterpret the concept.[24] The reason for commenting on it here is not to contribute to the discussion or to evaluate the merits or demerits of the concept but rather to show the relation between Marshall's treatment of consumer's surplus and my interpretation of his demand curve.

Marshall's treatment of consumer's surplus might, offhand, seem inconsistent with my interpretation of his demand curve for either of two different, and almost opposed, reasons. In the first place, consumer's surplus refers to a difference in real income under different situations. But, on my interpretation, all

contained in the *Pure Theory* "was considerably advanced"; that the *Pure Theory* itself was "substantially complete about 1873," though not printed even for private circulation until 1879; that "in 1877 he turned aside to write the *Economics of Industry* with Mrs. Marshall"; and that Mrs. Marshall said "Book III on Demand was largely thought out and written on the roof at Palermo, Nov. 1881—Feb. 1882" (*Memorials*, pp. 28, 21, 23, 39 n.). These dates are extremely suggestive, particularly since the constancy of the purchasing power of money is not explicitly mentioned in the *Pure Theory*, which Marshall was presumably working on at about the same time that he was developing his monetary theory, while it is explicitly mentioned in the 1879 *Economics of Industry*, begun some years later. See also nn. 37 and 38 below.

[23] See Alfred Marshall and Mary Paley Marshall, *Economics of Industry* (London: Macmillan & Co., 1st ed., 1879; 2d ed., 1881), Book III, chap. i, pp. 150–57. This and all later references are to the first edition. "Answers to Questions on the Subject of Currency and Prices Circulated by the Royal Commission on the Depression of Trade and Industry (1886)," *Official Papers by Alfred Marshall* (London: Macmillan & Co., Ltd., 1926), pp. 7–9. See also "Remedies for Fluctuations of General Prices" (1887), *Memorials*, pp. 189–92.

[24] See Hicks, *op. cit.*, pp. 38–41; "The Rehabilitation of Consumers' Surplus," *Review of Economic Studies*, VIII (February, 1941), 108–16; "Consumers' Surplus and Index Numbers," *ibid.* (summer, 1942), 126–37; "The Four Consumer's Surpluses," *ibid.*, XI (winter, 1943), 31–41. See also A. Henderson, "Consumer's Surplus and the Compensating Variation," *Review of Economic Studies*, VIII (February, 1941), 117–21; Knight, *op. cit.*; Kenneth E. Boulding, "The Concept of Economic Surplus," *American Economic Review*, XXXV (December, 1945), 851–69, reprinted in American Economic Association, *Readings in the Theory of Income Distribution* (Philadelphia: Blakiston Co., 1946), pp. 638–59; E. J. Mishan, "Realism and Relevance in Consumer's Surplus," *Review of Economic Studies*, XV (1947–48), 27–33.

points on the demand curve are to be regarded as corresponding to the same real income. A movement along such a demand curve cannot, therefore, involve a change in consumer's surplus. Does this not eliminate the entire notion of consumer's surplus and make Marshall's entire discussion of it pointless? The answer is clearly "No," the reason being that the two situations compared need not correspond to two points on the *same* demand curve, even though a single demand curve is used to *estimate* the difference in real income between the two situations.

In the second place, Marshall regarded his analysis of consumer's surplus as valid only for commodities that account for a small part of total expenditure. He makes this restriction in order to justify neglecting changes in the marginal utility of money. But, if all points on the demand curve correspond to the same real income, does it not then follow that the marginal utility of money is the same everywhere on the demand curve? And does it not also follow that his estimate of consumer's surplus is exact, so that the assumption that a negligible proportion of expenditures is devoted to the commodity in question becomes unnecessary? Again the answer is "No," and for much the same reason. If the two situations compared differ in real income, the fact that real income is the same along the demand curve becomes something of a vice in using it to measure consumer's surplus. The assumption that a negligible proportion of expenditures is devoted to the commodity in question cannot be dispensed with on my interpretation; indeed, if anything, it is even more necessary than on the current interpretation.

To explain and justify these cryptic answers, it will be necessary to examine Marshall's definition of consumer's surplus, his suggested estimate of its magnitude, and the relation of this estimate to the correct value under the two alternative interpretations of the demand curve.

Marshall is more explicit and complete in defining consumer's surplus than was his wont, and his definition admits of little ambiguity: "The excess of the price which he would be willing to pay rather than go without the thing, over that which he actually does pay, is the economic measure of this surplus satisfaction. It may be called *consumer's surplus*."[25]

Marshall then proceeds to argue that consumer's surplus can be *estimated* by the famous triangle under the demand curve. As Hicks remarks, this "association of Consumer's Surplus with the curvilinear triangle under the demand curve . . . is not a definition; it is a theorem, true under certain restrictive assumptions, but only true if these assumptions are granted."[26] The confusion of the suggested estimate with the definition is perhaps the chief source of misunderstanding on this exceedingly complex subject.

Figure 1, introduced in Section I*c* above to illustrate the relation between demand curves drawn on the current and on my interpretation, can also be used to show the relation between consumer's surplus as defined and estimates of it obtained from demand curves constructed according to the two interpretations. Curve *Cc*, it will be recalled, is a demand curve for the commodity *X* constructed according to the current interpretation. Money income and all other prices are the same for all points on it. *Aa* and *Cv*

[25] *Principles*, p. 124.

[26] "Rehabilitation of Consumers' Surplus," p. 109.

are demand curves constructed according to my interpretation—*Aa* for a real income the same as at *P* on *Cc; Cv* for a real income the same as at *C* on *Cc*. At point *P* on *Aa* and at point *C* on *Cv*, money income and all other prices are the same as on *Cc*. At other points other prices are sufficiently different, or money income is, to compensate for the difference in the price of *X* and thereby keep real income the same.

Now consider the consumer's surplus obtained from this commodity when the consumer is at *P*.[27] This is *defined* as "the excess of the price which he would be willing to pay rather than go without the thing, over that which he actually does pay." "Price" is here to be interpreted as "total amount" rather than "price per unit."[28] Further, it is clear that the sum he would pay rather than go without is to be determined for circumstances otherwise the same as at *P;* in particular, his money income and the other prices are to be the same as at *P*.[29] Now the amount that he actually does pay for *OM* of *X* is given by the rectangle *OHPM* in the figure. By the argument of Section I*c*, the maximum amount that he would be willing to pay for *OM* of *X* rather than go without any of it is given by the area under *Cv* between *O* and *M*, or *OCDGM*. The triangular area *CDH minus* the triangular area *DPG* therefore gives the consumer's surplus. This area is necessarily positive; we know he is willing to pay at least *OHPM* for *OM* of *X;* hence *OCDGM* must be greater than *OHPM*.

Marshall's *estimate* of the maximum sum is the area under the demand curve: *OCPM* if we use the current interpretation, *OAPM* if we use the alternative interpretation. For a "normal" commodity, the case for which the figure is drawn, both are clearly too large. How large the error is depends on the difference between *Aa* and *Cc*, on the one hand, and *Cv*, on the other. Now we have seen (in Sec. I*c*) that these differences arise entirely from differences in the real income associated with the different curves; if real incomes differ little, so will the curves. Here is where Marshall's assumption about the fraction of expenditures devoted to the commodity enters the picture. If this fraction is small, the differences in real income will tend to be small, and both estimates will approach the correct value.[30] Since the error is

[27] For simplicity, the discussion is restricted to the consumer's surplus obtained from the entire amount of *X* consumed; and to facilitate this, the demand curves have been drawn to cut the price axis.

[28] See Mathematical Note II of the *Principles* (p. 838), in which Marshall defines p as "the price which he is just willing to pay for an amount x of the commodity" and then differentiates p with respect to x to get the price per unit.

[29] None of the reasons cited earlier for keeping real income the same along the demand curve apply here. The question being asked is purely hypothetical; no other reactions need be allowed for. Further, to keep his real income the same when he has none of *X* as when he has *OM* of *X* would make the entire discussion of consumer's surplus pointless. The whole point of the discussion is to measure the difference in real income between the two situations.

[30] This statement is not rigorous. As the fraction of expenditures devoted to the commodity diminishes, so will aggregate consumer's surplus. It is not enough that the error become small in absolute terms; its ratio to the correct value must become small. This, in general, will occur, as is well known. The chief qualification has to do with the behavior of a demand curve constructed under the current interpretation (e.g., *Cc*) for small quantities of *X*. The crucial question is the difference in real income between *P* and *C*. Expenditure on the commodity might be a small fraction of total expenditure at *P;* yet, if the demand curve constructed under the current interpretation were extremely inelastic, not near *C*. In this case the difference in real income might be large.

This qualification is emphasized by Marshall. For example: "If however an amount b of the commodity is necessary for existence, $f(z)$ [*sic*] [ordinate of the demand curve] will be infinite, or at least indefinitely great, for values of x less than b. We must therefore take life for granted, and estimate separately the total utility of that part of the supply of

larger for Aa than for Cc, it is clear that Marshall's assumption is, if anything, even more necessary on my interpretation of the demand curve than on the current one.[31]

IV. TEXTUAL EVIDENCE ON WHAT MARSHALL REALLY MEANT

Marshall's writings on demand bear on three different problems: (1) the definition of the demand curve—the problem of form; (2) the shape of the demand curve—the problem of content; and (3) the use of the demand curve—the problem of application. In his usual manner Marshall gives precedence to the problem of content and does not explicitly separate his discussion of content from his discussion of form. His definitions are characteristically given parenthetically and implicitly. He went to extreme lengths to present his tools in the context of concrete problems, so that definitions grew out of the uses to be made of them.[32] His discussion of utility and diminishing utility in the chapter of the *Principles* which introduces the concept of a demand curve (Book III, chap. iii, "Gradations of Consumers' Demand") is part of the discussion of content, even though it precedes his definition. It is the means whereby he rationalizes his "one general *law of demand:*—The greater the amount to be sold, the smaller must be the price at which it is offered in order that it may find purchasers."[33] It is not part of his definition of the demand curve.

Similarly, one of the major applications that Marshall made of the demand curve was his analysis of consumer's surplus. This analysis, too, must be distinguished from his definition of the demand curve. Assumptions made in his

the commodity which is in excess of absolute necessaries" (p. 841). See also pp. 133 and 842. $f(z)$ clearly should be $f(x)$, as it is in the first four editions of the *Principles*. See appendix to this paper.

This discussion of the role of the assumption that the commodity absorbs only a small fraction of income throws some light on an issue about which there has been considerable discussion, namely, whether Marshall assumed the marginal utility of money to be roughly constant with respect to a change in price or a change in income. The above analysis suggests that he assumed constancy with respect to a change in income. This is also Hicks's conclusion (*Value and Capital*, p. 40; "Rehabilitation," p. 109). Samuelson denies this and asserts that he assumed constancy with respect to a change in price (see Paul A. Samuelson, "Constancy of the Marginal Utility of Income," in *Studies in Mathematical Economics and Econometrics*, p. 80).

[31] The argument can be easily extended to "inferior" goods. The order of the three curves in Fig. 1 is then reversed; the estimates then become too small, instead of too large; but the error under the alternative interpretation remains larger in absolute value than under the current interpretation.

In the terminology used by Hicks in "The Four Consumers' Surpluses," what I have called the consumer's surplus is what Hicks calls the "quantity-compensating variation." The estimate of consumer's surplus derived from the demand curve constructed under my interpretation (the area APH) Hicks calls the "quantity-equivalent variation." The area CDH in Fig. 1, Hicks calls the "price-compensating variation." Hicks's fourth concept, "price-equivalent variation," is not shown directly in Fig. 1. It is obtained by drawing a horizontal line through C. Designate by E the point at which this line cuts Aa. The "price-equivalent variation" is then equal to the area APH minus AEC. These relations can be checked by noting that curve *mep* in Hicks's Fig. 3 is Aa in our Fig. 1; his curve PCM is Cv in our Fig. 1. Further, in comparing the two figures, the part of Hicks's diagram for quantities less than hN should be neglected. That is, his point P is equivalent to our point C, his p to our P. Our Fig. 1 is also equivalent to Fig. 3B in Boulding, "The Concept of Economic Surplus."

[32] Cf. J. M. Keynes, *Memorials*, esp. pp. 33–38; see also Guillebaud, *op. cit.*

[33] *Principles*, p. 99. Note that on my interpretation this is truly a *general* law, not subject to the exceptions that have been made in recent literature. It depends for its validity only on (*a*) the postulate that consumers can be treated as if they behaved consistently and attempted to maximize some function of the quantity of commodities consumed; (*b*) the observed fact that consumers choose a higher income in preference to a lower, other things the same; and (*c*) the observed fact that consumers do not spend all their income on one commodity. For proof that a demand curve constructed on my interpretation must slope negatively see Slutsky, *op. cit.*, Sec. 8.

discussion of consumer's surplus cannot, without additional evidence, be supposed to apply equally to other applications of the "demand curve."

a) THE CENTRAL PASSAGES IN THE TEXT OF THE "PRINCIPLES"

The central passages in the text of the eighth and final edition of the *Principles* bearing on the other things to be kept the same seem to me to be three: one governing the entire volume, and two essentially parenthetical comments in his discussion of the demand curve:

> We may throughout this volume neglect possible changes in the general purchasing power of money. Thus the price of anything will be taken as representative of its exchange value relatively to things in general [p. 62].
>
> The larger the amount of a thing that a person has the less, other things being equal (i.e. *the purchasing power of money, and the amount of money at his command being equal*), will be the price which he will pay for a little more of it: or in other words his marginal demand price for it diminishes [p. 95; italics added].
>
> The demand prices in our list are those at which various quantities of a thing can be sold in a market *during a given time and under given conditions*. If the conditions vary in any respect the prices will probably require to be changed; and this has constantly to be done when the desire for anything is materially altered by a *variation of custom, or by a cheapening of the supply of a rival commodity, or by the invention of a new one* [p. 100; second set of italics added].

For our purposes the critical part of the second quotation is the italicized parenthesis and, of the third, the second set of italicized phrases.

Though these quotations are taken from the eighth edition of the *Principles*, their substantive content is contained in Marshall's earliest published work on the theory of demand. All except the constancy of the purchasing power of money is in *The Pure Theory of* (*Domestic*) *Values*, printed for private circulation in 1879[34] but, according to Keynes, "substantially complete about 1873";[35] and the constancy of the purchasing power of money is in his and Mrs. Marshall's *The Economics of Industry*, published in 1879.[36] The actual wording of the first and third quotations can be traced back to the first edition of the *Principles* (1890), of the second quotation, to the second edition (1891).[37]

[34] Reprinted, together with the companion paper, *The Pure Theory of Foreign Trade*, by the London School of Economics and Political Science (1930).

[35] *Memorials*, p. 23.

[36] This work should not be confused with the condensation of the *Principles*, published, under the same title but with Alfred Marshall as sole author, in 1892.

[37] In all editions of the *Principles* the statement corresponding to the first quotation is in a subsection dealing with the meaning of the word "value." In the first (1890), second (1891), and third (1895) editions, the subsection on "value" is at the end of Book I, "Preliminary Survey," chap. i, "Introduction," and contains the statement: "Throughout the earlier stages of our work it will be best to speak of the exchange value of a thing at any place and time as measured by its price, that is, the amount of money for which it will exchange then and there, and to assume that there is no change in the general purchasing power of money" (p. 9, all three editions). In the first edition this assumption is repeated at the beginning of the chapter on "The Law of Demand" (Book III, chap. ii): "The purchasing power of this money may vary from time to time; but in these early stages of our work we assume it to be constant" (1st ed., p. 151). This repetition was eliminated in later editions, apparently in the process of introducing into the second edition the chapter on "Wants in Relation to Activities." In the fourth edition (1898), the subsection on "value" was split, part remaining at the end of Book I, chap. i, the remainder, including the material on the purchasing power of money, being transferred to end of Book II, "Some Fundamental Notions," chap. ii, "Wealth." The wording was changed to essentially its final form; the only difference is that the first sentence is in the passive voice, reading: "Throughout this volume possible changes in the general purchasing power of money will be neglected" (4th ed., p. 130). In the fifth edition (1907), the rest of the subsection on "value" was transferred to the end of Book II, chap. ii, and the quotation revised to its present

b) THE BEARING OF THESE PASSAGES ON THE TWO INTERPRETATIONS

The "other things" listed in the three passages cited above are as follows:

1. "Purchasing power of money"
2. "Amount of money at his command"
3. "Custom"
4. Price of "a rival commodity" (to avoid "cheapening of the supply of a rival commodity")

form; even the page number is the same in the fifth and eighth editions (p. 62).

In both editions of *The Economics of Industry*, subsection 4 in Book II, "Normal Value," chap. i, "Definitions. Law of Demand," contains essentially the same material as the subsection on "value" in the *Principles* referred to in the preceding paragraph, including the following statement: "But while examining the theory of Normal value we shall, for convenience, assume that the purchasing power of money remains unchanged. So that a rise or fall in the price of a thing will always mean a rise or fall in its general purchasing power or exchange value" (pp. 68–69). No corresponding statement appears in *The Pure Theory*.

The italicized parenthesis in the second quotation is identical in the second and all later editions of the *Principles*. The remainder of the quotation was worded as follows in the second edition: "An increase in the amount of a thing that a person has will, other things being equal . . . diminish his Marginal Demand-price for it" (p. 152). In the third edition, the words "marginal" and "demand" were not capitalized, and the hyphen was eliminated after "Demand" (p. 170). In the fourth edition the end of the statement was expanded to read, "diminish the price which he will pay for a little more of it: or in other words diminishes his magrinal demand price for it" (pp. 169–70). In the fifth edition the quotation takes its present form, except for the addition of a comma, even the page number being the same as in the eighth edition (p. 95). In all editions from the second on, the indicated quotations are in Book III, chap. iii, the chapter first introducing the demand curve. This chapter is entitled "The Law of Demand" in the second and third editions, "Gradations of Demand" in the fourth, and "Gradations of Consumers' Demand" in the fifth and later editions.

The absence of the statement from the first edition reflects a difference in exposition, not in substance. As noted above, an explicit statement that the purchasing power of money is assumed constant appears in the chapter on "The Law of Demand" in the first edition. In all editions this chapter contains a statement covering the second part of the italicized parenthesis, which is worded as follows in the first edition: "Every increase in his resources increases the price which he is willing to pay for any given pleasure. And in the same way every diminution of his resources increases the marginal utility of money to him, and diminishes the price that he is willing to pay for any pleasure" (p. 156). The only change in this statement in later editions was the substitution of "benefit" for "pleasure" (8th ed., p. 96).

The Economics of Industry also contains a statement anticipating the second part of the italicized parenthesis: "The price which he is willing to pay for a thing depends not only on its utility to him but also on *his means;* that is, the amount of money or general purchasing power at his disposal" (p. 70).

In all editions of the *Principles* the statement corresponding to the third quotation is in the final subsection of the chapter first introducing the demand curve (1st ed., Book III, chap. ii; in later editions, Book III, chap. iii). In the first edition it reads: "It must be remembered that the demand schedule gives the prices at which various quantities of a thing can be sold in a market during a given time and under given conditions. If the conditions vary in any respect the figures of the schedule will probably require to be changed. One condition which it is especially important to watch is the price of rival commodities, that is, of commodities which can be used as substitutes for it" (p. 160). A footnote is attached to the word "rival," the first sentence of which reads: "Or to use Jevons' phrase (*Theory of Political Economy*, Ch. IV), commodities that are nearly 'equivalent' " (1st ed., p. 160, n. 2).

The part of the second sentence of the third quotation following the semicolon assumed its final form in the second edition (p. 157), the footnote reference to Jevons being dropped. The rest of the quotation is the same in the second and third editions as in the first and assumes its final form in the fourth (p. 174). The change made in the second sentence from the first to the second edition argues that the list was not intended to be exhaustive, but illustrative. No change in substance is involved (see 1st ed., p. 155). In all editions the quoted statement is followed by the example of tea and coffee to illustrate the necessity of assuming the prices of rival commodities to be known; in the second edition the example of gas and electricity was added, and in the third edition the example of different varieties of tea. The passage itself, the changes in it, and the examples all indicate that Marshall considered the price of "rival" commodities particularly important. The examples, together with the footnote in the first edition, make it clear that he meant "close" rivals.

For a statement in the *Pure Theory* covering the substance of these quotations, except the constancy of the purchasing power of money, see n. 38, below.

5. Range of rival commodities available (to avoid "invention of a new one")[38]

1. *The current interpretation.*—The current interpretation of Marshall's demand curve treats item 2 as referring to the money income of the group of purchasers to whom the demand curve relates, item 3 to their tastes and preferences, and item 4 to the price of every other commodity rather than of *rival* commodities alone. It ignores entirely items 1 and 5.

Item 2 is not entirely unambiguous. It might be interpreted as referring to the cash balances of the purchasers or to their wealth instead of, or in addition to, their income. On the whole, the most reasonable course seems to be to interpret it as referring to both income and wealth,[39] particularly since wealth qualifies for the list of "other things" by virtue of its possible importance as a factor affecting consumption. This expansion of the current interpretation does not alter it materially; it merely transfers "wealth" from the category of "other things" implicitly supposed to be the same to the list of things mentioned explicitly.

[38] The adequacy of this list as a summary of Marshall's views may be checked by comparing it with two others in Marshall's writings. In *The Pure Theory of (Domestic) Values*, he writes: "The periods with which we are concerned . . . are sufficiently long to eliminate . . . casual disturbances. . . . But they are sufficiently short to exclude fundamental changes in the circumstances of demand and in those of supply. On the side of demand for the ware in question it is requisite that the periods should not include (i) any very great change in the prosperity and purchasing power of the community; (ii) any important changes in the fashions which affect the use of the ware; (iii) the invention or the great cheapening of any other ware which comes to be used largely as a substitute for it; (iv) the deficiency of the supply of any ware for which the ware in question may be used as a substitute, whether this deficiency be occasioned by bad harvests, by war, or by the imposition of customs or excise taxes; (v) a sudden large requirement for the commodity, as e.g. for ropes in the breaking out of a maritime war; (vi) the discovery of new means of utilizing the ware, or the opening up of important markets in which it can be sold" (p. 15).

Item i in this list presumably corresponds with 2 in my list; ii corresponds with 3, and iii and iv with 4 and 5, iii excluding a fall in the price of a rival commodity and iv a rise. Items v and the first part of vi would seem to be contained in 3 and largely redundant with ii. The rest of vi is presumably covered by the restriction of the discussion to a demand curve for a particular market.

The other list is in Marshall's discussion in the *Principles* of the difficulties of the statistical study of demand (Book III, chap. iv), where he writes: "Other things seldom are equal in fact over periods of time sufficiently long for the collection of full and trustworthy statistics. . . . To begin with, [*a*] the purchasing power of money is continually changing. . . . Next come the changes in [*b*] the general prosperity and in the total purchasing power at the disposal of the community at large. . . . Next come the changes due to [*c*] the gradual growth of population and wealth. . . . Next, allowance must be made for changes in [*d*] fashion, and taste and habit, for [*e*] the opening out of new uses of a commodity, for [*f*] the discovery or improvement or cheapening of other things that can be applied to the same uses with it" (*Principles*, pp. 109–10; letters in brackets added). This statement dates from the first edition (pp. 170–71); only trivial editorial changes were made in later editions.

Item *a* in this list corresponds with 1 in my list; *b* with 2; *d* and presumably *e* with 3; and *f* with 4 and 5. Item *c* is presumably in part covered by restriction of the discussion to a demand curve for a particular market; in part it contains an item that may deserve to be added to the list, namely, "wealth." The wording of *f* is ambiguous, since it could refer to substitutes for the good in question, to complements, or to both. The subsequent text and the examples cited make it clear that it refers to substitutes; one example, of petroleum and petroleum lamps, itself ambiguously worded, suggests that it may refer to complements as well.

[39] In the quotations from Book III, chap. iv, in the preceding footnote, "wealth" is mentioned explicitly, though separately from "general prosperity" and "total purchasing power." See also the quotations in the fourth and fifth paragraphs of n. 37. Marshall repeatedly refers to "rich" and "poor" rather than to high- and low-income people (e.g., pp. 19, 95, 98). However, in an illustrative case, a rich man and a poor man are identified by their annual incomes (p. 19). And in Book III, chap. vi, he remarks: "We have throughout this and preceding chapters spoken of the rich, the middle classes and the poor as having respectively large, medium and small incomes—not possessions" (p. 134).

Item 3 requires no discussion, since the only reasonable interpretation of it is that it refers to tastes and preferences.[40]

The important defect of the current interpretation is its treatment of item 4, which is, in turn, responsible for the neglect of items 1 and 5. "Rival commodity" is replaced by, or read to mean, "any other commodity," and hence item 4 is taken to mean that the price of every other commodity is to be supposed the same. For example, Henry Schultz says, as if it were obvious and without citing any statements of Marshall: "Marshall also assumes, in giving definite form to the law of demand for any one commodity, that the prices of all other commodities remain constant."[41] Numerous other statements to the same effect could be cited. It is an amusing commentary on our capacity for self-delusion that the only references to Marshall for support that I have seen are to the page containing the third quotation in Section IV*a* above—the source of the words quoted in item 4.[42] The first set of italicized words in that quotation are the only words on the page even remotely supporting the substitution of "any other" for rival. The specific examples that follow the quotation—tea and coffee, gas and electric lighting, different varieties of tea, beef and mutton—make it clear that Marshall was using the word "rival" in a narrow sense and not in that broad sense in which it may be said that all commodities are "rivals" for the consumer's income.[43] Whatever the merits of the current interpretation, it cannot be found explicitly in Marshall.

The interpretation of item 4 as referring to all other commodities makes item 5 unnecessary and contradicts item 1. Item 5 is unnecessary because the introduction of a new commodity is equivalent to a decline in its price from infinity to a finite amount; hence is ruled out if the price of every other commodity is to be unchanged. Item 1 is contradicted because, if all other prices are unchanged, the purchasing power of money will be lower, the higher the price of the commodity in question. The purchasing power of money cannot, therefore, be the same for all points on the demand curve.

The redundancy of item 5 on this interpretation of item 4 is unimportant; this item is in a list that is illustrative rather than exhaustive, and there is no reason why Marshall should have scru-

[40] See n. 38, above. In discussing the law of diminishing marginal utility, Marshall says: "We do not suppose time to be allowed for any alteration in the character or tastes of the man himself" (p. 94).

[41] *Op. cit.*, p. 53. Immediately after making this statement he quotes from Edgeworth's article on "Demand Curves" cited in n. 5, above, not as evidence for the validity of his interpretation of Marshall but rather as an indication of the difficulties that it raises.

[42] Joan Robinson states without citation: "Marshall instructs us to draw up a demand schedule on the assumption that the prices of all other things are fixed" (*The Economics of Imperfect Competition* [London: Macmillan & Co., Ltd., 1934], p. 20). Paul Samuelson says, also without citation: "All other prices and income are held constant by *ceteris paribus* assumptions" in the "Marshallian partial equilibrium demand functions" (*Foundations of Economic Analysis* [Cambridge: Harvard University Press, 1947], p. 97). In an unpublished exposition of income and substitution effects prepared for class use about 1939, I stated, also without citation: "There is no question but that it [the Marshallian demand curve] was not intended to be . . . interpreted" as "showing the effect of *compensated* variations in price." Similar statements, all citing p. 100 of the *Principles* as authority, are made by Robert Triffin, *Monopolistic Competition and General Equilibrium Theory* (Cambridge: Harvard University Press, 1940), p. 44; Ruby Turner Norris, *The Theory of Consumer's Demand* (New Haven: Yale University Press, 1941), p. 82; and Weintraub, *op. cit.*, p. 539.

[43] If any doubt remains, it is removed by the footnote in the first edition attached to the word "rival" referring to Jevons' phrase "commodities that are nearly 'equivalent'" (see n. 37, above).

pulously avoided overlapping. The logical inconsistency between items 1 and 4 cannot, however, be dismissed so lightly. Retention of the current interpretation requires either that item 1 be eliminated, on the grounds that the quotations on which it is based are exceptional and peripheral, or that Marshall be convicted of logical inconsistency on a fundamental point in his theory of demand.[44] Item 1 cannot, I think, be eliminated. The constancy of the purchasing power of money is clearly fundamental in Marshall's thought, probably more fundamental than any other item on our list.[45]

One excuse for retaining the current interpretation of Marshall, despite the logical inconsistency that it introduces, is to suppose that Marshall intended to restrict the use of his demand curve to commodities that account for only a small fraction of total expenditures. A change in the price of such a commodity would have only a small effect on the purchasing power of money, and it could be argued that Marshall neglected it as a "second-order effect." On this rationalization, item 1 becomes redundant, but, in the limit, not logically inconsistent with an item 4 taken to refer to all other commodities.

I do not believe that Marshall intended to restrict the use of the demand curve to commodities accounting for only a small fraction of total expenditure. He speaks of a demand curve for wheat (p. 106), for houseroom (p. 107), and for other commodities that he cannot have regarded as unimportant. He first explicitly introduces the restriction to unimportant commodities in connection with his discussion of consumer's surplus, which comes well after the initial discussion of the demand curve—in the eighth edition, three chapters later; and the restriction is repeated at most points at which the argument depends on it. At one point the restriction is said to be "generally," not universally, justifiable. This evidence may not be conclusive but it certainly establishes a strong presumption that Marshall did not intend the restriction to carry over to all uses of the demand curve.[46]

[44] The extent to which the current interpretation dominates economic thought could not be more strikingly illustrated than by the fact that so acute an economic theorist as J. R. Hicks can write: "No doubt it [the constancy of the marginal utility of money] was . . . associated in his [Marshall's] mind with the assumption of a constant value of money (constant prices of other consumers' goods than the one, or sometimes ones, in question)" ("The Rehabilitation of Consumers' Surplus," p. 109). Hicks here treats constancy of all other prices as an alternative statement of item 1, when, in fact, it is logically inconsistent with item 1.

[45] See nn. 37 and 38, above. Note also that constancy of the purchasing power of money was a standard assumption of economic theory long before Marshall's day. It was made by Ricardo in his price theory, and Marshall refers to Cournot's discussion of the reasons for making this assumption (see Marshall, *Principles*, pp. ix, 62; Augustin Cournot, *Researches into the Mathematical Principles of the Theory of Wealth* [*1838*], Nathaniel Bacon translation [New York: Macmillan Co., 1897], p. 26).

[46] In connection with the discussion of consumer's surplus and the assumption of a constant marginal utility of money implicit in that discussion, Marshall says: "The assumption . . . underlies our whole reasoning, that the expenditure on any one thing . . . is only a small part of his whole expenditure" (p. 842). The first sentence of the paragraph from which this quotation is taken explicitly limits it to "the discussion of consumers' surplus" (p. 842). The quotation is followed by a cross-reference to the part of Marshall's famous analysis of the process by which equilibrium is reached in a corn-market in which he discusses "the latent assumption, that the dealers' willingness to spend money is nearly constant throughout" (p. 334). "This assumption," he says, "is justifiable with regard to most of the market dealings with which we are practically concerned. When a person buys anything for his own consumption, he generally spends on it a small part of his total resources" (p. 335).

Nowhere in Book III, chap. iii, does Marshall explicitly restrict his discussion to unimportant commodities. The one statement in that chapter that might be regarded as so restricting the dis-

It should be noted that Marshall's explicit introduction of the restriction to unimportant commodities has no bearing on the relative validity of the two interpretations of his demand curve. The restriction is necessary on either of the two interpretations at each point at which Marshall explicitly makes it. So the restriction cannot be regarded as called for by the inconsistency of items 1 and 4 on the current interpretation of 4.

2. *The alternative interpretation.*—My interpretation of the Marshallian demand curve resolves almost all the difficulties that plague the current interpretation, since it accepts at face value the five "other things" listed at the beginning of Section IV*b*. Marshall's words can be taken to mean what they say without uncomfortable stretching, and there is no logical inconsistency in the constancy of both item 1, the purchasing power of money, and item 4, the prices of rival commodities. Item 5, the range of rival commodities available, is still redundant, since, if "rival" has the same meaning in 4 and 5, the invention of a new rival commodity means a change in its price from infinity to a finite value.

My interpretation explains also the precise wording of the second quotation in Section IV*a*, which reads, in part: "The larger the amount of a thing that a person has the less . . . will be the price which he will pay for a little more of it." This is a curious form of phrasing on the current interpretation. Why emphasize the amount of a thing that a person has and the marginal expenditure that he can be induced to make rather than the amount he purchases and the average price he pays? On my interpretation, this phrasing follows directly from the argument of Section I*c* above (and Note II of Marshall's Mathematical Appendix), according to which a demand curve constructed on my interpretation can be viewed as showing the maximum price per unit that a person can be induced to pay for successive increments of the commodity.

One minor puzzle remains on my interpretation. Why does Marshall restrict his attention to "rival" commodities? Why not to "closely related" commodities, whether rivals or complements? His use of the word "rivals" in discussing the demand curve is apparently not a mere verbal accident. He uses the word repeatedly; almost all his examples deal with the effect of, or through, substitutes. I have no very good answer to this puzzle; the only one that seems at all persuasive is that he thought the concept of "joint demand" and the associated analytical apparatus better suited to problems involving complementary goods.[47]

My interpretation follows so directly

cussion is the statement on p. 95 that "the marginal utility of money to him is a fixed quantity." But the context argues and Note II in the Mathematical Appendix demonstrates that this is merely a verbal statement of an identity (if income is unchanged, so is marginal utility of money), and thus is not really relevant to the issue. In the eighth edition, Note II is referred to only at the end of the subsection following the paragraph containing the passage quoted. However, in the first edition, the corresponding note (Note III) is referred to at the end of the paragraph containing the passage quoted, and hence clearly covers it (pp. 155–56, 737–38).

The above quotations are essentially unchanged from the first edition on. The restriction to unimportant commodities is, however, mentioned neither in Marshall and Marshall, *Economics of Industry*, nor in the *Pure Theory*.

[47] In Note VII of the Mathematical Appendix, Marshall qualifies a suggested formula for combining consumer's surplus from different commodities by saying: "if we could find a plan for grouping together in one common demand curve all those things which satisfy the same wants, and are rivals; and also for every group of things of which the services are complementary (see Book V, chap. vi) . . ." (p. 842). Book V, chap. vi, contains the discussion of joint demand. The qualification quoted appears first in the third edition.

from Marshall's words that further defense of it would be unnecessary were it not for the unquestioned dominance of the current interpretation in the economic thinking and writing of the past half-century. This circumstance explains the presentation of additional textual evidence bearing on the validity of the alternative interpretation.

c) COUNTEREVIDENCE FROM THE TEXT OF THE "PRINCIPLES"

I have been able to find only one passage in the text of the eighth edition of the *Principles* that is in any way inconsistent with my interpretation of Marshall. This is the celebrated passage, adverted to above, which deals with the so-called "Giffen phenomenon" and which was first introduced in the third edition:

> For instance, as Sir R. Giffen has pointed out, a rise in the price of bread makes so large a drain on the resources of the *poorer labouring families* and raises so much the marginal utility of money to them, that they are forced to curtail their consumption of meat and the more expensive farinaceous foods: and bread being still the cheapest food which they can get and will take, they consume more, and not less of it [p. 132; italics added].

This passage clearly offsets an income effect against a substitution effect, whereas, on my interpretation of Marshall, real income is the same at all points on the demand curve, so there is no "income effect" (see Sec. II*b*, above). The passage is thus in the spirit of the current interpretation. Yet the words I have italicized indicate that it does not necessarily contradict my interpretation of Marshall. The purchasing power of money and the real income of the community at large may remain constant; yet the real income of a particular group in the community that has a special consumption pattern may be adversely affected by the rise in the price of a particular commodity.[48]

d) THE EVIDENCE OF THE MATHEMATICAL APPENDIX

The Mathematical Appendix to the *Principles* confirms and extends the evidence already presented from the text of the *Principles* and from Marshall's other writings. Note II (III in the first edition) explicitly derives a relation between price and quantity demanded that is identical with a demand curve on my interpretation, in which real income is kept constant by compensating variations in money income. Indeed, my derivation of such a demand curve in Section I*c* above is a verbal paraphrase of Marshall's mathematics. Marshall does not explicitly say that the relation he derives is a demand curve, but Note II is attached to his initial discussion of the demand curve (Book III, chap. iii, in the eighth edition) and is given as the authority for statements made about the demand curve; hence there can be no doubt that it presents the pure theory of his demand curve.

In all editions of the *Principles* Note VI, attached to Marshall's discussion of consumer's surplus, contains a sentence that is definitely wrong on the current interpretation of his demand curve but correct on my interpretation.

Finally, a sentence added to Note VI in the third edition, referred to in the text of the *Principles* in connection with the material added on the Giffen phenomenon, contains an implicit mathematical proposition that is correct on the current interpretation but incorrect on my interpretation. The mathematical point in question is considerably more

[48] See Marshall's explicit discussion of, and emphasis on, this possibility in "Remedies for Fluctuations of General Prices" (1887), *Memorials*, p. 207.

subtle than those referred to in the two preceding paragraphs, so it cannot be given the same weight.

These two notes are examined in some detail in the appendix to this paper, to which the reader is referred for proof of the above statements.

e) A SYNTHESIS OF THE EVIDENCE

There are two differences between the current interpretation of Marshall's demand curve and my interpretation: (1) On the current interpretation, account is taken of the price of each other commodity individually; on my interpretation, only of the average price of all commodities other than the one in question and its close rivals. (2) On the current interpretation, real income varies along the demand curve with the price of the good in question; on my interpretation, real income is constant along the demand curve.

On the first, and less important, point, it is mathematically convenient to consider each other price separately, and this procedure might well have recommended itself to the writer of mathematical Notes XIV and XXI. On the other hand, it is impossible to consider each price separately in a practical analysis; so the use of an average price would clearly have recommended itself to the writer of the text of the *Principles* and is entirely in the spirit of Marshall's explicit methodological statements (see Sec. II*a*, above). Marshall does not discuss this point explicitly; hence the textual evidence is all indirect.

On the second and basic point of difference the evidence leaves little room for doubt: Marshall's theory of demand, in the form in which it is presented in the first edition of the *Principles*, is explicitly based on constancy of real income along the demand curve. This interpretation not only is consistent with both the letter and the spirit of the entire text of the first edition of the *Principles* but is almost conclusively established by the evidence cited above from two notes in the Mathematical Appendix of the first edition. In his determined effort to be persuasive and to make his work accessible to educated laymen, Marshall might well have been vague in his verbal presentation, though even there it seems unlikely that he would have been logically inconsistent. It is hardly credible that he would have been not merely vague but downright wrong on simple mathematical points stated in mathematical language, especially since the mathematical points in question could hardly even have arisen if he had been explicitly using the current interpretation of the demand curve.

I am inclined to believe, however, that by the time Marshall made the revisions incorporated in the third edition of the *Principles*—presumably between 1891, when the second edition appeared, and 1895, when the third edition appeared—he had himself been influenced by the current interpretation, probably without realizing that it was different from his own. This conjecture is based primarily on the two passages cited above as inconsistent with my interpretation: the passage dealing with the Giffen phenomenon and the last sentence of Note VI of the Mathematical Appendix. Both were added in the third edition—and these are the only passages I have been able to find in any edition of the *Principles* that fit the current interpretation better than they fit my interpretation. Further, both show some evidence of confusion about the fine points of his theory of demand (see last paragraph of appendix to this paper).

The hypothesis that Marshall did not

recognize the contradiction between the current interpretation and his earlier work would hardly be tenable if the lapse of time between the work incorporated in the first and the third editions of the *Principles* were as short as between their publication. But, as already noted, this is not the case. The essence of both his theory of demand and his analysis of consumer's surplus is contained in the *Pure Theory of Domestic Values*, which, though not printed until 1879, "must have been substantially complete about 1873."[49] The one important point in the theory of demand that is not in the *Pure Theory*—explicit mention of constancy of the purchasing power of money—is in the 1879 *Economics of Industry*. The only important addition in the *Principles* is the concept of "elasticity of demand"; and even this concept, which is not relevant to the present problem, was worked out in 1881–82.[50] No important substantive changes were made in the theory of demand in successive editions of the *Principles*, though the exposition was amplified and rearranged, the wording changed in detail, and some examples modified. The only important change of substance introduced into the discussion of consumer's surplus (in the third edition) was in connection with a point that has no bearing on the present issue.[51]

Marshall himself writes: "My main position as to the theory of value and distribution was practically completed in the years 1867 to 1870. . . . By this time [from the context, 1874] I had practically completed the whole of the substance of my Mathematical Appendix."[52] Thus Marshall appears to have completed his fundamental work on the theory of demand in the early 1870's and to have made no important substantive changes thereafter. The third edition appeared some twenty or more years later—an ample lapse of time for the precise details of an essentially mathematical analysis to have become vague and their difference from a superficially similar set of details to pass unnoticed. This seems especially plausible in view of the acceptance of the current interpretation by others and the absence of controversy about it.

[49] Keynes, *Memorials*, p. 23.

[50] *Ibid.*, p. 39, n. 3.

[51] This change does not reflect favorably on Marshall's willingness to admit error. The first edition states: "Subject to these corrections then we may regard the aggregate of the money measures of the total utility of wealth as a fair measure of that part of the happiness which is dependent on wealth" (pp. 179–80), the corrections referred to being for "differences in the wealth of different purchasers" (p. 178) and "elements of collective wealth which are apt to be overlooked" (p. 179). A footnote to the first quotation refers to mathematical Note VII, in which he says, subject to the same two qualifications: "if a_1, a_2, a_3 . . . be the amounts consumed of the several commodities of which b_1, b_2, b_3 . . . are necessary for existence, if $y = f_1(x)$, $y = f_2(x)$, $y = f_3(x)$ . . . be the equations to their demand curves . . . , then the total utility of his wealth, subsistence being taken for granted, is represented by

$$\sum \int_b^a f(x)dx\text{"}$$

(1st ed., p. 741).

The eighth edition does not contain the first statement. Instead, the text contains an explicit warning against adding consumer's surpluses for different commodities, and a footnote says: "Some ambiguous phrases in earlier editions appear to have suggested to some readers the opposite opinion" (p. 131). Note VII in the Mathematical Appendix was modified by replacing "his wealth" by "income" and, of more importance, "is represented" by "might be represented" and by adding after the formula the significant qualification, "if we could find a plan for grouping together in one common demand curve all those things which satisfy the same wants, and are rivals; and also for every group of things of which the services are complementary. . . . But we cannot do this; and therefore the formula remains a mere general expression, having no practical application" (p. 842). As noted, these changes date from the third edition.

[52] Letter to J. B. Clark, *Memorials*, p. 416.

Further circumstantial evidence that Marshall did not recognize the contradiction between the current interpretation and his earlier work is provided by the apparent absence of any explicit discussion of the question in the writings of either Marshall or the more prominent of his students or even of any comments that could reasonably be interpreted as implying recognition of the existence of alternative interpretations of the demand curve. Yet, as noted earlier (n. 5), the current interpretation is explicitly given by Edgeworth as early as 1894 in an article on "Demand Curves" in *Palgrave's Dictionary of Political Economy* that Marshall must be presumed to have read. Though the assumption of constant prices of commodities other than the one in question is not explicitly attributed to Marshall, most of the article is based on Marshall; and there is no suggestion that this assumption does not apply to Marshall's demand curve. Further, Walras' definition of the demand curve, which presumably influenced Edgeworth, is identical with the current interpretation of Marshall's demand curve, and Marshall refers to Walras several times in the first edition of the *Principles*, though it seems clear that Marshall developed his theory of demand independently of Walras.[53] So Marshall must have been exposed to a definition of the demand curve corresponding to the current interpretation at a time when he was still making substantial revisions in the *Principles*. If he had recognized that this interpretation was incorrect, would he not have taken the opportunity to clarify his statements in later editions?

[53] *Principles* (1st ed.), pp. xi, xii, 425; Keynes, *Memorials*, pp. 19–24; Marshall's letter to J. B. Clark, *ibid.*, pp. 416–18.

V. ALTERNATIVE CONCEPTIONS OF ECONOMIC THEORY

There remains the mystery how the current interpretation of Marshall's demand curve gained such unquestioned dominance at so early a date and retained it so long, not only as an interpretation of Marshall, but also as "the" definition of "the" demand curve.

One obvious explanation is that mathematical economists were more likely than others to state explicitly and precisely their assumptions about the behavior of other prices; that mathematical economists were likely to be familiar with Walras' independent definition and to take it as a point of departure; and that, in any event, the current interpretation is mathematically more convenient. Other economists, it could be argued, followed the lead of the mathematical economists, and thus the current interpretation was taken for granted and accepted without question.

This explanation seems to me a significant part of the answer; however, I do not believe that it is the entire answer. If, as I have argued above, my interpretation of Marshall is more useful for most practical problems, why has its use been so rarely proposed; why has there been no general feeling of dissatisfaction with the current interpretation? There must, it would seem, be something about the role that has been assigned to economic theory that has made the current interpretation acceptable.

I am inclined to believe that this is, in fact, the case; that, by slow and gradual steps, the role assigned to economic theory has altered in the course of time until today we assign a substantially different role to theory than Marshall did. We curtsy to Marshall, but we walk with Walras.

The distinction commonly drawn between Marshall and Walras is that Marshall dealt with "partial equilibrium," Walras with "general equilibrium." This distinction is, I believe, false and unimportant. Marshall and Walras alike dealt with general equilibrium; partial equilibrium analysis as usually conceived is but a special kind of general equilibrium analysis—unless, indeed, partial equilibrium analysis is taken to mean erroneous general equilibrium analysis. Marshall wrote to J. B. Clark in 1908: "My whole life has been and will be given to presenting in realistic form as much as I can of my Note XXI."[54] Note XXI, essentially unchanged from the first edition of the *Principles* to the last, presents a system of equations of general equilibrium. It ends with the sentence: "Thus, however complex the problem may become, we can see that it is theoretically determinate, because the number of unknowns is always exactly equal to the number of equations which we obtain."[55] The explanation given above why Marshall might have decided to hold the purchasing power of money constant was entirely in terms of constructing the demand curve so that it would be consistent with general equilibrium in those parts of the system not under direct study.

The important distinction between the conceptions of economic theory implicit in Marshall and Walras lies in the purpose for which the theory is constructed and used. To Marshall—to repeat an expression quoted earlier—economic theory is "an engine for the discovery of concrete truth." The "economic organon" introduces "systematic and organized methods of reasoning." Marshall wrote:

> Facts by themselves are silent. . . . The most reckless and treacherous of all theorists is he who professes to let facts and figures speak for themselves, who keeps in the background the part he has played, perhaps unconsciously, in selecting and grouping them, and in suggesting the argument *post hoc ergo propter hoc*. . . . The economist . . . must be suspicious of any direct light that the past is said to throw on problems of the present. He must stand fast by the more laborious plan of interrogating facts in order to learn the manner of action of causes singly and in combination, applying this knowledge to build up the organon of economic theory, and then making use of the aid of the organon in dealing with the economic side of social problems.[56]

Economic theory, in this view, has two intermingled roles: to provide "systematic and organized methods of reasoning" about economic problems; to provide a body of substantive hypotheses, based on factual evidence, about the "manner of action of causes." In both roles the test of the theory is its value in explaining facts, in predicting the consequences of changes in the economic environment. Abstractness, generality, mathematical elegance—these are all secondary, themselves to be judged by the test of application. The counting of equations and unknowns is a check on the completeness of reasoning, the beginning of analysis, not an end in itself.

Doubtless, most modern economic theorists would accept these general statements of the objectives of economic theory. But our work belies our professions. Abstractness, generality, and mathematical elegance have in some measure become ends in themselves, criteria by which to judge economic theory. Facts are to be described, not explained. Theory is to be tested by the accuracy of its "assumptions" as photographic descrip-

[54] *Memorials*, p. 417.

[55] *Principles*, p. 856. This note was numbered XX in the first edition.

[56] The quotations are all taken from Marshall, "The Present Position of Economics" (1885), *Memorials*, pp. 159, 161, 164, 166, 168, 171.

tions of reality, not by the correctness of the predictions that can be derived from it. From this viewpoint the current interpretation of the demand curve is clearly the better. It is more general and elegant to include the price of every commodity in the universe in the demand function rather than the average price of a residual group. Any price may affect any other, so a demand equation including every price is a more accurate photographic description. Of course, it cannot be used in discovering "concrete truth"; it contains no empirical generalization that is capable of being contradicted—but these are Marshallian objections. From the "Walrasian" viewpoint, to take one other example from recent developments in economic theory, it is a gain to eliminate the concept of an "industry," to take the individual firm as the unit of analysis, to treat each firm as a monopoly, to confine all analysis to either the economics of the individual firm or to a general equilibrium analysis of the economy as a whole.[57] From the Marshallian viewpoint this logical terminus of monopolistic competition analysis is a blind alley. Its categories are rigid, determined not by the problem at hand but by mathematical considerations. It yields no predictions, summarizes no empirical generalizations, provides no useful framework of analysis.

Of course, it would be an overstatement to characterize all modern economic theory as "Walrasian" in this sense. For example, Keynes's theory of employment, whatever its merits or demerits on other grounds, is Marshallian in method. It is a general equilibrium theory containing important empirical content and constructed to facilitate meaningful prediction. On the other hand, much recent work based on Keynes's theory of employment is Walrasian.[58]

[57] See Triffin, *op. cit.*, pp. 188–89.

[58] O. Lange, *Price Flexibility and Employment* (Bloomington, Ind.: Principia Press, 1944), is perhaps as good an example as any.

VI. CONCLUSION

Modern economic theory typically defines the demand curve as showing the relation between the quantity of a commodity demanded and its price for given tastes, money income, and prices of other commodities. This definition has also been uniformly accepted as a correct interpretation of the demand curve defined and used by Alfred Marshall in his *Principles of Economics*. Rarely has the view been expressed that a different definition would be preferable.

Despite its unquestioned acceptance for over half a century, this interpretation of Marshall is, in my view, wrong. Marshall's early writings, the text of the *Principles*, and, even more definitely, the Mathematical Appendix provide almost conclusive proof that Marshall's demand curve differs in two respects from the one commonly used and attributed to him: first, commodities other than the one in question and its close rivals are treated as a group rather than individually, and only their average price is explicitly taken into account; second, and far more important, real income is considered the same at all points on the demand curve, whereas constant money income and other prices imply a higher real income, the lower the price of the commodity in question. Two variants of Marshall's demand curve can be distinguished: one, employed in the text of the *Principles*, uses variations in the prices of other commodities to compensate for variations in the price of the commodity in question and thereby keeps the purchasing power of money constant; the other, employed in the Mathematical

Appendix, uses variations in money income to compensate for variations in the price of the commodity in question.

The only textual evidence that conflicts with this interpretation is a passage in the text and a related sentence in the Mathematical Appendix that were added to the third edition of the *Principles*. The inconsistency of these with the rest of the *Principles* can be explained by the hypothesis that Marshall himself was after a point influenced by the current interpretation of the demand curve without recognizing its inconsistency with his earlier work. Some circumstantial evidence also supports this hypothesis.

The alternative interpretation of the demand curve not only is faithful to both the letter and the spirit of Marshall's work but also is more useful for the analysis of concrete problems than is the demand curve commonly employed. The acceptance of a less useful definition seems to me to be a consequence of a changed conception of the role of theory in economic analysis. The current interpretation of the demand curve is Walrasian; and so is current economic theory in general.

APPENDIX ON TWO NOTES IN THE MATHEMATICAL APPENDIX TO THE *PRINCIPLES*

I. NOTE II OF THE EIGHTH EDITION

This note is numbered III in the first edition of the *Principles*, II in the rest. In the first edition the relevant parts are worded as follows (pp. 737–38):

"If m is the amount of money or general purchasing power at a person's disposal at any time, and μ represents its total utility to him, then $d\mu/dm$ represents the marginal utility of money to him.

"If p is the price which he is just willing to pay for an amount x of the commodity which gives him a total pleasure u, then

$$\frac{d\mu}{dm}\Delta p = \Delta u \; ; \quad \text{and} \quad \frac{d\mu}{dm}\frac{dp}{dx} = \frac{du}{dx} \cdots .$$

"Every increase in his means diminishes the marginal utility of money to him; . . . .

"Therefore, du/dx, the marginal utility to him of an amount x of a commodity remaining unchanged, an increase in his means . . . increases dp/dx, that is, the rate at which he is willing to pay for further supplies of it. Treating u as a variable, that is to say, allowing for possible variations in the person's liking for the commodity in question, we may regard dp/dx as a function of m, u, and x. . . ."

The wording in the eighth edition is identical except that "marginal utility of money" is replaced by "marginal degree of utility of money" and that "du/dx" and the words "Treating u . . . in question" are omitted from the last paragraph quoted (pp. 838–39). The changes were first made in the third edition.

In the second sentence of this note, the word "price" is to be interpreted as "total amount" not as "price per unit." This is clear from the context and is demonstrated by the equation that follows and the designation of dp/dx as "the rate at which he is willing to pay for further supplies of it." The words "just willing" in the second sentence and the equations that follow demonstrate that p is the maximum amount he can pay for an amount x and have the same utility as if he had none of the commodity. Thus Marshall is describing a process like that outlined in Section I*c* of this paper, whereby the maximum possible amount is extracted from the individual for each successive increment of the commodity, the individual retaining the same "real income," that is, remaining on the same indifference curve, throughout the process.

The last sentence quoted shows that u is to be regarded as a parameter to allow for changes in tastes. The rest of that sentence simply describes a function like that obtained by eliminating y' from equations (5) and (6) of note 6 of this paper. The parameter m in Marshall's function takes the place of U_o in our footnote, since dp/dx is still to be regarded as the price per unit paid for an additional increment of the commodity rather than as the price per unit at which any amount can be purchased. In consequence, no explicit statement is needed as yet about the compensating variations in income that are implicit in Marshall's analysis.

The word "demand" does not appear in this note. But the note is attached to the chapter in the *Principles* in which Marshall first introduces the demand curve (Book III, chap. ii, in the first edition; Book III, chap. iii, in later editions) and is cited as proof of statements about the demand curve; hence there can be no doubt that the "function" mentioned in the last sentence quoted is the counterpart of Marshall's demand curve.

I have been able to construct no interpretation of this note that would render it consistent with the current interpretation of Marshall's demand curve.

2. NOTE VI

This note has the same number in all editions. In the first edition the relevant parts are worded as follows (p. 740):

"If y be the price at which an amount x of a commodity can find purchasers in a given market, and $y = f(x)$ be the equation to the demand-curve, then the total utility of the commodity is measured by $\int_0^a f(x)\,dx$, where a is the amount consumed.

"If however an amount b of the commodity is necessary for existence, $f(x)$ will be infinite, or at least indefinitely great, for values of x less than b. We must therefore take life for granted, and estimate separately the total utility of that part of the supply of the commodity which is in excess of absolute necessaries: it is of course $\int_b^a f(x)\,dx$ . . . .

"It should be noted that, in the discussion of Consumers' Rent, we assume that the marginal utility of money to the individual purchaser is the same throughout. . . ."

Only trivial changes were made in these sentences in subsequent editions: a typographical error in the fifth edition, which remained uncorrected thereafter, substituted $f(z)$ for $f(x)$ in the second sentence; and "consumers' surplus" replaced "Consumers' Rent." In the third edition the following sentence was added at the end of the note:

"If, for any reason it be desirable to take account of the influence which his expenditure on tea exerts on the value of money to him, it is only necessary to multiply $f(x)$, within the integral given above by that function of $xf(x)$ (i.e. of the amount which he has already spent on tea) which represents the marginal utility to him of money when his stock of it has been diminished by that amount" (3d ed., p. 795). The only subsequent changes were the addition of a comma after "reason" and the deletion of the comma before "within" (8th ed., p. 842).

In its final form Note VI seems internally inconsistent: the second sentence is wrong on the current interpretation of Marshall's demand curve, correct on my interpretation; the final sentence, added in the third edition, seems correct on the current interpretation, wrong on my interpretation.

a) THE SECOND SENTENCE

The second sentence is wrong on the current interpretation, which holds money income and other prices constant along the demand curve, since the ordinate of the demand curve for any quantity x cannot then exceed money income divided by x, and this is not "indefinitely great" for a fixed value of x—say, x_o—whether x_o is greater or less than b. True, $f(x)$ might approach infinity as x approaches zero, but this is not what Marshall says; he says it is "indefinitely great, for values of x less than b," i.e., for any particular value of x less than b—say, $x_o = 0.99b$.

On the variant of my interpretation involving compensating variations in money income—the variant that the note numbered II in the eighth edition leads me to believe Marshall used in the Mathematical Appendix—this sentence is entirely valid. As x declines from a value larger than b, the compensating variation in money income required to keep the individual's real income the same becomes larger and larger, approaching infinity as x approaches b, the minimum amount necessary for existence. This permits the ordinate of the demand curve likewise to approach infinity as x approaches b. On the variant involving compensating variations in other prices—the one Marshall used in the text—the definition of the demand curve breaks down for values of x less than b: for a finite price of the commodity in question, sufficiently high so that the given money income could purchase only a quantity x less than b, there will exist no set of nonnegative prices for the remaining commodities that will keep the purchasing power of money constant in the sense of enabling the same money income to provide the same level of utility; money income and real income cannot both be held constant and at the same time all prices be kept nonnegative. This sentence can therefore be defended as valid on either variant of my interpretation.

One possible ground for dismissing this sentence as evidence against the current interpretation is that the so-called "error" on that interpretation is of my own making, arising from a too subtle and too literal reading of the note. Marshall, it could be argued, was using "demand curve" to mean "utility curve" and $f(x)$ to mean "marginal utility," and therefore he did not consider whether the sentence would be valid if $f(x)$ were to be interpreted literally as the ordinate of the demand curve. A note that Marshall published in 1893 on "Consumer's Surplus" could be cited as evidence for this contention. In this note he quotes part of Note VI as follows: " 'If, however, an amount b of the commodity is necessary for existence, [the utility of the first element] a will be infinite.' "[59] The bracketed expression that Marshall substituted for $f(x)$ would support the notion that he was using "demand curve" and "utility curve" interchangeably.

I do not myself accept this argument; it seems to me to do much less than justice to Marshall. In the first place, I am inclined to give little weight to an incidental, explanatory, phrase inserted by Marshall as late as 1892 or 1893, some twenty years after the fundamental analysis incorporated in Note VI had been completed. I have noted above and shall presently cite evidence that Marshall may have been somewhat confused about the fine points of his own theory of demand by the early 1890's. In the second place, and more important, Marshall clearly distinguishes in the earlier notes in the Mathematical Appendix between a utility curve and a demand curve, repeatedly using the word "utility," and in the first sentence of Note VI says that "the total utility of the commodity is *measured by* $\int_0^a f(x)\,dx$" (1st ed., p. 740; italics added). If he had been using $f(x)$ to stand for marginal utility, the words I have italicized could have been omitted. Finally, Note VI, like most of the rest of the Mathematical Appendix, summarizes a subtle, closely reasoned, and by means obvious, mathematical argument, in which, so far as I know, few errors have ever been found. Is it credible that it would have been worded as loosely and carelessly as the argument being criticized requires; or that, if at one stage it had been, Marshall would have failed to see the simple mathematical error implicit in a literal reading of his words on the current interpretation of the demand curve? It seems to me far more credible that he meant what he said and that the correctness of what he said on my interpretation of his demand curve is strong evidence for that interpretation.

[59] "Consumer's Surplus," *Annals of the American Academy of Political and Social Science*, III (March, 1893), 618–21 (brackets in original). This note is a reply to some comments by Simon Patten. The letter a after the brackets which appears in the *Annals* note does not appear in the *Principles*, and I can explain it only as a typographical error.

b) THE FINAL SENTENCE

The explanation that follows of the final sentence added to Note VI in the third edition, though not completely satisfactory, is reasonably so, and I have been able to construct no other even remotely satisfactory explanation.

Let U be the utility function of the "individual purchaser" and U_x the marginal utility of x units of tea to him, i.e., the partial derivative of U with respect to x. Now the increase in utility attributable to having a rather than b units of tea—consumer's surplus in utility units—is given by

$$\int_b^a U_x dx\,, \tag{1}$$

where the integral is computed for constant quantities of other commodities equal to the amounts consumed when a units of tea are consumed and other conditions are those corresponding to the demand curve $y = f(x)$.

At every point along the demand curve,

$$U_x = ny = n(x)\,f(x)\,, \tag{2}$$

where n is the marginal utility of money—itself, of course, a function of x along the demand curve. Integrating both sides of equation (2) gives

$$\int_b^a U_x dx = \int_b^a n(x)\,f(x)\,dx\,. \tag{3}$$

The left-hand side of equation (3) is symbolically identical with equation (1); yet there is an important difference between them. In equation (1), U_x is computed, holding the quantities of other commodities constant as x varies; in equation (3), U_x is computed, holding constant whatever is held constant along the demand curve (money income and other prices on the current interpretation; real income on my interpretation). In general, quantities of other commodities vary along the demand curve (on either interpretation), and U_x may depend on the quantities of other commodities, so the

U_x in equation (3) may be numerically different from the U_x in equation (1) for a value of x other than a. This difficulty disappears if U_x is supposed to be independent of the quantities of other commodities—an assumption that Marshall pretty clearly makes as a general rule (e.g., see Nn. I and II of the Mathematical Appendix). On this assumption, then, the right-hand side of equation (3) measures consumer's surplus in utility units.

It is at this point that difficulties of interpretation arise; for the right-hand side of equation (3) is obtained by multiplying "$f(x)$ within the integral given above by that function of" x "which represents the marginal utility ... of money." Why does Marshall say "that function of $xf(x)$" rather than of x alone? And is it valid to make this substitution? One can argue that to each value of x there corresponds a value of $f(x)$ and hence of $xf(x)$, so that the two forms of statement are equivalent: Marshall has simply made the transformation $z = xf(x)$ and converted $n(x)$ into $n(z)$. This argument is not, however, rigorous. In general, x will not be a single-valued function of z; hence to any given value of z there may correspond more than one value of x and hence more than one value of n. The two forms of statement are equivalent if and only if n is a single-valued function of z, i.e., if $n(x)$ is the same for all values of x for which $xf(x)$ is the same.

Given independence between the marginal utility of tea and the quantity of other commodities, this condition is always satisfied on the current interpretation of the demand curve but not on the alternative interpretation. Let x' stand for the quantity of a composite commodity representing all commodities other than tea, y' for its price, and $U_{x'}$, for its marginal utility. At each point on the demand curve,

$$\frac{U_x}{y} = \frac{U_{x'}}{y'} = n \, .$$

On the current interpretation of the demand curve, money income and the prices of other commodities are the same for all points on the demand curve. It follows that, for all values of x that yield the same value of $xf(x)$, the same amount will be spent on other commodities; so x' is the same (since y' is by definition); so $U_{x'}$ is (since, on the assumption of independence, $U_{x'}$ depends only on x'); and so n is. Marshall's use of $xf(x)$ instead of x is thus valid on the current interpretation of the demand curve.

On my interpretation, either money income varies along the demand curve, so as to keep real income constant, or other prices do; hence the preceding argument is no longer valid. That the two forms of statement are no longer always equivalent can be shown by a counter-example. If other prices are held constant and compensating variations of income are used to keep real income constant, $U = \sqrt{x} + \sqrt{x'}$ is a utility function that gives different values of n for different values of x yielding the same value of $xf(x)$. If money income is held constant and compensating variations of other prices are used to keep real income constant, $U = 3 + x - \frac{1}{10}x^2 + \sqrt{x'}$ is such a utility function. Hence Marshall's use of $xf(x)$ instead of x is invalid on either variant of the alternative interpretation.

This explanation leaves a number of Marshall's verbal statements wrong or ambiguous, whichever interpretation of the demand curve is accepted. (1) The parenthetical explanation of the meaning of $xf(x)$ seems wrong—why the word "already"? If one is thinking of going through the process of extracting as much as possible from the consumer for each successive unit of tea and is supposing the maximum price that he will pay for successive units to be given by the demand curve, then $\int_b^x f(x)dx$ and not $xf(x)$ is the amount he has "already spent on tea." If one is thinking of the amount spent on tea at a given price for tea, then $xf(x)$ is the amount spent when the price is $f(x)$, not the amount "already spent." The explanation offered above accepts the latter rendering of the parenthesis, i.e., supposes the word "already" omitted. (2) The last clause—"when his stock of money has been diminished by that amount"—is ambiguous. To make it consistent with the explanation offered above, one must add "and tea is unavailable, so that the balance is spent solely on other commodities at the prices assumed in drawing the demand curve for tea." The reference to "stock of money" suggests that Marshall was supposing money income constant and so, independently of the rest of the quotation, would tend to rule out compensating variations in money income. It should be noted that there are no such ambiguities in the original version of Note VI, either in the parts quoted above or in the parts not quoted.

UNIVERSITY OF CHICAGO

[13]

The American Economic Review

Volume LVIII MARCH 1968 Number 1

THE ROLE OF MONETARY POLICY*

By MILTON FRIEDMAN**

There is wide agreement about the major goals of economic policy: high employment, stable prices, and rapid growth. There is less agreement that these goals are mutually compatible or, among those who regard them as incompatible, about the terms at which they can and should be substituted for one another. There is least agreement about the role that various instruments of policy can and should play in achieving the several goals.

My topic for tonight is the role of one such instrument—monetary policy. What can it contribute? And how should it be conducted to contribute the most? Opinion on these questions has fluctuated widely. In the first flush of enthusiasm about the newly created Federal Reserve System, many observers attributed the relative stability of the 1920s to the System's capacity for fine tuning—to apply an apt modern term. It came to be widely believed that a new era had arrived in which business cycles had been rendered obsolete by advances in monetary technology. This opinion was shared by economist and layman alike, though, of course, there were some dissonant voices. The Great Contraction destroyed this naive attitude. Opinion swung to the other extreme. Monetary policy was a string. You could pull on it to stop inflation but you could not push on it to halt recession. You could lead a horse to water but you could not make him drink. Such theory by aphorism was soon replaced by Keynes' rigorous and sophisticated analysis.

Keynes offered simultaneously an explanation for the presumed impotence of monetary policy to stem the depression, a nonmonetary interpretation of the depression, and an alternative to monetary policy

* Presidential address delivered at the Eightieth Annual Meeting of the American Economic Association, Washington, D.C., December 29, 1967.

** I am indebted for helpful criticisms of earlier drafts to Armen Alchian, Gary Becker, Martin Bronfenbrenner, Arthur F. Burns, Phillip Cagan, David D. Friedman, Lawrence Harris, Harry G. Johnson, Homer Jones, Jerry Jordan, David Meiselman, Allan H. Meltzer, Theodore W. Schultz, Anna J. Schwartz, Herbert Stein, George J. Stigler, and James Tobin.

for meeting the depression and his offering was avidly accepted. If liquidity preference is absolute or nearly so—as Keynes believed likely in times of heavy unemployment—interest rates cannot be lowered by monetary measures. If investment and consumption are little affected by interest rates—as Hansen and many of Keynes' other American disciples came to believe—lower interest rates, even if they could be achieved, would do little good. Monetary policy is twice damned. The contraction, set in train, on this view, by a collapse of investment or by a shortage of investment opportunities or by stubborn thriftiness, could not, it was argued, have been stopped by monetary measures. But there was available an alternative—fiscal policy. Government spending could make up for insufficient private investment. Tax reductions could undermine stubborn thriftiness.

The wide acceptance of these views in the economics profession meant that for some two decades monetary policy was believed by all but a few reactionary souls to have been rendered obsolete by new economic knowledge. Money did not matter. Its only role was the minor one of keeping interest rates low, in order to hold down interest payments in the government budget, contribute to the "euthanasia of the rentier," and maybe, stimulate investment a bit to assist government spending in maintaining a high level of aggregate demand.

These views produced a widespread adoption of cheap money policies after the war. And they received a rude shock when these policies failed in country after country, when central bank after central bank was forced to give up the pretense that it could indefinitely keep "the" rate of interest at a low level. In this country, the public denouement came with the Federal Reserve-Treasury Accord in 1951, although the policy of pegging government bond prices was not formally abandoned until 1953. Inflation, stimulated by cheap money policies, not the widely heralded postwar depression, turned out to be the order of the day. The result was the beginning of a revival of belief in the potency of monetary policy.

This revival was strongly fostered among economists by the theoretical developments initiated by Haberler but named for Pigou that pointed out a channel—namely, changes in wealth—whereby changes in the real quantity of money can affect aggregate demand even if they do not alter interest rates. These theoretical developments did not undermine Keynes' argument against the potency of orthodox monetary measures when liquidity preference is absolute since under such circumstances the usual monetary operations involve simply substituting money for other assets without changing total wealth. But they did show how changes in the quantity of money produced in other ways could affect total spending even under such circumstances. And, more fundamentally, they did undermine Keynes' key theoretical proposition, namely, that even in a world of flexible prices, a position of equilibrium at full employment might not exist. Henceforth, unemployment had again to be explained by rigidities or imperfections, not as the natural outcome of a fully operative market process.

The revival of belief in the potency of monetary policy was fostered also by a re-evaluation of the role money played from 1929 to 1933. Keynes and most other economists of the time believed that the Great Contraction in the United States occurred despite aggressive expansionary policies by the monetary authorities—that they did their best but their best was not good enough.[1] Recent studies have demonstrated that the facts are precisely the reverse: the U.S. monetary authorities followed highly deflationary policies. The quantity of money in the United States fell by one-third in the course of the contraction. And it fell not because there were no willing borrowers—not because the horse would not drink. It fell because the Federal Reserve System forced or permitted a sharp reduction in the monetary base, because it failed to exercise the responsibilities assigned to it in the Federal Reserve Act to provide liquidity to the banking system. The Great Contraction is tragic testimony to the power of monetary policy—not, as Keynes and so many of his contemporaries believed, evidence of its impotence.

In the United States the revival of belief in the potency of monetary policy was strengthened also by increasing disillusionment with fiscal policy, not so much with its potential to affect aggregate demand as with the practical and political feasibility of so using it. Expenditures turned out to respond sluggishly and with long lags to attempts to adjust them to the course of economic activity, so emphasis shifted to taxes. But here political factors entered with a vengeance to prevent prompt adjustment to presumed need, as has been so graphically illustrated in the months since I wrote the first draft of this talk. "Fine tuning" is a marvelously evocative phrase in this electronic age, but it has little resemblance to what is possible in practice—not, I might add, an unmixed evil.

It is hard to realize how radical has been the change in professional opinion on the role of money. Hardly an economist today accepts views that were the common coin some two decades ago. Let me cite a few examples.

In a talk published in 1945, E. A. Goldenweiser, then Director of the Research Division of the Federal Reserve Board, described the primary objective of monetary policy as being to "maintain the value of Government bonds. . . . This country" he wrote, "will have to adjust to

[1] In [2], I have argued that Henry Simons shared this view with Keynes, and that it accounts for the policy changes that he recommended.

a 2½ per cent interest rate as the return on safe, long-time money, because the time has come when returns on pioneering capital can no longer be unlimited as they were in the past" [4, p. 117].

In a book on *Financing American Prosperity,* edited by Paul Homan and Fritz Machlup and published in 1945, Alvin Hansen devotes nine pages of text to the "savings-investment problem" without finding any need to use the words "interest rate" or any close facsimile thereto [5, pp. 218-27]. In his contribution to this volume, Fritz Machlup wrote, "Questions regarding the rate of interest, in particular regarding its variation or its stability, may not be among the most vital problems of the postwar economy, but they are certainly among the perplexing ones" [5, p. 466]. In his contribution, John H. Williams—not only professor at Harvard but also a long-time adviser to the New York Federal Reserve Bank—wrote, "I can see no prospect of revival of a general monetary control in the postwar period" [5, p. 383].

Another of the volumes dealing with postwar policy that appeared at this time, *Planning and Paying for Full Employment,* was edited by Abba P. Lerner and Frank D. Graham [6] and had contributors of all shades of professional opinion—from Henry Simons and Frank Graham to Abba Lerner and Hans Neisser. Yet Albert Halasi, in his excellent summary of the papers, was able to say, "Our contributors do not discuss the question of money supply. . . . The contributors make no special mention of credit policy to remedy actual depressions. . . . Inflation . . . might be fought more effectively by raising interest rates. . . . But . . . other anti-inflationary measures . . . are preferable" [6, pp. 23-24]. *A Survey of Contemporary Economics,* edited by Howard Ellis and published in 1948, was an "official" attempt to codify the state of economic thought of the time. In his contribution, Arthur Smithies wrote, "In the field of compensatory action, I believe fiscal policy must shoulder most of the load. Its chief rival, monetary policy, seems to be disqualified on institutional grounds. This country appears to be committed to something like the present low level of interest rates on a long-term basis" [1, p. 208].

These quotations suggest the flavor of professional thought some two decades ago. If you wish to go further in this humbling inquiry, I recommend that you compare the sections on money—when you can find them—in the Principles texts of the early postwar years with the lengthy sections in the current crop even, or especially, when the early and recent Principles are different editions of the same work.

The pendulum has swung far since then, if not all the way to the position of the late 1920s, at least much closer to that position than to the position of 1945. There are of course many differences between then and now, less in the potency attributed to monetary policy than in the roles assigned to it and the criteria by which the profession believes monetary policy should be guided. Then, the chief roles assigned monetary policy were to promote price stability and to preserve the gold standard; the chief criteria of monetary policy were the state of the "money market," the extent of "speculation" and the movement of gold. Today, primacy is assigned to the promotion of full employment, with the prevention of inflation a continuing but definitely secondary objective. And there is major disagreement about criteria of policy, varying from emphasis on money market conditions, interest rates, and the quantity of money to the belief that the state of employment itself should be the proximate criterion of policy.

I stress nonetheless the similarity between the views that prevailed in the late 'twenties and those that prevail today because I fear that, now as then, the pendulum may well have swung too far, that, now as then, we are in danger of assigning to monetary policy a larger role than it can perform, in danger of asking it to accomplish tasks that it cannot achieve, and, as a result, in danger of preventing it from making the contribution that it is capable of making.

Unaccustomed as I am to denigrating the importance of money, I therefore shall, as my first task, stress what monetary policy cannot do. I shall then try to outline what it can do and how it can best make its contribution, in the present state of our knowledge—or ignorance.

I. *What Monetary Policy Cannot Do*

From the infinite world of negation, I have selected two limitations of monetary policy to discuss: (1) It cannot peg interest rates for more than very limited periods; (2) It cannot peg the rate of unemployment for more than very limited periods. I select these because the contrary has been or is widely believed, because they correspond to the two main unattainable tasks that are at all likely to be assigned to monetary policy, and because essentially the same theoretical analysis covers both.

Pegging of Interest Rates

History has already persuaded many of you about the first limitation. As noted earlier, the failure of cheap money policies was a major source of the reaction against simple-minded Keynesianism. In the United States, this reaction involved widespread recognition that the wartime and postwar pegging of bond prices was a mistake, that the abandonment of this policy was a desirable and inevitable step, and that it had none of the disturbing and disastrous consequences that were so freely predicted at the time.

The limitation derives from a much misunderstood feature of the relation between money and interest rates. Let the Fed set out to keep interest rates down. How will it try to do so? By buying securities. This raises their prices and lowers their yields. In the process, it also increases the quantity of reserves available to banks, hence the amount of bank credit, and, ultimately the total quantity of money. That is why central bankers in particular, and the financial community more broadly, generally believe that an increase in the quantity of money tends to lower interest rates. Academic economists accept the same conclusion, but for different reasons. They see, in their mind's eye, a negatively sloping liquidity preference schedule. How can people be induced to hold a larger quantity of money? Only by bidding down interest rates.

Both are right, up to a point. The *initial* impact of increasing the quantity of money at a faster rate than it has been increasing is to make interest rates lower for a time than they would otherwise have been. But this is only the beginning of the process not the end. The more rapid rate of monetary growth will stimulate spending, both through the impact on investment of lower market interest rates and through the impact on other spending and thereby relative prices of higher cash balances than are desired. But one man's spending is another man's income. Rising income will raise the liquidity preference schedule and the demand for loans; it may also raise prices, which would reduce the real quantity of money. These three effects will reverse the initial downward pressure on interest rates fairly promptly, say, in something less than a year. Together they will tend, after a somewhat longer interval, say, a year or two, to return interest rates to the level they would otherwise have had. Indeed, given the tendency for the economy to overreact, they are highly likely to raise interest rates temporarily beyond that level, setting in motion a cyclical adjustment process.

A fourth effect, when and if it becomes operative, will go even farther, and definitely mean that a higher rate of monetary expansion will correspond to a higher, not lower, level of interest rates than would otherwise have prevailed. Let the higher rate of monetary growth produce rising prices, and let the public come to expect that prices will continue to rise. Borrowers will then be willing to pay and lenders will then demand higher interest rates—as Irving Fisher pointed out decades ago. This price expectation effect is slow to develop and also slow to disappear. Fisher estimated that it took several decades for a full adjustment and more recent work is consistent with his estimates.

These subsequent effects explain why every attempt to keep interest rates at a low level has forced the monetary authority to engage in successively larger and larger open market purchases. They explain why, historically, high and rising nominal interest rates have been associated with rapid growth in the quantity of money, as in Brazil or Chile or in the United States in recent years, and why low and falling interest rates have been associated with slow growth in the quantity of money, as in Switzerland now or in the United States from 1929 to 1933. As an empirical matter, low interest rates are a sign that monetary policy *has been* tight—in the sense that the quantity of money has grown slowly; high interest rates are a sign that monetary policy *has been* easy—in the sense that the quantity of money has grown rapidly. The broadest facts of experience run in precisely the opposite direction from that which the financial community and academic economists have all generally taken for granted.

Paradoxically, the monetary authority could assure low nominal rates of interest—but to do so it would have to start out in what seems like the opposite direction, by engaging in a deflationary monetary policy. Similarly, it could assure high nominal interest rates by engaging in an inflationary policy and accepting a temporary movement in interest rates in the opposite direction.

These considerations not only explain why monetary policy cannot peg interest rates; they also explain why interest rates are such a misleading indicator of whether monetary policy is "tight" or "easy." For that, it is far better to look at the rate of change of the quantity of money.[2]

Employment as a Criterion of Policy

The second limitation I wish to discuss goes more against the grain of current thinking. Monetary growth, it is widely held, will tend to stimulate employment; monetary contraction, to retard employment. Why, then, cannot the monetary authority adopt a target for employment or unemployment—say, 3 per cent unemployment; be tight when unemployment is less than the target; be easy when unemployment is higher than the target; and in this way peg unemployment at, say, 3 per cent? The reason it cannot is precisely the same as for interest rates—the difference between the immediate and the delayed consequences of such a policy.

Thanks to Wicksell, we are all acquainted with the concept of a "natural" rate of interest and the possibility of a discrepancy between the "natural" and the "market" rate. The preceding analysis of interest rates can be translated fairly directly into Wicksellian terms. The monetary authority can make the market rate less than the natural rate

[2] This is partly an empirical not theoretical judgment. In principle, "tightness" or "ease" depends on the rate of change of the quantity of money supplied compared to the rate of change of the quantity demanded excluding effects on demand from monetary policy itself. However, empirically demand is highly stable, if we exclude the effect of monetary policy, so it is generally sufficient to look at supply alone.

only by inflation. It can make the market rate higher than the natural rate only by deflation. We have added only one wrinkle to Wicksell—the Irving Fisher distinction between the nominal and the real rate of interest. Let the monetary authority keep the nominal market rate for a time below the natural rate by inflation. That in turn will raise the nominal natural rate itself, once anticipations of inflation become widespread, thus requiring still more rapid inflation to hold down the market rate. Similarly, because of the Fisher effect, it will require not merely deflation but more and more rapid deflation to hold the market rate above the initial "natural" rate.

This analysis has its close counterpart in the employment market. At any moment of time, there is some level of unemployment which has the property that it is consistent with equilibrium in the structure of *real* wage rates. At that level of unemployment, real wage rates are tending on the average to rise at a "normal" secular rate, i.e., at a rate that can be indefinitely maintained so long as capital formation, technological improvements, etc., remain on their long-run trends. A lower level of unemployment is an indication that there is an excess demand for labor that will produce upward pressure on real wage rates. A higher level of unemployment is an indication that there is an excess supply of labor that will produce downward pressure on real wage rates. The "natural rate of unemployment," in other words, is the level that would be ground out by the Walrasian system of general equilibrium equations, provided there is imbedded in them the actual structural characteristics of the labor and commodity markets, including market imperfections, stochastic variability in demands and supplies, the cost of gathering information about job vacancies and labor availabilities, the costs of mobility, and so on.[3]

You will recognize the close similarity between this statement and the celebrated Phillips Curve. The similarity is not coincidental. Phillips' analysis of the relation between unemployment and wage change is deservedly celebrated as an important and original contribution. But, unfortunately, it contains a basic defect—the failure to distinguish between *nominal* wages and *real* wages—just as Wicksell's analysis failed to distinguish between *nominal* interest rates and *real* interest rates. Implicitly, Phillips wrote his article for a world in which everyone anticipated that nominal prices would be stable and in which that anticipation remained unshaken and immutable whatever happened to actual prices and wages. Suppose, by contrast, that everyone anticipates that prices will rise at a rate of more than 75 per cent a year—as, for exam-

[3] It is perhaps worth noting that this "natural" rate need not correspond to equality between the number unemployed and the number of job vacancies. For any given structure of the labor market, there will be some equilibrium relation between these two magnitudes, but there is no reason why it should be one of equality.

ple, Brazilians did a few years ago. Then wages must rise at that rate simply to keep real wages unchanged. An excess supply of labor will be reflected in a less rapid rise in nominal wages than in anticipated prices,[4] not in an absolute decline in wages. When Brazil embarked on a policy to bring down the rate of price rise, and succeeded in bringing the price rise down to about 45 per cent a year, there was a sharp initial rise in unemployment because under the influence of earlier anticipations, wages kept rising at a pace that was higher than the new rate of price rise, though lower than earlier. This is the result experienced, and to be expected, of all attempts to reduce the rate of inflation below that widely anticipated.[5]

To avoid misunderstanding, let me emphasize that by using the term "natural" rate of unemployment, I do not mean to suggest that it is immutable and unchangeable. On the contrary, many of the market characteristics that determine its level are man-made and policy-made. In the United States, for example, legal minimum wage rates, the Walsh-Healy and Davis-Bacon Acts, and the strength of labor unions all make the natural rate of unemployment higher than it would otherwise be. Improvements in employment exchanges, in availability of information about job vacancies and labor supply, and so on, would tend to lower the natural rate of unemployment. I use the term "natural" for the same reason Wicksell did—to try to separate the real forces from monetary forces.

Let us assume that the monetary authority tries to peg the "market" rate of unemployment at a level below the "natural" rate. For definiteness, suppose that it takes 3 per cent as the target rate and that the "natural" rate is higher than 3 per cent. Suppose also that we start out at a time when prices have been stable and when unemployment is higher than 3 per cent. Accordingly, the authority increases the rate of monetary growth. This will be expansionary. By making nominal cash

[4] Strictly speaking, the rise in nominal wages will be less rapid than the rise in anticipated nominal wages to make allowance for any secular changes in real wages.

[5] Stated in terms of the rate of change of nominal wages, the Phillips Curve can be expected to be reasonably stable and well defined for any period for which the *average* rate of change of prices, and hence the anticipated rate, has been relatively stable. For such periods, nominal wages and "real" wages move together. Curves computed for different periods or different countries for each of which this condition has been satisfied will differ in level, the level of the curve depending on what the average rate of price change was. The higher the average rate of price change, the higher will tend to be the level of the curve. For periods or countries for which the rate of change of prices varies considerably, the Phillips Curve will not be well defined. My impression is that these statements accord reasonably well with the experience of the economists who have explored empirical Phillips Curves.

Restate Phillips' analysis in terms of the rate of change of real wages—and even more precisely, anticipated real wages—and it all falls into place. That is why students of empirical Phillips Curves have found that it helps to include the rate of change of the price level as an independent variable.

balances higher than people desire, it will tend initially to lower interest rates and in this and other ways to stimulate spending. Income and spending will start to rise.

To begin with, much or most of the rise in income will take the form of an increase in output and employment rather than in prices. People have been expecting prices to be stable, and prices and wages have been set for some time in the future on that basis. It takes time for people to adjust to a new state of demand. Producers will tend to react to the initial expansion in aggregate demand by increasing output, employees by working longer hours, and the unemployed, by taking jobs now offered at former nominal wages. This much is pretty standard doctrine.

But it describes only the initial effects. Because selling prices of products typically respond to an unanticipated rise in nominal demand faster than prices of factors of production, real wages received have gone down—though real wages anticipated by employees went up, since employees implicitly evaluated the wages offered at the earlier price level. Indeed, the simultaneous fall *ex post* in real wages to employers and rise *ex ante* in real wages to employees is what enabled employment to increase. But the decline *ex post* in real wages will soon come to affect anticipations. Employees will start to reckon on rising prices of the things they buy and to demand higher nominal wages for the future. "Market" unemployment is below the "natural" level. There is an excess demand for labor so real wages will tend to rise toward their initial level.

Even though the higher rate of monetary growth continues, the rise in real wages will reverse the decline in unemployment, and then lead to a rise, which will tend to return unemployment to its former level. In order to keep unemployment at its target level of 3 per cent, the monetary authority would have to raise monetary growth still more. As in the interest rate case, the "market" rate can be kept below the "natural" rate only by inflation. And, as in the interest rate case, too, only by accelerating inflation. Conversely, let the monetary authority choose a target rate of unemployment that is above the natural rate, and they will be led to produce a deflation, and an accelerating deflation at that.

What if the monetary authority chose the "natural" rate—either of interest or unemployment—as its target? One problem is that it cannot know what the "natural" rate is. Unfortunately, we have as yet devised no method to estimate accurately and readily the natural rate of either interest or unemployment. And the "natural" rate will itself change from time to time. But the basic problem is that even if the monetary authority knew the "natural" rate, and attempted to peg the market rate at that level, it would not be led to a determinate policy. The "market" rate will vary from the natural rate for all sorts of reasons other than monetary policy. If the monetary authority responds to these variations, it will set in train longer term effects that will make any monetary growth path it follows ultimately consistent with the rule of policy. The actual course of monetary growth will be analogous to a random walk, buffeted this way and that by the forces that produce temporary departures of the market rate from the natural rate.

To state this conclusion differently, there is always a temporary trade-off between inflation and unemployment; there is no permanent trade-off. The temporary trade-off comes not from inflation per se, but from unanticipated inflation, which generally means, from a rising rate of inflation. The widespread belief that there is a permanent trade-off is a sophisticated version of the confusion between "high" and "rising" that we all recognize in simpler forms. A rising rate of inflation may reduce unemployment, a high rate will not.

But how long, you will say, is "temporary"? For interest rates, we have some systematic evidence on how long each of the several effects takes to work itself out. For unemployment, we do not. I can at most venture a personal judgment, based on some examination of the historical evidence, that the initial effects of a higher and unanticipated rate of inflation last for something like two to five years; that this initial effect then begins to be reversed; and that a full adjustment to the new rate of inflation takes about as long for employment as for interest rates, say, a couple of decades. For both interest rates and employment, let me add a qualification. These estimates are for changes in the rate of inflation of the order of magnitude that has been experienced in the United States. For much more sizable changes, such as those experienced in South American countries, the whole adjustment process is greatly speeded up.

To state the general conclusion still differently, the monetary authority controls nominal quantities—directly, the quantity of its own liabilities. In principle, it can use this control to peg a nominal quantity—an exchange rate, the price level, the nominal level of national income, the quantity of money by one or another definition—or to peg the rate of change in a nominal quantity—the rate of inflation or deflation, the rate of growth or decline in nominal national income, the rate of growth of the quantity of money. It cannot use its control over nominal quantities to peg a real quantity—the real rate of interest, the rate of unemployment, the level of real national income, the real quantity of money, the rate of growth of real national income, or the rate of growth of the real quantity of money.

II. *What Monetary Policy Can Do*

Monetary policy cannot peg these real magnitudes at predetermined levels. But monetary policy can and does have important effects on these real magnitudes. The one is in no way inconsistent with the other.

My own studies of monetary history have made me extremely sympathetic to the oft-quoted, much reviled, and as widely misunderstood, comment by John Stuart Mill. "There cannot . . . ," he wrote, "be intrinsically a more insignificant thing, in the economy of society, than money; except in the character of a contrivance for sparing time and labour. It is a machine for doing quickly and commodiously, what would be done, though less quickly and commodiously, without it: and like many other kinds of machinery, it only exerts a distinct and independent influence of its own when it gets out of order" [7, p. 488].

True, money is only a machine, but it is an extraordinarily efficient machine. Without it, we could not have begun to attain the astounding growth in output and level of living we have experienced in the past two centuries—any more than we could have done so without those other marvelous machines that dot our countryside and enable us, for the most part, simply to do more efficiently what could be done without them at much greater cost in labor.

But money has one feature that these other machines do not share. Because it is so pervasive, when it gets out of order, it throws a monkey wrench into the operation of all the other machines. The Great Contraction is the most dramatic example but not the only one. Every other major contraction in this country has been either produced by monetary disorder or greatly exacerbated by monetary disorder. Every major inflation has been produced by monetary expansion—mostly to meet the overriding demands of war which have forced the creation of money to supplement explicit taxation.

The first and most important lesson that history teaches about what monetary policy can do—and it is a lesson of the most profound importance—is that monetary policy can prevent money itself from being a major source of economic disturbance. This sounds like a negative proposition: avoid major mistakes. In part it is. The Great Contraction might not have occurred at all, and if it had, it would have been far less severe, if the monetary authority had avoided mistakes, or if the monetary arrangements had been those of an earlier time when there was no central authority with the power to make the kinds of mistakes that the Federal Reserve System made. The past few years, to come closer to home, would have been steadier and more productive of economic well-being if the Federal Reserve had avoided drastic and erratic changes of direction, first expanding the money supply at an unduly rapid pace, then, in early 1966, stepping on the brake too hard, then, at the end of 1966, reversing itself and resuming expansion until at least November, 1967, at a more rapid pace than can long be maintained without appreciable inflation.

Even if the proposition that monetary policy can prevent money itself from being a major source of economic disturbance were a wholly negative proposition, it would be none the less important for that. As it happens, however, it is not a wholly negative proposition. The monetary machine has gotten out of order even when there has been no central authority with anything like the power now possessed by the Fed. In the United States, the 1907 episode and earlier banking panics are examples of how the monetary machine can get out of order largely on its own. There is therefore a positive and important task for the monetary authority—to suggest improvements in the machine that will reduce the chances that it will get out of order, and to use its own powers so as to keep the machine in good working order.

A second thing monetary policy can do is provide a stable background for the economy—keep the machine well oiled, to continue Mill's analogy. Accomplishing the first task will contribute to this objective, but there is more to it than that. Our economic system will work best when producers and consumers, employers and employees, can proceed with full confidence that the average level of prices will behave in a known way in the future—preferably that it will be highly stable. Under any conceivable institutional arrangements, and certainly under those that now prevail in the United States, there is only a limited amount of flexibility in prices and wages. We need to conserve this flexibility to achieve changes in relative prices and wages that are required to adjust to dynamic changes in tastes and technology. We should not dissipate it simply to achieve changes in the absolute level of prices that serve no economic function.

In an earlier era, the gold standard was relied on to provide confidence in future monetary stability. In its heyday it served that function reasonably well. It clearly no longer does, since there is scarce a country in the world that is prepared to let the gold standard reign unchecked—and there are persuasive reasons why countries should not do so. The monetary authority could operate as a surrogate for the gold standard, if it pegged exchange rates and did so exclusively by altering the quantity of money in response to balance of payment flows without "sterilizing" surpluses or deficits and without resorting to open or concealed exchange control or to changes in tariffs and quotas. But again, though many central bankers talk this way, few are in fact willing to follow this course—and again there are persuasive reasons why they should not do so. Such a policy would submit each country to the vagaries not of an impersonal and automatic gold standard but of the policies—deliberate or accidental—of other monetary authorities.

In today's world, if monetary policy is to provide a stable background for the economy it must do so by deliberately employing its powers to that end. I shall come later to how it can do so.

Finally, monetary policy can contribute to offsetting major disturbances in the economic system arising from other sources. If there is an independent secular exhilaration—as the postwar expansion was described by the proponents of secular stagnation—monetary policy can in principle help to hold it in check by a slower rate of monetary growth than would otherwise be desirable. If, as now, an explosive federal budget threatens unprecedented deficits, monetary policy can hold any inflationary dangers in check by a slower rate of monetary growth than would otherwise be desirable. This will temporarily mean higher interest rates than would otherwise prevail—to enable the government to borrow the sums needed to finance the deficit—but by preventing the speeding up of inflation, it may well mean both lower prices and lower nominal interest rates for the long pull. If the end of a substantial war offers the country an opportunity to shift resources from wartime to peacetime production, monetary policy can ease the transition by a higher rate of monetary growth than would otherwise be desirable—though experience is not very encouraging that it can do so without going too far.

I have put this point last, and stated it in qualified terms—as referring to major disturbances—because I believe that the potentiality of monetary policy in offsetting other forces making for instability is far more limited than is commonly believed. We simply do not know enough to be able to recognize minor disturbances when they occur or to be able to predict either what their effects will be with any precision or what monetary policy is required to offset their effects. We do not know enough to be able to achieve stated objectives by delicate, or even fairly coarse, changes in the mix of monetary and fiscal policy. In this area particularly the best is likely to be the enemy of the good. Experience suggests that the path of wisdom is to use monetary policy explicitly to offset other disturbances only when they offer a "clear and present danger."

III. *How Should Monetary Policy Be Conducted?*

How should monetary policy be conducted to make the contribution to our goals that it is capable of making? This is clearly not the occasion for presenting a detailed "Program for Monetary Stability"—to use the title of a book in which I tried to do so [3]. I shall restrict myself here to two major requirements for monetary policy that follow fairly directly from the preceding discussion.

The first requirement is that the monetary authority should guide itself by magnitudes that it can control, not by ones that it cannot control. If, as the authority has often done, it takes interest rates or the current unemployment percentage as the immediate criterion of policy, it will be like a space vehicle that has taken a fix on the wrong star. No matter how sensitive and sophisticated its guiding apparatus, the space vehicle will go astray. And so will the monetary authority. Of the various alternative magnitudes that it can control, the most appealing guides for policy are exchange rates, the price level as defined by some index, and the quantity of a monetary total—currency plus adjusted demand deposits, or this total plus commercial bank time deposits, or a still broader total.

For the United States in particular, exchange rates are an undesirable guide. It might be worth requiring the bulk of the economy to adjust to the tiny percentage consisting of foreign trade if that would guarantee freedom from monetary irresponsibility—as it might under a real gold standard. But it is hardly worth doing so simply to adapt to the average of whatever policies monetary authorities in the rest of the world adopt. Far better to let the market, through floating exchange rates, adjust to world conditions the 5 per cent or so of our resources devoted to international trade while reserving monetary policy to promote the effective use of the 95 per cent.

Of the three guides listed, the price level is clearly the most important in its own right. Other things the same, it would be much the best of the alternatives—as so many distinguished economists have urged in the past. But other things are not the same. The link between the policy actions of the monetary authority and the price level, while unquestionably present, is more indirect than the link between the policy actions of the authority and any of the several monetary totals. Moreover, monetary action takes a longer time to affect the price level than to affect the monetary totals and both the time lag and the magnitude of effect vary with circumstances. As a result, we cannot predict at all accurately just what effect a particular monetary action will have on the price level and, equally important, just when it will have that effect. Attempting to control directly the price level is therefore likely to make monetary policy itself a source of economic disturbance because of false stops and starts. Perhaps, as our understanding of monetary phenomena advances, the situation will change. But at the present stage of our understanding, the long way around seems the surer way to our objective. Accordingly, I believe that a monetary total is the best currently available immediate guide or criterion for monetary policy—and I believe that it matters much less which particular total is chosen than that one be chosen.

A second requirement for monetary policy is that the monetary authority avoid sharp swings in policy. In the past, monetary authorities have on occasion moved in the wrong direction—as in the episode of the Great Contraction that I have stressed. More frequently, they have moved in the right direction, albeit often too late, but have erred by moving too far. Too late and too much has been the general practice. For example, in early 1966, it was the right policy for the Federal Reserve to move in a less expansionary direction—though it should have done so at least a year earlier. But when it moved, it went too far, producing the sharpest change in the rate of monetary growth of the postwar era. Again, having gone too far, it was the right policy for the Fed to reverse course at the end of 1966. But again it went too far, not only restoring but exceeding the earlier excessive rate of monetary growth. And this episode is no exception. Time and again this has been the course followed—as in 1919 and 1920, in 1937 and 1938, in 1953 and 1954, in 1959 and 1960.

The reason for the propensity to overreact seems clear: the failure of monetary authorities to allow for the delay between their actions and the subsequent effects on the economy. They tend to determine their actions by today's conditions—but their actions will affect the economy only six or nine or twelve or fifteen months later. Hence they feel impelled to step on the brake, or the accelerator, as the case may be, too hard.

My own prescription is still that the monetary authority go all the way in avoiding such swings by adopting publicly the policy of achieving a steady rate of growth in a specified monetary total. The precise rate of growth, like the precise monetary total, is less important than the adoption of some stated and known rate. I myself have argued for a rate that would on the average achieve rough stability in the level of prices of final products, which I have estimated would call for something like a 3 to 5 per cent per year rate of growth in currency plus all commercial bank deposits or a slightly lower rate of growth in currency plus demand deposits only.[6] But it would be better to have a fixed rate that would on the average produce moderate inflation or moderate deflation, provided it was steady, than to suffer the wide and erratic perturbations we have experienced.

Short of the adoption of such a publicly stated policy of a steady rate of monetary growth, it would constitute a major improvement if the monetary authority followed the self-denying ordinance of avoiding wide swings. It is a matter of record that periods of relative stability in the rate of monetary growth have also been periods of relative stability in economic activity, both in the United States and other countries. Periods of wide swings in the rate of monetary growth have also been periods of wide swings in economic activity.

[6] In an as yet unpublished article on "The Optimum Quantity of Money," I conclude that a still lower rate of growth, something like 2 per cent for the broader definition, might be better yet in order to eliminate or reduce the difference between private and total costs of adding to real balances.

By setting itself a steady course and keeping to it, the monetary authority could make a major contribution to promoting economic stability. By making that course one of steady but moderate growth in the quantity of money, it would make a major contribution to avoidance of either inflation or deflation of prices. Other forces would still affect the economy, require change and adjustment, and disturb the even tenor of our ways. But steady monetary growth would provide a monetary climate favorable to the effective operation of those basic forces of enterprise, ingenuity, invention, hard work, and thrift that are the true springs of economic growth. That is the most that we can ask from monetary policy at our present stage of knowledge. But that much—and it is a great deal—is clearly within our reach.

REFERENCES

1. H. S. Ellis, ed., *A Survey of Contemporary Economics.* Philadelphia 1948.
2. Milton Friedman, "The Monetary Theory and Policy of Henry Simons," *Jour. Law and Econ.*, Oct. 1967, *10*, 1-13.
3. ———, *A Program for Monetary Stability*. New York 1959.
4. E. A. Goldenweiser, "Postwar Problems and Policies," *Fed. Res. Bull.*, Feb. 1945, *31*, 112-21.
5. P. T. Homan and Fritz Machlup, ed., *Financing American Prosperity.* New York 1945.
6. A. P. Lerner and F. D. Graham, ed., *Planning and Paying for Full Employment.* Princeton 1946.
7. J. S. Mill, *Principles of Political Economy*, Bk. III, Ashley ed. New York 1929.

The Nature of the Firm

By R. H. Coase

Economic theory has suffered in the past from a failure to state clearly its assumptions. Economists in building up a theory have often omitted to examine the foundations on which it was erected. This examination is, however, essential not only to prevent the misunderstanding and needless controversy which arise from a lack of knowledge of the assumptions on which a theory is based, but also because of the extreme importance for economics of good judgment in choosing between rival sets of assumptions. For instance, it is suggested that the use of the word "firm" in economics may be different from the use of the term by the "plain man."[1] Since there is apparently a trend in economic theory towards starting analysis with the individual firm and not with the industry,[2] it is all the more necessary not only that a clear definition of the word "firm" should be given but that its difference from a firm in the "real world," if it exists, should be made clear. Mrs. Robinson has said that "the two questions to be asked of a set of assumptions in economics are: Are they tractable? and: Do they correspond with the real world?"[3] Though, as Mrs. Robinson points out, "more often one set will be manageable and the other realistic," yet there may well be branches of theory where assumptions may be both manageable and realistic. It is hoped to show in the following paper that a definition of a firm may be obtained which is not only realistic in that it corresponds to what is meant by a firm in the real world, but is tractable by two of the most powerful instruments of economic analysis developed by Marshall, the idea of the margin and that of substitution, together giving the idea of substitution at

[1] Joan Robinson, *Economics is a Serious Subject*, p. 12.
[2] See N. Kaldor, "The Equilibrium of the Firm," *Economic Journal*, March, 1934.
[3] Op. cit., p. 6.

the margin.[1] Our definition must, of course, "relate to formal relations which are capable of being *conceived* exactly."[2]

I

It is convenient if, in searching for a definition of a firm, we first consider the economic system as it is normally treated by the economist. Let us consider the description of the economic system given by Sir Arthur Salter.[3] "The normal economic system works itself. For its current operation it is under no central control, it needs no central survey. Over the whole range of human activity and human need, supply is adjusted to demand, and production to consumption, by a process that is automatic, elastic and responsive." An economist thinks of the economic system as being co-ordinated by the price mechanism and society becomes not an organisation but an organism.[4] The economic system "works itself." This does not mean that there is no planning by individuals. These exercise foresight and choose between alternatives. This is necessarily so if there is to be order in the system. But this theory assumes that the direction of resources is dependent directly on the price mechanism. Indeed, it is often considered to be an objection to economic planning that it merely tries to do what is already done by the price mechanism.[5] Sir Arthur Salter's description, however, gives a very incomplete picture of our economic system. Within a firm, the description does not fit at all. For instance, in economic theory we find that the allocation of factors of production between different uses is determined by the price mechanism. The price of factor *A* becomes higher in *X* than in *Y*. As a result, *A* moves from *Y* to *X* until the difference between the prices in *X* and *Y*, except in so far as it compensates for other differential advantages, disappears. Yet in the real world, we find that there are many areas where this does not apply. If a workman moves from department *Y* to department *X*, he does not go because of a change in relative prices, but because he is ordered to do so. Those who

[1] J. M. Keynes, *Essays in Biography*, pp. 223–4.
[2] L. Robbins, *Nature and Significance of Economic Science*, p. 63.
[3] This description is quoted with approval by D. H. Robertson, *Control of Industry*, p. 85, and by Professor Arnold Plant, "Trends in Business Administration," ECONOMICA, February, 1932. It appears in *Allied Shipping Control*, pp. 16–17.
[4] See F. A. Hayek, "The Trend of Economic Thinking," ECONOMICA, May, 1933.
[5] See F. A. Hayek, op. cit.

object to economic planning on the grounds that the problem is solved by price movements can be answered by pointing out that there is planning within our economic system which is quite different from the individual planning mentioned above and which is akin to what is normally called economic planning. The example given above is typical of a large sphere in our modern economic system. Of course, this fact has not been ignored by economists. Marshall introduces organisation as a fourth factor of production; J. B. Clark gives the co-ordinating function to the entrepreneur; Professor Knight introduces managers who co-ordinate. As D. H. Robertson points out, we find "islands of conscious power in this ocean of unconscious co-operation like lumps of butter coagulating in a pail of buttermilk."[1] But in view of the fact that it is usually argued that co-ordination will be done by the price mechanism, why is such organisation necessary? Why are there these "islands of conscious power"? Outside the firm, price movements direct production, which is co-ordinated through a series of exchange transactions on the market. Within a firm, these market transactions are eliminated and in place of the complicated market structure with exchange transactions is substituted the entrepreneur-co-ordinator, who directs production.[2] It is clear that these are alternative methods of co-ordinating production. Yet, having regard to the fact that if production is regulated by price movements, production could be carried on without any organisation at all, well might we ask, why is there any organisation?

Of course, the degree to which the price mechanism is superseded varies greatly. In a department store, the allocation of the different sections to the various locations in the building may be done by the controlling authority or it may be the result of competitive price bidding for space. In the Lancashire cotton industry, a weaver can rent power and shop-room and can obtain looms and yarn on credit.[3] This co-ordination of the various factors of production is, however, normally carried out without the intervention of the price mechanism. As is evident, the amount of "vertical" integration, involving as it does

[1] Op. cit., p. 85.

[2] In the rest of this paper I shall use the term entrepreneur to refer to the person or persons who, in a competitive system, take the place of the price mechanism in the direction of resources.

[3] *Survey of Textile Industries*, p. 26.

the supersession of the price mechanism, varies greatly from industry to industry and from firm to firm.

It can, I think, be assumed that the distinguishing mark of the firm is the supersession of the price mechanism. It is, of course, as Professor Robbins points out, "related to an outside network of relative prices and costs,"[1] but it is important to discover the exact nature of this relationship. This distinction between the allocation of resources in a firm and the allocation in the economic system has been very vividly described by Mr. Maurice Dobb when discussing Adam Smith's conception of the capitalist: "It began to be seen that there was something more important than the relations inside each factory or unit captained by an undertaker; there were the relations of the undertaker with the rest of the economic world outside his immediate sphere . . . . the undertaker busies himself with the division of labour inside each firm and he plans and organises consciously," but "he is related to the much larger economic specialisation, of which he himself is merely one specialised unit. Here, he plays his part as a single cell in a larger organism, mainly unconscious of the wider rôle he fills."[2]

In view of the fact that while economists treat the price mechanism as a co-ordinating instrument, they also admit the co-ordinating function of the "entrepreneur," it is surely important to enquire why co-ordination is the work of the price mechanism in one case and of the entrepreneur in another. The purpose of this paper is to bridge what appears to be a gap in economic theory between the assumption (made for some purposes) that resources are allocated by means of the price mechanism and the assumption (made for other purposes) that this allocation is dependent on the entrepreneur-co-ordinator. We have to explain the basis on which, in practice, this choice between alternatives is effected.[3]

[1] Op. cit., p. 71.

[2] *Capitalist Enterprise and Social Progress*, p. 20. Cf., also, Henderson, *Supply and Demand*, pp. 3–5.

[3] It is easy to see when the State takes over the direction of an industry that, in planning it, it is doing something which was previously done by the price mechanism. What is usually not realised is that any business man in organising the relations between his departments is also doing something which could be organised through the price mechanism. There is therefore point in Mr. Durbin's answer to those who emphasise the problems involved in economic planning that the same problems have to be solved by business men in the competitive system. (See "Economic Calculus in a Planned Economy," *Economic Journal*, December, 1936.) The important difference between these two cases is that economic planning is imposed on industry while firms arise voluntarily because they represent a more efficient method of organising production. In a competitive system, there is an "optimum" amount of planning!

II

Our task is to attempt to discover why a firm emerges at all in a specialised exchange economy. The price mechanism (considered purely from the side of the direction of resources) might be superseded if the relationship which replaced it was desired for its own sake. This would be the case, for example, if some people preferred to work under the direction of some other person. Such individuals would accept less in order to work under someone, and firms would arise naturally from this. But it would appear that this cannot be a very important reason, for it would rather seem that the opposite tendency is operating if one judges from the stress normally laid on the advantage of "being one's own master."[1] Of course, if the desire was not to be controlled but to control, to exercise power over others, then people might be willing to give up something in order to direct others; that is, they would be willing to pay others more than they could get under the price mechanism in order to be able to direct them. But this implies that those who direct pay in order to be able to do this and are not paid to direct, which is clearly not true in the majority of cases.[2] Firms might also exist if purchasers preferred commodities which are produced by firms to those not so produced; but even in spheres where one would expect such preferences (if they exist) to be of negligible importance, firms are to be found in the real world.[3] Therefore there must be other elements involved.

The main reason why it is profitable to establish a firm would seem to be that there is a cost of using the price mechanism. The most obvious cost of "organising" production through the price mechanism is that of discovering what the relevant prices are.[4] This cost may be reduced but it will not be eliminated by the emergence of specialists who will sell this information. The costs of negotiating and

[1] Cf. Harry Dawes, "Labour Mobility in the Steel Industry," *Economic Journal*, March, 1934, who instances "the trek to retail shopkeeping and insurance work by the better paid of skilled men due to the desire (often the main aim in life of a worker) to be independent" (p. 86).

[2] None the less, this is not altogether fanciful. Some small shopkeepers are said to earn less than their assistants.

[3] G. F. Shove, "The Imperfection of the Market: a Further Note," *Economic Journal*, March, 1933, p. 116, note 1, points out that such preferences may exist, although the example he gives is almost the reverse of the instance given in the text.

[4] According to N. Kaldor, "A Classificatory Note of the Determinateness of Equilibrium," *Review of Economic Studies*, February, 1934, it is one of the assumptions of static theory that "All the relevant prices are known to all individuals." But this is clearly not true of the real world.

concluding a separate contract for each exchange transaction which takes place on a market must also be taken into account.[1] Again, in certain markets, e.g., produce exchanges, a technique is devised for minimising these contract costs; but they are not eliminated. It is true that contracts are not eliminated when there is a firm but they are greatly reduced. A factor of production (or the owner thereof) does not have to make a series of contracts with the factors with whom he is co-operating within the firm, as would be necessary, of course, if this co-operation were as a direct result of the working of the price mechanism. For this series of contracts is substituted one. At this stage, it is important to note the character of the contract into which a factor enters that is employed within a firm. The contract is one whereby the factor, for a certain remuneration (which may be fixed or fluctuating), agrees to obey the directions of an entrepreneur *within certain limits*.[2] The essence of the contract is that it should only state the limits to the powers of the entrepreneur. Within these limits, he can therefore direct the other factors of production.

There are, however, other disadvantages—or costs—of using the price mechanism. It may be desired to make a long-term contract for the supply of some article or service. This may be due to the fact that if one contract is made for a longer period, instead of several shorter ones, then certain costs of making each contract will be avoided. Or, owing to the risk attitude of the people concerned, they may prefer to make a long rather than a short-term contract. Now, owing to the difficulty of forecasting, the longer the period of the contract is for the supply of the commodity or service, the less possible, and indeed, the less desirable it is for the person purchasing to specify what the other contracting party is expected to do. It may well be a matter of indifference to the person supplying the service or commodity which of several courses of action is taken, but not to the purchaser of that service or commodity. But the purchaser will not know which of these several courses he will want the supplier to take. Therefore,

[1] This influence was noted by Professor Usher when discussing the development of capitalism. He says: "The successive buying and selling of partly finished products were sheer waste of energy." (*Introduction to the Industrial History of England*, p. 13). But he does not develop the idea nor consider why it is that buying and selling operations still exist.

[2] It would be possible for no limits to the powers of the entrepreneur to be fixed. This would be voluntary slavery. According to Professor Batt, *The Law of Master and Servant*, p. 18, such a contract would be void and unenforceable.

the service which is being provided is expressed in general terms, the exact details being left until a later date. All that is stated in the contract is the limits to what the persons supplying the commodity or service is expected to do. The details of what the supplier is expected to do is not stated in the contract but is decided later by the purchaser. When the direction of resources (within the limits of the contract) becomes dependent on the buyer in this way, that relationship which I term a " firm " may be obtained.[1] A firm is likely therefore to emerge in those cases where a very short term contract would be unsatisfactory. It is obviously of more importance in the case of services—labour—than it is in the case of the buying of commodities. In the case of commodities, the main items can be stated in advance and the details which will be decided later will be of minor significance.

We may sum up this section of the argument by saying that the operation of a market costs something and by forming an organisation and allowing some authority (an " entrepreneur ") to direct the resources, certain marketing costs are saved. The entrepreneur has to carry out his function at less cost, taking into account the fact that he may get factors of production at a lower price than the market transactions which he supersedes, because it is always possible to revert to the open market if he fails to do this.

The question of uncertainty is one which is often considered to be very relevant to the study of the equilibrium of the firm. It seems improbable that a firm would emerge without the existence of uncertainty. But those, for instance, Professor Knight, who make the *mode of payment* the distinguishing mark of the firm—fixed incomes being guaranteed to some of those engaged in production by a person who takes the residual, and fluctuating, income—would appear to be introducing a point which is irrelevant to the problem we are considering. One entrepreneur may sell his services to another for a certain sum of money, while the payment to his employees may be mainly or wholly a share in profits.[2] The significant question would

[1] Of course, it is not possible to draw a hard and fast line which determines whether there is a firm or not. There may be more or less direction. It is similar to the legal question of whether there is the relationship of master and servant or principal and agent. See the discussion of this problem below.

[2] The views of Professor Knight are examined below in more detail.

appear to be why the allocation of resources is not done directly by the price mechanism.

Another factor that should be noted is that exchange transactions on a market and the same transactions organised within a firm are often treated differently by Governments or other bodies with regulatory powers. If we consider the operation of a sales tax, it is clear that it is a tax on market transactions and not on the same transactions organised within the firm. Now since these are alternative methods of "organisation"—by the price mechanism or by the entrepreneur—such a regulation would bring into existence firms which otherwise would have no *raison d'être*. It would furnish a reason for the emergence of a firm in a specialised exchange economy. Of course, to the extent that firms already exist, such a measure as a sales tax would merely tend to make them larger than they would otherwise be. Similarly, quota schemes, and methods of price control which imply that there is rationing, and which do not apply to firms producing such products for themselves, by allowing advantages to those who organise within the firm and not through the market, necessarily encourage the growth of firms. But it is difficult to believe that it is measures such as have been mentioned in this paragraph which have brought firms into existence. Such measures would, however, tend to have this result if they did not exist for other reasons.

These, then, are the reasons why organisations such as firms exist in a specialised exchange economy in which it is generally assumed that the distribution of resources is "organised" by the price mechanism. A firm, therefore, consists of the system of relationships which comes into existence when the direction of resources is dependent on an entrepreneur.

The approach which has just been sketched would appear to offer an advantage in that it is possible to give a scientific meaning to what is meant by saying that a firm gets larger or smaller. A firm becomes larger as additional transactions (which could be exchange transactions co-ordinated through the price mechanism) are organised by the entrepreneur and becomes smaller as he abandons the organisation of such transactions. The question which arises is whether it is possible to study the forces which determine the size of the firm. Why does the entrepreneur not organise one less transaction or one more? It is interesting to note that Professor Knight considers that:

> "the relation between efficiency and size is one of the most serious problems of theory, being, in contrast with the relation for a plant, largely a matter of personality and historical accident rather than of intelligible general principles. But the question is peculiarly vital because the possibility of monopoly gain offers a powerful incentive to *continuous and unlimited* expansion of the firm, which force must be offset by some equally powerful one making for decreased efficiency (in the production of money income) with growth in size, if even boundary competition is to exist."[1]

Professor Knight would appear to consider that it is impossible to treat scientifically the determinants of the size of the firm. On the basis of the concept of the firm developed above, this task will now be attempted.

It was suggested that the introduction of the firm was due primarily to the existence of marketing costs. A pertinent question to ask would appear to be (quite apart from the monopoly considerations raised by Professor Knight), why, if by organising one can eliminate certain costs and in fact reduce the cost of production, are there any market transactions at all?[2] Why is not all production carried on by one big firm? There would appear to be certain possible explanations.

First, as a firm gets larger, there may be decreasing returns to the entrepreneur function, that is, the costs of organising additional transactions within the firm may rise.[3] Naturally, a point must be reached where the costs of organising an extra transaction within the firm are equal to the costs involved in carrying out the transaction in the open market, or, to the costs of organising by another entrepreneur. Secondly, it may be that as the transactions which are organised increase, the entrepreneur fails to place the factors of production in the uses where their value

[1] *Risk, Uncertainty and Profit*, Preface to the Re-issue, London School of Economics Series of Reprints, No. 16, 1933.

[2] There are certain marketing costs which could only be eliminated by the abolition of "consumers' choice" and these are the costs of retailing. It is conceivable that these costs might be so high that people would be willing to accept rations because the extra product obtained was worth the loss of their choice.

[3] This argument assumes that exchange transactions on a market can be considered as homogeneous; which is clearly untrue in fact. This complication is taken into account below.

is greatest, that is, fails to make the best use of the factors of production. Again, a point must be reached where the loss through the waste of resources is equal to the marketing costs of the exchange transaction in the open market or to the loss if the transaction was organised by another entrepreneur. Finally, the supply price of one or more of the factors of production may rise, because the "other advantages" of a small firm are greater than those of a large firm.[1] Of course, the actual point where the expansion of the firm ceases might be determined by a combination of the factors mentioned above. The first two reasons given most probably correspond to the economists' phrase of "diminishing returns to management."[2]

The point has been made in the previous paragraph that a firm will tend to expand until the costs of organising an extra transaction within the firm become equal to the costs of carrying out the same transaction by means of an exchange on the open market or the costs of organising in another firm. But if the firm stops its expansion at a point below the costs of marketing in the open market and at a point equal to the costs of organising in another firm, in most cases (excluding the case of "combination"[3]), this will imply that there is a market transaction between these two producers, each of whom could organise it at less than the actual marketing costs. How is the paradox to be resolved? If we consider an example the reason for this will become clear. Suppose *A* is buying a product from *B* and that both *A* and *B* could organise this marketing transaction at less than its present cost. *B*, we can assume, is not organising one process or stage of production, but several. If *A* therefore wishes to avoid a market transaction, he will have to take over all the processes of production controlled by *B*. Unless *A* takes over all the processes of

[1] For a discussion of the variation of the supply price of factors of production to firms of varying size, see E. A. G. Robinson, *The Structure of Competitive Industry*. It is sometimes said that the supply price of organising ability increases as the size of the firm increases because men prefer to be the heads of small independent businesses rather than the heads of departments in a large business. See Jones, *The Trust Problem*, p. 531, and Macgregor, *Industrial Combination*, p. 63. This is a common argument of those who advocate Rationalisation. It is said that larger units would be more efficient, but owing to the individualistic spirit of the smaller entrepreneurs, they prefer to remain independent, apparently in spite of the higher income which their increased efficiency under Rationalisation makes possible.

[2] This discussion is, of course, brief and incomplete. For a more thorough discussion of this particular problem, see N. Kaldor, "The Equilibrium of the Firm," *Economic Journal*, March, 1934, and E. A. G. Robinson, "The Problem of Management and the Size of the Firm," *Economic Journal*, June, 1934.

[3] A definition of this term is given below.

production, a market transaction will still remain, although it is a different product that is bought. But we have previously assumed that as each producer expands he becomes less efficient; the additional costs of organising extra transactions increase. It is probable that *A*'s cost of organising the transactions previously organised by *B* will be greater than *B*'s cost of doing the same thing. *A* therefore will take over the whole of *B*'s organisation only if his cost of organising *B*'s work is not greater than *B*'s cost by an amount equal to the costs of carrying out an exchange transaction on the open market. But once it becomes economical to have a market transaction, it also pays to divide production in such a way that the cost of organising an extra transaction in each firm is the same.

Up to now it has been assumed that the exchange transactions which take place through the price mechanism are homogeneous. In fact, nothing could be more diverse than the actual transactions which take place in our modern world. This would seem to imply that the costs of carrying out exchange transactions through the price mechanism will vary considerably as will also the costs of organising these transactions within the firm. It seems therefore possible that quite apart from the question of diminishing returns the costs of organising certain transactions within the firm may be greater than the costs of carrying out the exchange transactions in the open market. This would necessarily imply that there were exchange transactions carried out through the price mechanism, but would it mean that there would have to be more than one firm? Clearly not, for all those areas in the economic system where the direction of resources was not dependent directly on the price mechanism could be organised within one firm. The factors which were discussed earlier would seem to be the important ones, though it is difficult to say whether "diminishing returns to management" or the rising supply price of factors is likely to be the more important.

Other things being equal, therefore, a firm will tend to be larger:

(*a*) the less the costs of organising and the slower these costs rise with an increase in the transactions organised.

(*b*) the less likely the entrepreneur is to make mistakes and the smaller the increase in mistakes with an increase in the transactions organised.

(*c*) the greater the lowering (or the less the rise) in the supply price of factors of production to firms of larger size.

Apart from variations in the supply price of factors of production to firms of different sizes, it would appear that the costs of organising and the losses through mistakes will increase with an increase in the spatial distribution of the transactions organised, in the dissimilarity of the transactions, and in the probability of changes in the relevant prices.[1] As more transactions are organised by an entrepreneur, it would appear that the transactions would tend to be either different in kind or in different places. This furnishes an additional reason why efficiency will tend to decrease as the firm gets larger. Inventions which tend to bring factors of production nearer together, by lessening spatial distribution, tend to increase the size of the firm.[2] Changes like the telephone and the telegraph which tend to reduce the cost of organising spatially will tend to increase the size of the firm. All changes which improve managerial technique will tend to increase the size of the firm.[3-4]

It should be noted that the definition of a firm which was given above can be used to give more precise meanings to the terms "combination" and "integration."[5] There is a combination when transactions which were previously

[1] This aspect of the problem is emphasised by N. Kaldor, op. cit. Its importance in this connection had been previously noted by E. A. G. Robinson, *The Structure of Competitive Industry*, pp. 83–106. This assumes that an increase in the probability of price movements increases the costs of organising within a firm more than it increases the cost of carrying out an exchange transaction on the market—which is probable.

[2] This would appear to be the importance of the treatment of the technical unit by E. A. G. Robinson, op. cit., pp. 27–33. The larger the technical unit, the greater the concentration of factors and therefore the firm is likely to be larger.

[3] It should be noted that most inventions will change both the costs of organising and the costs of using the price mechanism. In such cases, whether the invention tends to make firms larger or smaller will depend on the relative effect on these two sets of costs. For instance, if the telephone reduces the costs of using the price mechanism more than it reduces the costs of organising, then it will have the effect of reducing the size of the firm.

[4] An illustration of these dynamic forces is furnished by Maurice Dobb, *Russian Economic Development*, p. 68. "With the passing of bonded labour the factory, as an establishment where work was organised under the whip of the overseer, lost its *raison d'être* until this was restored to it with the introduction of power machinery after 1846." It seems important to realise that the passage from the domestic system to the factory system is not a mere historical accident, but is conditioned by economic forces. This is shown by the fact that it is possible to move from the factory system to the domestic system, as in the Russian example, as well as *vice versa*. It is the essence of serfdom that the price mechanism is not allowed to operate. Therefore, there has to be direction from some organiser. When, however, serfdom passed, the price mechanism was allowed to operate. It was not until machinery drew workers into one locality that it paid to supersede the price mechanism and the firm again emerged.

[5] This is often called "vertical integration," combination being termed "lateral integration."

organised by two or more entrepreneurs become organised by one. This becomes integration when it involves the organisation of transactions which were previously carried out between the entrepreneurs on a market. A firm can expand in either or both of these two ways. The whole of the " structure of competitive industry " becomes tractable by the ordinary technique of economic analysis.

III

The problem which has been investigated in the previous section has not been entirely neglected by economists and it is now necessary to consider why the reasons given above for the emergence of a firm in a specialised exchange economy are to be preferred to the other explanations which have been offered.

It is sometimes said that the reason for the existence of a firm is to be found in the division of labour. This is the view of Professor Usher, a view which has been adopted and expanded by Mr. Maurice Dobb. The firm becomes " the result of an increasing complexity of the division of labour . . . . The growth of this economic differentiation creates the need for some integrating force without which differentiation would collapse into chaos ; and it is as the integrating force in a differentiated economy that industrial forms are chiefly significant."[1] The answer to this argument is an obvious one. The " integrating force in a differentiated economy " already exists in the form of the price mechanism. It is perhaps the main achievement of economic science that it has shown that there is no reason to suppose that specialisation must lead to chaos.[2] The reason given by Mr. Maurice Dobb is therefore inadmissible. What has to be explained is why one integrating force (the entrepreneur) should be substituted for another integrating force (the price mechanism).

The most interesting reasons (and probably the most widely accepted) which have been given to explain this fact are those to be found in Professor Knight's *Risk, Uncertainty and Profit.* His views will be examined in some detail.

[1] Op. cit., p. 10. Professor Usher's views are to be found in his *Introduction to the Industrial History of England*, pp. 1–18.

[2] Cf. J. B. Clark, *Distribution of Wealth*, p. 19, who speaks of the theory of exchange as being the " theory of the organisation of industrial society."

Professor Knight starts with a system in which there is no uncertainty:

> "acting as individuals under absolute freedom but without collusion men are supposed to have organised economic life with the primary and secondary division of labour, the use of capital, etc., developed to the point familiar in present-day America. The principal fact which calls for the exercise of the imagination is the internal organisation of the productive groups or establishments. With uncertainty entirely absent, every individual being in possession of perfect knowledge of the situation, there would be no occasion for anything of the nature of responsible management or control of productive activity. Even marketing transactions in any realistic sense would not be found. The flow of raw materials and productive services to the consumer would be entirely automatic."[1]

Professor Knight says that we can imagine this adjustment as being "the result of a long process of experimentation worked out by trial-and-error methods alone," while it is not necessary "to imagine every worker doing exactly the right thing at the right time in a sort of 'pre-established harmony' with the work of others. There might be managers, superintendents, etc., for the purpose of co-ordinating the activities of individuals," though these managers would be performing a purely routine function, "without responsibility of any sort."[2]

Professor Knight then continues:

> "With the introduction of uncertainty—the fact of ignorance and the necessity of acting upon opinion rather than knowledge—into this Eden-like situation, its character is entirely changed . . . . With uncertainty present doing things, the actual execution of activity, becomes in a real sense a secondary part of life; the primary problem or function is deciding what to do and how to do it."[3]

This fact of uncertainty brings about the two most important characteristics of social organisation.

> "In the first place, goods are produced for a market, on the basis of entirely impersonal prediction of wants, not for the satisfaction of the wants of the producers themselves. The producer takes the responsibility of

[1] *Risk, Uncertainty and Profit*, p. 267.

[2] Op. cit., pp. 267–8.

[3] Op. cit., p. 268.

forecasting the consumers' wants. In the second place, the work of forecasting and at the same time a large part of the technological direction and control of production are still further concentrated upon a very narrow class of the producers, and we meet with a new economic functionary, the entrepreneur. . . . . When uncertainty is present and the task of deciding what to do and how to do it takes the ascendancy over that of execution the internal organisation of the productive groups is no longer a matter of indifference or a mechanical detail. Centralisation of this deciding and controlling function is imperative, a process of 'cephalisation' is inevitable."[1]
The most fundamental change is:
"the system under which the confident and venturesome assume the risk or insure the doubtful and timid by guaranteeing to the latter a specified income in return for an assignment of the actual results. . . . With human nature as we know it it would be impracticable or very unusual for one man to guarantee to another a definite result of the latter's actions without being given power to direct his work. And on the other hand the second party would not place himself under the direction of the first without such a guarantee. . . . The result of this manifold specialisation of function is the enterprise and wage system of industry. Its existence in the world is the direct result of the fact of uncertainty."[2]

These quotations give the essence of Professor Knight's theory. The fact of uncertainty means that people have to forecast future wants. Therefore, you get a special class springing up who direct the activities of others to whom they give guaranteed wages. It acts because good judgment is generally associated with confidence in one's judgment.[3]

Professor Knight would appear to leave himself open to criticism on several grounds. First of all, as he himself points out, the fact that certain people have better judgment or better knowledge does not mean that they can only get an income from it by themselves actively taking part in production. They can sell advice or knowledge. Every business buys the services of a host of advisers. We can imagine a system where all advice or knowledge was bought

[1] Op. cit., pp. 268–95.
[2] Op. cit., pp. 269–70.
[3] Op. cit., p. 270.

as required. Again, it is possible to get a reward from better knowledge or judgment not by actively taking part in production but by making contracts with people who are producing. A merchant buying for future delivery represents an example of this. But this merely illustrates the point that it is quite possible to give a guaranteed reward providing that certain acts are performed without directing the performance of those acts. Professor Knight says that " with human nature as we know it it would be impracticable or very unusual for one man to guarantee to another a definite result of the latter's actions without being given power to direct his work." This is surely incorrect. A large proportion of jobs are done to contract, that is, the contractor is guaranteed a certain sum providing he performs certain acts. But this does not involve any direction. It does mean, however, that the system of relative prices has been changed and that there will be a new arrangement of the factors of production.[1] The fact that Professor Knight mentions that the " second party would not place himself under the direction of the first without such a guarantee " is irrelevant to the problem we are considering. Finally, it seems important to notice that even in the case of an economic system where there is no uncertainty Professor Knight considers that there would be co-ordinators, though they would perform only a routine function. He immediately adds that they would be " without responsibility of any sort," which raises the question by whom are they paid and why? It seems that nowhere does Professor Knight give a reason why the price mechanism should be superseded.

IV

It would seem important to examine one further point and that is to consider the relevance of this discussion to the general question of the " cost-curve of the firm."

It has sometimes been assumed that a firm is limited in size under perfect competition if its cost curve slopes upward,[2] while under imperfect competition, it is limited

[1] This shows that it is possible to have a private enterprise system without the existence of firms. Though, in practice, the two functions of enterprise, which actually influences the system of relative prices by forecasting wants and acting in accordance with such forecasts, and management, which accepts the system of relative prices as being given, are normally carried out by the same persons, yet it seems important to keep them separate in theory. This point is further discussed below.

[2] See Kaldor, op. cit., and Robinson, *The Problem of Management and the Size of the Firm.*

in size because it will not pay to produce more than the output at which marginal cost is equal to marginal revenue.[1] But it is clear that a firm may produce more than one product and, therefore, there appears to be no *prima facie* reason why this upward slope of the cost curve in the case of perfect competition or the fact that marginal cost will not always be below marginal revenue in the case of imperfect competition should limit the size of the firm.[2] Mrs. Robinson[3] makes the simplifying assumption that only one product is being produced. But it is clearly important to investigate how the number of products produced by a firm is determined, while no theory which assumes that only one product is in fact produced can have very great practical significance.

It might be replied that under perfect competition, since everything that is produced can be sold at the prevailing price, then there is no need for any other product to be produced. But this argument ignores the fact that there may be a point where it is less costly to organise the exchange transactions of a new product than to organise further exchange transactions of the old product. This point can be illustrated in the following way. Imagine, following von Thunen, that there is a town, the consuming centre, and that industries are located around this central point in rings. These conditions are illustrated in the following diagram in which *A*, *B* and *C* represent different industries.

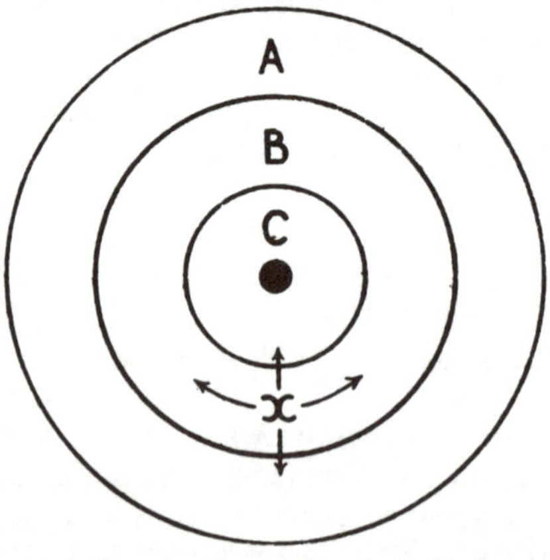

[1] Mrs Robinson calls this the Imperfect Competition solution for the survival of the small firm.

[2] Mrs Robinson's conclusion, op. cit., p. 249, note 1, would appear to be definitely wrong. She is followed by Horace J. White, Jr., "Monopolistic and Perfect Competition," *American Economic Review*, December, 1936, p. 645, note 27. Mr. White states "It is obvious that the size of the firm is limited in conditions of monopolistic competition."

[3] *Economics of Imperfect Competition.*

Imagine an entrepreneur who starts controlling exchange transactions from *x*. Now as he extends his activities in the same product (*B*), the cost of organising increases until at some point it becomes equal to that of a dissimilar product which is nearer. As the firm expands, it will therefore from this point include more than one product (*A* and *C*). This treatment of the problem is obviously incomplete,[1] but it is necessary to show that merely proving that the cost curve turns upwards does not give a limitation to the size of the firm. So far we have only considered the case of perfect competition; the case of imperfect competition would appear to be obvious.

To determine the size of the firm, we have to consider the marketing costs (that is, the costs of using the price mechanism), and the costs of organising of different entrepreneurs and then we can determine how many products will be produced by each firm and how much of each it will produce. It would, therefore, appear that Mr. Shove[2] in his article on "Imperfect Competition" was asking questions which Mrs. Robinson's cost curve apparatus cannot answer. The factors mentioned above would seem to be the relevant ones.

V

Only one task now remains; and that is, to see whether the concept of a firm which has been developed fits in with that existing in the real world. We can best approach the question of what constitutes a firm in practice by considering the legal relationship normally called that of "master and servant" or "employer and employee."[3] The essentials of this relationship have been given as follows:

"(1) the servant must be under the duty of rendering personal services to the master or to others on behalf

[1] As has been shown above, location is only one of the factors influencing the cost of organising.

[2] G. F. Shove, "The Imperfection of the Market," *Economic Journal*, March, 1933, p. 115. In connection with an increase in demand in the suburbs and the effect on the price charged by suppliers, Mr. Shove asks ". . . . why do not the old firms open branches in the suburbs?" If the argument in the text is correct, this is a question which Mrs. Robinson's apparatus cannot answer.

[3] The legal concept of "employer and employee" and the economic concept of a firm are not identical, in that the firm may imply control over another person's property as well as over their labour. But the identity of these two concepts is sufficiently close for an examination of the legal concept to be of value in appraising the worth of the economic concept.

> of the master, otherwise the contract is a contract for sale of goods or the like.
>
> (2) The master must have the right to control the servant's work, either personally or by another servant or agent. It is this right of control or interference, of being entitled to tell the servant when to work (within the hours of service) and when not to work, and what work to do and how to do it (within the terms of such service) which is the dominant characteristic in this relation and marks off the servant from an independent contractor, or from one employed merely to give to his employer the fruits of his labour. In the latter case, the contractor or performer is not under the employer's control in doing the work or effecting the service; he has to shape and manage his work so as to give the result he has contracted to effect."[1]

We thus see that it is the fact of direction which is the essence of the legal concept of "employer and employee," just as it was in the economic concept which was developed above. It is interesting to note that Professor Batt says further:

> "That which distinguishes an agent from a servant is not the absence or presence of a fixed wage or the payment only of commission on business done, but rather the freedom with which an agent may carry out his employment."[2]

We can therefore conclude that the definition we have given is one which approximates closely to the firm as it is considered in the real world.

Our definition is, therefore, realistic. Is it manageable? This ought to be clear. When we are considering how large a firm will be the principle of marginalism works smoothly. The question always is, will it pay to bring an extra exchange transaction under the organising authority? At the margin, the costs of organising within the firm will be equal either to the costs of organising in another firm or to the costs involved in leaving the transaction to be "organised" by the price mechanism. Business men will be constantly experimenting, controlling more or less, and in this way, equilibrium will be maintained. This gives the position of equilibrium for static analysis. But

[1] Batt, *The Law of Master and Servant*, p. 6.
[2] Op. cit., p. 7.

it is clear that the dynamic factors are also of considerable importance, and an investigation of the effect changes have on the cost of organising within the firm and on marketing costs generally will enable one to explain why firms get larger and smaller. We thus have a theory of moving equilibrium. The above analysis would also appear to have clarified the relationship between initiative or enterprise and management. Initiative means forecasting and operates through the price mechanism by the making of new contracts. Management proper merely reacts to price changes, rearranging the factors of production under its control. That the business man normally combines both functions is an obvious result of the marketing costs which were discussed above. Finally, this analysis enables us to state more exactly what is meant by the "marginal product" of the entrepreneur. But an elaboration of this point would take us far from our comparatively simple task of definition and clarification.

The Journal of

LAW & ECONOMICS

VOLUME III OCTOBER 1960

THE PROBLEM OF SOCIAL COST

R. H. COASE
University of Virginia

I. The Problem To Be Examined[1]

This paper is concerned with those actions of business firms which have harmful effects on others. The standard example is that of a factory the smoke from which has harmful effects on those occupying neighbouring properties. The economic analysis of such a situation has usually proceeded in terms of a divergence between the private and social product of the factory, in which economists have largely followed the treatment of Pigou in *The Economics of Welfare*. The conclusions to which this kind of analysis seems to have led most economists is that it would be desirable to make the owner of the factory liable for the damage caused to those injured by the smoke, or alternatively, to place a tax on the factory owner varying with the amount of smoke produced and equivalent in money terms to the damage it would cause, or finally, to exclude the factory from residential districts (and presumably from other

[1] This article, although concerned with a technical problem of economic analysis, arose out of the study of the Political Economy of Broadcasting which I am now conducting. The argument of the present article was implicit in a previous article dealing with the problem of allocating radio and television frequencies (The Federal Communications Commission, 2 J. Law & Econ. [1959]) but comments which I have received seemed to suggest that it would be desirable to deal with the question in a more explicit way and without reference to the original problem for the solution of which the analysis was developed.

areas in which the emission of smoke would have harmful effects on others). It is my contention that the suggested courses of action are inappropriate, in that they lead to results which are not necessarily, or even usually, desirable.

II. The Reciprocal Nature of the Problem

The traditional approach has tended to obscure the nature of the choice that has to be made. The question is commonly thought of as one in which A inflicts harm on B and what has to be decided is: how should we restrain A? But this is wrong. We are dealing with a problem of a reciprocal nature. To avoid the harm to B would inflict harm on A. The real question that has to be decided is: should A be allowed to harm B or should B be allowed to harm A? The problem is to avoid the more serious harm. I instanced in my previous article[2] the case of a confectioner the noise and vibrations from whose machinery disturbed a doctor in his work. To avoid harming the doctor would inflict harm on the confectioner. The problem posed by this case was essentially whether it was worth while, as a result of restricting the methods of production which could be used by the confectioner, to secure more doctoring at the cost of a reduced supply of confectionery products. Another example is afforded by the problem of straying cattle which destroy crops on neighbouring land. If it is inevitable that some cattle will stray, an increase in the supply of meat can only be obtained at the expense of a decrease in the supply of crops. The nature of the choice is clear: meat or crops. What answer should be given is, of course, not clear unless we know the value of what is obtained as well as the value of what is sacrificed to obtain it. To give another example, Professor George J. Stigler instances the contamination of a stream.[3] If we assume that the harmful effect of the pollution is that it kills the fish, the question to be decided is: is the value of the fish lost greater or less than the value of the product which the contamination of the stream makes possible. It goes almost without saying that this problem has to be looked at in total *and* at the margin.

III. The Pricing System with Liability for Damage

I propose to start my analysis by examining a case in which most economists would presumably agree that the problem would be solved in a completely satisfactory manner: when the damaging business has to pay for all damage caused *and* the pricing system works smoothly (strictly this means that the operation of a pricing system is without cost).

A good example of the problem under discussion is afforded by the case of straying cattle which destroy crops growing on neighbouring land. Let us suppose that a farmer and a cattle-raiser are operating on neighbouring proper-

[2] Coase, The Federal Communications Commission, 2 J. Law & Econ. 26–27 (1959).

[3] G. J. Stigler, The Theory of Price 105 (1952).

ties. Let us further suppose that, without any fencing between the properties, an increase in the size of the cattle-raiser's herd increases the total damage to the farmer's crops. What happens to the marginal damage as the size of the herd increases is another matter. This depends on whether the cattle tend to follow one another or to roam side by side, on whether they tend to be more or less restless as the size of the herd increases and on other similar factors. For my immediate purpose, it is immaterial what assumption is made about marginal damage as the size of the herd increases.

To simplify the argument, I propose to use an arithmetical example. I shall assume that the annual cost of fencing the farmer's property is $9 and that the price of the crop is $1 per ton. Also, I assume that the relation between the number of cattle in the herd and the annual crop loss is as follows:

Number in Herd (Steers)	Annual Crop Loss (Tons)	Crop Loss per Additional Steer (Tons)
1	1	1
2	3	2
3	6	3
4	10	4

Given that the cattle-raiser is liable for the damage caused, the additional annual cost imposed on the cattle-raiser if he increased his herd from, say, 2 to 3 steers is $3 and in deciding on the size of the herd, he will take this into account along with his other costs. That is, he will not increase the size of the herd unless the value of the additional meat produced (assuming that the cattle-raiser slaughters the cattle), is greater than the additional costs that this will entail, including the value of the additional crops destroyed. Of course, if, by the employment of dogs, herdsmen, aeroplanes, mobile radio and other means, the amount of damage can be reduced, these means will be adopted when their cost is less than the value of the crop which they prevent being lost. Given that the annual cost of fencing is $9, the cattle-raiser who wished to have a herd with 4 steers or more would pay for fencing to be erected and maintained, assuming that other means of attaining the same end would not do so more cheaply. When the fence is erected, the marginal cost due to the liability for damage becomes zero, except to the extent that an increase in the size of the herd necessitates a stronger and therefore more expensive fence because more steers are liable to lean against it at the same time. But, of course, it may be cheaper for the cattle-raiser not to fence and to pay for the damaged crops, as in my arithmetical example, with 3 or fewer steers.

It might be thought that the fact that the cattle-raiser would pay for all crops damaged would lead the farmer to increase his planting if a cattle-raiser came to occupy the neighbouring property. But this is not so. If the crop was previously sold in conditions of perfect competition, marginal cost was equal to price for the amount of planting undertaken and any expansion would have reduced the profits of the farmer. In the new situation, the existence of crop damage would mean that the farmer would sell less on the open market but his receipts for a given production would remain the same, since the cattle-raiser would pay the market price for any crop damaged. Of course, if cattle-raising commonly involved the destruction of crops, the coming into existence of a cattle-raising industry might raise the price of the crops involved and farmers would then extend their planting. But I wish to confine my attention to the individual farmer.

I have said that the occupation of a neighbouring property by a cattle-raiser would not cause the amount of production, or perhaps more exactly the amount of planting, by the farmer to increase. In fact, if the cattle-raising has any effect, it will be to decrease the amount of planting. The reason for this is that, for any given tract of land, if the value of the crop damaged is so great that the receipts from the sale of the undamaged crop are less than the total costs of cultivating that tract of land, it will be profitable for the farmer and the cattle-raiser to make a bargain whereby that tract of land is left uncultivated. This can be made clear by means of an arithmetical example. Assume initially that the value of the crop obtained from cultivating a given tract of land is $12 and that the cost incurred in cultivating this tract of land is $10, the net gain from cultivating the land being $2. I assume for purposes of simplicity that the farmer owns the land. Now assume that the cattle-raiser starts operations on the neighbouring property and that the value of the crops damaged is $1. In this case $11 is obtained by the farmer from sale on the market and $1 is obtained from the cattle-raiser for damage suffered and the net gain remains $2. Now suppose that the cattle-raiser finds it profitable to increase the size of his herd, even though the amount of damage rises to $3; which means that the value of the additional meat production is greater than the additional costs, including the additional $2 payment for damage. But the total payment for damage is now $3. The net gain to the farmer from cultivating the land is still $2. The cattle-raiser would be better off if the farmer would agree not to cultivate his land for any payment less than $3. The farmer would be agreeable to not cultivating the land for any payment greater than $2. There is clearly room for a mutually satisfactory bargain which would lead to the abandonment of cultivation.[4] But the same argument applies not only to the whole tract cultivated by the farmer but also to any

[4] The argument in the text has proceeded on the assumption that the alternative to cultivation of the crop is abandonment of cultivation altogether. But this need not be so. There may be crops which are less liable to damage by cattle but which would not be as profitable as the crop grown in the absence of damage. Thus, if the cultivation of a new crop would yield a return to the farmer of $1 instead of $2, and the size of the herd which would cause $3 damage with the old crop would cause $1 damage with the new crop, it would be profitable to the cattle-raiser to pay any sum less than $2 to induce the farmer

subdivision of it. Suppose, for example, that the cattle have a well-defined route, say, to a brook or to a shady area. In these circumstances, the amount of damage to the crop along the route may well be great and if so, it could be that the farmer and the cattle-raiser would find it profitable to make a bargain whereby the farmer would agree not to cultivate this strip of land.

But this raises a further possibility. Suppose that there is such a well-defined route. Suppose further that the value of the crop that would be obtained by cultivating this strip of land is $10 but that the cost of cultivation is $11. In the absence of the cattle-raiser, the land would not be cultivated. However, given the presence of the cattle-raiser, it could well be that if the strip was cultivated, the whole crop would be destroyed by the cattle. In which case, the cattle-raiser would be forced to pay $10 to the farmer. It is true that the farmer would lose $1. But the cattle-raiser would lose $10. Clearly this is a situation which is not likely to last indefinitely since neither party would want this to happen. The aim of the farmer would be to induce the cattle-raiser to make a payment in return for an agreement to leave this land uncultivated. The farmer would not be able to obtain a payment greater than the cost of fencing off this piece of land nor so high as to lead the cattle-raiser to abandon the use of the neighbouring property. What payment would in fact be made would depend on the shrewdness of the farmer and the cattle-raiser as bargainers. But as the payment would not be so high as to cause the cattle-raiser to abandon this location and as it would not vary with the size of the herd, such an agreement would not affect the allocation of resources but would merely alter the distribution of income and wealth as between the cattle-raiser and the farmer.

I think it is clear that if the cattle-raiser is liable for damage caused and the pricing system works smoothly, the reduction in the value of production elsewhere will be taken into account in computing the additional cost involved in increasing the size of the herd. This cost will be weighed against the value of the additional meat production and, given perfect competition in the cattle industry, the allocation of resources in cattle-raising will be optimal. What needs to be emphasized is that the fall in the value of production elsewhere which would be taken into account in the costs of the cattle-raiser may well be less than the damage which the cattle would cause to the crops in the ordinary course of events. This is because it is possible, as a result of market transactions, to discontinue cultivation of the land. This is desirable in all

to change his crop (since this would reduce damage liability from $3 to $1) and it would be profitable for the farmer to do so if the amount received was more than $1 (the reduction in his return caused by switching crops). In fact, there would be room for a mutually satisfactory bargain in all cases in which a change of crop would reduce the amount of damage by more than it reduces the value of the crop (excluding damage)—in all cases, that is, in which a change in the crop cultivated would lead to an increase in the value of production.

cases in which the damage that the cattle would cause, and for which the cattle-raiser would be willing to pay, exceeds the amount which the farmer would pay for use of the land. In conditions of perfect competition, the amount which the farmer would pay for the use of the land is equal to the difference between the value of the total production when the factors are employed on this land and the value of the additional product yielded in their next best use (which would be what the farmer would have to pay for the factors). If damage exceeds the amount the farmer would pay for the use of the land, the value of the additional product of the factors employed elsewhere would exceed the value of the total product in this use after damage is taken into account. It follows that it would be desirable to abandon cultivation of the land and to release the factors employed for production elsewhere. A procedure which merely provided for payment for damage to the crop caused by the cattle but which did not allow for the possibility of cultivation being discontinued would result in too small an employment of factors of production in cattle-raising and too large an employment of factors in cultivation of the crop. But given the possibility of market transactions, a situation in which damage to crops exceeded the rent of the land would not endure. Whether the cattle-raiser pays the farmer to leave the land uncultivated or himself rents the land by paying the land-owner an amount slightly greater than the farmer would pay (if the farmer was himself renting the land), the final result would be the same and would maximise the value of production. Even when the farmer is induced to plant crops which it would not be profitable to cultivate for sale on the market, this will be a purely short-term phenomenon and may be expected to lead to an agreement under which the planting will cease. The cattle-raiser will remain in that location and the marginal cost of meat production will be the same as before, thus having no long-run effect on the allocation of resources.

IV. The Pricing System with No Liability for Damage

I now turn to the case in which, although the pricing system is assumed to work smoothly (that is, costlessly), the damaging business is not liable for any of the damage which it causes. This business does not have to make a payment to those damaged by its actions. I propose to show that the allocation of resources will be the same in this case as it was when the damaging business was liable for damage caused. As I showed in the previous case that the allocation of resources was optimal, it will not be necessary to repeat this part of the argument.

I return to the case of the farmer and the cattle-raiser. The farmer would suffer increased damage to his crop as the size of the herd increased. Suppose that the size of the cattle-raiser's herd is 3 steers (and that this is the size of the herd that would be maintained if crop damage was not taken into account). Then the farmer would be willing to pay up to $3 if the cattle-raiser would reduce his herd to 2 steers, up to $5 if the herd were reduced to 1 steer and would pay up to $6 if cattle-raising was abandoned. The cattle-raiser would therefore receive $3 from the farmer if he kept 2 steers instead of 3. This $3 foregone is therefore part of the cost incurred in keeping the third steer. Whether the $3 is a payment which the cattle-raiser has to make if he adds the third steer to his herd (which it would be if the cattle-raiser was liable to the farmer for damage caused to the crop) or whether it is a sum of money which he would have received if he did not keep a third steer (which it would be if the cattle-raiser was not liable to the farmer for damage caused to the crop) does not affect the final result. In both cases $3 is part of the cost of adding a third steer, to be included along with the other costs. If the increase in the value of production in cattle-raising through increasing the size of the herd from 2 to 3 is greater than the additional costs that have to be incurred (including the $3 damage to crops), the size of the herd will be increased. Otherwise, it will not. The size of the herd will be the same whether the cattle-raiser is liable for damage caused to the crop or not.

It may be argued that the assumed starting point—a herd of 3 steers—was arbitrary. And this is true. But the farmer would not wish to pay to avoid crop damage which the cattle-raiser would not be able to cause. For example, the maximum annual payment which the farmer could be induced to pay could not exceed $9, the annual cost of fencing. And the farmer would only be willing to pay this sum if it did not reduce his earnings to a level that would cause him to abandon cultivation of this particular tract of land. Furthermore, the farmer would only be willing to pay this amount if he believed that, in the absence of any payment by him, the size of the herd maintained by the cattle raiser would be 4 or more steers. Let us assume that this is the case. Then the farmer would be willing to pay up to $3 if the cattle raiser would reduce his herd to 3 steers, up to $6 if the herd were reduced to 2 steers, up to $8 if one steer only were kept and up to $9 if cattle-raising were abandoned. It will be noticed that the change in the starting point has not altered the amount which would accrue to the cattle-raiser if he reduced the size of his herd by any given amount. It is still true that the cattle-raiser could receive an additional $3 from the farmer if he agreed to reduce his herd from 3 steers to 2 and that the $3 represents the value of the crop that would be destroyed by adding the third steer to the herd. Although a different belief on the part of the farmer (whether justified or not) about the size of the herd that the cattle-raiser would maintain in the absence of payments from him may affect the total payment he can be induced to pay, it is not true that this different belief would have any effect on the size of the herd that the cattle-raiser will actually keep. This will be the same as it would be if the cattle-raiser had to pay for damage caused by his cattle, since a receipt foregone of a given amount is the equivalent of a payment of the same amount.

It might be thought that it would pay the cattle-raiser to increase his herd above the size that he would wish to maintain once a bargain had been made, in order to induce the farmer to make a larger total payment. And this may be true. It is similar in nature to the action of the farmer (when the cattle-raiser was liable for damage) in cultivating land on which, as a result of an agreement with the cattle-raiser, planting would subsequently be abandoned (including land which would not be cultivated at all in the absence of cattle-raising). But such manoeuvres are preliminaries to an agreement and do not affect the long-run equilibrium position, which is the same whether or not the cattle-raiser is held responsible for the crop damage brought about by his cattle.

It is necessary to know whether the damaging business is liable or not for damage caused since without the establishment of this initial delimitation of rights there can be no market transactions to transfer and recombine them. But the ultimate result (which maximises the value of production) is independent of the legal position if the pricing system is assumed to work without cost.

V. The Problem Illustrated Anew

The harmful effects of the activities of a business can assume a wide variety of forms. An early English case concerned a building which, by obstructing currents of air, hindered the operation of a windmill.[5] A recent case in Florida concerned a building which cast a shadow on the cabana, swimming pool and sunbathing areas of a neighbouring hotel.[6] The problem of straying cattle and the damaging of crops which was the subject of detailed examination in the two preceding sections, although it may have appeared to be rather a special case, is in fact but one example of a problem which arises in many different guises. To clarify the nature of my argument and to demonstrate its general applicability, I propose to illustrate it anew by reference to four actual cases.

Let us first reconsider the case of *Sturges v. Bridgman*[7] which I used as an illustration of the general problem in my article on "The Federal Communications Commission." In this case, a confectioner (in Wigmore Street) used two mortars and pestles in connection with his business (one had been in operation in the same position for more than 60 years and the other for more than 26 years). A doctor then came to occupy neighbouring premises (in Wimpole Street). The confectioner's machinery caused the doctor no harm until, eight years after he had first occupied the premises, he built a consulting room at the end of his garden right against the confectioner's kitchen. It was then found that the noise and vibration caused by the confectioner's machin-

[5] See Gale on Easements 237–39 (13th ed. M. Bowles 1959).

[6] See Fontainebleu Hotel Corp. v. Forty-Five Twenty-Five, Inc., 114 So. 2d 357 (1959).

[7] 11 Ch. D. 852 (1879).

ery made it difficult for the doctor to use his new consulting room. "In particular . . . the noise prevented him from examining his patients by auscultation[8] for diseases of the chest. He also found it impossible to engage with effect in any occupation which required thought and attention." The doctor therefore brought a legal action to force the confectioner to stop using his machinery. The courts had little difficulty in granting the doctor the injunction he sought. "Individual cases of hardship may occur in the strict carrying out of the principle upon which we found our judgment, but the negation of the principle would lead even more to individual hardship, and would at the same time produce a prejudicial effect upon the development of land for residential purposes."

The court's decision established that the doctor had the right to prevent the confectioner from using his machinery. But, of course, it would have been possible to modify the arrangements envisaged in the legal ruling by means of a bargain between the parties. The doctor would have been willing to waive his right and allow the machinery to continue in operation if the confectioner would have paid him a sum of money which was greater than the loss of income which he would suffer from having to move to a more costly or less convenient location or from having to curtail his activities at this location or, as was suggested as a possibility, from having to build a separate wall which would deaden the noise and vibration. The confectioner would have been willing to do this if the amount he would have to pay the doctor was less than the fall in income he would suffer if he had to change his mode of operation at this location, abandon his operation or move his confectionery business to some other location. The solution of the problem depends essentially on whether the continued use of the machinery adds more to the confectioner's income than it subtracts from the doctor's.[9] But now consider the situation if the confectioner had won the case. The confectioner would then have had the right to continue operating his noise and vibration-generating machinery without having to pay anything to the doctor. The boot would have been on the other foot: the doctor would have had to pay the confectioner to induce him to stop using the machinery. If the doctor's income would have fallen more through continuance of the use of this machinery than it added to the income of the confectioner, there would clearly be room for a bargain whereby the doctor paid the confectioner to stop using the machinery. That is to say, the circumstances in which it would not pay the confectioner to continue to use the machinery and to compensate the doctor for the losses that this would bring (if the doctor had the right to prevent the confectioner's using his

[8] Auscultation is the act of listening by ear or stethoscope in order to judge by sound the condition of the body.

[9] Note that what is taken into account is the change in income after allowing for alterations in methods of production, location, character of product, etc.

machinery) would be those in which it would be in the interest of the doctor to make a payment to the confectioner which would induce him to discontinue the use of the machinery (if the confectioner had the right to operate the machinery). The basic conditions are exactly the same in this case as they were in the example of the cattle which destroyed crops. With costless market transactions, the decision of the courts concerning liability for damage would be without effect on the allocation of resources. It was of course the view of the judges that they were affecting the working of the economic system—and in a desirable direction. Any other decision would have had "a prejudicial effect upon the development of land for residential purposes," an argument which was elaborated by examining the example of a forge operating on a barren moor, which was later developed for residual purposes. The judges' view that they were settling how the land was to be used would be true only in the case in which the costs of carrying out the necessary market transactions exceeded the gain which might be achieved by any rearrangement of rights. And it would be desirable to preserve the areas (Wimpole Street or the moor) for residential or professional use (by giving non-industrial users the right to stop the noise, vibration, smoke, etc., by injunction) only if the value of the additional residential facilities obtained was greater than the value of cakes or iron lost. But of this the judges seem to have been unaware.

Another example of the same problem is furnished by the case of *Cooke v. Forbes*.[10] One process in the weaving of cocoa-nut fibre matting was to immerse it in bleaching liquids after which it was hung out to dry. Fumes from a manufacturer of sulphate of ammonia had the effect of turning the matting from a bright to a dull and blackish colour. The reason for this was that the bleaching liquid contained chloride of tin, which, when affected by sulphuretted hydrogen, is turned to a darker colour. An injunction was sought to stop the manufacturer from emitting the fumes. The lawyers for the defendant argued that if the plaintiff "were not to use . . . a particular bleaching liquid, their fibre would not be affected; that their process is unusual, not according to the custom of the trade, and even damaging to their own fabrics." The judge commented: ". . . it appears to me quite plain that a person has a right to carry on upon his own property a manufacturing process in which he uses chloride of tin, or any sort of metallic dye, and that his neighbour is not at liberty to pour in gas which will interfere with his manufacture. If it can be traced to the neighbour, then, I apprehend, clearly he will have a right to come here and ask for relief." But in view of the fact that the damage was accidental and occasional, that careful precautions were taken and that there was no exceptional risk, an injunction was refused, leaving the plaintiff to bring an action for damages if he wished. What the subsequent developments

[10] L. R. 5 Eq. 166 (1867–1868).

were I do not know. But it is clear that the situation is essentially the same as that found in *Sturges v. Bridgman,* except that the cocoa-nut fibre matting manufacturer could not secure an injunction but would have to seek damages from the sulphate of ammonia manufacturer. The economic analysis of the situation is exactly the same as with the cattle which destroyed crops. To avoid the damage, the sulphate of ammonia manufacturer could increase his precautions or move to another location. Either course would presumably increase his costs. Alternatively he could pay for the damage. This he would do if the payments for damage were less than the additional costs that would have to be incurred to avoid the damage. The payments for damage would then become part of the cost of production of sulphate of ammonia. Of course, if, as was suggested in the legal proceedings, the amount of damage could be eliminated by changing the bleaching agent (which would presumably increase the costs of the matting manufacturer) and if the additional cost was less than the damage that would otherwise occur, it should be possible for the two manufacturers to make a mutually satisfactory bargain whereby the new bleaching agent was used. Had the court decided against the matting manufacturer, as a consequence of which he would have had to suffer the damage without compensation, the allocation of resources would not have been affected. It would pay the matting manufacturer to change his bleaching agent if the additional cost involved was less than the reduction in damage. And since the matting manufacturer would be willing to pay the sulphate of ammonia manufacturer an amount up to his loss of income (the increase in costs or the damage suffered) if he would cease his activities, this loss of income would remain a cost of production for the manufacturer of sulphate of ammonia. This case is indeed analytically exactly the same as the cattle example.

Bryant v. Lefever[11] raised the problem of the smoke nuisance in a novel form. The plaintiff and the defendants were occupiers of adjoining houses, which were of about the same height.

> Before 1876 the plaintiff was able to light a fire in any room of his house without the chimneys smoking; the two houses had remained in the same condition some thirty or forty years. In 1876 the defendants took down their house, and began to rebuild it. They carried up a wall by the side of the plaintiff's chimneys much beyond its original height, and stacked timber on the roof of their house, and thereby caused the plaintiff's chimneys to smoke whenever he lighted fires.

The reason, of course, why the chimneys smoked was that the erection of the wall and the stacking of the timber prevented the free circulation of air. In a trial before a jury, the plaintiff was awarded damages of £40. The case then went to the Court of Appeals where the judgment was reversed. Bramwell, L.J., argued:

[11] 4 C.P.D. 172 (1878–1879).

> . . . it is said, and the jury have found, that the defendants have done that which caused a nuisance to the plaintiff's house. We think there is no evidence of this. No doubt there is a nuisance, but it is not of the defendant's causing. They have done nothing in causing the nuisance. Their house and their timber are harmless enough. It is the plaintiff who causes the nuisance by lighting a coal fire in a place the chimney of which is placed so near the defendants' wall, that the smoke does not escape, but comes into the house. Let the plaintiff cease to light his fire, let him move his chimney, let him carry it higher, and there would be no nuisance. Who then, causes it? It would be very clear that the plaintiff did, if he had built his house or chimney after the defendants had put up the timber on theirs, and it is really the same though he did so before the timber was there. But (what is in truth the same answer), if the defendants cause the nuisance, they have a right to do so. If the plaintiff has not the right to the passage of air, except subject to the defendants' right to build or put timber on their house, then his right is subject to their right, and though a nuisance follows from the exercise of their right, they are not liable.

And Cotton, L.J., said:

> Here it is found that the erection of the defendants' wall has sensibly and materially interfered with the comfort of human existence in the plaintiff's house, and it is said this is a nuisance for which the defendants are liable. Ordinarily this is so, but the defendants have done so, not by sending on to the plaintiff's property any smoke or noxious vapour, but by interrupting the egress of smoke from the plaintiff's house in a way to which . . . the plaintiff has no legal right. The plaintiff creates the smoke, which interferes with his comfort. Unless he has . . . a right to get rid of this in a particular way which has been interfered with by the defendants, he cannot sue the defendants, because the smoke made by himself, for which he has not provided any effectual means of escape, causes him annoyance. It is as if a man tried to get rid of liquid filth arising on his own land by a drain into his neighbour's land. Until a right had been acquired by user, the neighbour might stop the drain without incurring liability by so doing. No doubt great inconvenience would be caused to the owner of the property on which the liquid filth arises. But the act of his neighbour would be a lawful act, and he would not be liable for the consequences attributable to the fact that the man had accumulated filth without providing any effectual means of getting rid of it.

I do not propose to show that any subsequent modification of the situation, as a result of bargains between the parties (conditioned by the cost of stacking the timber elsewhere, the cost of extending the chimney higher, etc.), would have exactly the same result whatever decision the courts had come to since this point has already been adequately dealt with in the discussion of the cattle example and the two previous cases. What I shall discuss is the argument of the judges in the Court of Appeals that the smoke nuisance was not caused by the man who erected the wall but by the man who lit the fires. The novelty of the situation is that the smoke nuisance was suffered by the man who lit the fires and not by some third person. The question is not a trivial one since it lies at the heart of the problem under discussion. Who caused the smoke nuisance? The answer seems fairly clear. The smoke nuisance was caused both by the man who built the wall *and* by the man who lit the fires. Given the fires, there would have been no smoke nuisance without the wall; given the wall, there would have been no smoke nuisance without the fires. Eliminate the wall *or* the fires and the smoke nuisance would disappear. On the marginal principle it is clear that *both* were responsible and *both* should be forced to include the loss of amenity due to the smoke as a cost in deciding whether to continue the activity which gives rise to the smoke. And given the possibility of market transactions, this is what would in fact happen. Although the wall-builder was not liable legally for the nuisance, as the man with the smoking chimneys would presumably be willing to pay a sum equal to the monetary worth to him of eliminating the smoke, this sum would therefore become for the wall-builder, a cost of continuing to have the high wall with the timber stacked on the roof.

The judges' contention that it was the man who lit the fires who alone caused the smoke nuisance is true only if we assume that the wall is the given factor. This is what the judges did by deciding that the man who erected the higher wall had a legal right to do so. The case would have been even more interesting if the smoke from the chimneys had injured the timber. Then it would have been the wall-builder who suffered the damage. The case would then have closely paralleled *Sturges v. Bridgman* and there can be little doubt that the man who lit the fires would have been liable for the ensuing damage to the timber, in spite of the fact that no damage had occurred until the high wall was built by the man who owned the timber.

Judges have to decide on legal liability but this should not confuse economists about the nature of the economic problem involved. In the case of the cattle and the crops, it is true that there would be no crop damage without the cattle. It is equally true that there would be no crop damage without the crops. The doctor's work would not have been disturbed if the confectioner had not worked his machinery; but the machinery would have disturbed no one if the doctor had not set up his consulting room in that particular place. The matting was blackened by the fumes from the sulphate of ammonia manufacturer; but no damage would have occurred if the matting manufacturer had not chosen to hang out his matting in a particular place and to use a particular bleaching agent. If we are to discuss the problem in terms of causation, both parties cause the damage. If we are to attain an optimum allocation of resources, it is therefore desirable that both parties should take the harmful effect (the nuisance) into account in deciding on their course of action. It is one of the beauties of a smoothly operating pricing system that, as has already been explained, the fall in the value of production due to the harmful effect would be a cost for both parties.

Bass v. Gregory[12] will serve as an excellent final illustration of the problem. The plaintiffs were the owners and tenant of a public house called the Jolly Anglers. The defendant was the owner of some cottages and a yard adjoining the Jolly Anglers. Under the public house was a cellar excavated in the rock. From the cellar, a hole or shaft had been cut into an old well situated in the defendant's yard. The well therefore became the ventilating shaft for the cellar. The cellar "had been used for a particular purpose in the process of brewing, which, without ventilation, could not be carried on." The cause of the action was that the defendant removed a grating from the mouth of the well, "so as to stop or prevent the free passage of air from [the] cellar upwards through the well. . . ." What caused the defendant to take this step is not clear from the report of the case. Perhaps "the air . . . impregnated by the brewing operations" which "passed up the well and out into the open air" was offensive to him. At any rate, he preferred to have the well in his yard stopped up. The court had first to determine whether the owners of the public house could have a legal right to a current of air. If they were to have such a right, this case would have to be distinguished from *Bryant v. Lefever* (already considered). This, however, presented no difficulty. In this case, the current of air was confined to "a strictly defined channel." In the case of *Bryant v. Lefever*, what was involved was "the general current of air common to all mankind." The judge therefore held that the owners of the public house could have the right to a current of air whereas the owner of the private house in *Bryant v. Lefever* could not. An economist might be tempted to add "but the air moved all the same." However, all that had been decided at this stage of the argument was that there could be a legal right, not that the owners of the public house possessed it. But evidence showed that the shaft from the cellar to the well had existed for over forty years and that the use of the well as a ventilating shaft must have been known to the owners of the yard since the air, when it emerged, smelt of the brewing operations. The judge therefore held that the public house had such a right by the "doctrine of lost grant." This doctrine states "that if a legal right is proved to have existed and been exercised for a number of years the law ought to presume that it had a legal origin."[13] So the owner of the cottages and yard had to unstop the well and endure the smell.

[12] 25 Q.B.D. 481 (1890).

[13] It may be asked why a lost grant could not also be presumed in the case of the confectioner who had operated one mortar for more than 60 years. The answer is that until the doctor built the consulting room at the end of his garden there was no nuisance. So the nuisance had not continued for many years. It is true that the confectioner in his affidavit referred to "an invalid lady who occupied the house upon one occasion, about thirty years before" who "requested him if possible to discontinue the use of the mortars before eight o'clock in the morning" and that there was some evidence that the garden wall had been subjected to vibration. But the court had little difficulty in disposing of this line of argument: ". . . this vibration, even if it existed at all, was so slight, and the com-

The reasoning employed by the courts in determining legal rights will often seem strange to an economist because many of the factors on which the decision turns are, to an economist, irrelevant. Because of this, situations which are, from an economic point of view, identical will be treated quite differently by the courts. The economic problem in all cases of harmful effects is how to maximise the value of production. In the case of *Bass v. Gregory* fresh air was drawn in through the well which facilitated the production of beer but foul air was expelled through the well which made life in the adjoining houses less pleasant. The economic problem was to decide which to choose: a lower cost of beer and worsened amenities in adjoining houses or a higher cost of beer and improved amenities. In deciding this question, the "doctrine of lost grant" is about as relevant as the colour of the judge's eyes. But it has to be remembered that the immediate question faced by the courts is *not* what shall be done by whom *but* who has the legal right to do what. It is always possible to modify by transactions on the market the initial legal delimitation of rights. And, of course, if such market transactions are costless, such a rearrangement of rights will always take place if it would lead to an increase in the value of production.

VI. The Cost of Market Transactions Taken into Account

The argument has proceeded up to this point on the assumption (explicit in Sections III and IV and tacit in Section V) that there were no costs involved in carrying out market transactions. This is, of course, a very unrealistic assumption. In order to carry out a market transaction it is necessary to discover who it is that one wishes to deal with, to inform people that one wishes to deal and on what terms, to conduct negotiations leading up to a bargain, to draw up the contract, to undertake the inspection needed to make sure that the terms of the contract are being observed, and so on. These operations are often extremely costly, sufficiently costly at any rate to prevent many transactions that would be carried out in a world in which the pricing system worked without cost.

In earlier sections, when dealing with the problem of the rearrangement of legal rights through the market, it was argued that such a rearrangement would be made through the market whenever this would lead to an increase in the value of production. But this assumed costless market transactions. Once the costs of carrying out market transactions are taken into account it is clear that such a rearrangement of rights will only be undertaken when the increase in the value of production consequent upon the rearrangement

plaint, if it can be called a complaint, of the invalid lady . . . was of so trifling a character, that . . . the Defendant's acts would not have given rise to any proceeding either at law or in equity" (11 Ch.D. 863). That is, the confectioner had not committed a nuisance until the doctor built his consulting room.

is greater than the costs which would be involved in bringing it about. When it is less, the granting of an injunction (or the knowledge that it would be granted) or the liability to pay damages may result in an activity being discontinued (or may prevent its being started) which would be undertaken if market transactions were costless. In these conditions the initial delimitation of legal rights does have an effect on the efficiency with which the economic system operates. One arrangement of rights may bring about a greater value of production than any other. But unless this is the arrangement of rights established by the legal system, the costs of reaching the same result by altering and combining rights through the market may be so great that this optimal arrangement of rights, and the greater value of production which it would bring, may never be achieved. The part played by economic considerations in the process of delimiting legal rights will be discussed in the next section. In this section, I will take the initial delimitation of rights and the costs of carrying out market transactions as given.

It is clear that an alternative form of economic organisation which could achieve the same result at less cost than would be incurred by using the market would enable the value of production to be raised. As I explained many years ago, the firm represents such an alternative to organising production through market transactions.[14] Within the firm individual bargains between the various cooperating factors of production are eliminated and for a market transaction is substituted an administrative decision. The rearrangement of production then takes place without the need for bargains between the owners of the factors of production. A landowner who has control of a large tract of land may devote his land to various uses taking into account the effect that the interrelations of the various activities will have on the net return of the land, thus rendering unnecessary bargains between those undertaking the various activities. Owners of a large building or of several adjoining properties in a given area may act in much the same way. In effect, using our earlier terminology, the firm would acquire the legal rights of all the parties and the rearrangement of activities would not follow on a rearrangement of rights by contract, but as a result of an administrative decision as to how the rights should be used.

It does not, of course, follow that the administrative costs of organising a transaction through a firm are inevitably less than the costs of the market transactions which are superseded. But where contracts are peculiarly difficult to draw up and an attempt to describe what the parties have agreed to do or not to do (e.g. the amount and kind of a smell or noise that they may make or will not make) would necessitate a lengthy and highly involved document, and, where, as is probable, a long-term contract would be desir-

[14] See Coase, The Nature of the Firm, 4 Economica, New Series, 386 (1937). Reprinted in Readings in Price Theory, 331 (1952).

able;[15] it would be hardly surprising if the emergence of a firm or the extension of the activities of an existing firm was not the solution adopted on many occasions to deal with the problem of harmful effects. This solution would be adopted whenever the administrative costs of the firm were less than the costs of the market transactions that it supersedes and the gains which would result from the rearrangement of activities greater than the firm's costs of organising them. I do not need to examine in great detail the character of this solution since I have explained what is involved in my earlier article.

But the firm is not the only possible answer to this problem. The administrative costs of organising transactions within the firm may also be high, and particularly so when many diverse activities are brought within the control of a single organisation. In the standard case of a smoke nuisance, which may affect a vast number of people engaged in a wide variety of activities, the administrative costs might well be so high as to make any attempt to deal with the problem within the confines of a single firm impossible. An alternative solution is direct Government regulation. Instead of instituting a legal system of rights which can be modified by transactions on the market, the government may impose regulations which state what people must or must not do and which have to be obeyed. Thus, the government (by statute or perhaps more likely through an administrative agency) may, to deal with the problem of smoke nuisance, decree that certain methods of production should or should not be used (e.g. that smoke preventing devices should be installed or that coal or oil should not be burned) or may confine certain types of business to certain districts (zoning regulations).

The government is, in a sense, a super-firm (but of a very special kind) since it is able to influence the use of factors of production by administrative decision. But the ordinary firm is subject to checks in its operations because of the competition of other firms, which might administer the same activities at lower cost and also because there is always the alternative of market transactions as against organisation within the firm if the administrative costs become too great. The government is able, if it wishes, to avoid the market altogether, which a firm can never do. The firm has to make market agreements with the owners of the factors of production that it uses. Just as the government can conscript or seize property, so it can decree that factors of production should only be used in such-and-such a way. Such authoritarian methods save a lot of trouble (for those doing the organising). Furthermore, the government has at its disposal the police and the other law enforcement agencies to make sure that its regulations are carried out.

It is clear that the government has powers which might enable it to get some things done at a lower cost than could a private organisation (or at any

[15] For reasons explained in my earlier article, see Readings in Price Theory, n. 14 at 337.

rate one without special governmental powers). But the governmental administrative machine is not itself costless. It can, in fact, on occasion be extremely costly. Furthermore, there is no reason to suppose that the restrictive and zoning regulations, made by a fallible administration subject to political pressures and operating without any competitive check, will necessarily always be those which increase the efficiency with which the economic system operates. Furthermore, such general regulations which must apply to a wide variety of cases will be enforced in some cases in which they are clearly inappropriate. From these considerations it follows that direct governmental regulation will not necessarily give better results than leaving the problem to be solved by the market or the firm. But equally there is no reason why, on occasion, such governmental administrative regulation should not lead to an improvement in economic efficiency. This would seem particularly likely when, as is normally the case with the smoke nuisance, a large number of people are involved and in which therefore the costs of handling the problem through the market or the firm may be high.

There is, of course, a further alternative, which is to do nothing about the problem at all. And given that the costs involved in solving the problem by regulations issued by the governmental administrative machine will often be heavy (particularly if the costs are interpreted to include all the consequences which follow from the Government engaging in this kind of activity), it will no doubt be commonly the case that the gain which would come from regulating the actions which give rise to the harmful effects will be less than the costs involved in Government regulation.

The discussion of the problem of harmful effects in this section (when the costs of market transactions are taken into account) is extremely inadequate. But at least it has made clear that the problem is one of choosing the appropriate social arrangement for dealing with the harmful effects. All solutions have costs and there is no reason to suppose that government regulation is called for simply because the problem is not well handled by the market or the firm. Satisfactory views on policy can only come from a patient study of how, in practice, the market, firms and governments handle the problem of harmful effects. Economists need to study the work of the broker in bringing parties together, the effectiveness of restrictive covenants, the problems of the large-scale real-estate development company, the operation of Government zoning and other regulating activities. It is my belief that economists, and policy-makers generally, have tended to over-estimate the advantages which come from governmental regulation. But this belief, even if justified, does not do more than suggest that government regulation should be curtailed. It does not tell us where the boundary line should be drawn. This, it seems to me, has to come from a detailed investigation of the actual results of handling the problem in different ways. But it would be unfortunate if this investigation were undertaken with the aid of a faulty economic analysis. The aim of this article is to indicate what the economic approach to the problem should be.

VII. The Legal Delimitation of Rights and the Economic Problem

The discussion in Section V not only served to illustrate the argument but also afforded a glimpse at the legal approach to the problem of harmful effects. The cases considered were all English but a similar selection of American cases could easily be made and the character of the reasoning would have been the same. Of course, if market transactions were costless, all that matters (questions of equity apart) is that the rights of the various parties should be well-defined and the results of legal actions easy to forecast. But as we have seen, the situation is quite different when market transactions are so costly as to make it difficult to change the arrangement of rights established by the law. In such cases, the courts directly influence economic activity. It would therefore seem desirable that the courts should understand the economic consequences of their decisions and should, insofar as this is possible without creating too much uncertainty about the legal position itself, take these consequences into account when making their decisions. Even when it is possible to change the legal delimitation of rights through market transactions, it is obviously desirable to reduce the need for such transactions and thus reduce the employment of resources in carrying them out.

A thorough examination of the presuppositions of the courts in trying such cases would be of great interest but I have not been able to attempt it. Nevertheless it is clear from a cursory study that the courts have often recognized the economic implications of their decisions and are aware (as many economists are not) of the reciprocal nature of the problem. Furthermore, from time to time, they take these economic implications into account, along with other factors, in arriving at their decisions. The American writers on this subject refer to the question in a more explicit fashion than do the British. Thus, to quote Prosser on Torts, a person may

> make use of his own property or . . . conduct his own affairs at the expense of some harm to his neighbors. He may operate a factory whose noise and smoke cause some discomfort to others, so long as he keeps within reasonable bounds. It is only when his conduct is unreasonable, *in the light of its utility and the harm which results* [italics added], that it becomes a nuisance. . . . . As it was said in an ancient case in regard to candle-making in a town, "Le utility del chose excusera le noisomeness del stink."
>
> The world must have factories, smelters, oil refineries, noisy machinery and blasting, even at the expense of some inconvenience to those in the vicinity and the

plaintiff may be required to accept some not unreasonable discomfort for the general good.[16]

The standard British writers do not state as explicitly as this that a comparison between the utility and harm produced is an element in deciding whether a harmful effect should be considered a nuisance. But similar views, if less strongly expressed, are to be found.[17] The doctrine that the harmful effect must be substantial before the court will act is, no doubt, in part a reflection of the fact that there will almost always be some gain to offset the harm. And in the reports of individual cases, it is clear that the judges have had in mind what would be lost as well as what would be gained in deciding whether to grant an injunction or award damages. Thus, in refusing to prevent the destruction of a prospect by a new building, the judge stated:

> I know no general rule of common law, which . . . says, that building so as to stop another's prospect is a nuisance. Was that the case, there could be no great towns; and I must grant injunctions to all the new buildings in this town. . .[18]

In *Webb v. Bird*[19] it was decided that it was not a nuisance to build a schoolhouse so near a windmill as to obstruct currents of air and hinder the working of the mill. An early case seems to have been decided in an opposite direction. Gale commented:

> In old maps of London a row of windmills appears on the heights to the north of London. Probably in the time of King James it was thought an alarming circumstance, as affecting the supply of food to the city, that anyone should build so near them as to take the wind out from their sails.[20]

In one of the cases discussed in section V, *Sturges v. Bridgman*, it seems clear that the judges were thinking of the economic consequences of alternative decisions. To the argument that if the principle that they seemed to be following

[16] See W. L. Prosser, The Law of Torts 398–99, 412 (2d ed. 1955). The quotation about the ancient case concerning candle-making is taken from Sir James Fitzjames Stephen, A General View of the Criminal Law of England 106 (1890). Sir James Stephen gives no reference. He perhaps had in mind *Rex. v. Ronkett*, included in Seavey, Keeton and Thurston, Cases on Torts 604 (1950). A similar view to that expressed by Prosser is to be found in F. V. Harper and F. James, The Law of Torts 67–74 (1956); Restatement, Torts §§826, 827 and 828.

[17] See Winfield on Torts 541–48 (6th ed. T. E. Lewis 1954); Salmond on the Law of Torts 181–90 (12th ed. R.F.V. Heuston 1957); H. Street, The Law of Torts 221–29 (1959).

[18] Attorney General v. Doughty, 2 Ves. Sen. 453, 28 Eng. Rep. 290 (Ch. 1752). Compare in this connection the statement of an American judge, quoted in Prosser, op. cit. supra n. 16 at 413 n. 54: "Without smoke, Pittsburgh would have remained a very pretty village," Musmanno, J., in Versailles Borough v. McKeesport Coal & Coke Co., 1935, 83 Pitts. Leg. J. 379, 385.

[19] 10 C.B. (N.S.) 268, 142 Eng. Rep. 445 (1861); 13 C.B. (N.S.) 841, 143 Eng. Rep. 332 (1863).

[20] See Gale on Easements 238, n. 6 (13th ed. M. Bowles 1959).

were carried out to its logical consequences, it would result in the most serious practical inconveniences, for a man might go—say into the midst of the tanneries of *Bermondsey,* or into any other locality devoted to any particular trade or manufacture of a noisy or unsavoury character, and by building a private residence upon a vacant piece of land put a stop to such trade or manufacture altogether,

the judges answered that

whether anything is a nuisance or not is a question to be determined, not merely by an abstract consideration of the thing itself, but in reference to its circumstances; What would be a nuisance in *Belgrave Square* would not necessarily be so in *Bermondsey;* and where a locality is devoted to a particular trade or manufacture carried on by the traders or manufacturers in a particular and established manner not constituting a public nuisance, Judges and juries would be justified in finding, and may be trusted to find, that the trade or manufacture so carried on in that locality is not a private or actionable wrong.[21]

That the character of the neighborhood is relevant in deciding whether something is, or is not, a nuisance, is definitely established.

He who dislikes the noise of traffic must not set up his abode in the heart of a great city. He who loves peace and quiet must not live in a locality devoted to the business of making boilers or steamships.[22]

What has emerged has been described as "planning and zoning by the judiciary."[23] Of course there are sometimes considerable difficulties in applying the criteria.[24]

An interesting example of the problem is found in *Adams v. Ursell*[25] in which a fried fish shop in a predominantly working-class district was set up near houses of "a much better character." England without fish-and-chips is a contradiction in terms and the case was clearly one of high importance. The judge commented:

It was urged that an injunction would cause great hardship to the defendant and to the poor people who get food at his shop. The answer to that is that it does not follow that the defendant cannot carry on his business in another more suitable place somewhere in the neighbourhood. It by no means follows that because a fried fish shop is a nuisance in one place it is a nuisance in another.

In fact, the injunction which restrained Mr. Ursell from running his shop did not even extend to the whole street. So he was presumably able to move to other premises near houses of "a much worse character," the inhabitants

[21] 11 Ch.D. 865 (1879).

[22] Salmond on the Law of Torts 182 (12th ed. R.F.V. Heuston 1957).

[23] C. M. Haar, Land-Use Planning, A Casebook on the Use, Misuse, and Re-use of Urban Land 95 (1959).

[24] See, for example, Rushmer v. Polsue and Alfieri, Ltd. [1906] 1 Ch. 234, which deals with the case of a house in a quiet situation in a noisy district.

[25] [1913] 1 Ch. 269.

of which would no doubt consider the availability of fish-and-chips to outweigh the pervading odour and "fog or mist" so graphically described by the plaintiff. Had there been no other "more suitable place in the neighbourhood," the case would have been more difficult and the decision might have been different. What would "the poor people" have had for food? No English judge would have said: "Let them eat cake."

The courts do not always refer very clearly to the economic problem posed by the cases brought before them but it seems probable that in the interpretation of words and phrases like "reasonable" or "common or ordinary use" there is some recognition, perhaps largely unconscious and certainly not very explicit, of the economic aspects of the questions at issue. A good example of this would seem to be the judgment in the Court of Appeals in *Andreae v. Selfridge and Company Ltd.*[26] In this case, a hotel (in Wigmore Street) was situated on part of an island site. The remainder of the site was acquired by Selfridges which demolished the existing buildings in order to erect another in their place. The hotel suffered a loss of custom in consequence of the noise and dust caused by the demolition. The owner of the hotel brought an action against Selfridges for damages. In the lower court, the hotel was awarded £4,500 damages. The case was then taken on appeal.

The judge who had found for the hotel proprietor in the lower court said:

> I cannot regard what the defendants did on the site of the first operation as having been commonly done in the ordinary use and occupation of land or houses. It is neither usual nor common, in this country, for people to excavate a site to a depth of 60 feet and then to erect upon that site a steel framework and fasten the steel frames together with rivets. . . . Nor is it, I think, a common or ordinary use of land, in this country, to act as the defendants did when they were dealing with the site of their second operation—namely, to demolish all the houses that they had to demolish, five or six of them I think, if not more, and to use for the purpose of demolishing them pneumatic hammers.

Sir Wilfred Greene, M.R., speaking for the Court of Appeals, first noted

> that when one is dealing with temporary operations, such as demolition and re-building, everybody has to put up with a certain amount of discomfort, because operations of that kind cannot be carried on at all without a certain amount of noise and a certain amount of dust. Therefore, the rule with regard to interference must be read subject to this qualification. . . .

He then referred to the previous judgment:

> With great respect to the learned judge, I take the view that he has not approached this matter from the correct angle. It seems to me that it is not possible to say . . . that the type of demolition, excavation and construction in which the defendant company was engaged in the course of these operations was of such an abnormal and unusual nature as to prevent the qualification to which I have referred coming

[26] [1938] 1 Ch. 1.

into operation. It seems to me that, when the rule speaks of the common or ordinary use of land, it does not mean that the methods of using land and building on it are in some way to be stabilised for ever. As time goes on new inventions or new methods enable land to be more profitably used, either by digging down into the earth or by mounting up into the skies. Whether, from other points of view, that is a matter which is desirable for humanity is neither here nor there; but it is part of the normal use of land, to make use upon your land, in the matter of construction, of what particular type and what particular depth of foundations and particular height of building may be reasonable, in the circumstances, and in view of the developments of the day. . . . Guests at hotels are very easily upset. People coming to this hotel, who were accustomed to a quiet outlook at the back, coming back and finding demolition and building going on, may very well have taken the view that the particular merit of this hotel no longer existed. That would be a misfortune for the plaintiff; but assuming that there was nothing wrong in the defendant company's works, assuming the defendant company was carrying on the demolition and its building, productive of noise though it might be, with all reasonable skill, and taking all reasonable precautions not to cause annoyance to its neighbors, then the planitiff might lose all her clients in the hotel because they have lost the amenities of an open and quiet place behind, but she would have no cause of complaint. . . . [But those] who say that their interference with the comfort of their neighbors is justified because their operations are normal and usual and conducted with proper care and skill are under a specific duty . . . to use that reasonable and proper care and skill. It is not a correct attitude to take to say: 'We will go on and do what we like until somebody complains!' . . . Their duty is to take proper precautions and to see that the nuisance is reduced to a minimum. It is no answer for them to say: 'But this would mean that we should have to do the work more slowly than we would like to do it, or it would involve putting us to some extra expense.' All these questions are matters of common sense and degree, and quite clearly it would be unreasonable to expect people to conduct their work so slowly or so expensively, for the purpose of preventing a transient inconvenience, that the cost and trouble would be prohibitive. . . . In this case, the defendant company's attitude seems to have been to go on until somebody complained, and, further, that its desire to hurry its work and conduct it according to its own ideas and its own convenience was to prevail if there was a real conflict between it and the comfort of its neighbors. That . . . is not carrying out the obligation of using reasonable care and skill. . . . The effect comes to this . . . the plaintiff suffered an actionable nuisance; . . . she is entitled, not to a nominal sum, but to a substantial sum, based upon those principles . . . but in arriving at the sum . . . I have discounted any loss of custom . . . which might be due to the general loss of amenities owing to what was going on at the back. . . .

The upshot was that the damages awarded were reduced from £4,500 to £1,000.

The discussion in this section has, up to this point, been concerned with court decisions arising out of the common law relating to nuisance. Delimitation of rights in this area also comes about because of statutory enactments. Most economists would appear to assume that the aim of governmental action in this field is to extend the scope of the law of nuisance by designating as nuisances activities which would not be recognized as such by the common law. And there can be no doubt that some statutes, for example, the Public Health Acts, have had this effect. But not all Government enactments are of this kind. The effect of much of the legislation in this area is to protect businesses from the claims of those they have harmed by their actions. There is a long list of legalized nuisances.

The position has been summarized in *Halsbury's Laws of England* as follows:

> Where the legislature directs that a thing shall in all events be done or authorises certain works at a particular place for a specific purposes or grants powers with the intention that they shall be exercised, although leaving some discretion as to the mode of exercise, no action will lie at common law for nuisance or damage which is the inevitable result of carrying out the statutory powers so conferred. This is so whether the act causing the damage is authorised for public purposes or private profit. Acts done under powers granted by persons to whom Parliament has delegated authority to grant such powers, for example, under provisional orders of the Board of Trade, are regarded as having been done under statutory authority. In the absence of negligence it seems that a body exercising statutory powers will not be liable to an action merely because it might, by acting in a different way, have minimised an injury.

Instances are next given of freedom from liability for acts authorized:

> An action has been held not to be against a body exercising its statutory powers without negligence in respect of the flooding of land by water escaping from water-courses, from water pipes, from drains, or from a canal; the escape of fumes from sewers; the escape of sewage: the subsidence of a road over a sewer; vibration or noise caused by a railway; fires caused by authorised acts; the pollution of a stream where statutory requirements to use the best known method of purifying before discharging the effluent have been satisfied; interference with a telephone or telegraph system by an elctric tramway; the insertion of poles for tramways in the subsoil; annoyance caused by things reasonably necessary for the excavation of authorised works; accidental damage caused by the placing of a grating in a roadway; the escape of tar acid; or interference with the access of a frontager by a street shelter or safety railings on the edge of a pavement.[27]

The legal position in the United States would seem to be essentially the same as in England, except that the power of the legislatures to authorize what would otherwise be nuisances under the common law, at least without giving compensation to the person harmed, is somewhat more limited, as it is subject to constitutional restrictions.[28] Nonetheless, the power is there and cases more or less identical with the English cases can be found. The

[27] See 30 Halsbury, Law of England 690–91 (3d ed. 1960), Article on Public Authorities and Public Officers.

[28] See Prosser, op. cit. supra n. 16 at 421; Harper and James, op. cit. supra n. 16 at 86–87.

question has arisen in an acute form in connection with airports and the operation of aeroplanes. The case of *Delta Air Corporation v. Kersey, Kersey v. City of Atlanta*[29] is a good example. Mr. Kersey bought land and built a house on it. Some years later the City of Atlanta constructed an airport on land immediately adjoining that of Mr. Kersey. It was explained that his property was "a quiet, peaceful and proper location for a home before the airport was built, but dust, noises and low flying of airplanes caused by the operation of the airport have rendered his property unsuitable as a home," a state of affairs which was described in the report of the case with a wealth of distressing detail. The judge first referred to an earlier case, *Thrasher v. City of Atlanta*[30] in which it was noted that the City of Atlanta had been expressly authorized to operate an airport.

> By this franchise aviation was recognised as a lawful business and also as an enterprise affected with a public interest . . . all persons using [the airport] in the manner contemplated by law are within the protection and immunity of the franchise granted by the municipality. An airport is not a nuisance per se, although it might become such from the manner of its construction or operation.

Since aviation was a lawful business affected with a public interest and the construction of the airport was autorized by statute, the judge next referred to *Georgia Railroad and Banking Co. v. Maddox*[31] in which it was said:

> Where a railroad terminal yard is located and its construction authorized, under statutory powers, if it be constructed and operated in a proper manner, it cannot be adjudged a nuisance. Accordingly, injuries and inconveniences to persons residing near such a yard, from noises of locomotives, rumbling of cars, vibrations produced thereby, and smoke, cinders, soot and the like, which result from the ordinary and necessary, therefore proper, use and operation of such a yard, are not nuisances, but are the necessary concomitants of the franchise granted.

In view of this, the judge decided that the noise and dust complained of by Mr. Kersey "may be deemed to be incidental to the proper operation of an airport, and as such they cannot be said to constitute a nuisance." But the complaint against low flying was different:

> . . . can it be said that flights . . . at such a low height [25 to 50 feet above Mr. Kersey's house] as to be imminently dangerous to . . . life and health . . . are a necessary concomitant of an airport? We do not think this question can be answered in the affirmative. No reason appears why the city could not obtain lands of an area [sufficiently large] . . . as not to require such low flights. . . . For the sake of public convenience adjoining-property owners must suffer such inconvenience from noise and dust as result from the usual and proper operation of an airport, but their private rights are entitled to preference in the eyes of the law where the inconvenience is not one demanded by a properly constructed and operated airport.

[29] Supreme Court of Georgia. 193 Ga. 862, 20 S.E. 2d 245 (1942).

[30] 178 Ga. 514, 173 S.E. 817 (1934).

[31] 116 Ga. 64, 42 S.E. 315 (1902).

Of course this assumed that the City of Atlanta could prevent the low flying and continue to operate the airport. The judge therefore added:

From all that appears, the conditions causing the low flying may be remedied; but if on the trial it should appear that it is indispensable to the public interest that the airport should continue to be operated in its present condition, it may be said that the petitioner should be denied injunctive relief.

In the course of another aviation case, *Smith v. New England Aircraft Co.*,[32] the court surveyed the law in the United States regarding the legalizing of nuisances and it is apparent that, in the broad, it is very similar to that found in England:

It is the proper function of the legislative department of government in the exercise of the police power to consider the problems and risks that arise from the use of new inventions and endeavor to adjust private rights and harmonize conflicting interests by comprehensive statutes for the public welfare. . . . There are . . . analogies where the invasion of the airspace over underlying land by noise, smoke, vibration, dust and disagreeable odors, having been authorized by the legislative department of government and not being in effect a condemnation of the property although in some measure depreciating its market value, must be borne by the landowner without compensation or remedy. Legislative sanction makes that lawful which otherwise might be a nuisance. Examples of this are damages to adjacent land arising from smoke, vibration and noise in the operation of a railroad . . . ; the noise of ringing factory bells . . . ; the abatement of nuisances . . . ; the erection of steam engines and furnaces . . . ; unpleasant odors connected with sewers, oil refining and storage of naphtha. . . .

Most economists seem to be unaware of all this. When they are prevented from sleeping at night by the roar of jet planes overhead (publicly authorized and perhaps publicly operated), are unable to think (or rest) in the day because of the noise and vibration from passing trains (publicly authorized and perhaps publicly operated), find it difficult to breathe because of the odour from a local sewage farm (publicly authorized and perhaps publicly operated) and are unable to escape because their driveways are blocked by a road obstruction (without any doubt, publicly devised), their nerves frayed and mental balance disturbed, they proceed to declaim about the disadvantages of private enterprise and the need for Government regulation.

While most economists seem to be under a misapprehension concerning the character of the situation with which they are dealing, it is also the case that the activities which they would like to see stopped or curtailed may well be socially justified. It is all a question of weighing up the gains that would accrue from eliminating these harmful effects against the gains that accrue from allowing them to continue. Of course, it is likely that an extension of Government economic activity will often lead to this protection against

[32] 270 Mass. 511, 523, 170 N.E. 385, 390 (1930).

action for nuisance being pushed further than is desirable. For one thing, the Government is likely to look with a benevolent eye on enterprises which it is itself promoting. For another, it is possible to describe the committing of a nuisance by public enterprise in a much more pleasant way than when the same thing is done by private enterprise. In the words of Lord Justice Sir Alfred Denning:

> . . . the significance of the social revolution of today is that, whereas in the past the balance was much too heavily in favor of the rights of property and freedom of contract, Parliament has repeatedly intervened so as to give the public good its proper place.[33]

There can be little doubt that the Welfare State is likely to bring an extension of that immunity from liability for damage, which economists have been in the habit of condemning (although they have tended to assume that this immunity was a sign of too little Government intervention in the economic system). For example, in Britain, the powers of local authorities are regarded as being either absolute or conditional. In the first category, the local authority has no discretion in exercising the power conferred on it. "The absolute power may be said to cover all the necessary consequences of its direct operation even if such consequences amount to nuisance." On the other hand, a conditional power may only be exercised in such a way that the consequences do not constitute a nuisance.

> It is the intention of the legislature which determines whether a power is absolute or conditional. . . . [As] there is the possibility that the social policy of the legislature may change from time to time, a power which in one era would be construed as being conditional, might in another era be interpreted as being absolute in order to further the policy of the Welfare State. This point is one which should be borne in mind when considering some of the older cases upon this aspect of the law of nuisance.[34]

It would seem desirable to summarize the burden of this long section. The problem which we face in dealing with actions which have harmful effects is not simply one of restraining those responsible for them. What has to be decided is whether the gain from preventing the harm is greater than the loss which would be suffered elsewhere as a result of stopping the action which produces the harm. In a world in which there are costs of rearranging the rights established by the legal system, the courts, in cases relating to nuisance, are, in effect, making a decision on the economic problem and determining how resources are to be employed. It was argued that the courts are conscious of this and that they often make, although not always in a very explicit fashion, a comparison between what would be gained and what lost by preventing

[33] See Sir Alfred Denning, Freedom Under the Law 71 (1949).

[34] M. B. Cairns, The Law of Tort in Local Government 28-32 (1954).

actions which have harmful effects. But the delimitation of rights is also the result of statutory enactments. Here we also find evidence of an appreciation of the reciprocal nature of the problem. While statutory enactments add to the list of nuisances, action is also taken to legalize what would otherwise be nuisances under the common law. The kind of situation which economists are prone to consider as requiring corrective Government action is, in fact, often the result of Government action. Such action is not necessarily unwise. But there is a real danger that extensive Government intervention in the economic system may lead to the protection of those responsible for harmful effects being carried too far.

VIII. Pigou's Treatment in "The Economics of Welfare"

The fountainhead for the modern economic analysis of the problem discussed in this article is Pigou's *Economics of Welfare* and, in particular, that section of Part II which deals with divergences between social and private net products which come about because

> one person A, in the course of rendering some service, for which payment is made, to a second person B, incidentally also renders services or disservices to other persons (not producers of like services), of such a sort that payment cannot be exacted from the benefited parties or compensation enforced on behalf of the injured parties.[35]

Pigou tells us that his aim in Part II of *The Economics of Welfare* is

> to ascertain how far the free play of self-interest, acting under the existing legal system, tends to distribute the country's resources in the way most favorable to the production of a large national dividend, and how far it is feasible for State action to improve upon 'natural' tendencies.[36]

To judge from the first part of this statement, Pigou's purpose is to discover whether any improvements could be made in the existing arrangements which determine the use of resources. Since Pigou's conclusion is that improvements could be made, one might have expected him to continue by saying that he proposed to set out the changes required to bring them about. Instead, Pigou adds a phrase which contrasts "natural" tendencies with State action, which seems in some sense to equate the present arrangements with "natural" tendencies and to imply that what is required to bring about these improvements is State action (if feasible). That this is more or less Pigou's position is evident from Chapter I of Part II.[37] Pigou starts by referring to "optimistic

[35] A. C. Pigou, The Economics of Welfare 183 (4th ed. 1932). My references will all be to the fourth edition but the argument and examples examined in this article remained substantially unchanged from the first edition in 1920 to the fourth in 1932. A large part (but not all) of this analysis had appeared previously in Wealth and Welfare (1912).

[36] *Id.* at xii.

[37] *Id.* at 127–30.

followers of the classical economists"[38] who have argued that the value of production would be maximised if the Government refrained from any interference in the economic system and the economic arrangements were those which came about "naturally." Pigou goes on to say that if self-interest does promote economic welfare, it is because human institutions have been devised to make it so. (This part of Pigou's argument, which he develops with the aid of a quotation from Cannan, seems to me to be essentially correct.) Pigou concludes:

> But even in the most advanced States there are failures and imperfections. . . . there are many obstacles that prevent a community's resources from being distributed . . . in the most efficient way. The study of these constitutes our present problem. . . . its purposes is essentially practical. It seeks to bring into clearer light some of the ways in which it now is, or eventually may become, feasible for governments to control the play of economic forces in such wise as to promote the economic welfare, and through that, the total welfare, of their citizens as a whole.[39]

Pigou's underlying thought would appear to be: Some have argued that no State action is needed. But the system has performed as well as it has because of State action. Nonetheless, there are still imperfections. What additional State action is required?

If this is a correct summary of Pigou's position, its inadequacy can be demonstrated by examining the first example he gives of a divergence between private and social products.

> It might happen . . . that costs are thrown upon people not directly concerned, through, say, uncompensated damage done to surrounding woods by sparks from railway engines. All such effects must be included—some of them will be positive, others negative elements—in reckoning up the social net product of the marginal increment of any volume of resources turned into any use or place.[40]

The example used by Pigou refers to a real situation. In Britain, a railway does not normally have to compensate those who suffer damage by fire caused by sparks from an engine. Taken in conjunction with what he says in Chapter 9 of Part II, I take Pigou's policy recommendations to be, first, that there should be State action to correct this "natural" situation and, second, that the railways should be forced to compensate those whose woods are burnt. If this is a correct interpretation of Pigou's position, I would argue that the first recommendation is based on a misapprehension of the facts and that the second is not necessarily desirable.

[38] In Wealth and Welfare, Pigou attributes the "optimism" to Adam Smith himself and not to his followers. He there refers to the "highly optimistic theory of Adam Smith that the national dividend, in given circumstances of demand and supply, tends 'naturally' to a maximum" (p. 104).

[39] Pigou, op. cit. supra n. 35 at 129–30.

[40] *Id.* at 134.

Let us consider the legal position. Under the heading "Sparks from engines," we find the following in Halsbury's Laws of England:

> If railway undertakers use steam engines on their railway without express statutory authority to do so, they are liable, irrespective of any negligence on their part, for fires caused by sparks from engines. Railway undertakers are, however, generally given statutory authority to use steam engines on their railway; accordingly, if an engine is constructed with the precautions which science suggests against fire and is used without negligence, they are not responsible at common law for any damage which may be done by sparks. . . . In the construction of an engine the undertaker is bound to use all the discoveries which science has put within its reach in order to avoid doing harm, provided they are such as it is reasonable to require the company to adopt, having proper regard to the likelihood of the damage and to the cost and convenience of the remedy; but it is not negligence on the part of an undertaker if it refuses to use an apparatus the efficiency of which is open to bona fide doubt.

To this general rule, there is a statutory exception arising from the Railway (Fires) Act, 1905, as amended in 1923. This concerns agricultural land or agricultural crops.

> In such a case the fact that the engine was used under statutory powers does not affect the liability of the company in an action for the damage. . . . These provisions, however, only apply where the claim for damage . . . does not exceed £ 200, [£ 100 in the 1905 Act] and where written notice of the occurrence of the fire and the intention to claim has been sent to the company within seven days of the occurrence of the damage and particulars of the damage in writing showing the amount of the claim in money not exceeding £ 200 have been sent to the company within twenty-one days.

Agricultural land does not include moorland or buildings and agricultural crops do not include those led away or stacked.[41] I have not made a close study of the parliamentary history of this statutory exception, but to judge from debates in the House of Commons in 1922 and 1923, this exception was probably designed to help the smallholder.[42]

Let us return to Pigou's example of uncompensated damage to surrounding woods caused by sparks from railway engines. This is presumably intended to show how it is possible "for State action to improve on 'natural' tendencies." If we treat Pigou's example as referring to the position before 1905, or as being an arbitrary example (in that he might just as well have written "surrounding buildings" instead of "surrounding woods"), then it is clear that the reason why compensation was not paid must have been that the railway had statutory authority to run steam engines (which relieved it of liability for fires caused by sparks). That this was the legal position was

[41] See 31 Halsbury, Laws of England 474–75 (3d ed. 1960), Article on Railways and Canals, from which this summary of the legal position, and all quotations, are taken.

[42] See 152 H.C. Deb. 2622–63 (1922); 161 H.C. Deb. 2935–55 (1923).

established in 1860, in a case, oddly enough, which concerned the burning of surrounding woods by a railway,[43] and the law on this point has not been changed (apart from the one exception) by a century of railway legislation, including nationalisation. If we treat Pigou's example of "uncompensated damage done to surrounding woods by sparks from railway engines" literally, and assume that it refers to the period after 1905, then it is clear that the reason why compensation was not paid must have been that the damage was more than £100 (in the first edition of *The Economics of Welfare*) or more than £200 (in later editions) or that the owner of the wood failed to notify the railway in writing within seven days of the fire or did not send particulars of the damage, in writing, within twenty-one days. In the real world, Pigou's example could only exist as a result of a deliberate choice of the legislature. It is not, of course, easy to imagine the construction of a railway in a state of nature. The nearest one can get to this is presumably a railway which uses steam engines "without express statutory authority." However, in this case the railway would be obliged to compensate those whose woods it burnt down. That is to say, compensation would be paid in the absence of Government action. The only circumstances in which compensation would not be paid would be those in which there had been Government action. It is strange that Pigou, who clearly thought it desirable that compensation should be paid, should have chosen this particular example to demonstrate how it is possible "for State action to improve on 'natural' tendencies."

Pigou seems to have had a faulty view of the facts of the situation. But it also seems likely that he was mistaken in his economic analysis. It is not necessarily desirable that the railway should be required to compensate those who suffer damage by fires caused by railway engines. I need not show here that, if the railway could make a bargain with everyone having property adjoining the railway line and there were no costs involved in making such bargains, it would not matter whether the railway was liable for damage caused by fires or not. This question has been treated at length in earlier sections. The problem is whether it would be desirable to make the railway liable in conditions in which it is too expensive for such bargains to be made. Pigou clearly thought it was desirable to force the railway to pay compensation and it is easy to see the kind of argument that would have led him to this conclusion. Suppose a railway is considering whether to run an additional train or to increase the speed of an existing train or to install spark-preventing devices on its engines. If the railway were not liable for fire damage, then, when making these decisions, it would not take into account as a cost the increase in damage resulting from the additional train or the faster train or the failure to install spark-preventing devices. This is the source of the di-

[43] Vaughan v. Taff Vale Railway Co., 3 H. and N. 743 (Ex. 1858) and 5 H. and N. 679 (Ex. 1860).

vergence between private and social net products. It results in the railway performing acts which will lower the value of total production—and which it would not do if it were liable for the damage. This can be shown by means of an arithmetical example.

Consider a railway, which is *not* liable for damage by fires caused by sparks from its engines, which runs two trains per day on a certain line. Suppose that running one train per day would enable the railway to perform services worth $150 per annum and running two trains a day would enable the railway to perform services worth $250 per annum. Suppose further that the cost of running one train is $50 per annum and two trains $100 per annum. Assuming perfect competition, the cost equals the fall in the value of production elsewhere due to the employment of additional factors of production by the railway. Clearly the railway would find it profitable to run two trains per day. But suppose that running one train per day would destroy by fire crops worth (on an average over the year) $60 and two trains a day would result in the destruction of crops worth $120. In these circumstances running one train per day would raise the value of total production but the running of a second train would reduce the value of total production. The second train would enable additional railway services worth $100 per annum to be performed. But the fall in the value of production elsewhere would be $110 per annum; $50 as a result of the employment of additional factors of production and $60 as a result of the destruction of crops. Since it would be better if the second train were not run and since it would not run if the railway were liable for damage caused to crops, the conclusion that the railway should be made liable for the damage seems irresistable. Undoubtedly it is this kind of reasoning which underlies the Pigovian position.

The conclusion that it would be better if the second train did not run is correct. The conclusion that it is desirable that the railway should be made liable for the damage it causes is wrong. Let us change our assumption concerning the rule of liability. Suppose that the railway is liable for damage from fires caused by sparks from the engine. A farmer on lands adjoining the railway is then in the position that, if his crop is destroyed by fires caused by the railway, he will receive the market price from the railway; but if his crop is not damaged, he will receive the market price by sale. It therefore becomes a matter of indifference to him whether his crop is damaged by fire or not. The position is very different when the railway is *not* liable. Any crop destruction through railway-caused fires would then reduce the receipts of the farmer. He would therefore take out of cultivation any land for which the damage is likely to be greater than the net return of the land (for reasons explained at length in Section III). A change from a regime in which the railway is *not* liable for damage to one in which it *is* liable is likely therefore to lead to an increase in the amount of cultivation on lands adjoining the railway. It will also, of course, lead to an increase in the amount of crop destruction due to railway-caused fires.

Let us return to our arithmetical example. Assume that, with the changed rule of liability, there is a doubling in the amount of crop destruction due to railway-caused fires. With one train per day, crops worth $120 would be destroyed each year and two trains per day would lead to the destruction of crops worth $240. We saw previously that it would not be profitable to run the second train if the railway had to pay $60 per annum as compensation for damage. With damage at $120 per annum the loss from running the second train would be $60 greater. But now let us consider the first train. The value of the transport services furnished by the first train is $150. The cost of running the train is $50. The amount that the railway would have to pay out as compensation for damage is $120. It follows that it would not be profitable to run any trains. With the figures in our example we reach the following result: if the railway is not liable for fire-damage, two trains per day would be run; if the railway is liable for fire-damage, it would cease operations altogether. Does this mean that it is better that there should be no railway? This question can be resolved by considering what would happen to the value of total production if it were decided to exempt the railway from liability for fire-damage, thus bringing it into operation (with two trains per day).

The operation of the railway would enable transport services worth $250 to be performed. It would also mean the employment of factors of production which would reduce the value of production elsewhere by $100. Furthermore it would mean the destruction of crops worth $120. The coming of the railway will also have led to the abandonment of cultivation of some land. Since we know that, had this land been cultivated, the value of the crops destroyed by fire would have been $120, and since it is unlikely that the total crop on this land would have been destroyed, it seems reasonable to suppose that the value of the crop yield on this land would have been higher than this. Assume it would have been $160. But the abandonment of cultivation would have released factors of production for employment elsewhere. All we know is that the amount by which the value of production elsewhere will increase will be less than $160. Suppose that it is $150. Then the gain from operating the railway would be $250 (the value of the transport services) minus $100 (the cost of the factors of production) minus $120 (the value of crops destroyed by fire) minus $160 (the fall in the value of crop production due to the abandonment of cultivation) plus $150 (the value of production elsewhere of the released factors of production). Overall, operating the railway will increase the value of total production by $20. With these figures it is clear that it is better that the railway should not be liable for the damage it causes, thus enabling it to operate profitably. Of course, by altering the figures, it could be shown that there are other cases in which it would be desirable that the railway should be liable for the damage it causes. It is enough for my purpose to show that, from an economic point of view, a situation in which there is "uncompensated damage done to surrounding woods by sparks from railway engines" is not necessarily undesirable. Whether it is desirable or not depends on the particular circumstances.

How is it that the Pigovian analysis seems to give the wrong answer? The reason is that Pigou does not seem to have noticed that his analysis is dealing with an entirely different question. The analysis as such is correct. But it is quite illegitimate for Pigou to draw the particular conclusion he does. The question at issue is not whether it is desirable to run an additional train or a faster train or to install smoke-preventing devices; the question at issue is whether it is desirable to have a system in which the railway has to compensate those who suffer damage from the fires which it causes or one in which the railway does not have to compensate them. When an economist is comparing alternative social arrangements, the proper procedure is to compare the total social product yielded by these different arrangements. The comparison of private and social products is neither here nor there. A simple example will demonstrate this. Imagine a town in which there are traffic lights. A motorist approaches an intersection and stops because the light is red. There are no cars approaching the intersection on the other street. If the motorist ignored the red signal, no accident would occur and the total product would increase because the motorist would arrive earlier at his destination. Why does he not do this? The reason is that if he ignored the light he would be fined. The private product from crossing the street is less than the social product. Should we conclude from this that the total product would be greater if there were no fines for failing to obey traffic signals? The Pigovian analysis shows us that it is possible to conceive of better worlds than the one in which we live. But the problem is to devise practical arrangements which will correct defects in one part of the system without causing more serious harm in other parts.

I have examined in considerable detail one example of a divergence between private and social products and I do not propose to make any further examination of Pigou's analytical system. But the main discussion of the problem considered in this article is to be found in that part of Chapter 9 in Part II which deals with Pigou's second class of divergence and it is of interest to see how Pigou develops his argument. Pigou's own description of this second class of divergence was quoted at the beginning of this section. Pigou distinguishes between the case in which a person renders services for which he receives no payment and the case in which a person renders disservices and compensation is not given to the injured parties. Our main attention has, of course, centred on this second case. It is therefore rather astonishing to find, as was pointed out to me by Professor Francesco Forte, that the problem of the smoking chimney—the "stock instance"[44] or "classroom example"[45] of the second case—is used by Pigou as an example of the first case (services rendered without payment) and is never mentioned, at any rate explicitly, in connection with the second case.[46] Pigou points out that factory owners who devote resources to preventing their chimneys from smoking render services for which they receive no payment. The implication, in the light of Pigou's discussion later in the chapter, is that a factory owner with a smokey chimney should be given a bounty to induce him to install smoke-preventing devices. Most modern economists would suggest that the owner of the factory with the smokey chimney should be taxed. It seems a pity that economists (apart from Professor Forte) do not seem to have noticed this feature of Pigou's treatment since a realisation that the problem could be tackled in either of these two ways would probably have led to an explicit recognition of its reciprocal nature.

In discussing the second case (disservices without compensation to those damaged), Pigou says that they are rendered "when the owner of a site in a residential quarter of a city builds a factory there and so destroys a great part of the amenities of neighbouring sites; or, in a less degree, when he uses his site in such a way as to spoil the lighting of the house opposite; or when he invests resources in erecting buildings in a crowded centre, which by contracting the air-space and the playing room of the neighbourhood, tend to injure the health and efficiency of the families living there."[47] Pigou is, of course, quite right to describe such actions as "uncharged disservices." But he is wrong when he describes these actions as "anti-social."[48] They may or may not be. It is necessary to weigh the harm against the good that will result. Nothing could be more "anti-social" than to oppose any action which causes any harm to anyone.

The example with which Pigou opens his discussion of "uncharged disservices" is not, as I have indicated, the case of the smokey chimney but the case of the overrunning rabbits: ". . . incidental uncharged disservices are rendered to third parties when the game-preserving activities of one occupier involve the overrunning of a neighbouring occupier's land by rabbits. . . ." This example is of extraordinary interest, not so much because the economic

[44] Sir Dennis Robertson, I Lectures on Economic Principles 162 (1957).

[45] E. J. Mishan, The Meaning of Efficiency in Economics, 189 The Bankers' Magazine 482 (June 1960).

[46] Pigou, op. cit. supra n. 35 at 184.

[47] *Id.* at 185–86.

[48] *Id.* at 186 n.1. For similar unqualified statements see Pigou's lecture "Some Aspects of the Housing Problem" in B. S. Rowntree and A. C. Pigou, Lectures on Housing, in 18 Manchester Univ. Lectures (1914).

analysis of the case is essentially any different from that of the other examples, but because of the peculiarities of the legal position and the light it throws on the part which economics can play in what is apparently the purely legal question of the delimitation of rights.

The problem of legal liability for the actions of rabbits is part of the general subject of liability for animals.[49] I will, although with reluctance, confine my discussion to rabbits. The early cases relating to rabbits concerned the relations between the lord of the manor and commoners, since, from the thirteenth century on, it became usual for the lord of the manor to stock the commons with conies (rabbits), both for the sake of the meat and the fur. But in 1597, in *Boulston*'s case, an action was brought by one landowner against a neighbouring landowner, alleging that the defendant had made coney-burrows and that the conies had increased and had destroyed the plaintiff's corn. The action failed for the reason that

> . . . so soon as the coneys come on his neighbor's land he may kill them, for they are ferae naturae, and he who makes the coney-boroughs has no property in them, and he shall not be punished for the damage which the coneys do in which he has no property, and which the other may lawfully kill.[50]

As *Boulston*'s case has been treated as binding—Bray, J., in 1919, said that he was not aware that *Boulston*'s case has ever been overruled or questioned[51]—Pigou's rabbit example undoubtedly represented the legal position at the time *The Economics of Welfare* was written.[52] And in this case, it is not far from the truth to say that the state of affairs which Pigou describes came about because of an absence of Government action (at any rate in the form of statutory enactments) and was the result of "natural" tendencies.

Nonetheless, *Boulston*'s case is something of a legal curiousity and Professor Williams makes no secret of his distaste for this decision:

[49] See G. L. Williams, Liability for Animals—An Account of the Development and Present Law of Tortious Liability for Animals, Distress Damage Feasant and the Duty to Fence, in Great Britain, Northern Ireland and the Common Law Dominions (1939). Part Four, "The Action of Nuisance, in Relation to Liability for Animals," 236–62, is especially relevant to our discussion. The problem of liability for rabbits is discussed in this part, 238–47. I do not know how far the common law in the United State regarding liability for animals has diverged from that in Britain. In some Western States of the United States, the English common law regarding the duty to fence has not been followed, in part because "the considerable amount of open, uncleared land made it a matter of public policy to allow cattle to run at large" (Williams, *op. cit. supra* 227). This affords a good example of how a different set of circumstances may make it economically desirable to change the legal rule regarding the delimitation of rights.

[50] 5 Coke (Vol. 3) 104 b. 77 Eng. Rep., 216, 217.

[51] See Stearn v. Prentice Bros. Ltd., (1919) 1 K.B., 395, 397.

[52] I have not looked into recent cases. The legal position has also been modified by statutory enactments.

The conception of liability in nuisance as being based upon ownership is the result, apparently, of a confusion with the action of cattle-trespass, and runs counter both to principle and to the medieval authorities on the escape of water, smoke and filth. . . . The prerequisite of any satisfactory treatment of the subject is the final abandonment of the pernicious doctrine in *Boulston*'s case. . . . Once *Boulston*'s case disappears, the way will be clear for a rational restatement of the whole subject, on lines that will harmonize with the principles prevailing in the rest of the law of nuisance.[53]

The judges in *Boulston*'s case were, of course, aware that their view of the matter depended on distinguishing this case from one involving nuisance:

This cause is not like to the cases put, on the other side, of erecting a lime-kiln, dye-house, or the like; for there the annoyance is by the act of the parties who make them; but it is not so here, for the conies of themselves went into the plaintiff's land, and he might take them when they came upon his land, and make profit of them.[54]

Professor Williams comments:

Once more the atavistic idea is emerging that the animals are guilty and not the landowner. It is not, of course, a satisfactory principle to introduce into a modern law of nuisance. If A. erects a house or plants a tree so that the rain runs or drips from it on to B.'s land, this is A.'s act for which he is liable; but if A. introduces rabbits into his land so that they escape from it into B.'s, this is the act of the rabbits for which A. is not liable—such is the specious distinction resulting from *Boulston*'s case.[55]

It has to be admitted that the decision in *Boulston*'s case seems a little odd. A man may be liable for damage caused by smoke or unpleasant smells, without it being necessary to determine whether he owns the smoke or the smell. And the rule in *Boulston*'s case has not always been followed in cases dealing with other animals. For example, in *Bland v. Yates*,[56] it was decided that an injunction could be granted to prevent someone from keeping an *unusual and excessive* collection of manure in which flies bred and which infested a neighbour's house. The question of who owned the flies was not raised. An economist would not wish to object because legal reasoning sometimes appears a little odd. But there is a sound economic reason for supporting Professor Williams' view that the problem of liability for animals (and particularly rabbits) should be brought within the ordinary law of nuisance. The reason is not that the man who harbours rabbits is solely responsible for the damage; the man whose crops are eaten is equally responsible. And given that the costs of market transactions make a rearrange-

[53] Williams, op. cit. supra n. 49 at 242, 258.

[54] Boulston v. Hardy, Cro. Eliz., 547, 548, 77 Eng. Rep. 216.

[55] Williams, op. cit. supra n. 49 at 243.

[56] 58 Sol.J. 612 (1913–1914).

ment of rights impossible, unless we know the particular circumstances, we cannot say whether it is desirable or not to make the man who harbours rabbits responsible for the damage committed by the rabbits on neighbouring properties. The objection to the rule in *Boulston*'s case is that, under it, the harbourer of rabbits can *never* be liable. It fixes the rule of liability at one pole: and this is as undesirable, from an economic point of view, as fixing the rule at the other pole and making the harbourer of rabbits always liable. But, as we saw in Section VII, the law of nuisance, as it is in fact handled by the courts, is flexible and allows for a comparison of the utility of an act with the harm it produces. As Professor Williams says: "The whole law of nuisance is an attempt to reconcile and compromise between conflicting interests. . . ."[57] To bring the problem of rabbits within the ordinary law of nuisance would not mean *inevitably* making the harbourer of rabbits liable for damage committed by the rabbits. This is not to say that the sole task of the courts in such cases is to make a comparison between the harm and the utility of an act. Nor is it to be expected that the courts will always decide correctly after making such a comparison. But unless the courts act very foolishly, the ordinary law of nuisance would seem likely to give economically more satisfactory results than adopting a rigid rule. Pigou's case of the overrunning rabbits affords an excellent example of how problems of law and economics are interrelated, even though the correct policy to follow would seem to be different from that envisioned by Pigou.

Pigou allows one exception to his conclusion that there is a divergence between private and social products in the rabbit example. He adds: ". . . unless . . . the two occupiers stand in the relation of landlord and tenant, so that compensation is given in an adjustment of the rent."[58] This qualification is rather surprising since Pigou's first class of divergence is largely concerned with the difficulties of drawing up satisfactory contracts between landlords and tenants. In fact, all the recent cases on the problem of rabbits cited by Professor Williams involved disputes between landlords and tenants concerning sporting rights.[59] Pigou seems to make a distinction between the case in which no contract is possible (the second class) and that in which the contract is unsatisfactory (the first class). Thus he says that the second class of divergences between private and social net product

> cannot, like divergences due to tenancy laws, be mitigated by a modification of the contractual relation between any two contracting parties, because the divergence arises out of a service or disservice rendered to persons other than the contracting parties.[60]

[57] Williams, op. cit. supra n. 49 at 259.

[58] Pigou, op. cit. supra n. 35 at 185.

[59] Williams, op. cit. supra n. 49 at 244–47.

[60] Pigou, op. cit. supra n. 35 at 192.

But the reason why some activities are not the subject of contracts is exactly the same as the reason why some contracts are commonly unsatisfactory—it would cost too much to put the matter right. Indeed, the two cases are really the same since the contracts are unsatisfactory because they do not cover certain activities. The exact bearing of the discussion of the first class of divergence on Pigou's main argument is difficult to discover. He shows that in some circumstances contractual relations between landlord and tenant may result in a divergence between private and social products.[61] But he also goes on to show that Government-enforced compensation schemes and rent-controls will also produce divergences.[62] Furthermore, he shows that, when the Government is in a similar position to a private landlord, e.g. when granting a franchise to a public utility, exactly the same difficulties arise as when private individuals are involved.[63] The discussion is interesting but I have been unable to discover what general conclusions about economic policy, if any, Pigou expects us to draw from it.

Indeed, Pigou's treatment of the problems considered in this article is extremely elusive and the discussion of his views raises almost insuperable difficulties of interpretation. Consequently it is impossible to be sure that one has understood what Pigou really meant. Nevertheless, it is difficult to resist the conclusion, extroardinary though this may be in an economist of Pigou's stature, that the main source of this obscurity is that Pigou had not thought his position through.

IX. The Pigovian Tradition

It is strange that a doctrine as faulty as that developed by Pigou should have been so influential, although part of its success has probably been due to the lack of clarity in the exposition. Not being clear, it was never clearly wrong. Curiously enough, this obscurity in the source has not prevented the emergence of a fairly well-defined oral tradition. What economists think they learn from Pigou, and what they tell their students, which I term the Pigovian tradition, is reasonably clear. I propose to show the inadequacy of this Pigovian tradition by demonstrating that both the analysis and the policy conclusions which it supports are incorrect.

I do not propose to justify my view as to the prevailing opinion by copious references to the literature. I do this partly because the treatment in the literature is usually so fragmentary, often involving little more than a reference to Pigou plus some explanatory comment, that detailed examination would be inappropriate. But the main reason for this lack of reference is that the doctrine, although based on Pigou, must have been largely the product of an oral tradition. Certainly economists with whom I have discussed these problems have shown a unanimity of opinion which is quite

[61] *Id.* 174–75. [62] *Id.* 177–83. [63] *Id.* 175–77.

remarkable considering the meagre treatment accorded this subject in the literature. No doubt there are some economists who do not share the usual view but they must represent a small minority of the profession.

The approach to the problems under discussion is through an examination of the value of physical production. The private product is the value of the additional product resulting from a particular activity of a business. The social product equals the private product minus the fall in the value of production elsewhere for which no compensation is paid by the business. Thus, if 10 units of a factor (and no other factors) are used by a business to make a certain product with a value of $105; and the owner of this factor is not compensated for their use, which he is unable to prevent; and these 10 units of the factor would yield products in their best alternative use worth $100; then, the social product is $105 minus $100 or $5. If the business now pays for one unit of the factor and its price equals the value of its marginal product, then the social product rises to $15. If two units are paid for, the social product rises to $25 and so on until it reaches $105 when all units of the factor are paid for. It is not difficult to see why economists have so readily accepted this rather odd procedure. The analysis focusses on the individual business decision and since the use of certain resources is not allowed for in costs, receipts are reduced by the same amount. But, of course, this means that the value of the social product has no social significance whatsoever. It seems to me preferable to use the opportunity cost concept and to approach these problems by comparing the value of the product yielded by factors in alternative uses or by alternative arrangements. The main advantage of a pricing system is that it leads to the employment of factors in places where the value of the product yielded is greatest and does so at less cost than alternative systems (I leave aside that a pricing system also eases the problem of the redistribution of income). But if through some God-given natural harmony factors flowed to the places where the value of the product yielded was greatest without any use of the pricing system and consequently there was no compensation, I would find it a source of surprise rather than a cause for dismay.

The definition of the social product is queer but this does not mean that the conclusions for policy drawn from the analysis are necessarily wrong. However, there are bound to be dangers in an approach which diverts attention from the basic issues and there can be little doubt that it has been responsible for some of the errors in current doctrine. The belief that it is desirable that the business which causes harmful effects should be forced to compensate those who suffer damage (which was exhaustively discussed in section VIII in connection with Pigou's railway sparks example) is undoubtedly the result of not comparing the total product obtainable with alternative social arrangements.

The same fault is to be found in proposals for solving the problem of harmful effects by the use of taxes or bounties. Pigou lays considerable stress on this solution although he is, as usual, lacking in detail and qualified in his support.[64] Modern economists tend to think exclusively in terms of taxes and in a very precise way. The tax should be equal to the damage done and should therefore vary with the amount of the harmful effect. As it is not proposed that the proceeds of the tax should be paid to those suffering the damage, this solution is not the same as that which would force a business to pay compensation to those damaged by its actions, although economists generally do not seem to have noticed this and tend to treat the two solutions as being identical.

Assume that a factory which emits smoke is set up in a district previously free from smoke pollution, causing damage valued at $100 per annum. Assume that the taxation solution is adopted and that the factory owner is taxed $100 per annum as long as the factory emits the smoke. Assume further that a smoke-preventing device costing $90 per annum to run is available. In these circumstances, the smoke-preventing device would be installed. Damage of $100 would have been avoided at an expenditure of $90 and the factory-owner would be better off by $10 per annum. Yet the position achieved may not be optimal. Suppose that those who suffer the damage could avoid it by moving to other locations or by taking various precautions which would cost them, or be equivalent to a loss in income of, $40 per annum. Then there would be a gain in the value of production of $50 if the factory continued to emit its smoke and those now in the district moved elesewhere or made other adjustments to avoid the damage. If the factory owner is to be made to pay a tax equal to the damage caused, it would clearly be desirable to institute a double tax system and to make residents of the district pay an amount equal to the additional cost incurred by the factory owner (or the consumers of his products) in order to avoid the damage. In these conditions, people would not stay in the district or would take other measures to prevent the damage from occurring, when the costs of doing so were less than the costs that would be incurred by the producer to reduce the damage (the producer's object, of course, being not so much to reduce the damage as to reduce the tax payments). A tax system which was confined to a tax on the producer for damage caused would tend to lead to unduly high costs being incurred for the prevention of damage. Of course this could be avoided if it were possible to base the tax, not on the damage caused, but on the fall in the value of production (in its widest sense) resulting from the emission of smoke. But to do so would require a detailed knowledge of individual preferences and I am unable to imagine how the data needed for such a taxation system could be assembled. Indeed,

[64] *Id.* 192–4, 381 and Public Finance 94–100 (3d ed. 1947).

the proposal to solve the smoke-pollution and similar problems by the use of taxes bristles with difficulties: the problem of calculation, the difference between average and marginal damage, the interrelations between the damage suffered on different properties, etc. But it is unnecessary to examine these problems here. It is enough for my purpose to show that, even if the tax is exactly adjusted to equal the damage that would be done to neighboring properties as a result of the emission of each additional puff of smoke, the tax would not necessarily bring about optimal conditions. An increase in the number of people living or of business operating in the vicinity of the smoke-emitting factory will increase the amount of harm produced by a given emission of smoke. The tax that would be imposed would therefore increase with an increase in the number of those in the vicinity. This will tend to lead to a decrease in the value of production of the factors employed by the factory, either because a reduction in production due to the tax will result in factors being used elsewhere in ways which are less valuable, or because factors will be diverted to produce means for reducing the amount of smoke emitted. But people deciding to establish themselves in the vicinity of the factory will not take into account this fall in the value of production which results from their presence. This failure to take into account costs imposed on others is comparable to the action of a factory-owner in not taking into account the harm resulting from his emission of smoke. Without the tax, there may be too much smoke and too few people in the vicinity of the factory; but with the tax there may be too little smoke and too many people in the vicinity of the factory. There is no reason to suppose that one of these results is necessarily preferable.

I need not devote much space to discussing the similar error involved in the suggestion that smoke producing factories should, by means of zoning regulations, be removed from the districts in which the smoke causes harmful effects. When the change in the location of the factory results in a reduction in production, this obviously needs to be taken into account and weighed against the harm which would result from the factory remaining in that location. The aim of such regulation should not be to eliminate smoke pollution but rather to secure the optimum amount of smoke pollution, this being the amount which will maximise the value of production.

X. A Change of Approach

It is my belief that the failure of economists to reach correct conclusions about the treatment of harmful effects cannot be ascribed simply to a few slips in analysis. It stems from basic defects in the current approach to problems of welfare economics. What is needed is a change of approach.

Analysis in terms of divergencies between private and social products concentrates attention on particular deficiencies in the system and tends to nourish the belief that any measure which will remove the deficiency is necessarily desirable. It diverts attention from those other changes in the system which are inevitably associated with the corrective measure, changes which may well produce more harm than the original deficiency. In the preceding sections of this article, we have seen many examples of this. But it is not necessary to approach the problem in this way. Economists who study problems of the firm habitually use an opportunity cost approach and compare the receipts obtained from a given combination of factors with alternative business arrangements. It would seem desirable to use a similar approach when dealing with questions of economic policy and to compare the total product yielded by alternative social arrangements. In this article, the analysis has been confined, as is usual in this part of economics, to comparisons of the value of production, as measured by the market. But it is, of course, desirable that the choice between different social arrangements for the solution of economic problems should be carried out in broader terms than this and that the total effect of these arrangements in all spheres of life should be taken into account. As Frank H. Knight has so often emphasized, problems of welfare economics must ultimately dissolve into a study of aesthetics and morals.

A second feature of the usual treatment of the problems discussed in this article is that the analysis proceeds in terms of a comparison between a state of laissez faire and some kind of ideal world. This approach inevitably leads to a looseness of thought since the nature of the alternatives being compared is never clear. In a state of laissez faire, is there a monetary, a legal or a political system and if so, what are they? In an ideal world, would there be a monetary, a legal or a political system and if so, what would they be? The answers to all these questions are shrouded in mystery and every man is free to draw whatever conclusions he likes. Actually very little analysis is required to show that an ideal world is better than a state of laissez faire, unless the definitions of a state of laissez faire and an ideal world happen to be the same. But the whole discussion is largely irrelevant for questions of economic policy since whatever we may have in mind as our ideal world, it is clear that we have not yet discovered how to get to it from where we are. A better approach would seem to be to start our analysis with a situation approximating that which actually exists, to examine the effects of a proposed policy change and to attempt to decide whether the new situation would be, in total, better or worse than the original one. In this way, conclusions for policy would have some relevance to the actual situation.

A final reason for the failure to develop a theory adequate to handle the problem of harmful effects stems from a faulty concept of a factor of production. This is usually thought of as a physical entity which the businessman acquires and uses (an acre of land, a ton of fertiliser) instead of as a right to perform certain (physical) actions. We may speak of a person owning land and using it as a factor of production but what the land-owner in fact possesses is the right to carry out a circumscribed list of actions. The rights of a land-owner are not unlimited. It is not even always possible for him to remove the land to another place, for instance, by quarrying it. And although it may be possible for him to exclude some people from using "his" land, this may not be true of others. For example, some people may have the right to cross the land. Furthermore, it may or may not be possible to erect certain types of buildings or to grow certain crops or to use particular drainage systems on the land. This does not come about simply because of Government regulation. It would be equally true under the common law. In fact it would be true under any system of law. A system in which the rights of individuals were unlimited would be one in which there were no rights to acquire.

If factors of production are thought of as rights, it becomes easier to understand that the right to do something which has a harmful effect (such as the creation of smoke, noise, smells, etc.) is also a factor of production. Just as we may use a piece of land in such a way as to prevent someone else from crossing it, or parking his car, or building his house upon it, so we may use it in such a way as to deny him a view or quiet or unpolluted air. The cost of exercising a right (of using a factor of production) is always the loss which is suffered elsewhere in consequence of the exercise of that right—the inability to cross land, to park a car, to build a house, to enjoy a view, to have peace and quiet or to breathe clean air.

It would clearly be desirable if the only actions performed were those in which what was gained was worth more than what was lost. But in choosing between social arrangements within the context of which individual decisions are made, we have to bear in mind that a change in the existing system which will lead to an improvement in some decisions may well lead to a worsening of others. Furthermore we have to take into account the costs involved in operating the various social arrangements (whether it be the working of a market or of a government department), as well as the costs involved in moving to a new system. In devising and choosing between social arrangements we should have regard for the total effect. This, above all, is the change in approach which I am advocating.

[16]

The American Economic Review

VOLUME XXXV SEPTEMBER, 1945 NUMBER FOUR

THE USE OF KNOWLEDGE IN SOCIETY

By F. A. HAYEK*

I

What is the problem we wish to solve when we try to construct a rational economic order?

On certain familiar assumptions the answer is simple enough. *If* we possess all the relevant information, *if* we can start out from a given system of preferences and *if* we command complete knowledge of available means, the problem which remains is purely one of logic. That is, the answer to the question of what is the best use of the available means is implicit in our assumptions. The conditions which the solution of this optimum problem must satisfy have been fully worked out and can be stated best in mathematical form: put at their briefest, they are that the marginal rates of substitution between any two commodities or factors must be the same in all their different uses.

This, however, is emphatically *not* the economic problem which society faces. And the economic calculus which we have developed to solve this logical problem, though an important step toward the solution of the economic problem of society, does not yet provide an answer to it. The reason for this is that the "data" from which the economic calculus starts are never for the whole society "given" to a single mind which could work out the implications, and can never be so given.

The peculiar character of the problem of a rational economic order is determined precisely by the fact that the knowledge of the circumstances of which we must make use never exists in concentrated or integrated form, but solely as the dispersed bits of incomplete and frequently contradictory knowledge which all the separate individuals possess. The economic problem of society is thus not merely a problem

* The author is Tooke professor of political economy and statistics at the University of London (London School of Economics and Political Science).

of how to allocate "given" resources—if "given" is taken to mean given to a single mind which deliberately solves the problem set by these "data." It is rather a problem of how to secure the best use of resources known to any of the members of society, for ends whose relative importance only these individuals know. Or, to put it briefly, it is a problem of the utilization of knowledge not given to anyone in its totality.

This character of the fundamental problem has, I am afraid, been rather obscured than illuminated by many of the recent refinements of economic theory, particularly by many of the uses made of mathematics. Though the problem with which I want primarily to deal in this paper is the problem of a rational economic organization, I shall in its course be led again and again to point to its close connections with certain methodological questions. Many of the points I wish to make are indeed conclusions toward which diverse paths of reasoning have unexpectedly converged. But as I now see these problems, this is no accident. It seems to me that many of the current disputes with regard to both economic theory and economic policy have their common origin in a misconception about the nature of the economic problem of society. This misconception in turn is due to an erroneous transfer to social phenomena of the habits of thought we have developed in dealing with the phenomena of nature.

II

In ordinary language we describe by the word "planning" the complex of interrelated decisions about the allocation of our available resources. All economic activity is in this sense planning; and in any society in which many people collaborate, this planning, whoever does it, will in some measure have to be based on knowledge which, in the first instance, is not given to the planner but to somebody else, which somehow will have to be conveyed to the planner. The various ways in which the knowledge on which people base their plans is communicated to them is the crucial problem for any theory explaining the economic process. And the problem of what is the best way of utilizing knowledge initially dispersed among all the people is at least one of the main problems of economic policy—or of designing an efficient economic system.

The answer to this question is closely connected with that other question which arises here, that of *who* is to do the planning. It is about this question that all the dispute about "economic planning" centers. This is not a dispute about whether planning is to be done or not. It is a dispute as to whether planning is to be done centrally, by one authority for the whole economic system, or is to be divided among many individuals. Planning in the specific sense in which the term is used in contemporary controversy necessarily means central planning—direction of the whole economic system according to one unified plan. Competition, on the other hand, means decentralized planning by many separate persons. The half-way house between the two, about which many people talk but which few like when they see it, is the delegation of planning to organized industries, or, in other words, monopoly.

Which of these systems is likely to be more efficient depends mainly on the question under which of them we can expect that fuller use will be made of the existing knowledge. And this, in turn, depends on whether we are more likely to succeed in putting at the disposal of a single central authority all the knowledge which ought to be used but which is initially dispersed among many different individuals, or in conveying to the individuals such additional knowledge as they need in order to enable them to fit their plans in with those of others.

III

It will at once be evident that on this point the position will be different with respect to different kinds of knowledge; and the answer to our question will therefore largely turn on the relative importance of the different kinds of knowledge; those more likely to be at the disposal of particular individuals and those which we should with greater confidence expect to find in the possession of an authority made up of suitably chosen experts. If it is today so widely assumed that the latter will be in a better position, this is because one kind of knowledge, namely, scientific knowledge, occupies now so prominent a place in public imagination that we tend to forget that it is not the only kind that is relevant. It may be admitted that, so far as scientific knowledge is concerned, a body of suitably chosen experts may be in the best position to command all the best knowledge available—though this is of course merely shifting the difficulty to the problem of selecting the experts. What I wish to point out is that, even assuming that this problem can be readily solved, it is only a small part of the wider problem.

Today it is almost heresy to suggest that scientific knowledge is not the sum of all knowledge. But a little reflection will show that there is beyond question a body of very important but unorganized knowledge which cannot possibly be called scientific in the sense of knowledge of general rules: the knowledge of the particular circumstances of time and place. It is with respect to this that practically every individual has some advantage over all others in that he possesses unique information of which beneficial use might be made, but of which use can be made only if the decisions depending on it are left to him or are made with his active coöperation. We need to remember only how much we have to learn in any occupation after we have completed our theoretical training, how big a part of our working life we spend learning particular jobs, and how valuable an asset in all walks of life is knowledge of people, of local conditions, and special circumstances. To know of and put to use a machine not fully employed, or somebody's skill which could be better utilized, or to be aware of a surplus stock which can be drawn upon during an interruption of supplies, is socially quite as useful as the knowledge of better alternative techniques. And the shipper who earns his living from using otherwise empty or half-filled journeys of tramp-steamers, or the estate agent whose whole knowledge is almost exclusively one of temporary opportunities, or the *arbitrageur* who gains from local differences of commodity prices, are all performing eminently useful functions based on special knowledge of circumstances of the fleeting moment not known to others.

It is a curious fact that this sort of knowledge should today be generally regarded with a kind of contempt, and that anyone who by such knowledge gains an advantage over somebody better equipped with theoretical or technical knowledge is thought to have acted almost disreputably. To gain an advantage from better knowledge of facilities of communication or transport is sometimes regarded as almost dishonest, although it is quite as important that society make use of the best opportunities in this respect as in using the latest scientific discoveries. This prejudice has in a considerable measure affected the attitude toward commerce in general compared with that toward production. Even economists who regard themselves as definitely above the crude materialist fallacies of the past constantly commit the same mistake where activities directed toward the acquisition of such practical knowledge are concerned—apparently because in their scheme of things all such knowledge is supposed to be "given." The common idea now seems to be that all such knowledge should as a matter of course be readily at the command of everybody, and the reproach of irrationality leveled against the existing economic order is frequently based on the fact that it is not so available. This view disregards the fact that the method by which such knowledge can be made as widely available as possible is precisely the problem to which we have to find an answer.

IV

If it is fashionable today to minimize the importance of the knowledge of the particular circumstances of time and place, this is closely connected with the smaller importance which is now attached to change as such. Indeed, there are few points on which the assumptions made (usually only implicitly) by the "planners" differ from those of their opponents as much as with regard to the significance and frequency of changes which will make substantial alterations of production plans necessary. Of course, if detailed economic plans could be laid down for fairly long periods in advance and then closely adhered to, so that no further economic decisions of importance would be required, the task of drawing up a comprehensive plan governing all economic activity would appear much less formidable.

It is, perhaps, worth stressing that economic problems arise always and only in consequence of change. So long as things continue as before, or at least as they were expected to, there arise no new problems requiring a decision, no need to form a new plan. The belief that changes, or at least day-to-day adjustments, have become less important in modern times implies the contention that economic problems also have become less important. This belief in the decreasing importance of change is, for that reason, usually held by the same people who argue that the importance of economic considerations has been driven into the background by the growing importance of technological knowledge.

Is it true that, with the elaborate apparatus of modern production, economic decisions are required only at long intervals, as when a new factory is to be erected or a new process to be introduced? Is it true that, once a plant has been built, the rest is all more or less mechanical, determined by the character of the plant, and leaving little to be changed in adapting to the ever-changing circumstances of the moment?

The fairly widespread belief in the affirmative is not, so far as I can ascertain, borne out by the practical experience of the business man. In a competitive industry at any rate—and such an industry alone can serve as a test—the task of keeping cost from rising requires constant struggle, absorbing a great part of the energy of the manager. How easy it is for an inefficient manager to dissipate the differentials on which profitability rests, and that it is possible, with the same technical facilities, to produce with a great variety of costs, are among the commonplaces of business experience which do not seem to be equally familiar in the study of the economist. The very strength of the desire, constantly voiced by producers and engineers, to be able to proceed untrammeled by considerations of money costs, is eloquent testimony to the extent to which these factors enter into their daily work.

One reason why economists are increasingly apt to forget about the constant small changes which make up the whole economic picture is probably their growing preoccupation with statistical aggregates, which show a very much greater stability than the movements of the detail. The comparative stability of the aggregates cannot, however, be accounted for—as the statisticians seem occasionally to be inclined to do—by the "law of large numbers" or the mutual compensation of random changes. The number of elements with which we have to deal is not large enough for such accidental forces to produce stability. The continuous flow of goods and services is maintained by constant deliberate adjustments, by new dispositions made every day in the light of circumstances not known the day before, by *B* stepping in at once when *A* fails to deliver. Even the large and highly mechanized plant keeps going largely because of an environment upon which it can draw for all sorts of unexpected needs; tiles for its roof, stationery for its forms, and all the thousand and one kinds of equipment in which it cannot be self-contained and which the plans for the operation of the plant require to be readily available in the market.

This is, perhaps, also the point where I should briefly mention the fact that the sort of knowledge with which I have been concerned is knowledge of the kind which by its nature cannot enter into statistics and therefore cannot be conveyed to any central authority in statistical form. The statistics which such a central authority would have to use would have to be arrived at precisely by abstracting from minor differences between the things, by lumping together, as resources of one kind, items which differ as regards location, quality, and other particulars, in a way which may be very significant for the specific decision. It follows from this that central planning based on statistical information by its nature cannot take direct account of these circumstances of time and place, and that the central planner will have to find some way or other in which the decisions depending on them can be left to the "man on the spot."

V

If we can agree that the economic problem of society is mainly one of rapid adaptation to changes in the particular circumstances of time and place, it would seem to follow that the ultimate decisions must be left to the people who are familiar with these circumstances, who know directly of the relevant changes and of the resources immediately available to meet them. We cannot expect that this problem will be solved by first communicating all this knowledge to a central board which, after integrating *all* knowledge, issues its orders. We must solve it by some form of decentralization. But this answers only part of our problem. We need decentralization because only thus can we ensure that the knowledge of the particular circumstances of time and place will be promptly used. But the "man on the spot" cannot decide solely on the basis of his limited but intimate knowledge of the facts of his immediate surroundings. There still remains the problem of communicating to him such further information as he needs to fit his decisions into the whole pattern of changes of the larger economic system.

How much knowledge does he need to do so successfully? Which of the events which happen beyond the horizon of his immediate knowledge are of relevance to his immediate decision, and how much of them need he know?

There is hardly anything that happens anywhere in the world that *might* not have an effect on the decision he ought to make. But he need not know of these events as such, nor of *all* their effects. It does not matter for him *why* at the particular moment more screws of one size than of another are wanted, *why* paper bags are more readily available than canvas bags, or *why* skilled labor, or particular machine tools, have for the moment become more difficult to acquire. All that is significant for him is *how much more or less* difficult to procure they have become compared with other things with which he is also concerned, or how much more or less urgently wanted are the alternative things he produces or uses. It is always a question of the relative importance of the particular things with which he is concerned, and the causes which alter their relative importance are of no interest to him beyond the effect on those concrete things of his own environment.

It is in this connection that what I have called the economic calculus proper helps us, at least by analogy, to see how this problem can be solved, and in fact is being solved, by the price system. Even the single controlling mind, in possession of all the data for some small, self-contained economic system, would not—every time some small adjustment in the allocation of resources had to be made—go explicitly through all the relations between ends and means which might possibly be affected. It is indeed the great contribution of the pure logic of choice that it has demonstrated conclusively that even such a single mind could solve this kind of problem only by constructing and constantly using rates of equivalence (or "values," or "marginal rates of substitution"), *i.e.*, by attaching to each kind of scarce resource a numerical index which cannot be derived from any property possessed by that particular thing, but which reflects, or in which is condensed, its significance in view of the whole means-end structure. In any small change he will have to consider only these quantitative indices (or "values") in which all the relevant information is concentrated; and by adjusting the quantities one by one, he can appropriately rearrange his dispositions without having to solve the whole puzzle *ab initio*, or without needing at any stage to survey it at once in all its ramifications.

Fundamentally, in a system where the knowledge of the relevant facts is dispersed among many people, prices can act to coördinate the separate actions of different people in the same way as subjective values help the individual to coördinate the parts of his plan. It is worth contemplating for a moment a very simple and commonplace instance of the action of the price system to see what precisely it accomplishes. Assume that somewhere in the world a new opportunity for the use of some raw material, say tin, has arisen, or that one of the sources of supply of tin has been eliminated. It does not matter for our purpose—and it is very significant that it does not matter—which of these two causes has made tin more scarce. All that the users of tin need to know is that some of the tin they used to consume is now more profitably employed elsewhere, and that in consequence they must economize tin. There is no need for the great majority of them even to know where the more urgent need has arisen, or in favor of what other needs they ought to husband the supply. If only some of them know directly of the new demand, and switch resources over to it, and if the people who are aware of the new gap thus created in turn fill it from still other sources, the effect will rapidly spread throughout the whole economic system and influence not only all the uses of tin, but also those of its substitutes and the substitutes of these substitutes, the supply of all the things made of tin, and their substitutes, and so on; and all this without the great majority of those instrumental in bringing about these substitutions knowing anything at all about the original cause of these changes. The whole acts as one market, not because any of its members survey the whole field, but because their limited individual fields of vision sufficiently overlap so that through many intermediaries the relevant information is communicated to all. The mere fact that there is one price for any commodity—or rather that local prices are connected in a manner determined by the cost of transport, etc.—brings about the solution which (it is just conceptually possible) might have been arrived at by one single mind possessing all the information which is in fact dispersed among all the people involved in the process.

VI

We must look at the price system as such a mechanism for communicating information if we want to understand its real function—a function which, of course, it fulfills less perfectly as prices grow more rigid. (Even when quoted prices have become quite rigid, however, the forces which would operate through changes in price still operate to a considerable extent through changes in the other terms of the contract.) The most significant fact about this system is the economy of knowledge with which it operates, or how little the individual participants need to know in order to be able to take the right action. In abbreviated form, by a kind of symbol, only the most essential information is passed on, and passed on only to those concerned. It is more than a metaphor to describe the price system as a kind of machinery for registering change, or a system of telecommunications which enables individual producers to watch merely the movement of a few pointers, as an engineer might watch the hands of a few dials, in order to adjust their activities to changes of which they may never know more than is reflected in the price movement.

Of course, these adjustments are probably never "perfect" in the sense in which the economist conceives of them in his equilibrium analysis. But I fear that our theoretical habits of approaching the problem with the assumption of more or less perfect knowledge on the part of almost everyone has made us somewhat blind to the true function of the price mechanism and led us to apply rather misleading standards in judging its efficiency. The marvel is that in a case like that of a scarcity of one raw material, without an order being issued, without more than perhaps a handful of people knowing the cause, tens of thousands of people whose identity could not be ascertained by months of investigation, are made to use the material or its products more sparingly; *i.e.*, they move in the right direction. This is enough of a marvel even if, in a constantly changing world, not all will hit it off so perfectly that their profit rates will always be maintained at the same constant or "normal" level.

I have deliberately used the word "marvel" to shock the reader out of the complacency with which we often take the working of this mechanism for granted. I am convinced that if it were the result of deliberate human design, and if the people guided by the price changes understood that their decisions have significance far beyond their immediate aim, this mechanism would have been acclaimed as one of the greatest triumphs of the human mind. Its misfortune is the double one that it is not the product of human design and that the people guided by it usually do not know why they are made to do what they do. But those who clamor for "conscious direction"—and who cannot believe that anything which has evolved without design (and even without our understanding it) should solve problems which we should not be able to solve consciously—should remember this: The problem is precisely how to extend the span of our utilization of resources beyond the span of the control of any one mind; and, therefore, how to dispense with the need of conscious control and how to provide inducements which will make the individuals do the desirable things without anyone having to tell them what to do.

The problem which we meet here is by no means peculiar to economics but arises in connection with nearly all truly social phenomena, with language and most of our cultural inheritance, and constitutes really the central theoretical problem of all social science. As Alfred Whitehead has said in another connection, "It is a profoundly erroneous truism, repeated by all copy-books and by eminent people when they are making speeches, that we should cultivate the habit of thinking what we are doing. The precise opposite is the case. Civilization advances by extending the number of important operations which we can perform without thinking about them." This is of profound significance in the social field. We make constant use of formulas, symbols and rules whose meaning we do not understand and through the use of which we avail ourselves of the assistance of knowledge which individually we do not possess. We have developed these practices and institutions by building upon habits and institutions which have proved successful in their own sphere and which have in turn become the foundation of the civilization we have built up.

The price system is just one of those formations which man has learned to use (though he is still very far from having learned to make the best use of it) after he had stumbled upon it without understanding it. Through it not only a division of labor but also a coördinated utilization of resources based on an equally divided knowledge has become possible. The people who like to deride any suggestion that this may be so usually distort the argument by insinuating that it asserts that by some miracle just that sort of system has spontaneously grown up which is best suited to modern civilization. It is the other way round: man has been able to develop that division of labor on which our civilization is based because he happened to stumble upon a method which made it possible. Had he not done so he might still have developed some other, altogether different, type of civilization, something like the "state" of the termite ants, or some other altogether unimaginable type. All that we can say is that nobody has yet succeeded in designing an alternative system in which certain features of the existing one can be preserved which are dear even to those who most violently assail it—such as particularly the extent to which the individual can choose his pursuits and consequently freely use his own knowledge and skill.

VII

It is in many ways fortunate that the dispute about the indispensability of the price system for any rational calculation in a complex society is now no longer conducted entirely between camps holding different political views. The thesis that without the price system we could not preserve a society based on such extensive division of labor as ours was greeted with a howl of derision when it was first advanced by von Mises twenty-five years ago. Today the difficulties which some still find in accepting it are no longer mainly political, and this makes for an atmosphere much more conducive to reasonable discussion. When we find Leon Trotsky arguing that "economic accounting is unthinkable without market relations"; when Professor Oscar Lange promises Professor von Mises a statue in the marble halls of the future Central Planning Board; and when Professor Abba P. Lerner rediscovers Adam Smith and emphasizes that the essential utility of the price system consists in inducing the individual, while seeking his own interest, to do what is in the general interest, the differences can indeed no longer be ascribed to political prejudice. The remaining dissent seems clearly to be due to purely intellectual, and more particularly methodological, differences.

A recent statement by Professor Joseph Schumpeter in his *Capitalism, Socialism and Democracy* provides a clear illustration of one of the methodological differences which I have in mind. Its author is preeminent among those economists who approach economic phenomena in the light of a certain branch of positivism. To him these phenomena accordingly appear as objectively given quantities of commodities impinging directly upon each other, almost, it would seem, without any intervention of human minds. Only against this background can I account for the following (to me startling) pronouncement. Professor Schumpeter argues that the possibility of a rational calculation in the absence of markets for the factors of production follows for the theorist "from the elementary proposition that consumers in evaluating ('demanding') consumers' goods *ipso facto* also evaluate the means of production which enter into the production of these goods."[1]

Taken literally, this statement is simply untrue. The consumers do nothing of the kind. What Professor Schumpeter's "*ipso facto*" presumably means is that the valuation of the factors of production is

[1] J. Schumpeter, *Capitalism, Socialism, and Democracy* (New York, Harper, 1942), p. 175. Professor Schumpeter is, I believe, also the original author of the myth that Pareto and Barone have "solved" the problem of socialist calculation. What they, and many others, did was merely to state the conditions which a rational allocation of resources would have to satisfy, and to point out that these were essentially the same as the conditions of equilibrium of a competitive market. This is something altogether different from showing how the allocation of resources satisfying these conditions can be found in practice. Pareto himself (from whom Barone has taken practically everything he has to say), far from claiming to have solved the practical problem, in fact explicitly denies that it can be solved without the help of the market. See his *Manuel d'économie pure* (2nd ed., 1927), pp. 233-34. The relevant passage is quoted in an English translation at the beginning of my article on "Socialist Calculation: The Competitive 'Solution,'" in *Economica*, New Series, Vol. VIII, No. 26 (May, 1940), p. 125.

implied in, or follows necessarily from, the valuation of consumers' goods. But this, too, is not correct. Implication is a logical relationship which can be meaningfully asserted only of propositions simultaneously present to one and the same mind. It is evident, however, that the values of the factors of production do not depend solely on the valuation of the consumers' goods but also on the conditions of supply of the various factors of production. Only to a mind to which all these facts were simultaneously known would the answer necessarily follow from the facts given to it. The practical problem, however, arises precisely because these facts are never so given to a single mind, and because, in consequence, it is necessary that in the solution of the problem knowledge should be used that is dispersed among many people.

The problem is thus in no way solved if we can show that all the facts, *if* they were known to a single mind (as we hypothetically assume them to be given to the observing economist), would uniquely determine the solution; instead we must show how a solution is produced by the interactions of people each of whom possesses only partial knowledge. To assume all the knowledge to be given to a single mind in the same manner in which we assume it to be given to us as the explaining economists is to assume the problem away and to disregard everything that is important and significant in the real world.

That an economist of Professor Schumpeter's standing should thus have fallen into a trap which the ambiguity of the term "datum" sets to the unwary can hardly be explained as a simple error. It suggests rather than there is something fundamentally wrong with an approach which habitually disregards an essential part of the phenomena with which we have to deal: the unavoidable imperfection of man's knowledge and the consequent need for a process by which knowledge is constantly communicated and acquired. Any approach, such as that of much of mathematical economics with its simultaneous equations, which in effect starts from the assumption that people's *knowledge* corresponds with the objective *facts* of the situation, systematically leaves out what is our main task to explain. I am far from denying that in our system equilibrium analysis has a useful function to perform. But when it comes to the point where it misleads some of our leading thinkers into believing that the situation which it describes has direct relevance to the solution of practical problems, it is time that we remember that it does not deal with the social process at all and that it is no more than a useful preliminary to the study of the main problem.

[17]

THE JOURNAL OF
POLITICAL ECONOMY

Volume LXIX JUNE 1961 *Number 3*

THE ECONOMICS OF INFORMATION[1]

GEORGE J. STIGLER
University of Chicago

One should hardly have to tell academicians that information is a valuable resource: knowledge *is* power. And yet it occupies a slum dwelling in the town of economics. Mostly it is ignored: the best technology is assumed to be known; the relationship of commodities to consumer preferences is a datum. And one of the information-producing industries, advertising, is treated with a hostility that economists normally reserve for tariffs or monopolists.

There are a great many problems in economics for which this neglect of ignorance is no doubt permissible or even desirable. But there are some for which this is not true, and I hope to show that some important aspects of economic organization take on a new meaning when they are considered from the viewpoint of the search for information. In the present paper I shall attempt to analyze systematically one important problem of information—the ascertainment of market price.

I. THE NATURE OF SEARCH

Prices change with varying frequency in all markets, and, unless a market is completely centralized, no one will know all the prices which various sellers (or buyers) quote at any given time. A buyer (or seller) who wishes to ascertain the most favorable price must canvass various sellers (or buyers)—a phenomenon I shall term "search."

The amount of dispersion of asking prices of sellers is a problem to be discussed later, but it is important to emphasize immediately the fact that dispersion is ubiquitous even for homogeneous goods. Two examples of asking prices, of consumer and producer goods respectively, are displayed in Table 1. The automobile prices (for an identical model) were those quoted with an average amount of "higgling": their average was $2,436, their range from $2,350 to $2,515, and their standard deviation $42. The prices for anthracite coal were bids for federal government purchases and had a mean of $16.90 per ton, a range from $15.46 to $18.92, and a standard deviation of $1.15. In both cases the range of

[1] I have benefited from comments of Gary Becker, Milton Friedman, Zvi Griliches, Harry Johnson, Robert Solow, and Lester Telser.

prices was significant on almost any criterion.

Price dispersion is a manifestation—and, indeed, it is the measure—of ignorance in the market. Dispersion is a biased measure of ignorance because there is never absolute homogeneity in the commodity if we include the terms of sale within the concept of the commodity. Thus, some automobile dealers might perform more service, or carry a larger range of varieties in stock, and a portion of the observed dispersion is presumably attributable to such differences. But it would be metaphysical, and fruitless, to assert that all dispersion is due to heterogeneity.

TABLE 1

ASKING PRICES FOR TWO COMMODITIES

A. CHEVROLETS, CHICAGO, FEBRUARY, 1959*

Price (Dollars)	No. of Dealers
2,350–2,400	4
2,400–2,450	11
2,450–2,500	8
2,500–2,550	4

B. ANTHRACITE COAL, DELIVERED (WASHINGTON, D.C.), APRIL, 1953†

Price per Ton (Dollars)	No. of Bids
15.00–15.50	2
15.50–16.00	2
16.00–16.50	2
16.50–17.00	3
17.00–18.00	1
18.00–19.00	4

* Allen F. Jung, "Price Variations Among Automobile Dealers in Metropolitan Chicago," *Journal of Business*, XXXIII (January, 1960), 31–42.

† Supplied by John Flueck

At any time, then, there will be a frequency distribution of the prices quoted by sellers. Any buyer seeking the commodity would pay whatever price is asked by the seller whom he happened to canvass, if he were content to buy from the first seller. But, if the dispersion of price quotations of sellers is at all large (relative to the cost of search), it will pay, on average, to canvass several sellers. Consider the following primitive example: let sellers be equally divided between asking prices of \$2 and \$3. Then the distribution of minimum prices, as search is lengthened, is shown in Table 2. The buyer who canvasses two sellers instead of one has an expected saving of 25 cents per unit, etc.

The frequency distributions of asking (and offering) prices have not been studied sufficiently to support any hypothesis as to their nature. Asking prices are probably skewed to the right, as a rule, because the seller of reproducible goods will have some minimum but no maximum limit on the price he can accept. If

TABLE 2

DISTRIBUTION OF HYPOTHETICAL MINIMUM PRICES BY NUMBERS OF BIDS CANVASSED

No. of Prices Canvassed	Probability of Minimum Price of \$2.00	Probability of Minimum Price of \$3.00	Expected Minimum Price
1	.5	.5	\$2.50
2	.75	.25	2.25
3	.875	.125	2.125
4	.9375	.0625	2.0625
∞	1.0	0	2.00

the distribution of asking prices is normal, the distributions of minimum prices encountered in searches of one, two, and three sellers will be those displayed in Figure 1. If the distribution is rectangular, the corresponding distributions would be those shown in Panel B. The latter assumption does not receive strong support from the evidence, but it will be used for a time because of its algebraic simplicity.

In fact, if sellers' asking prices (p) are uniformly distributed between zero and one, it can be shown that:[2] (1) The dis-

[2] If $F(p)$ is the cumulative-frequency function of p, the probability that the minimum of n observations will be greater than p is

$$[1 - F(p)]^n = \left[\int^1 dx\right]^n$$

tribution of minimum prices with n searches is

$$n(1-p)^{n-1}, \qquad (1)$$

(2) the average minimum price is

$$\frac{1}{n+1},$$

and (3) the variance of the average minimum price is

$$\frac{n}{(n+1)^2(n+2)}.$$

Whatever the precise distribution of prices, it is certain that increased search will yield diminishing returns as measured by the expected reduction in the minimum asking price. This is obviously true of the rectangular distribution, with an expected minimum price of $1/(n+1)$ with n searches, and also of the normal distributions.[3] In fact, if a distribution of asking prices did not display this property, it would be an unstable distribution for reasons that will soon be apparent.[4]

For any buyer the expected savings from an additional unit of search will be approximately the quantity (q) he wishes to purchase times the expected reduction in price as a result of the search,[5] or

$$q\left|\frac{\partial P_{\min}}{\partial_n}\right|. \qquad (2)$$

The expected saving from given search will be greater, the greater the dispersion of prices. The saving will also obviously be greater, the greater the expenditure on the commodity. Let us defer for a time the problem of the time period to which the expenditure refers, and hence the amount of expenditure, by considering the purchase of an indivisible, infrequently purchased good—say, a used automobile.

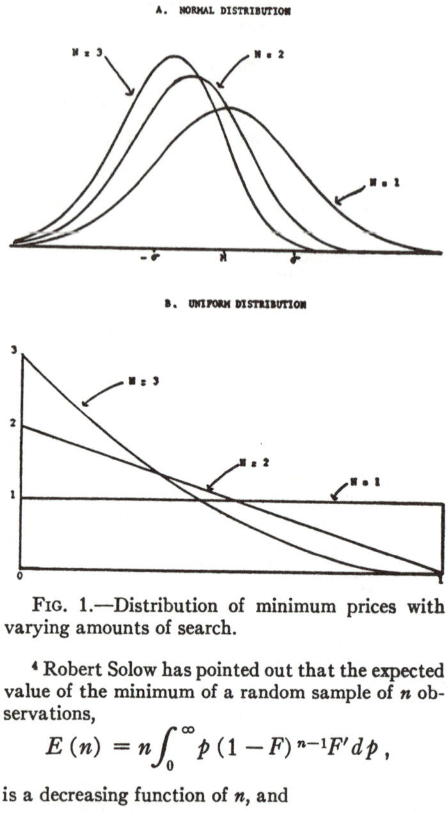

FIG. 1.—Distribution of minimum prices with varying amounts of search.

[3] The expected minimum prices with a normal distribution of mean M and standard deviation σ are

Search	Expected Minimum Price
1	M
2	$M - .564\sigma$
3	$M - .846\sigma$
4	$M - 1.029\sigma$
5	$M - 1.163\sigma$
6	$M - 1.267\sigma$
7	$M - 1.352\sigma$
8	$M - 1.423\sigma$
9	$M - 1.485\sigma$
10	$M - 1.539\sigma$

[4] Robert Solow has pointed out that the expected value of the minimum of a random sample of n observations,

$$E(n) = n\int_0^{\infty} p(1-F)^{n-1}F'dp,$$

is a decreasing function of n, and

$$[E(n+2) - E(n+1)] - [E(n+1) - E(n)]$$

is positive so the minimum decreases at a decreasing rate. The proofs involve the fact that the density function for the rth observation from the maximum in a sample of n is

$$n\binom{n-1}{r-1}F^{n-r}(1-F)^{r-1}F'dp.$$

[5] The precise savings will be (a) the reduction in price times the quantity which would be purchased at the higher price—the expression in the text—*plus* (b) the average saving on the additional purchases induced by the lower price. I neglect this quantity, which will generally be of a smaller order of magnitude.

The cost of search, for a consumer, may be taken as approximately proportional to the number of (identified) sellers approached, for the chief cost is time. This cost need not be equal for all consumers, of course: aside from differences in tastes, time will be more valuable to a person with a larger income. If the cost of search is equated to its expected marginal return, the optimum amount of search will be found.[6]

Of course, the sellers can also engage in search and, in the case of unique items, will occasionally do so in the literal fashion that buyers do. In this—empirically unimportant—case, the optimum amount of search will be such that the marginal cost of search equals the expected increase in receipts, strictly parallel to the analysis for buyers.

With unique goods the efficiency of personal search for either buyers or sellers is extremely low, because the identity of potential sellers is not known—the cost of search must be divided by the fraction of potential buyers (or sellers) in the population which is being searched. If I plan to sell a used car and engage in personal search, less than one family in a random selection of one hundred families is a potential buyer of even a popular model within the next month. As a result, the cost of search is increased more than one hundredfold per price quotation.

The costs of search are so great under these conditions that there is powerful inducement to localize transactions as a device for identifying potential buyers and sellers. The medieval markets commonly increased their efficiency in this respect by prohibiting the purchase or sale of the designated commodities within a given radius of the market or on non-market days. The market tolls that were frequently levied on sellers (even in the absence of effective restrictions on non-market transactions) were clear evidence of the value of access to the localized markets.

Advertising is, of course, the obvious modern method of identifying buyers and sellers: the *classified* advertisements in particular form a meeting place for potential buyers and sellers. The identification of buyers and sellers reduces drastically the cost of search. But advertising has its own limitations: advertising itself is an expense, and one essentially independent of the value of the item advertised. The advertising of goods which have few potential buyers relative to the circulation of the advertising medium is especially expensive. We shall temporarily put advertising aside and consider an alternative.

The alternative solution is the development of specialized traders whose chief service, indeed, is implicitly to provide a meeting place for potential buyers and sellers. A used-car dealer, turning over a thousand cars a year, and presumably encountering three or five thousand each of buying and selling bids, provides a substantial centralization of trading activity. Let us consider these dealer markets, which we shall assume to be competitive in the sense of there being many independent dealers.

Each dealer faces a distribution of (for example) buyers' bids and can vary his selling prices with a corresponding effect upon purchases. Even in the markets for divisible (and hence non-unique) goods there will be some scope for higgling (discrimination) in each individual transaction: the buyer has a maximum price given by the lowest price he encounters among the dealers he has searched (or

[6] Buyers often pool their knowledge and thus reduce the effective cost of search; a few remarks are made on this method below.

plans to search), but no minimum price. But let us put this range of indeterminacy aside, perhaps by assuming that the dealer finds discrimination too expensive,[7] and inquire how the demand curve facing a dealer is determined.

Each dealer sets a selling price, p, and makes sales to all buyers for whom this is the minimum price. With a uniform distribution of asking prices by dealers, the number of buyers of a total of N_b possible buyers who will purchase from him is

$$N_i = KN_b n(1-p)^{n-1}, \quad (3)$$

where K is a constant.[8] The number of buyers from a dealer increases as his price is reduced, and at an increasing rate.[9] Moreover, with the uniform distribution of asking prices, the number of buyers increases with increased search if the price is below the reciprocal of the amount of search.[10] We should generally expect the high-price sellers to be small-volume sellers.

The stability of any distribution of asking prices of dealers will depend upon the costs of dealers. If there are constant returns to scale, the condition of equal rates of return dictates that the difference between a dealer's buying and selling prices be a constant. This condition cannot in general be met: any dealer can buy low, and sell high, provided he is content with a small volume of transactions, and he will then be earning more than costs (including a competitive rate of return). No other dealer can eliminate this non-competitive rate of profit, although by making the same price bids he can share the volume of business, or by asking lower prices he can increase the rewards to search and hence increase the amount of search.

With economies of scale, the competition of dealers will eliminate the profitability of quoting very high selling and very low buying prices and will render impossible some of the extreme price bids. On this score, the greater the decrease in average cost with volume, the smaller will be the dispersion of prices.[11] Many distributions of prices will be inconsistent with any possible cost conditions of dealers,[12] and it is not evident that strict equalities of rates of return for dealers are generally possible.

If economies of scale in dealing lead to

[7] This is the typical state of affairs in retailing xcept for consumer durable goods.

[8] Since $n(1-p)^{n-1}$ is a density function, we must multiply it by a dp which represents the range of prices between adjacent price quotations. In addition, if two or more sellers quote an identical price, they will share the sales, so $K = dp/r$, where r is the number of firms quoting price p.

[9] For

$$\frac{\partial N_i}{\partial p} = -\frac{(n-1)N_i}{(1-p)} < 0,$$

and

$$\frac{\partial^2 N_i}{\partial p^2} = \frac{(n-1)(n-2)N_i}{(1-p)^2} > 0$$

if $n > 2$.

[10] Let

$$\log N_i = \log K + \log N_b + \log n + (n-1)\log(1-p).$$

Then

$$\frac{1}{N_i}\frac{\partial N_i}{\partial n} = \frac{1}{n} + \log(1-p) = \frac{1}{n} - p,$$

approximately.

[11] This argument assumes that dealers will discover unusually profitable bids, given the buyers' search, which is, of course, only partly true: there is also a problem of dealers' search with respect to prices.

[12] With the rectangular distribution of asking prices, if each buyer purchases the same number of units, the elasticity of demand falls continuously with price, so that, if average cost equaled price at every rate of sales (with one seller at each price), marginal costs would have to be negative at large outputs. But, of course, the number of sellers can be less at lower prices.

a smaller dispersion of asking prices than do constant costs of dealing, similarly greater amounts of search will lead to a smaller dispersion of observed selling prices by reducing the number of purchasers who will pay high prices. Let us consider more closely the determinants of search.

DETERMINANTS OF SEARCH

The equation defining optimum search is unambiguous only if a unique purchase is being made—a house, a particular used book, etc. If purchases are repetitive, the volume of purchases based upon the search must be considered.

If the correlation of asking prices of dealers in successive time periods is perfect (and positive!), the initial search is the only one that need be undertaken. In this case the expected savings of search will be the present value of the discounted savings on all future purchases, the future savings extending over the life of the buyer or seller (whichever is shorter).[13] On the other hand, if asking prices are uncorrelated in successive time periods, the savings from search will pertain only to that period,[14] and search in each period is independent of previous experience. If the correlation of successive prices is positive, customer search will be larger in the initial period than in subsequent periods.[15]

The correlation of successive asking prices of sellers is usually positive in the handful of cases I have examined. The rank correlation of anthracite price bids (Table 1) in 1953 with those in 1954 was .68 for eight bidders; that for Chevrolet dealers in Chicago February and August of 1959 was .33 for twenty-nine dealers—but, on the other hand, it was zero for Ford dealers for the same dates. Most observed correlations will, of course, be positive because of stable differences in the products or services, but our analysis is restricted to conditions of homogeneity.

As a rule, positive correlations should exist with homogeneous products. The amount of search will vary among individuals because of differences in their expenditures on a commodity or differences in cost of search. A seller who wishes to obtain the continued patronage of those buyers who value the gains of search more highly or have lower costs of search must see to it that he is quoting relatively low prices. In fact, goodwill may be defined as continued patronage by customers without continued search (that is, no more than occasional verification).

A positive correlation of successive asking prices justifies the widely held view that inexperienced buyers (tourists)

[13] Let the expected minimum price be $p_1 = f(n)_1$ in period 1 (with $f' < 0$) and let the expected minimum price in period 2, with r a measure of the correlation between sellers' successive prices, be

$$p_2 = \left(\frac{p_1}{f(n_2)}\right)^r f(n_2) .$$

If the cost of search is λ per unit, total expenditures for a fixed quantity of purchases (Q) per unit of time are, neglecting interest,

$$E = Q(p_1 + p_2) + \lambda(n_1 + n_2) .$$

Expenditures are a minimum when

$$\frac{\partial E}{\partial n_1} = Qf'(n_1) + Qr[f(n_1)]^{r-1} \times [f(n_2)]^{1-r} f'(n_1) + \lambda = 0$$

and

$$\frac{\partial E}{\partial n_2} = (1-r)Q[f(n_1)]^r \times [f(n_2)]^{-r} f'(n_2) + \lambda = 0 .$$

If $r = 1$, $n_2 = 0$, and n_1 is determined by $Qf'(n_1) = -\lambda/2$, the cost of search is effectively halved.

[14] See n. 13; if $r = 0$, $n_1 = n_2$.

[15] Let $f(n) = e^{-n}$. Then, in the notation of our previous footnotes,

$$n_1 - n_2 = \frac{2r}{1-r},$$

approximately.

pay higher prices in a market than do experienced buyers.[16] The former have no accumulated knowledge of asking prices, and even with an optimum amount of search they will pay higher prices on average. Since the variance of the expected minimum price decreases with additional search, the prices paid by inexperienced buyers will also have a larger variance.

If a buyer enters a wholly new market, he will have no idea of the dispersion of prices and hence no idea of the rational amount of search he should make. In such cases the dispersion will presumably be estimated by some sort of sequential process, and this approach would open up a set of problems I must leave for others to explore. But, in general, one approaches a market with some general knowledge of the amount of dispersion, for dispersion itself is a function of the average amount of search, and this in turn is a function of the nature of the commodity:

1. The larger the fraction of the buyer's expenditures on the commodity, the greater the savings from search and hence the greater the amount of search.
2. The larger the fraction of repetitive (experienced) buyers in the market, the greater the effective amount of search (with positive correlation of successive prices).
3. The larger the fraction of repetitive sellers, the higher the correlation between successive prices, and hence, by condition (2), the larger the amount of accumulated search.[17]
4. The cost of search will be larger, the larger the geographical size of the market.

An increase in the number of buyers has an uncertain effect upon the dispersion of asking prices. The sheer increase in numbers will lead to an increase in the number of dealers and, *ceteris paribus*, to a larger range of asking prices. But, quite aside from advertising, the phenomenon of pooling information will increase. Information is pooled when two buyers compare prices: if each buyer canvasses s sellers, by combining they effectively canvass $2s$ sellers, duplications aside.[18] Consumers compare prices of some commodities (for example, liquor) much more often than of others (for example, chewing gum)—in fact, pooling can be looked upon as a cheaper (and less reliable) form of search.

SOURCES OF DISPERSION

One source of dispersion is simply the cost to dealers of ascertaining rivals' asking prices, but even if this cost were zero the dispersion of prices would not vanish. The more important limitation is provided by buyers' search, and, if the conditions and participants in the market were fixed in perpetuity, prices would immediately approach uniformity. Only those differences could persist which did not remunerate additional search. The condition for optimum search would be (with perfect correlation of successive prices):

$$q\left|\frac{\partial p}{\partial n}\right| = i \times \text{marginal cost of search},$$

where i is the interest rate. If an additional search costs \$1, and the interest rate is 5 per cent, the expected reduction in price with one more search would at equilibrium be equal to $\$0.05/q$—a quantity which would often be smaller than the smallest unit of currency. But, indivisibilities aside, it would normally be

[16] For that matter, a negative correlation would have the same effects.

[17] If the number of sellers (s) and the asking-price distributions are the same in two periods, but k are new sellers, the average period-1 buyer will have lost proportion k/s of his period-1 search.

[18] Duplications will occur more often than random processes would suggest, because pooling is more likely between buyers of similar location, tastes, etc.

unprofitable for buyers or sellers to eliminate all dispersion.

The maintenance of appreciable dispersion of prices arises chiefly out of the fact that knowledge becomes obsolete. The conditions of supply and demand, and therefore the distribution of asking prices, change over time. There is no method by which buyers or sellers can ascertain the new average price in the market appropriate to the new conditions except by search. Sellers cannot maintain perfect correlation of successive prices, even if they wish to do so, because of the costs of search. Buyers accordingly cannot make the amount of investment in search that perfect correlation of prices would justify. The greater the instability of supply and/or demand conditions, therefore, the greater the dispersion of prices will be.

In addition, there is a component of ignorance due to the changing identity of buyers and sellers. There is a flow of new buyers and sellers in every market, and they are at least initially uninformed on prices and by their presence make the information of experienced buyers and sellers somewhat obsolete.

The amount of dispersion will also vary with one other characteristic which is of special interest: the size (in terms of both dollars and number of traders) of the market. As the market grows in these dimensions, there will appear a set of firms which specialize in collecting and selling information. They may take the form of trade journals or specialized brokers. Since the cost of collection of information is (approximately) independent of its use (although the cost of dissemination is not), there is a strong tendency toward monopoly in the provision of information: in general, there will be a "standard" source for trade information.

II. ADVERTISING

Advertising is, among other things, a method of providing potential buyers with knowledge of the identity of sellers. It is clearly an immensely powerful instrument for the elimination of ignorance—comparable in force to the use of the book instead of the oral discourse to communicate knowledge. A small $5 advertisement in a metropolitan newspaper reaches (in the sense of being read) perhaps 25,000 readers, or fifty readers per penny, and, even if only a tiny fraction are potential buyers (or sellers), the economy they achieve in search, as compared with uninstructed solicitation, may be overwhelming.

Let us begin with advertisements designed only to identify sellers; the identification of buyers will not be treated explicitly, and the advertising of price will be discussed later. The identification of sellers is necessary because the identity of sellers changes over time, but much more because of the turnover of buyers. In every consumer market there will be a stream of new buyers (resulting from immigration or the attainment of financial maturity) requiring knowledge of sellers, and, in addition, it will be necessary to refresh the knowledge of infrequent buyers.

Suppose, what is no doubt too simple, that a given advertisement of size a will inform c per cent of the potential buyers in a given period, so $c = g(a)$.[19] This contact function will presumably show diminishing returns, at least beyond a certain size of advertisement. A certain fraction, b, of potential customers will be "born" (and "die") in a stable population, where "death" includes not only

[19] The effectiveness of the advertisement is also a function of the skill with which it is done and of the fraction of potential buyers who read the medium, but such elaborations are put aside.

departure from the market but forgetting the seller. The value of b will obviously vary with the nature of the commodity; for example, it will be large for commodities which are seldom purchased (like a house). In a first period of advertising (at a given rate) the number of potential customers reached will be cN, if N is the total number of potential customers. In the second period $cN(1 - b)$ of these potential customers will still be informed, cbN new potential customers will be informed, and

$$c[(1 - b)N - cN(1 - b)]$$

old potential customers will be reached for the first time, or a total of

$$cN[1 + (1 - b)(1 - c)] .$$

This generalizes, for k periods, to

$$cN[1 + (1 - b)(1 - c) + \ldots + (1 - b)^{k-1}(1 - c)^{k-1}] ,$$

and, if k is large, this approaches

$$\frac{cN}{1 - (1 - c)(1 - b)} = \lambda N . \quad (4)$$

The proportion (λ) of potential buyers informed of the advertiser's identity thus depends upon c and b.

If each of r sellers advertises the same amount, λ is the probability that any one seller will inform any buyer. The distribution of N potential buyers by the number of contacts achieved by r sellers is given by the binomial distribution:

$$N(\lambda + [1 - \lambda])^r ,$$

with, for example,

$$\frac{Nr!}{m!(r - m)!} \lambda^m (1 - \lambda)^{r-m}$$

buyers being informed of exactly m sellers' identities. The number of sellers known to a buyer ranges from zero to r, with an average of $r\lambda$ sellers and a variance of $r\lambda(1 - \lambda)$.[20]

The amount of relevant information in the market, even in this simple model, is not easy to summarize in a single measure—a difficulty common to frequency distributions. If all buyers wished to search s sellers, all buyers knowing less than s sellers would have inadequate information, and all who knew more than s sellers would have redundant information, although the redundant information would not be worthless.[21] Since the value of information is the amount by which it reduces the expected cost to the buyer of his purchases, if these expected reductions are $\Delta C_1, \Delta C_2, \ldots$, for searches of $1, 2, \ldots$, the value of the information to buyers is approximately

$$\sum_{m=1}^{r} \frac{r!}{m!(r - m)!} \lambda^m (1 - \lambda)^{r-m} \Delta C_m .$$

The information possessed by buyers, however, is not simply a matter of chance; those buyers who spend more on the commodity, or who search more for a given expenditure, will also search more for advertisements. The buyers with more information will, on average, make more extensive searches, so the value of information will be greater than this last formula indicates.

We may pause to discuss the fact that advertising in, say, a newspaper is normally "paid" for by the seller. On our analysis, the advertising is valuable to the buyer, and he would be willing to pay

[20] This approach has both similarities and contrasts to that published by S. A. Ozga, "Imperfect Markets through Lack of Knowledge," *Quarterly Journal of Economics*, LXXIV (February, 1960), 29–52.

[21] The larger the number of sellers known, the larger is the range of prices among the sellers and the lower the expected minimum price after s searches. But this effect will normally be small.

more for a paper with advertisements than for one without. The difficulty with having the sellers insert advertisements "free" and having the buyer pay for them directly is that it would be difficult to ration space on this basis: the seller would have an incentive to supply an amount of information (or information of a type) the buyer did not wish, and, since numerous advertisements are supplied jointly, the buyer could not register clearly his preferences regarding advertising. (Catalogues, however, are often sold to buyers.) Charging the seller for the advertisements creates an incentive for him to supply to the buyer only the information which is desired.

It is commonly complained that advertising is jointly supplied with the commodity in the sense that the buyer must pay for both even though he wishes only the latter. The alternative of selling the advertising separately from the commodity, however, would require that the advertising of various sellers (of various commodities) would be supplied jointly: the economies of disseminating information in a general-purpose periodical are so great that some form of jointness is inescapable. But the common complaint is much exaggerated: the buyer who wishes can search out the seller who advertises little (but, of course, enough to be discoverable), and the latter can sell at prices lower by the savings on advertising.

These remarks seem most appropriate to newspaper advertisements of the "classified" variety; what of the spectacular television show or the weekly comedian? We are not equipped to discuss advertising in general because the problem of quality has been (and will continue to be) evaded by the assumption of homogeneous goods. Even within our narrower framework, however, the use of entertainment to attract buyers to information is a comprehensible phenomenon. The assimilation of information is not an easy or pleasant task for most people, and they may well be willing to pay more for the information when supplied in an enjoyable form. In principle, this complementary demand for information and entertainment is exactly analogous to the complementary demand of consumers for commodities and delivery service or air-conditioned stores. One might find a paradox in the simultaneous complaints of some people that advertising is too elaborate and school *houses* too shoddy.

A monopolist will advertise (and price the product) so as to maximize his profits,

$$\pi = Npq\lambda - \phi(N\lambda q) - ap_a ,$$

where $p = f(q)$ is the demand curve of the individual buyer, $\phi(Nq\lambda)$ is production costs other than advertising, and ap_a is advertising expenditures. The maximum profit conditions are

$$\frac{\partial \pi}{\partial q} = N\lambda\left(p + q\frac{\partial p}{\partial q}\right) - \phi' N\lambda = 0 \quad (5)$$

and

$$\frac{\partial \pi}{\partial a} = Npq\frac{\partial \lambda}{\partial a} - \phi' Nq\frac{\partial \lambda}{\partial a} - p_a = 0 . \quad (6)$$

Equation (5) states the usual marginal cost–marginal revenue equality, and equation (6) states the equality of (price − marginal cost) with the marginal cost $[p_a/Nq(\partial\lambda/\partial a)]$ of advertising.[22]

[22] The marginal revenue from advertising expenditure,

$$\frac{Npq}{p_a}\frac{\partial \lambda}{\partial a},$$

equals the absolute value of the elasticity of demand by equations (5) and (6); see R. Dorfman and P. O. Steiner, "Optimal Advertising and Optimal Quality," *American Economic Review*, XLIV (1954), 826.

With the Cournot spring (where production costs $\phi = 0$) the monopolist advertises up to the point where price equals the marginal cost of informing a buyer: the monopolist will not (cannot) exploit ignorance as he exploits desire. The monopolist will advertise more, the higher the "death" rate (b), unless it is very high relative to the "contact" rate (c).[23] The monopolistic situation does not invite comparison with competition because an essential feature—the value of search in the face of price dispersion—is absent.

A highly simplified analysis of advertising by the competitive firm is presented in the Appendix. On the assumption that all firms are identical and that all buyers have identical demand curves and search equal amounts, we obtain the maximum-profit equation:

$$\text{Production cost} = p\left(1 + \frac{1}{\eta_{qp} + \eta_{Kp}}\right), \quad (7)$$

where η_{qp} is the elasticity of a buyer's demand curve and η_{K_p} is the elasticity of the fraction of buyers purchasing from the seller with respect to his price. The latter elasticity will be of the order of magnitude of the number of searches made by a buyer. With a uniform distribution of asking prices, increased search will lead to increased advertising by low-price sellers and reduced advertising by high-price sellers. The amount of advertising by a firm decreases as the number of firms increases.

Price advertising has a decisive influence on the dispersion of prices. Search now becomes extremely economical, and the question arises why, in the absence of differences in quality of products, the dispersion does not vanish. And the answer is simply that, if prices are advertised by a large portion of the sellers, the price differences diminish sharply. That they do not wholly vanish (in a given market) is due simply to the fact that no combination of advertising media reaches all potential buyers within the available time.

Assuming, as we do, that all sellers are equally convenient in location, must we say that some buyers are perverse in not reading the advertisements? Obviously not, for the cost of keeping currently informed about all articles which an individual purchases would be prohibitive. A typical household probably buys several hundred different items a month, and, if, on average, their prices change (in some outlets) only once a month, the number of advertisements (by at least several sellers) which must be read is forbiddingly large.

The seller's problem is even greater: he may sell two thousand items (a modest number for a grocery or hardware store), and to advertise each on the occasion of a price change—and frequently enough thereafter to remind buyers of his price—would be impossibly expensive. To keep the buyers in a market informed on the current prices of all items of consumption would involve perhaps a thousandfold increase of newspaper advertising.

From the manufacturer's viewpoint, uncertainty concerning his price is clearly disadvantageous. The cost of search is a cost of purchase, and consumption will therefore be smaller, the greater the dispersion of prices and the greater the optimum amount of search. This is presumably one reason (but, I conjecture, a very minor one) why uniform prices are set by

[23] Differentiating equation (6) with respect to b, we find that $\partial a/\partial b$ is positive or negative according as

$$b \lessgtr \frac{c}{1-c}.$$

If $c \geq \frac{1}{2}$, the derivative must be positive.

sellers of nationally advertised brands: if they have eliminated price variation, they have reduced the cost of the commodity (including search) to the buyer, even if the dealers' margins average somewhat more than they otherwise would.

The effect of advertising prices, then, is equivalent to that of the introduction of a very large amount of search by a large portion of the potential buyers. It follows from our discussion in Section I that the dispersion of asking prices will be much reduced. Since advertising of prices will be devoted to products for which the marginal value of search is high, it will tend to reduce dispersion most in commodities with large aggregate expenditures.

III. CONCLUSIONS

The identification of sellers and the discovery of their prices are only one sample of the vast role of the search for information in economic life. Similar problems exist in the detection of profitable fields for investment and in the worker's choice of industry, location, and job. The search for knowledge on the quality of goods, which has been studiously avoided in this paper, is perhaps no more important but, certainly, analytically more difficult. Quality has not yet been successfully specified by economics, and this elusiveness extends to all problems in which it enters.

Some forms of economic organization may be explicable chiefly as devices for eliminating uncertainties in quality. The department store, as Milton Friedman has suggested to me, may be viewed as an institution which searches for the superior qualities of goods and guarantees that they are good quality. "Reputation" is a word which denotes the persistence of quality, and reputation commands a price (or exacts a penalty) because it economizes on search. When economists deplore the reliance of the consumer on reputation—although they choose the articles they read (and their colleagues) in good part on this basis—they implicitly assume that the consumer has a large laboratory, ready to deliver current information quickly and gratuitously.

Ignorance is like subzero weather: by a sufficient expenditure its effects upon people can be kept within tolerable or even comfortable bounds, but it would be wholly uneconomic entirely to eliminate all its effects. And, just as an analysis of man's shelter and apparel would be somewhat incomplete if cold weather is ignored, so also our understanding of economic life will be incomplete if we do not systematically take account of the cold winds of ignorance.

APPENDIX

Under competition, the amount of advertising by any one seller (i) can be determined as follows. Each buyer will engage in an amount s of search, which is determined by the factors discussed above (Sec. 1). He will on average know

$$(r-1)\lambda+\lambda_i$$

sellers, where λ_i is defined by equation (4) for seller i. Hence,

$$\frac{\lambda_i}{(r-1)\lambda+\lambda_i}$$

per cent of buyers who know seller i will canvass him on one search, and

$$\left(1-\frac{\lambda_i}{(r-1)\lambda+\lambda_i}\right)^s$$

per cent of the buyers who know i will not canvass him in s searches,

$$s\leq (r-1)\lambda+\lambda_i\,.$$

Therefore, of the buyers who know i, the proportion who will canvass him at least once is[24]

$$1-\left(1-\frac{\lambda_i}{(r-1)\lambda+\lambda_i}\right)^s.$$

If we approximate

$$\frac{\lambda_i}{(r-1)\lambda+\lambda_i}$$

by

$$\frac{\lambda_i}{r\lambda}$$

and take only the first two terms of the binomial expansion, this becomes

$$\frac{s\lambda_i}{r\lambda}.$$

The receipts of any seller then become the product of (1) The number of buyers canvassing him,

$$\frac{s\lambda_i}{r\lambda}\lambda_i N = T_i,$$

(2) the fraction K of those canvassing him who buy from him, where K depends upon his relative price (and the amount of search and the number of rivals), and (3) sales to each customer, pq. If $\phi(T_i Kq)$ is production costs and ap_a advertising costs, profits are

$$\pi = T_i K p q - \phi(T_i K q) - a p_a .$$

The conditions for maximum profits are

$$\frac{\partial\pi}{\partial p} = T_i\left(K\frac{\partial pq}{\partial p}+pq\frac{\partial K}{\partial p}\right) - T_i\phi'\left(K\frac{\partial q}{\partial p}+q\frac{\partial K}{\partial p}\right)=0 \qquad (8)$$

and

$$\frac{\partial\pi}{\partial a} = Kpq\frac{\partial T_i}{\partial a} - \phi' Kq\frac{\partial T_i}{\partial a} - p_a = 0. \qquad (9)$$

[24] The formula errs slightly in allowing the multiple canvass of one seller by a buyer.

The former equation can be rewritten in elasticities as

$$\phi' = p\left(1+\frac{1}{\eta_{qp}+\eta_{Kp}}\right) \qquad (8a)$$

Price exceeds marginal cost, not simply by $(-p/\eta_{qp})$ as with monopoly, but by the smaller amount

$$\frac{-p}{\eta_{qp}+\eta_{Kp}},$$

where η_{Kp} will generally be of the order of magnitude of the number of searches made by a buyer.[25] Equation (2) states the equality of the marginal revenue of advertising with its marginal cost. By differentiating equation (2) with respect to s and taking ϕ' as constant, it can be shown that increased search by buyers will lead to increased advertising by low-price sellers and reduced advertising by high-price sellers (with a uniform distribution of prices).[26]

By the same method it may be shown that the amount of advertising by the firm will decrease as the number of rivals increases.[27] The aggregate amount of advertising by the industry may either increase or decrease with an increase in the number of firms, s, depending on the relationship between λ and a.

[25] In the case of the uniform distribution, η_{Kp} is

$$\frac{-(s-1)p}{1-p}.$$

[26] The derivative $\partial a/\partial s$ has the sign of $(1+\eta_{Ks})$, and this elasticity equals

$$1+s\log[1-p]$$

with a uniform distribution of prices.

[27] By differentiation of equation (2) with respect to r one gets

$$r\frac{\partial a}{\partial r}\left\{\lambda_i\frac{\partial^2\lambda_i}{\partial a^2}+\left(\frac{\partial\lambda_i}{\partial a}\right)^2\right\} = \lambda_i\frac{\partial\lambda_i}{\partial a}\left(1-\frac{r}{K}\frac{\partial K}{\partial r}\right).$$

The term in brackets on the left side is negative by the stability condition; the right side is positive.

[18]

ON WELFARE THEORY AND PARETO REGIONS*

By RAGNAR FRISCH

1. Introduction

The following considerations constitute an attempt at discussing—and questioning—certain basic propositions of welfare theory which are frequently taken more or less for granted. They are, I believe, very much in need of being scrutinized more cautiously. In particular I shall discuss the way in which *conditions* enter into the argument about optimality. I shall concentrate on these basic points without making any attempt at surveying the whole field of welfare economics.[1]

* * *

The purpose of a macro-economic decision model[2] is to discuss which economic policy or policies might be designated as "good" or perhaps as "the best" under given circumstances. In this connection it becomes necessary to consider *criteria* which may, in point of principle, be used to define the meaning of these words as applied to an economic policy.

An essential problem in this connection is how to *reconcile* the desires of those in power (the dictator, the democratic public authority, the influential non-official personalities, etc.) with those of the mass of citizens. A conflict may arise on this point. This conflict is formally similar to the conflict between the interests of individual citizens. The discussion of the general problem may therefore well take as its starting-point a theoretical device for describing the preferences of *any* economic entity, whether a person, a family, a business enterprise, a public authority, etc. Such a device is the *preference function* of that entity.[3] In what follows we assume the existence of such a function for each such entity. For shortness such an entity will be referred to as an "individual". In other words, we assume that each individual acts *as if* there exists a function which this individual tries to maximize.

In the most general case the preference function of any individual may be envisaged as depending not only on the values assumed by all the *variables* of

* This paper was worked out in the main in the autumn of 1950; it was subsequently revised and presented as an appendix to a paper "From National Accounts to Macro-economic Decision Models", read at the meeting of the International Association for Research in Income and Wealth, Rome, September 1953. That paper has since appeared in *Income and Wealth*, Series IV, London, 1955, pp. 1-26, but the appendix reproduced below, although written in English by Professor Frisch, has so far been published only in French: "La Théorie de l'avantage collectif et les régions de Pareto", translated by Georges T. Guilbaud, *Économie Appliquée*, vol. VII, No. 3, July/September 1954. The original English version has so far been available only in mimeographed form at the *Universitetets Socialøkonomiske Institutt* at Oslo, which is headed by Professor Frisch.

[1] An excellent survey of the opinions of different authors is given by Tibor Scitovsky in the *American Economic Review*, 1951.

[2] The concept of a decision model is studied at length in two papers in the *Revue d'Économie Politique*, 1951.

[3] The application of this concept to the "homme d'état" is considered in a very interesting article by Maurice Fréchet: "Sur les fonctions de bien-être", which I have had an opportunity to read in manuscript.

the theoretical model used, but as depending also explicitly on the nature of the various *relations* that form part of the model (*i.e.* on the parameters of these relations). This means that the value of the preference function will depend on the nature of these relations in a manner which is so complicated that it is not sufficient to indicate the *result* of the relations, that is, the values of the various variables as they *actually exist*. In what follows we shall, for simplicity, only consider the case where the preference functions *can* be expressed simply in terms of these variables.

Some of the conditions—in the form of equations or inequalities—which we impose on the variables of a model are more or less *obligatory*, unavoidable. For instance, certain definitional equations between the variables, certain technically given production functions depending on the laws of nature, certain existing limitations on natural resources, etc. Others of the conditions we impose on the variables of the model are of a more or less *facultative* sort. They may be changed if man changes the "rules of the game", *i.e.* changes the rules and regulations by which production and distribution take place. The choice of an economic policy just consists in choosing a specific form of these facultative conditions. On closer scrutiny it might in border cases be found difficult to draw the line of demarcation between obligatory and facultative conditions in a hard and fast way, but some sort of distinction between these two kinds of conditions has to be made if it shall be possible at all to discuss the question of economic policy in a systematic way. The distinction between obligatory and facultative conditions is more important than a distinction between "technical" and "behaviouristic" conditions.

A certain variable or a certain set of variables may belong to a given individual as his *parameter(s) of action* (variable(s) of action).[4] That is, the individual in question is free to choose whatever magnitude he wishes of this or these parameters; *e.g.* the quantity bought by a buyer in an atomistic market, or the price fixed by a monopolistic seller who is not under public regulation, etc. In choosing a specific magnitude of this or these parameters the individual will be guided by the nature of his preferences—as expressed by his preference function—and by the conditions that are *conjectural* to him, that is, the conditions which he *believes* will hold good *while he makes his choice*. For instance, the buyer in the atomistic market believes that by changing the quantity which he buys, he will not affect the price, the monopolistic seller believes that if he changes his price by so much, the quantity demanded will be changed by so much, etc.

The conjectural conditions are not the same thing as the *objective* (obligatory or facultative) conditions referred to above, but the conjectural conditions will, in general, depend on some of these objective conditions and on the psychology of the individual in question. The set of *all* these conditions: the objective conditions (the obligatory and facultative ones) and the conjectural conditions, we

[4] M. Lutfalla, editor of the *Revue d'Économie Politique*, has suggested the term *variable potestative*, which would refer to the meaning of the term *potestas* in Roman law.

shall call *a régime*. Thus a régime is simply the complete set of conditions which the variables of a model will satisfy under a given type of economic policy. If nothing is said to the contrary, we assume that the régime is specified in such a way as to lead to a uniquely determined point or at any rate to a pointset of measure zero.

When speaking of a purpose to be realized by an economic policy, two types of problems should be distinguished: the *selection* problems and the *realization* problems (problems of régime).

In the first type of problems we ask whether *there exist* points (a pointset of zero or higher measure) satisfying some preassigned set of conditions. Some of these conditions may be objective (obligatory or facultative) and some may be conjectural and, perhaps, some may be *additional* conditions imposed by the policy-makers in the manner discussed in detail in the paper on decision models already referred to (*e.g.* "the part of the national income that goes to the workers shall not decrease").

If such points exist, we classify them according to their desirability defined in some way or another. We may, for instance, pick out one specific *subset* of points which we consider particularly desirable. The consideration of *Pareto conditions* is an example of a principle by which to select such a subset.

In the second type of problems we ask whether there exists *a régime* that will lead to a point in the selected subset.

The distinction between these two types of problems is absolutely fundamental if it shall be possible at all to attach any meaning to a statement about whether a régime is "good" or not. First we must define what we mean by "good". This is the selection problem. Secondly, we must define the régime and find out whether it leads to a point that has the property which was defined as "good". The distinction between these two types of problems brings out very forcibly the necessity of being fully aware of the significance of *conditions*. Indeed in the selection problem, *i.e.* in the definition of what is "good" and in the definition of a régime, two entirely different sets of conditions enter and fundamental fallacies may be introduced if we are not aware of the difference in the meaning of an "optimality" produced under these two sets of conditions.

This classification of the problems in the two categories: selection problems and realization problems, is discussed fully in Section 9 of the article in the *Revue d'Économie Politique*. In that article a number of examples of formulations are also given. In what follows the rôle of conditions will be considered.[5]

2. The Rôle of Conditions in Problems of Choice

In the discussion of welfare problems, the reasoning about Pareto conditions is not always carried through as carefully as one could wish. A brief systematic

[5] *Note added in March* 1959. It should be stressed that the main purpose of the paper is to elucidate the basic rôle of conditions, and to warn against the errors which may creep into the reasoning if this rôle is not clearly recognized.

discussion of some essential points—starting from a rigorous statement of definitions—might therefore be useful.

Consider a model containing the m variables $X_i(i=1, 2 \dots m)$ and the n individuals Nos. $j=1, 2 \dots n$, each of whom has a preference function $\Omega_j(X_1, X_2 \dots X_m)$. A point in m-dimensional space with cartesian co-ordinates $(X_1, X_2 \dots X_m)$ we denote for shortness by X. Sometimes we may speak of "the space X".

Let C be any given set of compatible conditions (constraints) imposed on the variables $X_1, X_2 \dots X_m$. The set of points X satisfying these conditions we denote by

(2.1) $$X[C]$$

In particular the total space we denote $X[O]$. $X[C]$ may be called the admissible region under the conditions C.

If the conditions consist of s independent *equations*, the normal case will be the one where the locus of points satisfying C is of dimensionality $m-s$. On the other hand, if the condition consists of any number of independent *inequalities*, the locus of points satisfying C will, in the normal case, still be of dimensionality m. That is, a set of inequalities will, in general, not restrict the dimensionality of the admissible space (but it will restrict its volume). If the conditions are in the form of s equations and any number of inequalities, the dimensionality of the admissible space will in the normal case be $m-s$.

Definition (2.2). Let X and X' be any two points. If X' is such that for *any* of the individuals whose preference functions are $\Omega_1 \dots \Omega_n$, X' is either preferred to X or indifferent to X, and for *at least one* of the individuals X' is actually preferred to X, we shall say that X' is *Pareto-preferred* to X under the preference function $\Omega_1 \dots \Omega_n$, *i.e.* by the individuals Nos. $1 \dots n$.

The property of Pareto-preference is *transitive* provided the individual comparisons are completely transitive. This means that for *any* of the individuals the comparison of points is transitive with respect to preference and also

From the criteria discussed there follow also certain conclusions which have a practical bearing on the question of régime. It is true that the régime needed to produce *exactly* a Pareto-optimal solution may be so complicated that we do not find it feasible to organize it. This simply means that in practice we should choose a solution that does not deviate *too grossly* from one that has the criteria in question. This can often be done *ad hoc*. Or, if a more refined analysis is wanted, we can formulate the problem of choosing amongst a set of feasible régimes that (or those) coming *closest* to Pareto optimality.

Such extensions of the theory may, in particular, be needed in cases where it is found necessary to let the utility of one individual depend not only on the quantities received by him, but also on those received by other individuals. Similar complications may be considered in the technical field. (The subsequent general parts of the argument do take account of such complications, but the examples which are discussed in detail do not.)

It is, of course, perfectly proper to try to improve the analysis by proceeding to a closer scrutiny of more general cases, provided one can do it in such a way as actually to reach precise conclusions and to show that the simplified treatment *eliminated something that is quantitatively important*. This cannot be done by general philosophical discussions, but demands a precise mathematical analysis. One should not be led to the negative, perfectionist attitude of saying that, since the principle of Pareto optimality does not solve all intricacies, the principle should be abandoned altogether. If we did abandon it, we would lose a lot of relevant—although approximate—insight.

transitive with respect to indifference and transitive with respect to comparisons with one preferent and one indifferent term, preference being in this case dominant (if X'' is preferred to X' and X' indifferent to X, X'' is preferred to X, and similarly if X'' is indifferent to X' and X' preferred to X). Then the property defined in Definition (2.2) is transitive. Indeed, suppose that X'' is Pareto-preferred to X' and X' Pareto-preferred to X. Then there can be no individual for whom X is preferred to X'' (because for any individual X'' is preferred or indifferent to X', and X' preferred or indifferent to X, hence X'' preferred or indifferent to X). Furthermore, there must be at least one individual who prefers X'' to X'. For this particular individual X' is either preferred or indifferent to X, hence this individual will actually prefer X'' to X. Consequently X'' is Pareto-preferred to X.

The property of Pareto-preference being transitive, if X' is Pareto-preferred to X, and if we determine the set of points which are Pareto-preferred to X and the set of points that are Pareto-preferred to X', we will find that the latter set is included in the first.

Definition (2.3). Let X and X' be any two points. If X is *not* Pareto-preferred to X' and X' *not* Pareto-preferred to X (with respect to a given set of preference functions), we shall say that X and X' are non-distinguishable in the Pareto-sense (with respect to these preference functions). Otherwise we shall say that X and X' are distinguishable in the Pareto-sense.

The property of being non-distinguishable in the Pareto-sense is not transitive. Indeed, even if X'' and X' are non-distinguishable and also X' and X non-distinguishable, it might well be that X'' and X are distinguishable, for instance X'' Pareto-preferred to X. It is therefore not possible to build up a theory of "indifference curves for Pareto-preference" in the same way as we do for individual preference. Some useful concepts may, however, be derived from the above definitions, as, for instance, the concept of a positive Pareto-pressure indicated in Section 5.

Definition (2.4). A point X will be called *locally Pareto-optimal under the condition C* and with respect to the preference functions $\Omega_1 \ldots \Omega_n$—or shorter with respect to the individuals Nos. $1 \ldots n$—if there exists *no other point* in the vicinity of X and satisfying C, which is Pareto-preferred to X with respect to the preference functions $\Omega_1 \ldots \Omega_n$—*i.e.* for the individuals Nos. $1 \ldots n$.

Definition (2.5). A point X will be called *globally Pareto-optimal under the condition C* if (2.4) applies when the words "in the vicinity of X" are replaced by "in the whole permissible space".

The locus of points that are globally Pareto-optimal under the conditions C will be said to form the Pareto region or the Pareto-optimal region (or space) under the conditions C and with respect to the preference function $\Omega_1 \ldots \Omega_n$—*i.e.* for the individuals Nos. $1 \ldots n$.

This region will be denoted

(2.6) $Par[C]$ or more explicitly $Par[C; \Omega_1 \ldots \Omega_n]$

If the variables $X_1 \ldots X_m$ are independent under the search for points that are—locally or globally—Pareto-optimal, that is, if *no* conditions are imposed on $X_1 \ldots X_m$ during this search (apart from trivial conditions), we shall say that the points obtained are *unconditionally* Pareto-optimal—locally or globally as the case may be. The region of points having this property will be denoted

(2.7) $Par\ [O]$ or, more explicitly, $Par\ [O; \Omega_1 \ldots \Omega_n]$

The above definition includes the limiting cases where there exist one or more other points, different from X, which are *for each individual* indifferent to the original point X. If necessary, we may characterize this formulation of the definition as Pareto-optimality in the *general* sense.

A slightly more restrictive definition is obtained if we call a point Pareto-optimal only in the case where all other points are such as to make at least one of these individuals worse off than in the original point X. This point may be called *strong* Pareto-optimality—local or global as the case may be.

The distinction between general and strong optimality will not play an important rôle in what follows. If nothing is said to the contrary, the optimality is to be understood in the general sense.

I shall not at this point take up a full discussion of how "correct" it is to require that a point must be—locally or globally—Pareto-optimal in order that it shall be considered a "good" or "efficient" point. I only want to take exception to one particular type of argument which does not, I think, render justice to the principle under discussion. The principle has been criticized on the ground that it makes "the initial position" a sacred one from which we are not allowed to depart if such a departure should make any individual worse off. As I see it, this way of arguing is misinterpreting the meaning of the principle. The principle does not single out any point as an "initial position". The Pareto-principle is a principle of *negation*, not one of *affirmation*. It states that if a point is *not* Pareto-optimal, then it cannot be said to be a "good" or "efficient" point. And this must be our conclusion *regardless* of how in detail we have formulated our desiderata for a "good" or "efficient" point. In other words, the principle gives a necessary condition, it segregates a class of points to which our "good" or "efficient" point must belong, if any such points shall be fixed at all. Taken in this sense it would seem that it is next to impossible not to accept the principle—unless by saying that the individuals do not know what is best for them. Indeed, if they do know this, and we want to respect it, how could we maintain a point as a "good" or "efficient" point if there exist one or more other points that are Pareto-preferred to it? Only the dictator could maintain it: "I know better than you what is best for you".

To adopt this principle is, of course, by no means the same as to say that any "initial" point which we have happened to run across and which we find on scrutiny to be Pareto-optimal, is a point from which we should not depart. Many other points may, of course, also have the property of being Pareto-optimal.

Since the Pareto-principle only forms a necessary, not a sufficient, criterion —a fact which will be clearly illustrated by some of the subsequent examples— the principle does not lead to a final fixation of what should be considered the "best" or "most efficient" point, it leaves considerable *leeway in the fixation of economic policies*. An analysis of the consequences produced by adopting some specific way of handling this leeway is just the purpose of the macro-economic decision model.

Obviously the property of a point of being globally Pareto-optimal under a given set of conditions is a special case of the property of being locally Pareto-optimal under these same conditions. In other words, any point which is globally Pareto-optimal must necessarily be locally Pareto-optimal, but the inverse does not hold. If it is wanted to construct the Pareto-optimal region in an actual case, we may therefore—if this is found convenient—begin by constructing the locus of points that are *locally* Pareto-optimal under the conditions considered. Out of this pointset we may then pick out the points that have the global property. However, in any case where it is possible to use a graphical representation it will, as a rule, be safer and more illuminating to proceed directly to an analysis from the global viewpoint. This is exemplified in the figures of Sections 4 and 5. Whenever we speak of a point or a region as being Pareto-optimal without further specification, we have the global property in mind.

It should be emphasized that it is absolutely essential to indicate explicitly the *conditions* under which the search for Pareto-optimal points is to take place. If these conditions are not indicated, the definition of a Pareto-optimal region has no sense. It is as if one would speak of "the derivative" of a function of several variables without indicating the variable *with respect to which* the derivation is to be performed.

This necessity of specifying conditions when speaking of Pareto-optimal points is only a special manifestation of a basic principle underlying the whole theory of choice. The absurdities which may be produced by carelessness on this point may, perhaps, be illustrated by the following "theoretical analysis" of the "régime" which consists in forcing people to do abominable things under the threat of being shot. Firstly: this régime has the important property that any person subject to it is *perfectly free to choose* himself the alternative which he likes. Secondly: this being so, everybody will, of course, choose the alternative which gives him *the highest possible satisfaction*. Thirdly: any régime which allows everybody subject to it to reach the highest possible satisfaction must be *a very desirable régime* for these persons. Therefore: the régime considered must be a very desirable régime for those concerned. *Quod erat demonstrandum*.

I am not suggesting that all attempts at "proving theoretically" the superiority of the régime of free competition proceed on logical lines similar to the above, but I think it is fair to say that some of these attempts come dangerously close to this form of logic. Translated into economic terms: "the régime of free competition is the best of all régimes within the class of régimes which consists of the régime of free competition". It is even possible that Pareto himself has at one time been thinking more or less along such lines, but has at a later stage recognized the fallacy. My suspicion in this direction has been confirmed by prolonged conversations with such an eminent *connaisseur* of Pareto as Professor Gustavo Del Vecchio. The essence of our conversations on this point is given in Section 7.

3. The Unconditional Pareto Region

To simplify we only consider points where all the preference functions have continuous first order partial derivatives and none of the preference functions has all its first order partial derivatives equal to zero. Any point where the conditions are not fulfilled would need a special investigation which is not necessary for the present purpose.

Proposition (3.1). If all the preference functions have continuous first order partial derivatives and none of the preference functions has all its first order partial derivates equal to zero, a necessary and sufficient condition for a point X' to be unconditionally locally Pareto-optimal is that there exists at least one set of n numbers $\Theta_1 \ldots \Theta_n$, functions of the point X, all of them effectively positive (*i.e.* none of the Θ equal to zero), such that

(3.2) $$\Theta_1 d\Omega_1 + \ldots + \Theta_n d\Omega_n = 0 \quad (\Theta_j > 0)$$

for all variations $d\Omega_1 \ldots d\Omega_n$ around the given point X, *i.e.* for all values of $dX_1 \ldots dX_m$ around the point X.

The proposition holds no matter whether $m > n$, $m = n$ or $m < n$.

Another way to express the criterion (when the indifference surfaces have the usual convexity property) is to say that it is necessary and sufficient that there exists at least one set of n numbers $\Theta_1 \ldots \Theta_n$ with the specified properties, such that

(3.3) $$\Theta_1 \omega_{1i} + \Theta_2 \omega_{2i} + \ldots + \Theta_n \omega_{ni} = 0 \text{ for } i = 1, 2 \ldots m$$

where

(3.4) $$\omega_{ji} = \frac{\partial \Omega_j}{\partial X_i}$$

If we consider $\omega_1 \ldots \omega_n$ as n *vectors*—preference vectors—in m-dimensional space, with components $(\omega_{11} \ldots \omega_{1m}) \ldots (\omega_{n1} \ldots \omega_{nm})$, we can interpret (3.3) by saying that it is necessary and sufficient that *any* of the n preference vectors $\omega_1 \ldots \omega_n$ is expressible as a linear form in the *other* $(n-1)$ preference vectors, with coefficients all of which are effectively negative.

Another symbolic way to express (3.3) is to say that for a *given* point X, the n "variables" $\omega_1 \ldots \omega_n$ (so far without specification of the secondary subscript) shall be perfectly correlated (around their natural origin) over the "field of variation" generated by maintaining X fixed, but putting successively $i=1$, $2 \ldots m$, all the "perfect regression coefficients" in the homogeneous form of the equation, *i.e.* all the $\Theta_1 \ldots \Theta_n$ (constants under the variation over i) being effectively positive. In the terminology of confluence analysis we may say that the variables $\omega_1 \ldots \omega_n$ form a *closed* set of variables.

Finally, we may interpret the situation by saying that if there exists a convex corner on X such that all the n preference vectors $\omega_1 \ldots \omega_n$ from X lie in this corner or on its boundary, and at least one of them lies in the interior of it (as a limiting case the convex corner may be a half-space), then, and only then, will there exist points in the vicinity of X that are Pareto-preferred to X. Consequently the necessary and sufficient condition that no such points shall exist in the vicinity of X is that the n preference vectors $\omega_1 \ldots \omega_n$ do *not* have the property in question, a condition that is precisely expressed by the existence of the n effectively positive numbers $\Theta_1 \ldots \Theta_n$.

The *sufficiency* of the criterion in (3.1) follows immediately when the proposition is considered in the form (3.2), that is, when the variations around the given point X are expressed in terms of the increments $d\Omega_1 \ldots d\Omega_n$. Indeed, if $\Theta_1 \ldots \Theta_n$ is any set of n numbers, all of which are positive, non-zero, it is impossible to find a set of non-negative numbers $d\Omega_1 \ldots d\Omega_n$, at least one of them different from zero, such that the linear form written in the left member of (3.2) vanishes. Hence, if there actually exist n effectively positive numbers $\Theta_1 \ldots \Theta_n$ such that (3.2) holds for *any* variations around the given point X, this point must be unconditionally locally Pareto-optimal.

The *necessity* of the criterion in (3.1) is most easily discussed in terms of (3.3), which we now prefer to look upon as a vector equation in the n preference vectors $\omega_1 \ldots \omega_n$. We may first note that in any point which is unconditionally locally Pareto-optimal the preference vectors must be *linearly dependent*. This is trivial in the case $m<n$ because any set of more than m vectors are necessarily linearly dependent in m-dimensional space. In the case $m \gtreqless n$, suppose that the n preference vectors $\omega_1 \ldots \omega_n$ in the given point X are *not* linearly dependent. Hence the matrix $[\omega_{ji}]$ $(m \gtreqless n)$ is of rank n and the equations

$$(3.5) \qquad \omega_{j1}dX_1 + \ldots + \omega_{jm}dX_m = \delta_j \quad j=1, 2 \ldots n \; (\lesseqgtr m)$$

has solutions $dX_1 \ldots dX_m$ for arbitrarily given $\delta_1 \ldots \delta_n$. In particular we may choose all the δ_j non-negative and at least one of them positive. Any set of values $dX_1 \ldots dX_m$ satisfying the equations (3.5) with this choice of the δ's, will produce increments $d\Omega_j = \omega_{j1}dX_1 + \ldots + \omega_{jm}dX_m$, $j=1, 2 \ldots n$, which are non-negative and at least one of them positive.

Thus, in any point X that is unconditionally locally Pareto-optimal, there must exist at least one set of n numbers $\Theta_1 \ldots \Theta_n$, independent of i and at least one of them different from zero, such that (3.3) holds for all i (and consequently (3.2) holds for all variations of $d\Omega_1 \ldots d\Omega_n$ around X). This applies no matter whether $m>n$, $m=n$ or $m<n$.

To complete the proof of the necessity of the criterion in (3.1) it therefore suffices to consider the *sign condition* for the Θ's and dispense with all cases where at least one of the Θ's is zero or of different sign from the other Θ's. The necessity of the sign condition for the Θ's in (3.1) follows from a general principle of the signs of the coefficients in linear vector aggregates. However, rather than to approach the problem from this general and abstract viewpoint, we prefer to discuss the meaning of the sign condition in terms of some simple examples, maintaining all the time the concrete interpretation of the vectors as preference vectors. From these examples the necessity of the sign conditions in (3.1) in the general case will follow more or less intuitively.

To simplify the wording we shall say that a given point X' is *deferred* to X (by a given individual) if it is such that X is preferred to X'. We shall say that the point is *non-deferred* to X if it is either indifferent to X or preferred to X (by a given individual).

Example 1. In the case m arbitrary ($\gtreqless 1$), $n=2$, we have an immediate geometric interpretation of the necessity and sufficiency of (3.3). Indeed, in this case a point X, where none of the preference functions has all its partial derivatives equal to zero, is obviously unconditionally locally Pareto-optimal when, and only when, the preference vector of one of the two individuals points exactly in the *opposite* direction of the preference vector of the other individual, that is, when, and only when, there exist two effectively positive numbers Θ_1 and Θ_2 such that $\Theta_1\omega_{1i}+\Theta_2\omega_{2i}=0$ for all i.

Example 2. Next consider the case $m=2$, $n=3$. Consider the two preference vectors ω_1 and ω_2 going out from a given point X (none of these preference vectors having both its preference components equal to zero). First suppose that they form an angle different from 0 and from 180° as indicated in Figure 1 (3.6). Extend these two vectors forwards and backwards (towards A and B). We have the proposition:

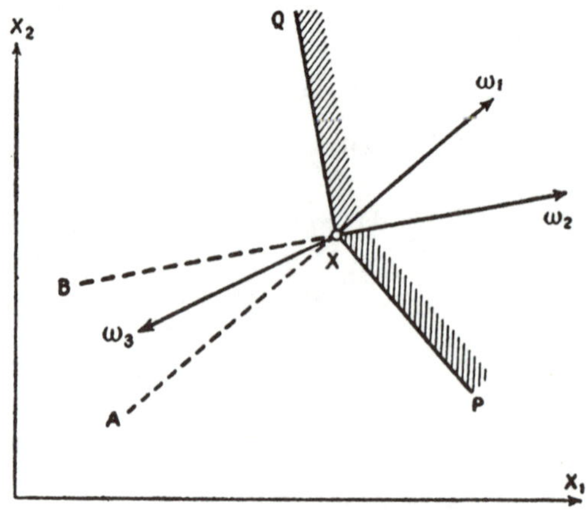

FIG. 1 (3.6)

Proposition (3.7). In order that the point X shall be unconditionally locally Pareto-optimal for the three individuals Nos. 1, 2, 3—when the two preference vectors ω_1 and ω_2 are given (and all the indifference surfaces have the usual convexity property)—it is necessary and sufficient that the third preference vector ω_3 is directed to a point in the *interior* of the opposite of the (infinite) convex corner formed by the vectors ω_1 and ω_2, *i.e.* it is necessary and sufficient that ω_3 is directed to a point in the interior of the (infinite) convex corner AXB in Figure 1 (3.6), not to a point on the boundary lines AX or BX of this corner, and not to a point in any other sector of the plane.

Indeed, draw the straight half-line XP perpendicular to ω_1 and the straight half-line XQ perpendicular to ω_2. The local region around X which is non-deferred by both individuals 1 and 2 and actually preferred by at least one of them is the convex corner PXQ (North-East of X), the boundary lines XP and XQ included. No point (except X itself) has the property of being indifferent to X for both individuals as long as we confine our attention to the vicinity of X. Hence, in order that the point X shall be unconditionally locally Pareto-optimal with respect to all three individuals—when the two preference vectors ω_1 and ω_2 are given and form an angle different from 0 and from 180°—it is necessary that the preference vector ω_3 is such that all points in the convex corner PXQ, boundary lines included, become actually deferred to X for individual No. 3. This happens when, and only when, the preference vector ω_3 is directed to some point in the interior of the (infinite) convex corner AXB, boundary lines not included. This happens when, and only when, the vector $(-\omega_3)$ is directed to some point in the *interior* of the (infinite) convex corner formed by the two preference vectors ω_1 and ω_2, boundary lines *not* included. According to a familiar proposition in vector algebra, this happens when, and only when, the vector $(-\omega_3)$ can be written as a linear form in the two vectors ω_1 and ω_2 with coefficients, each of which is positive, not zero. In other words, if the point X shall be unconditionally locally Pareto-optimal when the two vectors ω_1 and ω_2 are given and form an angle different from 0 and from 180°, it is *necessary* that there exist at least one equation of the form

$$\Theta_1\omega_1+\Theta_2\omega_2+\Theta_3\omega_3=0 \tag{3.8}$$

where all the coefficients Θ are positive, not zero. In the case now considered these coefficients are obviously uniquely determined apart from a common factor which is positive, but otherwise arbitrary.

If the two vectors ω_1 and ω_2 point in the *same* direction (*i.e.* form an angle of 0 degrees), the point X will obviously be unconditionally locally Pareto-optimal when, and only when, the vector ω_3 points in the opposite direction of ω_1 and ω_2, *i.e.* when, and only when, $\omega_3=-\alpha\omega_1$ where α is positive. If ω_1 and ω_2 point in the *same* direction, the condition on ω_3 can also be expressed by saying that we must have $\omega_3=-\beta\omega_2$ where β is positive. Multiplying these two equations by arbitrary positive constants and adding, we see that in order that the point X shall be unconditionally locally Paretian it is also now necessary that there exist at least one equation of the form (3.8) with all the Θ's positive, not zero. In the present case those Θ's have a two-dimensional arbitrariness.

If the two vectors ω_1 and ω_2 point in *opposite* directions, *i.e.* form an angle of 180°, the point X will be unconditionally locally Pareto-optimal for the two individuals 1 and 2. This applies no matter whether we define the local structure of the preferences as a linear structure expressed through the single datum consisting of the preference vectors, or we define it more exactly in its curved form depending also on the higher order derivatives (with the usual convexity assumption). The difference between the two viewpoints is only of avail if we attribute importance to a refined distinction between limiting cases. In the formulation (3.2) no assumption about first order approximation—*i.e.* linearity—is implied, but in (3.3)—where only the first order derivatives are involved—such an approximation is involved. In a point X, where the preference vectors ω_1 and ω_2 of two individuals point in opposite directions, the situation is as follows: when due account is taken of the curvature of the indifference lines (with the usual convexity assumption), any point in the vicinity of X will make at least one of the individuals worse off than he is in X. When first order derivatives only are considered, any point in the vicinity will make at least one of the individuals worse off, *except* points on the straight line through X which is normal to the direction of ω_1 and ω_2. Along this line any point will—in terms of the linear approximation—be indifferent to both individuals. Whichever of the two ways of looking at the situation we use, the point X will in the general sense (compare the definitions (2.4)–(2.5)) be locally Pareto-optimal for the two individuals. If we introduce a third individual, we must take account of the difference between the curvilinear and the linear way of looking at the situation. From the curvilinear point of view the point X will be strongly Pareto-optimal for the two individuals 1 and 2, and consequently also be strongly Pareto-optimal for the three individuals 1, 2, 3 (compare Proposition (3.13) below). From the linear point of view the point X is only Pareto-optimal in the general sense (not in the strong sense) for the two individuals 1 and 2. If in this case the preference vector ω_3 does not fall in the direction line of ω_1 and ω_2, the point X is *not* Pareto-optimal (neither in the general nor in the strong sense) for the three individuals 1, 2, 3. Indeed, if the vectors ω_1 and ω_2 point in opposite directions and the vector ω_3 does not fall in the line defined by ω_1 and ω_2, then some points along the line through X normal to ω_1 and ω_2 will be Pareto-preferred by the three individuals, namely the points on that half of the perpendicular considered which is situated to the same side of X as ω_3. In this case it is impossible to satisfy (3.3) which is the appropriate formula to consider when the linear viewpoint is adopted. Only if ω_3 falls in the same line as ω_1 and ω_2 (no matter whether it is to the side of ω_1 or to that of ω_2), will the point X be unconditionally locally Pareto-optimal for the three individuals. When this happens, we put $\omega_2 = -\alpha\omega_1$ and $\omega_3 = \beta\omega_1$, where α is effectively positive and β either effectively positive or effectively negative. Multiplying these two equations by effectively positive numbers Θ_2 and Θ_3

and adding, we get (3.8) with $\Theta_3 = \alpha\Theta_2 - \beta\Theta_3$. If β is negative, Θ_3 will be effectively positive for any choice of the two positive numbers Θ_2 and Θ_3. If β is positive, we only have to impose the condition $\frac{\Theta_2}{\Theta_3} > \frac{\beta}{\alpha}$. Thus we reach the conclusion that there must exist at least one equation of the form (3.8) where all the coefficients are positive, not zero. This checks with (3.3).

The above difference in interpretation of the point X according to whether we adopt the exact, curvilinear, or the approximate, linear, point of view, only applies to the point X itself, not to some *near-by* point such as, for instance, X' in Figure 2 (3.9) with preference vectors ω_1', ω_2' and ω_3'. This near-by point X' will, as a rule, appear as non-Pareto-optimal for the three individuals 1,2, 3, no matter whether we adopt the exact, curvilinear, or the approximate, linear, point of view. This illustrates the fact that the difference between the two viewpoints is only of avail when we want to classify in detail limiting cases, and in

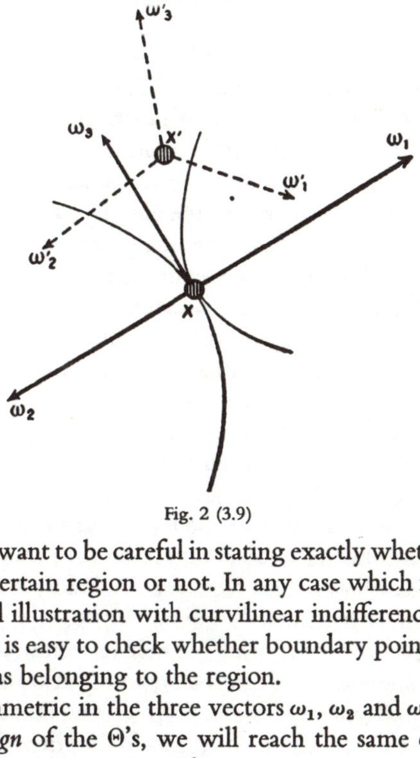

Fig. 2 (3.9)

particular when we want to be careful in stating exactly whether some boundary points belong to a certain region or not. In any case which is simple enough to admit of a graphical illustration with curvilinear indifference lines—such as the examples below—it is easy to check whether boundary points should, or should not, be considered as belonging to the region.

Since (3.8) is symmetric in the three vectors ω_1, ω_2 and ω_3, and the criterion only specifies the *sign* of the Θ's, we will reach the same criterion no matter which set of two vectors we start with.

From the above analysis we conclude that in all cases where the point X in two-dimensional space is unconditionally locally Pareto-optimal with respect to three individuals, there must exist at least one equation of the form (3.8) where each of the three coefficients Θ is positive, not zero.

We can also express the conclusions of Example 2 in the following proposition:

Proposition (3.10). If the point X is unconditionally locally Pareto-optimal, the preference vectors must be distributed around X in such a way that *any* vector around the point X which can be written as a linear form in the preference vectors can be written as such a form with all the coefficients *positive*, not zero.

If we had wanted to, we could have aimed at first proving (3.10) and from (3.10) deduce (3.8). It is easily seen that if (3.10) holds, the existence of an equation of the form (3.8) is assured. Indeed, if ω is any vector which can be written as a linear combination of the preference vectors, the vector $(-\omega)$ has the same property. Write each of these two vectors as a linear combination of the preference vectors with coefficients that are *positive*, not zero. The sum of these two vector equations is a vector equation of the form (3.8) with all the Θ's positive, not zero.

Example 3. $m=2$, n arbitrary>2. If all the n preference vectors are situated in the same line, the point X is unconditionally locally Pareto-optimal when, and only when, there is at least one vector pointing in one direction along this line, and at least one vector pointing in the other direction. In this case obviously any vector that can be written as a linear combination of the preference vectors (*i.e.* any vector directed to a point on the line considered) can be written as such a combination with coefficients that are positive, not zero, hence by the same argument as in (3.10) there must exist an equation of the form (3.3).

If not all the preference vectors are situated in the same line, draw a circle around X and follow the circumference. If the point X shall be locally Pareto-optimal, we must nowhere pass as much as 180° between one preference vector and the next. Indeed, suppose that somewhere we pass exactly 180°. There would then be at least two preference vectors pointing in opposite directions and at least one preference vector pointing in the sector covered by the 180° which we have *not* passed. Any points in this sector and situated on the line which is perpendicular to the line of the two preference vectors that point in opposite directions would be Pareto-preferred by the group consisting of all the individuals. If we passed *more* than 180°, there would even be a whole convex corner of Pareto-preferred points.

Thus we only have to consider the case where we nowhere pass as much as 180° when going from one preference vector to the next. In this case there must exist a set of three preference vectors $\omega_1, \omega_2, \omega_3$, such that the counterclockwise angle between any two consecutive vectors is less than 180°; as indicated in Figure 3 (3.11). Such a triple of vectors is, for instance, constructed by starting with any preference vector ω_1 and moving counterclockwise until we reach the *last* (one of the last) preference vectors that form an angle of less than 180° with ω_1. Let it be ω_2. From ω_2 we continue the counterclockwise movement until we reach the first (one of the first) vectors ω_3 such that the counterclockwise angle from ω_1 to ω_3 is more than 180°. Since there is no empty angle of as much as 180°, ω_3 must be situated somewhere in the interior of the counterclockwise angle between A_1 (the negative of ω_1) and ω_1. Hence the counterclockwise angle from ω_3 to ω_1 is less than 180°. Any vector around X can be expressed

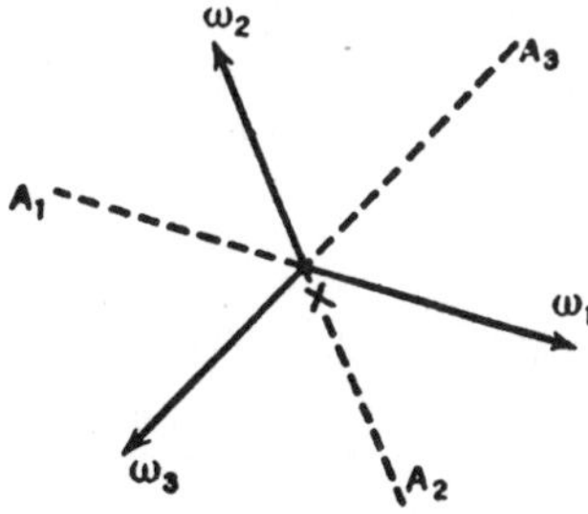

FIG. 3 (3.11)

as a linear form in the three vectors ω_1, ω_2, ω_3, with coefficients all of which are *effectively negative*. Indeed, consider first a vector directed along A_1. It can be expressed in the form $-\alpha\omega_1$, with α effectively positive, but it can also be expressed in the form $\beta_2\omega_2+\beta_3\omega_3$ with β_2 and β_3 effectively positive. Hence it can be expressed in the form $p(-\alpha)\omega_1+q(\beta_2\omega_2+\beta_3\omega_3)$ with $p+q=1$. Choosing q negative (and consequently p positive) the vector in question will be expressed in terms of ω_1, ω_2, ω_3 with coefficients all of which are effectively negative. Similarly for any vector along A_2 or along A_3 or for any vector along ω_1 or ω_2 or ω_3. Next consider a vector in the interior of the convex corner $(A_1\omega_3)$. It can be expressed in the form $\alpha_2\omega_2+\alpha_3\omega_3$ with α_2 and α_3 effectively positive, but it can also be expressed in the form $-(\beta_1\omega_1+\beta_2\omega_2)$ with the β_1 and β_2 positive; hence it can be expressed in the form $p(\alpha_2\omega_2+\alpha_3\omega_3)-q(\beta_1\omega_1+\beta_2\omega_2)$ with $p+q=1$. Choosing p negative (and consequently q positive) the vector will be expressed as a linear form in ω_1, ω_2, ω_3, with coefficients all of which are effectively negative. Similarly for vectors situated in the other sectors of Figure 3 (3.11). Thus, any vector around X can be expressed as a linear form in ω_1, ω_2, ω_3 with coefficients, each of which is effectively negative. Applying this in particular to all the *other* preference vectors $\omega_4, \omega_5 \ldots \omega_n$ around X, we get an equation of the form (3.3). Hence (3.1) holds for $m=2$, $n>2$.

These examples will be enough to exhibit the meaning of the general proposition (3.1).

The conditions on the signs of the Θ's are not important from the viewpoint of manipulation of formulae in the *first stages* of the work when we wish to construct the unconditional local Pareto region in an actual case. Indeed, in this case we might begin by *eliminating* the Θ's and thus deriving a set of conditions on the point X which will be well defined when the shape of the indicators Ω_j are given. Since the Θ's enter in a homogeneous and linear fashion, the conditions after elimination of the Θ's will appear as $(m-n+1)$ equations between the derivatives of the indicator, when $m \gtreqless n$. The dimensionality of the subspace of the points that are Pareto-optimal will consequently—apart from degenerate cases—be

$$(3.12) \qquad m-(m-n+1)=n-1 \quad (\text{when } m \gtreqless n)$$

In the *further discussion* of the properties of the pointset X which is Paretian, it becomes essential to add the sign conditions. These sign conditions can then be formulated by saying that the expressions obtained for the Θ's—expressions only involving the partial derivatives of the indicators—shall be effectively positive.

* * *

If $m<n$ the unconditional Pareto region will, in general, form a closed subspace whose dimensionality is independent of n, namely equal to m, but whose volume will, in general, be all the *larger* the larger is n. In degenerate cases special situations may emerge, but the general rule is that the volume of the Pareto-optimal region increases as the number of individuals increases. One general proposition that illustrates this is the following.

Proposition (3.13). The region that is *strongly* Pareto-optimal for a group of individuals consists at least of all points that have the property of belonging to any region that is *strongly* Pareto-optimal for a subgroup of these individuals.

This proposition follows immediately from the fact that a point X, which belongs to a region that is strongly Pareto-optimal for a subgroup of the individuals, is by definition such that in any *other* point at least one of the individuals in the subgroup must be worse off. This is saying that at least one of the individuals of the total group must be worse off. In other words, the point X must belong to the region that is strongly Pareto-optimal for the total group.

A graphical illustration of a simple case will suggest the nature of the possibilities that exist. See Figure 4 (3.14). By a global analysis of Pareto conditions, such as given in Figure 4 (3.14), we get a much more elucidating picture of the situation than by a formal application of Lagrange multipliers.

The case illustrated in Figure 4 (3.14) is $m=2$, $n=3$. The two independent variables X_1 and X_2 are measured along the horizontal and vertical axis, respectively. Each individual is represented by a system of contour-lines for his preference function. The maximum points are at (1), (2), (3), respectively.

We begin by considering the individuals 1 and 2 only. Take the point A. The shaded region between A and B (enclosed by the indifference lines for individual 1 and that for individual 2, that pass through A), represents points that the individuals 1 and 2 Pareto-prefer to the initial point A. The endpoint B is not Pareto-preferred, but Pareto-indifferent to A. This, however, is unessential in this connection. What is essential is that there exist points that are Pareto-preferred to A by the individuals 1 and 2. In other words, A is not Pareto-optimal for the two individuals 1 and 2. Take any point C *in the interior* of the shaded area between A and B. A similar argument applies here. That is, the doubly-shaded area *CD*—situated entirely inside of the area *AB*—represents (with the exception of the endpoint *D*) points that the individuals 1 and 2 Pareto-prefer to *C*. Hence *C* is not Pareto-optimal for the two individuals 1 and 2. Continuing in this way, we end up by reaching a point where there is

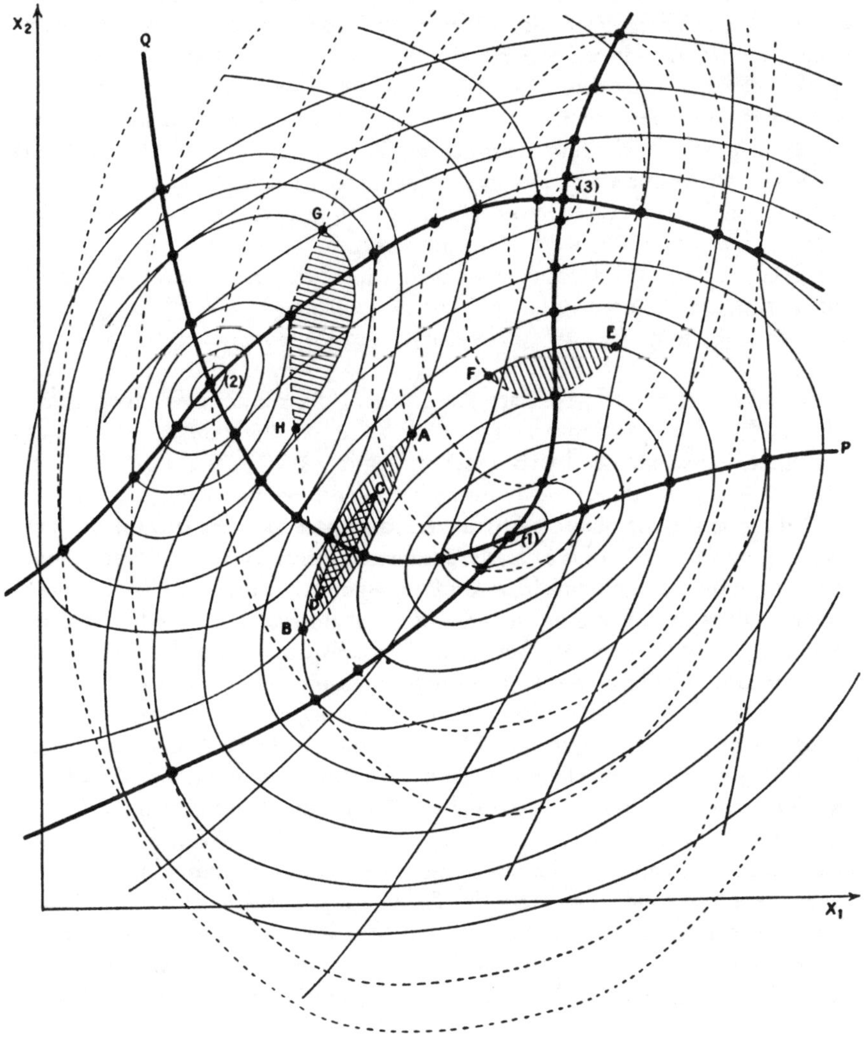

FIG. 4 (3.14)

tangency between a preference line of the individual 1 and a preference line of the individual 2 (assuming continuous variation of the partial derivatives of the preference functions). The locus of points where such a tangency exists is the heavily drawn curve *P*(1)(2)*Q*. This curve is defined as the set of points satisfying (3.3) for $i=1, 2$ (with $n=2$) *and no condition* put on the Θ's. Introducing the additional condition that the two Θ's involved shall be of the same sign, we get the points of the curve $P(1)(2)Q$ that are situated on the *finite segment* between the points (1) and (2). To the right of the point (1) and to the left of the point (2) the two Θ's are of opposite signs. Hence: any point belonging to the finite segment of the heavily drawn curve between the points (1) and (2) is unconditionally Pareto-optimal for the two individuals 1 and 2. This optimality is to be taken in the general sense if we adopt the viewpoint of a locally linear preference structure, but it is even a strong optimality from the exact curvilinear viewpoint. Furthermore, no other point in space has this property which the points on the finite segment (1)(2) have. In other words, any point on this segment—the endpoints included—is such that there is no other point in space which would be Pareto-preferred to it by the two individuals 1 and 2. And no other point in space has this property.

Similar interpretations are possible for the finite segments of the heavily drawn curves between the points (1) and (3) and between (2) and (3), respectively. The construction of the curve between (1) and (3) is suggested by the shaded area *EF* and that of the curve between (2) and (3) by the shaded area *GH*.

The region of points which are Pareto-optimal simultaneously for all three individuals—when no constraints are imposed on the points—is the two-dimensional area enclosed by the three curves (1) (2), (1) (3) and (2) (3). If we adopt the exact curvilinear viewpoint, we may add: boundary included. Indeed, take, for instance, the point *A*. Divide the total space in two parts: the one outside and the one inside of the closed indifference curve for the individual 3 that passes through *A*. The points that are Pareto-preferred by 1 and 2 are situated entirely in the outside region, namely in the shaded area *AB* (endpoint *B* not included), while those points that are preferred by 3 are situated entirely in the inside region. The only point that is indifferent to both 1 and 2 is *B* and this point is for individual 3 on a lower level of satisfaction than *A*. Since no other point can be Pareto-preferred to *A* by the group of the three individuals than points that are either Pareto-preferred to *A* by the two individuals 1 and 2 or indifferent to *A* for these two individuals, we see that there does not exist any point which is Pareto-preferred to *A* by the three individuals 1, 2, 3. Hence *A* is unconditionally globally Pareto-optimal for these three individuals.

On the other hand, take the point *B*. Again divide the space in two parts: the one inside and the one outside the closed indifference line for 3 that passes through *B*. There are points in the inside region, namely the points in the shaded area *AB*, that are preferred by all three individuals. Hence *B* is not Pareto-optimal.

Considering in this way one by one all the 6 regions: SW. of the line (1) (2), NW. of the point (2), NW. of the line (2) (3), NE. of the point (3), E. of the line (3) (1), S. and SE. of the point (1), we see that each of these regions will be characterized in a certain way with respect to the preferences of the individuals and always such that a point in the region becomes non-Pareto-optimal for the group of the three individuals. Hence: a necessary and sufficient condition for a point to be Pareto-optimal for the group of three individuals 1, 2, 3, is that it is situated in the closed area (1), (2), (3)—boundary included if we adopt the exact curvilinear viewpoint of the indifference lines.

By changing the nature of the indifference lines, for instance by moving the point (3) towards (2), one may produce a situation where the curve segment (1) (3) coincides with the line segment (1) (2). This would reduce the dimensionality of the Pareto-optimal region to unity, *i.e.* the region which is Pareto-optimal for all the three individuals would now become a curve segment. This and similar situations would represent degenerate cases.

4. The Region which is Pareto-optimal under a Set of Conditions expressed by Equations

Consider first the *dimensionality* (the number of degrees of freedom) of the Pareto-optimal region. A full discussion of all possible limiting and degenerate cases would be a tedious and, perhaps, not a very important task. Apart from degenerate cases a simple rule may be formulated. We notice first that in the case where no constraints are imposed on m variables to be preference-evaluated by n individuals, the Pareto-optimal region will—apart from degenerate cases—be of dimensionality (number of degrees of freedom) $min[m, n-1]$, where $min[\quad]$ indicates the smaller of the two numbers written in brackets. From what has been mentioned, this follows by noticing that (3.3) gives m equations. If we eliminate from these m equations, the $(n-1)$ *ratios* between the Θ's, we are left with $m-(n-1)$ equations, hence $(n-1)$ degrees of freedom. This assumes that $(n-1)$ does not exceed m. If it does, the number of degrees of freedom is, of course, limited by m.

In the case where s constraints are imposed, we may re-formulate the problem by expressing everything in terms of $(m-s)$ independent parameters. In the new setting of the problem we can apply the above reasoning. Hence we have the proposition:

Proposition (4.1). The region which is Pareto-optimal under a set of constraints exposed by s independent equations between m variables that are preference-evaluated by n individuals has a dimensionality (number of degrees of freedom) which—apart from degenerate cases—is equal to $min[m-s, n-1]$.

Thus, so far as the dimensionality of the Pareto-optimal region is concerned, the addition of constraints in the form of equations tends to reduce the content of the region. But when it comes to the *volume* of the region within its given dimensionality, the addition of constraints tends to *widen* the region—just as the addition of more individuals tends to widen the Pareto-optimal region (see Section 3). The precise meaning of the above statement is given in Figure 5 (4.2) and Proposition (4.3) and in the examples discussed in connection with the proposition. Before proceeding to this more detailed discussion, I would like to state that in my opinion the fact here considered is of fundamental importance for the whole welfare analysis. It has far-reaching consequences for our interpretation of *what is really meant* when we say that a point is "good" because it is Pareto-optimal. A slipslop way of passing over the basic logical principle here involved is, as I see it, the main cause for so much of the unprecise and unwarranted reason that has been given about the superiority of the régime of free competition—amongst others by Pareto himself and his immediate followers.

Let C and c be two sets of constraints such that c is included in C. That is to say, any point X that satisfies C must necessarily satisfy c, but the inverse is not true. For shortness we may call C the strong and c the weak condition. The general argument leading to Proposition (4.3) applies to any type of condition whether expressed by equations or inequalities, but the subsequent example is concerned with the case where the conditions are expressed by equations.

Since C is the stronger of the two sets of conditions, the points X that satisfy C form a region $X[C]$ that is entirely included in the region $X[c]$ of the points that satisfy c. This is illustrated in Figure 5 (4.2). For simplicity the region

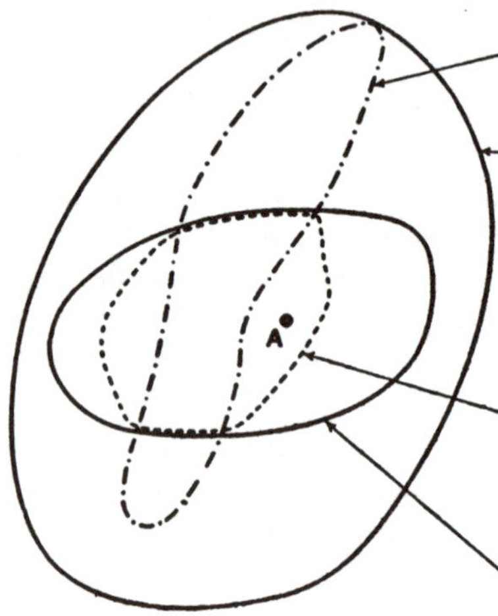

FIG. 5 (4.2)

$X[c]$ is here drawn as one continuous region, but the argument is general and applies no matter what the structure of the point set $X[c]$ is. Similar remark on $X[C]$.

The region $Par[c]$ must, of course, be situated in $X[c]$ and the region $Par[C]$ in $X[C]$. The region $Par[c]$ may, or may not, have points in $X[C]$. If it does have points in $X[C]$, these points must belong to $Par[C]$. On the other hand, there are, in general, points that are Pareto-optimal under C without being Pareto-optimal under c, as, for instance, the point A in Figure 5 (4.2). That is to say, if we confine our attention to points in $X[C]$, we find that the points that are Pareto-optimal under the stronger condition C form *a more inclusive* set than the points that are Pareto-optimal under the *weaker* condition c. This idea that a stronger condition leads to a more inclusive set is a bit unfamiliar and it takes a little attention to incorporate it correctly in a reasoning about "good" points and "good" régimes.

We may formulate the fact referred to in the following proposition:

Proposition (4.3). *Par*[*c*] . *X*[*C*] is included in *Par*[*C*] but not inversely, *i.e.* those points that are strongly Pareto-optimal under the weaker condition *c* and lie within the region of points that satisfy the stronger condition *C*, must be included in the points that are strongly Pareto-optimal under the stronger condition *C*. But the inverse is not true.

To give a formal proof of (4.3) let *X* be any point in *X*[*C*] and consider the following three cases—which form an exhaustive list of all possibilities:

1. There exists a point in *X*[*C*]—and consequently in *X*[*c*]—which is Pareto-preferred to *X*.	Then *X* is *not Par*[*C*] and *not Par*[*c*].
2. There exists no point in *X*[*C*], but a point in *X*[*c*] which is Pareto-preferred to *X*.	Then *X is Par*[*C*] but *not Par*[*c*].
3. There exists no point in *X*[*c*]—and consequently no point in *X*[*C*]—which is Pareto-preferred to *X*.	Then *X is Par*[*C*] and *is Par*[*c*].

In other words, for any given point *X* which belongs to *X*[*C*] it is true that *if* it is *Par*[*c*], it must be *Par*[*C*], but it may be *Par*[*C*] without being *Par*[*c*]. In this formulation *Par* stands for "strongly Pareto-optimal".

As a special case *all* the points that are Pareto-optimal under the weak condition *c* may fall in the region of points that satisfy the strong condition *C*, but that is of no particular importance. In any case will Proposition (4.3) hold.

As an example consider the case where *c* is a production constraint given, say, by the limitation of natural resources and the technical situation, in short a set of what might be called *obligatory* conditions, while *C* is a more inclusive set of conditions, consisting of the obligatory conditions and a set of *facultative* conditions expressing, say, conditions to the effect that the total output shall be distributed amongst the individuals in certain proportions. In short, we may term these conditions the production and distribution constraints, respectively.

If we are to use the concept of Pareto-optimality on this set-up, we must keep in mind that Pareto-optimality under the production constraint is not the same thing as Pareto-optimality under the production and distribution constraints. For instance, if we want to say something about the distribution system from the viewpoint of Pareto-optimality, the pertinent question is whether some point *X* which shows the prescribed distribution ratios, is Pareto-optimal under a constraint which consists of the *production constraint only*. If a choice is to be made between different systems of distribution, we must, of course, not evaluate a given point in terms of an optimality definition that imposes one particular distribution as a necessity. In other words, if we ascertain that some point *X*, which has been reached in some way or another, has the property of being

Pareto-optimal under the inclusive set of constraints consisting of the production and distribution constraints, this does not say anything about whether this point is "good" in the sense of giving an "effective" utilization of the resources. If we only know that our point X is Pareto-optimal under the inclusive condition C, it may, perhaps, fall in A of Figure 5 (4.2) and thus not be Pareto-optimal under the production constraints. In all cases we must be very careful to impose only the *obligatory* conditions and not any condition pertaining to the alternatives between which we want to select.

The nature of the pitfall might perhaps be illustrated by an analogy in partial derivatives.[6] Suppose we have a function $f(x, y, z)$ of three variables and we want to find the value of its partial derivative $f_x'(x, y, z)=\frac{\partial f(x, y, z)}{\partial x}$ (under constant y and z) in a point (x_0, y_0, z_0) that satisfies $z_0=g(x_0, y_0)$ where g is a given function of two variables. The value sought is

$$f_x'(x_0, y_0, z_0)$$

and *not* the value that would be obtained by imposing the relation $z=g(x, y)$ *under the derivation process*. This latter value would be

$$f_x'(x_0, y_0, z_0)+f_z'(x_0, y_0, z_0)\, g_x'(x_0, y_0)$$

One way to approach the problem correctly would be first to seek all points that are Pareto-optimal under the production constraints only, and then within this set to pick out those points that show some desired distribution ratios. It may then, of course, happen that it is *impossible* to realize the desired distribution ratios by confining the point to lying in the region that is Pareto-optimal under the production constraint. If so, this simply shows that the goals put up are inconsistent.

A simple example will illustrate the situation.

Example (4.5)

Consider two goods Nos. $i=1, 2$ and two individuals Nos. $j=1, 2$. Let each good be produced in an independent production process with only one factor of production which we may call labour. We use the following notation:

N= total quantity of labour.
N_1 and N_2= quantities of labour used in the two industries.
X_1 and X_2= quantities produced in the two industries.
X_{1j} and X_{2j}= volumes of these goods received by the two individuals ($j=1, 2$).
$\Omega_j=\Omega_j(X_{1j}, X_{2j})$= preference function of individual j ($j=1, 2$).
$X_i=f_i(N_i)$= production function of industry i ($i=1, 2$).

[6] *Note added in March* 1959. The essence of the matter is that the stronger the conditions, the easier will it be to find points which do *not* satisfy these conditions. My friends and colleagues Professors Trygve Haavelmo and B. Thalberg have produced another example to illustrate the nature of the above pitfall:

Given a function $F(x,y,p,q)$ of four variables. Consider three subsets in space (x,y).

(1) Maximize F over x and y under fixed p and q. To a given p,q region there will correspond a well-defined (x,y) region. Let this be subset S_1.

By definition we have

(4.6) $$N_1+N_2=N$$

(4.7) $$X_i=X_{i1}+X_{i2} \quad (i=1, 2)$$

The marginal preferences and the marginal productivities will be denoted

(4.8) $$\omega_{ji}=\omega_{ji}(X_{1j}, X_{2j})=\frac{\partial\Omega_j(X_{1j}, X_{2j})}{\partial X_{ij}} \quad (i=1, 2;\ j=1, 2)$$

(4.9) $$f_i'=\frac{df_i(N_i)}{dN_i} \quad (i=1, 2)$$

Marginal labour cost in industry No. i is $\frac{1}{f_i'}$

The inverse production functions will be denoted

(4.10) $$N_i=f_i^{-1}(X_i) \quad (i=1, 2)$$

Reducing the model to its lowest terms by eliminating all unnecessary variables, we can say that we have a problem in the four variables

(4.11) $$X_{11},\ X_{12},\ X_{21},\ X_{22}$$

on which is imposed the single condition

(4.12) $$f_1^{-1}(X_{11}+X_{12})+f_2^{-1}(X_{21}+X_{22})=N$$

where N is given. The shapes of the two functions f_1^{-1} and f_2^{-1} are also assumed to be given.

We shall first determine the region that is Pareto-optimal for the two individuals, one constraint in the form of an equation being imposed on the four variables ($m=4$, $n=2$, $s=1$).

We take X_{11}, X_{12} and X_{21} as free variables and consider X_{22} as a function of the three free variables, the relationship being defined through (4.12).

Letting now ∂ indicate partial derivation in the model of three degrees of freedom, we can formulate the necessary and sufficient condition for a Pareto-optimal point as

(4.13) $$\frac{\frac{\partial\Omega_1}{\partial X_{11}}}{\frac{\partial\Omega_2}{\partial X_{11}}}=\frac{\frac{\partial\Omega_1}{\partial X_{12}}}{\frac{\partial\Omega_2}{\partial X_{12}}}=\frac{\frac{\partial\Omega_1}{\partial X_{21}}}{\frac{\partial\Omega_2}{\partial X_{21}}}=\text{negative (compare (3.3))}$$

This is a set of conditions formed by two equations and a sign condition. In other words, the dimensionality of the solution will be one, and out of this one-dimensional pointset there will, in general, be a finite segment that answers the requirement. This checks with $min[m-s, n-1]=min[3, 1]=1$.

(2) Add the condition $g(x,y)=0$. This gives S_2. It is a subset of S_1.

(3) Maximize F over x and y under the constraint $g(x,y)=0$, the values of p and q being given. To the same p,q region as in case (1), there will correspond a well-defined (x,y) region. Let it be S_3.

It is *not* true that S_3 will in general be identical with S_2. In general it will be larger than S_2.

By implicit derivation of (4.12) we find

$$(4.14)\qquad \frac{\partial X_{22}}{\partial X_{11}}=\frac{\partial X_{22}}{\partial X_{12}}=-\frac{f_2'}{f_1'} \qquad \frac{\partial X_{22}}{\partial X_{21}}=-1$$

and hence

$$(4.15)\qquad \begin{matrix} \frac{\partial \Omega_1}{\partial X_{11}}=\omega_{11} & \frac{\partial \Omega_1}{\partial X_{12}}=0 & \frac{\partial \Omega_1}{\partial X_{21}}=\omega_{21} \\ \frac{\partial \Omega_2}{\partial X_{11}}=-\frac{\omega_{22}f_2'}{f_1'} & \frac{\partial \Omega_2}{\partial X_{12}}=\omega_{21}-\frac{\omega_{22}f_2'}{f_1'} & \frac{\partial \Omega_2}{\partial X_{21}}=-\omega_{22} \end{matrix}$$

The conditions (4.13) can therefore be written

$$(4.16)\qquad \frac{\omega_{11}f_1'}{\omega_{22}f_2'}=\frac{0}{\omega_{22}f_2'-\omega_{21}f_1'}=\frac{\omega_{12}}{\omega_{22}}=\text{positive}$$

Rearranging the terms and writing out all the variables, we get (the central denominator must be zero)

$$(4.17)\qquad \frac{\omega_{11}(X_{11},X_{21})}{\omega_{12}(X_{11},X_{21})}=\frac{\omega_{21}(X_{12},X_{22})}{\omega_{22}(X_{12},X_{22})}=\frac{f_2'[f_2^{-1}(X_{21}+X_{22})]}{f_1'[f_1^{-1}(X_{11}+X_{12})]}$$

ω_{12} and ω_{22} of the same sign (in the regular case both positive).

The result can be summarized in the formula

$$(4.18)\qquad Par[12]=X[17,12]$$

In words: the region (of the four-dimensional space X_{11}, X_{12}, X_{21}, X_{22}) which is Pareto-optimal for the two individuals under the constraint (4.12) (with given N), consists of the points where (4.17) and (4.12) are satisfied.

Since the region which is Pareto-optimal under the production constraint has one degree of freedom, there is still room for adding a condition without giving up the requirements that the point shall be Pareto-optimal under the production constraint. Suppose that we try to dispose of the remaining degree of freedom by requesting that a certain *distribution ratio* shall prevail between the two individuals. This way of disposing of the remaining *degree of freedom is purely conventional* and not derived by any sort of consideration on Pareto-optimality.

In order to be able to compare the part that one of the individuals gets of the total product with the part that the other individual gets, we must in some way or another introduce a principle for comparing quantities of the two goods. Suppose we do it by using labour costs as value coefficients. *This too is a purely conventional criterion not derived by any consideration on Pareto-optimality.*

If labour costs are used as value coefficients, the relative part which the individual 2 gets of the total product will be

$$(4.19)\qquad \frac{\dfrac{X_{12}}{f_1'}+\dfrac{X_{22}}{f_2'}}{\dfrac{X_{11}+X_{12}}{f_1'}+\dfrac{X_{21}+X_{22}}{f_2'}}=L(X_{11},\ X_{12},\ X_{21},\ X_{22})$$

If we insert in the left member of (4.19) the expressions for f_1' and f_2' in terms of the four variables X_{11}, X_{12}, X_{21}, X_{22} (the same expressions as those written in the right member of (4.17)), we get a certain function L of the point in four-dimensional space. The shape of this function L is uniquely determined through the shape of the production functions. Hence, the requirement that the distribution ratio shall have a preassigned value λ is expressed by

$$(4.20)\qquad L(X_{11},\ X_{12},\ X_{21},\ X_{22})=\lambda$$

This is simply a one-dimensional condition on the point and may consequently be considered as a means of taking out the one degree of freedom that remained after imposing the condition that the point shall be Pareto-optimal under the production constraint.

Is it possible to assign an arbitrary value to λ? Certainly not if the point shall be Pareto-optimal in the above sense. Since the value of the function $L(X_{11}, X_{12}, X_{21}, X_{22})$ in any point of the four-dimensional space is given directly from the shape of the two production functions and from nothing else, we may follow the variation of this function as the point moves over the one-dimensional pointset *Par*[12] defined by (4.18). For simplicity assume continuous variation and let L_{max} and L_{min} be the maximum and minimum respectively, assumed by the function L under this variation. The two numbers L_{max} and L_{min} depend on the shapes of the two production functions and the two preference functions and on nothing else. Obviously, if we require that the distribution coefficient shall have a value between L_{max} and L_{min}, the problem of finding a point that gives this ratio and at the same time is Pareto-optimal *under the production constraint*, has a solution (at least one). But if we choose a distribution ratio that falls *outside* of the interval (L_{max}, L_{min}), no point can be found that is Pareto-optimal under the production constraint and has the distribution ratio chosen.

This simplified example illustrates the principle according to which a *selection problem—i.e.* a problem of *how to formulate the goal* for economic policy—may be handled. The goal in the example has been formulated in such a way as to conform to Pareto-optimality *under those constraints that it is not possible to change simply by a human decision.* And the remaining degrees of freedom have been handled by a *postulate* in the form of a social value judgement. This social value judgement is something which the economist as scientist and technician simply has to take as a datum. But *all the rest* is within his sphere of competence. It would seem that even with the above limitation of the economist's field, there is more than enough for him to do.

So far I have not discussed the problem of *the régime*, that is the problem of how actually to organize production and trade in order to make the equilibrium point fix itself in the desired position. Before proceeding to a discussion of this I shall work through the above example once more and now determine explicitly the region that is Pareto-optimal under a set of conditions that consist simultaneously of the production constraint *and* the distribution constraints. The resulting region will prove to be very different from the one that is Pareto-optimal under the production constraint only.

We now have to consider a model with two degrees of freedom, namely the same four variables X_{11}, X_{12}, X_{21}, X_{22} as before, but now with two constraints (4.12) and (4.20) with N and λ given.

We take X_{11} and X_{21} as free variables and determine first the elements of the Jacobian $\frac{\partial(X_{12}, X_{22})}{\partial(X_{11}, X_{21})}$. Letting ∂ indicate partial derivation within the two degrees of freedom now considered, we get

$$(4.21)\qquad \begin{aligned} \frac{\partial f_1^{-1}}{\partial X_{11}} &= \frac{df_1^{-1}}{dX_1} \cdot \frac{\partial(X_{11}+X_{12})}{\partial X_{11}} = \frac{1}{f_1'}\left(1+\frac{\partial X_{12}}{\partial X_{11}}\right) \\ \frac{\partial f_2^{-1}}{\partial X_{11}} &= \frac{df_2^{-1}}{dX_2} \cdot \frac{\partial(X_{21}+X_{22})}{\partial X_{11}} = \frac{1}{f_2'}\frac{\partial X_{22}}{\partial X_{11}} \end{aligned}$$

and hence by implicit derivation of (4.12)

$$(4.22)\qquad \begin{aligned} \frac{\partial X_{12}}{\partial X_{11}} + \Phi\frac{\partial X_{22}}{\partial X_{11}} &= -1 \\ \frac{\partial X_{12}}{\partial X_{21}} + \Phi\frac{\partial X_{22}}{\partial X_{21}} &= -\Phi \end{aligned}$$

where

$$(4.23)\qquad \Phi = \frac{f_1'}{f_2'}$$

Since

$$(4.24)\qquad \begin{aligned} \frac{\partial}{\partial X_{11}}\left[\frac{1}{f_1'}\right] &= -\frac{1}{(f_1')^2}\frac{\partial f_1'}{\partial X_{11}} = -\frac{1}{(f_1')^2}\frac{df_1'}{dN_1}\frac{dN_1}{dX_1}\frac{\partial(X_{11}+X_{12})}{\partial X_{11}} = -\frac{f_1''}{(f_1')^3}\left(1+\frac{\partial X_{12}}{\partial X_{11}}\right) \\ \frac{\partial}{\partial X_{11}}\left[\frac{1}{f_2'}\right] &= -\frac{1}{(f_2')^2}\frac{\partial f_2'}{\partial X_{11}} = -\frac{1}{(f_2')^2}\frac{df_2'}{dN_2}\frac{dN_2}{dX_2}\frac{\partial(X_{21}+X_{22})}{\partial X_{11}} = -\frac{f_2''}{(f_2')^3}\frac{\partial X_{22}}{\partial X_{11}} \end{aligned}$$

we get by implicit derivation of (4.20)

$$\delta_1\frac{\partial X_{12}}{\partial X_{11}} + \Phi\delta_2\frac{\partial X_{22}}{\partial X_{11}} = 1-\delta_1$$

(4.25)

$$\delta_1 \frac{\partial X_{12}}{\partial X_{21}} + \Phi\delta_2 \frac{\partial X_{22}}{\partial X_{21}} = \Phi(1-\delta_2)$$

where

(4.26) $$\delta_i = \delta_i(\lambda;\, X_{i1},\, X_{i2}) = 1 - \lambda + \frac{f_i''}{(f_i')^2}\,[\lambda X_{i1} - (1-\lambda)X_{i2}] \quad (i=1,\, 2)$$

Hence

(4.27)

$$\frac{\partial X_{12}}{\partial X_{11}} = -(1-\Delta) \qquad \frac{\partial X_{22}}{\partial X_{11}} = -\frac{\Delta}{\Phi}$$

$$\frac{\partial X_{12}}{\partial X_{21}} = \Phi\Delta \qquad \frac{\partial X_{22}}{\partial X_{21}} = -(1+\Delta)$$

where

(4.28) $$\Delta = \Delta(\lambda;\, X_{11},\, X_{12},\, X_{21},\, X_{22}) = \frac{1}{\delta_1 - \delta_2}$$

In the two degrees of freedom model now considered we have

(4.29)

$$\frac{\partial \Omega_1}{\partial X_{11}} = \omega_{11} \qquad \frac{\partial \Omega_1}{\partial X_{21}} = \omega_{12}$$

$$\frac{\partial \Omega_2}{\partial X_{11}} = \omega_{21}\frac{\partial X_{12}}{\partial X_{11}} + \omega_{22}\frac{\partial X_{22}}{\partial X_{11}} \qquad \frac{\partial \Omega_2}{\partial X_{21}} = \omega_{21}\frac{\partial X_{12}}{\partial X_{21}} + \omega_{22}\frac{\partial X_{22}}{\partial X_{21}}$$

Furthermore, the condition for Pareto-optimality is now

(4.30) $$\frac{\dfrac{\partial \Omega_1}{\partial X_{11}}}{\dfrac{\partial \Omega_2}{\partial X_{11}}} = \frac{\dfrac{\partial \Omega_1}{\partial X_{21}}}{\dfrac{\partial \Omega_2}{\partial X_{21}}} = \text{negative}$$

Inserting in (4.29) from (4.27), and further inserting the expressions thus obtained in (4.30), we finally get

(4.31) $$\frac{\omega_{11}}{\omega_{12}} = \frac{\omega_{21}(1-\Delta) + \omega_{22} \cdot \dfrac{\Delta}{\Phi}}{\omega_{22}(1+\Delta) - \omega_{21}\Phi\Delta}$$

ω_{11} and $\left[\omega_{21}(1-\Delta) + \omega_{22}\frac{\Delta}{\Phi}\right]$ of the same sign (in the regular case both positive).

The formula (4.31) expresses a constraint consisting of one equation and a sign condition.

The result may be summarized in the following proposition:

Proposition (4.32)

$$Par[12,\, 20] = X[31,\, 12,\, 20]$$

In words: the region (of the four-dimensional space X_{11}, X_{12}, X_{21}, X_{22}) that is Pareto-optimal simultaneously under the production constraint (4.12)—

with given N—and the distribution constraint (4.20)—with given λ and the function L being defined by (4.19)—is the one-dimensional segment of points satisfying (4.31), (4.12) and (4.20).

Already a glance at the conditions (4.31) and (4.17) shows that we have here two fundamentally different kinds of regions. For instance, (4.31) depends on the second order derivatives of the production function while (4.17) depends only on the first order derivatives of these functions.

Any point that satisfies (4.17)—the Pareto condition under the weak constraint—must satisfy (4.31). Indeed, noticing that the right member of (4.17) is $\frac{1}{\Phi}$, we see that if (4.17) holds, so that $\omega_{22}=\Phi\omega_{21}$, (4.31) reduces to the first equation in (4.17). This applies no matter what magnitude has been fixed for λ. That is to say, any point that is *Par*[12] must satisfy *that* part of the conditions for *Par*[12, 20] which is expressed by (4.31). In other words, if we take any point in *Par*[12] and verify that it gives a certain value λ of the distribution ratio defined by (4.19), this is sufficient to make sure that the point in question is also *Par*[12, 20] under *this particular* value of λ.

Or again we may say: let λ be any given value of the distribution ratio (between the maximum and minimum assumed by the function L over *Par*[12]). Consider any point in *Par*[12] that gives this value of the distribution ratio. This point must also be *Par*[12, 20] with this value of λ. This checks with the general structure exhibited in Figure 5 (4.2).

On the other hand, let λ be any given number and consider the set of points which satisfy (4.31), (4.12) and (4.20) with this particular value of λ. We have no guarantee that this point will satisfy (4.17). In other words, within the set of points that give a certain distribution ratio, any point that is Pareto-optimal under the production constraint will be so also under the more inclusive set of constraints which consist of the production and distribution constraint with the given distribution ratio. But it is not true that any point which is Pareto-optimal under this more inclusive set of constraints is also Pareto-optimal under the production constraint. This checks with Figure 5 (4.2), where we may have a point such as A. No importance should be attached to the dimensionality of the regions in Figure 5 (4.2), they do not correspond to the dimensionalities in the example under consideration. Only the inclusion or non-inclusion of one region in another is important in Figure 5 (4.2).

In the discussion on Pareto-optimum, one way of reasoning which is frequently used is this: suppose that the individuals act on the assumption that prices are constant and let us determine Pareto-optimality under this condition. We can do it by introducing a system of prices and be careful to specify that they constitute *any* system of relative prices, the precise magnitude of them being determined *afterwards* through the equilibrium process itself.

As I see it, this specification does not help in the least to correct the fundamental logical fallacy involved. Any analysis of this sort means that the assumption of some sort of free competition is smuggled into the analysis already from the outset so that the conclusion can only be formulated by saying that "free competition is the best possible of all régimes in the class of régimes which consists of the régime of free competition". In other words: in the course of the analysis Pareto-optimality is determined under the *stronger* condition, while it should have been determined under the weaker condition. The example under consideration can illustrate what I have in mind.

Suppose that we do not begin by attributing any *specific* value to the distribution ratio λ, but let it have *any* value. Afterwards we may dispose of this value in some way which we find convenient, for instance we may just put it equal to the value which the function L assumes in the final point to which we may be led possibly by some sort of régime.

Let us determine the points that are Pareto-optimal under the set of conditions which consist first of the production constraint where the total labour input N is some *given* magnitude not to be determined by the equilibrium point, and second, *some* value λ of the distribution ratio, this value, however, to be determined afterwards as the value of the function L in the point in which we arrive, no matter what it might be. This formulation of the problem resembles, I think, in all logical essentials a type of reasoning frequently encountered in the discussion on Pareto-optimality.

As our example will show, the above proviso that the magnitude of the distribution ratio is to be taken as it emerges afterwards, does *not* correct the fundamental fallacy. Indeed, the solution to the present problem is obtained simply by inserting in (4.31) instead of λ the explicit expression for the function L in terms of its four variables, and *drop* the condition (4.20) that the distribution ratio shall have a given magnitude λ. This will lead to a two-dimensional point-set, namely the region in the four-dimensional space $(X_{11}, X_{12}, X_{21}, X_{22})$ which satisfies (4.12) and the single equation obtained from (4.31) by inserting $L(X_{11}, X_{12}, X_{21}, X_{22})$ instead of λ.[7]

Let $\delta_1(L)$ and $\delta_2(L)$ be the functions of $X_{11}, X_{12}, X_{21}, X_{22}$ obtained when we replace λ in (4.26) by the left member of (4.19). We get

$$\delta_1(L)=(1-\lambda)+\frac{\Phi\,.\,(X_{11}X_{22}-X_{12}X_{21})}{(X_{11}+X_{12})+\Phi\,.\,(X_{21}+X_{22})}\cdot\frac{f_1''}{(f_1')^2}$$

(4.33)

$$\delta_2(L)=(1-\lambda)-\frac{(X_{11}X_{22}-X_{21}X_{12})}{(X_{11}+X_{12})+\Phi\,.\,(X_{21}+X_{22})}\cdot\frac{f_2''}{(f_2')^2}$$

Inserting these expressions for δ_1 and δ_2 in the right member of (4.28), we get Δ as a function of the point $(X_{11}, X_{12}, X_{21}, X_{22})$, hence the whole right member of (4.31) becomes a function of the point.

[7] The fact that we now have a two-dimensional Pareto-optimal region is not in contradiction with the formula *min*[*m*—*s*, *n*—1] because this formula is to be applied *before* the optimization takes place. Any additional degrees of freedom that come in afterwards by letting certain previously fixed parameters become variable, must be added.

It is obvious that the pointset determined by the production constraint (4.12) and the constraint expressed by the new form of (4.31) will, in general, not belong to the pointset determined by the production constraint and (4.17), while on the other side any point in the latter set must belong to the first. In other words, if we ascertain that a point is Pareto-optimal in the special meaning now considered, *that does not tell us anything about whether it is Pareto-optimal under the production constraint or not.* Consequently it gives no criterion for whether the point represents an "effective" utilization of resources or not.

The question may be raised whether it might not be possible to escape the above antagonism between Pareto-optimality under different kinds of constraints by making special sorts of assumptions about the *shape of the production functions.*

In particular, it might be interesting to look into a special case which so frequently produces a particular sort of situation, namely the case where the production functions are homogeneous of the first order. In the present example this simply means that the marginal productivities f_1' and f_2' are *constant*, *i.e.* that f_1'' and f_2'' are zero. It will turn out that this particular case does not introduce any modification in the conclusions reached about the antagonism between the two types of Pareto-optimality.

The solution in the case now considered is obtained from (4.31) simply by letting Δ tend towards infinity. In this case the condition for Pareto-optimality under the production and distribution constraint reduces to

(4.34) $$(\omega_{11}\Phi-\omega_{12})\,(\omega_{21}\Phi-\omega_{22})=0$$

If the first parenthesis in (4.34) is different from zero, the second must be equal to zero, and *vice versa*. In other words, the optimality condition in the present case can be expressed by saying that *at least* one of the two expressions $(\omega_{11}\Phi-\omega_{12})$ and $(\omega_{21}\Phi-\omega_{22})$ must be equal to zero. When the condition is expressed in this form, we get a simple and very illustrative comparison with the condition (4.17) for Pareto-optimality under the production constraint only. The condition (4.17) states that *both* expressions $(\omega_{11}\Phi-\omega_{12})$ and $(\omega_{21}\Phi-\omega_{22})$ must be equal to zero. Thus, also in the case of homogeneous production functions of the first degree, it is true that a Pareto-optimality determined under the production *and* distribution constraint does *not* entail a Pareto-optimality determined under the production constraint only, while the inverse is true (for all points having the desired distribution ratio). Pareto-optimality under a stronger condition leads to a *more inclusive* pointset than Pareto-optimality under a weaker condition.

5. The Region which is Pareto-optimal under a Set of Conditions expressed partly or wholly by Inequalities. The Pareto-pressure

The examples so far have only been concerned with conditions expressed in the form of equations. We now turn to the more complex case where some of, or all, the conditions are expressed by inequalities. By introducing one more variable for each inequality, any system involving inequalities can, of course, be reduced to a system involving only equations and *sign conditions* on one or more variables. (This re-formulation of the problem is, for instance, sometimes found useful in linear programming.)

We will illustrate the case now considered by studying rather carefully a simplified example.

Let the quantities of two goods X_1 and X_2—say "public health service" and "public radio entertainment"—be evaluated by two individuals Nos. 1 and 2. Let the indifference lines be as indicated in Figure 6 (5.1). The figure indicates a

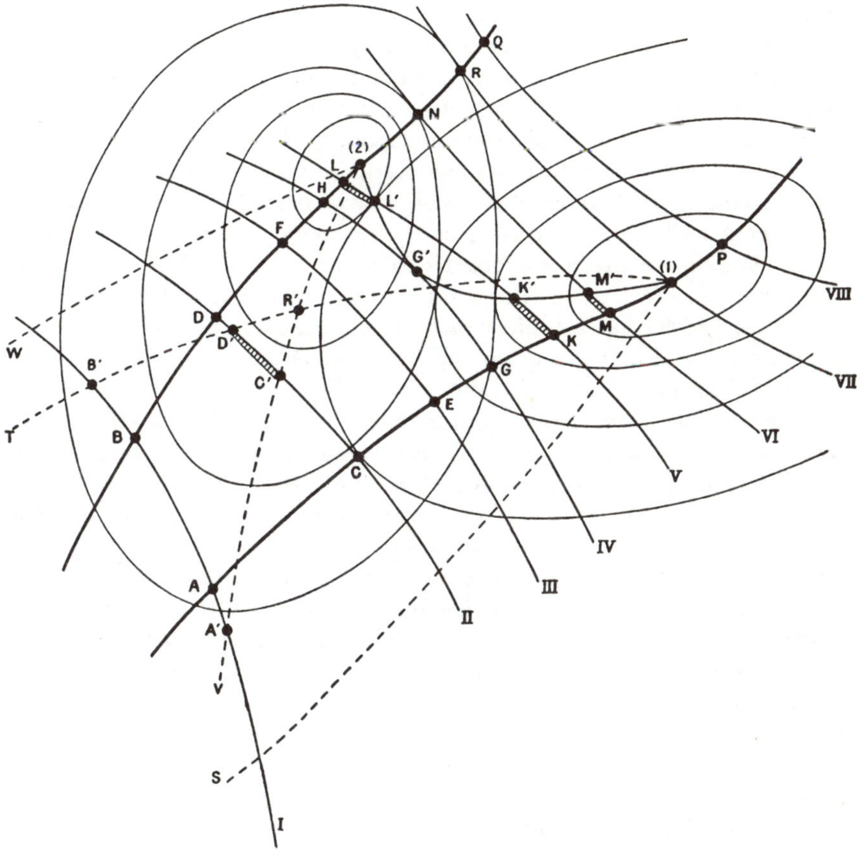

FIG. 6 (5.1)

situation where the individual No. 1 attributes greater weight to health service and smaller weight to radio entertainment than No. 2 does. Let $\Omega_1(X_1, X_2)$ and $\Omega_2(X_1, X_2)$ be the indicators of choice, and suppose there exists between X_1 and X_2 a production constraint such that for given magnitudes of some common factor of production—say "labour"—one gets the isoquants Nos. I, II, ... VIII. Let the curve *ACE* ... *P* be determined by the tangency of isoquants with the indifference curves of individual No. 1. Similarly we get the curve *BDF* ... Q for individual No. 2. Let (1)*S* and (1)*T* be the locus of points where the indifference lines for No. 1 are horizontal and vertical, respectively. The curve (2)*V* and (2)*W* has a similar meaning for individual No. 2. Thus: in the region *S*(1)*T* the preference direction for individual No. 1 has both its components positive, in the region *V*(2)*W* the preference direction for individual No. 2 has both its components positive, and in the region *TR'V* all four preference components are positive. The finite curve segment (1)M'*K'G'L'*(2) is—as follows from the reasoning in connection with Figure 4 (3.14)—the region that is Pareto-optimal under no constraint.

We start by considering the case where it is *prescribed* that exactly so much of the common factor of production shall be used that the (X_1, X_2) point falls somewhere on the isoquant marked I—*i.e.* somewhere on the curve *A'ABB'*. The finite segment *AB* of this isoquant represents the points that are Pareto-optimal for the group of the two individuals 1 and 2 under the constraint that exactly so much of the common factor of production shall be used as is indicated by the isoquant I. Indeed any point on this segment—and no point outside of it—has the property that it is impossible to depart from it without making one of the individuals worse off. Along this segment the interests of the two individuals are directly opposed. No. 1 wants to go in the direction of *A* and No. 2 in the direction of *B*. The segment *AB* is situated entirely in the region *TR'V* where all four preference components are positive.

If the quantity used of the common factor is increased so much that the isoquant becomes II, the region which is Pareto-optimal under the production constraint becomes the finite segment *CD*. Of this segment only the part *C'D'* is situated in the region where all the four preference components are positive. On the isoquant III the Pareto-optimal segment is *EF*. Here there are *no points* where all preference components are positive. The requirement that exactly so much *shall* be used of the common factor, entails that at least one of the preference components for one of the individuals must become negative. We must either produce so much public radio-entertainment that it becomes a nuisance to individual No. 1, or so much public health service that it becomes a nuisance to No. 2.[8]

On the isoquant IV—where the conditional Pareto-optimal region is the finite segment *GH*—there is *one point*, namely *G'*, which is at the same time Pareto-optimal under no constraint. This gives another example of the fact that Pareto-optimality under a weak condition plus the additional requirement that the point shall satisfy a certain constraint, is sufficient to ensure that the point is Pareto-optimal under the stronger condition obtained by appending the additional requirement to the original weak condition.

[8] A supplement to the Pareto-criterion might perhaps be to *require* that all the preference components of all the individuals shall be non-negative. I shall, however, not go into this question here.

On the isoquant V—where the conditional Pareto-optimal region is the segment *LK*—there are two points, namely *L′* and *K′*, that are at the same time unconditionally Pareto-optimal.

On the isoquant VI the conditional Pareto-segment is *MN*. This isoquant is different from the isoquants so far considered in one respect: there is one individual, No. 2, who can find no point on the Pareto-optimal segment of VI, which is as preferable to him as the most preferable point on the preceding isoquant V.

The isoquant VII—where the conditional Pareto-optimal region is *PQ*—is even such that *none* of the individuals can find a point in the Pareto region on this isoquant, which to him is more preferable than the most preferable point on the preceding isoquant VI.

On the isoquant VIII we can make a similar statement—in relation to VII—and we can even replace the term "more preferable" by "equally preferable".

Each of the above Pareto-optimal regions was defined under the condition that the quantity used of the common factor should be *exactly* the quantity represented by the isoquant in question.

Let us now go through the same alternatives, but each time replace the condition exactly equal to by *not larger than*. This means that in the first case—isoquant I—the condition is that the point may be anywhere on this isoquant or *South-West of it*. Which points in this area are Pareto-optimal for the two individuals? Obviously, again the segment *AB*. Similar reasoning for all the isoquants II-IV.

For the isoquant V the situation becomes different. The region which is Pareto-optimal under the condition that the quantity used of the common factor shall be equal to, or less than, that represented by the isoquant V, is the curve made up of the segments *LL′* and *L′G′K′* and *K′K*. This is easily seen by a method of analysis similar to the one used in connection with Figure 4 (3.14).

For the isoquant VI the Pareto region will be made up of the two segments (2)*L′G′K′M′* and *M′M*. Here again we see an example of the fact that the points (namely, the segment *K′G′L′*) that are Pareto-optimal under the weak condition (VI) and satisfy the strong condition (V) must also be Pareto-optimal under the strong condition (V). And we see that there are points (namely, the segments *KK′* and *LL′*, endpoints *K′* and *L′* not included) that are Pareto-optimal under the strong condition (V) without being Pareto-optimal under the weak condition (VI).

For the constraint defined by the isoquant VII the Pareto-optimal region will be the segment (2)*L′G′K′M′*(1), *i.e.* the same as the region which is Pareto-optimal under no constraint. The same will be true for any of the higher isoquants, such as, for instance, VIII.

We will now study these various situations from the point of view of the *sequence* which they form. That is, we consider the sequence of situations that is characterized by the isoquants I, II, III ... VIII, each of these isoquants now being interpreted not as a locus of admissible points, but as the North-East boundary of a set of admissible points. This means that the conditions considered form a sequence of conditions that become weaker and weaker. We shall say that a condition C_2 is effectively weaker than a condition C_1 if the set of points that satisfies C_2 contains all the points satisfying C_1 and at least one other point. The sequence of conditions now considered obviously satisfies this criterion.

In the sequence now considered, the isoquant IV—or more precisely the region whose North-East boundary is isoquant IV—occupies a special position. There is indeed a distinct difference between the isoquants *lower* than IV and those *higher* than IV. Any isoquant in the range below IV has the property that if we pass from this isoquant to a higher one in the sequence, we find that the Pareto region corresponding to this higher isoquant *contains no point* that belongs to the Pareto region corresponding to the lower isoquant. This means that to any point X in the Pareto region obtained by taking the lower isoquant as a constraint, there corresponds at least one point X' situated within the boundary given by the higher isoquant, but not within that given by the lower isoquant, which is Pareto-preferred to X under the new (and weaker) conditions. We can therefore say that from the Pareto viewpoint *an unquestionable gain is obtained by weakening the condition.*

This does *not* apply to isoquant IV itself or to any of the higher isoquants. True enough, *something* is gained by passing, say, from IV to V, namely *a larger variety* of points that are Pareto-optimal, but, to use a simplified expression, "none of these points are any Pareto-better than the best point attainable under the old (and stronger) condition". More precisely expressed: each point X' obtainable under the new (and weaker) condition is such that we can indicate at least one point X which was attainable already under the old (and stronger) conditions and which is such that X' is not Pareto-preferred to X under the new (and weaker) conditions.

Starting with the isoquant VII, we see that this and the higher isoquants even have the property that the Pareto-optimal region remains *unchanged* as the condition is weakened. We may generalize these considerations in the form of the following definition :

Definition (5.2). Let $C(\alpha)$ be a one-dimensional pencil of conditions, that is, a sequence of conditions depending on a parameter α, such that an effective increase in α means an effective *weakening* of the condition, *i.e.* if $\alpha_2>\alpha_1$, any point that satisfies $C(\alpha_1)$ will also satisfy $C(\alpha_2)$ and there exists at least one point which satisfies $C(\alpha_2)$ but not $C(\alpha_1)$. If the pointset $Par[C(\alpha_2)]$ contains *no point* belonging to $Par[C(\alpha_1)]$, when $\alpha_2>\alpha_1$, we shall say that there exists a positive Pareto-pressure on α from α_1 to α_2.

An essential feature of this definition is that $Par[C(\alpha_2)]$ shall contain *no point* belonging to $Par[C(\alpha_1)]$. We do not use the weaker formulation that $Par[C(\alpha_2)]$ shall contain *some points* that do *not* belong to $Par[C(\alpha_1)]$. If we want to use only the kind of criteria that are genuine to a Pareto-optimality way of thinking, we can indeed not say that any point within a given Pareto region is any better than another point in this region. Therefore, if by weakening the condition we have found a new Pareto region that contains one or more points that belonged already to the old Pareto region, we cannot say that we have found something that is actually better than what we had before.

Nor can we approach the definition of a Pareto pressure, for instance, by saying that there exists a positive Pareto pressure on the parameter that generates the conditions, if at least one of the points that satisfy the new (weaker) condition, but not the old (stronger) condition, is Pareto-preferred—under the new conditions—to all points that satisfy the old condition. If such a situation should occur, we would certainly be led to say that there exists a pressure of an extremely heavy sort. But this idea of looking for a point that *is actually Pareto-preferred to all other points* (in a certain admissible region) is not genuine to the way of thinking in Pareto-optimality analysis. Such a point would exist only in cases that are so extremely particular as to be virtually trivial. The definition (5.2) on the contrary builds on ideas that are natural in Pareto-optimality analysis.

An obvious generalization is to consider a set of conditions depending on two or more parameters. This would lead to the concept of *directional* Pareto pressure, that is Pareto pressure defined by changing one of the parameters while keeping all the others constant. The concept of the region of the parameter space where all the directional Pareto pressures are positive would then indicate a situation where all the parameters are far from being "free goods" in the Pareto sense.

6. The Problem of the Régime

All the above arguments pertained to the *selection* problem, that is, to the definition of the point X which it is considered "desirable" to reach. Having decided on such a point or on a class of such points, the next question is to indicate a *régime* or a class of régimes which will achieve this goal.

From the analysis of the previous section we know that a point X that shall be Pareto-optimal under the production constraint (when a change in quantities is possible) must have the marginal preferences proportional for all the individuals and proportional to marginal costs. Contrary to what is commonly believed, such a point *cannot* be reached under a system of production and distribution possessing the characteristics which are commonly associated with free competition and a system of income taxes and capital taxes of the usual type and a "neutral" monetary system.

I shall discuss this by considering a number of *special cases* that are constructed on several different assumptions. From these special cases I shall extract certain conclusions that will seem to hold under very general conditions.

In all the subsequent discussions it is vitally important to be fully aware of the nature of the *constraints* under which Pareto-optimality is defined. When it comes to discussing the optimality-conditions of a régime, any reasoning that is not built on a terminology and mathematical symbolism that express the *kind* of

Pareto-optimality involved in the argument (the nature of the constraints), is *a waste of time*. Just as it would be a waste of time to discuss the "derivative" of a function of several variables without indicating the variable with respect to which the derivative is to be taken.

Can abstract discussions on Pareto-optimality be of any practical significance at all for questions of economic policy? Yes, I am convinced that they do have great practical significance. Even though this reasoning involves many quantitative concepts that cannot be measured *directly* through actual observation, certain important *conclusions* can be drawn which are of paramount practical importance. These conclusions show amongst others that most present-day taxation systems are in one particular respect extremely questionable—to say the least.

In a general way we may say that the useful result that can be deduced from discussions of this type, consists in asserting that certain economic régimes do *not* satisfy certain optimality criteria which would seem to be of such a nature that we *must* accept them. In other words, Pareto-optimality is a principle of *negation*, not one of affirmation. In this it has the same logical structure as the statistical testing of hypotheses. What statistical testing can do, is to *reject* a hypothesis.

Logically the first step in a discussion of Pareto-optimality is to formulate the *obligatory conditions*, that is certain conditions which we will accept as the basis of the analysis. For instance, certain fundamentals regarding the technical aspects of production, or certain basic human rights, etc. The formulation of these obligatory conditions has logically much in common with the circumscription of the class of *admissible* hypotheses in statistical testing.

Once the obligatory conditions are formulated, we are by pure logic, without the intervention of any social value judgements, led to formulate the criterion that no régime can be accepted as satisfactory if it is *not* Pareto-optimal under the obligatory constraints.

This criterion may exclude a great number of particular régimes, but it will, in general, not lead to the selection of *one* particular régime. In general, there will be a whole class of régimes which are Pareto-optimal under the obligatory constraints. Here is where the spectrum of social value judgements comes in.

The economist as scientist and technician simply has to take these judgements as *data*. As citizen he has as much as, but nothing more, to say about these value judgements than other citizens. When the supplementary conditions derived from social value judgements are given, all the rest is within the sphere of competence of the economist. This limitation of the economist's field is necessary for the maintenance of his objectivity and self-respect *as a scientist*. It would seem that even with this healthy limitation of the economist's field, there is more than enough for him to do.

With this general philosophy in mind I now turn to a study of some models of régimes.

Case 1

Consider first the model defined by (4.6)-(4.12). If it is humanly possible to impose a sufficiently strong *control-system* and one is willing to take the inconveniences that go with this régime, one could produce a preassigned combination of X_{11}, X_{12}, X_{21} and X_{22}. By choosing this combination in an appropriate way, it would seem that one could always reach a point that has a *preassigned* distribution ratio (within certain objectively given limits) and at the same time satisfies (4.12) and (4.17), which by (4.18) means that the point is Pareto-optimal under the production constraint. The following will illustrate this and also illustrate that such a situation cannot be realized by decontrolling the market completely.

Suppose, for instance, that forced labour is used so as to ensure a given magnitude of N. Suppose that a certain sum of money R_1 is given to the first individual and another sum R_2 to the second individual and that prices of the two goods are not controlled but left to be determined by the play of forces in the market. Suppose that each individual acts as a quantity adapter under the conjectural assumption that prices are constant. Finally, suppose that the central production authority has full knowledge of the preference functions of the individuals so that it is able to calculate what the prices will become under a given set of conditions, and also suppose that the authority distributes the available labour force between the two industries so as to achieve proportionality between marginal labour costs and prices. Under this régime we will have

(6.1) For individual 1: $\frac{\omega_{12}}{\omega_{11}}=\frac{p_2}{p_1} \qquad p_1X_{11}+p_2X_{21}=R_1$

(6.2) For individual 2: $\frac{\omega_{22}}{\omega_{21}}=\frac{p_2}{p_1} \qquad p_1X_{12}+p_2X_{22}=R_2$

(6.3) Production policy equation: $\frac{p_2}{p_1}=\frac{f_1'(f_1^{-1}(X_{11}+X_{12}))}{f_2'(f_2^{-1}(X_{21}+X_{22}))}$

Finally we have the production constraint (4.12). This gives a total of six independent equations which determine the six variables X_{11}, X_{12}, X_{21}, X_{22}, p_1 and p_2. In the present case where the absolute magnitudes of R_1 and R_2 are given, the absolute prices—not only the relative prices—will be determined. Thus, the régime considered leads, in general, to a well-defined equilibrium point. The equilibrium point now considered satisfies the conditions (4.12) and (4.17), hence is Pareto-optimal under the production constraint (4.12). This applies whatever the magnitudes of R_1 and R_2 (within admissible limits); hence the equilibrium point will show a prescribed distribution coefficient.[9]

The pure exchange market *without* production but with given initial quantities can also easily be analysed in terms of this example with a central authority

[9] By (6.1)-(6.3) the ratio between R_1 and R_2 is a technically given function of the four quantities X_{ij}. Maximizing and minimizing this expression, we *may* get upper and/or lower limits for the ratio R_1/R_2.

that gives certain amounts R_1 and R_2 to the two individuals. This is a distribution condition expressed by

(6.4) $$R_1 = \text{given} \qquad R_2 = \text{given}$$

The "production" constraint is now expressed by (6.18). Necessary and sufficient for Pareto-optimality under this condition is easily seen to be simply the proportionality of marginal utilities (see (6.21)), *i.e.* the first member of (4.17), with the appropriate sign condition. A point of this character is alway reached if the central authority gives arbitrarily given amounts R_1 and R_2 to the two individuals. The equilibrium point will then be given by the six equations (6.1), (6.2) and (6.4). This determines the four X and the two p. In this case the absolute prices are determined. On the other hand, if the central authority fixes the *real* expenditures R_1/p_1 and R_2/p_2, only the relative prices are determined. The quantity combination is determined and is the same as before. The exchange market with given initial quantities is only a verbal reformulation of this case.

This case has not much in common with "free competition" under realistic circumstances. Indeed, who shall determine the *given* initial quantities that characterize the real income distribution? Some dictator?

The crucial question in a modern society is, of course, just this: does the excessively skew income distribution that is produced by the "free play of the forces", represent a state of affairs that in some sense of the word can be considered as optimal within a certain class of states *between which we choose*? The case with given initial quantities has therefore no realistic relevance whatsoever for a discussion of whether the régime of free competition can be considered an "optimal" system or not.

But suppose that the income distribution is corrected, say, by an *income tax* system? Would it not then be an "optimal" procedure to leave the market to the free play of the forces? It would not. As will appear from the examples below, *no régime* of "free competition" with an income tax on labour can produce an equilibrium point that is Pareto-optimal under the production constraint.

Case 2

We will now change the model somewhat in the direction of a free economy, but still maintain it within the framework of (4.6)-(4.12), for which we have determined the region that is Pareto-optimal under the production constraint. We assume that there has by custom or by regulation of working hours or in some other way been fixed certain amounts of work N_{11} and N_{21} which the individual No. 1 performs in the industries 1 and 2, respectively. Similarly we assume certain fixed amounts N_{12} and N_{22} for individual No. 2. These four magnitudes, which we prefer to write in the order

(6.5) $$N_{11}, \quad N_{12}, \quad N_{21}, \quad N_{22}$$

are for the time being assumed given. That is to say, no adaptation of the working hours is supposed to take place as a consequence of changes in prices and wages, etc. Consequently the total amounts of work performed in the two industries are also given, namely

$$N_i = N_{i1} + N_{i2} \qquad (i=1,\ 2) \tag{6.6}$$

Suppose that we now let the prices of the two goods, *i.e.* p_1 and p_2, as well as the wage rates in the two industries, q_1 and q_2, be determined by the play of the forces in the market, each of the two industries acting as a quantity adapter trying to maximize profit.[10] Each of the two individuals will, as before, try to maximize his preference function, but the budget equation is now obtained by expressing that the value of the goods purchased is equal to the value of the wages received—after correction for taxes.

We consider a *tax* T imposed as a certain constant—a *per capita* tax—on individual No. 1, the proceeds of the tax to be given to individual No. 2. The magnitude T may be positive or negative, it may be looked upon simply as an *income redistribution parameter*. Under this régime the following equations will hold:

$$\frac{\omega_{12}}{\omega_{11}} = \frac{p_2}{p_1} \qquad p_1 X_{11} + p_2 X_{21} = q_1 N_{11} + q_2 N_{21} - T \tag{6.7}$$

$$\frac{\omega_{22}}{\omega_{21}} = \frac{p_2}{p_1} \qquad p_1 X_{12} + p_2 X_{22} = q_1 N_{12} + q_2 N_{22} + T \tag{6.8}$$

$$f_1' = \frac{q_1}{p_1} \tag{6.9}$$

$$f_2' = \frac{q_2}{p_2} \tag{6.10}$$

(6.7) and (6.8) are the adaptation equations of the first and second individuals respectively, (6.9) and (6.10) are the adaptation equations of the two industries. In addition we have to reckon with the two production equations

$$X_{11} + X_{12} = f_1(N_{11} + N_{12}) \qquad X_{21} + X_{22} = f_1(N_{21} + N_{22}) \tag{6.11}$$

This gives a total of eight independent equations.

We may attribute to the nominal value of the income redistribution parameter T an *arbitrary* value, with the proviso, however, of distinguishing fundamentally between a zero and a non-zero value of T as explained below. To any such given value of T there will correspond an equilibrium point under the régime (6.7)-(6.11), and a comparison of the form of these equations with those of (4.18) shows that the equilibrium point now reached is Pareto-optimal under the single production constraint (4.12). Since (4.12) is a weaker constraint than (6.11) and we know that the point now considered satisfies this stronger condition (6.11), we can conclude that it is Pareto-optimal under the stronger production constraint (6.11).

[10] The fact that total labour in the industries is *objectively* given does not prevent bidding by the entrepreneurs under a *conjectural* variation where they take account of marginal productivities.

This fact, however, must not be interpreted to mean that under the régime considered it is possible to reach an equilibrium point which is Pareto-optimal under the production constraint (6.11) and gives a preassigned *real*-income distribution as defined by the distribution coefficient λ in (4.20). To believe this would be an error of the "homogeneity-kind", that is an error which has emerged by not being sufficiently aware of the particular form of the equations with respect to homogeneity.

The situation under the régime (6.7)-(6.11) is as follows: *by changing the value of* T *one would simply change proportionally all prices and wage rates.* Hence the *real value* of T, that is, its *deflated* value, would remain unchanged. This deflated value of T is determined by the régime (6.7)-(6.11). That is to say, under the régime considered it is *necessary to perform a specific real-income redistribution, in order that the system of equations shall have a solution.* The amount of this income redistribution, reckoned in real, *i.e.* deflated, values *must* be a specific number in order that the equations shall be solvable. In other words, if the production functions and the preference functions have arbitrarily given shapes, we can *not* influence the real income distribution.

This follows from the nature of the solution. First consider the equation obtained by taking the sum of the two budget equations for the two individuals. This equation is

$$(6.12) \qquad p_1(X_{11}+X_{12})+p_2(X_{21}+X_{22})=q_1(N_{11}+N_{12})+q_2(N_{21}+N_{22})$$

In other words, the two industries taken together must produce with a zero profit. That this emerges as a consequence of the two budget equations of the individuals shows that the régime now considered is a plausible one for discussing distribution as a problem *between the two individuals.* If we should introduce the concept of a surplus going to the industries, *i.e.* a part of the national income which did *not* go to one or the other of the two individuals, the whole problem of the Pareto region would have to be reconsidered, now with (at least) one third party besides the two individuals (compare Case 7). What sorts of concrete arrangements one could apply in the industries in order to assure the fulfilment of (6.12) is not relevant in this connection.

Equation (6.12) together with the first two equations of (6.7) and (6.8) and the equations (6.9)-(6.11) give a total of seven independent equations in the seven variables $X_{11}, X_{12}, X_{21}, X_{22}$ and $\frac{p_2}{p_1}, \frac{q_1}{p_1}, \frac{q_2}{p_2}$. Eliminating the last three of these variables, we get the following set of four independent equations between the four variables X_{11}, X_{12}, X_{21}, X_{22}: the two production equations (6.11) and the two equations

$$(6.13) \qquad \frac{\omega_{11}}{\omega_{12}}=\frac{\omega_{21}}{\omega_{22}} \text{ which may also be written } \begin{vmatrix} \omega_{11} & \omega_{12} \\ \omega_{21} & \omega_{22} \end{vmatrix}=0$$

and

$$(6.14) \qquad \omega_{i1}(X_{11}+X_{12}).(1-\epsilon_1)+\omega_{i2}(X_{21}+X_{22}).(1-\epsilon_2)=0 \text{ (for an arbitrary } i)$$

The equation (6.14) may be taken for an arbitrary i. If it holds for one i, it will by (6.13) hold also for the other i.

The functions ϵ_1 and ϵ_2 are the passus-coefficients of the two production functions, *i.e.*

$$\epsilon_i = \frac{f_i' \cdot N_i}{X_i} \qquad (i=1, 2) \tag{6.15}$$

ϵ_i, like f_i, is a function of one variable. As its argument we may take N_i or X_i. Over a region where the production function $f_i(N_i)$ is monotonic, it does not matter whether we take N_i or X_i as the argument of ϵ_i.

The four equations (6.11), (6.13) and (6.14) contain—when the four N are given—only the four variables X_{11}, X_{12}, X_{21}, X_{22}. This set of equations will therefore—apart from degenerate cases—define the point X in four-dimensional space that will be realized under the régime (6.7)-(6.11). By means of the four equations mentioned, this definition of the point X is achieved *directly* without any reference to how prices and wages will work out or how the income transfer T is fixed. The point X determined by these four equations is not subject to any argument of the form: "it cannot hold because then this price—or this wage rate—would change". It is a great advantage to have the point X fixed by such a system of equations.

When the point X in four-dimensional space is fixed, we derive from, say, the first of the budget equations of the individuals

$$\frac{T}{p_1} = X_1\left[\frac{X_{11}}{X_1} - \epsilon_1\frac{N_{11}}{N_1}\right] + \frac{\omega_{12}}{\omega_{11}}X_2\left[\frac{X_{21}}{X_2} - \epsilon_2\frac{N_{21}}{N_2}\right] \tag{6.16}$$

The right member of (6.16) depends *only on the point* X (and the given values of the N_{ij}). Hence, since the point X is fixed by the régime, the real (deflated) value of T is also fixed.

This argument shows immediately what conditions must be put on T from the viewpoint of zero or non-zero values. If the nature of the preference functions and the production functions is such that under the given values of the N_{ij} the equilibrium point in X_{ij}, as determined by the four equations mentioned, turns out to make the right member of (6.16) zero, then only zero-values of T are permissible. That is to say, if under these conditions we tried to impose any form of income transfers, we would run into an incompatible system. That is to say, the model could not give a realistic picture of what would actually happen. We could only say that some of the relations considered would in the world of realities have to break down. The most effective way to discuss this situation might be the introduction of the pressure coefficients of the decision-model—they can describe the tension towards "instability" and "crisis"—but I shall not enter into details on this here.

On the other hand, if in the equilibrium point the right member of (6.16) is different from zero, then only non-zero values of the income transfer T are permissible. More precisely: only values of T are permissible which are of the *same sign* as the value which the right member of (6.16) assumes in the equilibrium point (and it is wanted to have a regime with a positive price p_1).

The wage-rate ratio $\frac{q_1}{q_2}$ is also determined as a function of the equilibrium point. From (6.7), (6.9) and (6.10) we get indeed

$$\frac{q_1}{q_2} = \frac{\omega_{11}}{\omega_{12}} \cdot \frac{f_1'}{f_2'} \tag{6.17}$$

The price ratio $\frac{p_2}{p_1}$ is given as a function of the equilibrium point by any of the equations (6.7) or (6.8).

To see whether the equilibrium point now reached is Pareto-optimal under the production constraint, let us determine the region of points that now have this property. The production constraint can now be written

$$X_{11}+X_{12}=X_1 \text{ (given)} \qquad X_{21}+X_{22}=X_2 \text{ (given)} \tag{6.18}$$

Taking X_{11} and X_{21} as independent variables, we have

$$\begin{aligned} \frac{\partial \Omega_1}{\partial X_{11}} &= \omega_{11} \qquad & \frac{\partial \Omega_1}{\partial X_{21}} &= \omega_{12} \\ \frac{\partial \Omega_2}{\partial X_{11}} &= -\omega_{21} \qquad & \frac{\partial \Omega_2}{\partial X_{21}} &= -\omega_{22} \end{aligned} \tag{6.19}$$

The condition for Pareto-optimality under the production constraint in the present case, namely

$$\frac{\dfrac{\partial \Omega_1}{\partial X_{11}}}{\dfrac{\partial \Omega_2}{\partial X_{11}}} = \frac{\dfrac{\partial \Omega_1}{\partial X_{21}}}{\dfrac{\partial \Omega_2}{\partial X_{21}}} = \text{negative}, \tag{6.20}$$

can therefore be written

$$\frac{\omega_{11}}{\omega_{12}} = \frac{\omega_{21}}{\omega_{22}} \qquad \omega_{12} \text{ and } \omega_{22} \text{ of the same sign.} \tag{6.21}$$

Thus Pareto-optimality in the present case does *not* require proportionality between marginal utilities and marginal productivities as, for instance, in (4.17).

The fulfilment of (6.21) is assured by (6.7) and (6.8) (apart from the sign condition, which we may assume to hold except in pathological cases).

To summarize: if the *real* value of the income transfer is fixed at the magnitude which it must have in order to make equilibrium possible, the equilibrium point produced by the régime considered will be Pareto-optimal under the production constraint. If the real value of the income transfer is not fixed at this magnitude, no point satisfying the régime exists.

In the *pari passu* case, that is, in the case where both production functions are homogeneous of the first order, *i.e.* both ϵ_1 and ϵ_2 identically equal to 1, the equation (6.14) *drops out* and the régime considered has a solution with one degree of freedom. In this case a certain leeway is left in the fixation of the real value of the income transfer. If we note the maximum and minimum assumed by the right member of (6.16) over the one-dimensional region that now gives the solution, the real value of the income transfer (the deflation being done by p_1) may be fixed arbitrarily at any magnitude between this maximum and minimum.

If a model of this sort is to be reasonably realistic, we will have to assume that there is only a small span between the maximum and minimum referred to. The *pari passu* case is, indeed, not a realistic one, as witnessed by the fact that so much of the discussion in other sectors of distribution theory proceeds on the assumption that output is *not* for all values of the input proportional to input. In the present case we must therefore take *arbitrarily given* shapes of the production functions and discuss what consequences will follow from such a general assumption. These consequences are contained in the above remarks on the real value of the income transfer.

Case 3

One might perhaps think that if the amounts N_{ij} of the labour inputs were considered as *variables* to be adapted by the individuals according to the price and wage structure, the situation would be radically changed and then it would be possible to achieve an equilibrium point which is Pareto-optimal under a condition which simply consists of the production constraint, and at the same time gives a preassigned distribution of the national income. Closer examination will reveal, however, that this is not so. It will turn out that the above conclusions about the real value of the income transfer are valid also under the new régime now considered.

Indeed, consider a model with X_{11}, X_{12}, X_{21}, X_{22} and N_{11}, N_{12}, N_{21}, N_{22}, as basic variables. Suppose that each individual has a preference function

$$(6.22) \qquad \Omega_j(X_{1j}, X_{2j}, N_{1j}, N_{2j}) \qquad (j=1, 2)$$

with continuous partial derivatives

$$(6.23) \qquad \omega_{ji}=\frac{\partial\Omega_j}{\partial X_{ij}} \qquad \omega_{j(i)}=\frac{\partial\Omega_j}{\partial N_{ij}} \qquad \begin{pmatrix} i=1, 2 \\ j=1, 2 \end{pmatrix}$$

As before, let the production functions be given. The production constraints are then given by the two equations (6.11). Since the distribution of the labour force between the two industries is now to be considered explicitly in the optimization process, we have to take the production constraint in the form (6.11), not only in the form (4.12).

Let us first determine the region which is Pareto-optimal under the production constraint (6.11). We have $n=2$, $m=8$, $s=2$, hence $min[m-s, n-1]=1$, so that the region to be looked for is one-dimensional.

Disregarding for a moment the sign conditions for derivatives, we make a simple analysis by means of Lagrange multipliers. This leads to maximizing the function

$$(6.24) \quad (\Theta_1\Omega_1+\Theta_2\Omega_2)+\mu_3[X_{11}+X_{12}-f_1(N_{11}+N_{12})]+ \\ +\mu_4[X_{21}+X_{22}-f_2(N_{21}+N_{22})]$$

on the assumption that the four X and the four N are free variables while the four parameters Θ_1, Θ_2, μ_3 and μ_4 are constants. Equating the eight partial derivatives to zero, we get

$$(6.25) \quad \begin{array}{ll} \Theta_1\omega_{11}+\mu_3=0 & \Theta_1\omega_{1(1)}-\mu_3 f_1'=0 \\ \Theta_1\omega_{12}+\mu_4=0 & \Theta_1\omega_{1(2)}-\mu_4 f_2'=0 \\ \Theta_2\omega_{21}+\mu_3=0 & \Theta_2\omega_{2(1)}-\mu_3 f_1'=0 \\ \Theta_2\omega_{22}+\mu_4=0 & \Theta_2\omega_{2(2)}-\mu_4 f_2'=0 \end{array}$$

That is

$$(6.26) \quad \begin{array}{ll} \dfrac{\mu_3}{\Theta_1}=-\omega_{11}=\dfrac{\omega_{1(1)}}{f_1'} & \dfrac{\mu_3}{\Theta_2}=-\omega_{21}=\dfrac{\omega_{2(1)}}{f_1'} \\ \dfrac{\mu_4}{\Theta_1}=-\omega_{12}=\dfrac{\omega_{1(2)}}{f_2'} & \dfrac{\mu_4}{\Theta_2}=-\omega_{22}=\dfrac{\omega_{2(2)}}{f_2'} \end{array}$$

If we eliminate from the system the ratios between the multipliers (this takes out three equations), we get the following five equations:

$$(6.27) \quad \frac{-\omega_{1(i)}}{\omega_{1i}}=\frac{-\omega_{2(i)}}{\omega_{2i}}=f_i' \qquad (i=1,2)$$

$$(6.28) \quad \frac{\omega_{11}}{\omega_{12}}=\frac{\omega_{21}}{\omega_{22}}$$

These five equations together with the two equations (6.11) determine the one-dimensional region which is Pareto-optimal under the production constraint in the present case. For the argument which follows it is not necessary to discuss the sign condition on the derivatives.

Now let us consider the following régime: as in Case 2, we assume prices p_1 and p_2 as well as wage rates q_1 and q_2 to be determined by the free play of the forces in the market, each of the two industries acting as a quantity adapter trying to maximize profits, and each of the two individuals trying to maximize his preference function under the same kind of budget equations as in (6.7) and (6.8), but now not only with the X, but also the N as free variables. This régime leads to the following equilibrium equations:

$$(6.29) \quad \frac{q_i}{p_i}=\frac{-\omega_{1(i)}}{\omega_{1i}}=\frac{-\omega_{2(i)}}{\omega_{2i}}=f_i' \qquad (i=1,2)$$

$$(6.30) \quad \frac{p_1}{p_2}=\frac{\omega_{11}}{\omega_{12}}=\frac{\omega_{21}}{\omega_{22}}$$

These eight equations together with the two budget equations—the same as those written to the right in (6.7) and (6.8)—and the two production constraints (6.11) give a total of twelve independent equations to determine the eight basic variables X_{ij} and N_{ij} together with the four variables $\frac{q_1}{p_1}, \frac{q_2}{p_2}, \frac{p_2}{p_1}$ and $\frac{T}{p_1}$. In other words, we have exactly the same kind of solution as in Case 2. Also in the present case will the equilibrium values of X_{ij} and N_{ij} be independent of the choice of the nominal value of T, a change in T only entailing a corresponding proportional change in the prices and wages rates. The formula for the *real value* of the income transfer will also now be (6.16). All the rest of the discussion can be repeated practically word by word as in Case 2.

Case 4

This case will illustrate a general proposition which can best be brought out by a still more simplified example.

Consider the case where there is only one individual (one typical individual representing the whole working population) and one industry (representing the whole production activity of the nation). Let X be the quantity produced and N the input of labour. Let $\Omega(X,N)$ be the preference function of the representative individual and $f(N)$ the production function of the representative industry.

The region which is Pareto-optimal under the production constraint in the present case is simply the social optimum point defined by seeking the unconditional maximum of the function $\Omega(f(N), N)$ of the single variable N. This point is obviously determined by

(6.31) $$\frac{-\omega_N}{\omega_X}=f'$$

where $\omega_X=\frac{\partial\Omega}{\partial X}$, $\omega_N=\frac{\partial\Omega}{\partial N}$ and $f'=\frac{df}{dN}$. Both members of (6.31) may be looked upon as depending on the single variable N. Its optimum value is determined as a root of this equation.

What sorts of *régimes* will lead to this social optimum point?

We shall assume that the representative worker is not necessarily remunerated at a fixed wage rate, but at a wage rate that may depend on the input of labour (a progressive or degressive wage rate). This means that the total wage bill $B(N)$ will be *some* function of the total input N, not necessarily a magnitude proportional to N as in the case of a fixed wage rate. We assume that B is measured in terms of the good produced, *i.e.* the price of the good is conventionally put equal to 1.

Consider the following régime:

(6.32) *Consumption equals production*, *i.e.* the magnitude X that enters into $\Omega(X, N)$ is equal to $X=f(N)$.

(6.33) *The representative worker consumes all he earns*, *i.e.* $X=B(N)$ (which is only another way of saying that the profit of the industry is zero).

(6.34) *The representative worker tries to maximize his preference function under the constraint* (6.33), *i.e.* he will try to maximize $\Omega(B(N), N)$ with N as a free variable.

(6.35) *The representative enterprise will try to maximize profit, i.e.* it will try to maximize $f(N)-B(N)$.

The two institutionally determined types of behaviour (6.34) and (6.35) lead to

$$\frac{-\omega_N}{\omega_X}=B'(N) \tag{6.36}$$

$$f'(N)=B'(N) \tag{6.37}$$

(6.32), (6.33), (6.36) and (6.37) give four conditions on the two variables X and N. Hence, in order that the system shall have a solution (under arbitrarily given shapes of the preference function Ω and the production function f), the wage-bill function $B(N)$ must satisfy two point conditions. One of these may be thought of as corresponding to the fixing of the wage rate in the orthodox theory, the other is a condition which in the orthodox theory is generally overlooked.

The necessary and sufficient condition which the wage-bill function must satisfy, can be obtained as follows.

If $B(N)$ does have a shape such that a solution is possible, the equilibrium point must satisfy (6.31). This is seen by combining (6.36) and (6.37). In other words, if a solution exists, it must be the same as the social optimum defined by (6.31). In this social optimum point—which can be characterized by the corresponding magnitude N_0 of N—it is by (6.32), (6.33), (6.36), (6.37) *necessary* that we have

$$B(N_0)=f(N_0) \quad \text{and} \quad B'(N_0)=f'(N_0) \tag{6.38}$$

The fulfilment of (6.38) in the point N_0—where $f'(N_0)$ by (6.31) is equal to $\frac{-\omega_N}{\omega_X}$—is obviously also *sufficient* for the existence of an equilibrium point.

We can summarize this in the following proposition:

Proposition (6.39). In order that the régime (6.32)-(6.35) shall be *consistent* and lead to an equilibrium point, it is necessary and sufficient that the wage-bill function $B(N)$ satisfies (6.38), *i.e.* that it has *first order contact with the production function in the special input point* N_0 *that corresponds to the social optimum.* If the wage-bill function has this property, the equilibrium point of the régime will coincide with the social optimum.

From this proposition we deduce, for example, immediately that if the production function in the vicinity of the social optimum point is homogeneous of the first degree, *i.e.* gives an output that is proportional to the input, the wage-bill function must have the same property, that is, it must be on the basis of a fixed wage rate in the vicinity of thé social optimum point. If the production function does *not* have this character, the remuneration of the representative worker can *not* be on the basis of a fixed wage rate.

Although this example is simplified to the extreme, it does illustrate something of considerable importance. What is here taken account of in the form of a wage-bill function would, of course, in the world of realities have to be worked out in the form of social transfers, an appropriate form of a non-proportional (positive or negative) income tax or some similar device.

Case 5

Let us reconsider Case 3, but now assume that the income transfer T is a *function* of the four variables N_{11}, N_{12}, N_{21}, N_{22}. This might illustrate the case where the income transfer is achieved through some sort of *income tax* system. To indicate this, T may now be called the tax function. The other assumptions about the régime remain the same as in Case 3.

Assuming autonomous adaptation on the part of individual No. 1, we have to maximize $\Omega_1(X_{11}, X_{21}, N_{11}, N_{21})$ under the budget constraint written to the right in (6.7) where now T is a function of the four variables N_{11}, N_{12}, N_{21}, N_{22} of which N_{12} and N_{22} are conjecturally constant for individual No. 1. *Vice versa* for individual No. 2. This gives

(6.40) Adaptation of individual 1: $$\frac{\omega_{11}}{p_1}=\frac{\omega_{12}}{p_2}=\frac{-\omega_{1(1)}}{q_1-T_{(11)}}=\frac{-\omega_{1(2)}}{q_2-T_{(21)}}.$$

(6.41) Adaptation of individual 2: $$\frac{\omega_{21}}{p_1}=\frac{\omega_{22}}{p_2}=\frac{-\omega_{2(1)}}{q_1-T_{(12)}}=\frac{-\omega_{2(2)}}{q_2-T_{(22)}}$$

where

(6.42) $$T_{(ij)}=\frac{\partial T(N_{11}, N_{12}, N_{21}, N_{22})}{\partial N_{ij}} \qquad \begin{pmatrix} i=1, 2 \\ j=1, 2 \end{pmatrix}$$

We further have

(6.43) Adaptation of the two enterprises: $$\frac{q_i}{p_i}=f_i' \qquad (i=1, 2)$$

In addition we have the two budget equations (6.7)-(6.8) and the two production constraints (6.11). This gives a total of twelve equations on the 11 unknowns X_{ij}, N_{ij}, $\frac{q_1}{p_1}$, $\frac{q_2}{p_2}$ and $\frac{p_2}{p_1}$. Hence the function T must satisfy one point condition if there shall exist a point that satisfies the régime. If T is assumed constant, we get back to Case 3.

So much for the consistency of the régime. Now let us see what additional conditions this function T of the four variables N_{ij} must satisfy in order that the point produced by the régime shall be Pareto-optimal under the production constraint. This means that the function T must satisfy four additional point conditions, namely (6.27). This entails

(6.44) $T_{(11)}=T_{(12)}=T_{(21)}=T_{(22)}=0$ in the equilibrium point.

In other words, it is necessary that the tax function is *constant* in the vicinity of the equilibrium point, *i.e.* it must have the character of a *per capita* tax in this vicinity. This can be expressed in the following proposition:

Proposition (6.45). No régime of the type (6.40)-(6.43) with a tax function T that *actually depends* on the labour inputs N_{ij} in the vicinity of the equilibrium point, can lead to a point that is Pareto-optimal under the production constraint.

In particular, any régime that *includes an income tax* (which in the vicinity of the equilibrium point depends effectively on the income) is ruled out. Only a régime with a tax which in the vicinity of the equilibrium point has the character of a *per capita* tax, can produce an equilibrium point that is Pareto-optimal under the production constraint. If the tax *has* this property and its real value has the precise magnitude which it must have in order that a point satisfying the régime shall exist, then this point *is* Pareto-optimal under the production constraint. The magnitude of the real value of the tax can also in the present case be discussed in the same way as in Case 3.

Case 6

Now consider the case of m goods Nos. $i=1, 2\dots m$, and n individuals Nos. $j=1, 2\dots n$. Each good is assumed to be produced in a single process using only labour. Let

(6.46) $X_{i1}+X_{i2}+\dots+X_{in}=f_i(N_{i1}+N_{i2}+\dots+N_{in})$ $(i=1, 2\dots m)$

be the production functions, N_{ij} being the amounts of work furnished by individual j to industry i, and X_{ij} being the output of industry i which is received by individual j. Also in this case will the main conclusions of Case 5 apply.

Pareto-optimality under the production constraint (6.46) is now—with an analogous notation as before—expressed by

(6.47) $$\frac{-\omega_{j(i)}}{\omega_{ji}}=f_i' \text{ for all } i \text{ and } j$$

(6.48) $$\frac{\omega_{ji}}{\omega_{jk}}=\text{independent of } j \text{ for all } i, j \text{ and } k$$

Not all the equations (6.47)-(6.48) are independent, but all of them must be satisfied in a point that shall be Pareto-optimal under (6.46).

This being so, consider a régime where each individual and each industry behaves as in Case 5, the individual j being subject to a tax of the form

(6.49) $T_j(N_{1j}, N_{2j}\dots N_{mj})$ $(j=1, 2\dots n)$

and a budget equation of the form

(6.50) $q_1N_{1j}+q_2N_{2j}+\dots+q_mN_{mj}=p_1X_{1j}+p_2X_{2j}+\dots+p_mX_{mj}+T_j$ $(j=1, 2\dots n)$

The prices $p_1, p_2 \dots p_m$ and the wage rates $q_1, q_2 \dots q_m$ are assumed constant from the viewpoint of any individual or any industry.

This régime leads to

(6.51) Adaptation of the individuals: $\frac{q_i - T_{j(i)}}{p_i} = \frac{-\omega_{j(i)}}{\omega_{ji}}$ for all i and j

(6.52) Adaptation of the industries: $\frac{q_i}{p_i} = f_i'$ for all i

where

(6.53) $$T_{j(i)} = \frac{\partial T_j(N_{1j}, N_{2j} \dots N_{mj})}{\partial N_{ij}} \qquad \begin{pmatrix} i=1, 2 \dots m \\ j=1, 2 \dots n \end{pmatrix}$$

From (6.47), (6.51) and (6.52) follows

(6.54) $T_{j(i)} = 0$ for all i and j in the equilibrium point.

This shows that if the régime shall lead to a point that is Pareto-optimal under the production constraint, it is *necessary* that the taxes have the character of *per capita* taxes, *not income taxes*, in the vicinity of the equilibrium point. In other words, the essence of proposition (6.45) holds good also in the case of m industries and n individuals.

This conclusion is rather far-reaching. It is independent of whether or not the sum of the taxes is zero or not. That is, we need not assume

(6.55) $$T_1(N_{11}, N_{21} \dots N_{m1}) + \dots + T_n(N_{1n}, N_{2n} \dots N_{mn}) = 0$$

If the taxes have the character of *per capita* taxes in a certain region, will an equilibrium point of the régime exist in this region? More specifically: under what further conditions on the income transfers $T_1 \dots T_n$ will such a point exist?

In the problem we have $2mn$ variables X_{ij} and N_{ij}, further m prices p_i, m wage rates q_i and n income transfers T_j, all reckoned in nominal, *i.e.* undeflated, values. These $2m+n$ nominal magnitudes enter, however, in the equations in such a way that only their *relative* values—expressed, say, in terms of p_1—count as unknowns. That is, the total number of unknowns is

(6.56) $$2mn + 2m + n - 1$$

In order to rewrite the equilibrium equations in the form of a system of *independent* equations, we first put

(6.57) $$\frac{\omega_{j1}}{p_1} = \frac{\omega_{j2}}{p_2} = \dots = \frac{\omega_{jm}}{p_m} = \frac{-\omega_{j(1)}}{q_1} = \frac{-\omega_{j(2)}}{q_2} = \dots = \frac{-\omega_{j(m)}}{q_m} \qquad (j=1, 2 \dots n)$$

This gives $(2m-1)n$ equations. When these are fulfilled, we have (6.51)—in view of (6.54). Adding the m equations (6.52) is sufficient to assure the fulfilment also of (6.47). We further have m production equations (6.46) and budget equations (6.50), in other words, a total of

(6.58) $$2mn + 2m$$

independent equations, hence $(n-1)$ degrees of freedom. If we further add the condition (6.55), the number of degrees of freedom is reduced to $(n-2)$. In the case $n=2$, there is no degree of freedom. An example of this is Case 3 where the real value of the income transfer is determined by the régime.

In the general case, $(n-1)$ of the *per capita* income transfers may, in principle, be fixed arbitrarily. There may, however, by the nature of the preference functions and production functions involved, be very close upper and lower limits to how the choice can be made if an equilibrium point shall exist. Whether the range is small or large, the income transfers must have the character of *per capita* taxes in the vicinity of the equilibrium point of the régime in order that this point shall be Pareto-optimal under the production constraint.

Case 7

So far we have considered only régimes where the industries taken as a totality work with zero profit. Now let us drop this assumption. Consider a single industry—"industry as a whole"—producing a single commodity—"the national output"—with a single factor of production which is supplied by a single individual—"the labour class".

As in Case 4, let

$$X=f(N) \tag{6.59}$$

be the production function and let Y be the amount consumed by labour. This means that the residual $X-Y$ is retained by the industry. It is immaterial whether we call it "profit", "investment" or "consumption of the entrepreneur". The essential point is that by considering the two variables X and Y separately, we get two degrees of freedom. If labour tries to maximize an indicator $\Omega(Y,N)$ subject to the budget equation

$$pY-qN=0 \tag{6.60}$$

with the product price p and the wage rate q constant, and industry tries to maximize the profit $(pX-qN)$ on the same assumption about the constancy of p and q, the equilibrium point is determined by:

$$\frac{\omega_1}{p}=\frac{-\omega_{(1)}}{q} \tag{6.61}$$

$$pf'=q \tag{6.62}$$

where

$$\omega_1=\frac{\partial\Omega}{\partial Y} \qquad \omega_{(1)}=\frac{\partial\Omega}{\partial N} \tag{6.63}$$

The two equations (6.61)-(6.62) in conjunction with (6.59) determine the equilibrium point. In this case there is no over-determinateness because industry takes up whatever may be left over in the equilibrium point as a residuum $X-Y$, positive or negative. In other words, no condition on the *magnitude* of the (real value of the) profit $X-Y$ is imposed besides the *marginal* condition (6.62).

The real value of the profit in the equilibrium point is

$$X-Y=(1-\epsilon)X \tag{6.64}$$

where

$$\epsilon=\frac{d\log X}{d\log N}=\frac{f'N}{X} \tag{6.65}$$

This expression (6.64) for the real value of the profit in the equilibrium point follows immediately by noticing that in this point we have

$$f'=\frac{Y}{N} \tag{6.66}$$

because both sides in (6.66) are equal to $\frac{q}{p}$ in the equilibrium point.

If the production function f and the indicator Ω have arbitrarily given shapes, nothing prevents the equilibrium profit from being negative. If such a situation is considered unrealistic, *another régime must be introduced.* If we proceed more or less on Marshallian neo-classical lines, it would be natural to assume that ϵ is decreasing as N increases, and that there is some institutionally or conventionally fixed "normal profit"

$$\gamma=\frac{X-Y}{Y} \tag{6.67}$$

which "industry as a whole" must be assured in the equilibrium point. If (6.62) is actually *replaced* by (6.67) where γ is given, we have again, in general, a well-defined equilibrium point. But in this point we will, of course, *not* necessarily have (6.62), that is, marginal productivity will not necessarily be equal to the real wage rate. If we would require *at the same time* that (6.62) is fulfilled and that the "normal profit" γ takes on a preassigned value in the equilibrium point, we would get an *over-determinate* system. In a system where labour is assumed to act as a quantity adapter and we do not have any taxes that can be manipulated, it is—under arbitrarily given shapes of the production function f and the preference function Ω—impossible to impose both a *marginal* and a *total* condition on the adaptation of industry.

If we find that it is unrealistic to drop the assumption (6.62) in a market that is reasonably atomistic, we shall have to look for still another régime.

We can always assure a given "normal profit" γ and an atomistic marginal adaptation on the part of the entrepreneurs if we put a *point condition* on the shape of the production function. In our case this point condition will have to be that

$$\epsilon=1-\gamma \text{ in the equilibrium point} \tag{6.68}$$

where γ is institutionally or conventionally given. Personally, I don't think that this is a very realistic approach. If we want to be realistic, we do not have very much freedom in the choice of assumptions about our technical production function.

To me it would seem much more realistic to introduce a *tax system* and shape this tax system in such a way that we can maintain our assumption about atomistic marginal adaptation on the part of industry and still be able to produce an equilibrium point which satisfies certain desiderata about "normal profit". If we do this, and discuss the character which the tax system must have in order that the equilibrium point shall be Pareto-optimal under the production constraint, we will find that we get back to *the same fundamental properties* which we found in the previous examples which were constructed in a rather different way. Also in the present case must taxation of the workers have the character of a *per capita* tax in the vicinity of the equilibrium point. And if the disposable "normal profit" of industry shall have a given rate γ, the real value of the *per capita* tax on labour must have a *specific magnitude* in order that an equilibrium point shall exist. The previous examples illustrated the case $\gamma=0$. For the question of determinateness or over-determinateness it is, of course, immaterial whether we put γ equal to zero or to some other given value.

To verify the above conclusions let $T(qN)$ be the tax function on labour and $t(pX-qN)$ that on industry. We do not assume that we necessarily have

(6.69) $$T+t=0$$

T is a function of one variable, and so is t.

The budget equation for labour is now

(6.70) $$qN-pY=T(qN)$$

and the equilibrium equation for labour now becomes

(6.71) $$\frac{-\omega_{(1)}}{\omega_1}=\frac{q}{p}(1-T')$$

where $T'=\dfrac{dT}{d(qN)}$ is the marginal tax on labour.

The equilibrium equation for industry is now

(6.72) $$(1-t')(pf'-q)=0$$

If t' is not greater than unity, that is, if the tax on industry is not "over-progressive", (6.72) reduces to the same condition as before, namely (6.62). Thus, the equilibrium point of the régime is now determined by the three equations (6.59), (6.62) and (6.71) between the three unknowns X, Y and N.

Will the equilibrium thus determined be Pareto-optimal under the production constraint? Pareto-optimality is now determined by maximizing

(6.73) $$\theta\Omega(Y, N)+\nu\Phi(X-Y)+\mu[X-f(N)]$$

where θ, ν, μ are constant multipliers, θ and ν positive. Φ is an indicator of utility to the industries. This leads to

(6.74) $$\nu\Phi'+\mu=0 \qquad \theta\omega_1-\nu\Phi'=0 \qquad \theta\omega_{(1)}-\mu f'=0$$

where Φ' is the derivative of Φ with respect to its argument. These equations entail amongst others

(6.75) $$\frac{-\omega_{(1)}}{\omega_1}=f'$$

Comparing this with (6.62) and (6.71), we see that it is *necessary* that

(6.76) $$T'=0 \text{ in the equilibrium point}$$

That is to say, T must have the character of a *per capita* tax in the vicinity of the equilibrium point of the régime. If T does not have this property, the equilibrium point of the régime cannot be Pareto-optimal under the production constraint. This, of course, is in essence the same as Proposition (6.45). For the tax on industry, t, no condition ensues (apart from $t'<1$).

7. What did Pareto prove on Welfare?

During my stay in Rome in the late fall of 1950, I had several intensely interesting talks with Professor Gustavo Del Vecchio on welfare economics and in particular on how Pareto's work in this connection should be interpreted. There is probably no living economist who knows the way of thinking of Pareto so well as Professor Del Vecchio. Some of Del Vecchio's views have been incorporated in his introductory remarks to Volume IV of the *Nuova collana di economisti* (pp. x-xi). On certain points he gave valuable further comments in the course of our talks. I am authorized to bring these points before the public.

First it might be well to restate Pareto's own definition of what we would now call a Pareto-optimal position. To do this one should not take as a starting-point *Corso di economia politica*, Lausanne, 1896. The approach in these lectures represents precisely what Pareto later tried to get away from. If one shall discuss the Pareto optimum, one should refer to his *Manuale*, 1909. On p. 337 of this work we find the definition which in English translation (checked by Del Vecchio) can be rendered as follows: "Let us begin by defining a term which is very convenient to use in order to save words. We shall say that the individuals (*i componenti*) of a group (*una collettività*) in a given position have *maximum ophelimity* (*massimo di ophelimità*) if it is impossible to depart some small distance (*allontanarsi pochissimo*) from this position in such a way that this departure is useful for all the individuals of the group. Every small displacement from this position would necessarily have the effect of being useful to some of the individuals of the society and detrimental to some others."

Professor Del Vecchio comments that Pareto had the habit of working fast and not to bother too much with limiting cases. Therefore when Pareto here says "useful for all individuals of the group" it should be interpreted "useful to at least one of them and for the rest of them either useful or indifferent".

In the appendix to the French edition of the *Manuel d'économie politique*, 1909, Pareto not only developed the mathematical theory of free competition, but also gave what Pareto himself seems to think is a mathematical demonstration that the régime of free competition leads to maximum satisfaction. In the subsequently published article in the *Encyclopédie des sciences mathématiques** Pareto only develops the mathematical theory of free competition and *stops short*, without adding anything on maximum satisfaction. The *Encyclopédie* was published in instalments, and from all appearances—not least from a comparison between the structure of the *Encyclopédie* article and that of the mathematical appendix to the French *Manuel*—it would seem that a section on maximum satisfaction was to follow in a subsequent instalment of the *Encyclopédie* article. However, this continuation never appeared. Del Vecchio thinks that this was an *advantage*. He thinks that Pareto attributed too far-reaching consequences to his analysis on this point. Pareto wrote in terms which must lead the reader to believe that Pareto has proved a proposition to the effect that a régime of free competition produces a higher level of satisfaction than other régimes. It is difficult to escape the conclusion that Pareto himself believed that he had actually demonstrated this. See, for instance, the phrasing used in the Italian *Manuale*, 1909, p. 544: "Quindi le conclusioni . . ." ("hence the conclusions . . ."). At any rate it is an indisputable fact that many people have thought that Pareto's demonstration was of this general character. This applies certainly to Barone in his "Il ministro della produzione nello stato collettivista",** 1908, and to a great number of mathematical economists.

This being so, a logical explanation of the fact that the continuation of the *Encyclopédie* article never appeared, would be that Pareto—who frequently worked over his manuscripts many times—had in the meantime become aware that the demonstration in his previous works was *not* a general demonstration of the sort he was in search of and had believed that he had produced.

In spite of all efforts made by Del Vecchio to find out definitely the reason for the discontinuation of the *Encyclopédie* article, an authentic answer has not been found. Pareto's own manuscript for a possible continuation has never been unearthed.

As the matter now stands, we must say that Pareto has not established any mathematical proof of a general proposition that free competition produces maximum satisfaction. What Pareto has done is only to give *a particular sort of definition* of maximum satisfaction. This definition in itself is one of great value and we should all be grateful for the analytical tool it has provided.

* Published in English as "Mathematical Economics", *International Economic Papers* No. 5, 1955—Ed.

** Published in English as "The Ministry of Production in the Collectivist State", Appendix A of *Collectivist Economic Planning*, edited by F. A. Hayek, London, 1935—Ed.

[19]

The Impossibility of a Paretian Liberal

Amartya Sen

Delhi School of Economics and Harvard University

I. Introduction

The purpose of this paper is to present an impossibility result that seems to have some disturbing consequences for principles of social choice. A common objection to the method of majority decision is that it is illiberal. The argument takes the following form: Given other things in the society, if you prefer to have pink walls rather than white, then society should permit you to have this, even if a majority of the community would like to see your walls white. Similarly, whether you should sleep on your back or on your belly is a matter in which the society should permit you absolute freedom, even if a majority of the community is nosey enough to feel that you must sleep on your back. We formalize this concept of individual liberty in an extremely weak form and examine its consequences.

II. The Theorem

Let R_i be the ordering of the ith individual over the set X of all possible social states, each social state being a complete description of society including every individual's position in it. There are n individuals. Let R be the social preference relation that is to be determined.

DEFINITION 1: *A collective choice rule* is a functional relationship that specifies one and only one social preference relation R for any set of n individual orderings (one ordering for each individual).

A special case of a collective choice rule is one that Arrow (1951) calls a social welfare function, namely, a rule such that R must be an ordering.

DEFINITION 2: *A social welfare function* is a collective choice rule, the range of which is restricted to orderings.

A weaker requirement is that each R should generate a "choice function," that is, in every subset of alternatives there must be a "best"

For comments and criticisms I am grateful to Kenneth Arrow, Peter Diamond, Milton Friedman, Tapas Majumdar, Stephen Marglin, and Thomas Schelling.

alternative, or, in other words, there must be some (but not necessarily only one) alternative that is at least as good as all the other alternatives in that subset. This may be called a "social decision function."

DEFINITION 3: *A social decision function* is a collective choice rule, the range of which is restricted to social preference relations that generate a choice function.

It was shown in Sen (1969) that the conditions that were proven to be inconsistent by Arrow (1951, 1963) in his justly famous "impossibility theorem" in the context of a social welfare function are in fact perfectly consistent if imposed on a social decision function. The impossibility theorem to be presented here holds, however, for social decision functions as well.

Arrow's condition of collective rationality (Condition 1′) can be seen to be merely a requirement that the domain of the collective choice rule should not be arbitrarily restricted.

CONDITION U (Unrestricted Domain): Every logically possible set of individual orderings is included in the domain of the collective choice rule.

Arrow used a weak version of the Pareto principle.

CONDITION P: If every individual prefers any alternative x to another alternative y, then society must prefer x to y.

Finally, we introduce the condition of individual liberty in a very weak form.

CONDITION L (Liberalism): For each individual i, there is at least one pair of alternatives, say (x, y), such that if this individual prefers x to y, then society should prefer x to y, and if this individual prefers y to x, then society should prefer y to x.[1]

The intention is to permit each individual the freedom to determine at least one social choice, for example, having his own walls pink rather than white, other things remaining the same for him and the rest of the society.[2]

The following impossibility theorem holds.

THEOREM I: There is no social decision function that can simultaneously satisfy Conditions U, P, and L.

[1] The term "liberalism" is elusive and is open to alternative interpretations. Some uses of the term may not embrace the condition defined here, while many uses will. I do not wish to engage in a debate on the right use of the term. What is relevant is that Condition L represents a value involving individual liberty that many people would subscribe to. Whether such people are best described as liberals is a question that is not crucial to the point of this paper.

[2] Even this informal statement, which sounds mild, is much more demanding than Condition L. If the individual's preference over a personal choice (like choosing the color of his wall) is to be accepted by the society, other things remaining the same, then this gives the individual rights not only over one pair, which is all that is required by Condition L, but over many pairs (possibly an infinite number of pairs) varying with the "other things." If it is socially all right for me to have my walls either pink or white as I like in a social state where you smoke cigars, it should be socially all right for me to do the same where you indulge yourself in ways other than smoking cigars. Even this is not required by Condition L, which seems to demand very little.

In fact, we can weaken the condition of liberalism further. Such freedom may not be given to all, but to a proper subset of individuals. However, to make sense the subset must have more than one member, since if it includes only one then we might have a dictatorship. Hence, we demand such freedom for at least two individuals.

CONDITION L* (Minimal Liberalism): There are at least two individuals such that for each of them there is at least one pair of alternatives over which he is decisive, that is, there is a pair of x, y, such that if he prefers x (respectively y) to y (respectively x), then society should prefer x (respectively y) to y (respectively x).

The following theorem is stronger than Theorem I and subsumes it.

THEOREM II: There is no social decision function that can simultaneously satisfy Conditions U, P, and L^*.

PROOF: Let the two individuals referred to in Condition L^* be 1 and 2, respectively, and the two pairs of alternatives referred to be (x, y) and (z, w), respectively. If (x, y) and (z, w) are the same pair of alternatives, then there is a contradiction. They have, therefore, at most one alternative in common, say $x = z$. Assume now that person 1 prefers x to y, and person 2 prefers w to $z(=x)$. And let everyone in the community including 1 and 2 prefer y to w. There is in this no inconsistency for anyone, not even for 1 and 2, and their respective orderings are: 1 prefers x to y and y to w, while 2 prefers y to w and w to x. By Condition U this should be in the domain of the social decision mechanism. But by Condition L^*, x must be preferred to y, and w must be preferred to x $(=z)$, while by the Pareto principle, y must be preferred to w. Thus, there is no best element in the set $(x=z, y, w)$ in terms of social preference, and every alternative is worse than some other. A choice function for the society does not therefore exist.

Next, let x, y, z, and w, be all distinct. Let 1 prefer x to y, and 2 prefer z to w. And let everyone in the community including 1 and 2 prefer w to x and y to z. There is no contradiction for 1 or 2, for 1 simply prefers w to x, x to y, and y to z, while 2 prefers y to z, z to w, and w to x. By Condition U this configuration of individual preferences must yield a social choice function. But by Condition L^* society should prefer x to y and z to w, while by the Pareto principle society must prefer w to x, and y to z. This means that there is no best alternative for this set, and a choice function does not exist for any set that includes these four alternatives. Thus, there is no social decision function satisfying Conditions U, P, and L^*, and the proof is complete.[3]

[3] We can strengthen this theorem further by weakening Condition L^* by demanding only that 1 be decisive for x against y, but not vice versa, and 2 be decisive for z against w, but not vice versa, and require that $x \neq z$, and $y \neq w$. This condition, too, can be shown to be inconsistent with Condition U and P, but the logical gain involved in this extension does not, alas, seem to be associated with any significant increase of relevance that I can think of.

III. An Example

We give now a simple example of the type of impossibility that is involved in Theorem II by taking a special case of two individuals and three alternatives. There is one copy of a certain book, say *Lady Chatterly's Lover*, which is viewed differently by 1 and 2. The three alternatives are: that individual 1 reads it (x), that individual 2 reads it (y), and that no one reads it (z). Person 1, who is a prude, prefers most that no one reads it, but given the choice between either of the two reading it, he would prefer that he read it himself rather than exposing gullible Mr. 2 to the influences of Lawrence. (Prudes, I am told, tend to prefer to be censors rather than being censored.) In decreasing order of preference, his ranking is z, x, y. Person 2, however, prefers that either of them should read it rather than neither. Furthermore, he takes delight in the thought that prudish Mr. 1 may have to read Lawrence, and his first preference is that person 1 should read it, next best that he himself should read it, and worst that neither should. His ranking is, therefore, x, y, z.

Now if the choice is precisely between the pair (x, z), i.e., between person 1 reading the book and no one reading it, someone with liberal values may argue that it is person 1's preference that should count; since the prude would not like to read it, he should not be forced to. Thus, the society should prefer z to x. Similarly, in the choice exactly between person 2 reading the book (y) and no one reading it (z), liberal values require that person 2's preference should be decisive, and since he is clearly anxious to read the book he should be permitted to do this. Hence y should be judged socially better than z. Thus, in terms of liberal values it is better that no one reads it rather than person 1 being forced to read it, and it is still better that person 2 is permitted to read the book rather than no one reading it. That is, the society should prefer y to z, and z to x. This discourse could end happily with the book being handed over to person 2 but for the fact that it is a Pareto inferior alternative, being worse than person 1 reading it, in the view of both persons, i.e., x is Pareto superior to y.

Every solution that we can think of is bettered by some other solution, given the Pareto principle and the principle of liberalism, and we seem to have an inconsistency of choice. This is an example of the type of problem that is involved in Theorems I and II.

IV. Relevance

The dilemma posed here may appear to be somewhat disturbing. It is, of course, not necessarily disturbing for every conceivable society, since the conflict arises with only particular configurations of individual preferences. The ultimate guarantee for individual liberty may rest not on rules for social choice but on developing individual values that respect each other's personal choices. The conflict posed here is concerned with societies where such a condition does not hold and where pairwise choice based on liberal values may conflict with those based on the Pareto principle. Like Arrow's "General Possibility Theorem," here also the Condition of Unrestricted Domain is used.

However, unlike in the theorem of Arrow, we have not required transitivity of social preference. We have required neither transitivity of strict preference, nor transitivity of indifference, but merely the existence of a best alternative in each choice situation.[4] Suppose society prefers x to y, and y to z, and is indifferent between z and x. Arrow would rule this out, since there is an intransitivity; but we do not, for here alternative x is "best" in the sense of being at least as good as both the other alternatives. Our requirements are, in this respect, very mild, and we still have an impossibility.

Second, we have not imposed Arrow's much debated condition of "the independence of irrelevant alternatives."[5] Many people find the relaxation of this condition to be an appealing way of escaping the Arrow dilemma. This way out is not open here, for the theorem holds without imposing this condition.

The Pareto principle is used here in a very weak version, as in Arrow. We do not necessarily require that if someone prefers x to y and everyone regards x to be at least as good as y, then x is socially better. We permit the possibility of having collective choice rules that will violate this provided everyone strictly preferring x to y must make x socially better than y.

[4] It may appear that one way of solving the dilemma is to dispense with the social choice function based on a binary relation, that is, to relax not merely transitivity but also *acyclicity*. A choice function that need not correspond to any binary relation has undoubtedly a wider scope. But then Condition P and Condition L would have to be redefined, for example, (1) x should not be chosen when y is available, if everyone prefers y to x, and (2) for each individual there is a pair (x_i, y_i) such that if he prefers x_i (respectively y_i) to y_i (respectively x_i), then y_i (repectively x_i) should not be chosen if x_i (respectively y_i) is available. Thus redefined, the choice set for the set of alternatives may be rendered empty even without bringing in acyclicity, and the contradiction will reappear. This and other possible "ways out" are discussed more fully in my forthcoming book (Sen, in press, chap. 6).

[5] Using the condition of the independence of irrelevant alternatives, A. Gibbard, in an unpublished paper, has recently proved the following important theorem: Any social decision function that must generate social preferences that are all transitive in the strict relation (quasi-transitive) and which must satisfy Conditions U, P, nondictatorship, and the independence of irrelevant alternatives, must be an oligarchy in the sense that there is a unique group of individuals each of whom, by preferring x to y, can make the society regard x to be at least as good as y, and by all preferring x to y can make the society prefer x to y, irrespective of the preferrences of those who are not in this group. Gibbard's Theorem is disturbing, for the conditions look appealing but the resultant oligarchy seems revolting, and it is a major extension of the problem posed by Arrow (1951, 1963). Gibbard argues against the simultaneous insistence on a binary relation of social preference generating a choice function and on the condition of the independence of irrelevant alternatives. We have not imposed the latter.

Nevertheless it turns out that a principle reflecting liberal values even in a very mild form cannot possibly be combined with the weak Pareto principle, given an unrestricted domain. If we do believe in these other conditions, then the society cannot permit even minimal liberalizm. Society cannot then let more than one individual be free to read what they like, sleep the way they prefer, dress as they care to, etc., *irrespective* of the preferences of others in the community.

What is the moral? It is that in a very basic sense liberal values conflict with the Pareto principle. If someone takes the Pareto principle seriously, as economists seem to do, then he has to face problems of consistency in cherishing liberal values, even very mild ones.[6] Or, to look at it in another way, if someone does have certain liberal values, then he may have to eschew his adherence to Pareto optimality. While the Pareto criterion has been thought to be an expression of individual liberty, it appears that in choices involving more than two alternatives it can have consequences that are, in fact, deeply illiberal.

References

Arrow, K. J. *Individual Values and Social Choice*. New York: Wiley, 1951; 2d ed., 1963.

Sen, A. K. "Quasi-transitivity, Rational Choice and Collective Decisions." Discussion paper no. 45, Harvard Institute of Economic Research 1968. *Rev. Econ. Studies* 36, no. 3 (July 1969): 381–93.

———. *Collective Choice and Social Welfare*. San Francisco: Holden-Day; and Edinburgh: Oliver & Boyd, in press.

[6] The difficulties of *achieving* Pareto optimality in the presence of externalities are well known. What is at issue here is the *acceptability* of Pareto optimality as an objective in the context of liberal values, given certain types of externalities.

[20]

ON THE RATIONALE OF GROUP DECISION-MAKING

DUNCAN BLACK

When a decision is reached by voting or is arrived at by a group all of whose members are not in complete accord, there is no part of economic theory which applies. This paper is intended to help fill this gap; to provide a type of reasoning which will contribute to the development of the theory of trade-unions, the firm, and the cartel; and to provide the basis for a theory of the equilibrium distribution of taxation or of public expenditure. Still other uses of the theory might be not less important. For reasons of space we avoid discussion of many points that demand fuller treatment and only attempt to indicate the course of the argument.[1]

I. GENERAL ASSUMPTIONS

Let us suppose that a decision is to be determined by vote of a committee. The members of the committee may meet in a single room, or they may be scattered over an area of the country as are the electors in a parliamentary constituency. Proposals are advanced, we assume, in the form of motions on a particular topic or in favor of one of a number of candidates. We do not inquire into the genesis of the motions but simply assume that given motions have been put forward. In the case of the selection of candidates, we assume that determinate candidates have offered themselves for election and that one is to be chosen by means of voting. For convenience we shall speak as if one of a number of alternative motions, and not candidates, was being selected.

To develop our theory, we must make some further assumptions. Our major assumption will be that each member of the committee ranks the motions in a definite order of preference, whatever that order may be. To take a simple illustration, if there are four motions denoted by a_1, a_2, a_3, a_4, say, before a committee, the member A may prefer a_2 to any of the others, may be indifferent between a_3 and a_4, and may prefer either of them to a_1.

If so, A's valuation of the motions could be represented by the schedule of preferences on the left hand side of Fig. 1, in which a_2 stands highest; a_3 and a_4 next highest, each at the same level; and a_1 lowest. And similar scales could be drawn for other members of the committee with $a_1 \ldots a_4$ appearing in some definite order on each scale, though the ordering of the motions might be different on the scale of each member.

We are here using the theory of relative valuation of orthodox Economic Science, whether the theory of relative utility or the theory of indifference curves. The only points which have significance on the directed straight line representing a member's schedule of preferences are those at which motions are marked, and his scale really consists of a number of points placed in a certain order in relation to each other. No significance attaches to the distance between the points on the scale, and any two scales would be equivalent on which the motions occurred in the same order.

When a member values the motions before a committee in a definite order, it is reasonable to assume that, when these motions are put against each other,

[1] The theory will be set out at greater length in a forthcoming book on *The Pure Science of Politics*.

he votes in accordance with his valuation, i.e., in accordance with his schedule of preferences. Thus the member *A* would be assumed to vote for a_2 when it was put in a vote against a_1; or if a_3 were put against a_4—since he is indifferent between the two and it would be irrational for him to support either against the other—he would be assumed to abstain from voting.

A member's level of preference between the different motions may also be shown by denoting the motions put forward by particular points on a horizontal axis, while we mark level of preference along the vertical axis. For instance, the same set of valuations of the individual *A* is shown in the right and left parts of Fig. 1. The only points in the diagram having significance would be those for the values a_1, a_2, a_3, a_4, on the horizontal axis, corresponding to the motions actually put forward. We have joined these points standing at various levels of preference by straight-line segments, but this is done merely to assist the eye, since the curve would be imaginary except at the four points. In this diagram, as in the case of the preference schedule, it is only the relative heights of different points which have meaning, not their absolute heights.[2]

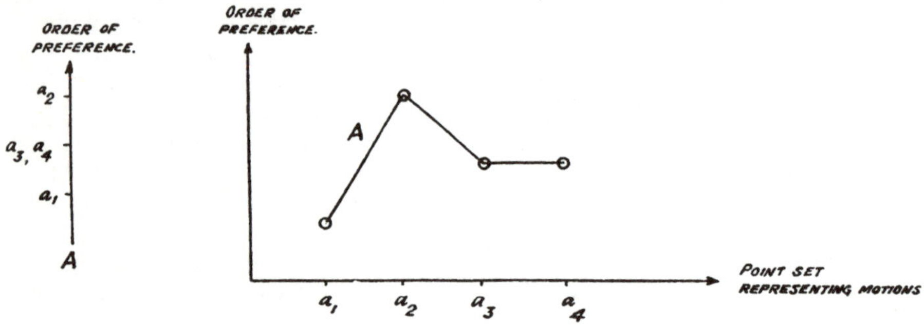

FIG. 1

[2] Cf. F. H. Knight, *Risk, Uncertainty and Profit*, pp. 68–70.

While a member's preference curve may be of any shape whatever, there is reason to expect that, in some important practical problems, the valuations actually carried out will tend to take the form of isolated points on single-peaked curves. This would be particularly likely to happen were the committee considering different possible sizes of a numerical quantity and choosing one size in preference to the others. It might be reaching a decision, say, with regard to the price of a product to be marketed by a firm, or the output for a future period, or the wage rate of labor, or the height of a particular tax, or the legal school-leaving age, and so on.

In such cases the committee member, in arriving at an opinion on the matter, would often try initially to judge which size is for him the optimum. Once he had arrived at his view of the optimum size, the farther any proposal departed from it on the one side or the other, the less he would favor it. The valuations carried out by the member would then take the form of points on a single-peaked or ∩-shaped curve.

In working out our theory we shall devote considerable attention to this class of curves which slope continuously upward to a peak and slope continuously downward from that peak. We shall refer to the motion corresponding to the peak of any curve—the most-preferred motion for the member concerned—as his optimum.

Another case likely to be of frequent occurrence in practice—especially, again, where the committee is selecting a particular size of a numerical quantity—is that in which the valuations carried out by a member take the form of points on a single-peaked curve with a truncated top. Such a case would arise when the individual feels uncertain as to which of two or more numerical quantities proposed represents his optimum choice. He cannot discriminate in choice between (say) two of these numerical quantities; but the farther the proposal made falls below the lower of these values, or the higher it rises above the larger of them, the less he esteems the motion concerned.

We shall work out the theory first for the case in which the members' preference curves are single-peaked, and, after that, we shall show how the answer to any problem can be obtained no matter what the shape of the members' curves may be. When any matter is being considered in a committee, only a finite number of motions will be put forward and only a finite number of valuations will be carried out by each member. If three motions or six motions were put forward, each member would be assumed to value each of them in relation to the others. When we are drawing our preference curves, however, we will draw continuous curves and—since there are an infinite number of points on any continuous curve—we imply that the person for whom the curve is drawn has carried out an evaluation of each of an infinite number of motions in regard to each of the others. This is unrealistic, it is true, but, when the theory is worked out for this case, we can easily get the answer for any case in which only a finite number of motions is put forward and valued by the members.

We assume that the committee with which we are concerned makes use of a simple majority in its voting. In practice, voting would be so conducted that, after discussion, one motion would be made and, after further discussion, another motion (an "amendment," that is) might be moved. If so, the original motion and amendment would be placed against each other in a vote. One of the two motions having been disposed of, leaving a single motion in the field, a further amendment to it might be moved; then a further vote would be taken between the survivor of the first vote and the new motion; and so on. If 2 motions were put forward, 1 vote would be taken; if 3 motions, 2 votes; and, in general, if m motions were put forward, there would be $(m - 1)$ votes.[3]

Now it will be found to simplify the development of the theory if, in the first instance, we suppose that the voting procedure is different from this. We wish to make the assumption that when m motions $a_1, a_2, \ldots a_m$ (say) have been put forward, the committee places each of these motions against every other in a vote and picks out that motion, if any, which is able to get a simple majority against *every* other motion. The motion a_1 is to be envisaged as being put against all the other motions $a_2 \ldots a_m$; a_2 will already have been put against a_1, and we assume that it will then be put against $a_3 \ldots a_m$; and so on, a_{m-1} finally being pitted against a_m. On this assumption the number of votes taken will be the number of ways of choosing 2 things out

[3] In addition, the motion which is selected by this process is usually put to the meeting for final acceptance or rejection. This is equivalent to putting it against the motion "that there be no change in the existing state of affairs." The step in theory to correspond to this stage in the procedure could easily be supplied.

of m, i.e., $m(m-1)/2$ votes, instead of the $(m - 1)$ votes which would be taken in practice.

This assumption enables the theory to proceed more smoothly and quickly than the assumption that only $(m - 1)$ votes are held. When we have worked out the theory on this basis, we can go on to prove that—in the class of cases in which we are mainly interested—the same answer would be given whether $m(m-1)/2$ votes were held, as we assume, or only the $(m - 1)$ votes of reality. The assumption is a kind of theoretical scaffolding which can be discarded once it has served its turn.

These, then, are our assumptions: that in a committee m motions are put forward, that each member carries out an evaluation of each motion in regard to every other, that in the voting each motion is put against every other, and that the committee adopts as its decision ("resolution") that motion, if any, which is able to get a simple majority over every other.

It can be shown that, at most, only one motion will be able to get a simple majority over every other. To prove this, let us assume that a_h is such a motion, i.e., that a_h can get a simple majority over every other. And let us assume that this is also true of some other motion, a_k. By our first assumption, however, a_h can get a simple majority over every other motion, including a_k. Therefore a_k cannot get a simple majority over a_h. Hence, at most, only one motion can get a simple majority over every other.

II. MEMBERS' PREFERENCE CURVES ALL SINGLE-PEAKED

The method of reasoning which we employ can be seen most easily from a particular example. Figure 2 shows the preference curves of the 5 members of a committee. Only part of each curve has been drawn, and the curves are supposed to extend over a common range of the horizontal axis.

Then if a_h is put against a_k (where $a_h < a_k \leqslant O_1$), the preference curve of each member—irrespective of what its precise shape may be—is upsloping from a_h to a_k; and a_k, standing at a higher level of preference on the curve of each member, will get a 5:5 (5 out of 5) majority against a_h. If a_h is put against a_k, (where $a_h < a_k \leqslant O_2$), at least 4 members—viz., those with optimums at or above O_2—will have preference curves which are upsloping from a_h to a_k; and a_k will get at least a 4:5 majority against a_h. If $a_h < a_k \leqslant O_3$, a_k will get at least a 3:5 majority against a_h. And similar relations hold for motions corresponding to values above O_3. If two values above O_3 are placed against each other in a vote, the nearer of the two values to O_3 will get a majority of at least 3:5 against the other.

If a value a_h (where $a_h < O_3$) is put against a value a_k (where $a_k > O_3$), before we could find which of the values would win in a vote, we would have to draw the complete preference curve for each member, find whether a_h or a_k stood higher on the preference curve of each member and count up the votes cast for a_h and a_k. But even though a value below the median optimum O_3 should defeat all values to the left of itself, and should defeat some of the values above O_3, this would be without significance. What we are looking for is that motion which can defeat every other by at least a simple majority. And we notice that the preference curves of at least 3 members are downsloping from O_3 leftward, and the preference curves of at least 3 members are downsloping from O_3 rightward. Therefore O_3 can defeat any other value in the entire range by at least a simple majority. And, as we have already seen (end of Sec. I), this can be true of only a single value. The resolution adopted by the committee must be the motion corresponding to the value O_3.

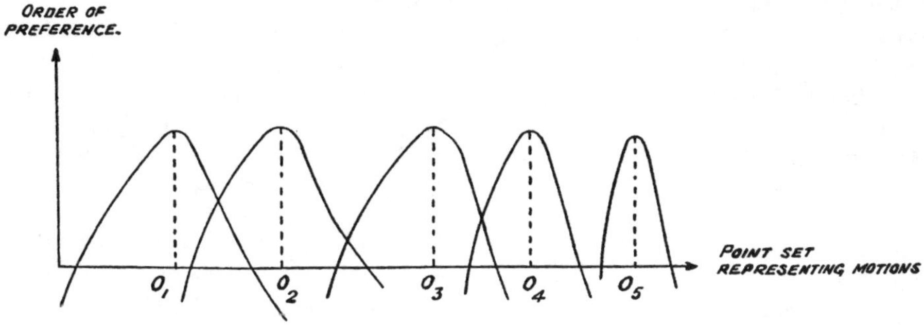

FIG. 2

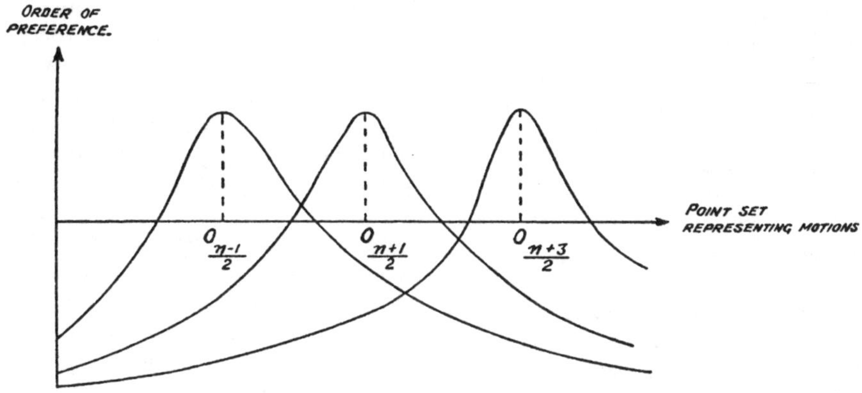

FIG. 3

To give the general proof, two cases must be worked out—that in which the number of members in the committee is odd and that in which it is even. We will consider each in turn.

Let there be n members in the committee, where n is odd. We suppose that an ordering of the points on the horizontal axis representing motions exists, rendering the preference curves of all members single-peaked. The points on the horizontal axis corresponding to the members' optimums are named O_1, O_2, O_3, . . . , in the order of their occurrence. The middle or median optimum will be the $(n + 1)/2^{th}$, and, in Figure 3, only this median optimum, the one immediately above it and the one immediately below it are shown.

Then $O_{(n+1)/2}$ will be the motion adopted by the committee. Suppose $O_{(n+1)/2}$ were placed against any lower value, say, a_h. Since $(n + 1)/2$ members have optimums at or above $O_{(n+1)/2}$, as we move from left to right from a_h to $O_{(n+1)/2}$, at least $(n + 1)/2$ curves are upsloping, viz., those of members with optimums at or to the right of $O_{(n+1)/2}$. At least $(n + 1)/2$ members prefer $O_{(n+1)/2}$ to a_h and, in a vote against a_h, $O_{(n+1)/2}$ will get a majority of at least $(n + 1)/2:n$, and this is sufficient to give it at least a simple majority. Therefore $O_{(n+1)/2}$ can get at least a simple majority against any lower value which is put against it. Similarly it can get at least a simple majority against any higher value. Thus it can get a simple majority against any other value which can be proposed. And by previous argument, it is the only value which can do so.

When the number of members, n, in the committee, is even, there may be a tie in the voting; and we will suppose that an additional person acting as chairman, in the event of a tie has the right to cast a deciding vote.

Let us suppose, first, that this member who acts as chairman has his optimum at $O_{n/2}$ or at one of the lower optimums. It can be shown that the motion corresponding to the value $O_{n/2}$ will be able to defeat any lower value (Fig. 4). Let a_h be such a value, that is, $a_h < O_{n/2}$. Then $(n/2 + 1)$ members have optimums at or above $O_{n/2}$; and at least $(n/2 + 1)$ preference curves will be upsloping as we move from left to right from a_h to $O_{n/2}$. At least $(n/2 + 1)$ members will vote for $O_{n/2}$ against a_h, and this is sufficient to give $O_{n/2}$ a simple majority.

If $O_{n/2}$ is put against any value a_k (where $a_k > O_{n/2}$)—since there are $n/2$ optimums at or below $O_{n/2}$—the preference curves of at least $n/2$ members will be downsloping from $O_{n/2}$ to a_k, and $O_{n/2}$ will get at least $n/2$ votes against a_k, i.e., will at least tie with a_k. In the event of a tie $O_{n/2}$ will defeat a_k with the aid of the chairman's deciding vote because, by hypothesis, his optimum is situated at or below $O_{n/2}$ and his preference curve must be downsloping from $O_{n/2}$ to a_k.

Thus, when the chairman's optimum is situated at or below $O_{n/2}$, $O_{n/2}$ will be able to get at least a simple majority against any other value which may be proposed.

Similarly when n, the number of members in the committee, is even, and the chairman's optimum is at or above $O_{(n/2)+1}$, it can be shown that $O_{(n/2)+1}$ will be able to get at least a simple majority against every other value.

One cannot leave the theorem of the preceding paragraphs without pointing out its analogy with the central principle of economics—that showing how price is fixed by demand and supply. The theorem we have proved shows that the decision adopted by the committee becomes determinate as soon as the position of one optimum—which we can refer to conveniently enough as the median optimum—is given. No matter in what manner the preference curves or optimums of the other members alter or move about, if it is given that one optimum remains the median optimum, the decision of the committee must remain fixed. The analogy with economic science is that, in the determination of price in a market, price remains unchanged so long as the point of intersection of the demand and supply curves is fixed and given, irrespective of how these curves may alter their shapes above and below that point. Or, in the version of the theory due to Böhm-Bawerk, which brings out the point very clearly, price remains unaltered so long as the "marginal pairs" of buyers and sellers and their price attitudes remain unchanged.

But the analogy exists only between the two theories; there is a marked difference in the materials to which they relate. In the case of market price, when the price of a commodity is being determined, a series of adjustments on the part of the consumers will bring into existence a state of affairs in which this commodity, and all others which they purchase, will have the same significance at the margin for each consumer. This is one of the several grand harmonies running through the material of economic life, a harmony by which no one who understands it can fail to be impressed—and by which the economists of the last generation were perhaps overimpressed. In the material of committee decisions, (or of political phenomena in general) on the other hand, no such grand harmony exists. The possibility of the persistence of disharmony and discord is as striking in the one case as is the certainty of harmony in the other.

In reaching the foregoing conclusions, we assumed that a member of the committee voted on the various motions put forward in accordance with their order on his schedule of preferences. It can be shown that, when a motion exists which would defeat every other if the members voted in this way, it is not open to any member, or any number of members acting in concert, to alter their voting so that some other motion which is more preferred by them can be adopted as the resolution of the committee.[4] It is open to them, however, to vote in such a way that no motion will be able to get a majority over all the others.

If all members voted as we have supposed, the motion adopted by the committee would be that corresponding to the median optimum, O_{med}, say. Let us suppose now that one or more members with optimums above O_{med}—by voting otherwise than directly in accordance with their schedule of preferences—attempt to give some other value, say a_h, a majority over all the others, where $a_h > O_{\text{med}}$.

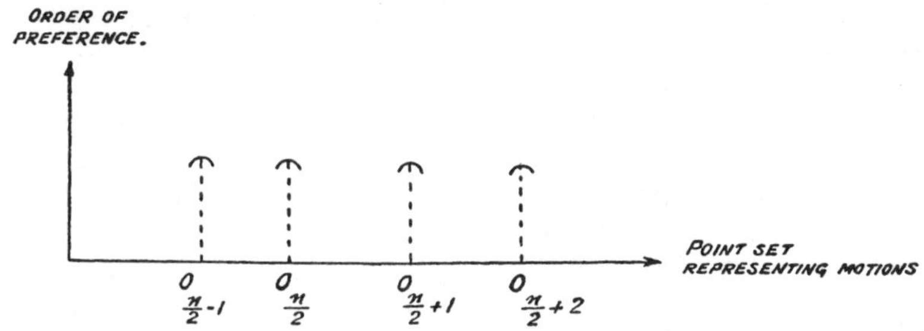

FIG. 4

But when the members vote directly in accordance with their preference scales, those who have a_h higher on their scales than O_{med} would already be supporting a_h against O_{med} and, even so, a_h would be defeated by O_{med}. Before it could defeat O_{med}, a_h would require the support of members whose optimums lie below O_{med}. The only members who—by voting otherwise than in accordance with their scales of preferences—could make a_h the resolution of the committee, are those with optimums below O_{med}, i.e., those against whose interest it is to do so.

It would be possible, of course, for a number of members to vote so that no motion would get a majority over every other. If, for example, a sufficient number of voters with optimums above O_{med} were to vote against O_{med} when it was placed against some value which stood

[4] If only $(m-1)$ votes are held, this conclusion no longer holds.

lower on their scales of preferences, O_{med} might be defeated. At most, therefore, a group of voters would have it in their power to prevent any resolution at all being adopted by the committee.

When the members' preference curves are single-peaked, as we suppose, it can be shown that voting between the different motions obeys the transitive property[5] and that if—of any three values a_1, a_2, a_3—a_1 can defeat a_2 in a vote and a_2 can defeat a_3, then, of necessity, a_1 can defeat a_3.

This can be proved by consideration of the orderings of the points a_1, a_2, a_3, in relation to the median optimum. It can be shown that each ordering of the 4 points a_1, a_2, a_3, and the median optimum, either renders the assumption impossible that a_1 defeats a_2 and a_2 defeats a_3 or else satisfies the assumption and, at the same time, necessitates that a_1 defeats a_3.

The transitive property can easily be extended to show that, if a_1 can defeat a_2, a_2 can defeat a_3, . . . and a_{l-1} can defeat a_l, then a_1 can defeat a_l.

It follows from the transitive property that a_1 can defeat a_3. By hypothesis, a_3 can defeat a_4. Hence a_1 can defeat a_4. Proceeding by successive applications we can see that a_1 can defeat a_l.

In arriving at the above-mentioned results, we assumed that every motion was placed against every other and that in all $m(m - 1)/2$ votes were held. We can now remove this assumption and show that the same motion will be adopted by a committee when only $(m - 1)$ votes are taken as in the committee practice of real life.

For the case when n is odd, $O_{(n+1)/2}$ is one of the motions put forward and it must enter into the series of votes at some point. When it does, it will defeat the first motion which it meets. It will likewise defeat the second and every other motion which is put against it. That is, $O_{(n+1)/2}$ must enter the voting process at some stage, and, when it does, it will defeat the other motions put against it and become the decision of the committee. The conclusion we reached holds good not only for the imaginary procedure of placing every motion against every other but also for the actual committee procedure of real life. The same is true of the conclusions we reached for the case in which the number of members in the committee was even. In the committee procedure of real life $O_{n/2}$ or $O_{(n/2)+1}$ will be the motion actually adopted.

The assumption, that $m(m - 1)/2$ votes were held, enabled us to give a mathematical proof which was both definite and short. But our conclusions are true independently of this assumption.

As an example of the use of this technique, we may suppose that the three directors of a monopolistic firm are fixing the price of their product for a forthcoming period. Let us further assume that neither future sales nor future costs can be calculated with certainty and that there is no possibility of a choice of price being made purely by means of cost accounting. Subjective factors enter, and varying estimates of the future position are formed by the different directors. If, on their different views of the situation, the directors' scales of preference are as shown (Fig. 5), the price fixed will be that corresponding to the motion a_3.

[5] The transitive property is defined in L. S. Stebbing, *A Modern Introduction to Logic*, pp. 112 and 168.

III. WHEN THE MEMBERS' PREFERENCE CURVES ARE SUBJECT TO NO RESTRICTION

When the members' preference curves are not of the single-peaked variety, a solution to any problem can always be arrived at arithmetically, provided the number of motions put forward is finite.

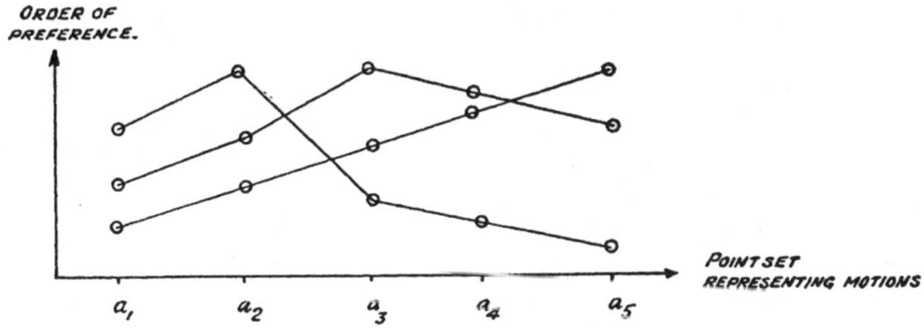

FIG. 5

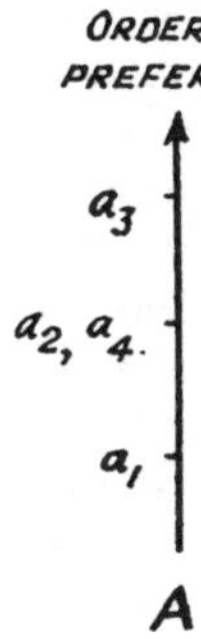

(against)

(for)	a_1	a_2	a_3	a_4
a_1		(0, 1)	(0, 1)	(0, 1)
a_2	(1, 0)		(0, 1)	(0, 0)
a_3	(1, 0)	(1, 0)		(1, 0)
a_4	(1, 0)	(0, 0)	(0, 1)	

FIG. 6

To begin with, we return to the assumption that every motion is placed in a vote against every other. The results of the series of votes can be shown very readily by the construction of a voting matrix.[6]

The construction of a matrix is illustrated in Figure 6, which gives the matrix corresponding to the schedule of preferences of the single member *A* who is voting in a committee in which the four motions $a_1 \ldots a_4$ have been put forward. Along the top row and down the left-hand column are shown the motions $a_1, \ldots a_4$. In each cell of the matrix, we record the individual's vote for one motion when it is placed against another. Looking to the topmost row of figures, when a_1 is placed against a_2, *A* votes for a_2, and we enter in the cell (a_1, a_2) the figures (0, 1). When a_1 is placed against a_3, he votes for a_3 and, in the cell (a_1, a_3), we enter the figures (0, 1) standing for 0 votes for and 1 against. The other cells are filled in the same way. Since *A* is indifferent in choice between a_2 and a_4, he will abstain from voting when a_2 is placed against a_4, and the cell (a_2, a_4) will show (0, 0). The figures in the cell(a_4, a_2) will also be (0, 0).

[6] I am indebted to Dr. R. A. Newing for suggesting the use of a matrix notation.

Along the main diagonal of the matrix, instead of having cells of the usual type, we have simply placed a series of zeros and joined them by a straight line. This is to indicate that the cells (a_1, a_1), (a_2, a_2), . . . , which would denote that a_1 was placed against a_1, a_2 against a_2, . . . , have no meaning. In constructing the matrix in practice, it is usually easiest to enter these zeros along the main diagonal first and join them by a straight line.

Each row to the right of the main diagonal is a reflection in the diagonal of the column immediately beneath, with the figures in the cells reversed. Thus the cell (a_2, a_3) immediately to the right of the diagonal shows (0, 1), the reflection in the diagonal of the figure (1, 0) immediately below the diagonal. The cell (a_2, a_4), two places to the right of the diagonal, is the reflection of the cell (a_4, a_2) two places below the diagonal. The reason for this is that the figures in any cell (a_h, a_k) must be those of the cell (a_k, a_h) on the other side of the diagonal, placed in the reverse order. This feature roughly halves the work of constructing a matrix: we can fill in the figures on one side of the diagonal and then complete the matrix by reflection of these figures in the diagonal.

The construction of an individual matrix would be gratuitous labor since it merely gives, in a clumsier form, information which is shown clearly enough in the member's schedule of preference. When, however, we have a group of individuals voting on a particular topic and the preference schedule of each is known, the matrix for the group presents in very convenient form the information that we need. For instance, for the group of schedules shown in Figure 7, the accompanying matrix has been constructed precisely as described above. Along the main diagonal, as before, we enter zeros and join them by a straight line. In the cell (a_1, a_2) we enter the figure (2, 3) because on the scales of 2 members a_1 stands higher than a_2, and on the scales of the remaining 3 members a_2 stands higher. The other cells are filled in the same way and, as before, the half of the matrix on one side of the diagonal can be obtained by reversal of the frequencies in the corresponding cells on the other side.

From the group matrix we can read off immediately that—when the motions a_1 . . . a_6 are placed each against every other, as we suppose—a_3 will be able to get a simple majority over each of the other motions put forward. For this committee a_3 would be the resolution adopted.

If a motion exists which would be able to get a simple majority over all the others when the members voted directly in accordance with their schedules of preferences, it would not be open to any member or group of members—by voting in some other fashion—to bring into existence as the resolution of the committee a motion which stood higher on the scales of all of them. Proof of this proposition is almost identical with that of our earlier analysis (see above, p. 26).

If, when $m(m - 1)/2$ votes are held, a motion exists which is able to get at least a simple majority over each of the other motions put forward, it can be proved, as before, that, when the members vote directly in accordance with their schedules of preferences, this would be bound to be the motion adopted even though only $(m - 1)$ votes had been held.

But when the members' preference curves are not single-peaked, no motion need exist which is able to get at least a simple majority over every other. This can be seen very quickly from the accompanying group of schedules (Fig. 8) in which the arrangement of the motions a_1, a_2, a_3, on the members' scales is symmetrical. When a_1 is put forward, it is defeated by a_3, which gets the votes of *B* and *C*; when a_2 is put forward, it is defeated by a_1; when a_3 is put forward, it is defeated by a_2. That is, no one of the three motions is able to get a simple majority over the other two.

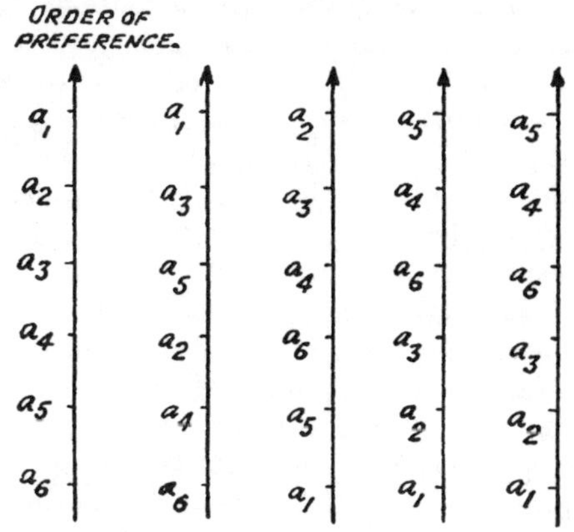

	a_1	a_2	a_3	a_4	a_5	a_6
a_1		(2, 3)	(2, 3)	(2, 3)	(2, 3)	(2, 3)
a_2	(3, 2)		(2, 3)	(3, 2)	(2, 3)	(3, 2)
a_3	(3, 2)	(3, 2)		(3, 2)	(3, 2)	(3, 2)
a_4	(3, 2)	(2, 3)	(2, 3)		(2, 3)	(5, 0)
a_5	(3, 2)	(3, 2)	(2, 3)	(3, 2)		(4, 1)
a_6	(3, 2)	(2, 3)	(2, 3)	(0, 5)	(1, 4)	

FIG. 7

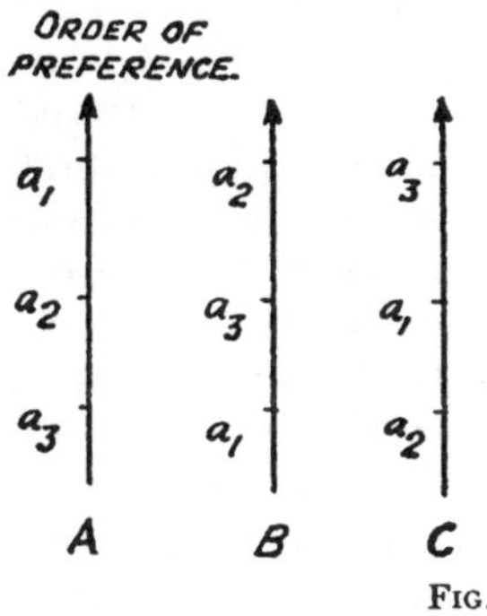

	a_1	a_2	a_3
a_1		(2, 1)	(1, 2)
a_2	(1, 2)		(2, 1)
a_3	(2, 1)	(1, 2)	

FIG. 8

By writing down groups of schedules in which 6 or 7 motions are arranged in various ways and by constructing the group matrices, the reader can quickly satisfy himself that such cases—in which no motion exists which can get a simple majority over each of the others—are by no means exceptional. The greater the number of motions put forward in a committee of any given size, the greater will be the percentage of the total number of possible cases in which there exists no motion which is able to get a simple majority over each of the others.

In this state of affairs, when no one motion can obtain a simple majority over each of the others, the procedure of a committee which holds only $(m - 1)$ votes *will* arrive at the adoption of a particular motion, whereas—if the requirement were that a motion should be able to get a simple majority over every other—no motion would be adopted. The particular motion which is adopted by the committee using the procedure of practice will depend on chance—the chance of particular motions coming earlier or later into the voting process. For Figure 8, if only $(m - 1 = 2)$ votes were taken, that motion, a_1 or a_2 or a_3, would be adopted which was introduced last into the voting process. If, for example, a_1 were first put against a_2, a_2 would be eliminated; and, with the field thus cleared, a_3 would defeat a_1.

If, then, only $(m - 1)$ votes are held and if no motion exists which is able to get a simple majority over every other, we cannot read off directly from the matrix the decision adopted by the committee. But when, in addition to the matrix, we know the order in which the motions are put against one another in a vote, again we can deduce what the decision of the committee must be.

Reference to Figure 8 will show that, when the shapes of the preference curves are subject to no restriction, the transitive property does not necessarily hold good.

IV. CONCLUSION

The technique of this paper applies irrespective of the topic to which the motions may relate. They may refer to price, quantity, or other economic phenomena; they may relate to motions put forward in regard to colonial government, to the structure of a college curriculum, and so on. The theory applies to a decision taken on any topic by means of voting—so far, of course, as the assumptions which are made correspond to reality. And it is possible to widen the assumptions, for example, to include cases of complementary valuation; to make allowance for the time element; and to cover the cases of committees making use of special majorities of any stipulated size. With these extensions in the assumptions there would be a widening of the field of phenomena to which the theory applies.

The theory, indeed, would appear to present the basis for the development of a pure science of politics. This would employ the same theory of relative valuation as economic science. It would employ a different definition of equilibrium. Equilibrium would now be defined in terms of voting, in place of the type of definition employed in economic science. We could move from the one science to the other with the alteration of a single definition. This, in the view of the writer, would be the main function of the theory. It fairly obviously, too, enables some parts of economics—those which relate to decisions taken by groups—to be carried a stage beyond their present development.

Glasgow University

[21]

PROBLEMS OF MAJORITY VOTING

GORDON TULLOCK
University of South Carolina

ECONOMISTS have devoted a great deal of thought to problems of governmental policy and, in particular, to the question of proper allocation of resources between the public and private sectors.[1] On the other hand, little attention has been given to the actual process of decision-making or to the type of policy likely to come out of the process.[2] It is the purpose of this article to discuss one particular method of making governmental decisions—majority voting—and to attempt to derive conclusions about its implications for resource allocation and government policy. It is hoped that the conclusions will be more realistic than current doctrine, which is based on an essentially economic view of what "ought" to happen.

Since it is impossible to talk about everything at once, the demonstration will be confined to certain features of the majority process. A number of other serious problems raised by the voting system will be disregarded. The most important of these concerns a series of difficulties and paradoxes in the voting process itself.[3] I will also disregard the fact that voters are frequently very poorly informed or even deceived in voting, the great oversimplification of issues necessary in order to reduce them to a form such that they can be determined by vote, and innumerable other possible limitations on the functional efficiency of the democratic process.

I shall consider the operation of majority rule under two different restrictions: logrolling (i.e., vote-trading) permitted and logrolling not permitted, starting with the latter. Since logrolling is the norm, discussion of the non-logrolling case must start with consideration of the institutional structure which eliminates logrolling. The standard referendum on a simple issue is the best example. The voter cannot trade his vote on one issue for votes on others because he and his acquaintances represent too small a part of the total electorate for this to be worth the effort involved. Further, the use of the secret ballot makes it impossible to tell whether voting promises are carried out. In these circumstances the voter will simply vote in accord with his preferences on each individual issue.

The contrary case, logrolling permitted, occurs under two circumstances. First, it occurs where a rather small body of voters vote openly on each measure; this is normally to be found in representative assemblies, but it may also be found in very small "direct democracy" units. Under these circumstances trades of votes are easy to arrange and observe and significantly affect the outcome. It

[1] See Julius Margolis, "The Economic Evaluation of Federal Water Resource Development," *American Economic Review*, XLIX (March, 1959), 69–111, for a review of some of the recent literature on the subject.

[2] Pioneers have begun to appear. See Anthony Downs, *An Economic Theory of Democracy* (New York: Harper & Bros., 1957), and Duncan Black, *The Theory of Committees and Elections* (Cambridge: Cambridge University Press, 1958).

[3] See Black (*op. cit.*) for a comprehensive view of the difficulties discovered to date.

is probable that this fact is one of the major reasons for the widespread use of representative democracy. The second type of logrolling, which may be called implicit logrolling, occurs when large bodies of voters are called on to decide complex issues, such as which party shall rule, or a complex set of issues presented as a unit for a referendum vote. Here there is no formal trading of votes, but an analogous process goes on. The "entrepreneurs" who offer candidates or programs to the voter make up a complex mix of policies to attract support.[4] In doing so, they keep firmly in mind the fact that the voter may be so interested in the outcome of some issue that he will vote for the party which supports it, although the party opposes him on other issues. This implicit logrolling will not be discussed further.

In the system in which logrolling is not permitted every voter simply indicates his preference, and the preference of the majority of the voters is carried out. The defect, and it is a serious one, of this procedure is that it ignores the various intensities of the desires of the voters. A man who is passionately opposed to a given measure and a man who does not much care but is slightly in favor of it are weighted equally. Obviously, both could very easily be made better off if the man who felt strongly were permitted to give a present to the man who had little preference in return for a reversal of his decision. The satisfaction of both would be improved, and the resulting situation would, on strictly Paretian grounds, be superior to the outcome of voting that weighed their votes equally. By way of illustration it is conceivable that a proposal to send all Negroes to Africa (or all Jews to Israel) would be passed by referendum. It would have not the slightest chance of passing Congress because the supporters of these two minorities would be willing to promise to support almost any other measure in return for votes against such a bill. In the absence of vote-trading, the support for it might reach 51 per cent, but it would not be intense, at least in the marginal cases, and hence the trading process would insure its defeat.

Even voters who are more or less indifferent to a given issue may find their votes on it counting as much as those of the most highly concerned individuals. The fact that a voter votes normally proves that he is not completely indifferent, but many voters are motivated to vote on referendum issues more by a sense of duty to vote than by any real concern with the matter at hand. Under these circumstances even the tiniest preference for one side or the other may determine the issue. Permitting the citizens who feel very strongly about an issue to compensate those whose opinion is only feebly held can result in a great increase of the well-being of both groups, and prohibiting such transactions is to prohibit a movement toward the optimum surface.

Note that the result under logrolling and under non-logrolling differs only if the minority feels more intensely about the issue than the majority; if the feeling of the majority is equal to or more intense than the minority, then the majority would prevail both with and without logrolling. It is only when the intensity of feeling of the minority is enough greater than that of the majority so that they are willing to make sacrifices in other areas sufficient to detach the

[4] This problem is discussed in a paper presented by Julius Margolis before the Conference on Public Finances: Needs, Sources, and Utilization, of the Universities–National Bureau of Economic Research Committee, held April 10 and 11, 1959, at Charlottesville, Virginia.

marginal voters from the majority (intense members of the majority might make counteroffers if they wished) that the logrolling process will change the outcome.

As an introduction to logrolling, let us consider a simple model. A township inhabited by one hundred farmers who have more or less similar farms is cut by a number of main roads maintained by the state. However, these roads are limited-access roads, and the farmers are permitted to enter the primary network only at points where local roads intersect it. The local roads are built and maintained by the township. Maintenance is simple. Any farmer who wishes to have a specific road repaired puts the issue up to vote. If the repairing is approved, the cost is assessed to the farmers as part of the real property tax. The principal use of the local roads by the farmers is to get to and from the major state roads. Since these major roads cut through the district, generally there are only four or five farmers dependent on any particular bit of local road to reach the major roads.

Under these circumstances the referendum system would result in no local roads being repaired, since an overwhelming majority would vote against repairing any given road. The logrolling system, however, permits the roads to be kept in repair through bargains among voters. The bargaining might take a number of forms, but most of these would be unstable, and the "equilibrium" involves overinvestment of resources.

One form that the implicit bargain among the farmers might take is this: each individual might decide, in his own mind, the general standard that should be maintained. That is, he would balance, according to his own schedule of preferences, the costs of maintaining his own road at various levels of repair with the benefits to be received from it and reach a decision as to the point where the margins were equal. He could then generalize this decision: he could vote on each proposal to repair a given road in the same way as he would vote for repairs on his own road. If every voter followed this rule, we would find a schedule of voting behavior such as that illustrated in Figure 1. Each mark on the horizontal line represents the standard of one voter for maintenance of all roads. If a proposal for repairing a given road falls to the left of his position, he would vote for it; if it falls to his right, against. If each road has at least one farmer whose preference for road repairs falls to the right of the median (*A* in Fig. 1)

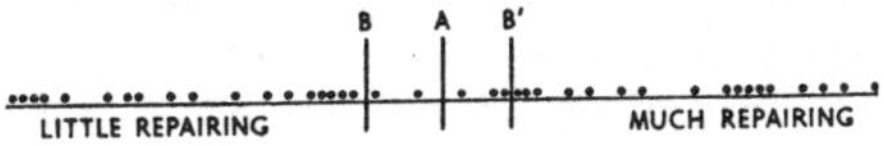

FIG. 1

then a proposal for repairs would be made as soon as a given road fell below his preferred degree of repair and successive further such proposals as the road gradually deteriorated. When it reached the median level, a repair proposal would pass; hence all roads would be repaired at the median preference.

Although this result would not be a Paretian optimum, it would be possible to argue for it in ethical terms. In fact, I believe that this is the result that most proponents of democracy in such situations have in the back of their minds. In any event, I intend to use this result, which I shall call "Kantian" as the "correct" result with which I shall contrast what actually happens. Since my Kantian result differs from the "equal marginal cost and marginal benefit" system used by most economists in this field, it is incumbent on me to explain why I use it. The reason is simple—it is the best I can do. I have been unable to find any system of voting which would lead to a social matching of costs and benefits at the margin.

If the farmers generally followed this policy in voting, then any individual farmer could benefit himself simply by voting against all proposals to repair roads other than his own and voting for proposals to repair his road at every opportunity. This would shift the median of the schedules slightly so that his taxes would be reduced or his road kept in better-than-average repair. If the other farmers on his road followed his example (we shall call farmers who follow this rule "maximizers"), they would be able to shift the standards of repair so that the roads on which they lived would be repaired at level B' while reducing the standard of repair on other roads to B. Since the largest share of the cost of keeping their road up falls on other taxpayers, while the largest share of their taxes goes for the repair of other roads, this change would be greatly to the advantage of the maximizers and greatly to the disadvantage of the Kantians.

If the farmers along another road also switched to a maximizing pattern, this would bring the level of road-repairing on the two maximizing roads down toward about that which would prevail under the Kantian system, while still further lowering the standards on the Kantian roads. However, it is likely that the two groups of maximizers could benefit by forming a coalition in order to raise the standards of road maintenance on their own roads. Let us consider the situation of an individual maximizer debating whether or not to enter such a coalition. Since he will pay only about 1/100th of the cost, practically any proposal to repair his own road is to his benefit. If, however, in order to obtain support for some repair project on his own road, he must also vote for the repair of another road, then he must also count the cost to him of this other repair project as part of the cost of his own road. In weighing the costs and benefits, he must consider not only the tax cost to himself of the repair of his own road but the tax cost of the other repair job which he must vote for in order to get his road done. In the particular case we are now discussing, when the farmers on all the roads except two are still Kantian, this would put few restraints on feasible projects, but it would still have to be considered. However, as more and more Kantians become tired of being exploited by the maximizers and switch to a maximizing pattern of behavior, this consideration would become more and more important.

Let us now examine a rather unlikely, but theoretically important, special case. Suppose that exactly 51 of our 100 farmers were maximizers, while 49 were Kantians. Further suppose that all the maximizers lived on some roads while all the Kantians lived on others. Under these circumstances the Kantians clearly would never get their roads repaired, but the level of repair on the maximizers' roads presents a more difficult problem. In order to simplify it, let us assume (plausibly) that they are maintained on a high enough level so that all the Kantians vote against any project for further repair. Under these circumstances it would be necessary to obtain the votes of all the maximizers for each repair project. A farmer considering whether he wants to have his road repaired must consider the whole cost, including the taxes he must pay in order to repair the roads of the other parties to the bargain. He can, however, simply compare his own marginal benefits and costs, and this requires no knowledge of anyone else's utility. He need only decide whether the total bargain is to his advantage or not.[5]

Note, however, that, while no roads leading to the Kantian farmers' houses will be repaired, they are required to contribute to the repair of the roads leading to the houses of the maximizers. Thus part of the cost of the road-repair projects will be paid by persons not party to the bargain, and, since the maximizers only count the costs to themselves of their votes, the general standard of road maintenance on the roads on which they live should be higher than if they had to count also the cost of maintaining the roads on which the Kantians lived. Under such conditions, where virtue so conspicuously is not paying, it seems likely that at least some of the Kantian farmers would decide to switch to a minimizing policy. For simplicity, let us assume that all of them do this at once. Since they would still be in a minority, their change of policy would not immediately benefit them, but surely they could find two of the original maximizers who would, in return for very good maintenance, desert their former colleagues. It is again obvious that the new majority would be susceptible to similar desertions; a permanent coalition of 51 farmers for the purpose of exploiting the remaining 49 could thus not be maintained. In terms of game theory any combination of 51 voters dominates any other size of combination, but no combination of 51 dominates all other combinations of 51.[6]

The outcome is clear. Each farmer would enter into bilateral agreements with enough farmers on other roads to insure that his own was repaired. He would then be forced to count as part of the cost of getting his road repaired the cost (to him) of repairing the roads of the other 50 farmers. These bilateral agreements, however, would overlap. Farmer A (more precisely the farmers on road A) would bargain with Farmers B, . . . , M. Farmer M, on the other hand, might make up his majority from Farmer A and Farmers N, . . . , Z.

Counting the cost to himself of the maintenance of his road in terms of support for other road-repair projects, each farmer would consider only those projects for which he voted. Thus his expenditure pattern would count the tax payments of 49 voters as a free gift. The natural result would be that each road would be maintained at a level considerably higher and at greater expense than is rational from the standpoint of the farmers living along it. Each individual behaves rationally, but the outcome is irrational. This apparent paradox may be explained as follows: each voter pays enough in support for repair of other roads to equalize the benefit he receives from the repair of his own road. But his payments counted under this system include only part of the road repair jobs undertaken.[7]

[5] In practice the problem of getting the unanimous agreement of 51 persons might be insoluble. Since we are now only discussing a rather unlikely special case, we can ignore the point. Alternatively, the reader can assume that there are 53 or 54 maximizers, and those who set their terms too high can simply be left out.

[6] In the "Theory of the Reluctant Duelist" (*American Economic Review*, XLVI [December, 1956], 909–23) Daniel Ellsberg contends that game theory really only applies to "reluctant" players. Our case is a particularly pure example. The voter must "play the game" by entering into bargains with 50 of his fellows, even though this leads to rather unsatisfactory results, simply because any other course of action is even worse.

[7] The fact that he is taxed for other roads not part of his bargain reduces his real income and hence, to some extent, reduces the amount of road repairing he would wish to consume.

There are others which are the result of bargains to which he is not a party. Taken as a group, the road-repair projects for which he votes represent a good bargain for him, but other *ad hoc* bargains to repair other roads will also take place. He will vote against these, but, as he will be in the minority, he will have to pay for them. The result is a sizable loss to him.

Any farmer following any other course of action will be even worse off. A Kantian farmer, for example, would never have his own road repaired but would pay heavy taxes for the support of repair jobs on other roads. The whole process will proceed through elaborate negotiations; the man who is the most effective bargainer will have a considerable advantage, but the general pattern will be less than optimal for all parties.

This seems a rather unsatisfactory result, and we should consider whether there are not ways of improving it. First, however, I should like to discuss certain possible objections to my reasoning.[8] It may be said that the maximizers are behaving wickedly and that ethical considerations will prevent the majority of the population from following such a course. Ethical systems vary greatly from culture to culture, and I do not wish to rule out the possible existence somewhere of an ethical system which could bar logrolling, but surely the American system does not. Under our system logrolling is normally publicly characterized as "bad," but no real stigma attaches to those who practice it. The press describes such deals without any apparent disapproval, and, in fact, all our political organizations bargain in this fashion.

A second argument asserts that each farmer in our community would realize that, if he adopted a maximizing policy, this would lead all other farmers to do the same. Since the "maximizing equilibrium" is worse for all[9] the farmers than the "Kantian median," each farmer would, on the basis of cold selfish calculation, follow the Kantian system. This argument is similar to the view that no union will force its wage rate up because each union realizes that such action will lead other unions to do the same, the eventual outcome being higher prices and wage rates but no increase in real income. There seems to be overwhelming empirical evidence that men do not act this way; in addition, the argument contains a logical flaw. This is the observation that, in any series of actions by a number of men, there must be a first one. If this can be prevented, then the whole series can be prevented. This is true, of course, but there also must be a second, a third, etc. If any one of these is prevented, then the whole series cannot be carried out. If all our 100 farmers would refrain from a maximizing course of action because each one felt that his personal adoption of such a course would lead to a switch to the "maximizing equilibrium," then, if one of them had done so, we could construct an exactly similar argument "proving" that no 1 of the 99 remaining farmers would follow his example. But if this second argument is true, then the first is false; and hence the chain of reasoning contains an inconsistency.

[8] James Buchanan kindly permitted me to present this paper before his graduate seminar in public finance, and the objections made by some of the students tended to follow these lines.

[9] Not necessarily for all. There might well be one or more farmers whose personal preference schedules called for a large enough investment in roads so that the "maximizing equilibrium" was preferable to the "Kantian median."

I turn now to possible methods of improving the results. Could the members of a community somehow enter into an enforceable bargain under which they act according to the Kantian model? In the very narrow special case of our model, it is at least conceivable that they could. It is possible that a clear, unambiguous formula for telling when a road needed repair might be agreed upon, and then the exact figures to be inserted in the formula determined by general voting. Probably even in our case this would not be practical, but the theoretical possibility must be admitted.

In the more general and realistic case where governmental units deal with a continuing stream of radically different projects, no such agreed formula would be possible. A formula which would permit weighing such diverse programs as building giant irrigation projects in the West to increase farm production, paying large sums of money to farmers in the Midwest to reduce farm production, giving increased aid to Israel, and dredging Baltimore's harbor is inconceivable. There could not, therefore, be any agreement on an automatic system of allocating resources, and this throws us back to making individual decisions with the use of logrolling.

This is by no means a tragedy. If it were possible to set up some system by present voting to determine future resource allocation, it is more likely that this determination would take a form favored by a simple majority of the voters than a form favored by the whole group unanimously. This is likely to result in a worse decision than that resulting from logrolling. The problem of intensity must also be considered. The Kantian system makes no allowance for the differential intensities of the voters' preferences. If the voters who wanted more resources spent on road-repairing felt more intensely about it than the voters who wanted less, then the Kantian system would not result in an optimum distribution of resources. Permitting logrolling would take care of this problem.

Requiring more than a simple majority would reduce the resources spent on roads, since more people would have to be included in each bargain, and the cost to each voter of repair to this road would consequently be increased. The larger the majority required, the more closely would the result approach a Pareto optimum. Practically, however, the difficulty of negotiating a bargain would increase exponentially as the number of required parties increased, and this might make such a solution impossible. The provision in so many constitutions for a two-house legislature, each house elected according to a different system, raises much the same issues.

Our next problem is to inquire to what extent the results obtained in our simple model can be generalized. It would appear that any governmental activity which benefits a given individual or group of voters and which is paid for from general taxation could be fitted into our model. It is not necessary that the revenues used to pay for the projects be collected equally from all voters. All that is necessary is that the benefits be significantly more concentrated than the costs. This is a very weak restraint, and a very large number of budgetary patterns would fit it. If the taxes were collected by some indirect method so that individuals could not tell just how much they were paying for any given project, then this fact would accentuate the process. In the marginal case the individual might be indifferent about projects benefiting other people whose cost to him was slight and difficult to calculate.

One requirement of the process has not yet been emphasized. It is necessary that the voting on the various projects be a continuing process. A number of different projects or groups of projects must be voted on at different times. If all projects were inserted in a single bill to be accepted or rejected for all time, then 51 per cent of the voters could fix the bill permanently to exploit the remainder. In fact, of course, since government is a continuing process, our condition is fulfilled.

The process which we have been discussing can be generalized to cover other types of government activity. We shall start by generalizing it to cover other types of taxation-expenditure problems and then turn to other types of governmental problems. First, let us suppose that we have some governmental activity of general benefit, police work, for example, which is paid for by some general type of taxation. By reasoning paralleling that which we have done so far, we can demonstrate that special tax exemptions to special groups at the expense of the general efficiency of the police force would be carried on to a degree which would far exceed the Kantian median. Similarly, if a given sum of money is to be spent on two different types of governmental activity, one of which is of general benefit and one of which benefits a series of special groups, too much will be spent on the latter. Defense, for example, will be slighted in favor of river and harbor work.

The same reasoning can be applied to the tax structure. If a given amount of money had to be raised, we would expect it to be raised by general taxes that were "too heavy" but riddled by special exemptions for all sorts of groups. This would greatly reduce the effect of any general tax policy, such as progression, that had been adopted. This pattern appears to be very realistic. On the basis of our theory, we would predict general and diffuse taxes, riddled with special exceptions, and governmental functions of general benefit sacrificed in favor of the interests of particular groups. I see no great conflict between the prediction and reality.

To apply our theory generally to all types of governmental activity, however, we must radically generalize it. For any individual voter all possible measures can be arranged according to the intensity of his feeling. His welfare can be improved if he accepts a decision against his desire in an area where his feelings are comparatively weak in return for a decision in his favor in an area where his feelings are strong. Bargains between voters, therefore, can be mutually beneficial. Logically, the voter should enter into such bargains until the marginal "cost" of voting for something he disapproves of but about which his feelings are weak exactly matches the marginal benefit of the vote on something else which he receives in return. Thus he will benefit from the total complex of issues which enter into the set of bargains which he makes with other people. In making these bargains, however, he must gain the assent of a majority of the voters only, not of all of them. On any given issue he can safely ignore the desires of 49 per cent. This means that he can afford to "pay" more to people for voting for his measures because part of the inconvenience imposed by the measure will fall on parties not members of the bargains.

Unfortunately, the converse also applies. Bargains will be entered into in which our voter does not participate but part of the cost of which he will have to bear. As a result, the whole effect of the measures which result from his bargains and on which he votes on the winning side will be beneficial to him. But this will be only slightly more than half of all the "bargained" measures passed, and the remainder will be definitely contrary to his interest. The same would be true for the *average* voter under a pure referendum system. In fact, the whole problem discussed in this paper arises from the system of compelling the minority to accept the will of the majority.

Although this paper so far has been an exercise in "positive politics," the analysis does raise important policy problems, and at least some comment on them seems desirable. It seems clear that the system of majority voting is not by any means an optimal method of allocating resources. This fact should be taken into account in considering whether some aspect of our economy would be better handled by governmental or market techniques. On the other hand, these problems and difficulties do not materially reduce the advantage which voting procedures have over despotism as a system of government. The primary lesson would appear to be the need for further research. Majority voting plays the major role in the governments of all the nations in which the social sciences are comparatively advanced. It seems likely that careful analysis of the process would lead to the discovery of improved techniques and a possible increase in governmental efficiency.

[22]

THE WELFARE COSTS OF TARIFFS, MONOPOLIES, AND THEFT

GORDON TULLOCK

RICE UNIVERSITY

In recent years a considerable number of studies have been published that purport to measure the welfare costs of monopolies and tariffs.[1] The results have uniformly shown very small costs for practices that economists normally deplore. This led Mundell to comment in 1962 that "Unless there is a thorough theoretical re-examination of the validity of the tools upon which these studies are founded . . . someone will inevitably draw the conclusion that economics has ceased to be important."[2] Judging from conversations with graduate students, a number of younger economists are in fact drawing the conclusion that tariffs and monopolies are not of much importance. This view is now beginning to appear in the literature. On the basis of these measurements Professor Harvey Leibenstein has argued "Microeconomic theory focuses on allocative efficiency to the exclusion of other types of efficiencies that, in fact, are much more significant in many instances."[3]

It is my purpose to take the other route suggested by Mundell and demonstrate that the "tools on which these studies are founded" produce an underestimation of the welfare costs of tariffs and monopolies. The classical economists were not concerning themselves with trifles when they argued against tariffs, and the Department of Justice is not dealing with a miniscule problem in its attacks on monopoly.

STATICS

The present method for measuring these costs was pioneered by Professor Harberger.[4] Let us, therefore, begin with a very simple use of his diagram to analyze a tariff. Figure 1 shows a commodity that can be produced

[1]These studies are conveniently listed with a useful table of the welfare losses computed in each in Harvey Leibenstein, "Allocative Efficiency vs. 'X-Efficiency'," *Am. Econ. Rev.*, June 1966, *56*, 392-415.

[2]R. A. Mundell, Review of L. H. Janssen, *Free Trade, Protection and Customs Union*, *Am. Econ. Rev.*, June 1962, *52*, 622.

[3]*Op. cit.*, p. 392. In this article Leibenstein consistently uses the phrase "allocative efficiency" to refer solely to the absence of tariffs and monopolies.

[4]A. C. Harberger, "Using the Resources at Hand More Effectively," *Am. Econ. Rev.*, May 1959, *49*, 134-46. It should be noted that Harberger suggested the method for the measurement of the welfare costs of monopoly, but its extension to cover tariffs was the work of other scholars. The more careful scholars who have measured the welfare costs of tariffs have not all used this very simple application of Harberger's method, but a method such as illustrated in Figure 2. I have chosen to begin with this method of measurement partly because it simplifies the exposition and partly because this procedure is the "conventional wisdom" on the matter. *(Cf.* Leibenstein, *op. cit.)*

domestically at the constant cost of P_1 and imported at P_0. With the given demand and no tariff Q_0 units will be purchased at a price of P_0. If a prohibitive tariff is imposed Q_1 units will be bought at a price of P_1. The increase in price, it is argued, is merely a transfer from some members of the community to others, and the only welfare loss is consequently the shaded triangle. The studies purporting to measure the welfare costs of tariffs have simply computed the value of this triangle. From the geometry it is fairly obvious that the amount would normally be small.

Figure 1

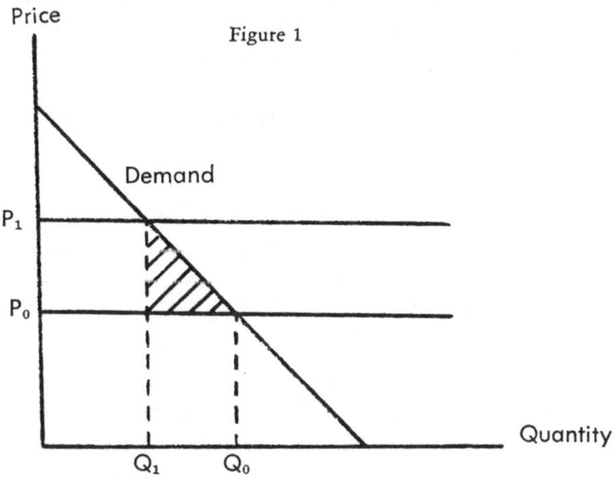

There are a considerable number of costs that are ignored by this procedure. As a starter, collection of a tariff involves expenditure on customs inspectors, etc., who do the actual collection and coast guards who prevent smuggling. Further, customs brokers are normally hired by the shipper to expedite the movement of their goods through customs.[5] Normally we pay little attention to collections costs because they are small, but in this case they may well be larger than the welfare triangle which is also small. Thus by simply adding in collection costs we significantly increase the "social cost" of the tariff.

For a more significant criticism of this method of measuring the welfare cost let us apply the procedure to a standard excise tax instead of a tariff. Assume that Figure 1 shows a constant supply cost and a declining demand for some commodity in some country. Q_0 units are bought at a price, P_0. Now suppose that a tax is imposed, raising the price to P_1, and reducing sales to Q_1. The welfare cost of this tax is measured by the shaded triangle. But suppose further, that the revenues raised by this tax are completely wasted, building tunnels, for example, which go nowhere. Now the social

[5]Strictly speaking, the customs brokerage should be added on to the tax thus producing a larger welfare triangle.

cost of the total package of tax and wasteful expenditure is the welfare triangle plus the total tax revenue, or the trapezoid bounded by the lines showing cost, the cost-plus-tax, and the demand function. The people buying the product pay more than the cost, but no one benefits from the expenditure.[6] The funds are not transferred because no one benefits from the existence of the tax. The whole economy is poorer not just by the triangle, but by the whole amount of wasted resources.

The tariff involves a similar waste of resources and consequently its social cost cannot be measured simply by the welfare triangle. Figure 1 can also be used to show the foreign and domestic costs of some type of good and the national demand for it. Since domestic cost is higher than the (delivered) cost of the foreign good, none would be produced domestically in the absence of a tariff. Q_0 units would be imported and consumed at a price shown by P_0. The country now puts on a prohibitive tariff and the higher cost domestic production takes over the complete market. Q_1 units are sold at P_1. The welfare triangle has been used to measure the welfare cost of this operation.[7] The argument for this procedure is, essentially, that the higher prices paid by the consumers represent a transfer payment, not a real loss to the economy. But who receives this transfer? The owners of the resources now engaged in inefficiently producing the commodity receive no more than they would have received had the tariff never been introduced and they had been employed in other industries.[8] These resources, however, are being inefficiently utilized, and the rectangle between P_1 and P_0 and bounded by the vertical axis and Q_1 measures the social cost of this waste. Thus the total welfare cost of the tariff is the triangle plus the much larger rectangle to its left.

The situation is identical to that which would arise if the government required an established domestic industry to abandon an efficient method of production and adopt an inefficient. This could be graphed on the same diagram, and it would be generally agreed that the welfare loss would not be just the welfare triangle, but would also include the inefficient use of resources required by the governmental regulation shown in the rectangle to the left of the triangle. Since a tariff shifting production from the production of export goods to import-replacement goods where the country has a comparative disadvantage is, in fact, a governmental requirement that the goods be obtained in an inefficient manner, the cases are identical. The cost of a protective tariff is the triangle plus the difference between domestic cost of production and the price at which the goods could be purchased abroad.

[6]The government action might slightly increase the rents on the resources used to build the tunnel, and thus the owners of specialized resources might benefit slightly, but clearly this is a very trivial effect.

[7]Tibor Scitovsky, *Economic Theory and Western European Integration*, Stanford 1958.

[8]There might be sizable but temporary rents to the firstcomers when the industry was first established.

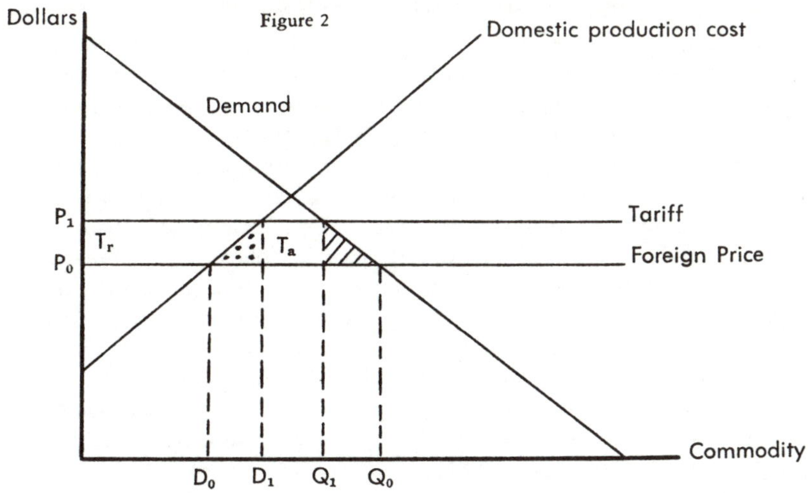

Let us, however, consider the situation in which there is some domestic production before the imposition of a tariff. Figure 2 shows a commodity part of the consumption of which is imported and part produced domestically. The supply elasticity of the commodity from foreign sources is assumed infinite, but domestic production is carried on in conditions of increasing costs. Without the tariff, the price is P_0, domestic producers turn out D_0 units and $Q_0 - D_0$ units are imported to make up the total consumption of Q_0. Suppose now, that Mr. Gladstone is prime minister and imposes a tariff on imports and an excise tax of the same amount on domestic production. With the new price, P_1, consumers will want only Q_1 units, and the shaded triangle measures the excess burden. Domestic production will remain D_0, but imports will shrink from $Q_0 - D_0$ to $Q_1 - D_0$. The government will receive a tax revenue equivalent to the entire rectangle bounded by the two price lines, the vertical axis and Q_1.

Let us now change our example by assuming that the domestic excise tax is repealed, so that we have only a protective tariff. Domestic consumption and price would remain the same, but domestic production would expand to D_1 and imports would shrink accordingly. There would be an inefficient use of resources in producing things which would be better imported represented by the dotted triangle. Governmental revenues would shrink to the rectangle marked T_a and the owners of the resources in the domestic industry would receive an amount of resources equal to the area of the trapezoid T_r.[9] Clearly the social cost of the tariff is not just the shaded triangle, but also the dotted triangle which shows a net waste of resources in inefficient production.

[9]See J. Wemelsfelder, "The Short Term Effect of the Lowering of Import Duties in Germany," *Econ. Jour.*, March 1960, *70*, 94-104.

DYNAMICS: THE COST OF TRANSFERS

The trapezoid T_r, however, would appear to be a pure transfer, and hence not to be included in the computation of the cost of the tariff. Strictly speaking this is so, but looking at the matter dynamically, there is another social cost involved, and its magnitude is a function of the size of this transfer trapezoid. Generally governments do not impose protective tariffs on their own. They have to be lobbied or pressured into doing so by the expenditure of resources in political activity. One would anticipate that the domestic producers would invest resources in lobbying for the tariff until the marginal return on the last dollar so spent was equal to its likely return producing the transfer. There might also be other interests trying to prevent the transfer and putting resources into influencing the government in the other direction. These expenditures, which may simply offset each other to some extent, are purely wasteful from the standpoint of society as a whole; they are spent not in increasing wealth, but in attempts to transfer or resist transfer of wealth. I can suggest no way of measuring these expenditures, but the potential returns are large, and it would be quite surprising if the investment was not also sizable.

Monopolies involve costs of a somewhat similar nature, and it follows that I will not be able to produce a method to measure their social costs. I will, however, be able to demonstrate that the welfare triangle method greatly underestimates these costs. The argument is customarily explained with the aid of a figure like Figure 1. The monopolist charges the monopoly price P_1 instead of the cost P_0 for the commodity, and consumption is reduced from Q_0 to Q_1. The welfare triangle is a clear loss to the community but the rectangle to its left is merely a transfer from the consumers to the owners of the monopoly. We may object to the monopolist getting rich at the expense of the rest of us, but this is not a reduction in the national product.

In order to demonstrate that this line of reasoning ignores important costs, I should like to take a detour through the economics of theft.[10] Theft, of course, is a pure transfer, and therefore might be assumed to have no welfare effects at all. Like a lump sum tax, it produces no welfare triangle at all, and hence would show a zero social cost if measured by the Harberger method. This would, of course, be incorrect. In spite of the fact that it involves only transfers, the existence of theft has very substantial welfare costs. Our laws against theft do not deal with a trivial and/or unimportant problem any more than our laws against monopoly.

[10]The economics of illegal activities is an underdeveloped area, but Harold Demsetz discusses the subject briefly in "The Exchange and Enforcement of Property Rights," *Jour. of Law and Econ.*, October 1964, 7, 11-26. J. Randolph Norsworthy's Doctoral Dissertation, *A Theory of Tax Evasion and Collection*, Virginia, 1966, is a more comprehensive examination of one type of illegal activity. Two unpublished items have been circulated among a few scholars. Gary Becker's "A Theory of Government Punishments and Rewards," and my own *Law and Morals*, the unfinished manuscript of a book which I began four years ago and which has languished in draft form for almost all of those four years.

Figure 3 shows the situation confronting the potential thief. On the horizontal axis is shown the quantity of effort and capital (burglars' tools, etc.) he might invest in a career of crime. On the vertical axis are shown potential returns. The "opportunity cost" line shows the returns he could get for the same investment of work and material in other occupations. It is assumed to be constant. Let us begin by assuming that taking another's property is not illegal. Under these circumstances the returns on various amounts of investment in the activity are shown by line *R*. The potential thieves would invest the quantity of resources shown at *A* in theft, the cost to him would be the rectangle AA'DC, and his net return on the investment would be the triangular area above A'D.

Figure 3

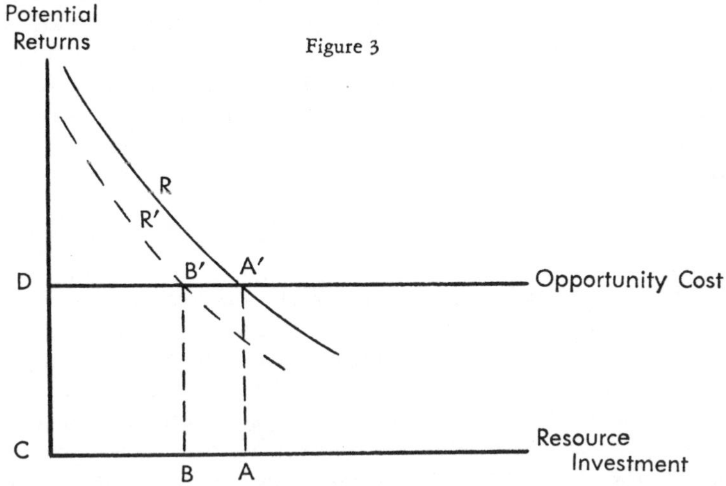

The situation of a person who wished to guard his own assets, who might, of course, be the thief hoping to hold onto his loot, may also be shown on Figure 3. On the horizontal axis are shown the resources invested in loss minimizing activities.[11] The cost of each unit of resources put to this use is shown by the horizontal opportunity line, and the savings are on the vertical axis. The line *R* now shows the returns in the form of savings for each unit of "theft prevention." The total amount of resources invested would again be *A*.

The two situations are interrelated by more than the fact that they can be shown on the same diagram. The height of the *R* curve for the thief would depend upon the amount of resources invested by other members of the community in locks and other protections. Similarly, the individual in considering how many locks to buy would find that his *R* curve

[11]The word "activities" may be misleading. One way of minimizing loss by theft is to have little or nothing to steal. In a world in which theft was legal we could expect this fact to lead to a reduction in productive activities and a great expansion in leisure.

depended upon the resources being invested in attempts at theft by the rest of the population. When a potential thief invests money, say, in an improved lock pick, the *R* curve for people trying to protect their property moves downward. Similarly, hiring an armed guard to watch your valuables moves the *R* curve for potential thieves down. Putting a new lock on my door reduces the chance that I will be robbed, but whether the gain will be worth the cost will depend upon the effort the thieves are willing to put into getting in. Over time the interaction between the investment in locks, the payoff on lock picks and the investment in nitroglycerine and safes would come to equilibrium.

This equilibrium, however, would be extremely costly to the society in spite of the fact that the activity of theft only involves transfers. The cost to society would be the investments of capital and labor in the activity of theft and in protection against theft. If we consider Figure 3 as representing the entire society instead of individuals, then the social costs would be the area covered by the rectangle AA′DC. Transfers themselves cost society nothing, but for the people engaging in them they are just like any other activity, and this means that large resources may be invested in attempting to make or prevent transfers. These largely offsetting commitments of resources are totally wasted from the standpoint of society as a whole.

This lesson has been learned by almost all societies that have adopted a collective method of reducing this sort of income transfer. This collective procedure, laws against theft and police and courts to enforce them, can also be shown on Figure 3. On the horizontal axis we now have resources invested by police and courts, with their opportunity cost shown as a horizontal line. The "protection" given by each unit of resources invested in these activities is shown by the *R* line. The society would purchase *A* amount of protective services, and the total cost would be the usual rectangle. The effect of this would be to reduce the expected returns on theft and the savings to be made by private investment in locks, etc. The new returns are shown by *R′* on Figure 3, and there is a corresponding reduction in the resources invested in each of these fields to *B′*. Whether the establishment of a police force is wise or not, depends upon an essentially technological question. If police activities are, for a range, more efficient than private provision of protection, then the *R* line will have the shape shown, and the police and court rectangle will have an area smaller than the sum of the two "savings" rectangles, for theft and locks.[12] This is, of course, what we normally find in the real world.

Note, however, that we do not carry investment in police protection to the extent that it totally replaces private protective expenditures. Clearly

[12]It may be suggested that society should not be interested in the saving of the resources of thieves, and hence that the value of the protection afforded by the police should be measured by the lock rectangle only. This, however, would be correct only to the extent that the resources would not be reallocated to socially acceptable production.

it is more efficient to have some protective expenditures by the owners of property. Automobiles are equipped with locks and keys, presumably because the expansion of the police force which could be paid for from the cost of leaving them off would be less effective in preventing theft than they are.[13] The total social cost of theft is the sum of the efforts invested in the activity of theft, private protection against theft, and the public investment in police protection. The theft itself is a pure transfer, and has no welfare cost, but the existence of theft as a potential activity results in very substantial diversion of resources to fields where they essentially offset each other, and produce no positive product. The problem with income transfers is not that they directly inflict welfare losses, but that they lead people to employ resources in attempting to obtain or prevent such transfers. A successful bank robbery will inspire potential thieves to greater efforts, lead to the installation of improved protective equipment in other banks, and perhaps result in the hiring of additional policemen. These are its social costs, and they can be very sizable.

But this has been a detour through the criminal law, our major subject is monopoly. To return to Figure 1, the rectangle to the left of the welfare triangle is the income transfer that a successful monopolist can extort from the customers. Surely we should expect that with a prize of this size dangling before our eyes, potential monopolists would be willing to invest large resources in the activity of monopolizing. In fact the investment that could be profitably made in forming a monopoly would be larger than this rectangle, since it represents merely the income transfer. The capital value, properly discounted for risk, would be worth much more. Entrepreneurs should be willing to invest resources in attempts to form a monopoly until the marginal cost equals the properly discounted return.[14] The potential customers would also be interested in preventing the transfer and should be willing to make large investments to that end. Once the monopoly is formed, continual efforts to either break the monopoly or muscle into it would be predictable. Here again considerable resources might be invested. The holders of the monopoly, on the other hand, would be willing to put quite sizable sums into the defense of their power to receive these transfers.

As a successful theft will stimulate other thieves to greater industry and require greater investment in protective measures, so each successful establishment of a monopoly or creation of a tariff will stimulate greater diversion of resources to attempts to organize further transfers of income. In Gladstone's England few resources were put into attempts to get favorable

[13]James Buchanan and Gordon Tullock, "Public and Private Interaction Under Reciprocal Externality," in *The Public Economy of Urban Communities,* Julius Margolis, Ed., Washington, D.C. 1964, pp. 52-73.

[14]The margin here is a rather unusual one. Additional units of resources invested in attempting to get a monopoly do not increase the value of the potential monopoly, but the likelihood of getting it. Thus they change the discount rate, rather than the payoff.

tariff treatment. In present day United States large and well financed lobbies exist for this purpose. The welfare cost in the first case was very low, in the second it must be quite sizable. An efficient police force reduces the resources put into the activity of theft, and free trade or an active antitrust policy will reduce the resources invested in lobbying or attempting to organize monopolies.

The problem of identifying and measuring these resources is a difficult one, partly because the activity of monopolizing is illegal. The budget of the antitrust division and the large legal staffs maintained by companies in danger of prosecution would be clear examples of the social cost of monopoly, but presumably they are only a small part of the total. That very scarce resource, skilled management, may be invested to a considerable extent in attempting to build, break, or muscle into a monopoly. Lengthy negotiations may be in real terms very expensive, but we have no measure of their cost. Similarly, a physical plant may be designed not for maximum efficiency in direct production, but for its threat potential. Again, no measure is possible. As a further problem, probably much of the cost of monopoly is spread through companies that do not have a monopoly, but have gambled resources on the hopes of one. The cost of a football pool is not measured by the cost of the winner's ticket, but by the cost of all tickets.[15] Similarly the total costs of monopoly should be measured in terms of the efforts to get a monopoly by the unsuccessful as well as the successful. Surely most American businessmen know that the odds are against their establishing a paying monopoly, and they therefore discount the potential gain when investing resources in attempting to get one. The successful monopolist finds that his gamble has paid off, and the unsuccessful "bettor" in this particular lottery will lose, but the resources put into the "pool" would be hard to find by economic techniques. But regardless of the measurement problem, it is clear that the resources put into monopolization and defense against monopolization would be a function of the size of the prospective transfer. Since this would be normally large, we can expect that this particular socially wasteful type of "investment" would also be large. The welfare triangle method of measurement ignores this important cost, and hence greatly understates the welfare loss of monopoly.

[15]This helpful analogy was suggested to me by Dr. William Niskanen.

[23]

Uncertainty, Costs, and Collectivist Economic Planning[1]

By JACK WISEMAN

I. INTRODUCTION

The purpose of this paper is to consider the possibility, in conditions of uncertainty, of utilising a marginal cost ' rule ' to distribute resources between uses in an economy in which there is consumers' sovereignty, with freedom of choice of goods and occupations, but in which factors of production cannot be privately owned and exploited.[2]

It will be argued that in conditions of uncertainty (i.e. once the fact of time is admitted), the marginal cost rule, as normally framed, gives no clear guidance to those responsible for the organisation of production in such an economy. Attempts to reinterpret the rule in such a way as to take account of uncertainty preclude the possibility of a direct check on the efficiency of collectivist managers in obeying that rule. Any indirect, *objective*, check used as a supplement to the marginal rule will in fact supplant that rule as the directive for managerial effort, and in any case no completely objective check is possible. Further, whatever rule or check is adopted, imperfectly competitive behaviour is to be expected in the absence of detailed regulation to control it.

In these circumstances, the most satisfactory distribution of resources seems likely to be obtained by an instruction to collectivist managers similar to the profit maximisation ' rule ' of the market economy. Identification of the managerial and the public interest would then have to be sought through the detailed regulation of managerial behaviour, in much the way that the government in a market economy attempts to regulate imperfectly competitive behaviour by entrepreneurs.[3]

II. THE NATURE OF THE RULE

(*a*) *The Competitive Market Economy*

The ' rule ' to be discussed derives from the classical model of the perfectly competitive market economy, and is best understood in relation to that model. It was elucidated in the course of controversy as to

[1] I am particularly indebted to the valuable suggestions and criticisms of Mr. G. F. Thirlby, and to my colleagues who commented on the article in draft.

[2] Such an economy will be referred to hereafter as a ' liberal collectivist ' economy.

[3] While the argument presented is related to the functioning of a liberal collectivist economy, it has a direct bearing on problems arising in a ' mixed ' society such as our own. It is relevant, for example, to a consideration of the pricing policy of public utilities which is normally discussed in relation to similar ' rules '. This is a question the writer hopes to take up in a later paper.

the possibility of distributing productive factors efficiently between uses in an economy in which such factors were owned collectively.[1]

In this competitive market economy, resources are privately owned and exploited. They are also, in the perfectly competitive model, perfectly divisible and perfectly mobile between uses. Producers are assumed to act in the light of known data; i.e., their task is the combination of factors of production with known prices in the production of products to be sold at known prices. The distribution of resources between uses is carried out by an administrative mechanism, the characteristics of which are profit maximisation and a system of competitive markets in which buyers and sellers compete. With such a mechanism, producers' decisions about the use of resources are determined by *opportunity cost;* i.e., the use of resources in the chosen way is the result of an assessment of the revenues to be obtained by their use in any other way, the greatest of these foregone alternative revenues being the opportunity cost.

With the conditions of the model, the process described must result in an ' efficient ' distribution of resources between uses in the sense that, with given consumer incomes, no reallocation of factors or products between uses could increase the satisfaction of any one consumer without reducing that of another. Since all relevant factor- and product-values are assumed known, there is no *doubt* about the production decisions to be taken by individual producers. The subjective (opportunity) costs have an objective counterpart in lists of known factor prices, which are in effect the sole content of the opportunity cost decision. The producers' task is simply the pricing of money inputs (i.e., sums of known factor prices) and product outputs, in the case of some production plan, and the relating of this certain result to the money values of products foregone, the prices of these products also being known. Different individuals in similar circumstances should make identical assessments and reach identical decisions. That is, the opportunity cost concept in such conditions is merely a reassertion of the fundamental economic problem of *scarcity;* it contains no element either of uncertainty or of judgment.

The competitive model as normally set out nevertheless contains an indirect check on efficiency in resource distribution, implicit in the mechanism of competitive profit maximisation. It is a property of the ideally efficient situation that producers' total money revenues will equal their total money outlays (including payment for their own services). Inefficiency in production (and hence in resource distribution)

[1] Much of the early discussion has been brought together in two sets of reprints of relevant articles: *Collectivist Economic Planning*, ed. F. A. Hayek (which includes L. von Mises' pioneer article, "Economic Calculus in the Socialist Commonwealth"), and *On the Economic Theory of Socialism*, ed. Benjamin E. Lipincott (which includes reprints of articles by O. Lange and F. M. Taylor suggesting and elaborating the use of marginal criteria). A number of other papers on the subject were published in the *Economic Journal* and *Review of Economic Studies* during the 1930's, and a marginal ' rule ' was elaborated by (*inter alia*) A. P. Lerner in *Economics of Control* (1944).

results in a money loss which indicates a need to redistribute resources. That is, the final check on the efficiency of the individual firm would be the bankruptcy court. However, the idea that firms can be ' extra-marginal ' (in this sense of money outlays exceeding money revenues) requires the introduction of time into the analysis in some form, since otherwise it is difficult to explain, in the light of the assumptions of the competitive model, how the resources came to be in that use, or why there is not an instantaneous readjustment removing all extra-marginal production. This difficulty is usually circumvented, not by introducing a problem of *judgment* by relaxing the assumptions about knowledge, but by retaining the assumptions about knowledge and introducing time only as a modification of the assumptions about mobility. Only some of the productive factors are now fully free to move; losses can therefore be incurred as a result of the use of temporarily immobile factors, if the data on which the decisions were taken change after that use was decided upon.

A solution along these lines is uncomfortable in two important and related respects. The producer plans his productive activities in terms of factor and product prices of which it is assumed he has knowledge. It appears that he does not take possible future changes into account in reaching his decisions. If this is because the assumptions imply *knowledge* of future prices, and these are the prices which influence decisions whenever relevant, then how can the data change so as to create extra-marginality, since the change was foreseen? If, on the other hand, future conditions are not assumed known, then how can the producer plan in terms of known prices? Associated with this problem is the difficulty of establishing a precise relationship between mobility and time: the concept of the long period as a period in which all factors are free to move seems to make sense only if regarded as a planning period—i.e., a subjective notion about future activity sufficiently distant for all resource uses to be replanned. But such an interpretation appears to imply the need for foresight and judgment, which are ruled out by the perfect competition assumptions.

(b) The Liberal Collectivist Economy

This, then, is the model from which the cost rule of the liberal collectivist economy derives. As has been said, a liberal collectivist economy is one in which resources cannot be privately owned and exploited. With this reservation, the same freedom of choice of goods and occupations pertains as in a competitive market economy.[1]

The administrative mechanism of profit maximisation is replaced in the liberal collectivist economy by a ' marginal rule '. This rule has several formulations;[2] the most general one is the rule that

[1] An economy of this kind is discussed (e.g.) by A. P. Lerner, *Economics of Control*, and E. F. M. Durbin, *Problems of Economic Planning*.

[2] e.g. Lerner (*idem*) formulates five conditions relating marginal private and social benefit, cost, etc. Durbin (*idem*, Paper VIII), has suggested the use of marginal-value products. These differences do not affect the substance of the argument.

managers of collectivist enterprises, working through a system of competitive markets similar to that of the market economy, should produce that output which makes marginal (money) cost equal to price. The origins of this rule are to be found in the model of the competitive market economy. It is a property of the 'efficient' situation in such an economy that marginal money cost (i.e. the sum of known prices of marginal factor inputs) of producing each product must be equal to the price for which the product can be sold. This equality is merely another way of expressing the fact that profit is being maximised, since in the conditions postulated a maximum profit (excess of revenues over outlays) is made when marginal cost is equal to price.

This is a *property of the market economy model*, an incidental result of the operation of the administrative mechanism of profit maximisation in the rarified conditions of perfect competition. It is no one's purpose to make marginal cost equal to price. But in the liberal collectivist economy this incidental property becomes a principle of administration, by following which, it is argued,[1] a liberal collectivist economy could not only effect an efficient distribution of resources, but could do so more quickly and accurately than a market economy, because a broader survey of the data relevant to his decisions could be made available to each collectivist manager.

III. Time and Uncertainty

Once we admit that the future is unknown, analysis of the behaviour of producers in terms of adaptation to *known* future conditions becomes irrelevant. It is therefore necessary to ask how the admission of time and uncertainty affects the administrative mechanism of the market economy and of the liberal collectivist economy. The task of the producer is now to decide, on the basis of *his own estimates* about likely future conditions, between the possible alternative courses of action open to him at any point in time. Present prices and conditions are relevant only in so far as they provide a basis for judgments about the future. There is now no reason to suppose that individuals in similar circumstances will make the same assessments and hence reach the same decisions.

The administrative mechanism of competitive profit maximisation can still function in the market economy, but the 'efficient' distribution of resources between uses must now take account of the use of *new* resources and of the development of *new* products. An excess of money revenues over money outlays, once the element of judgment inevitable with uncertainty is admitted, is no longer necessary evidence of an inefficient distribution of resources ; it may be due simply to exceptional skill in forecasting. But, at the same time, the fact of uncertainty makes the association of competitive behaviour and profit maximisation, on which the market economy model depends, less

[1] e.g. Lange (*idem*, pp. 89–90), Durbin (*idem*, p. 50), P. M. Sweezy, *Socialism*, p. 231.

generally acceptable. The desire to reduce uncertainty by gaining control of the uncertain variables must be an important motive in attempts to eliminate competition. Uncertainty thus implies the need for positive government policy to ensure *competitive* behaviour in pursuit of profit maximisation, since only such behaviour conduces to an efficient distribution of resources. The difficulty in framing such a policy lies in distinguishing those factors which are the inevitable accompaniment of ignorance and uncertainty and those which arise simply out of a desire to maximise net revenue in an environment characterised by these things.

It is no longer possible, once uncertainty is admitted, to interpret the opportunity cost problem as one of scarcity alone, to be solved by a choice between alternative factor inputs and product outputs with all prices known. That is, opportunity cost is no longer a simple question of summation and comparison of known data. Prices and other variables have to be estimated: opportunity cost decisions involve uncertainty (and therefore judgment) as well as scarcity. The cost problem now arises as a *choice between alternative plans of action*, i.e., a choice between a series of estimates of the outlays likely to be incurred and the revenues likely to be obtained as a result of the adoption of particular alternative courses of action. Costs are in fact incurred when decisions are made; to understand the use of resources over time it is necessary to go back to the decisions which decided that use, and to understand cost, requires consideration of the *estimated foregone alternative revenue* associated with the decision when taken. These foregone alternatives (i.e. discarded plans) not then implemented may in fact never be implemented at all.[1] But in the circumstances of the market economy, errors in the alternatives considered by any one producer do tend to be adjusted by the ability of others to take advantage of his oversight.

Since opportunity costs cannot be treated simply as known money costs, but must be considered as estimates of foregone alternative revenues, it is no longer very useful in conditions of uncertainty to speak of equality of marginal money cost and price as a property of an efficient resource distribution. This is unimportant in a market economy, since the equality comprises no part of its administrative mechanism. Uncertainty creates conditions in which it is to be expected that the mechanism of profit maximisation in competitive markets will function imperfectly and will require positive government action to support it. But the final check on efficiency is still the bankruptcy court, and difficulties about the interpretation of the marginal cost price equation are unimportant to its functioning. In fact, the admission of uncertainty disposes of those difficulties of the competitive market economy model which arise out of the association of time with resource

[1] A decision to build a particular type of bridge over a river, for example, is likely to mean that alternative plans concerned with other types of bridges, considered *ex ante*, will never be implemented.

mobility only. Once the assumptions about knowledge are dropped, 'extra-marginality' becomes reasonable; it is a function both of accuracy in forecasting and of speed of reaction to change (i.e. flexibility in co-ordination and the replanning of activities).

The problem is of greater importance in a liberal collectivist economy: it follows from the nature of the opportunity cost problem that an instruction to equate marginal money cost and money price in conditions of uncertainty gives no clear guidance to collectivist managers as to their productive behaviour. Thus the rule requires reformulation. The most appropriate reformulation would appear to be in terms of *anticipated objective outlays*. The marginal cost of any decision must be the displaced alternative revenue which would have accrued from some alternative use of the resources concerned. To obtain this figure requires a comparison of alternative sets of *ex ante* budget calculations. Each set of calculations gives the expected revenues and outlays involved in the production of each of the two relevant outputs of some product. The *budgeted* marginal cost is the difference between the outlay and revenue calculations in the case of the best foregone alternative budget.[1]

The question is whether the rule, thus reinterpreted, can provide an unambiguous guide for collectivist managers, and whether it enables a check to be made on the efficiency of the distribution of resources between uses similar to that provided by profit in the market economy.

IV. The Rule as Reformulated

If no rule other than the marginal cost rule is used,[2] and that rule is interpreted as a relationship between *budgeted* marginal cost (as defined) and *budgeted* price, is there any check on the efficiency of the distribution of resources between uses?

A *direct* check on efficiency requires a check on decisions in relation to results. But only one of the *budgeted* outlays becomes a *realised objective* outlay, since only one plan can in fact be decided upon. Thus the 'marginal cost' with which we are concerned rests upon a judgment by the manager as to the accuracy of his estimates about the revenues which would have accrued had the foregone alternatives in fact been chosen. That is, estimation of marginal cost involves an inevitable element of personal judgment. There may in some cases be a check upon the 'reasonableness' of estimates. This is the more likely to be so the more the alternatives considered relate to the production of known things by known methods. The imponderables, and with them the difficulty of a direct check on efficiency, become the greater the more unique or novel are the matters with which decisions are concerned. All decisions about new and major investments of

[1] This formulation is based upon that used by G. F. Thirlby: "The Ruler," *South African Journal of Economics*, December 1946.

[2] i.e., no relation between total revenues and total outlays is postulated (see section VI).

resources seem likely to involve important imponderables of this kind; it appears that those decisions likely to be most important to efficiency will be those upon which no adequate check can be made with the rule as now interpreted.

There is a further difficulty not yet considered. How is it to be decided whether the plans considered are the relevant ones? Suppose, for example, there is a difference of opinion about market prospects between the manager and the checking authority. If the checking authority can impose its views on the manager, then decisions about resource distribution (i.e. about costs) inhere in the checking authority; the decisions of that authority become the ones relevant to a check on efficiency, and the same questions have to be asked about them as about the decisions of the collectivist manager. The removal of investment decisions from managers robs them of their primary function from an economic viewpoint: the concentration of decisions in another authority shifts the relevance of the analysis towards that authority. It becomes appropriate to consider the *joint* decisions of the two bodies, in so far as any decisions are left with the manager at all. In effect, the vesting of such powers in the checking authority carries with it the need to abandon rules of the kind considered here, and to adopt some kind of Centralist Scheme[1] for the distribution of resources.

If the check is made at intervals, it must also be taken into account by the checking authority that estimates are subject to constant revision; skill and speed in revision must in effect be recognised as factors in efficient behaviour. But the existence of, and need for, such revision of plans is a further obstacle to a sensible check by an outside authority.

Thus, if the only criterion used is a marginal-cost: marginal-revenue relationship, as now defined, there can be no possibility of an unambiguous check on managerial efficiency through the use of these magnitudes. The most that can be done is to check efficiency, in the limited sense of correct forecasting, in the plan actually chosen. If both the manager's *planned* results and his *realised* results can be stated in unambiguously objective (empirical) terms, and if the plan is unambiguously his own, the comparison of planned and realised results provides (*ex post*) a check on *forecasting* efficiency *in respect only of the plan actually chosen.* But this provides only a very partial check, since it cannot explain whether that plan should have been chosen at all.

There seems little possibility of a direct check upon whether the marginal-cost rule has been obeyed: can the liberal collectivist economy then function without such a check? There are two possibilities: abandonment of any attempt to check obedience to the 'rule', and the use of some other 'indirect' check, in the form of a relationship

[1] cf. H. D. Dickinson, "Price Formation in a Socialist Economy", *Economic Journal*, December 1933, and *The Economics of Socialism*, pp. 104–5, and M. Dobb, *Political Economy and Capitalism*, ch. VIII. Dobb advocates such a scheme in preference to the competitive solution using a marginal rule; Dickinson merely suggests it as a possible practical alternative.

between total revenues and total outlays, *ex post*, arising out of the plan actually implemented.

V. The Rule without a Check

The rule as reformulated does not carry with it any relationship between total revenues and total outlays. In the absence of some further instruction there seems no reason why a manager should not obey it whilst producing continuously at a loss.[1] The manager can check his own efficiency (i.e. the extent to which his activity conduces to an efficient distribution of resources, as defined), or can have it checked by someone else, only through the fulfilment or non-fulfilment of the plans he elects to implement. And even the meaning of the results of this limited check is not unambiguous: what degree of non-fulfilment should suggest to a manager (e.g.) that he should cease producing?

The manager is not told what things to take into account in drawing up budgets. As a result, it is to be expected that he will often base his policy partly upon judgments about the policy of his close rivals, since he considers this to be realistic budgeting, unless he is instructed to ignore such related policies when compiling his own. But how could such an instruction be formulated or enforced? Would it be conducive to efficiency, in any case, to attempt to make managers act on the basis of assumptions they believed to be unrealistic? But, in the absence of any guidance or control beyond the 'rule', it is a short step from this 'oligopolistic competition' to attempts to make budgeting easier by reaching policy agreements with rivals—that is, to collusive, imperfectly competitive behaviour.

Knowledge of rivals' reactions gained in this way is not, of course, what is envisaged by those who suggest that a liberal collectivist economy could reach an equilibrium more quickly and efficiently because more data on which to base decisions could be placed at the disposal of each manager. Their argument is quite other: its basis is the idea that more information could be made available to all managers by the use of some kind of central information service. But there is a logical fallacy here. What each manager wants is knowledge of the firm plans of other managers, on which to base his own plans. But, plainly, not *all* managers can have such information unless either all plans are imposed from above (a possibility already rejected) or the plans are made *jointly* through some form of collusive (non-competitive) behaviour.

If there is to be no check on the efficiency of managers in attempting to obey the 'rule', the choice of the managers themselves becomes particularly important to efficiency. The market economy depends, for the correction of errors of judgment, upon the ability of any producer to take advantage of the oversights of others. From this point

[1] i.e., if no plan considered is expected to yield a surplus of revenues over outlays.

of view, any restriction of the field of choice of managers is a restriction upon possibly useful entrants and hence a curb upon efficiency. On the other hand, if *anyone* can be a collectivist manager, how are the managers of banking institutions to decide who is to have control over liquid resources, and how much ?[1] Presumably they would have to try to judge whether the applicant was capable of equating marginal cost and marginal revenue, although once the funds have been granted and used, those granting them become dependent upon the applicants' view as to whether this has been done or not.

It has sometimes been suggested, as an alternative, that managers should qualify by some kind of competitive examination.[2] Apart from the difficulty of formulating a suitable test, it still has to be decided what those who have qualified become entitled to. Can they all demand control over the same volume of liquid resources, or does the volume controlled vary with seniority, or is there some other means of deciding ?

In the absence of a check on the *outcome* of managerial behaviour, then, managers will be uncertain as to the implications of the consequences of their own acts, no other authority will be in a position to check the efficiency of those acts, oligopolistic and collusive behaviour is to be expected, and there is no clear criterion for the allocation of control over resources between managers. Therefore, while there can be no direct check on efficiency in resource distribution through the marginal relationship, an indirect objective check is plainly desirable ; the problem is to discover one.

VI. Checks through Net Revenue

Since the marginal check is ineffective, the only possibility remaining lies in a check on efficiency depending upon the relationship between total money revenues and total money outlays. There are two possible relationships between total revenues and total outlays which might be accepted as a standard of efficiency: equality of total outlays and total revenues, and maximisation of the excess of receipts over outlays.

The equality criterion is indicative of an efficient resource distribution only in the conditions of the perfectly competitive model. Uncertainty introduces the possibility of a difference between revenues and outlays due to exceptional ability in forecasting, and such a difference cannot be considered incompatible with efficiency. Thus to use such a check might entail the abandonment of plans which producers would expect to yield greater revenues for the same outlays. Since such plans would be implemented if the marginal rule were followed, a criterion of equality of total revenues and total outlays is incompatible with the marginal rule, as reformulated to take account of uncertainty. A check on the equality of total revenues and total outlays would not operate as a

[1] I leave aside the question of where *these* managers come from, and whether they can interpret the marginal rule, if they are expected to follow it.

[2] e.g. Durbin appears to envisage 'Planning' of this kind being taken care of by extension of the Civil Service—*idem*, Paper VI.

supplement, for the checking authority, to the marginal rule to be followed by managers, but would in fact replace that marginal rule as the directive to managerial effort.

The most likely result of the use of an equality criterion is secret budgeting for revenue surpluses on the part of managers. These surpluses can then be ' lost ' if they seem likely to materialise, so that the required equality is always achieved. There is also an inducement to non-competitive behaviour. Oligopolistic situations arise for reasons already argued, and the realisation of interdependence must lead to a realisation that the equality of total revenues and total outlays is more easily budgeted for and achieved if some variables can be ruled out of account by collusive action.

The seeming objectivity of a check on the equality of total receipts and total outlays is in any case misleading. The check must by its nature be periodic, and to obtain the requisite receipt and outlay figures for any period, it is necessary to place a valuation upon the *physical resources* of the organisation at the beginning and end of the period concerned. This valuation rests upon a judgment about possibilities of future revenues from the use of the resources in question—a judgment incapable of complete check by another person or body.[1]

An instruction to managers to maximise the excess of money receipts over money outlays raises fewer problems. It is compatible with the marginal rule, in that the latter would lead to the same choice of plan as does the instruction to maximise net revenues. But the marginal rule is no longer needed; once net revenue is accepted as the guide, the marginal rule is no more important to a check on efficiency than it is in the market economy. On grounds of convenience it is therefore better dispensed with. There is with this revenue rule some kind of check on efficiency, in the size of the net revenue, and some possibility of formulating a criterion for the allocation of resources between producers, probably in terms of the size of past net revenues. The utility of the net-revenue rule does, however, depend upon two preconditions.[2] First, there must be similar opportunity for individual producers to take advantage of the oversight of others as was the case in the market economy, so that absence of net revenue is a clear indication of a need to redistribute resources and its persistence in the case of any one manager an indication of the inefficiency of that manager. Second, the behaviour of managers in maximising net revenue must be conducive to efficiency, i.e. it must be competitive. But since, in conditions of uncertainty, the net-revenue rule provides the same kind of incentive to imperfectly competitive, collusive and monopolistic behaviour as in the market economy, the net-revenue rule could only hope to function

[1] A valuation problem similar to this arises, of course, in a market economy. In either economy there is more possibility of an approximate check than was the case with the marginal rule, since wide fluctuations in successive valuations of particular assets appear reasonably clearly and need to be explained.

[2] It also depends upon a reasonably satisfactory solution of the valuation problem, which is still relevant (see note 1, above).

reasonably efficiently given detailed government regulation of revenue maximising behaviour of kinds incompatible with efficiency in the distribution of resources.

Conclusions

The most effective general rule for managers of enterprises in a liberal collectivist economy would seem to be one similar in nature to the profit maximisation 'rule' of the market economy. This appears to be the only rule offering the possibility of any external check on managerial efficiency; the 'marginal' rule is of no value in this respect. The 'net-revenue' rule also makes possible the formulation of a criterion for the allocation of resources to producers in the future, in terms of achieved past net revenues. The use of the 'net-revenue' rule (or, for that matter, any other of the rules examined) provides an incentive for non-competitive behaviour on the part of producers, which would need to be tackled by detailed regulation similar to that required in a market economy.[1]

It may be that imperfectly competitive behaviour would be less of a problem in a liberal collectivist economy, because the link between personal income and net revenue is less direct and the desire to act in the public interest more important. But it must be borne in mind that in the case of joint-stock organisation the link is also indirect, and also that it is implicit in the whole liberal collectivist pattern that the incentive to obey the rule (in this case to maximise net revenue), whatever that incentive might be, is such that producers treat it seriously.

If the preceding argument is sound, and the need for a net-revenue rule is accepted, then the only difference of economic importance between the two systems lies in this possibility of greater simplicity in the control of imperfectly competitive behaviour in the liberal collectivist economy, balanced against the loss of the 'unparalleled simplicity and force' of the motive of private profit in the market economy. It becomes relevant at least to consider whether a competitive market economy might not function more efficiently even while accepting such impairment of the force of the profit motive as resulted from policies of income redistribution satisfactory to collectivists.

London School of Economics.

[1] Where, in the nature of things, competition cannot function (e.g. for technological, reasons), revenue maximisation with detailed regulation may be unsatisfactory; a combination of regulation and some given net-revenue objective might operate more efficiently. This is the public utility pricing problem of the market economy.

[24]

THE THEORY OF PUBLIC UTILITY PRICE —AN EMPTY BOX[1]

By J. WISEMAN

CRITICISM of the analytical validity of public utility pricing 'rules' has resulted over a period of years in the introduction of successive modifications to the original simple (though not unambiguous) marginal-cost 'rule', culminating in advocacy of the two-part tariff and of the 'club' principle.[2] While these pricing rules have been regarded with scepticism as practical guides to public utility pricing policy,[3] however, there has perhaps been a less general appreciation of the cumulative weight of the theoretical objections to all such rules; there is still interest in the discovery of a 'right' rule, and in the estimation of the 'marginal' or other costs of particular public utility enterprises.

It will be argued in this article that no general pricing rule or rules can be held unambiguously to bring about an 'optimum' use of resources by public utilities, even in theory. Indeed, failing some universally acceptable theory of the public economy, the economist can offer no *general* guidance at all to a government having to decide a price policy for such utilities. To demonstrate this, it will be necessary to begin with a brief survey of the criticisms of the simple marginal-cost rule. This will provide the basis for a demonstration of the possibly less familiar (though no less decisive) analytical shortcomings of the two-part tariff rule, both in its simple form

[1] I am grateful to Professor H. G. Johnson, to Mr. T. Wilson, and to colleagues at the London School of Economics for reading and criticizing drafts of this article.

[2] There is a good deal of literature on this subject. For a useful first list, the reader is referred to the end of the lucid survey of the topic by Professor E. H. Phelps Brown in chapter viii of his book, *A Course in Applied Economics*. Cf. also G. F. Thirlby, 'The Ruler', *South African Journal of Economics*, Dec. 1946; William Vickrey, 'Some Objections to Marginal Cost Pricing', *Journal of Political Economy*, vol. lvi (1948); Gabriel Dessus, 'The General Principles of Rate Fixing in Public Utilities', *International Economic Papers*, No. 1 (translation of a report presented to the Congress of the Union Internationale des Producteurs et Distributeurs d'Energie Electrique, 1949); and T. Wilson, 'The Inadequacy of the Theory of the Firm as a Branch of Welfare Economics', *Oxford Economic Papers*, Feb. 1952. This list is not comprehensive.

The historical development of the 'rules' and their analytical origins is set out in two articles by Nancy Ruggles: 'The Welfare Basis of the Marginal Cost Pricing Principle' and 'Recent Developments in the Theory of Marginal Cost Pricing', *Review of Economic Studies*, 1949–50, nos. 42 and 43.

Specific references have been given in the text only where articles are of particular relevance to the issue concerned.

[3] The scepticism is by no means universal: e.g. the *Report of the Committee on National Policy for the use of Fuel and Power Resources* (Cmd. 8647), 1952 (Ridley Report), considered the question of whether coal should be priced at marginal cost, and half the members of the Committee in fact favoured the use of some form of marginal-cost pricing.

and as modified by a 'club' principle. In conclusion, the effect of uncertainty on the analysis will be examined, and the broad implications of the whole argument for public policy will be suggested.

I. The Marginal-cost Rule

Any discussion of a 'right' price presupposes criteria of the public interest against which alternative suggested prices can be judged. The criteria from which the marginal-cost rule stems are derived from the analytical model of a perfectly competitive market economy, in which entrepreneurs are assumed to have perfect foresight[1] and it is a property of the long-run equilibrium situation that, given the distribution of income between consumers, no transfer of factors between uses could increase the satisfactions of one consumer without reducing those of another. The optimum conditions of 'economic welfare' are consequently said to be fulfilled by the model. For the competitive firm, it is an incidental property of the long-run situation that marginal cost (money outlay on factors) = average cost = price of product. Consequently, this equality can be regarded as evidence of the existence of an 'ideal' situation, and pricing at marginal cost has accordingly been proposed as a general pricing rule (e.g. as the 'principle of administration' of a collectivist economy).[2] But public utility enterprises are not perfectly competitive firms. By the usual definition, an important part of the factors they employ are not perfectly divisible; they can be obtained only in large physical units, or in a durable or specific form, or both. Also, the technically efficient production unit is large relative to the possible size of the market, and the utilities are public bodies, often with considerable powers of monopoly protected by law. In such circumstances, there may be no possible price equal both to marginal cost (the money outlay required to increase output marginally) and average cost (which includes outlays on the 'indivisible' factors excluded from marginal cost). It therefore appears to be necessary to decide whether price should be fixed equal to the one or to the other.

The argument for pricing such public utility products at average cost is, simply, that 'each tub should stand on its own bottom'; all money outlays which would have been avoided if a product had not been produced should be recovered in the price charged by the utility. But the advocates of marginal-cost pricing find this unconvincing. Some of the outlays included

[1] This assumption is of course highly unrealistic; there are also tenable arguments for the view that it is internally inconsistent (cf., e.g., J. Wiseman, 'Uncertainty, Costs, and Collectivist Economic Planning', *Economica*, May 1953, p. 120). For the purposes of this article, the model is accepted for the present and criticism is developed within its assumptions. Section III discusses the consequences of relaxation of the foresight assumption.

[2] For a critique of this collectivist 'rule' and of the model from which it derives, cf. Wiseman, idem.

in average cost, they argue, are not current opportunity costs but are either payments for technically indivisible factors or past out-payments for durable and specific factors. The inclusion of these outlays in the price charged therefore prevents the achievement of the optimum welfare conditions, which (it is said) require that additional consumption of a good or service should be possible at a price not greater than the additional costs (money outlays) necessarily incurred in providing for that consumption. Accordingly, such outlays should be ignored, and the product priced at marginal cost, even though the enterprise runs at a loss as a result.

Clearly, the proposal for pricing at marginal cost requires an explanation of how the consequent losses are to be financed. Hotelling, who originated much of the discussion,[1] suggested the use of particular types of taxes. The inclusion of charges for 'overheads' (past outlays on indivisible factors) was itself, he said, of the nature of a tax. But there were other and preferable taxes (lump sum taxes on inheritance, income taxes, &c.) which did not offend against the welfare criteria since they affected only the *distribution* and not the *size* of the national income. If such taxes were used, and public utility prices were equated with marginal cost, the optimum welfare conditions would be achieved. Later writers have been justifiably sceptical of the possibility of a tax-system that would meet Hotelling's conditions.[2] In particular, income taxes (on which he expected to have to rely) can be shown to affect the marginal welfare conditions directly. In any case, the proposal is open to an even more fundamental objection: the welfare 'ideal' relates to a *given* distribution of income, and that distribution of income must be altered by the proposed taxes (unless these fall on consumers of public utility products in proportion to their consumption, which is effectively a return to average-cost pricing). Thus to advocate marginal-cost pricing and the meeting of losses out of taxation is to advocate acceptance of income redistribution from non-consumers to consumers of public utility products. The welfare criteria provide no justification for an interpersonal comparision of this kind. In other words, any government deciding upon a pricing policy for public utilities has to take simultaneously into

[1] H. Hotelling, 'The General Welfare in Relation to Problems of Taxation and of Railway and Utility Rates', *Econometrica*, 1938. Hotelling's paper was stimulated by the much earlier work of Dupuit, around 1844. The relevant papers have been collected and reprinted with comments by Mario di Bernardi and Luigi Einaudi, 'De l'Utilite et de sa Mesure', *La Riforma Soziale*, Turin, 1932. One of the most interesting papers, 'On the Measurement of Utility of Public Works', *Annales des Ponts et Chaussees*, 1844, is published in translation in *International Economic Papers*, no. 2.

[2] Cf. (*inter alia*) J. E. Meade, 'Price and Output Policy of State Enterprise', *Economic Journal*, 1944, pp. 321–8, and 'Rejoinder', pp. 337–9; P. A. Samuelson, *The Foundations of Economic Analysis*, p. 240; R. H. Coase, 'The Marginal Cost Controversy', *Economica*, n.s., 1946, pp. 169–82; H. P. Wald, 'The Classical Indictment of Indirect Taxation', *Quarterly Journal of Economics*, 1945, pp. 577–97; I. M. D. Little, 'Direct *v.* Indirect Taxes', *Economic Journal*, 1951, pp. 577–84.

account the effects of its decisions upon the fulfilment of the welfare optima (and hence the size of the national product) and upon the distribution of incomes, and there is nothing in the welfare analysis that provides guidance as to the 'right' policy about the second of these.[1]

The reason why marginal-cost pricing raises these difficulties is to be found in the fact that the arguments for the marginal-cost rule are logically unsatisfactory in that they attempt to apply welfare criteria derived from an analysis concerned with marginal variations in factor-use to a problem whose essence is discrete change; the whole basis of the public utility discussion is the indivisibility of the factors employed by such utilities. The results of this attempt are not only of dubious relevance to policy; they are also uncertain in themselves.

The type of indivisibility most emphasized in the discussion is that created by the durability and specificity of factors (*temporal* indivisibility).[2] It is enlightening to examine the nature of such indivisibility more closely. It has been shown that the marginal-cost 'rule' distinguishes between 'current' and 'past' opportunity-cost problems. Once the sacrifices necessary to create a durable and specific asset have been made, it is argued, no further opportunity costs are created by its later use. The opportunity costs having been borne in the past, no account should be taken of them in deciding current prices,[3] even though, as has been demonstrated, this results in losses and in income redistribution. Such an argument rests upon a dubious interpretation of the welfare criteria. The long period, from which the welfare postulates derive, is a situation in which all factors of

[1] There is implicit in Hotelling's argument (and in that of writers who have supported him) the view that the welfare criteria can be extended to cover situations involving changes in the distribution of income. Some attempt has been made to support this position by reformulating the compensation principle (that a decision about a particular measure can be made only if all who would lose by it can be, and in fact are, compensated for their loss) in such a way that only the *possibility* and not the *fact* of compensation is necessary for an economic policy to be accepted as beneficial. However, it has been amply demonstrated that interpersonal comparisons cannot be avoided in this way (cf. M. W. Reder, *Studies in the Theory of Welfare Economics*; I. M. D. Little, *Critique of Welfare Economics*; W. J. Baumol, *Welfare Economics and the Theory of the State*, and the references cited therein). The debate will not be discussed in the text; all that has to be established is that the simultaneous decisions referred to therein are unavoidable, and that the welfare criteria provide guidance about only one of these decisions.

[2] The distinction between this type of indivisibility and *technical* indivisibility is not always made clear in the literature (for a clear separation, cf., e.g., Phelps Brown (op. cit.) and Coase (idem)).

In contrast with the present section, the discussion of the 'club' principle in Section II will be conducted with reference mainly to technical indivisibility. Such indivisibility amounts to no more than the fact that the whole of a productive factor must be employed in order to obtain *any part* of the total product of that factor, so that if the factor is an economic good it must have *current* alternative uses, and therefore a price (e.g. if a railway carriage can be attached to different trains, opportunity costs are incurred in attaching it to any one train. But no opportunity costs may be incurred in allowing one more passenger to travel once the carriage is attached).

[3] Dupuit's argument against bridge tolls (op. cit.) is the *locus classicus* of this argument.

production are considered to be perfectly mobile; this would seem to imply consideration of a time-period at least as long as the lowest common multiple of the life-span of all the factors of production concerned. If the marginal-cost rule is conceived in terms of a time-period shorter than this, then not all the opportunity costs requisite to the manufacture of the product concerned can be imputed to that product, and the time-period chosen must itself be arbitrary, so that the marginal-cost rule becomes simply a statement that outlays on factors of some specified durability should be ignored in deciding prices (i.e. should be treated as 'past' outlays). The figure treated as marginal cost will thus depend upon the time-period selected.[1]

The division of outlays into 'past' and 'current' is clearly unsatisfactory, and the implications of durability and specificity become less obscure if such a division is abandoned and the problem is presented in the form of a planning process through time. All opportunity-cost decisions, taken at one moment in time, fix the use of factors during some future period of time. All factors embodied in plans implemented by entrepreneurs, that is, become durable and specific to some degree; new opportunity costs arise in respect of them only when their use can be replanned. This being so, it is not possible to separate opportunity costs into two groups, 'past' and 'current'. The most that can be said is that some kinds of factors lend themselves more readily than do others to frequent replanning. There is a difference, for example, between the extent to which factor-use will be 'fixed' over time by the implementation of a decision to build a railway bridge and by a decision to hire a railway porter. But the difference is one not of kind but of degree; it is possible to conceive of an 'ordering' of opportunity-costs decisions in accordance with the length of time for which they commit factors to particular uses (i.e. create specificity and durability), but it is not possible to divide such decisions into a group that involves a commitment over time and another group that does not.

Marginal (opportunity) cost in these circumstances is represented by a foregone revenue. The use of factors of production in the entrepreneur's selected plan excludes them from use in some other plan; marginal cost is the foregone marginal revenue from the best plan necessarily excluded because the chosen plan is selected. But the alternative uses to which factors can be put, and hence the opportunity-cost valuation imputed to them in the planning process, will depend on the time-period in terms of which the entrepreneur's plans are themselves conceived; marginal cost will consequently vary according to the time-span of the production plans considered. Thus, the meaning and results of an instruction to equate marginal cost and price will be determined by the length of the planning

[1] Cf. T. Wilson, idem.

period to which the marginal cost is intended to refer. At one extreme, the period chosen may be as long as the lowest common multiple of the life-periods of the assets required to produce the public utility product, and the marginal-cost rule would then give a price that took into account the whole of the sacrifice of alternative consumption caused by the implementation of plans to manufacture the utility product. At the other extreme, the consideration of 'current' opportunity costs only, if interpreted rigorously, would seem to require that products should be given away. Between these two extremes, there is a range of possible marginal-cost rules, differing from each other in the planning time-period chosen as appropriate and hence in the 'durable' assets they ignore and in the opportunity costs they treat as relevant to decisions about price and output.

The only time-period in which all factor-use can be clearly attributed is one as long as the lowest common multiple of the life-periods of the assets concerned; the designation of any other (shorter) time-period as the one appropriate to the rule must involve both an arbitrary decision that that period is one relevant to the computation of marginal cost and a value judgement that income should be redistributed over time towards the consumers of goods produced with relatively durable assets. The marginal-cost principle thus becomes, not the assertion of a general welfare 'ideal', *but the expression of a particular value judgement, that certain long-run opportunity costs for the community as a whole should be ignored in the interests of the greater short-run utilization by consumers of specific factors of some stated degree of durability.*[1]

The only defence offered against criticism of the marginal-cost rule on such grounds lies in the introduction of a supplementary criterion: the investment principle. This requires that marginal-cost pricing should be used to decide the selling prices of public utility products once the utilities are in existence, but that the public investment necessary to create a utility initially should be considered justified only if a perfectly discriminating monopolist could (notionally) recover its cost by charging prices that would maximize his returns. The need for such a supplementary principle to a 'general' rule is implausible. In any case, the investment principle does not answer the criticisms. It still has to be decided which economic decisions are to be treated as 'investment' decisions and which as subject to the marginal-cost rule, and no principle has been suggested by reference to which such decisions might be made. Further, since the prices actually charged are to be determined by the marginal-cost rule, the discussion of the effects of that rule (e.g. on income distribution) is unaffected by the introduction of the supplementary principle. It is worth pointing out,

[1] It will be appreciated that arguments based on *technical* indivisibility raise similar considerations.

further, that the investment criterion itself has redistributive implications: certainly it does not appear to meet the welfare conditions in the same fashion as would a perfectly competitive market.[1]

The foregoing criticisms of marginal-cost pricing have been fairly widely accepted, although the precise nature of the value judgements implied in the treatment of temporal indivisibility is perhaps not generally recognized. Despite this acceptance, there still seems to be considerable support for marginal-cost pricing from those who feel that policies affecting only the *distribution* of the national income both are possible and are in some sense superior to alternative policies that would also affect its *size*. In the absence of some generally acceptable basis for preference between different income distributions, it is clear that such a position cannot be supported by logic. The two issues cannot be separated, and policies desirable in terms of the welfare criteria may therefore reasonably be rejected because a government chooses to obtain a 'preferred' distribution of income even at the cost of some diminution of its total size. There is no escape from the very special value judgements that marginal-cost pricing implies.[2]

II. The Multi-part Tariff and the 'Club'

The two- (or more) part tariff is intended to avoid the anomalies of marginal-cost pricing, in that it is designed to meet the marginal 'welfare' conditions and also to avoid problems of interpersonal comparison by raising revenues large enough to cover all outlays. The essence of the proposal is that the price to be charged should be the sum of two parts:[3] a 'marginal-cost' element determined by the increase in costs necessarily

[1] In the competitive market case, all consumers are faced with the same system of prices: in Wicksteed's phrase, the 'terms on which alternatives are offered' are the same for all. In the other, since discrimination is admitted, each individual is considered to be faced with a different price for the purpose of deciding whether or not to make the investment. If such prices were subsequently charged, they would involve a change in the distribution of real income, and would fall under the same strictures about interpersonal comparison as the marginal-cost rule. That is, a decision taken in accordance with the investment principle might be considered as being partly concerned with the consequences for consumption of the public utility product in question of a change in the distribution of real income. But it would appear that in this respect, as with the advocacy of marginal-cost pricing, the income redistribution is treated as a problem separable from, and in some way inferior to, that of income size (as expressed in the welfare 'ideal').

[2] An illustration may help to make the point clear:

A government, having decided to build a bridge out of revenue raised by taxation, might offer the services of the bridge free and ignore the source of the initial revenues in framing subsequent tax policy. Alternatively, it might decide to charge tolls for (say) 20 years, accepting the reduction in use (i.e. in total income) in the interests of compensating those who had to make the initial sacrifice, or it might decide upon some other combination of current financing and compensation. The economist is without adequate criteria to judge between these alternatives.

[3] There could of course be more than two parts, depending upon the nature of the fixed factors. To introduce more simply adds complexity without affecting the logic of the argument.

incurred in providing further consumption for an individual consumer, and a 'fixed charge' to cover costs which do not vary with consumption but which must be incurred if the consumer in question is to be enabled to consume at all. In this way, total costs are covered and the payments made for additional consumption are kept equal to the extra costs of provision (marginal cost) alone. The problem appears to be solved, since the 'welfare' conditions are satisfied and no income redistribution seems to be implied.[1]

Unfortunately, multi-part pricing provides an unambiguous solution only if the two types of costs concerned can be clearly imputed to individual consumers. In fact, when this can be done the two 'parts' of the price can logically be treated as the prices of separate products, each capable of clear determination by a normal market process. When these conditions do not obtain, however, the situation becomes very different. This can be seen by introducing the possibility of common costs. If problems of time are disregarded, these are simply current costs that do not vary with total output, but are necessarily incurred if *any* output is to be produced at all and *are not imputable directly to individual consumers.*[2] How should these current 'fixed and common' costs be shared between consumers? In principle, limits can be set to the charges that individual consumers can and should be asked to pay, by reference to the cost of providing the indivisible service for them if other consumers ceased to consume, on the one hand, and the minimum possible cost of providing their addition to total consumption on the other.[3] But there may still remain a variety of possible methods of charging, and some non-arbitrary means

[1] A model used by R. H. Coase (idem) gives the essentials of the argument very clearly. The model is concerned with current (technical) indivisibility only, problems of time and of common costs being abstracted therefrom. In the model, a number of roads radiate from a central market, and there is one consumer on each road. All costs are assumed to be currently incurred, and each consumer purchases a combination of the market product and the transport service necessary to deliver it. Transport units are sufficiently large to carry any one consumer's requirements. Thus, while the transport service is *indivisible*, in that extra units of product can be carried without cost, yet there are *no common costs* since one van serves only one customer and the transport cost is attributable to that consumer. In these conditions, Coase argued, the price charged should comprise a fixed charge for the transport service and a price per unit for the product. Total costs are then covered, and the additional payment for extra consumption is equal to the price of the product only (i.e. to marginal cost).

[2] Indivisibility need not imply the existence of such costs, though their presence must imply indivisibility.

The nature of the complications caused by common costs can be illustrated by replacing Coase's road-system (n. 1 above) by a ring road, with the market at the centre and one van serving a number of customers around the circumference, which the van can join at any point. Clearly, the pricing problem now becomes much more complex.

[3] In the conditions of the modification of the Coase model (n. 2 above), these limits (for any one consumer) would be the total cost of providing the service ('indivisible' transport cost plus cost of goods purchased), on the one hand, and the cost of the goods alone on the other. If there were also variable costs associated with the transport service (e.g. petrol cost), then the lower limit would have to be increased by the minimum cost of transport between the consumer in question and the next nearest consumer.

of choosing between them is required if the multi-part tariff is to provide an unambiguous solution to the public utility pricing problem.[1]

There is a suggested means of meeting this common-cost problem that seems to be fairly widely accepted. This is the use of the 'club' principle. This principle is not usually stated with precision; its essence appears to be the proposition that the consumers of the utility product can be treated as a 'club', created by the consumers to arrange both the amount of the good each individual shall consume and the amount that he shall pay for it. Then, if all 'members' (potential consumers) are asked what they would voluntarily pay as a fixed charge rather than go without the possibility of consuming a particular product at a price per unit equal to marginal cost (money outlay), and if the sum of the amounts offered would be great enough to cover the total outlays required, the service should be provided and each consumer charged that part of the common cost that he has stated his willingness to bear. It follows that the 'club' principle is likely to give rise to price discrimination, in that different individuals need not be required to pay the same amount for a similar volume of consumption. That is, the principle must imply a redistribution of real income, since consumers with given money incomes purchase a technically homogeneous product at money prices differing from one consumer to another. But, it is argued, the 'club' principle allows consumers themselves to make a voluntary decision whether to accept the good and the consequent income redistribution in preference to having neither. If they, as consumers, take the first course, then this must produce a more satisfactory situation from the point of view of consumers' choice, and the optimum 'welfare' conditions must therefore be better satisfied as a result of the use of the 'club' principle despite the consequent redistribution of income.

The 'club' principle has deficiencies serious enough to make the extent of its acceptance a matter for some surprise. The deficiencies are of two kinds. First, the value judgements being made in relation to income redistribution are difficult to justify. Second, the 'club' proposals require an unusual (and peculiar) interpretation of the concept of voluntary choice.

Income Redistribution and the 'Club' Principle.

No one suggests that the 'club' principle avoids the need for value judgements about income distribution.[2] Rather, what is implied is that

[1] The problem becomes even more intractable if time is introduced into the analysis, so that the 'common costs' being considered can become past outlays on *temporally* indivisible assets. This kind of question cannot suitably be discussed without relaxing the assumptions of the competitive model. The present section therefore ignores these questions of time, which are more fully treated in the following section of the article. It will be appreciated that the criticisms of the two-part tariff and the 'club' principle in the present section are in no way invalidated by this simplification.

[2] The 'club' argument might indeed be stated in the form that there is some distribution

'welfare' can unambiguously be said to have been improved by a policy which meets the marginal welfare conditions, even though there is a consequent change in the distribution of income, *provided that the changed income distribution is the consequence of the 'voluntary' action of consumers.* This extension of the welfare criteria is less innocuous than might at first appear. Economic welfare, as normally defined, is concerned solely with the optimum conditions of individual choice, given the distribution of income; the objective of the public utility discussion might be described as the discovery of a pricing policy to meet those conditions, in the special circumstances of public utility production. But if a suggested principle of pricing would affect economic magnitudes other than the conditions of choice, then it becomes necessary to establish further policy criteria concerned with these other magnitudes, by reference to which the proposed principle can be assessed. In the present case, since income distribution is affected by the 'club' principle, criteria for choice between income distributions are required. Moreover, these criteria must take the form of a statement about the *income-redistributive objectives of a government*, since it has to be recognized that the public utility discussion (although itself conceived in relation to the conditions of individual choice) is concerned to recommend policies to be implemented by a government. *That is, income distribution is a question of public policy, and it is the attitude of the government to it, and not the attitude of particular groups of consumers, that is of significance for policy.* The value judgement implied in the 'club' principle is that if the members of the public utility 'club' agree to a particular redistribution of income, then the government must necessarily think such a redistribution desirable. This is not plausible; there are likely to be many cases in which the 'voluntary' redistribution would be of a kind that the government disapproved.[1] In short, once a government is committed, by the creation of a utility and the existence of common costs, to a decision about income distribution, there is no reason why it should prefer public utility pricing policies that cover total costs by use of the 'club' principle to other policies which may or may not cover costs, but which accord better with its own attitude to redistribution. A government permitting utilities to use the 'club' principle in effect substitutes the authorities of the utility

of income, different from the existing one, which would induce consumers to cover the costs of the utility without the need for differential charges, and that this distribution must be superior to the existing one because consumers will 'voluntarily' bring it about if allowed to do so. This form of statement brings out the similarity between the 'club' principle and the investment criterion and compensation principle (n. 1, p. 59) discussed earlier; it is therefore not surprising to find that they have similar weaknesses.

[1] An illustration used by Phelps Brown (op. cit., p. 260) makes the point very well; poor families in an area may be willing to pay more towards the provision of a playground than richer families in the same area, but there is no presumption that a government will agree that they should. The welfare criteria provide no guidance in such cases since they offer no means of choice between income distributions.

for itself as the final arbiter in matters of income distribution in this particular context.[1]

'Voluntary' Choice and the 'Club' Principle

The argument for the 'club' principle depends upon the fact that the charges to which it gives rise are 'voluntarily' agreed by consumers. In general, this agreement will be 'voluntary' only in the special sense that a malefactor voluntarily goes away to prison after a judge has sentenced him; he chooses the best alternative still available. To appreciate this, it is necessary to look more closely at the form these 'clubs' can take and at the nature of their 'regulations' (i.e. the powers they have to take and enforce decisions about such matters as the payments to be made by members). Three broad types of 'club' can be envisaged.

The first type might be called the *direct production club*: it is created and administered by the consumers themselves. Thus, if factor services are available for purchase in free competitive markets, groups of consumers may find it convenient to join together to hire certain services whose products will be consumed by all the group, although it would not be worth the while of individual consumers to hire them separately. Effectively, the consumers *ask themselves* whether it is worth their while to create a 'club' to provide the good concerned, and agree together (in deciding to create it) upon the volume of their individual consumption and upon the payments each shall make. The illustrations given of the 'club' principle are usually of this direct-production character.[2] Provided that there are alternative

[1] These criticisms are the more striking when the restrictive assumptions of the analysis are recalled; the 'offers' made by consumers must be quite independent, since otherwise there may be no possibility of an 'agreed' set of prices because 'club' members insist on relating their own offers to the amounts others will be expected to pay. Further, there is no *logical* reason why only one system of prices should satisfy the 'club' principle; what happens, e.g., if the amounts offered to meet standing charges are greater than the total of common costs, but only total cost is to be recovered? In these cases, where more than one set of prices would satisfy the conditions, someone will have to choose between them. Value judgements must be made in the process, and it is difficult to understand why the government should accept those of the utility as superior to its own.

The false plausibility of the argument for voluntary redistribution through the 'club' arises from the application of a logical system concerned solely with individual choice and taking no account of the existence of a government with coercive powers, to a situation where governments have to take decisions involving economic matters outside the scope of individual choice. Some attempt has indeed been made to 'fit' the behaviour of the public economy into the individual choice (welfare) analysis, by treating the whole of the economy as a 'club'. This brings out the weakness and unrealism of the 'club' argument even more forcefully than the discussion above; it leads to advocacy of an 'ethically neutral' system of government income and expenditure, such that the size of the taxes paid and the public services consumed by individuals would be determined by the free agreement of the citizens (taxpayers and consumers) themselves, and to the suggestion that those unwilling to pay such taxes should be treated as 'pathological' (see F. Benham, 'Notes on the Pure Theory of Public Finance', *Economica*, 1934, pp. 453–4, and, for a critical discussion, Musgrave, 'The Voluntary Exchange Theory of the Public Economy', *Quarterly Journal of Economics*, Nov. 1949).

[2] If, for example, a man wishes to fly to Scotland to visit a sick relative, but cannot quite

competing means of satisfying the demand in question without recourse to a 'club', then the possibility of forming a 'club' simply represents a widening in the range of choices made available by the competitive market, and so increases satisfactions ('welfare').[1] This is true even though members of the 'club' pay different amounts for what is technically the same service. However, such cases of direct production would seem unlikely to be of widespread importance, though there may be special instances in which the conditions are quite well satisfied.[2]

The second form that the 'club' might take is one in which the organization of production is undertaken, not by the eventual consumers, but by independent producers, who find the use of standing charges advantageous but whose freedom in deciding the charges that consumers ('members') shall be asked to pay is restricted by the presence in the market of other, similar clubs competing for the consumer's membership. An example of this type of 'club' (the *competitive producer club*) is provided by the book clubs, offering supplies of books at differential rates related to total guaranteed consumption, but with the discretion of any one club in deciding its rates circumscribed by the policies adopted (or able to be adopted) by the other book clubs, and by the ability of consumers to transfer their 'membership'. There is a case for the existence of this type of 'club' also, on grounds of economic welfare. But it must be noticed that the consumers are not now taking decisions about how much they are willing to contribute to a venture in joint production; their 'voluntary' decisions are concerned solely with the nature and amount of their personal consumption at the prices thrown up by the market. The production decisions are taken by independent producers, and the fulfilment of the welfare conditions depends upon the protection provided for the consumers by competition between these producers.[3]

afford to charter an aeroplane at £30 for the trip, it may be possible to find a prospective rail traveller who is willing to pay £10 to share the air trip. The same (physical) service thus costs each traveller a different amount, but each prefers to make the payment and take the service rather than take the services to be obtained by using the market in any other way.

[1] e.g., in the illustration given (n. 2, p. 66) the travellers could themselves decide whether to travel separately or together, could choose between a variety of competing means of transport, and could decide between various offers of aeroplanes for hire.

[2] A good example is given in Part III (pp. 94–145) of R. S. Edwards, *Co-operative Industrial Research*. Here the common service is research for a group of firms with a common interest in the results. Firms can, within broad limits, control the direction of research activity, the distribution of benefits between members, and the methods by which common costs are covered. There is also a possibility of using the market as an alternative to the 'club'. But it is also not without interest, in view of the earlier argument about the role of government (see p. 65), that a decision had to be made as to whether membership should be made compulsory, because the benefits of the co-operative research are not always easily confined to members of the 'club'.

[3] The difference between the two types of 'club' might be put in this way: in the second type, unlike the first, the members of the 'club' are not automatically members of the committee, although they are still in a strong position to influence its decisions.

The third type of 'club', *the discriminating monopoly club*, occurs when neither direct production (with factor services provided by a competitive market) nor competition between 'club'-type producers is present. Only one 'club' is in a position to provide the good or service, so that consumers must join this 'club' and pay the discriminatory charges asked, or go without the good. In such cases, where the producer has a considerable degree of monopoly power, it is difficult to see how discriminatory charges can be justified by appeal to the 'club' principle. The differential charges are fixed by the producer without reference to consumers, who must accept them as a datum when deciding how much to consume—the only 'voluntary' decision left with them. Consumers in these circumstances are protected neither by direct association with pricing and production decisions nor by the existence of competition among producers of the good concerned. The distinction between this last formulation of the 'club' principle and the earlier ones is clear; it is the difference between my offer (choice) to pay two-thirds of the cost of a particular taxi shared with a friend, in preference to travelling by bus, and my choice whether or not to consume electricity at the particular set of discriminatory prices that a monopolistic electricity utility decides to apply to me. Cases of the latter type are clearly not justifiable on 'welfare' grounds; if all that is required to satisfy the 'club' principle is that some consumers should pay rather than go without, then any private discriminating monopolist might meet the conditions.

Unfortunately, it is only the last and most unsatisfactory type of 'club' that is likely to be relevant to the pricing policy of public utilities, whose products often have no close substitutes and whose monopoly power is protected by law, so that the 'club' becomes effectively a method of coercion operated by a sole producer.

In summary, there are clear arguments for a multi-part pricing rule only where the services of the indivisible factors (and therefore the 'standing charges') can be imputed directly to individual consumers. In such conditions the method avoids the need for interpersonal utility comparisons. This is not so if there are common costs, which is likely to be the general case. In these cases, the decision taken about the prices to be charged must involve a value judgement about the distribution of income, and this cannot in general be avoided by an instruction to make use of the 'club' principle.

III. The Welfare Model and Uncertainty[1]

In the simplified conditions of the competitive model so far postulated, the pricing 'rules' could be implemented simply on the basis of objective

[1] The method of analysis adopted in this section is similar to that used by G. F. Thirlby, idem. Cf. also T. Wilson, idem, and J. Wiseman, idem.

cost computations made by utility managers. The assumptions about knowledge that lie behind the model are such that it does not matter who takes the decisions about the use of factors in production, nor is there any need for economic activity concerned with the discovery of information, framing of expectations, or considering and choosing between alternative and speculative courses of action. Any departure from the 'ideal' situation in which the price of any factor (including 'entrepreneurship' as rewarded by normal profit) is equal to its value in another use or to another user must be explained solely by reference to the short-term immobility of factors of production.

A simple model of this kind is inadequate for the derivation of pricing rules intended to have relevance to practical policy. This can be seen by considering the effects of uncertainty.[1] Once uncertainty is admitted, it becomes necessary to distinguish between the process of decision-taking by which the use of resources is determined (the *ex ante* planning process), and the *ex post* distribution of factors between uses that is the consequence of that process. The opportunity cost problems arise at the *ex ante* planning stage: costs are incurred when decisions committing factors to particular uses are taken. With uncertainty, this *ex ante* planning process must involve judgement as well as a capacity for arithmetic; there is no longer any reason why different individuals, working as they must in an atmosphere of doubt and with incomplete information, should make the same assessments or reach the same decisions even in the unlikely event of their acting on the basis of identical data. That is, the *ex post* distribution of factors between uses at any time is determined not only by factor-mobility but also by the skill of those who plan the use of those factors *ex ante*.

In these circumstances, the entrepreneurial function cannot be treated simply as a factor of production rewarded in similar fashion to other factors. The decision-taking process is concerned with the selection and implementation of the production plans which, in the view of those taking the decisions, offer combinations of riskiness and expected net revenue superior to those offered by any alternative plans considered. But the implementation of any plan at all involves a risk that the actual revenues and outlays achieved *ex post* will differ from the *ex ante* forecasts that provided a basis for action. This risk is borne by those whose resources are utilized in implementing the plan (the 'owners'). The 'owners' and the

[1] It is not suggested that the unsatisfactory treatment of uncertainty is the only reason for objection to the perfectly competitive model and to the welfare criteria. In particular, there has been considerable and cogent criticism of the validity of the simple welfare model as an explanation of the process and nature of individual choice (cf., e.g., I. M. D. Little, op. cit., and W. J. Baumol, op. cit.). However, such criticism need not concern us here. There is still point in discussing the use of resources in terms of choice, and the logic of the 'rules' can be destroyed even accepting the conceptions of the simplest welfare analysis.

'decision-takers' need not be identical. The possible combinations of the functions of ownership and planning control (decision-taking) are clearly very numerous, and the returns to risk-bearing and to the planning function are difficult if not impossible to separate in practice, since individuals may share both functions in varying degrees. But the separation is clear in principle.

The reward of the decision-taking function will be that part of the earnings of decision-takers that is not directly dependent upon the *ex post* success of their *ex ante* planning activities. So regarded, the return to such decision-taking can be treated, like normal profit in the competitive model, as an outlay on a productive factor. But the rewards offered to individual decision-takers will reflect the view taken by owners of their relative abilities; there can be no question of their being treated as homogeneous. The return to risk-bearing, on the other hand, cannot be treated as an outlay at all; its reward is the *ex post* (achieved) excess of revenues over outlays (net revenue) in plans actually implemented. It is in no sense a hire-payment for a factor, depending as it does upon the ability to obtain a return from the utilization of factors greater than the hire-payments that have to be made to those factors. The size of the return obtained is directly determined by the efficiency with which planning decisions are taken *ex ante* and by the attitude of risk-bearers to ventures of different degrees of riskiness.

Since net revenue is the return to the essential economic function of risk-bearing, but cannot be treated as an outlay on a factor, it follows that, if factors of production are to be ideally distributed between uses, the total revenues obtained by firms (*ex post*) should be greater than their total outlays and not equal to such outlays as in the conditions of the perfectly competitive model. Also, the 'normal profit' principle cannot be satisfactorily replaced, as a condition of the welfare 'ideal', by a requirement that the net revenues obtained by different firms should be equated *ex post*. The competitive process does provide a check on the undue divergence of the net revenues actually obtained from different kinds of productive activity, by directing activity towards avenues in which large net revenues seem likely. But even with complete freedom for potential producers to enter any market they wish there is no reason to expect that competition will, or (from the point of view of an 'ideal' factor-distribution) should, result in a general equality of achieved net revenues. Net revenue depends upon the individual skill of risk-bearers and decision-takers and upon their attitude to risk. If the abilities and risk-attitudes of these individuals differ, then net revenues must also be expected to differ. A welfare principle of net-revenue equalization, in accord with the general principle of factor-price equalization, would thus be valid only in a society in which risk-bearers and decision-takers were of precisely equal ability and took the same attitude to risk. Such a situation being unlikely, it seems better to substitute the more realistic, if less precise, formula that some net revenue must be obtained if the employment of factors of production in any use is to be justified, and that some means (such as the competitive process) is necessary to limit the extent of the divergences between the net revenue obtained from different kinds of productive activity.

If this argument is accepted, then a new dilemma arises for public utility pricing policy. The need for skill in making production plans, and the risks involved in implementing those plans, are not peculiar to one form of economic organization. They do not disappear because an industry becomes a public utility; simply, the risks are transferred from private owners to the community as a whole. In respect of decision-taking, no insuperable difficulties need arise; so long as there is a large private sector, suitable individuals can be hired at prices determined by their earnings in private industry, and their hire-prices treated as outlays. The only difficulty in this respect is the discovery of an incentive to efficient *ex ante* planning activity that will replace the association of reward with achieved net revenue generally used in private industry. But risk-payments cannot be treated in this way; they are not simply factor-outlays. If public utilities are not expected to earn some net revenue, as is the case with the 'rules' so far discussed, then factors of production will be utilized in plans that would not be implemented in private industry because the expected returns were too small. On the other hand, public utilities will often have considerable powers of monopoly, so that the competitive process is not available as a check upon the means utilized to obtain revenues. Consequently, if they are required to earn a net revenue, utilities may do so simply by using their monopoly power to raise prices. Some increase in *ex ante* planning efficiency may (but need not) also be stimulated, by the need to reach a more difficult target. Thus there would appear to be some justification for the view that if a public utility, required to achieve a specified net revenue, did so solely by exercise of its monopoly power over prices, yet the need to raise the revenue might serve a useful 'welfare' purpose by checking the over-expansion of the public utility enterprise relative to enterprises in private industry of a similar degree of riskiness. But there seems to be no 'right' net revenue that all utilities should be required to earn in all circumstances, since public utilities differ both in riskiness and in the extent of their monopoly power.

The introduction of considerations of uncertainty also draws attention to the problems that would arise for utility managers concerned with interpreting and administering 'rules' of the type so far discussed. These problems are particularly important in the case of rules that do not require costs to be covered. For example, the investment principle, interpreted in *ex ante* planning terms, requires that managers, when deciding whether or not to create an asset, should base their revenue estimate upon the system of prices (discriminatory or not) that they would expect to maximize such revenues. The asset should be created if any plan shows a potential (*ex ante*) excess of revenues over outlays. But if no charge is made for the use of the asset once created, then the plans that prompted its creation will never be implemented. There will therefore be no means of checking upon the efficiency with which the investment decisions are made. This position will be aggravated by the fact that once charges for the use of durable assets cease to be made, no guidance can be obtained from the success of *ex post* (implemented) plans when considering newly current (*ex ante*) plans, since the revenues obtained from implemented plans are not an indication of the valuations placed upon the durable factors by consumers. It is difficult to believe that such a situation would be conducive to efficiency in planning the use of factors and hence in the *ex post* (achieved) distribution of factors between uses. Similar problems arise with the marginal-cost rule. The marginal-cost–price relationship becomes a manager's opinion about the results of a marginal increase in factor-use in the alternative *ex ante* plans considered by him.[1] There is consequently no possibility of any outside authority checking upon whether a general instruction to implement the marginal-cost rule is being followed, quite apart from the other shortcomings of such a policy. Considered together with the proposition advanced earlier, that what is treated as marginal cost must depend upon the length of the planning period specified, this suggests that the marginal-cost rule could only be made intelligible in an environment of uncertainty if the general rule were replaced by specific individual directions to managers. Such directions would take the form of an instruction to ignore the estimated replacement costs of particular specified durable assets when deciding price policy, which should otherwise aim at the recovery of all outlays. But this would amount to the replacement of the marginal-cost rule by average cost (or multi-part) pricing, associated with a specific subsidy.

Summary and Conclusions

It must be concluded that the welfare criteria give rise to no unambiguous general rule for the price and output policy of public utilities, such that for the given distribution of income to which the welfare model refers obedience to that rule must achieve an ideal use of resources by the utility. An instruction to price at marginal cost, if it was to be intelligible, would need to be supplemented by a specific statement of what costs were to be

[1] For further discussion of this cf. T. Wilson, idem, and 'Price and Outlay Policy of State Enterprise', *Economic Journal*, Dec. 1945, G. F. Thirlby, idem, and J. Wiseman, idem.

ignored when fixing prices, in the case of each utility, so that the general 'rule' would effectively be replaced by average cost (or multi-part) pricing and specific subsidies decided separately for each utility. Furthermore, value judgements about income distribution are unavoidable with marginal-cost pricing. Average cost or multi-part pricing can solve some of the problems, but only if there are no important common costs, or if the 'club' principle can be justified in individual cases. In any case, any policy 'rule' adopted would need adjustment to take account of uncertainty; an optimum use of resources requires that utilities should earn an excess of revenues over outlays, and there is no simple principle by reference to which the appropriate net revenue to be earned on account of the risk-factor can be decided. Failure to require an excess of revenues over outlays encourages the use of resources by utilities that could be better employed elsewhere, but a net revenue requirement may be met by the exploitation of the monopolistic position of the utility concerned. Consequently, uncertainty considerations also require the abandonment of general 'rules' and the separate determination of pricing policy in respect of each individual utility.

These negative conclusions have an important positive aspect. The failure to establish general pricing rules does not mean that the government need take no pricing decisions. Rather, given the existence of public utilities, it has to consider each utility individually, and decide policy in respect of some or all of the following matters in respect of each one:

1. The net revenue that the utility should be expected to earn.

2. Whether it is considered desirable explicitly to encourage the short-period use of particular durable and specific factors and, if so, what form the requisite subsidization shall take.[1]

3. The nature and extent of the discriminatory pricing to be permitted. That is, if there are common costs, whether these can be satisfactorily allocated by the free use of a 'club' principle without this implying a compulsory and undesirable redistribution of income by the utility managers. If the 'club' principle is not appropriate, then a decision has to be taken as to what system of charges would best accord with the government's general policy in regard to income distribution.

4. Whether, quite apart from the considerations at (2) and (3), the industry concerned is thought suitable for use as a means of redistributing income, as a part of the general system of indirect taxes and subsidies. In this regard, of course, public utilities differ from other industries only in

[1] In general the desire of governments to give this type of encouragement seems likely to be greater the longer the relevant planning period and the more random and imprecise the distribution of the benefits and losses concerned.

An example of a suitable case might be a change of a permanent nature in the geographical environment, as through the diversion of a river.

that they are more likely to become the subject of government policy for other reasons,[1] and in that they provide a convenient method of achieving those 'indirect' income redistributions that some economists consider must be one of the purposes of public finance.[2]

Clearly, the decisions taken in the case of each utility must be a reflection of the particular attitude of the government concerned. It would therefore appear that, failing some universally acceptable theory of the *public* economy by reference to which policy could be decided (and the possibility of such a theory is doubtful), economists would find their efforts better rewarded if they ceased to seek after general pricing rules and devoted attention to the examination of the policies actually adopted by governments, in order to discover their effects and make clear to the government and to the electorate the nature and consequences of the policies actually being pursued. That is, the economists' *general* recommendations need to be concerned not with general pricing rules, but rather with the availability of information about policy and with the methods adopted to keep that policy under review.[3]

LONDON SCHOOL OF ECONOMICS.

[1] A question of this type inevitably arises, e.g., when a utility ceases to be able to cover costs at its present size as a consequence of changes in the economic environment, so that a decision has to be taken as to whether it should be subsidized, or should simply cease to be treated as a public utility at all, and competition allowed to determine its future size and operations. This is perhaps a not unrealistic way of describing the current position of the British railway industry.

[2] Cf., e.g., J. Margolis, 'A Comment on the Pure Theory of Public Expenditures', *Review of Economics and Statistics*, Nov. 1955.

[3] The preceding analysis would appear to furnish sound arguments, for example, for treating British public utility pricing policy as part of indirect tax policy, and (possibly), for providing opportunity for review and discussion of the policies of important utilities along with the rest of tax policy at the time of the annual budget.

[25]

Risk and the Social Rate of Discount

By MARK V. PAULY*

A step toward clearing up controversy about the proper rate of discount to use in evaluating benefit and cost streams from public investment was provided by a recent article by William Baumol. But Baumol has left us with an uncomfortable indeterminancy. He claims that there is not and cannot be a single "optimal" social rate of discount. This is because private aversion to risk causes the rate of return r' on private investment to diverge from the rate r at which individuals are willing to loan money to the government.[1] Since public and private investments are equally riskless when the operation of the law of large numbers is considered, Baumol recommends, but does not expect to see, a subsidy to private investment to offset what investors (mistakenly) perceive as increased riskiness.

I will show in this paper that the rate r at which individuals are willing to loan money to the government necessarily understates the true social cost of the investment, and so should not be used as a measure of the social rate of discount. Hence, divergence between r and r' does not necessarily indicate the absence of an optimal rate. I will also show that, if taxation-induced distortions are ignored, the "correct" rate for evaluating government investment opportunities may be equal to, or greater than, the private rate r'. In such cases, risk does not provide grounds for a differential subsidy to private investment.

The standard argument for the lesser riskiness of public investment is based on the law of large numbers. William Vickrey and Paul Samuelson, among others, have claimed that since government is able to spread its funds over a large number of investments, it can reduce the variance in the stream of income from those investments to a greater extent than can be done with the returns from private investments. Baumol claims that this argument is not strictly correct because from the viewpoint of society, either public or private investment is equally risk-free, owing to the fact that there are large numbers of both types of investment. But since investors behave *as if* private investment is differentially risky, he argues that a divergence, a risk-premium is introduced between r and r'. Baumol therefore suggests that private investment be subsidized to bring r' down to r. If such a risk-premium does indeed exist, the suggested use of various analogous private discount rates (see Hirshleifer, DeHaven, and Milliman), or of a rate which is weighted average of public and private rates (see Arnold Harberger), would amount to treating some or all of risk as a social as well as a private cost.

In fact, however, there may be no reason why investors need to treat private investment as differentially risky. Pooling of private investment is possible, and it may be possible on at least as large a scale as is pooling of public investment. In part, pooling is provided by purchase of the securities of a large diversified firm. But, it is also provided by diversification of portfolios to include the shares of many firms. Investors with relatively large amounts of funds can engage in pooling directly through purchase of diversified portfolios, and smaller investors can purchase slices of such portfolios by such devices as mutual funds or insurance annuities. The government spreads

* The author is assistant professor of economics at Northwestern University. Helpful comments were received from Kenneth Arrow, William Baumol, Jack Hirshleifer, Richard Kihlstrom, and Colin Wright. Research support was provided by the Health Services Research Center.

[1] Differential taxes on income from private investment, especially the corporate income tax, cause a similar divergence, but integration of the corporate with the individual income tax, which is probably desirable on other grounds, would avoid this problem. The effect of taxation on rates of return will be ignored in this paper.

risk by making many wholly-owned investments, and a private investor can spread risk by purchasing small shares of many investments.[2] Hence, pooling via the financial markets takes place in the private sector.

It may be that private markets for risk bearing are imperfect, and that perfect diversification is impossible, so that private pooling of individual investments is imperfect. Yet, Peter Diamond has shown that security markets may be relatively effective in pooling risks. Moreover, it is also not true that the government in fact is a perfect pooler, in the sense that it provides all possible commodity options (see J. Hirshleifer and D. L. Shapiro). In terms of its own overall accounts the government may be able to count upon the operation of the law or large numbers. But, as Diamond has suggested, this is by no means the necessary case for beneficiaries of particular risky government projects.

Suppose there is perfect pooling of individual investments in both the public and private sectors. One might conclude that the rate at which individuals would be willing to loan money for diversified private investments should, in the absence of tax distortions, approximate the rate at which individuals are willing to loan money to the government. But there is another reason why the public rate will tend to be below the private rate. Government bonds are safe or certain because the government can always tax, either explicitly or implicitly by printing money, in order to pay the interest on them. Private investment, even diversified private investments of the type just discussed, does not have such a characteristic. Its diversification guards against fluctuations in the earnings of individual firms, but the return is not protected against the variability that arises from conditions which affect all of its component firms in more or less the same way. This risk, which Hirshleifer (1966) calls "social variability", arises from occurrences such as depression, war, etc. Such a national disaster (or good fortune) affects the return on almost all investment, and would cause the mean of private rates of return to fluctuate over time. If prospective lenders are risk-averters, the rate of return on private investment would then include a "risk premium."

The return from public investment is guaranteed not to fluctuate by the taxing power of the government. Risk-averting individuals would therefore be willing to lend government money at a lower rate, and so it appears that there is a divergence between private and public costs.

This divergence is only apparent, however, because risk is also associated with government investment. Suppose government bonds finance public investment. This investment is also subject to the social variability of depression and war. A depression, if it occurred, would make public investment in waterways, human capital, or whatever, yield a low or zero return. If something did occur which made returns on all public investments decline, the interest on the bonds sold to raise the funds would still be paid, but it would be paid by general taxpayers out of their consumption or their returns, if any, from private investment. In short, public investment implies assumption by taxpayers of the social risk associated with that investment. There is no reason to suppose that the correlation of the return from public investment with "general economic and social conditions" is any less than that of diversified private investment of equal term.[3] In any event, public investment

[2] It is true, as Baumol argues, that for society the stock of investments includes both public and private investment, and that the number of such investments is a "large number." The number of private investments in any private pooling will be less than this totality, but it can be very large, so that in such a case the divergence between marginal private risk and marginal social risk is of the smallest order of smalls. Perhaps more importantly, the existence of a large number of investments, whether made by "society" or by the private sector of society, is only a *necessary*, not a *sufficient* condition for Pareto optimality in the sense of provision of all possible commodity options and the insurance of all risks.

[3] Arrow (1966) seems to maintain that returns on new public investments tend to be uncorrelated or negatively correlated (as in the case of flood control) with social risk. I see no basis for such an assertion. Surely many public investments do vary directly with social risk, and some private investment are negatively correlated with it.

is certainly not completely free of variability in return. This means that the cost of public investment is not just the interest cost of funds to the government, but must also include the cost of assumption of social risk by risk-averting taxpayers.

To complete the argument, we need to consider the prospective purchaser of bonds. His willingness to make funds available to the government at r percent measures his pure time preference. But the interest rate r certainly understates the cost of a public investment. The cost of that investment is the sum of the return for sacrificing present consumption by bondholders plus the incremental risk imposed upon taxpayers in general.[4] It is this sum, not the rate of time preference alone, which optimally ought to be equated to the expected rate of return from public investment. The rate $r'>r$ at which individuals are willing to make funds available for a diversified private investment, on the other hand, already includes a risk premium for general risk.[5] Hence, the rate at which individuals are willing to lend money to the government necessarily understates the true cost of public investment if taxpayers are risk-averters. It is not appropriate to use the riskless rate in a world risky in the large as well as the small.

[4] It might be suggested that, insofar as bond purchasers are also taxpayers, they will consider the risk they will suffer as taxpayers when deciding whether or not to purchase bonds, and so r will reflect some of the risk associated with government investment. This is not correct, however, because in a competitive market each bond purchaser will take the amount of bonds to be sold as given, and will not think that his purchase of a bond increases the risk he bears as a taxpayer.

[5] Contrary to Arrow (1966), if this sort of risk, which cannot be eliminated, is the source of the divergence in rates and risk, then observation that all risk to private firms has not been eliminated by the private market is not sufficient to prove that the private market is inefficient in pooling of individual (not social) variability risk. Nor does the fact that the return on first quality corporate bonds approximates the government rate indicate that private pooling of individual investment is less perfect than public pooling. The relevant rate is the the return on private investment. The seniority of corporate debt protects the return on that *security* from a large part of individual and social risk, but this does not reflect any characteristic of the return on private real *investment*.

Baumol regards imperfect pooling of private investment to be (in a tax-free world) the source of the divergence between r and r'. I contend that even with perfect pooling of individual private investments social variability would still cause a divergence to persist. The returns from government investment are subject to much the same social variability, even though the return from money individuals lend to the government is not. If private and public individual-investment pooling are perfect, as has been assumed, then the expected divergence between observed rates does not provide grounds for a differential subsidy to private investment, since the divergence only reflects understatement of the social cost of public investment. Instead, in such a case no subsidy is warranted, and the "correct" rate of discount, for both public and private investment, is the private rate r' (or more precisely, a series of various private rates corresponding to the risk-class of the investment).[6] It is important to note that these same conclusions also follow if private pooling is imperfect, in the sense of not providing all possible commodity options, but is no more imperfect than public pooling and provision through the political process.

Of course, the assumption of equal efficiency of public and private pooling is not the only assumption possible. If, as seems likely, not all of the risk can be eliminated from the benefit streams of government investment, then we can be sure that the "correct" rate of discount lies above the government rate r. If the government is more efficient than the private market at pooling and at providing commodity options, but is not perfect (either because of social risk or because political decision costs preclude provision of some commodity options), then the appropriate rate, ***which will not be observable***, will be above the rate at which individuals are willing to loan money to the government but below the private rate. A subsidy to private investment would be warranted in such a case. If, however, the government is less efficient at

[6] I am indebted to Hirshleifer for this point.

pooling than is the private market, then the appropriate discount rate for public investment returns would be above the private rate and a subsidy to private investment would be unwarranted. "Efficiency" in this sense is ultimately an empirical question, depending upon the number of investments made, the correlation of their returns with each other and with social risk, and the availability of possible commodity options. Empirical research on public market and private market imperfections would be useful to help provide the answer.

REFERENCES

K. J. Arrow, "The Role of Securities in the Optimal Allocation of Risk-Bearing," *Rev. Econ. Stud.*, Apr. 1964, *31*, 91–96.

———, "Discounting and Public Investment Criteria," in A. V. Kneese and S. C. Smith, eds., *Water Research*, Baltimore 1966.

W. J. Baumol, "On the Social Rate of Discount," *Amer. Econ. Rev.*, Sept. 1958, *58*, 788–802.

P. A. Diamond, "The Role of a Stock Market in a General Equilibrium Model with Technological Uncertainty," *Amer. Econ. Rev.*, Sept. 1967, *57*, 759–76.

A. Harberger, "The Social Opportunity Cost of Capital: A New Approach." Paper presented at the Annual Meeting of the Water Resources Research Committee, Western Agricultural Research Council, Denver, Dec. 11, 1968.

J. Hirshleifer, "Investment Decision under Uncertainty," *Quart. J. Econ.*, May 1966, *80*, 252–76.

———, J. C. DeHaven, and J. W. Milliman, *Water Supply: Economics, Technology, and Policy*. Chicago 1960.

——— and D. L. Shapiro, "The Treatment of Risk and Uncertainty," paper prepared for Joint Economic Committee, *Economic Analysis of Public Expenditure Decision*, 90th Cong., 2nd Sess., Washington 1969.

P. A. Samuelson, "Principles of Efficiency—Discussion," *Amer. Econ. Rev. Proc.*, May 1964, *54*, 93–96.

W. Vickrey, "Principles of Efficiency—Discussion," *Amer. Econ. Rev. Proc.*, May 1964, *54*, 88–92.

[26]

MACROECONOMICS OF UNBALANCED GROWTH: THE ANATOMY OF URBAN CRISIS*

By William J. Baumol

There are some economic forces so powerful that they constantly break through all barriers erected for their suppression. Such, for example, are the forces of supply and demand which have resisted alike medieval efforts to abolish usury and contemporary attempts to control prices. In this paper I discuss what I believe to be another such mechanism which has colored the past and seems likely to stamp its character on the future. It helps us to understand the prospective roles of a wide variety of economic services: municipal government, education, the performing arts, restaurants, and leisure time activity. I will argue that inherent in the technological structure of each of these activities are forces working almost unavoidably for progressive and cumulative increases in the real costs incurred in supplying them. As a consequence, efforts to offset these cost increases, while they may succeed temporarily, in the long run are merely palliatives which can have no significant effect on the underlying trends.

The justification of a macroeconomic model should reside primarily in its ability to provide insights into the workings of observed phenomena. Its aggregation of diverse variables usually deny it the elegance and the rigor that are provided by microeconomic analysis at its best. Yet macro models have succeeded in explaining the structure of practical problems and in offering guidance for policy to a degree that has so far eluded the more painstaking modes of economic analysis. This article hopes to follow in the tradition—the structure of its basic model is rudimentary. Yet it can perhaps shed some light on a variety of economic problems of our generation.

1. *Premises*

Our model will proceed on several assumptions, only one of which is really essential. This basic premise asserts that economic activities can, not entirely arbitrarily, be grouped into two types: technologically progressive activities in which innovations, capital accumulation, and economies of large scale all make for a cumulative rise in output per

* The author is professor of economics, Princeton University. He wishes to thank the Ford Foundation and the National Science Foundation whose grants greatly facilitated completion of this paper. The basic hypothesis was originally developed jointly with William G. Bowen in the study of the performing arts conducted for the Twentieth Century Fund. In this paper there is no attempt to document the illustrative empirical observations though in every case the data have been examined and appear to support the assertions.

man hour and activities which, by their very nature, permit only sporadic increases in productivity.

Of course, one would expect that productivity would not grow at a uniform rate throughout the economy so it is hardly surprising that, given any arbitrarily chosen dividing line, one can fit all goods and services into one or the other of two such categories in whatever way the dividing line is drawn. I am, however, making a much stronger assertion: that the place of any particular activity in this classification is not primarily a fortuitous matter determined by the particulars of its history, but rather that it is a manifestation of the activity's technological structure, which determines quite definitely whether the productivity of its labor inputs will grow slowly or rapidly.

The basic source of differentiation resides in the role played by labor in the activity. In some cases labor is primarily an instrument—an incidental requisite for the attainment of the final product, while in other fields of endeavor, for all practical purposes the labor is itself the end product. Manufacturing encompasses the most obvious examples of the former type of activity. When someone purchases an air conditioner he neither knows nor cares how much labor went into it. He is not concerned one way or the other with an innovation that reduces the manpower requirements for the production of his purchase by 10 per cent if the price and the quality of the product are unaffected. Thus it has been possible, as it were, behind the scenes, to effect successive and cumulative decreases in the labor input coefficient for most manufactured goods, often along with some degree of improvement in the quality of the product.

On the other hand there are a number of services in which the labor is an end in itself, in which quality is judged directly in terms of amount of labor. Teaching is a clear-cut example, where class size (number of teaching hours expended per student) is often taken as a critical index of quality. Here, despite the invention of teaching machines and the use of closed circuit television and a variety of other innovations, there still seem to be fairly firm limits to class size. We are deeply concerned when elementary school classes grow to 50 pupils and are disquieted by the idea of college lectures attended by 2000 underclassmen. Without a complete revolution in our approach to teaching there is no prospect that we can ever go beyond these levels (or even up to them) with any degree of equanimity. An even more extreme example is one I have offered in another context: live performance. A half hour horn quintet calls for the expenditure of $2\frac{1}{2}$ man hours in its performance, and any attempt to increase productivity here is likely to be viewed with concern by critics and audience alike.

The difference between the two types of activity in the flexibility of their productivity levels should not be exaggerated. It is a matter of degree rather than an absolute dichotomy. The jet airplane has increased the productivity per man hour of a faculty member who is going from New York to California to give a lecture. Certainly the mass media have created what may be considered a new set of products that are close substitutes for live performance and by which productivity was increased spectacularly. In addition, there are, as the reader will recognize, all sorts of intermediate activities which fall between the two more extreme varieties. Yet, the distinction between the relatively constant productivity industries and those in which productivity can and does rise is a very real one, and one which, we shall see, is of considerable practical importance.

In addition to the separability of activities into our two basic categories I shall utilize three other assumptions, two of them primarily for ease of exposition. The reader will recognize, as we proceed, that neither is essential to the argument. The first of the incidental premises consists simply in the assertion that all outlays other than labor costs can be ignored. This assertion is patently unrealistic but it simplifies greatly our mathematical model. A second, far more important, and more realistic assumption is that wages in the two sectors of the economy go up and down together. In the long run there is some degree of mobility in all labor markets and consequently, while wages in one activity can lag behind those in another, unless the former is in process of disappearing altogether we cannot expect the disparity to continue indefinitely. For simplicity I will in the next section take hourly wages to be precisely the same in both sectors, but the model is easily complicated to allow for some diversity in wage levels and their movements.

A final inessential assumption which is, however, not altogether unrealistic, asserts that money wages will rise as rapidly as output per man hour in the sector where productivity is increasing. Since organized labor is not slow to learn of increases in its productivity it is likely to adjust its wage demands accordingly. This assumption affects only the magnitude of the absolute price level in our model, and does not influence the relative costs and prices that are the critical elements in the analysis.

2. *A Model of Unbalanced Expansion*

Assume that the economy is divided into two sectors, sector one, in which the productivity of labor is constant, while in sector two output per man hour grows cumulatively at a constant compounded rate, r. Thus we have for the respective values of outputs Y_{1t} and Y_{2t} in the two sectors at time t:

$$Y_{1t} = aL_{1t} \tag{1}$$

$$Y_{2t} = bL_{2t}e^{rt} \tag{2}$$

where L_{1t} and L_{2t} are the quantities of labor employed in the two sectors and a and b are constants.

We suppose wages are equal in the two sectors and are fixed at W_t dollars per unit of labor, where W_t itself grows in accord with the productivity of sector 2, our "progressive" sector, so that

(3) $$W_t = We^{rt}. \qquad (W = \text{some constant})$$

We may now derive several properties of such a system. First and most fundamental is *Proposition 1:* The cost per unit of output of sector 1, C_1, will rise without limit while C_2, the unit cost of sector 2, will remain constant.

proof:

$$C_1 = W_tL_{1t}/Y_{1t} = We^{rt}L_{1t}/aL_{1t} = We^{rt}/a$$
$$C_2 = W_tL_{2t}/Y_{2t} = We^{rt}L_{2t}/bL_{2t}e^{rt} = W/b.$$

Note that the *relative* costs will behave in this manner whether or not wages increase in accord with (3) for we have

$$C_1/C_2 = (L_{1t}/Y_{1t})/(L_{2t}/Y_{2t}) = be^{rt}/a.$$

In practice, we would expect in these circumstances that market demand for the output of sector 1 would decline. Suppose, for example, the elasticity of demand for the two outputs were unity in terms of prices which were proportionate to costs. Then relative outlays on the two commodities would remain constant, i.e., we would have

$$\frac{C_1Y_1}{C_2Y_2} = \frac{We^{rt}L_{1t}}{We^{rt}L_{2t}} = \frac{L_{1t}}{L_{2t}} = A(\text{constant}).$$

Hence the output ratio of the two sectors would be given by

$$Y_1/Y_2 = aL_{1t}/bL_{2t}e^{rt} = aA/be^{rt}$$

which declines toward zero with the passage of time. Thus we have *Proposition 2:* In the model of unbalanced productivity there is a tendency for the outputs of the "nonprogressive" sector whose demands are not highly inelastic to decline and perhaps, ultimately, to vanish.

We may inquire, however, what would happen if despite the change in their relative costs and prices the magnitude of the relative outputs of the two sectors were maintained, perhaps with the aid of government subsidy, or if demand for the product in question were sufficiently price inelastic or income elastic. Then we would have

$$(b/a)\ Y_1/Y_2 = L_1/L_2e^{rt} = K.$$

Let $L = L_1 + L_2$ be the total labor supply. It follows that

(4) $$L_1 = (L - L_1)Ke^{rt} \quad \text{or} \quad L_1 = LKe^{rt}/(1 + Ke^{rt})$$

and

$$L_2 = L - L_1 = L/(1 + Ke^{rt}). \tag{5}$$

Hence, as t approaches infinity, L_1 will approach L and L_2 will approach zero. Thus we have *Proposition 3:* In the unbalanced productivity model, if the ratio of the outputs of the two sectors is held constant, more and more of the total labor force must be transferred to the nonprogressive sector and the amount of labor in the other sector will tend to approach zero.

Finally, we may note what happens to the overall rate of growth of output in the economy if the output ratio for the two sectors is not permitted to change. We may take as an index of output a weighted average of the outputs of the two sectors:

$$I = B_1Y_1 + B_2Y_2 = B_1aL_1 + B_2bL_2e^{rt}$$

so that by (4) and (5)

$$I = L(KB_1a + B_2b)e^{rt}/(1 + Ke^{rt}) = Re^{rt}/(1 + Ke^{rt})$$

where

$$R = L(KB_1a + B_2b).$$

Therefore

$$\begin{aligned} dI/dt &= R[re^{rt}(1 + Ke^{rt}) - Kre^{2rt}]/(1 + Ke^{rt})^2 \\ &= rRe^{rt}/(1 + Ke^{rt})^2. \end{aligned}$$

As a result, the percentage rate of growth of output will be

$$(dI/dt)/I = r/(1 + Ke^{rt})$$

which declines asymptotically toward zero as t increases. We have, then, arrived at *Proposition 4:* An attempt to achieve balanced growth in a world of unbalanced productivity must lead to a declining rate of growth relative to the rate of growth of the labor force. In particular, if productivity in one sector and the total labor force remain constant the growth rate of the economy will asymptotically approach zero.

3. *Discussion of the Propositions*

The logic of the entire analysis can be restated rather simply in intuitive terms. If productivity per man hour rises cumulatively in one sector relative to its rate of growth elsewhere in the economy, while wages rise commensurately in all areas, then relative costs in the nonprogressive sectors must inevitably rise, *and these costs will rise cumulatively and without limit.* For while in the progressive sector productivity increases will serve as an offset to rising wages, this offset must be smaller in the nonprogressive sectors. For example (ignoring nonwage costs) if wages and productivity in the progressive sector both go up 2 per cent per year, costs there will not rise at all. On the other hand, if in the nonprogressive sector productivity is constant, every rise in wages must yield a corresponding addition to costs—a two per cent cumulative rise in wages means that, year in year out, costs must be two per cent above those of the preceding year. Thus, the very progress of the technologically progressive sectors inevitably adds to the costs of the technologically unchanging sectors of the economy, unless somehow the labor markets in these areas can be sealed off and wages held absolutely constant, a most unlikely possiblity.

We see then that costs in many sectors of the economy will rise relentlessly, and will do so for reasons that are for all practical purposes beyond the control of those involved. The consequence is that the outputs of these sectors may in some cases tend to be driven from the market. If their relative outputs are maintained, an ever increasing proportion of the labor force must be channeled into these activities and the rate of growth of the economy must be slowed correspondingly.

4. *Some Applications*[1]

These observations can be used at once to explain a number of observed phenomena. For example, there is evidence that an ever increasing portion of the nation's labor force has been going into retailing and that a rising portion of the cost of commodities is accounted for by outlays on marketing. Now there have been several pronounced changes in the technology of marketing in recent decades: self service, the supermarket, and prewrapping have all increased the productivity per man hour of the retailing personnel. But ultimately, the activity involved is in the nature of a service and it does not allow for constant and cumulative increases in productivity through capital accumulation, innovation, or economies of large-scale operation. Hence it is neither mismanagement nor lack of ingenuity that accounts for the relatively constant productivity of this sector. Since some sort of marketing effort is an inescapable element in economic activity, demand for this service is quite income elastic. Our model tells us what to expect in this case—cumulatively increasing costs relative to those of other economic activities, and the absorption of an ever growing proportion of society's resources by this sector—precisely what seems to have been observed.

Higher education is another activity the demand for whose product seems to be relatively income elastic and price inelastic. Higher tuition charges undoubtedly impose serious hardships on lower-income stu-

[1] Some of the ideas in this section arose out of discussions with Eugene Beem of Sperry and Hutchinson.

dents. But, because a college degree seems increasingly to be a necessary condition for employment in a variety of attractive occupations, most families have apparently been prepared to pay the ever larger fees instituted in recent years. As a result higher education has been absorbing a constantly increasing proportion of per capita income. And the relatively constant productivity of college teaching leads our model to predict that rising educational costs are no temporary phenomenon—that they are not a resultant of wartime inflation which will vanish once faculty salaries are restored to their prewar levels. Rather, it suggests that, as productivity in the remainder of the economy continues to increase, costs of running the educational organizations will mount correspondingly, so that whatever the magnitude of the funds they need today, we can be reasonably certain that they will require more tomorrow, and even more on the day after that.

But not all services in the relatively constant productivity sector of the economy face inelastic demands. Many of them are more readily dispensable than retailing and education as far as individual consumers are concerned. As their costs increase, their utilization tends therefore to decrease and they retreat into the category of luxury goods with very limited markets or disappear almost completely. Fine pottery and glassware produced by the careful labor of skilled craftsmen sell at astronomical prices, though I am told the firms that produce them earn relatively little profit from these product lines which they turn out primarily for prestige and publicity, obtaining the bulk of their earnings from their mass production activities. Fine restaurants and theaters are forced to keep raising their prices, and at least in the case of the latter we know that volume is dwindling while it becomes ever more difficult for suppliers (the producers) to make ends meet.

An extreme example of an activity that has virtually disappeared is the construction (and, indeed, the utilization) of the large and stately houses whose operation even more than their construction allows for little in the way of enhanced productivity, and whose rising costs of operation have apparently decreased their salability even to the wealthy.

These observations suggest something about the likely shape of our economy in the future. Our model tells us that manufactures are likely to continue to decline in relative cost and, unless the income elasticity of demand for manufactured goods is very large, they may absorb an ever smaller proportion of the labor force, which, if it transpires, may make it more difficult for our economy to maintain its overall rate of output growth.

The analysis also suggests that real cost in the "nonprogressive" sectors of the economy may be expected to go on increasing. Some of the services involved—those whose demands are inelastic—may continue viable on the free market. Some, like the theater, may be forced to leave this market and may have to depend on voluntary public support for their survival. Our hospitals, our institutions of private education and a variety of other nonprofit organizations have already long survived on this basis, and can continue to do so if the magnitude of contributions keeps up with costs. Some activities will either disappear or retreat to a small scale of operation catering primarily to a luxury trade. This fate may be in store for restaurants offering true *haute cuisine* and it is already the case for fine hand-worked furniture and for clothes made to measure. Some activities, perhaps many of the preceding among them, will fall increasingly into the hands of the amateurs who already play a considerable role in theatrical and orchestral performances, in gastronomy, in crafts such as woodworking and pottery. Finally, there is a considerable segment of nonprogressive activity that is dependent on tax support. Some of the problems that go with this position will be considered in the remainder of this paper.

In all the observations of this section there is one implicit underlying danger that should not escape the reader: the inherent threat to quality. Amateur activity has its virtues, as an educational device, as a good use for leisure time and so forth. But in a variety of fields it offers a highly imperfect substitute for the highly polished product that can be supplied by the professional. Unbalanced productivity growth, then, threatens to destroy many of the activities that do so much to enrich our existence, and to give others over into the hands of the amateurs. These are dangers which many of us may feel should not be ignored or taken lightly.

5. *On the Financial Problem of the Cities*

One of the major economic problems of our times is the crisis of the larger cities. Together with their suburban periphery the cities are attracting ever greater segments of our population. Yet at least the core of the metropolis is plagued by a variety of ills including spreading blight as entire neighborhoods deteriorate, increasing pollution of its atmosphere, worsening traffic, critical educational problems, and, above all, mounting fiscal pressures. The financial troubles are perhaps central to the entire issue because without adequate funds one cannot hope to mount an effective attack on the other difficulties. More than one reform mayor has taken office determined to undertake a radical program to deal with the city's difficulties and found himself baffled and stymied by the monstrous deficit which he discovered to be hanging over him, a deficit whose source appeared to have no reasonable explanation. There seems in these cases to be no way to account for the growth in the city's financial needs—for the fact that a municipal budget far above that which was roughly adequate a decade earlier threatens to disrupt seriously the city's most vital services today. Where the political process is involved it is easy to blame growing costs on inefficiency and corruption but when they take office, reform administrations seem consistently puzzled by their inability to wring out the funds they require through the elimination of these abuses.

A critical element in the explanation becomes clear when we recognize how large a proportion of the services provided by the city are activities falling in the relatively nonprogressive sector of the economy. The bulk of our municipal expenditures is devoted to education which, as we have already seen, offers very limited scope for cumulative increases in productivity. The same is true of police, of hospitals, of social services, and of a variety of inspection services. Despite the use of the computer in medicine and in traffic planning, despite the use of closed circuit television and a variety of other devices, there is no substitute for the personal attention of a physician or the presence of a police patrol in a crime-ridden neighborhood. The bulk of municipal services is, in fact, of this general stamp and our model tells us clearly what can be expected as a result. Since there is no reason to anticipate a cessation of capital accumulation or innovation in the progressive sectors of the economy, the upward trend in the real costs of municipal services cannot be expected to halt; inexorably and cumulatively, whether or not there is inflation, administrative mismanagement or malfeasance, municipal budgets will almost certainly continue to mount in the future, just as they have been doing in the past. This is a trend for which no man and no group should be blamed, for there is nothing that can be done to stop it.

6. *The Role of Static Externalities*

Though these may be troubles enough for the municipal administrator, there are other compelling forces that plague him simultaneously. Among them are the general class of externality problems which have so long been the welfare economist's stock in trade.

Since the appearance of Marshall's and Pigou's basic writing in the area a most significant development has been the growing impact of external costs on urban living. No longer are road crowding and smoke nuisance only quaint cases serving primarily as textbook illustrations. Rather, they have become pressing issues of public concern—matters discussed heatedly in the daily press and accorded serious attention by practical politicians. Newspapers devote headlines to an engineer's prediction that the human race is more likely to succumb to its own pollutants than through a nuclear holocaust, and report with glee the quip that Los Angeles is the city in which one is wakened by the sound of birds coughing.

Now there are undoubtedly many reasons for the explosion in external costs but there is a pertinent observation about the relationship between population size in a given area and the cost of externalities that seems not to be obvious. It is easy to assume that these costs will rise roughly in proportion with population but I shall argue now that a much more natural premise is that they will rise more rapidly—perhaps roughly as the square of the number of inhabitants. For example, consider the amount of dirt that falls into the house of a typical urban resident as a result of air pollution, and suppose that this is equal to kn where n is the number of residents in the area. Since the number of homes in the area, an, is also roughly proportionate to population size, total domestic soot-fall will be equal to soot per home times number of homes $= kn \cdot an = akn^2$. Similarly, if delays on a crowded road are roughly proportionate to n, the number of vehicles traversing it, the total number of man hours lost thereby will increase roughly as n^2, since the number of passengers also grows roughly as the number of cars. The logic of the argument is simple and perhaps rather general: if each inhabitant in an area imposes external costs on every other, and if the magnitude of the costs borne by each individual is roughly proportionate to population size (density) then since these costs are borne by each of the n persons involved, the total external costs will vary not in proportion with n but with n^2. Of course I do not maintain that such a relationship is universal or even that it is ever satisfied more than approximately. Rather I am suggesting that, typically, increases in population size may plausibly be expected to produce disproportionate increases in external costs—thus pressures on the municipality to do something about these costs may then grow correspondingly.

7. *Cumulative Decay and Dynamic Pareto Optimality*

Economic theory indicates yet another source of mounting urban problems. These are the processes of cumulative urban decay which once set in motion induce matters to go from bad to worse. Since I have discussed these elsewhere I can illustrate the central proposition rather briefly. Public transportation is an important example. In many urban areas with declining utilization, frequency of service has been sharply reduced and fares have been increased. But these price rises have only served to produce a further decline in traffic, leading in turn to yet another deterioration in schedules and another fare increase and so on, apparently *ad infinitum*. More important, perhaps, is the logic of the continued flight to the suburbs in which many persons who apparently would otherwise wish to remain in the city are driven out by growing urban deterioration—rising crime rates, a growing number of blighted neighborhoods, etc. Once again, the individuals' remedy intensifies the community's problems and each feeds upon the other. Those who leave the city are usually the very persons who care and can afford to care—the ones who maintain their houses, who do not commit crimes, and who are most capable of providing the taxes needed to arrest the process of urban decay. Their exodus therefore leads to further deterioration in urban conditions and so induces yet another wave of emigration, and so on.[2]

It is clear that these cumulative processes can greatly increase the financial pressures besetting a municipality and can do so in a variety of ways: they can increase directly municipal costs by adding to the real quantities of inputs required for the upkeep of buildings, to maintain levels of urban sanitation, to preserve the level of education attained by an average resident, etc.; they can reduce the tax base—the exodus of more affluent urban inhabitants cause a decline in the financial resources available to the city; and with the passage of time the magnitude of the resources necessary to arrest and reverse the cumulative processes itself is likely to grow so that the city may find it increasingly difficult to go beyond programs that slow the processes slightly.[3]

[2] As is to be expected, such dynamic processes may be monotonic or oscillatory, stable or unstable. As examples we might expect the public transportation scheduling problem to grow monotonically while automotive road crowding may be inherently oscillatory. More specifically, let f represent frequency of public bus departure and p be the number of bus passengers. We would expect the relevant relationships to be something such as

$$p_t = a + bf_t \quad \text{(demand for public transport) and}$$
$$f_{t+1} = w + vp_t \quad \text{(lagged public transport supply response)}$$

so that

$$f_{t+1} = w + av + vbf_t$$

in which the coefficient vb is presumably positive. On the other hand, if D represents average delay on some road and A is the volume of automotive traffic, the corresponding relationships would be

$$D_t = a' + b'A_t \quad \text{(delay grows with traffic volume) and}$$
$$A_{t+1} = w' - v'D_t \quad \text{(delays today lead to lower traffic tomorrow)}$$

so that we have a negative coefficient $-b'v'$ in the difference equation

$$A_{t+1} = w' - a'v' - b'v'A_t.$$

Since monotonic and oscillatory time paths correspond respectively to positive and negative variable coefficients in a first-order difference equation, our result follows. An intuitive explanation is fairly simple in each case: increased automotive traffic today causes delays and so may reduce traffic tomorrow. But a decline in number of passengers which causes a deterioration in service leads to still another fall in volume.

As stated, the time path in each case may be stable. But in the latter case, even though the declines will not be unbounded, the limit toward which they tend may be very low and totally unacceptable as a matter of public policy.

[3] I have argued that the cumulative processes involve what may be considered dynamic externalities. Each passenger who uses public transportation less frequently imposes the increased likelihood of poorer schedules not only on himself but on others as well. As a result these processes will yield results that do not maximize social welfare. For the private and social marginal rates of transformation between present and future will then differ from one another. The individual will tend to cut down on his use of public transportation by an amount greater

8. *Conclusion—The Financial Problems of the Large City*

The story is perhaps completed if we add to the preceding observations the fact that each city is in competition with others and with its own surrounding areas for industry and for people with the wherewithal to pay taxes. No city government acting alone can afford to raise its tax rates indefinitely. Even if they were politically feasible, mounting tax rates must eventually produce diminishing and perhaps even negative returns as they depress the tax base further.

We can now quickly pull the pieces of our story together. We have just seen that our municipalities are perhaps unavoidably subject to a variety of growing financial pressures: the limited sources of tax funds, the pressures imposed by several processes of cumulative decay, the costs of externalities which seem to have a built-in tendency to rise more rapidly than the population. These phenomena imply that the activities of the municipality will have to be expanded if standards of city life are to be maintained. But the funds available for the purpose are extremely limited. And over all this hangs the shadow cast by our model of unbalanced growth which has shown that the costs of even a constant level of activity on the part of a municipal government can be expected to grow constantly higher.

The picture that has been painted is bleak. It suggests strongly that self-help offers no way out for our cities. All of this would then appear to offer stronger theoretical support for the Heller-Pechman proposal that the federal government can provide the resources necessary to prevent the serious crisis that threatens our larger urban communities and whose effects on the quality of life in our society may become one of the nation's most serious economic problems.

References

1. W. J. Baumol and W. G. Bowen, *Performing Arts: The Economic Dilemma*. New York 1966.
2. Jean Fourastié, *The Causes of Wealth*. Glencoe, Ill., 1960.
3. Tibor and Anne Scitovsky, "What Price Economic Progress?" *Yale Review*, Autumn 1959, *49*, 95–110.

than that which is optimal because he himself does not bear all of the costs of his action. There is a marginal rate of transformation between the utility derived from public transportation today and that obtainable from transportation tomorrow. If relative prices do not equal that marginal rate of transformation a misallocation of resources is likely to result. The consequences may even be what might be called Pareto-nonoptimal. That is, everyone may be harmed. For example, when automobile traffic becomes sufficiently bad it may become clear that everyone will be better off if passenger cars are banned completely from the downtown area in order to make possible a faster, more efficient public transportation system.

[27]

A NOTION OF EQUILIBRIUM AND ITS POSSIBILITY UNDER MAJORITY RULE

By CHARLES R. PLOTT*

Consider a committee that is faced with the task of deciding on how to change the magnitude of several variables. It is assumed that agreement is defined by majority rule. The decision-making body could be a board of directors attempting to decide on the magnitude of several investment projects, or a group of individuals deciding upon the allocation of a budget among several public goods. The setting makes no difference as long as the variables could conceivably be changed by any amount. If a change in the variables is proposed and the change does not receive a majority vote, then the "existing state" of the variables remains. If no possible change in the variables could receive a majority vote, then the "existing state" of the variables is an "equilibrium."[1]

The purpose of this paper is to make clear such a notion of equilibrium and to investigate the possibility of its existence. Section I sets forth the general setting, definitions, and assumptions. Section II pertains to situations where there is no constraint on the possible magnitude of the variables. Section III pertains to situations where there is one constraint (such as a fixed amount that the committee may spend). Section IV contains some general observations, possible applications, and questions brought forth by the procedure. An appendix contains an outline to the proofs of the propositions in the text.

Before continuing, it may be best to indicate some of the things ***not*** considered except by way of observation in the final section, if at all. Only "local" equilibriums are considered. Of course, "global" equilibriums must be special cases of these. There is no real theory of the path to equilibrium or even, for that matter, a convincing assurance that an equilibrium, if it exists, will be attained. Strategic considerations are ignored as are all second order conditions. These omissions are especially important in light of the results.

I. *The Basic Model*

Assume there are m individuals $(1, 2, \cdots, i, \cdots, m)$ who are attempting to decide on the magnitude of n variables $(x_1, x_2, \cdots, x_j,$

* The author is assistant professor of economics at Purdue University. He wishes to thank James M. Buchanan of the University of Virginia and James Quirk of the University of Kansas for their helpful comments and criticisms. Financial support was provided in part from a National Science Foundation grant under the general supervision of Gordon Tullock and from a research grant provided by the Krannert Graduate School of Industrial Administration.

[1] This notion of equilibrium was first examined by Duncan Black and R. A. Newing. Special cases of some of the theorems are implied by the diagrams in [1, pp. 19–28] and [2, pp. 137–39].

$\cdots, x_n)$. Each individual is assumed to have a differentiable utility function $U^i = U^i(x_1, x_2, \cdots, x_n)$ defined on the n variables.[2]

Consider now a specific, small change in the variables $(dx_1^*, dx_2^*, \cdots, dx_n^*)$ from some "existing situation" (say $\overline{X}$ in Euclidean n-space, E_n). This change in the variables shall be called a "motion."[3] Individual i would "vote for" the motion over the existing situation $\overline{X}$ if

$$\frac{\partial U^i}{\partial x_1} dx_1^* + \frac{\partial U^i}{\partial x_2} dx_2^* + \cdots + \frac{\partial U^i}{\partial x_n} dx_n^* > 0.$$

That is, he favors the motion if it would increase his utility. Adopting the notation to be used, we can say that he "votes for" the motion b_k if

$$\nabla U^i b_k > 0$$

where

$$\nabla U^i = \left(\frac{\partial U^i}{\partial x_1}, \frac{\partial U^i}{\partial x_2}, \cdots, \frac{\partial U^i}{\partial x_n}\right)$$

is the gradient vector of individual i's utility function, b_k is some *particular* "motion" $(dx_1^k, dx_2^k, \cdots, dx_n^k)$ from the infinite set of "small moves away from $\overline{X}$.[4] Further, if $\nabla U^i b_k < 0$, we say he is "indifferent." It shall be assumed that indifferent individuals behave in the same specified manner, i.e., always "vote for," always "vote against," or "never vote" as the case may be.

Graphically the situation is represented by Figure 1. The curve I is an indifference curve or level surface of the utility function. Suppose $\overline{X}$ represents the "existing state." This individual would "vote for" a proposed move from $\overline{X}$ such as b_f, vote "against" a motion such as b_a, and be indifferent toward a proposal such as b_i.

Consider now a group of individuals $(1, 2, \cdots, m)$ and the associated gradient vectors $\nabla U^i = (a_{i1}, a_{i2}, \cdots, a_{in})$. Ignoring problems of strategic behavior, all individuals would "vote for" any proposal, b, which satisfies[5]

$$Ab > 0 \tag{1}$$

[2] The variables are such that they behave as "collective goods." See [5].

[3] We shall assume the "motion" vector is normalized, i.e., where $(dx_1^*, \cdots, dx_n^*) = b^*$, then $|b^*| = 1$. For notational purposes, some particular motion, say j, will be denoted as b_j and the components will be denoted as $(b_{j1}, b_{j2}, \cdots, b_{jn})$.

[4] He votes for any motion for which the directional derivative, in that direction, is positive. ab, where a and b are vectors, denotes an inner product.

[5] The problem of finding such "acceptable proposals" is simply a linear programming problem. See [4].

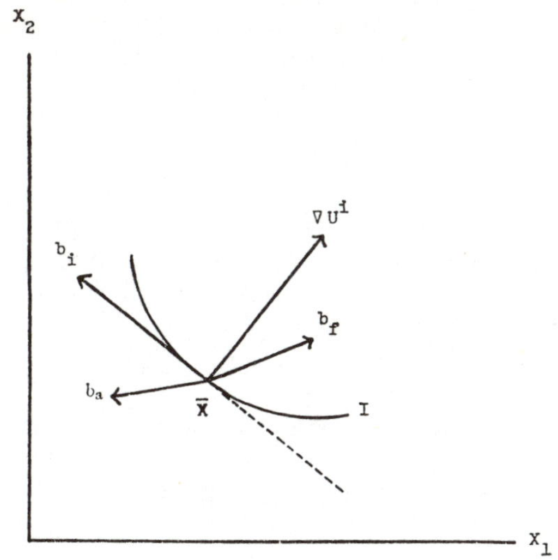

FIGURE 1

where

$$A = \begin{bmatrix} a_{11} & a_{12} & \cdots & a_{1n} \\ \vdots & & & \\ a_{m1} & a_{m2} & \cdots & a_{mn} \end{bmatrix}.$$

It is well known that this system of inequalities has a solution, b, if and only if the system

(2) $\quad yA = 0 \qquad y = (y_1, \cdots, y_m)$ and $y_i \geq 0$ not all $= 0$

has no semipositive solution y (see appendix).

Suppose the committee was operating under unanimity. Suppose further that an individual will vote "against" a motion that does not increase his utility (indifferent people vote "no"). Then any point in the space where (2) is satisfied would be an "equilibrium point." There would not exist a "motion" that could receive the required vote because, for any of the infinite possible motions, at least one person would vote "no."[6]

Suppose the committee was operating under majority rule. The committee would be at an equilibrium if and only if there does not exist a "motion" that could receive a favorable vote from a majority. This notion of equilibrium seems to accord well with the usual meanings of

[6] If it is supposed that individuals would "permit" a motion to which they are indifferent, an equilibrium point must be one where (2) has a strictly positive solution y. Every "motion" would either decrease the utility of at least one individual or leave everyone indifferent.

equilibriums. Certainly if the magnitude of the variables was such that some change in them could receive the required vote there is no a priori reason to suppose that the variables would not be so changed.

II. *Equilibrium: No Constraint*

The conditions for majority rule equilibrium when there exists no constraint on permissible motions will be given. Such a constraint is added in the following section. It will be assumed that there are m (an odd number) decision makers. Simple modifications can be made to account for situations where the number of people is even.

A. Existence of an unconstrained equilibrium requires that indifrerent individuals do not vote "yes."

If individuals who are indifferent are assumed to abstain from voting, such activities cannot be considered as "yes" votes. Otherwise, an equilibrium cannot exist. To prove this point, let M be an $(m+1)/2\times n$ matrix, the rows of which come from the rows of A. Since indifferent people vote "yes," equilibrium must be a situation where $Mb<0$[7] for all possible M that can be formed from the rows of A and all possible b. Pick an M and b that satisfy this equilibrium condition (say M_i and b_i). Then, where $b_k=-b$, $M_ib_k>0$. The motion b_k would receive a majority contrary to the assumption of equilibrium. Indifferent people cannot vote "yes."

The remaining equilibrium conditions must be satisfied by the gradient vectors. The proofs are in the appendix.

B. Any equilibrium must be a point of maximum utility for at least one individual.

If the point is a maximum for one and only one individual,[8] the gradients of the remaining individuals must satisfy C.

C. The remaining (even number of) rows of A can be divided into pairs for which there exists a strictly positive solution to

$$\begin{bmatrix} y_i \\ y_j \end{bmatrix} \begin{bmatrix} a_{i1} & a_{i2} & \cdots & a_{in} \\ a_{j1} & a_{j2} & \cdots & a_{jn} \end{bmatrix} = 0 \qquad y_i, y_j > 0. \tag{3}$$

The last condition means that all individuals for which the point is not a maximum can be divided into pairs whose interests are diametrically opposed. The situation is shown diagrammatically by Figure 2. Points 1, 2, 3, 4, and 5 are the points of maximum utility for individuals 1, 2, 3, 4, and 5 respectively. The lines connecting the points are those

[7] The notation $Mb>0$ means that the inner product of b with each row of M is strictly positive.

[8] The conditions can be modified to account for the point being a maximum for more than one individual.

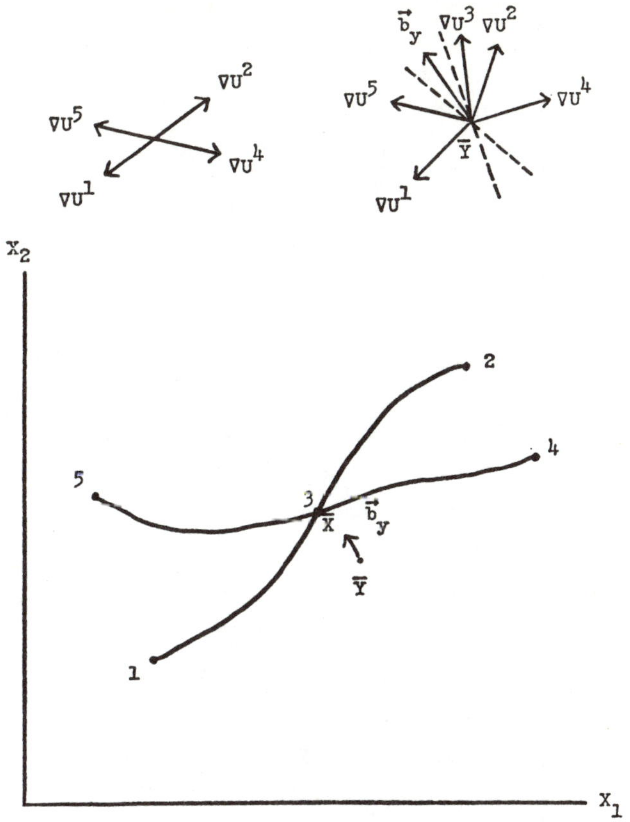

FIGURE 2

points for which (3) is satisfied—the "contract curves" as traditionally termed in economics. The only point which is an equilibrium point is $\overline{X}$, the point corresponding to the maximum of individual 3. At any other point there exists a motion which would receive a majority vote. For example, consider $\overline{Y}$. The motion b_y would receive the "yes" votes of individuals 2, 3, and 5.

The above conditions, as qualified, are both necessary and sufficient for a point to be an equilibrium.

Notice that any majority rule equilibrium is obviously Pareto Optimal (almost by definition). But, certainly not all Pareto Optimals are majority rule equilibriums. The condition for Pareto Optimality is simply condition (2), or the condition described in footnote number 6, depending upon how you choose to define Pareto Optimality.

The most important point is that there is certainly nothing inherent

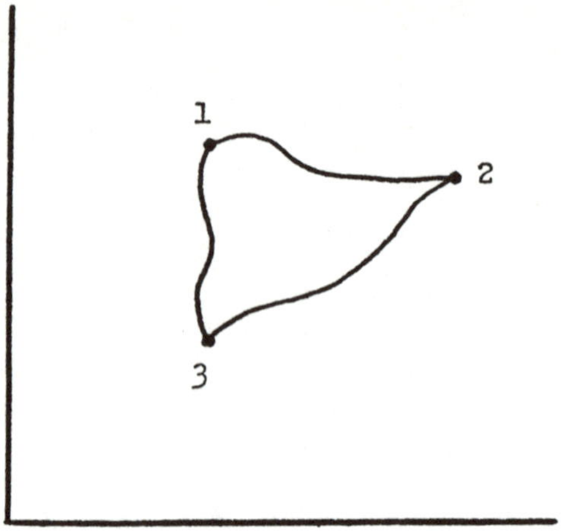

FIGURE 3

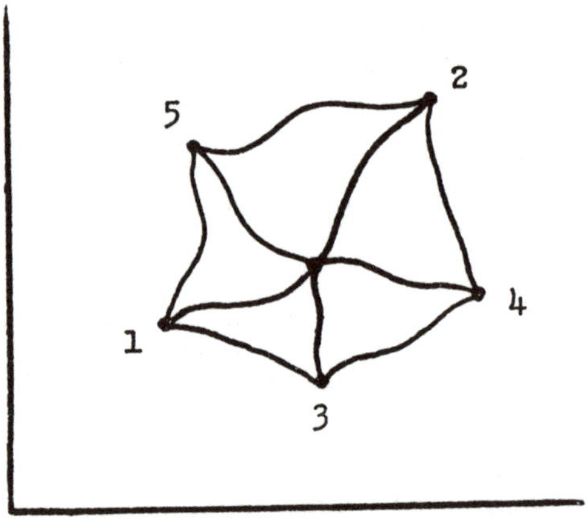

FIGURE 4

in utility theory which would assure the existence of an equilibrium. In fact, it would only be an accident (and a highly improbable one) if an equilibrium exists at all. For example, in Figures 3 and 4 there exists no equilibrium. And, it will be shown below that the addition of a constraint does little to relieve the situation if there are more than two variables to be determined.

III. *Equilibrium: One Constraint*

Suppose the committee was operating under a single constraint such as a budget constraint. Each of the variables has an associated price and the committee has only a fixed amount (I) to spend. The constraint is of the form

$$\sum_{i=1}^{n} P_i x_i \leq I. \tag{4}$$

If the committee is at a point such that

$$\sum_{i=1}^{n} P_i x_i < I$$

the constraint does not alter the range of possible motions and an equilibrium must satisfy the conditions A, B, and C above. Therefore, only points such that

$$\sum_{i=1}^{n} P_i x_i = I$$

are of interest.

The constraint can be treated as an individual who has veto power. Where the price vector, or the gradient of the constraint is denoted as P, the only admissible (or feasible) motions are those in a set β where

$$\beta = \{b \in E_n \mid Pb \leq 0\}.$$

The problem of finding majority rule equilibrium conditions is simply one of finding conditions on the gradients of the individuals such that

$$Mb \leq 0$$

for all M and all $b \in \beta$ where M again ranges over all $(m+1)/2 \times n$ matrices that can be formed from the rows of A, the matrix of all gradient vectors.

Again, just as in the unconstrained case, it is assumed that all indifferent individuals behave in the same manner. This assumption gives rise to the following behavioral condition.

D. If a constrained equilibrium exists, people cannot "vote for" a motion to which they are indifferent.[9]

Again the remaining conditions are on the gradient vectors of the individuals.

E. For a point to be an equilibrium, the gradient of at least one individual must satisfy

$$\begin{bmatrix} y_1 \\ y_p \end{bmatrix} \begin{bmatrix} a_{i1} & a_{i2} & & a_{in} \\ -P_1 & -P_2 & \cdots & -P_n \end{bmatrix} = 0 \qquad y_i > 0 \qquad y_P \geq 0. \tag{5}$$

[9] The proof is analogous to the proof of A above. The only difference is that rather than *any* b, one must be chosen from the set β' where $\beta' = \{b \in E_n \mid Pb = 0\}$.

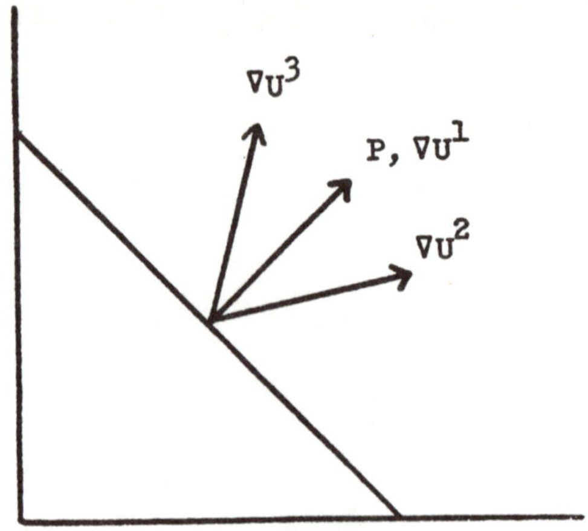

FIGURE 5

This says that the point is either a constrained maximum or a maximum for at least one individual. We shall assume for the following conditions that this is true for one and only one individual. Again, the conditions can easily be modified to account for other cases.

E. For a point to be an equilibrium point, those gradients (even in number) for which D does not hold can be divided into pairs such that there exists a solution to

$$\begin{bmatrix} y_i \\ y_j \\ y_p \end{bmatrix} \begin{bmatrix} a_{i1} & a_{i2} \cdots & a_{in} \\ a_{j1} & a_{j2} \cdots & a_{jn} \\ -P_1 & -P_2 \cdots & -P_n \end{bmatrix} = 0 \qquad \begin{matrix} y_i, y_j > 0 \\ y_P \geq 0. \end{matrix} \tag{6}$$

In words this means that the individuals can be divided into pairs such that they are either diametrically opposed or at least opposed on every motion in the set β' defined in footnote 9. On Figure 5, the vectors P and ∇U^1 are parallel and lie in the same direction thus satisfying (5). P can be found as a positive combination of ∇U^2 and ∇U^3 thus satisfying (6).

It is certainly no trick to find a situation where there is no equilibrium at all. For example, there is no equilibrium on Figure 6, where points 1, 2, and 3 are points of constrained maximum for individuals 1, 2, and 3 respectively. Again there is nothing in utility theory that would guarantee the existence of an equilibrium. And again, if an equilibrium exists, it would be purely accidental. This result leads, at this stage of analysis, to rather pessimistic conclusions about the allocation of public goods. Samuelson [5] has demonstrated that the equilibrium attained by a market mechanism for public goods will, in general, fail to be an optimum. The analysis here implies that a majority rule political process

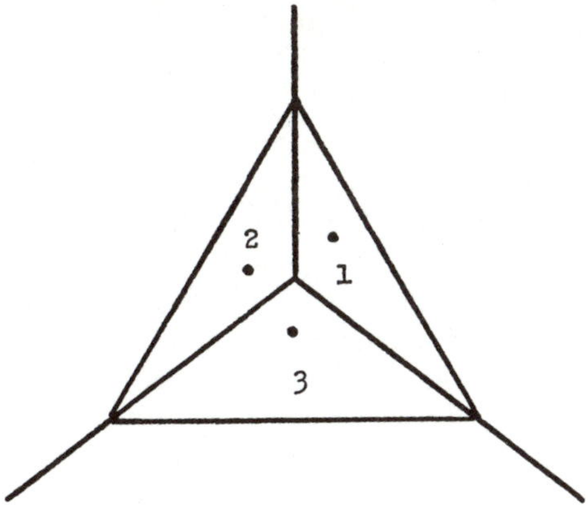

FIGURE 6

will fail to reach an equilibrium at all. Thus, in the case of public goods, society can count upon neither the market nor a majority rule political process to be a desirable allocative device.

IV. *Observations and Conjectures*

The results thus far seem rather negative in that equilibrium under majority rule would seem to be an almost nonexistent phenomenon. In view of this, a review of the concept of equilibrium used, and an inquiry into whether or not any important ingredients were left out should be useful.

Of great importance is the process by which motions are proposed. The decision process *itself* may dictate that some motions cannot be proposed. Often, before a motion can be voted on by a decision body, it must pass through a subcommittee. Unless proposals and amendments can be made from the floor, the subcommittee determines what motions can be voted on. In such cases, the equilibrium conditions would apply only to members of this committee. When the members of such a committee are in equilibrium, the complete voting body is in equilibrium regardless of the preferences of those not on the subcommittee.

This brings up an additional observation on coalitions. Where there exists a majority coalition which, itself, operates under a rule of unanimity, condition (2), when satisfied for the members of this coalition, defines the equilibrium points. If there exists a constraint, the traditional requirements on utility functions are sufficient to assure the existence of an equilibrium in such cases.

A third observation pertains to the role of time in the analysis. Certainly there may be great costs of indecision—if nothing else, simply sitting. As time passes, the utility functions as reflected in the commodity space may tend to "flatten." That is, with time, the marginal utility associated with an additional unit of a variable may tend to diminish. The points of maximum may extend to a neighborhood around the original maximum and the "contract curves" may tend to become "broad" as the time taken to reach a decision increases. This type of phenomenon would certainly tend to increase the possibility of the existence of an equilibrium.

Associated with the possibility of a change in evaluations through time is the possibility of a change in preference due to the decision process itself. The exchange of information associated with any decision process may serve actually to change the utility functions. A "persuasive" individual may be successful in changing the utility functions of others so that all of the orderings, in the end, resemble his. Or, the process may tend to cause all utility functions to change to a "similar" ordering but one which is not "similar" to any of the original functions.

The model outlined here lends itself to the possible testing of all of these speculations. If the original utility functions are known, the contract curves can be described as a system of equations and solved (at least theoretically) for an equilibrium. In the absence of such detailed information one might assume that the contract curves are linear. The only information then needed would be the points of maximum for the various individuals (or constrained maximums as the case may be). The contract curves would then be the curves L of the form

$$L = tC + A \qquad 0 \leq t \leq 1$$

where

$$B - A = C$$

assuming B is the maximum for individual B and A is the maximum for individual A.

Having obtained this information the experimenter can estimate the equilibrium. The decision process can then be observed. The resulting equilibrium can be compared with the "theoretical" equilibrium and the final utility functions compared with the originals. The path to equilibrium can be observed along with associated strategic behavior, etc. It may be the case that strategic considerations influence individuals to vote against some motion which would increase their utility. Such observations could, in principle, lead to the identification of variables which systematically contribute to the final outcome of group decisions.

Mathematical Appendix

The proofs for the various statements and conditions given in the text are presented below. The propositions given below follow in the same order as the corresponding descriptions in the text.

Definitions

A is an $m \times n$ (m, n finite and m an odd number) matrix.

(m) is the set of vectors which serve as rows of A. The elements of (m) are $(a_1, \cdots, a_i, \cdots, a_m)$.

M is an $(m+1)/2 \times n$ submatrix of A. (M) is the set of all M that can be formed from A.

A^* is a $r \times n$ submatrix of $A(r=m-1)$.

(r) is the set of vectors which serve as rows of A^*.

In general, except for specifically defined submatrices such as those above, if (ξ) is a set of row vectors of some matrix with ξ elements, then $[\xi]$ is the submatrix with the ξ members of (ξ) as rows.

For *any* matrix $[\xi]$ and vector b the notation $[\xi]\ b>0$ means that the inner product of b with every row of $[\xi]$ is strictly greater than zero. The complement of a set (ξ) is denoted as $(\bar{\xi})$. E_n denotes Euclidean n-space. The notation ab represents an inner product. Define A to be an $\hat{A}$ if and only if for any $b \in E_n \exists M \in (M)$ such that $Mb \leq 0$.

Lemma 1. A is an $\hat{A}$ if and only if for *no* $M \in (M)$ there is a $b \in E_n$ such that $Mb>0$.

Proof. Examine first the "if" part. Assume that for $M_i \exists b_i$ such that $M_i b_i > 0$. Since M_i has $(m+1)/2$ rows, there are at most $m-(m+1)/2 = (m-1)/2$ remaining rows of A for which $ab_i \leq 0$ so A cannot be $\hat{A}$.

Assume that for $b_i \nexists$ an $M \in (M)$ such that $Mb_i \leq 0$. At most, there could be $(m-1)/2$ rows of A such that $ab_i \leq 0$ is the case. For the remaining $(m+1)/2$ rows—call them M_i—it must be the case that $ab_i>0$. Thus, for M_i there exists a solution to $M_i b>0$.

Lemma 2. If A is an $\hat{A}$, then for every $b \in E_n \exists$ an $a \in (m)$ such that $ab=0$.

PROOF. Assume A is an $\hat{A}$. Assume that for b_i there does not exist an $a \in (m)$ such that $ab_i=0$. By the definition of $\hat{A} \exists$ some $M_j \in (M)$ such that $M_j b_i < 0$. But, by letting $b_k = -b_i$, we find $M_j b_k > 0$, thus contradicting the assumption that A is an $\hat{A}$.

Theorem 1. If A is an $\hat{A}$, then there exists at least one $a_i \in (m)$ such that $a_i=0$.

PROOF. For any $b \in E_n$ there must exist an orthogonal row of A by Lemma 2. To prove the theorem, it is sufficient to show that if at least one row of A is not the zero vector, then there exists a solution, say b^*, to $Ab \neq 0$. This will be shown by induction.

Assume A has only one column, no element of which is zero. Then any non-zero scalar satisfies the requirements of b^*.

Assume A has n columns. Assume further that there exists a solution, say b, to

$$\sum_{j=1}^{n-1} a_{ij} b_j = \alpha_i \neq 0 \qquad i = 1, \cdots, m.$$

Now, if there exists b_n such that $a_{in} b_n \not\rightarrow -\alpha_i$ for $i=1, \cdots, m$, we are finished. Certainly such a number exists. Just choose b_n not equal to any of the numbers

$$\left(-\frac{\alpha_1}{a_{1n}}, \ldots, -\frac{\alpha_n}{a_{nn}}\right).$$

By the theorem, at least one row of A must be the zero vector. The reduced matrix A^* is formed from A by the elimination of a row which is the zero vector. The remaining discussion pertains to A^* which has $r=m-1$ rows called the set (r).

Lemma 3. The equation

$$[\xi]x > 0$$

has a solution x if and only if the equation

$$y[\xi] = 0$$

has no semipositive solution y.[10]

Corollary. The equation

$$[\xi]x < 0$$

has a solution, x, if and only if the equation

$$y[\xi] < 0$$

has no semipositive solution y.

Proof. It is sufficient to show that $[\xi]x<0$ has a solution if and only if $[\xi]x>0$ has a solution. Suppose x is a solution to $[\xi]x>0$. Then $x'=-x$ is a solution to $[\xi]x'<0$. If x is a solution to $[\xi]x<0$, then $x'=-x$ is a solution to $[\xi]x'>0$.

Lemma 4. If A is an $\hat{A}$ then for any $b\in E_n$ such that $a_i b_i=0$ for some non-zero $a_i\in(r)$, then there exists at least one $a_j\in(r)$, where $i\neq j$, such that $a_j b_i=0$.

PROOF. Let A be an $\hat{A}$ and assume that for b_i, $ab_i=0$ for one and only one non-zero $a\in(r)$. Since A is an $\hat{A}$, we know the following:

$ab_i=0$ for one and only one non-zero $a\in(r)$, by assumption. Call it a_i.

$ab_i>0$ for $\frac{r}{2}$ rows of A^*. Call them the set (P).

$ab_i<0$ for $\frac{r}{2}-1$ rows of A^*. Call them the set (D).

The last two statements are valid because otherwise either b_i or $-b_i$ would be a solution to $Mb>0$ contrary to the assumption that A is an $\hat{A}$. It makes no difference whether (P) or (D) contains $r/2$ elements since (D) becomes (P) for $-b_i$. By Lemma 3, there exists no semipositive solution to

$$y[P] = 0.$$

[10] For the proof, see [3, p. 48]. "Semipositive" is taken to mean that $y_i\geq 0$ and not all $y_i=0$.

This is forced by the definition of (P). There also exists no semipositive solution to

$$y\begin{bmatrix} P \\ a_i \end{bmatrix} = 0. \tag{1}$$

Assume that there does exist a semipositive solution to (1). This implies that $-a_i$ can be expressed as a positive combination of some of the elements of (P). Assume them to be the first k elements. That is

$$-a_i = \sum_{j=1}^{k} y_j a_j \quad \text{where} \quad y_j > 0.$$

Multiplying by b_i, we find

$$0 \geqq -a_i b_i = y_1 a_1 b_i + \cdots + y_k a_k b_i \qquad y_i > 0.$$

But, this contradicts the fact that $ab_i > 0$ for all $a \in (P)$. Because (1) has no solution, by Lemma 3 there must exist a solution to

$$\begin{bmatrix} P \\ a_i \end{bmatrix} \quad b > 0 \tag{2}$$

and, since there are $(m+1)/2$ rows of the matrix in (2), A cannot be an $\hat{A}$. The lemma is proved.

Lemma 5. If A is an $\hat{A}$, then for each row vector a_i of A^* there exists at least one row vector a_j, $j \neq i$, of A^* and scalars α_i and α_j (not both zero) such that $\alpha_j a_j + \alpha_i a_i = 0$.

Proof. If some $a \in (r)$ is the zero vector, the condition of the lemma is satisfied. If no $a \in (r)$ is the zero, then any b such that $a_i b = 0$ must be orthogonal to at least one other row of A^*. The finite condition on the rows forces there to be at least one row, say a_j, which is orthogonal to every vector b which is orthogonal to a_i. This means a_i and a_j are parallel and the lemma is proved. The formal proof follows closely the proof of Theorem 1.

Theorem 2. If one and only one row of A is the zero vector, then A is an $\hat{A}$ if and only if the rows of A^* can be partitioned into two element sets such that there exists a solution to

$$y_i a_i + y_j a_j = 0 \qquad y_i, y_j > 0.$$

Proof. By Lemma 5, if A is an $\hat{A}$, then the rows of A^* can be divided into sets which are parallel. It will be shown that each such set contains an even number of vectors and that half lie in one direction and the other half lie in the opposite direction. This is simply another way of stating the theorem.

Choose any row of A^*, say a_i, and divide all rows of A^* into the sets with respect to a_i as defined below.

s = the number of vectors in a set (s) where $(s) = \{a_j \in (r) \mid \alpha_i a_i + \alpha_j a_j = 0$

has a solution α_i and α_j}. Note that (s) contains a_i. Recall also that by assumption, (r) contains no zero.

q = the number of vectors in a set (q) where $(q) = \{a_j \in (s) \mid a_j = \lambda a_i$ has a solution $\lambda > 0\}$. Note that (q) contains a_i.

l = the number of vectors in a set (l) where $(l) = \{a \in (s) \mid a \notin (q)\}$. Notice that $s - q = l$.

b_i = some vector in E_n such that $ab_i = 0$ for all $a \in (s)$ and $ab_i \neq 0$ for all $a \in (r) \cap (\bar{s})$.

p = the number of vectors in a set (p) where $(p) = \{a \in (r) \cap (\bar{s}) \mid ab_i > 0\}$.

d = the number of vectors in a set (d) where $(d) = \{a \in (r) \cap (\bar{s}) \mid ab_i < 0\}$.

Observe that

$$r = p + d + l + q.$$

By Lemma 3 and its corollary there exists no semipositive solution, y, to

$$y[p] = 0 \quad \text{or} \quad y[q] = 0.$$

Also, there exists no semipositive solution, y, to

$$y\begin{bmatrix} p \\ q \end{bmatrix} = 0. \tag{3}$$

A solution to (3) would imply that the negative of some member of (q) can be expressed as a positive combination of a subset of (p) or vice versa. Assume $a_q \in (q)$ can be expressed as a positive combination of the first k elements of (p), i.e.,

$$-a_q = y_1 a_1 + \cdots + y_k a_k \qquad y_i > 0.$$

Multiply by b_i and obtain

$$0 = -a_q b_i = y_1 a_1 b_i + \cdots + y_k a_k b_i \qquad y_i > 0.$$

But, by the definition of (p), all members on the right of the equation are positive thus establishing a contradiction. Since there is no semi-positive solution to (3), there must exist a solution to

$$\begin{bmatrix} p \\ q \end{bmatrix} \qquad b > 0. \tag{4}$$

If A is to be an $\hat{A}$, (4) dictates that

$$p + q \leq \frac{r}{2}\cdot \tag{5}$$

Otherwise, $\begin{bmatrix} p \\ q \end{bmatrix}$ would be an M for which there is a solution to $Mb > 0$

thus violating Lemma 1. By the same reasoning, we know that

$$p + l \leq \frac{r}{2} \tag{6}$$

and, since (d) becomes (p) for $-b_i$, the same argument gives

$$d + l \leq \frac{r}{2} \tag{7}$$

$$d + q \leq \frac{r}{2} \cdot \tag{8}$$

Recalling that $r=p+d+l+q$ and solving equations 5 through 8, one can derive

$$q \leq l \quad \text{and} \tag{9}$$

$$l \leq q. \tag{10}$$

Therefore, $l=q$ and the "only if" part of the theorem is proved.

Now the "if" part. Assume the conditions of the theorem are satisfied. Choose any $b_i \in E_n \cdot ab_i = 0$ for the zero vector. For every $a \in ab_i > 0$, there is an $a \in ab_i \leq 0$. Therefore $ab_i \leq 0$ for $(m+1)/2$ elements of (m) and A is an $\hat{A}$.

The theorems below are related to the discussion contained in Section Three of the text. Recall that the discussion there is about majority decisions which must satisfy a single constraint such as

$$\sum_{i=1}^{n} p_i x_i \leq I.$$

It is assumed that the "existing position" is one which satisfies

$$\sum_{i=1}^{k} p_i x_i = I.$$[11]

The following definitions are needed.

Let C be a specific, non-zero vector (the negative of the gradient of the constraint).

$$G = \{b \in E_n \mid b \in J \cup K\}$$
$$J = \{b \in E_n \mid Cb > 0\}$$
$$K = \{b \in E_n \mid Cb = 0\}.$$

Let A be an $\hat{A}$ if and only if for every $b \in G$ there exists an $M \in (M)$ such that $Mb \leq 0$.

[11] See the discussion in the text.

Lemma 6. A is an $\hat{A}$ if and only if for *no* $M \in (M)$ does there exist a $b \in G$ which is a solution to $Mb > 0$. (proof omitted)

Lemma 7. If A is an $\hat{A}$, then there must exist some $a \in (m)$ and a set of scalars (α_i, a_c) with at least one $\alpha \neq 0$ such that

$$\alpha_i a + \alpha_c C = 0.$$

PROOF. Assume no $a \in (m)$ satisfies the conditions of Lemma 7. Then there exists $b_i \in K$ such that $ab = 0$ for *no* $a \in (m)$. The elements of (m) can be partitioned into two sets according to whether $ab_i > 0$ or $ab_i < 0$. One of these sets must contain at least $(m+1)/2$ elements. Since these sets reverse positions for $-b_i$, A cannot be an $\hat{A}$ by Lemma 6.

Theorem 3. If A is an $\hat{A}$, then there exists some $a \in (m)$ such that a solution exists to

$$y_i a + y_c C = 0 \qquad y_i > 0,\ y_c \geq 0.$$

PROOF. The following definitions are needed.

H = the number of elements in the set (H) where $(H) = \{a \in (m) \mid \alpha_i a + \alpha_c C = 0 \text{ not all } \alpha = 0\}$.

By Lemma 7, the set (H) is not empty. If a member of (H) is the zero vector, it also satisfies the conditions of the theorem. So only the case where (H) contains no zero vector need be examined.

Assume A to be an $\hat{A}$ and assume that no member of (H) satisfies the condition of the theorem.

b_i = some $b \in K$ such that $ab_i \neq 0$ for all $a \in (\overline{H})$.

P = the number of elements in (P) where $(P) = \{a \in (\overline{H}) \mid ab_i > 0\}$.

D = the number of elements in (D) where $(D) = \{a \in (\overline{H}) \mid ab_i < 0\}$. Note that $P + D + H = m$.

If A is an $\hat{A}$, then

$$P < \frac{m+1}{2} \quad \text{and} \quad D < \frac{m+1}{2} \cdot$$

Otherwise either $[P]b$ or $[D](-b)$ would satisfy $Mb > 0$ contrary to Lemma 6.

Now, there can exist no semipositive solution to

$$y \begin{bmatrix} P \\ H \\ C \end{bmatrix} = 0.$$

A solution to this implies that any $a_k \in (H) \cup C$ with $y_k \neq 0$ can be expressed as

$$\sum y_j a_j = -a_k \qquad y_j \geq 0.$$

Multiply this equation by b_i and observe

$$\sum_{j=1}^{P} y_j a_j b_i = -a_k b_i = 0 \qquad y_j \geq 0$$

which contradicts the fact that $a_j b_i > 0$ for $j = 1, \cdots, P$.

So, by Lemma 3, there does exist a solution to

$$\begin{bmatrix} P \\ H \\ C \end{bmatrix} \qquad b > 0.$$

The same argument shows there is a solution to

$$\begin{bmatrix} D \\ H \\ C \end{bmatrix} \qquad b > 0.$$

But, since $P+D+H=m$, either $P+H \geq (m+1)/2$ or $D+H \geq (m+1)/2$ so either one or the other satisfies $Mb>0$. By Lemma 6, A cannot be an $\hat{A}$.

If A is an $\hat{A}$ at least one element of (m) must satisfy the condition of Theorem 3. Elimination of this element yields a set called (r) with $r=m-1$ elements.

Lemma 8. If A is an $\hat{A}$ and if the condition of Theorem 3 is satisfied by one and only one row of A, then for *every* $a_i \in (r)$ there exists at least one $a_j \in (r)$, $i \neq j$, such that a solution exists to

$$\alpha_i a_i + \alpha_j a_j + \alpha_c C = 0 \qquad \alpha_i, \alpha_j \neq 0.$$

PROOF. It can be shown that if the condition of this Lemma is *not* satisfied for some row, say a_i, then there exists a $b \in K$ such that $a_i b = 0$ and $a_j b \neq 0$ for all $j \in (r)$, $j \neq i$.[12]

Assume A is an $\hat{A}$, no $a \in (r)$ satisfies the condition of Theorem 3, and that for a_i there exists a $b \in K$, say b_i, such that $a_i\, b_i = 0$ and $a_j b_i \neq 0$ for all $a_j \in (r)$, $i \neq j$. We let

P = the number of elements in a set (P) where $(P) = \{a \in (r) \mid ab_i > 0\}$

D = the number of elements in a set (D) where $(D) = \{a \in (r) \mid ab_i < 0\}$.

If A is an $\hat{A}$ then one set contains $r/2$ elements and the other contains $r/2-1$. Otherwise, either b_i or $-b_i$ would be a solution to $Mb>0$. Assume $P=r/2$. By the same argument used previously there exists no semipositive solution to

$$y \begin{bmatrix} P \\ a_i \\ C \end{bmatrix} = 0.$$

[12] Use corollary to Theorem 2.3 in [3, p. 37].

Thus, by Lemma 3, there exists a solution to

$$\begin{bmatrix} P \\ a_i \\ C \end{bmatrix} \qquad b > 0.$$

But the set $(P) \cup a_i$ contains $(m+1)/2$ elements and is therefore an M. So A cannot be an $\hat{A}$. Recalling that (D) becomes (P) for $-b_i$ proves the Lemma.

Lemma 9. If A is an $\hat{A}$ and if the condition of Theorem 3 is satisfied by one and only one row of A, then the elements of (r) can be partitioned into mutually exclusive sets each containing two elements such that there exists a solution to

$$\alpha_i a_i + \alpha_j a_j + \alpha_c C = 0 \qquad \alpha_i, \alpha_j \neq 0.$$

PROOF. Assume A is an $\hat{A}$ and that the condition of Theorem 3 is satisfied by one and only one row of A. Choose any member of (r), say a_i, and partition the members of (r) with respect to a_i as follows.

H = the number of elements in a set (H) where $(H) = \{a_j \in (r) \mid$ a solution exists to $\alpha_i a_i + \alpha_j a_j + \alpha_c C = 0$, $\alpha_i, \alpha_j \neq 0\}$. Notice that $a_i \in (H)$ and by Lemma 8, (H) contains more than one element.

$b_i = \{\text{some } b \in K \mid \text{for all } a \in (H),\ ab_i = 0 \text{ and for all } a \in (r) \cap (\overline{H}),\ ab_i \neq 0\}$.
$b_j = \{\text{some } b \in K \mid \text{for all } a \in (H),\ ab_j \neq 0\}$.[13]
P = the number of elements in a set (P) where $(P) = \{a \in (r) \cap (\overline{H}) \mid ab_i > 0\}$.
D = the number of elements in a set (D) where $(D) = \{a \in (r) \cap (\overline{H}) \mid ab_i < 0\}$.
Q = the number of elements in a set (Q) where $(Q) = \{a \in (H) \mid ab_j > 0\}$.
L = the number of elements in a set (L) where $(L) = \{a \in (H) \mid ab_j < 0\}$.

Observe that

$$r = Q + L + P + D.$$

By arguments used previously, there exists no semipositive solution to

$$y \begin{bmatrix} P \\ Q \\ C \end{bmatrix} = 0.$$

So, if A is to be an $\hat{A}$

$$P + Q \leq \frac{r}{2} \cdot \tag{11}$$

[13] The existence of such a b_j involves an assumption that $\alpha_i a + \alpha_i C = 0$ has no solution for any $a \epsilon (H)$. No confusion should result since a_i could be so chosen.

The same argument gives

(12) $$P + L \leq \frac{r}{2} \cdot$$

Since (D) becomes (P) for $-b_i$, we have

(13) $$D + L \leq \frac{r}{2}$$

(14) $$D + Q \leq \frac{r}{2} \cdot$$

Recalling that $r = Q + L + P + D$, it can be shown that

(15) $$L = Q.$$

Since $L + Q = H$, the lemma is proved.

Theorem 4. If the condition of Theorem 3 is satisfied by one and only one row of A, A is an $\hat{A}$ if and only if the elements of (r) can be partitioned into pairs such that there exists a solution to

$$y_i a_i + y_j a_j + y_c C = 0 \qquad \begin{matrix} y_i, y_j > 0 \\ y_c \geq 0. \end{matrix}$$

PROOF. Choose some element of (r), say a_k. The elements of (r) can be partitioned with respect to a_k as follows.

H = the number of elements in a set (H) where $(H) = \{a_i \in (r) \mid$ a solution exists to $\alpha_i a_i + \alpha_k a_k + \alpha_c C = 0 \ \alpha_i, \alpha_k \neq 0\}$.

By Lemma 8 and Lemma 9, the number of elements in (H) is greater than zero and even. Notice that $a_k \in (H)$.

Now partition (H) into pairs such that for the maximum possible number of pairs a solution exists to

$$v_i a_i + y_j a_j + y_c C = 0 \qquad y_i, y_j > 0, \ y_c \geq 0.$$

Call the set of pairs for which this condition is satisfied $(H_p) \cdot (H_p)$ is a subset of (H) and contains H_p (an even number) elements.

H_n = the (even) number of elements in (H_n) where $(H_n) = (H) \cap (\overline{H}_p)$.

$b_i = \{$some $b \in K \mid ab_i = 0$ for all $a \in H$ and $ab_i \neq 0$ for all $a \in (r) \cap (\overline{H})\}$.

P = the number of elements in a set (P) where $(P) = \{a \in (r) \cap (\overline{H}) \mid ab_i > 0\}$.

D = the number of elements in a set (D) where $(D) = \{a \in (r) \cap (\overline{H}) \mid ab_i < 0\}$.

There exists no semipositive solution to $y \begin{bmatrix} P \\ H_n \\ C \end{bmatrix} = 0$. This can be shown by the method used previously. By eliminating the proper elements ($H_p/2$ in number) from (H_p) a set (H_p') containing $H_p/2$ elements can be formed such that there exists no semipositive solution to

$$y\begin{bmatrix} P \\ H_n \\ H_p' \\ C \end{bmatrix} = 0.$$

Therefore, if A is an $\hat{A}$

$$P + \frac{H_p}{2} + H_n \leq \frac{r}{2}\cdot$$

The same argument gives

$$D + \frac{H_p}{2} + H_n \leq \frac{r}{2}\cdot$$

By noting that $r = P + D + H_p + H_n$, it can be shown that

$$H_n \leq 0.$$

The "only if" part is proved. Proof of the "if" is omitted.

REFERENCES

1. D. BLACK AND R. A. NEWING, *Committee Decisions with Complementary Valuation*. Andover 1951.
2. D. BLACK, *The Theory of Committees and Elections*. Cambridge 1958.
3. D. GALE, *The Theory of Linear Economic Models*. New York 1960.
4. C. R. PLOTT, "A Method for Finding 'Acceptable Proposals' in Group Decision Processes," *Papers on Non-Market Decision Making*, 1967, *2*, 45–59.
5. P. A. SAMUELSON, "The Pure Theory of Public Expenditures," *Rev. Econ. Stud.*, Nov. 1954, *36*, 378–89.

[28]

Journal of Public Economics 24 (1984) 373–380. North-Holland

SEPARATION OF THE REDISTRIBUTIVE AND ALLOCATIVE FUNCTIONS OF GOVERNMENT

A public choice perspective

Marilyn R. FLOWERS

The University of Oklahoma, Norman, OK 73019, USA

Patricia M. DANZON*

Center for Health Policy, Duke University, Durham, NC 27706, USA

Received March 1983, revised version received February 1984

The implications of not separating the redistributive and allocative functions of government are examined from a public choice perspective. Many democratic governments lump transfers and public services into a single unified budget. This can distort voter perceptions of the marginal cost of public services relative to the marginal tax price embodied in the taxing institutions employed to generate public revenue. If the median voter's perception of marginal cost is affected, the majority rule outcome with respect to public goods spending will be altered correspondingly.

1. Introduction

The methodological propriety of separate consideration of the allocative and redistributive activities of government has been subject to some debate in the public finance literature [Musgrave (1959), Samuelson (1969), and Hochman and Rogers (1969)]. In this paper we examine, from a public choice perspective, the implication of *not separating* the redistributive and allocative activities of government.

Many democratic governments lump together transfers and public services in a single unified budget. We will argue that this can distort voter perception of the marginal cost of public services relative to the marginal tax prices embodied in the taxing institution employed to generate public revenue. If the median voter's perception of marginal cost is affected, the majority rule outcome with respect to the level of spending for public goods will be altered correspondingly. This distortion arises if budgeting institutions cause voters to perceive that marginal units of a public good are financed out of reduced transfer spending rather than higher taxes. Relevant rules

*Both authors gratefully acknowledge research support from the Hoover Institution on War, Revolution and Peace. Initial work on this paper occurred while Flowers was a National Fellow, and Danzon a Senior Research Fellow at the Hoover Institution.

from this perspective include constraints on total government outlays, earmarked taxes, the order in which budget choices are made and the manner in which the transfer process is institutionalized.

2. A simple three-voter model

We begin with a simple model in which there are three voters, all of whom are identical with respect to preferences and income. The government provides a single public good, defense, which is financed by a taxing institution which assigns equal tax shares to the three voters. We assume initially that no income redistribution is carried out through the public sector. Suppose that defense is produced under conditions of constant marginal cost of \$3. Each voter then confronts a marginal tax price of \$1. Given our assumption of identical preferences, these equal tax prices correspond to a Lindahl benefit tax. Consequently, there will be unanimous agreement among the voters on a Pareto efficient level of defense spending. We assume this to be \$30 (10 units).

Now suppose that, in addition to defense outlays, any majority coalition of voters has the option of voting transfer payments for its members out of public revenue. We assume initially that voter support for transfers is motivated by a self-interested desire to increase own consumption rather than any altruistic concern with increasing the consumption of others. The government budget can now contain both public good and transfer components. We are interested in whether and how different voting rules can affect outlays for each activity. Specifically we ask whether use of the fisc for redistributive purposes can prevent an efficient level of spending on defense despite an allocation of tax shares in accordance with the benefit principle. For simplicity, we assume that defense is characterized by zero income elasticity of demand. This insures that the government's redistributive activity does not effect the efficient level of defense consumption.

There are a variety of voting rules and procedures which might be employed to determine the government budget. The first to be examined is a two-stage process in which voters are asked first to choose a total level of government spending (and taxing) and then to allocate that total between outlays for defense and for transfers. It is the second stage of this procedure which is of primary concern.

Suppose that two voters form a majority coalition to control the allocation of some fixed level of expenditure. Money not spent on defense is divided equally between the two voters. These two voters would not choose to spend \$30 on defense even if the total budget were large enough to accommodate that level of expenditure. The requirement to finance defense out of what otherwise would be transfer income has changed the marginal cost of defense to each coalition member. Marginal cost is now \$1.50 rather than the \$1 which would be required if the marginal unit of defense were financed by levying additional taxes.

In the preceding example, membership in the transfer coalition was established prior to the vote on defense spending. How might the outcome be altered if voters were uncertain about who would be the beneficiaries of the transfer process? Suppose, for example, that budgeting rules required that the decision on defense spending be made first with any residual funds to be allocated as transfers to whatever majority coalition is successful in forming. Assume also that this reversal of the temporal ordering of the votes on defense and transfers has the effect, as it obviously might, of preventing a transfer coalition from forming until after the vote on defense outlays. If, at the time the defense vote is taken, each of our three voters views each of the three possible majority transfer coalitions as equally likely, the expected individual marginal cost of defense is \$1. For every \$3 not allocated to defense, each voter perceives a two-thirds chance of receiving \$1.50 and a one-third chance of receiving nothing from the transfer process. If voters are risk neutral, uncertainty about membership in the transfer coalition restores efficiency to the decision on public goods spending. If voters are risk averse, uncertainty might actually result in a decision to collectively purchase more than 10 units of defense.

An alternative procedure for determining budget size and composition requires separate decisions by voters regarding how much to tax and to spend for each function. Separation of the financing decisions on defense and transfers can result in voter perception that marginal units of defense will be financed by increasing tax burden rather than at the expense of transfer spending. Given our assumption that the existing tax system imposes the 'correct' set of marginal tax prices on voters vis-à-vis defense expenditures, this change in the rules might restore efficiency to the defense decision.

However, if the same tax base is used to finance defense and transfers and if, in addition, the transfer coalition knows its identity in advance of the vote on defense spending, the separation of decisions on transfer and defense spending may be nominal rather than real. It is in the interest of the transfer coalition to impose the revenue maximizing tax rate on whatever base is being employed.[1] If this occurs, the coalition, in effect, is able to secure the maximum transfer to themselves through the fiscal process and then to 'choose' to allocate some portion of their post-transfer income to defense expenditure. Because marginal units of defense again are effectively financed out of what would otherwise be transfer income, the distorted perception of marginal cost which occurred in our first example reappears. One way of avoiding this problem and achieving a true separation of the taxing–spending decisions on defense and transfers is to employ earmarked taxes. A require-

[1]It should be noted that once we have allowed the kind of voter response to tax rates which limits the maximum from a particular base we have departed from a pure benefit tax.

ment that each activity be financed from its own tax base imposes an institutional barrier which prevents one activity from being financed at the expense of the other.

3. Transfers with interdependent utility functions

Thus far we have assumed that the motivation for transfer spending was purely selfish. What if voters have an altruistic demand for use of the fisc to transfer from themselves to others? The basic implication of our model is not changed. If total revenue is fixed, voters still must choose between selfish transfers or allocating revenue to a public good which, in this case, is a benevolent transfer to the poor. However, because the poor can become members of the transfer coalition, they receive more transfer income than our previous analysis would suggest, but still less than would be the case if the potential for selfish transfers were removed.

Consider a society of five individuals, four rich and one poor. The four rich individuals have some concern for the welfare of the poor person. In fig. 1 we have mapped the preferences of a typical wealthy individual, measuring own income on the horizontal axis and transfers to the poor on the vertical axis. With equal tax shares the rich individual must pay 25¢ for every \$1 of transfer to the poor person. The slope of budget constraint *AA* is −4. Without the option for selfish transfers, the wealthy individual would support a public transfer of \$120 at a tax cost to himself of \$30. Assume that tax rates have been set to generate this \$120 from the four wealthy persons. Now suppose that this money can either be transferred completely to the poor individual — a public good — or can be siphoned by a majority coalition into selfish transfers.

If the majority coalition consists of the three wealthy individuals who share equally in selfish transfers, the marginal cost to each of increasing the income of the poor rises to 33¢ per dollar transfer. In fig. 1 the effective budget constraint for a wealthy coalition member is *bcd*, with an optimum at point *c*. In response to the higher marginal cost, the majority coalition will devote only a portion of the \$120 in tax revenue to the poor person. The rest will go to selfish transfers.

The solution at *c* in fig. 1 is based on an assumption that the majority transfer coalition consists of three wealthy individuals. However, a coalition of two rich and one poor person provides all coalition members with a higher level of utility. This is because spillover benefits accompany transfers to the poor individual. If, for example, the poor person receives a pro rata share of selfish transfers, the effective budget constraint for a wealthy coalition member is *bf* instead of *bcd*. Even if all public funds were diverted to selfish transfers, the poor person would receive \$40. This is the situation at point *f*.

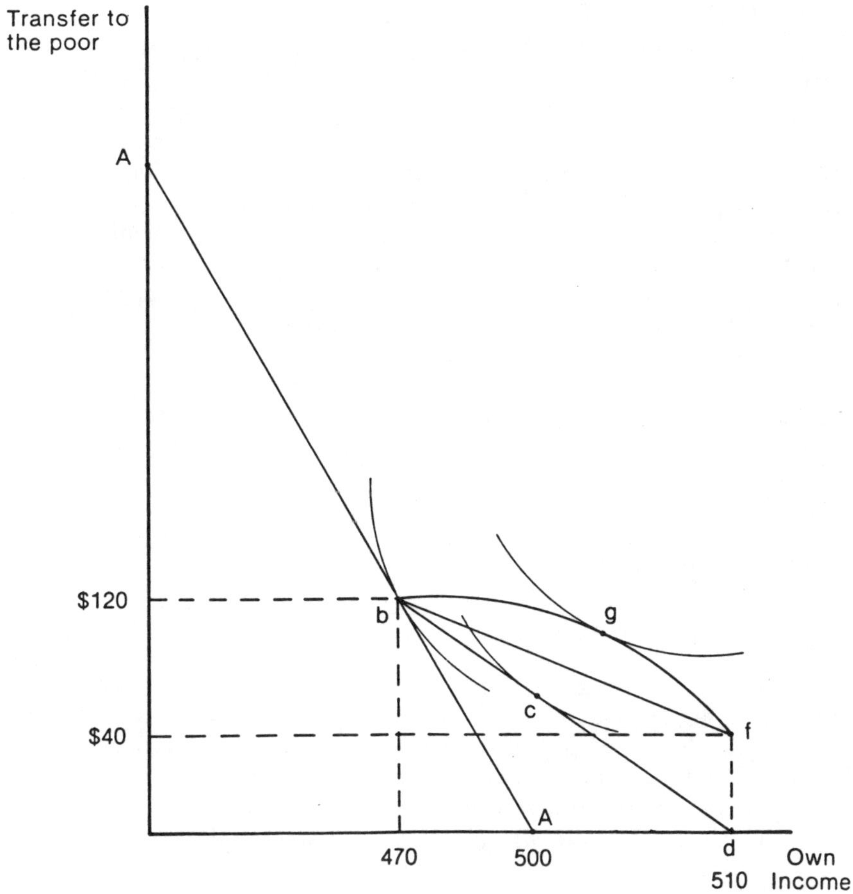

Fig. 1

Not only is the poor individual a more attractive member of the coalition than a non-poor individual, wealthy coalition members may even grant the poor member a greater than equal share of the funds diverted to the transfer coalition. In fig. 1, *bgf* depicts the possible combinations of own income and transfers to the poor available to the non-poor coalition member. Movement along that constraint to the left of point *f* represents increasingly larger shares of the coalition's transfer income going to the poor member, with point *b*, of course, representing a 100 percent share. As depicted in fig. 1, the wealthy member of the coalition would be willing to give the poor member a larger than equal share, such as that depicted at point *g*.

4. The large number setting

Regardless of the number of voters, if a stable, identifiable majority transfer coalition exists, its members will perceive higher costs to them if incremental units of the public good are financed by reducing transfer spending rather than increasing taxes. However, an increase in the number of voters should make it more difficult for such a stable coalition to form, especially if potential members of that coalition can be chosen at random from the voting population. This suggests that with large numbers, uncertainty about coalition membership and net gains from the transfer process is likely to dominate voter perceptions of the marginal cost of a public good.

Suppose that there are N voters and that n denotes the number required for a simple majority. Assume, as in our earlier example, that some fixed level of total expenditure must be allocated between defense and transfers and that voters must choose defense spending first, with residual funds allocated to transfer recipients. If voters regard any of the possible majority coalitions as equally likely, the probability that any individual will be a transfer beneficiary is n/N.[2] Given equal sharing among coalition members and denoting the marginal cost of defense as C, the expected value of the individual marginal cost of defense is

$$(n/N)(C/n) = C/N.$$

C/N is also the average individual tax price if defense is financed on the margin from higher taxes. If the median voter on defense were assigned a tax share of $1/N$, his 'tax price' of defense and the expected marginal cost of defense measured in terms of forgone transfer income are equal.

A particular taxing institution may not assign a tax price to the median voter which is equal to the average tax price. Thus, the potential for selfish transfers can create a difference between the perceived cost of financing marginal units of defense out of increased taxes as opposed to reduced transfers even if all transfer coalitions are regarded as equiprobable. However, there is no systematic bias of the sort incurred in the certainty model. Such a bias might appear if the median voter were to perceive some probability greater than n/N of being a beneficiary of the transfer process. This could occur if budgeting institutions make some transfer coalitions more likely than others.

[2] $\binom{N}{n}$ is the number of possible majority coalitions. $\binom{N-1}{n-1}$ is the number of coalitions containing a specific voter.

$$\binom{N-1}{n-1} \Big/ \binom{N}{n} = \frac{N}{n}$$

is the probability that a specific voter will be included in the majority.

As a result of several features of U.S. political institutions, the likely beneficiaries of government transfer spending are not a randomly selected 51 percent of the voting population. In reality, spending votes are taken by elected representatives, not directly by the voters, as in our simple model. Indirect voting enhances the relative influence of special interest groups — those with a comparative advantage in organizing to exert political influence. The majority is likely to consist of a coalition of such minorities. In the U.S. budget, several such specific minority groups — the poor, the elderly, farmers, etc. — have succeeded in institutionalizing transfers to their members through a set of 'entitlement' programs. Entitlements are not subject to annual budget review, but rather are funded for indefinite periods through permanent appropriations. These factors should reduce considerably the costs of maintaining a stable, identifiable transfer coalition. The coalition is not required to re-establish itself every year in order to maintain its claim on budget funds. Once having established benefit levels, it has a prior claim on public revenue for an indefinite number of future budget years.

Those programs, which are subject to the annual appropriations process, tend to be the more traditional public goods such as national defense, environmental protection and the like. If the budget is subject to either an implicit or explicit constraint on total spending, these services must be funded from the residual which remains after entitlements have claimed their share. Proposals to increase public goods spending beyond this residual level must come at the expense of reduced outlays for existing transfer programs with identifiable beneficiaries. This suggests that a bias in the perceived marginal cost of public goods is especially likely to occur in times of budget stringency when increased demands for public goods outlays can only be accommodated by reductions in existing transfer programs.

The analysis in this paper has some interesting potential implications for current U.S. policy. Proposals to place formal and explicit constitutional limits on total federal government spending are receiving serious consideration. Such proposals, if adopted, would formally require that marginal units of public good expenditure be financed from reduced transfer spending rather than higher taxes. Some supporters of spending limits are also desirous of increasing total outlays for national defense. Our analysis suggests that total spending limits and higher defense outlays may be mutually incompatible rather than complementary policy objectives.

Social security financing is another policy issue for which the analysis of this paper has some relevance. Social security, which is the largest entitlement program in the budget, is financed by an earmarked payroll tax. As noted above, earmarking is one means of forcing a separation of public goods and transfer spending. Current proposals to allow at least partial general revenue financing of social security would weaken this separation between transfer and public goods outlays in the budget process and should be carefully considered in view of the potential consequences. With regard to this issue, it should be noted that a total spending constraint would also tie together transfers and public goods outlays even if earmarking were retained.

References

Hochman, H.H. and J.D. Rogers, 1969, Pareto optimal redistribution, American Economic Review 59 (4), 542–557.

Musgrave, Richard, 1959, The theory of public finance (McGraw-Hill Book Company, New York).

Samuelson, Paul, 1969, Pure theory of public expenditure and taxation, in: J. Margolis and H. Guitton, eds, Public economics (St. Martin's Press, New York).

[29]

The Political Economy of the Rent-Seeking Society

By Anne O. Krueger*

In many market-oriented economies, government restrictions upon economic activity are pervasive facts of life. These restrictions give rise to rents of a variety of forms, and people often compete for the rents. Sometimes, such competition is perfectly legal. In other instances, rent seeking takes other forms, such as bribery, corruption, smuggling, and black markets.

It is the purpose of this paper to show some of the ways in which rent seeking is competitive, and to develop a simple model of competitive rent seeking for the important case when rents originate from quantitative restrictions upon international trade. In such a case 1) competitive rent seeking leads to the operation of the economy inside its transformation curve; 2) the welfare loss associated with quantitative restrictions is unequivocally greater than the loss from the tariff equivalent of those quantitative restrictions; and 3) competitive rent seeking results in a divergence between the private and social costs of certain activities. Although the analysis is general, the model has particular applicability for developing countries, where government interventions are frequently all-embracing.

A preliminary section of the paper is concerned with the competitive nature of rent seeking and the quantitative importance of rents for two countries, India and Turkey. In the second section, a formal model of rent seeking under quantitative restrictions on trade is developed and the propositions indicated above are established. A final section outlines some other forms of rent seeking and suggests some implications of the analysis.

I. Competitive Rent Seeking

A. *Means of Competition*

When quantitative restrictions are imposed upon and effectively constrain imports, an import license is a valuable commodity. It is well known that under some circumstances, one can estimate the tariff equivalents of a set of quantitative restrictions and analyze the effects of those restrictions in the same manner as one would the tariff equivalents. In other circumstances, the resource-allocational effects of import licensing will vary, depending upon who receives the license.[1]

It has always been recognized that there are *some* costs associated with licensing: paperwork, the time spent by entrepreneurs in obtaining their licenses, the cost of the administrative apparatus necessary to issue licenses, and so on. Here, the argument is carried one step further: in many circumstances resources are devoted to competing for those licenses.

The consequences of that rent seeking are examined below. First, however, it will be argued that rent-seeking activities are often competitive and resources are devoted to competing for rents. It is difficult, if not impossible, to find empirically observable measures of the degree to which rent seeking is competitive. Instead, some

* Professor of economics, University of Minnesota.
I am indebted to James M. Henderson for invaluable advice and discussion on successive drafts. Jagdish Bhagwati and John C. Hause made helpful comments on earlier drafts of this paper.

[1] This phenomenon is explored in detail in Bhagwati and Krueger.

mechanisms under which rent seeking is almost certain to be competitive are examined. Then other cases are considered in which it is less obvious, but perhaps equally plausible, that competition results.

Consider first the results of an import-licensing mechanism when licenses for imports of intermediate goods are allocated in proportion to firms' capacities. That system is frequently used, and has been analyzed for the Indian case by Jagdish Bhagwati and Padma Desai. When licenses are allocated in proportion to firms' capacities, investment in additional physical plant confers upon the investor a higher expected receipt of import licenses. Even with initial excess capacity (due to quantitative restrictions upon imports of intermediate goods), a rational entrepreneur may still expand his plant if the expected gains from the additional import licenses he will receive, divided by the cost of the investment, equal the returns on investment in other activities.[2] This behavior could be perfectly rational even if, for all entrepreneurs, the total number of import licenses will remain fixed. In fact, if imports are held constant as domestic income grows, one would expect the domestic value of a constant quantity of imports to increase over time, and hence installed capacity would increase while output remained constant. By investing in additional capacity, entrepreneurs devote resources to compete for import licenses.

A second sort of licensing mechanism frequently found in developing countries is used for imports of consumer goods. There, licenses are allocated *pro rata* in proportion to the applications for those licenses from importers-wholesalers. Entry is generally free into importing-wholesaling, and firms usually have U-shaped cost curves. The result is a larger-than-optimal number of firms, operating on the downward sloping portion of their cost curves, yet earning a "normal" rate of return. Each importer-wholesaler receives fewer imports than he would buy at existing prices in the absence of licensing, but realizes a sufficient return on those licenses he does receive to make it profitable to stay in business. In this case, competition for rents occurs through entry into the industry with smaller-than-optimally sized firms, and resources are used in that the same volume of imports could be efficiently distributed with fewer inputs if firms were of optimal size.

A third sort of licensing mechanism is less systematic in that government officials decide on license allocations. Competition occurs to some extent through both mechanisms already mentioned as businessmen base their decisions on expected values. But, in addition, competition can also occur through allocating resources to influencing the probability, or expected size, of license allocations. Some means of influencing the expected allocation—trips to the capital city, locating the firm in the capital, and so on—are straightforward. Others, including bribery, hiring relatives of officials or employing the officials themselves upon retirement, are less so. In the former case, competition occurs through choice of location, expenditure of resources upon travel, and so on. In the latter case, government officials themselves receive part of the rents.

Bribery has often been treated as a transfer payment. However, there is competition for government jobs and it is reasonable to believe that expected total remuneration is the relevant decision variable for persons deciding upon careers. Generally, entry into government service requires above-average educational at-

[2] Note that: 1) one would expect to find greater excess capacity in those industries where rents are higher; and 2) within an industry, more efficient firms will have greater excess capacity than less efficient firms, since the return on a given amount of investment will be higher with greater efficiency.

tainments. The human capital literature provides evidence that choices as to how much to invest in human capital are strongly influenced by rates of return upon the investment. For a given level of educational attainment, one would expect the rate of return to be approximately equated among various lines of endeavor. Thus, if there appear to be high official-plus-unofficial incomes accruing to government officials and higher education is a prerequisite for seeking a government job, more individuals will invest in higher education. It is not necessary that government officials earn the same total income as other college graduates. All that is necessary is that there is an excess supply of persons seeking government employment, or that highly educated persons make sustained efforts to enter government services. Competition takes place through attaining the appropriate credentials for entry into government service and through accepting unemployment while making efforts to obtain appointments. Efforts to influence those in charge of making appointments, of course, just carry the argument one step further back.

To argue that competition for entry into government service is, in part, a competition for rents does not imply that all government servants accept bribes nor that they would leave government service in their absence. Successful competitors for government jobs might experience large windfall gains even at their official salaries. However, if the possibility of those gains induces others to expend time, energy, and resources in seeking entry into government services, the activity is competitive for present purposes.

In all these license-allocation cases, there are means, legal and illegal, for competing for rents. If individuals choose their activities on the basis of expected returns, rates of return on alternative activities will be equated and, in that sense, markets will be competitive.[3] In most cases, people do not perceive themselves to be rent seekers and, generally speaking, individuals and firms do not specialize in rent seeking. Rather, rent seeking is one part of an economic activity, such as distribution or production, and part of the firm's resources are devoted to the activity (including, of course, the hiring of expediters). The fact that rent seeking and other economic activities are not generally conducted by separate economic entities provides the motivation for the form of the model developed below.

B. *Are Rents Quantitatively Important?*

Granted that rent seeking may be highly competitive, the question remains whether rents are important. Data from two countries, India and Turkey, suggest that they are. Gunnar Myrdal believes India may "... on the balance, be judged to have somewhat less corruption than any other country in South Asia" (p. 943). Nonetheless, it is generally believed that "corruption" has been increasing, and that much of the blame lies with the proliferation of economic controls following independence.[4]

Table 1 presents crude estimates, based on fairly conservative assumptions of the value of rents of all sorts in 1964. One important source of rents—investment licensing—is not included for lack of any valid basis on which to estimate its value. Many smaller controls are also excluded. Nonetheless, it is apparent from Table 1 that

[3] It may be objected that illegal means of competition may be sufficiently distasteful that perfect competition will not result. Three comments are called for. First, it requires only that enough people at the margin do not incur disutility from engaging in these activities. Second, most lines of economic activity in many countries cannot be entered without some rent-seeking activity. Third, risks of detection (especially when bribery is expected) and the value judgments associated with illegal activities differ from society to society. See Ronald Wraith and Edgar Simpkins.

[4] Santhanam Committee, pp. 7–8.

TABLE 1—ESTIMATES OF VALUE OF RENTS: INDIA, 1964

Source of Rent	Amount of Rent (Rs. million)
Public investment	365
Imports	10,271
Controlled commodities	3,000
Credit rationing	407
Railways	602
Total	14,645

Sources:

1) Public investment: The Santhanam Committee, pp. 11–12, placed the loss in public investment at *at least* 5 percent of investment. That figure was multiplied by the average annual public investment in the *Third Five Year Plan*.

2) Imports: The Santhanam Committee, p. 18, stated that import licenses were worth 100 to 500 percent of their face value. Seventy-five percent of the value of 1964 imports was used here as a conservative estimate.

3) Controlled commodities: These commodities include steel, cement, coal, passenger cars, scooters, food, and other price—and/or distribution-controlled commodities, as well as foreign exchange used for illegal imports and other unrecorded transactions. The figure is the lower bound estimate given by John Monteiro, p. 60. Monteiro puts the upper bound estimate at Rs. 30,000 billion, although he rejects the figure on the (dubious) ground that notes in circulation are less than that sum.

4) Credit rationing: The bank rate in 1964 was 6 percent; Rs. 20.3 billion of loans were outstanding. It is assumed that *at least* an 8 percent interest rate would have been required to clear the market, and that 3 percent of bank loans outstanding would be equivalent to the present value of new loans at 5 percent. Data source: Reserve Bank of India, Tables 534 and 554.

5) Railways: Monteiro, p. 45, cites commissions of 20 percent on railway purchases, and extra-official fees of Rs. 0.15 per wagon and Rs. 1.4 per 100 maunds loaded. These figures were multiplied by the 1964 traffic volume; 203 million tons of revenue-paying traffic originated in that year. Third plan expenditure on railroads was Rs. 13,260 million. There were 350,000 railroad goods wagons in 1964–65. If a wagon was loaded once a week, there were 17,500,000 wagons of freight. At Rs. 0.15 per load, this would be Rs. 2.6 million; 100 maunds equal 8,228 pounds so at 1.4 Rs. per 100 maunds, Rs. 69 million changed hands; if one-fifth of railroad expenditures were made in 1964–65, Rs. 2652 million was spent in 1964; at 20 percent, this would be Rs. 530 million, for a total of Rs. 602 million.

import licenses provided the largest source of rents. The total value of rents of Rs. 14.6 billion contrasts with Indian national income of Rs. 201 billion in 1964. At 7.3 percent of national income, rents must be judged large relative to India's problems in attempting to raise her savings rate.

For Turkey, excellent detailed estimates of the value of import licenses in 1968 are available.[5] Data on the c.i.f. prices of individual imports, their landed cost (c.i.f. price plus all duties, taxes, and landing charges), and wholesale prices were collected for a sizeable sample of commodities representing about 10 percent of total imports in 1968. The c.i.f. value of imports in the sample was TL 547 million and the landed cost of the imports was TL 1,443 million. The value at the wholesale level of these same imports was TL 3,568 million. Of course, wholesalers incur some handling, storage, and transport costs. The question, therefore, is the amount that can be attributed to normal wholesaling costs. If one assumes that a 50 percent markup would be adequate, then the value of import licenses was TL 1,404 million, or almost three times the c.i.f. value of imports. Imports in 1968 were recorded (c.i.f.) as 6 percent of national income. On the basis of Aker's data, this would imply that rents from import licenses in Turkey in 1968 were about 15 percent of *GNP*.

Both the Indian and the Turkish estimates are necessarily somewhat rough. But they clearly indicate that the value of import licenses to the recipients was sizeable. Since means were available of competing for the licenses, it would be surprising if competition did not occur for prizes that large. We turn, therefore, to an examination of the consequences of competitive rent seeking.

[5] I am indebted to Ahmet Aker of Robert College who kindly made his data available to me. Details and a description of the data can be found in my forthcoming book.

II. The Effects of Competitive Rent Seeking

The major proposition of this paper is that competitive rent seeking for import licenses entails a welfare cost in addition to the welfare cost that would be incurred if the same level of imports were achieved through tariffs. The effects of tariffs upon production, trade, and welfare are well known, and attention is focussed here upon the additional cost of competitive rent seeking. A simple model is used to develop the argument. Initially, free trade is assumed. Then, a tariff or equivalent import restriction is introduced. Finally, an equal import restriction with competitive rent seeking is examined.

A. *The Basic Model*

Two commodities are consumed by the country under investigation: food and consumption goods. Food is produced domestically and exported. Consumption goods are imported. Distribution is a productive activity whereby food is purchased from the agricultural sector, exported, and the proceeds are used to import consumption goods which are sold in the domestic market. Labor is assumed to be the only domestic factor of production.[6] It is assumed that the country under consideration is small and cannot affect its international terms of trade. Physical units are selected so that the fixed international prices of both goods are unity.

The agricultural production function is

$$(1) \quad A = A(L_A) \qquad A' > 0,\ A'' < 0$$

where A is the output of food and L_A is the quantity of labor employed in agriculture. The sign of the second derivative reflects a diminishing marginal physical product of labor in agriculture, due, presumably, to fixity in the supply of land.

The level of distribution output, D, is defined to equal the level of consumption-goods imports, M:

$$(2) \quad D = M$$

One unit of distributive services entails exchanging one unit of imports for food with the agricultural sector at the domestic terms of trade, and exporting the food in exchange for imports at the international terms of trade. Constant returns to scale are assumed for the distribution activity; one unit of distribution requires k units of labor. Total labor employed in distribution, L_D, is

$$(3) \quad L_D = kD$$

A distribution charge of p_D per unit is added to the international price of imports:

$$(4) \quad p_M = 1 + p_D$$

where p_M is the domestic price of imports. The domestic price of food is assumed to equal its unit international price.[7]

Society's demand for imports depends upon the domestic price of imports and total income generated in agriculture:[8]

$$(5) \quad M = M(p_M, A)$$

where $\partial M/\partial p_M < 0$ and $\partial M/\partial A > 0$. Demand decreases with increases in the price of imports, and increases with increases in agricultural output (income). Equation (5) is derived from micro utility maximization with the assumption that farmers, distributors, and rent seekers all have the same consumption behavior. Domestic

[6] Labor could be regarded as a composite domestic factor of production. Extensions to two or more factors would complicate the analysis, but would not alter its basic results.

[7] These assumptions establish a domestic numeraire. The real analysis would be unaffected by proportional changes in the domestic prices.

[8] Food and imports are consumed. But, by choice of food as the numeraire (see equation (6)) and the assumed constancy of international prices, agricultural output serves as a measure of income.

food consumption, F, is simply the quantity not exported:

(6) $$F = A - M$$

Since the fixed international terms of trade equal unity, food exports equal consumption goods imports.

Finally, it is assumed that the economy under consideration has a fixed labor supply, $\bar{L}$:

(7) $$\bar{L} = L_A + L_D + L_R$$

where L_R is the quantity of labor engaged in rent seeking.

B. *Free Trade*

Under free trade, there is free entry into both agriculture and distribution and competition equates the wage in the two activities:

(8) $$A' = p_D/k$$

Equations (1) to (8) constitute the free-trade system. These eight equations contain the eight variables A, M, D, F, L_A, L_D, p_M, and p_D. Since there is no rent seeking under free trade, $L_R \equiv 0$.

It is easily established that free trade is optimal in the sense that the domestic price ratio under free trade equals the marginal rate of transformation between food consumption and imports. The consumption possibility locus is obtained by substituting into (6) from (1) and (7)

$$F = A(\bar{L} - kM) - M$$

The locus has a marginal rate of transformation greater than one:

(9) $$\frac{-dF}{dM} = kA' + 1 > 1$$

which reflects the positive distribution cost of substituting imports for food consumption. The locus is concave:

$$\frac{d^2F}{dM^2} = k^2A'' < 0$$

since $A'' < 0$, which follows from diminishing returns in food production. Substituting from (8) into (9),

$$\frac{-dF}{dM} = 1 + p_D$$

which establishes the aforementioned equality.

A free-trade solution is depicted in Figure 1. Domestic food consumption and import consumption are measured along OF and OM, respectively. The consumption possibility locus is $\hat{F}\hat{M}$. At the point $\hat{F}$ no imports are consumed and hence there is no distribution. If distribution were costless, society could choose its consumption point from the line $\hat{F}A$. However, to consume one unit of import requires exchanging one unit of food *and* withdrawing k workers from agriculture to provide the requisite distributive services. With diminishing marginal product of labor in agriculture, the cost of additional imports in terms of foregone food production rises. Thus, the price of distribution, and hence the domestic price of imports, increases in moving northwest from $\hat{F}$. The consump-

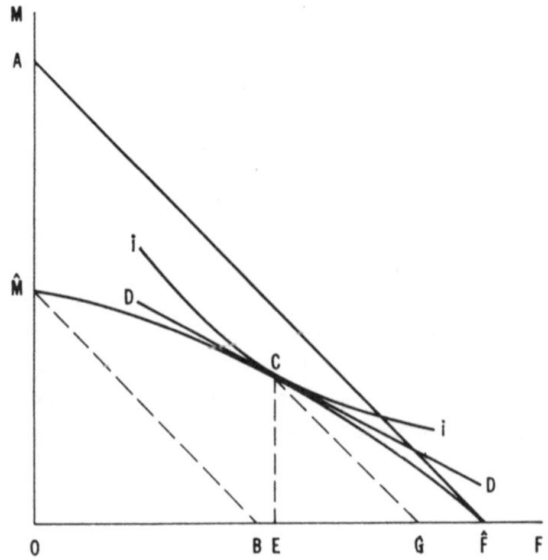

FIGURE 1. FREE TRADE

tion point $\hat{M}$ has OB food exchanged for $O\hat{M}$ of imports. The distance $\hat{F}B$ is the agricultural output foregone to distribute $O\hat{M}$ imports.

If society's preferences are given by the indifference curve *ii*, point *C* is optimal. The price of distribution is reflected in the difference between the slope of $\hat{F}A$ and the slope of *DD* at *C*. At the point *C*, *OG* food would be produced, with *EG* (=*EC*) exported, and the rest domestically consumed.

C. *A Tariff or an Import Restriction Without Rent Seeking*

Consider now a case in which there is a restriction upon the quantity of imports

$$M = \overline{M} \tag{10}$$

where $\overline{M}$ is less than the import quantity that would be realized under free trade. Since entry into distribution is now limited, the competitive wage equality (8) will no longer hold. The relevant system contains (1) to (7) and (10). The variables are the same as in the free-trade case and again $L_R=0$. The system may be solved sequentially: given (10), *D* follows from (2), L_D from (3), L_A from (7), *A* from (1), *F* from (6), p_M from (5), and p_D from (4). Since equations (1), (6), and (7) remain intact, the solution for this case is also on the consumption possibility locus.

It is useful to establish the directions of change for the variables following a switch from free trade to import restriction. The reduced import level will reduce the labor employed in distribution and increase the labor force in agriculture. Diminishing returns will reduce the agricultural wage. The domestic price of imports, the distributive margin, and the wage of distributors will increase. Distributors will earn a rent in the sense that their wage will exceed the wage of those engaged in agriculture.

In the absence of rent seeking, a tariff

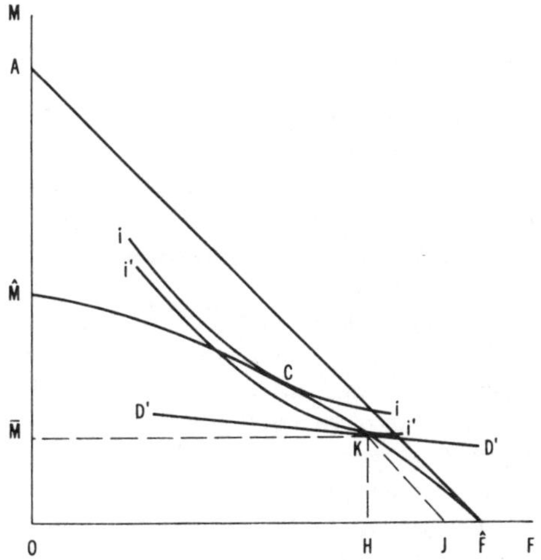

FIGURE 2. IMPORT RESTRICTION WITHOUT RENT SEEKING

and a quantitative restriction are equivalent[9] aside from the resultant income distribution. Under a quantitative restriction the distributive wage is higher than the agricultural. If instead there were an equivalent tariff with redistribution of the proceeds, the marginal product of labor in agriculture would be unchanged, but agricultural workers would benefit by the amount of tariff proceeds redistributed to them whereas traders' income would be lower. Since the allocation of labor under a tariff and quantitative restriction without rent seeking is the same and domestic prices are the same, the only difference between the two situations lies in income distribution.

The solution under a quantitative restriction is illustrated in Figure 2, where $\hat{F}\hat{M}$ is again the consumption possibility locus and *C* the free-trade solution. With a quantitative restriction on imports in the amount $O\overline{M}$, the domestic prices of

[9] The change in the price of the import from the free-trade solution is the tariff equivalent of the quantitative restriction described here.

imports, and hence of distribution, rise from free trade to import restriction. Food output (OJ) and domestic consumption of food increase, and exports decline to HJ $(=OM)$. The indifference curve $i'i'$ lies below ii (and the point C), and the welfare loss may be described by the consumption and production cost measure given by Harry Johnson.

The wage rate in distribution unequivocally rises for a movement from free trade to a quantitative restriction. The total income of distributors will increase, decrease, or remain unchanged depending upon whether the proportionate increase in p_D is greater than, less than, or equal to the absolute value of the proportionate decrease of imports. For the moment, let p_D, p_M, and M represent free-trade solution values, and let p_D^*, p_M^*, and $\overline{M}$ represent import-restriction solution values. The total arc elasticity of demand for imports for the interval under consideration, η, is

$$\eta = \frac{-(\overline{M} - M)}{\overline{M} + M} \cdot \frac{\overset{*}{p}_M + p_M}{\overset{*}{p}_M - p_M} \tag{11}$$

Total expenditures on imports will increase, decrease, or remain unchanged as η is less than one, greater than one, or equal to one. The total income of distributors will increase if

$$\overset{*}{p}_D\overline{M} > p_D M$$

Multiplying both sides of this inequality by $(p_M^* + p_M)/(p_M^* - p_M)$, substituting from (11), and using (4),

$$1 + 2/(\overset{*}{p}_D + p_D) > \eta \tag{12}$$

Hence, distributors' total income can increase even if the demand for imports is price elastic.[10] The smaller is the free-trade distributive markup, the more likely it is that the distributors' total income will increase with a curtailment of imports. The reason is that an increase in the domestic price of imports results in a proportionately greater increase in the price of distribution.

D. *An Import Restriction with Competitive Rent Seeking*

In the import-restriction model just presented, the wage in distribution p_D/k exceeds the wage in agriculture A'. Under this circumstance, it would be surprising if people did not endeavor to enter distribution in response to its higher return. Resources can be devoted to rent seeking in all the ways indicated in Section IA. This rent-seeking activity can be specified in a number of different ways. A simple and intuitively plausible specification is that people will seek distributive rents until the average wage in distribution and rent seeking equals the agricultural wage:[11]

$$A' = \frac{p_D\overline{M}}{L_D + L_R} \tag{13}$$

One can regard all distributors and rent seekers as being partially engaged in each activity or one can think of rent seekers as entering in the expectation of receiving import licenses. In the latter case, the final solution classifies the successful seekers in L_D and the unsuccessful ones in L_R. Equation (13) implies risk neutrality in this circumstance.

The model for import restriction with rent seeking contains the same equations,

[10] Proof of (12) uses the step that $p_D^*\overline{M} > p_D M$ implies $(p_D^* - p_D)/(p_D^* + p_D) > -(\overline{M} - M)/(\overline{M} + M)$. Note that in the continuous case, (12) reduces to $1 + 1/p_D > \eta$.

[11] As an alternative, the distributive production function (3) can be altered to treat all persons competing for import licenses as distributors so that L_D also encompasses L_R and $A' = p_D\overline{M}/L_D$. Another alternative is to introduce a rent-seeking activity distinct from distribution with a wage determined from total rents $(p_D - A'k)\overline{M}/L_R$, and require that this wage equal the wages in distribution and agriculture. These specifications give results equivalent to those that follow from (13).

(1) to (7) and (10), and the same variables as the model for import restrictions without rent seeking. In addition, the new model contains (13) and the introduction of L_R as a variable. The essential factor of rent seeking is that L_R becomes positive.

Let us start with a solution for an import restriction without rent seeking and ask what happens to the values of the variables when rent seeking is introduced. By assumption $M=\overline{M}$ is unchanged, so that L_D is unchanged. Therefore, $dL_A = -dL_R$, because the labor that enters rent seeking can only come from agriculture. Substituting into the total differential of (1) and using (6),

$$dF = dA = -A'dL_R < 0 \tag{14}$$

Agricultural production and food consumption are reduced by the introduction of rent seeking. Since the import level remains unchanged, rent seeking entails a welfare loss beyond that for an import restriction without rent seeking. The concavity of the agricultural production function results in a food loss that is less than proportional to decrements in L_A. Differentiating (5) totally,

$$0 = M_1 dp_M + M_2 dA \tag{15}$$

where M_1 and M_2 are the partial derivatives of (5) with respect to p_M and A, respectively. Solving (15) for dp_M, and substituting from (4) and (14),

$$dp_D = dp_M = \frac{M_2}{M_1} A'dL_R < 0 \tag{16}$$

since $M_1 < 0$ and $M_2 > 0$. The domestic cost of imports will be lower under rent-seeking competition. This follows from the decrease in the consumption of food relative to imports.

The results of (14) and (16) are not dependent upon the particular form of the equilibrium of the labor market. They hold for any specification of competitive rent seeking. Equation (13) serves to determine particular values for L_R and other variables of the system. The mere existence of competitive rent seeking is enough to determine the directions of change of the variables.

The above results are sufficient to indicate that, for any given level of import restrictions, competition among rent seekers is clearly inferior to the tariff equivalent of the restrictions, in that there could be more food consumed with no fewer imports under the latter case than the former. To the extent that rent seeking is competitive, the welfare cost of import restrictions is equal to the welfare cost of the tariff equivalent *plus the additional cost of rent-seeking activities*. Measurement of that excess cost is considered below.

The tariff-equivalent and rent-seeking equilibria are contrasted in Figure 3. Equilibrium under rent seeking will be at some point such as L, with the same consumption of imports, but smaller production and consumption of food than occurs under a tariff. The points K and C are the tariff-equivalent and free-trade equilibria, respectively. The line $D'D'$ cor-

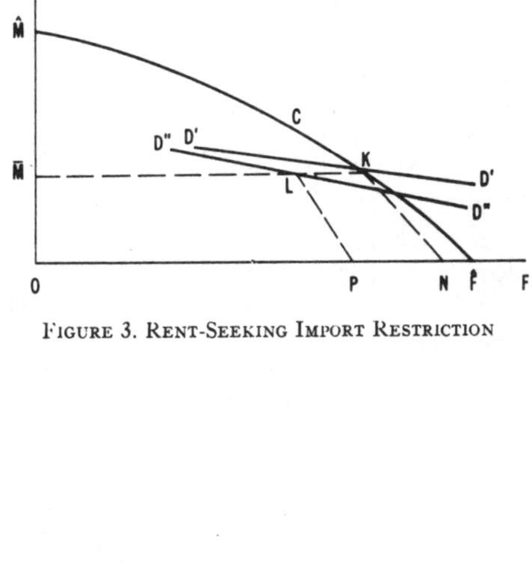

FIGURE 3. RENT-SEEKING IMPORT RESTRICTION

responds to the domestic price of imports in Figure 2, and the steeper line $D''D''$ corresponds to the lower domestic price of imports under competitive rent seeking.

So far, it has been shown that for any given level of import restriction, a tariff is Pareto-superior to competitive rent seeking, and the properties of rent-seeking equilibrium have been contrasted with those of the tariff-equivalent case in the absence of competition for the rents. A natural question is whether anything can be said about the properties of rent-seeking equilibrium in contrast to those of a free-trade equilibrium, which is, after all, the optimal solution. It has been seen that the number of persons engaged in distribution declines from free trade to import restriction without rent seeking, and increases as one goes from that situation to competition for import licenses. Likewise, agricultural output increases between free trade and the tariff-equivalent case, and declines between that and rent seeking. The question is whether any unambiguous signs can be placed on the direction of these changes between free trade and rent seeking and, in particular, is it possible that society might produce and consume less of both goods under rent seeking than under free trade?

The answer is that if inequality (12) is satisfied, the absolute number of persons (L_D+L_R) in distribution will increase going from a free-trade to a rent-seeking equilibrium. If import demand is more elastic, the number of persons in distribution will decline. Contrasted with a free-trade equilibrium, there would be less agricultural output *and* fewer imports when inequality (12) holds. If, with import restriction, the income from distribution $p_D^*\overline{M}$ is greater than distributors' income at free trade, more persons will be employed in distribution-cum-rent seeking with import restriction than are employed under free trade.

E. *Measuring the Welfare Loss from Rent Seeking*

A tariff has both production and consumption costs, and it has already been shown that rent seeking entails costs in addition to those of a tariff. Many forms of competition for rents, however, are by their nature difficult to observe and quantify and one might therefore question the empirical content of the result so far obtained.

Fortunately, there is a way to estimate the production cost of rent seeking. That cost, in fact, is equal to the value of the rents. This can be shown as follows. The rent per import license, r, is:

$$r = p_D - kA' \tag{17}$$

This follows because the labor required to distribute one unit of imports is k, which could be used in agriculture with a return A'. Note that at free trade r equals zero. A distributor could efficiently distribute an import and earn his opportunity cost in agriculture with zero rent. The total value of rents, R, with competitive rent seeking is thus the rent per unit of imports times the amount imported.

$$R = r\overline{M} = (p_D - kA')\overline{M} \tag{18}$$

Using (3) and (13),

$$\begin{aligned} R &= \left(p_D - \frac{kp_D\overline{M}}{L_D + L_R}\right)\overline{M} \\ &= p_D\left(1 - \frac{L_D}{L_D + L_R}\right)\overline{M} \\ &= \frac{p_D\overline{M}L_R}{L_D + L_R} \end{aligned} \tag{19}$$

Thus the total value of rents reflects the agricultural wage (A') times the number of rent seekers.

The value of rents reflects the value (at current prices) of the domestic factors of production which could be extracted from the economy with no change in the final goods and services available for society's utilization. Thus, if the value of rents is known, it indicates the volume of resources that could be transferred out of distribution and into other activities, with no loss of distributive services from an initial position of rent-seeking activity. The estimates of rents in India and Turkey, therefore, may be interpreted as the deadweight loss from quantitative restrictions in addition to the welfare cost of their associated tariff equivalents if one believes that there is competition for the rents.

The value of the rents overstates the increase in food output and consumption that could be attained with a tariff to the extent that the marginal product of labor in agriculture is diminishing, since the equilibrium wage will rise between the tariff and the competitive rent-seeking situation. In the case of a constant marginal product of labor in alternative uses, the value of rents will exactly measure foregone output.

F. *The Implications of Rent Seeking for Trade Theory*

Recognition of the fact of rent seeking alters a variety of conclusions normally obtained in the trade literature and examination of such cases is well beyond the scope of this paper. A few immediately derivable results are worth brief mention, however.

First, an import prohibition might be preferable to a nonprohibitive quota if there is competition for licenses under the quota. This follows immediately from the fact that a prohibition would release resources from rent seeking and the excess cost of domestic production might be less than the value of the rents. Second, one could not, in general, rank the tariff-equivalents of two (or more) quotas, since the value of rents is a function of both the amount of rent per unit (the tariff equivalent) and the volume of imports of each item.[12] Third, it has generally been accepted that the more inelastic domestic demand the less is likely to be the welfare cost of a given tariff. For the quota-cum-rents case, the opposite is true: the more price inelastic is demand, the greater will be the value of rents and the greater, therefore, the deadweight loss associated with rent seeking. Fourth, it is usually believed that competition among importers will result in a better allocation of resources than will a monopoly. If rent seeking is a possibility, however, creating a monopoly position for one importer will generally result in a higher real income if not in a preferable income distribution for society. Finally, devaluation under quantitative restrictions may have important allocation effects because it diminishes the value of import licenses, and hence the amount of rent-seeking activity, in addition to its effects upon exports.

III. Conclusions and Implications

In this paper, focus has been on the effects of competition for import licenses under a quantitative restriction of imports. Empirical evidence suggests that the value of rents associated with import licenses can be relatively large, and it has been shown that the welfare cost of quantitative restrictions equals that of their tariff equivalents plus the value of the rents.

While import licenses constitute a large and visible rent resulting from government intervention, the phenomenon of rent seeking is far more general. Fair trade laws result in firms of less-than-optimal size. Minimum wage legislation generates equilibrium levels of unemployment above the optimum with associated deadweight losses, as shown by John Harris and

[12] I am indebted to Bhagwati for pointing out this implication.

Michael Todaro, and Todaro. Ceilings on interest rates and consequent credit rationing lead to competition for loans and deposits and/or high-cost banking operations. Regulating taxi fares affects the average waiting time for a taxi and the percent of time taxis are idle, but probably not their owners' incomes, unless taxis are also licensed. Capital gains tax treatment results in overbuilding of apartments and uneconomic oil exploration. And so on.

Each of these and other interventions lead people to compete for the rents although the competitors often do not perceive themselves as such. In each case there is a deadweight loss associated with that competition over and above the traditional triangle. In general, prevention of that loss can be achieved only by restricting entry into the activity for which a rent has been created.

That, in turn, has political implications. First, even if they *can* limit competition for the rents, governments which consider they must impose restrictions are caught on the horns of a dilemma: if they do restrict entry, they are clearly "showing favoritism" to one group in society and are choosing an unequal distribution of income. If, instead, competition for the rents is allowed (or cannot be prevented), income distribution may be less unequal and certainly there will be less appearance of favoring special groups, although the economic costs associated with quantitative restrictions will be higher.

Second, the existence of rent seeking surely affects people's perception of the economic system. If income distribution is viewed as the outcome of a lottery where wealthy individuals are successful (or lucky) rent seekers, whereas the poor are those precluded from or unsuccessful in rent seeking, the market mechanism is bound to be suspect. In the United States, rightly or wrongly, societal consensus has been that high incomes reflect—at least to some degree—high social product. As such, the high American per capita income is seen as a result of a relatively free market mechanism and an unequal distribution is tolerated as a by-product. If, instead, it is believed that few businesses would survive without exerting "influence," even if only to bribe government officials to do what they ought in any event to do, it is difficult to associate pecuniary rewards with social product. The perception of the price system as a mechanism rewarding the rich and well-connected may also be important in influencing political decisions about economic policy. If the market mechanism is suspect, the inevitable temptation is to resort to greater and greater intervention, thereby increasing the amount of economic activity devoted to rent seeking. As such, a political "vicious circle" may develop. People perceive that the market mechanism does not function in a way compatible with socially approved goals because of competitive rent seeking. A political consensus therefore emerges to intervene further in the market, rent seeking increases, and further intervention results. While it is beyond the competence of an economist to evaluate the political impact of rent seeking, the suspicion of the market mechanism so frequently voiced in some developing countries may result from it.

Finally, all market economies have some rent-generating restrictions. One can conceive of a continuum between a system of no restrictions and a perfectly restricted system. With no restrictions, entrepreneurs would seek to achieve windfall gains by adopting new technology, anticipating market shifts correctly, and so on. With perfect restrictions, regulations would be so all-pervasive that rent seeking would be the only route to gain. In such a system, entrepreneurs would devote all their time and resources to capturing windfall rents.

While neither of these extreme types could ever exist, one can perhaps ask whether there might be some point along the continuum beyond which the market fails to perform its allocative function to any satisfactory degree. It will remain for further work to formalize these conjectures and to test their significance. It is hoped, however, that enough has been said to stimulate interest and research on the subject.

REFERENCES

J. Bhagwati, "On the Equivalence of Tariffs and Quotas," in his *Trade, Tariffs and Growth,* London 1969.

——— **and P. Desai,** *Planning for Industrialization: A Study of India's Trade and Industrial Policies Since 1950,* Cambridge 1970.

——— **and A. Krueger,** *Foreign Trade Regimes and Economic Development: Experience and Analysis,* New York forthcoming.

J. R. Harris and M. P. Todaro, "Migration, Unemployment, and Development: A Two-Sector Analysis," *Amer. Econ. Rev.,* Mar. 1970, *60,* 126–42.

H. G. Johnson, "The Cost of Protection and the Scientific Tariff," *J. Polit. Econ.,* Aug. 1960, *68,* 327–45.

A. Krueger, *Foreign Trade Regimes and Economic Development: Turkey,* New York 1974.

J. B. Monteiro, *Corruption,* Bombay 1966.

G. Myrdal, *Asian Drama,* Vol. III, New York 1968.

M. P. Todaro, "A Model of Labor Migration and Urban Employment in Less Developed Countries," *Amer. Econ. Rev.,* Mar. 1969, *59,* 138–48.

R. Wraith and E. Simpkins, *Corruption in Developing Countries,* London 1963.

Government of India, Planning Commission, *Third Five Year Plan,* New Delhi, Aug. 1961.

Reserve Bank of India, *Report on Currency and Finance,* 1967–68.

Santhanam Committee, *Report on the Committee on Prevention of Corruption,* Government of India, Ministry of Home Affairs, New Delhi 1964.

Name Index